RECKONING WITH PINOCHET

A book in the series

LATIN AMERICA OTHERWISE: LANGUAGES, EMPIRES, NATIONS

Series editors:

Walter D. Mignolo, Duke University

Irene Silverblatt, Duke University

Sonia Saldívar-Hull, University of Texas, San Antonio

LATIN AMERICA OTHERWISE: LANGUAGES, EMPIRES, NATIONS
is a critical series. It aims to explore the emergence and consequences of concepts
used to define "Latin America" while at the same time exploring the broad interplay of political, economic, and cultural practices that have shaped Latin American
worlds. Latin America, at the crossroads of competing imperial designs and local
responses, has been construed as a geocultural and geopolitical entity since the
nineteenth century. This series provides a starting point to redefine Latin America
as a configuration of political, linguistic, cultural, and economic intersections that
demands a continuous reappraisal of the role of the Americas in history, and of the
ongoing process of globalization and the relocation of people and cultures that
have characterized Latin America's experience. *Latin America Otherwise: Languages,
Empires, Nations* is a forum that confronts established geocultural constructions,
that rethinks area studies and disciplinary boundaries, that assesses convictions
of the academy and of public policy, and that, correspondingly, demands that the
practices through which we produce knowledge and understanding about and from
Latin America be subject to rigorous and critical scrutiny.

※

September 11 brought terror to Chile when General Augusto Pinochet, in 1973, led a coup to overthrow the country's elected president, Salvador Allende. With the backing of the United States, Pinochet used the machinery of state to intimidate Chile's citizenry and unspeakable acts of state violence—torture and murder—became life's daily fare. Steve Stern here asks piercing questions of historical memory—how those who suffered as well as how those who caused such inhuman suffering recalled those terrible times.

Steve Stern has written an extraordinary trilogy, "The Memory Box of Pinochet's Chile," devoted to those years and how they were understood by participants in the horrors. He has delivered the third volume on Chilean memories of Augusto Pinochet's regime with the erudition, flair, and creativity with which the reader is already familiar from the first two volumes. This final volume covers the years from 1989 (the beginning of transition from totalitarian regime) to 2006, the year that Pinochet died.

Stern not only accomplished what historians are expecting, but has gone beyond the canon of historical narrative by inserting layers of documentation, analysis, and reflections (such as found in the "Afterwords" closing each chapter). In addition to his main object of analysis (the Pinochet regime), Stern focuses on the impact it had on all Chileans, an impact that is perceptible in the fact that memories of Pinochet's years became an integral part of everyday life. The historian meets the anthropologist in the following pages, as Stern's reliance on the historical archives is complemented by the experiences of living Chileans for whom Pinochet's regime is not only an event of the past but lives on in the memories through which Chileans in the present are coping with that past.

Reckoning with Pinochet: The Memory Question in Democratic Chile, 1989–2006, closes a monumental narrative of the period in which the world saw, without realizing it at the time, that Pinochet was a key agent in the turn from liberalism (the end of the welfare state) to neoliberalism. In this regard, the memory of Pinochet is relevant not only for Chileans but for all Latin Americans who endured the consequences of neoliberal regimes (Carlos Menem's in Argentina; Gonzalo Sánchez de Losada's in Bolivia), as well as for the rest of the world, which had witnessed the instauration of neoliberal doctrines in the 1980s (Reagan-Thatcher) and their failure in 2008–09 with the collapse of Wall Street.

STEVE J. STERN

Reckoning with Pinochet

The Memory Question in Democratic Chile, 1989–2006

BOOK THREE OF THE TRILOGY: *The Memory Box of Pinochet's Chile*

Duke University Press Durham & London 2010

© 2010 Duke University Press

Printed in the United States of America

on acid-free paper

Designed by C. H. Westmoreland

Typeset in Scala by Keystone Typesetting, Inc.

Library of Congress Cataloging-in-Publication

Data appear on the last printed page of

this book.

✻

Para mi tan querida Florencia,

mi chilenita de corazón,

corazón sin fronteras . . .

Contents

Acknowledgments

If the measure of one's riches is people—the help and friendship one receives from others—I am one of the richest persons on earth. I have so many people to thank for making this project possible, and for improving how it turned out.

In Chile, the numbers of people who helped are so many I cannot list them all. I am deeply grateful to every person who consented to an interview, a conversation, or an argument; to the people who provided documents from their personal archives; to the staffs of the archives, documentation centers, and libraries; to the human rights activists and the victim-survivors who inspired and challenged me. My colleagues at Facultad Latinoamericana de Ciencias Sociales (FLACSO)—Chile provided an office base, intellectual exchanges, and contacts; a library and network of expert transcribers of interview tapes; and a supportive human environment. I owe particular thanks to Claudio Fuentes, José Olavarría, and Marisa Weinstein for support, intellectual advice, sharing of research, and, in Marisa's case, research assistance; to Magaly Ortíz for organizing a network of people, including herself, to produce interview transcripts; to María Inés Bravo for her amazing FLACSO library and ability to find materials; to Enrique Correa and Francisco Rojas for institutional support; and, most especially, to Alicia Frohmann and Teresa Valdés, for their intellectual engagement and suggestions, their generosity with useful contacts, and their personal affection and friendship. Alicia's help extended from everyday discussions in her office at FLACSO, to comments and critical suggestions after reading a first draft of the first and third books of the trilogy. Teresa worked through ideas at almost every stage of the way, generously shared contacts and her Mujeres Por La Vida archive, and offered a helpful critique of an early formulation of ideas. At the Fundación de Documentación y Archivo de la Vicaría de la Solidaridad, the most important memory and human rights archive and library in Chile, I owe a special thanks to three amazing women who offered warmth, knowledge, and access to their documentary treasure: Carmen Garretón, María Paz Vergara, and Mariana Cáceres. I owe similar thanks to Teresa Rubio, a dear friend and dedicated bibliographer and custodian of documents at the Fundación Salvador Allende, and to my close friend Helen Hughes, photographer extraordinaire, for sharing her photojournalism collection and reproduction of numerous photographs in Books Two and Three of this trilogy.

Among my other colleagues and friends in Chile whose intellectual guidance and personal support meant more than they may know, I thank Roberta Bacic, Mario Garcés, my cousin Gastón Gómez Bernales, Elizabeth Lira, Pedro Matta, Juan O'Brien, Anne Perotin and Alex Wilde, Julio Pinto and Verónica Valdivia Ortiz de Zárate, Alfredo Riquelme, Claudio Rolle, Gonzalo Rovira, Sol Serrano, María Elena Valenzuela, Augusto Varas, Pilar Videla and her family, and José Zalaquett. Sol Serrano was a model colleague and warm friend. She shared her astute historical mind, her experiences and social contacts, materials from her library, her interpretations and disagreements. Sol and Pepe Zalaquett also demonstrated extraordinary generosity by reading and critiquing the entire first draft of the trilogy.

Among the busy public figures who made time for interviews and discussion, I must especially thank the late Sola Sierra, president of the Association of Relatives of the Detained and Disappeared (Agrupación de Familiares de Detenidos-Desaparecidos), and former Chilean president Patricio Aylwin Azócar. I did not see eye to eye with either on every point, nor did they agree with one another on every point. But precisely for that reason, each taught me a great deal and each proved generous, direct, and inspiring.

A number of persons anchored in varied countries and disciplinary perspectives enriched my learning process. After the initial stage of research, it was my privilege to work as a collaborating faculty member on a Social Science Research Council (ssRc) project to train and mentor young Latin American intellectuals—from Argentina, Brazil, Chile, Paraguay, Peru, and Uruguay—on issues of memory, repression, and democratization. The inspired idea behind the project was to build a critical mass of transnationally networked young intellectuals able to research and reflect vigorously on the wave of violent military dictatorships, and attendant memory struggles and legacies, that had shaped Brazil and the Southern Cone countries in recent times, and on related memory issues that emerged in the wake of the Shining Path war period in Peru. Involvement in this work enhanced my thought process, intellectual exchange networks, and feedback enormously. I wish to thank Elizabeth Jelin, the Argentine faculty director of the project; Eric Hershberg, the ssRc organizer and codirector of the project; Carlos Iván Degregori, who took on a codirecting role as Peruvian experiences were integrated into the project; and the fellows and other faculty collaborators, especially Susana Kaufman, who worked during one or another phase of the project.

I also wish to thank my colleagues in the University of Wisconsin Legacies of Authoritarianism study circle, especially Leigh Payne and Louis Bickford, Ksenija Bilbija, Al McCoy, Cynthia Milton, and Thongchai Winichakul, for opportunities for comparative and interdisciplinary thinking on memory issues. Additional Wisconsin colleagues who offered helpful insights, encouragement, suggestions, and critiques included Florence Bernault, Alda Blanco, Stanley Kutler, Gerda Lerner, the late George Mosse, Francisco Scarano, Thomas Skidmore (now at Brown University), Jeremi Suri, and Joseph Thome. I wish to thank, too, various colleagues and students who heard talks, engaged the issues, and offered suggestions at international meetings and workshops in Buenos Aires, Cape Town, Lima, London, Lucila del Mar (Argentina), Montevideo, Piriápolis (Uruguay), and Santiago; in Latin American Studies Association panels in the United States; and in lectures and seminars at various U.S. universities. Finally, I must thank two of the leading senior historians of Chile, Paul Drake and Peter Winn, for warm encouragement and valuable ideas during various phases of the project, and the graduate students at the University of Wisconsin, for the intellectual energy and insight they bring to our learning community and its seminars on violence and memory.

I received indispensable material assistance. I thank the Fulbright-Hays Faculty Research Abroad Program, the Social Science Research Council, the American Council of Learned Societies, and the University of Wisconsin at Madison for generous grants without which this project could not have happened. I also thank Nancy Appelbaum, Claudio Barrientos, Gavin Sacks, and Marisa Weinstein for valuable research assistance and good cheer in various phases of the project; and Onno Brouwer and Marieka Brouwer of the Cartographic Laboratory of the University of Wisconsin at Madison, for production of the maps, accompanied by expert technical and aesthetic counsel. I also thank Carrie Ryan for her superb help in the final phases of preparation of the manuscript of Book Three.

My editor at Duke University Press, Valerie Millholland, has been a source of wisdom throughout this project. Valerie helped clarify a host of intellectual, practical, and aesthetic issues, and the particular demands of a trilogy project. Her astute professional advice, her understanding of the human issues at stake, and her enthusiasm for the project have added up to an extraordinary experience and a valued friendship. I am deeply grateful, also, to the many people at the Press who brought the project to fruition and to my patient and skilled copy editor, Sonya Manes.

Two anonymous readers for Duke University Press offered meticulous and thoughtful advice in response to the first draft of the trilogy. A third reader offered equally pertinent advice on a subsequent draft. I thank them, along with Chilean readers Alicia Frohmann, Sol Serrano, and José Zalaquett, for taking the time to review and critique the manuscript. I have not responded successfully to every point or suggestion, but my readers saved me from specific mistakes and offered ideas and insights that helped me improve the larger analysis. I accept full responsibility for the shortcomings that remain despite their best efforts.

Finally, I must also thank my family. The large Chilean family I acquired by marriage to Florencia Mallon offered affection, friendship, contacts, and experiences. My deepest thanks to *mis tíos y tías* Tenca and the late Roberto, Celina and Gastón, the late Alfredo and Smyrna, and Nieves; *mis primos* Polencho and Gabriela, Diego, Gastón and Tita, Pablo and Sol, Ignacio and Alejandra, Chimina and Gonzalo; my parents-in-law Nacha and Dick, with whom we enjoyed a wonderful family reunion in Chile; my nieces and nephews who scampered around during family gatherings; and my own children, Ramón and Rafa, for navigating an international life and its challenges together, supporting the idea of the project, and reminding me of what is enduring and important. My own large U.S.-based family of siblings and parents also provided important support, and I must especially thank my mother, Adel Weisz Rosenzweig Stern. Mom, in a sense you raised me to write this trilogy. The treasured stories of life in Hungary with my grandparents and aunts and uncles, the fears and nightmares of Auschwitz and Buchenwald you also shared despite your desire not to do so, the spoken and unspoken memories and anxieties that permeated our lives, the fierce love and closeness we always experienced, these kindled a fire. Someday, I would have to confront and write about the most challenging and paradoxical aspects of twentieth-century history—the way modern times brought forth a horrifying human capacity to organize, and implement systematically, political projects of mind-bending absoluteness, violence, destructiveness, and hatred; and the way modernity *also* brought forth an amazing human capacity to build or reassert values of universal caring, dignity, rights, and solidarity, even in trying and terrifying times.

I dedicate this trilogy to my brilliant colleague and beloved partner for life, Florencia E. Mallon. The intellectual ideas and information and support you contributed to this work were fundamental, yet they constitute only a modest fraction of the many reasons for a thank you and a dedication. Our journey together has been a wondrous gift. May the journey never end.

1. Chile in the Pinochet Era.

This map shows major cities, towns, and sites of memory struggle mentioned in the trilogy text. It excludes the Juan Fernández Islands, Easter Island, and Chilean Antarctic territory. For a more detailed geography of places and memory sites in the central and southern regions, see map 2 (opposite).
Cartographic Laboratory, University of Wisconsin, Madison.

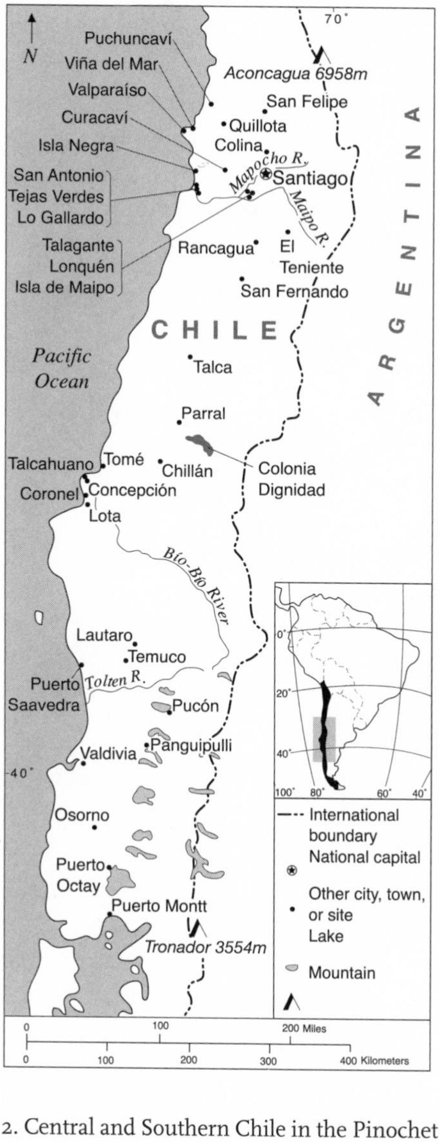
70°
N
Puchuncaví
Viña del Mar
Valparaíso
Curacaví
Isla Negra
San Antonio
Tejas Verdes
Lo Gallardo
Talagante
Lonquén
Isla de Maipo
Aconcagua 6958m
San Felipe
Quillota
Colina
Mapocho R.
Santiago
Maipo R.
Rancagua
El Teniente
San Fernando
ARGENTINA
CHILE
Pacific Ocean
Talca
Parral
Talcahuano
Tomé
Chillán
Colonia Dignidad
Coronel
Concepción
Lota
Bío-Bío River
Lautaro
Temuco
Puerto Saavedra
Tolten R.
Pucón
Valdivia
Panguipulli
40°
Osorno
Puerto Octay
Puerto Montt
Tronador 3554m
0°
20°
40°
100°
80°
60°
40°
International boundary
National capital
Other city, town, or site
Lake
Mountain
0
100
200 Miles
0
100
200
300
400 Kilometers

2. Central and Southern Chile in the Pinochet Era.
This map shows major cities, towns, and sites of memory struggle mentioned in the trilogy text, and corresponding to central and southern Regions (Regions V through X and the Metropolitan Region). *Cartographic Laboratory, University of Wisconsin, Madison.*

Introduction to
the Trilogy

✸

The Memory Box of Pinochet's Chile

This trilogy, The Memory Box of Pinochet's Chile, studies how Chileans have struggled to define the meaning of a collective trauma: the military action of 11 September 1973, when a junta composed of Augusto Pinochet and three other generals toppled the elected socialist government of Salvador Allende, and the massive political violence unleashed against perceived enemies and critics of the new regime.

The time frame under analysis corresponds to Pinochet's period as a major figure in public life—from 1973, when he stepped into rule as the army's commanding general in the new military junta, to 2001, when a Chilean court ruling on his health released him from jeopardy in criminal proceedings but completed his marginalization from public life. Many of the tensions and dilemmas analyzed for the 1990–2001 postdictatorship period, however, continued to shape national life and power after 2001. Precisely for this reason, the third volume of the trilogy carries the story forward through 2006. It thereby takes account of the major new cycle that opened up in memory reckonings from 2002 onward. The new cycle influenced responses to Pinochet's death in 2006, and set the stage for the paradox of memory politics—unprecedented advance, alongside heightened risk of marginality—in the new administration of Michelle Bachelet. In sum, "Pinochet's Chile" and its attendant memory struggles remained a strong legacy, even as Pinochet the person receded. The trilogy considers an arc of time—1973 to 2006—sufficient to analyze the implications of memory reckoning beyond the period when Pinochet was personally powerful in defining public life and culture.

The crisis of 1973 and the violence of the new order generated a contentious memory question in Chilean life. The memory question proved central to the remaking of Chilean politics and culture, first under the military regime that ruled until 1990, and subsequently under a democracy shadowed by legacies of dictatorship and a still-powerful military. As a result, the study of memory cannot be disentangled from an account of wider political, economic, and cultural contexts. Indeed, the making of memory offers a useful new lens on the general course of Chilean history in the last quarter of the twentieth century and beyond. To my knowledge, although excellent studies have established a reliable chronicle of basic political and economic events (some of them related to collective memory themes) under the rule of Pinochet, there still does not exist an account that systematically traces the long process of making and disputing memory by distinct social actors within a deeply divided society, across the periods of dictatorship and democratic transition.

The memory question is not only a major subject in its own right; its history opens up the underexplored "hearts and minds" aspect of the dictatorship experience. We often see the history and legacy of recent dictatorships in South America, especially Chile, in terms of several now-obvious and well-analyzed aspects: the facts of brute force and repression, and the attending spread of fear; the imposition of neoliberal economic policy, and the corresponding dismantling of statist approaches to social welfare and economic development; the rise of a depoliticized technocratic culture, within and beyond the state, and its consequences for social movements and political activism; and the political pacts and continuing power of militaries that conditioned transitions and the quality of democracies in South America in the 1980s and 1990s. These are crucial themes (and many were not at first obvious). A superb social science literature has emerged over the years to analyze them—a key early wave on "bureaucratic authoritarianism" led by Guillermo O'Donnell among others, followed by more recent waves on transitions and democratization. This literature has also illuminated relationships between modernity, technocracy, and state terror—that is, South America's version of a central disturbing issue of twentieth-century world history, posed forcefully by reflections on the Holocaust, and reinforced by regimes of terror and mass atrocity that arose in various world regions after World War II.[1]

The history of "memory" enables us to see an additional aspect of Chilean life that is subtle yet central: the making and unmaking of political and cultural legitimacy, notwithstanding violent rule by terror. In the struggle for hearts and minds in Chile, the memory question became strategic—politically, morally, existentially—both during and after dictatorship. In this way "memory, which by the 1980s crystallized as a key cultural idea, code word, and battleground, casts fresh light on the entire era of dictatorship and constrained democracy from the 1970s through the early 2000s. Its study complements the fine scholarly analyses that have given more attention to the facts of force and imposition than to the making of subjectivity and legitimacy within an era of force. Indeed, the lens of memory struggle invites us to move beyond rigid conceptual dichotomy between a top-down perspective oriented to elite engineering, and a bottom-up perspective that sees its obverse: suppression, punctuated by outbursts of protest. In this scheme, the moments of protest render visible the frustration, desperation, organizing, and resilience that often have an underground or marginalized aspect in conditions of repressive dictatorship or constrained democracy.

Tracing the history of memory struggles invites us to consider not only the genuine gap and tensions between top-down and bottom-up perspectives but also more subtle interactive dynamics within a history of violence and repression. We see efforts of persuasion from above to shore up or expand a social base from below, not simply to solidify support and concentrate power from above; grassroots efforts to seek influence among, split off, or pressure the elites of state, church, and political parties, not simply to organize networks, influence, and protest among subaltern groups and underdogs; specific collaborations in media, human rights, cultural, or political projects that yield both tension and synergy among actors in distinct "locations" in the social hierarchy, from respectable or powerful niches in state, church, and professional institutions, to precarious or stigmatized standing as street activists, victim-survivors, the poor and unemployed, and alleged subversives. Memory projects—to record and define the reality of the Allende era and its culminating crisis of 1973, to record and define the reality of military rule and its human rights drama—ended up becoming central to the logic by which people sought and won legitimacy in a politically divided and socially heterogeneous society that experienced a great turn and trauma.[2]

The repression in Pinochet's Chile was large in scale and layered in its implementation. In a country of only 10 million people in 1973, individually proved cases of death or disappearance by state agents (or persons in their hire) amount to about 3,000; torture victims run in the dozens of thousands; documented political arrests exceed 82,000; the exile flow amounts to about 200,000. These are lower-end figures, suitable for a rock-bottom baseline. Even using a conservative methodology, a reasonable estimated toll for deaths and disappearances by state agents is 3,500–4,500, for political detentions 150,000–200,000. Some credible torture estimates surpass the 100,000 threshold; some credible exile estimates reach 400,000.[3]

The experience of a state turning violently against a portion of its own citizenry is always dramatic. In a society of Chile's size, these figures translate into pervasiveness. A majority of families, including supporters and sympathizers of the military regime, had a relative, a friend, or an acquaintance touched by one or another form of repression. Just as important, from political and cultural points of view, Pinochet's Chile pioneered a new technique of repression in the Latin American context: systematic "disappearance" of people. After the point of abduction, people vanished in a cloud of secrecy, denial, and misinformation by the state. Also important was cultural shock. Many Chileans believed such violence by the state—beyond margins set by legal procedure and human decency—to be an impossibility. Fundamentally, their society was too civilized, too law abiding, too democratic. In 1973, many victims voluntarily turned themselves in when they appeared on arrest lists.[4]

The Chilean story of memory struggle over the meanings and truths of a violent collective shock is part of a larger story of "dirty war" dictatorships in South America. During the 1960s and 1970s, at the height of the Cold War, ideas of social justice and revolution sparked significant sympathy and social mobilization. Urban shantytowns were populated by poor laborers, street sellers, and migrants in search of a better life. Many rural regions evinced systems of land tenure, technology, and social abuse that seemed anachronistic as well as violent and unjust. Educated youths and progressive middle-class sectors saw in the young Cuban revolution either an inspiring example or a wake-up call that argued for deep reforms. Presidents of influential countries such as Brazil and Chile announced agrarian reform —an idea whose political time had finally arrived. On the fringes of established politics, some middle-class youths began to form guerrilla groups, hoping to produce a revolution through sheer audacity.

Not surprisingly, proponents of deep change—whether they considered themselves "reformers" or "revolutionaries"—ran up against entrenched opposition, fear, and polarization. The obvious antagonists included the socially privileged under the status quo, that is, wealthy families and social circles under fire in the new age of reform, middle-class sectors who either identified with conservative social values or were frightened by possible upheaval, and notable landowning families and their local intermediaries in rural regions facing agrarian reform. There were unexpected antagonists, too, including persons of modest means and backgrounds. Some poor and lower middle-class residents of urban shantytowns, for example, proved nervous and interested in order as they saw polarization unfold, were dubious about the viability of grand reforms, or had aligned themselves on one side or another of the political squabbles among competing reformers and revolutionaries.[5]

Most important for the political and cultural future, however, the antagonists included militaries whose doctrines of national security, consistent with the ideology of the Cold War, came to define the internal enemy as the fundamental enemy of the nation. In this line of thinking, the whole way of understanding politics that had arisen in Latin America was a cancerous evil. The problem went beyond that of achieving transitory relief by toppling a government if it went too far in threatening the military forces' institutional cohesion or interests, or if it went too far in upsetting the status quo, mobilizing the downtrodden, tolerating self-styled revolutionaries or guerrillas, or sparking economic crisis or social disorder. The "political class" of elites who worked the body politic had become addicted to demagoguery, and civil society included too many people addicted to the idea of organizing politically to end injustice. The result was fertile ground for the spread of Marxism and subversion that would destroy society from within.

As military regimes displaced civilian ones, they defined a mission more ambitious than transitory relief from an untenable administration. They would create a new order. The new military regimes would conduct a "dirty war" to root out subversives and their sympathizers once and for all, to frighten and depoliticize society at large, to lay the foundation for a technocratic public life. To a greater or lesser degree, such regimes spread over much of South America—Brazil in 1964 (with notable "hardening" in 1968), Bolivia in 1971, Chile and Uruguay in 1973, and Argentina in 1976. Paraguay, ruled by General Alfredo Stroessner since 1954, followed a distinct political dynamic but aligned itself with the transnational aspect of the new scheme—"Operation Condor," a program of secret police cooperation across South American borders. To a greater or lesser degree, all these regimes also generated contentious struggles over "memory"—truth, justice, meaning.[6]

The Chilean version of struggles over collective memory is worth telling in its own right. It is a dramatic story, filled with heroism and disappointment on matters of life and death. It is a story of moral consciousness, as human beings attempted to understand and to convince compatriots of the meaning of a great and unfinished trauma and its ethical and political implications. It is a story that lends itself to serious historical research, because it has unfolded over a long stretch of time, because survivors and witnesses are still alive, and because it generated substantial and diverse documentary trails. Indeed, this trilogy draws on three streams of sources: written documents—archival, published, and, more recently, electronic—that constitute the traditional heart of historical research; audio and visual traces of the past, in television and video archives, photojournalism, radio transcripts, and sound recordings; and oral history, including formal semi-structured interviews, less formal interviews and exchanges, and field notes from participant-observation experiences and focus groups. The "Essay on Sources" offers a more technical guide to these sources, as well as a reflection on oral history method and debates.

The Chilean version of the memory question is also worth telling because of its international significance. For better or worse, the long and narrow strip of western South America we call Chile has constituted an influential symbol in world culture in the last half century. As the model "Alliance for Progress" country of the 1960s, it constituted the Kennedy and Johnson administrations' best example of a Latin American society that could stop "another Cuba" through democratic social reforms assisted by the United States. When Salvador Allende was elected president in 1970, his project—an electoral road to socialism and justice in a Third World society—exerted almost irresistible symbolism. The blending of a Western-style electoral political culture with socialist idealism and economic policies had obvious resonance in Western Europe and its labor-oriented parties, and it provoked extreme hostility from the Nixon administration. The David-versus-Goliath aspect of relations between Chile and the United States proved compelling across the conventional fault lines of international politics. Allende's Chile drew sympathetic attention not only among radicals, social democrats, and solidarity-minded activists in the West but also in the Soviet bloc countries and in the "Non-aligned Movement" then influential in the Third World and the United Nations. Chile, a small country determined to achieve social justice by democratic means, against odds set by a monstrous power spreading death and destruction in Vietnam, stood as the beleaguered yet proud symbol of a wider yearning.

After 1973, Chile continued to occupy a large symbolic place in world culture. For critics and admirers alike the new regime became a kind of laboratory, an example of early neoliberalism in Latin America and its power to transform economic life. Most of all and most controversially, Pinochet and the Chile he created became icons of the "dirty war" dictatorships spreading over South America. For many, Pinochet was also the icon of U.S. government (or Nixon-Kissinger) complicity with evil in the name of anti-Communism.

In short, the symbolic power of Augusto Pinochet's Chile crossed national borders. For the world human rights movement, as Kathryn Sikkink has shown, Chile's 1973 crisis and violence constituted a turning point. It marked a "before" and "after" by galvanizing new memberships in human rights organizations such as Amnesty International; by sparking new organizations, such as Washington Office on Latin America; by spreading "human rights" as an international vocabulary and common sense—a public concern voiced in transnational networks from the United Nations, to churches and nongovernmental organizations including solidarity groups, to influential media and political leaders including the U.S. Congress. The symbolism of Pinochet and Chile's 1973 crisis proved more than a short-lived blip. For many (including baby boomers in Europe and the United States, who became politically and culturally influential in the 1990s) it had been a defining moment of moral growth and awareness. The symbolism was reactivated in October 1998, when London police detained Pinochet by request of a Spanish judge investigating crimes against humanity. It has been reinforced by the precedent set by his arrest for international human rights law.[7]

What has given memory of Chile's 1973 crisis and the violence it unleashed such compelling value? As a story in its own right, and as a symbol beyond its borders? The answers are many, and they include the value of work undertaken by many Chileans in exile—to mobilize international solidarity, to work professionally on themes of human rights, to build circuits of political dialogue, with Europeans and North Americans as well as among themselves, about the meaning of the Chilean experience. Among many valid reasons, however, one cuts to the core. Chile is Latin America's example of the "German problem." The Holocaust and the Nazi experience bequeathed to contemporary culture a profoundly troubling question. How does a country capable of amazing achievement in the realm of science or culture also turn out to harbor amazing capacity for barbarism? Can one reconcile—or better, disentangle—the Germany that produced and appreciated Beethoven and Wagner from the Germany that produced and appreciated Hitler and Goebbels?

In the case of Latin America, tragic historical patterns and international cultural prejudices may incline the foreign citizen-observer to view violent repression and the overthrow of elected civilian governments as in some way "expected"—part of Latin America's "normal" course of history. After all, Latin America has not been notable for the resilience of democratic institutions, nor for hesitation about using strong-arm methods of political rule.

In the case of Chile, however, both Chileans and outsiders believed in a myth of exceptionalism. Chile was, like other Latin American societies, afflicted by great social needs and great social conflicts. But it was also a land of political and cultural sophistication. Its poets (Gabriela Mistral, Pablo Neruda) won Nobel Prizes. Its Marxist and non-Marxist leaders were veterans of a parliamentary tradition resonant with Western Europe. Its intellectuals worked out respected new approaches to international economics with the United Nations Economic Commission on Latin America. Its soldiers understood not to intervene in the political arrangements of civilians. In Chile, social mobilization and turbulence could be reconciled with the rule of law and competitive elections. The political system was democratic and resilient. Over time it had incorporated once-marginalized social sectors—the urban middle class, workers, women, peasants, and the urban poor. Its leaders and polemicists knew how to retreat into the conserving world of gentlemen politicians, where cultural refinement could be appreciated, a drink or a joke could be shared, the heat of verbal excess and battle pushed aside for another day. In this clublike atmosphere, personal confidences were reestablished to navigate the next round of conflict and negotiation. Compared to other Latin American countries, military intervention was rare and had not happened since the early 1930s. Chile's "amazing achievement," in the Latin American context, was precisely its resilient democratic constitutionalism.

Not only did the myth of democratic resilience finally break apart under the stresses of the 1960s and early 1970s. The country also descended into a world of brutality beyond the imaginable, at least not in a Chilean urban or middle-class context. The assumed core of Chile, civilized and democratic and incapable of trampling law or basic human decency, would not resurface for a very long time. What happened after the military takeover of 11 September 1973 was more shocking than the takeover itself.[8]

Beyond the argument that a history of memory offers insight into the "hearts and minds" drama, still present and unfinished, of Pinochet's Chile, a brief statement of how I specifically approach memory—what I am arguing against, what I am arguing for—may be useful. Two influential ideas hover over discussions of memory in Chile. The first invokes the dichotomy of memory against forgetting (*olvido*). In essence, memory struggles are struggles against oblivion. This dichotomy, of course, is pervasive in many studies of collective memory in many parts of the world and not without reason. The dialectic of memory versus forgetting is an inescapable dynamic, perceived as such by social actors in the heat of their struggles. In regimes of secrecy and misinformation, the sense of fighting oblivion, especially in the human rights community, is powerful and legitimate. In recent years, influential criticism of the postdictatorship society of the 1990s has invoked the dichotomy of remembering against forgetting to characterize Chile as a culture of oblivion, marked by a tremendous compulsion to forget the past and the uncomfortable. A second influential idea, related to the first, is that of the Faustian bargain. In this idea, amnesia occurs because the middle classes and the wealthy, as beneficiaries of economic prosperity created by the military regime, developed the habit of denial or looking the other way on matters of state violence. They accept moral complacency as the price of economic comfort—the Faustian bargain that seals "forgetting."[9]

The interpretation in this trilogy argues against these ideas. The dissent is partial; I do not wish to throw out the baby with the bathwater. At various points in the analysis, I too invoke the dialectic of memory versus forgetting and attend to the influence of economic well-being in political and cultural inclination to forget. The problem with the memory-against-forgetting dichotomy, and the related idea of a Faustian bargain, is not that they are "wrong" or "untrue" in the simple sense. It is that they are insufficient— profoundly incomplete and in some ways misleading.

What I am arguing *for* is a study of contentious memory as a process of competing selective remembrances, ways of giving meaning to and drawing legitimacy from human experience. The memory-against-forgetting dichotomy is too narrow and restrictive; it tends to align one set of actors with memory and another with forgetting. In the approach I have taken, the social actors behind distinct frameworks are seeking to define that which is truthful and meaningful about a great collective trauma. They are necessarily selective as they give shape to memory, and they may all see themselves as struggling, at one point or another, against the oblivion propagated by their antagonists.

Historicizing memory in this way blurs an old conceptual distinction, given a new twist by the distinguished memory scholar Pierre Nora, between "history" as a profession or science purporting to preserve or recon-struct the unremembered or poorly remembered past; and "memory" as a subjective, often emotionally charged and flawed, awareness of a still-present past that emerges within a community environment of identity and experience. Insofar as the historian must take up memory struggles and frameworks as a theme for investigation in its own right—as a set of rela-tionships, conflicts, motivations, and ideas that *shaped* history—the distinc-tion begins to break down. The point of oral history research becomes not only to establish the factual truth or falsehood of events in a memory story told by an informant but also to understand what social truths or processes led people to tell their stories the way they do, in recognizable patterns. When examining the history of violent "limit experiences," moreover, the historian cannot escape the vexing problems of representation, interpreta-tion, and "capacity to know" that attach to great atrocities. Conventional narrative strategies and analytical languages seem inadequate; professional history itself seems inadequate—one more "memory story" among others.[10]

The metaphor I find useful—to picture memory as competing selective remembrances to give meaning to, and find legitimacy within, a devastating community experience—is that of a giant, collectively built memory box. The memory chest is foundational to the community, not marginal; it sits in the living room, not in the attic. It contains several competing scripted albums, each of them works in progress that seek to define and give shape to a crucial turning point in life, much as a family album may script a wedding or a birth, an illness or a death, a crisis or a success. The box also contains "lore" and loose memories, that is, the stray photos and mini-albums that seem important to remember but do not necessarily fit easily in the larger scripts. The memory chest is a precious box to which people are drawn, to which they add or rearrange pictures and scripts, and about which they quarrel and even scuffle. This trilogy asks how Chileans built and struggled over the "memory box of Pinochet's Chile," understood as the holder of truths about a traumatic turning point in their collective lives.

When considering the consequences of such memory struggles for poli-tics, culture, and democratization, I argue that Chile arrived at a culture of "memory impasse," more complex than a culture of oblivion, by the mid-to-late 1990s. The idea of a culture of forgetting, facilitated by Faustian com-placency, is useful up to a point, but it simplifies the Chilean path of mem-ory struggles and distorts the cultural dynamics in play. The problem turned out to be more subtle and in some ways more horrifying. On the one hand, forgetting itself included a conscious component—political and cultural decisions to "close the memory box," whether to save the political skin of those implicated by "dirty" memory, or in frustration because memory politics proved so intractable and debilitating. It is this conscious component of "remembering to forget" that is often invoked when human rights activists cite a famous phrase by Mario Benedetti, "oblivion is filled with memory." On the other hand, memory of horror and rupture also proved so unforgettable or "obstinate," and so important to the social actors and politics of partial redemocratization in the 1990s, that it could not really be buried in oblivion.[11]

What emerged instead was impasse. Cultural belief by a majority in the truth of cruel human rupture and persecution under dictatorship, and in the moral urgency of justice, unfolded alongside political belief that Pinochet, the military, and their social base of supporters and sympathizers remained too strong for Chile to take logical "next steps" along the road of truth and justice. The result was not so much a culture of forgetting, as a culture that oscillated—as if caught in moral schizophrenia—between prudence and convulsion. To an extent, this was a "moving impasse." Specific points of friction in the politics of truth, justice, and memory changed; the immobilizing balance of power did not simply remain frozen. But travel to logical "next steps" in memory work proved exceedingly slow and arduous, and the process often turned back, as in a circle, to reencounter with impasse between majority desire and minority power.

As we shall see in Book Three, the structure of impasse unraveled substantially after 1998. It remains, however, an open question—a possible focal point of future struggles—whether reinvigorated impasse or marginalization of the memory question will prove debilitating and decisive in the future. If so, new generations in the twenty-first century may well come of age in a culture of oblivion, and have trouble understanding why the memory question was a fire that burned so powerfully between the 1970s and early 2000s.

A brief guide to organization may prove useful. I have designed the trilogy to function at two levels. On the one hand, the trio may be viewed as an integrated three-volume work. The books unfold in a sequence that builds a cumulative, multifaceted history of—and argument about—the Pinochet era, the memory struggles it unleashed, and its legacy for Chilean democracy since 1990. On the other hand, each volume stands on its own and has a distinct focus and purpose. Each has its own short introduction (which incorporates in schematic form any indispensable background from preceding volumes) and its own conclusions. Each reproduces, as a courtesy to readers of any one book who wish to understand its place within the larger project and its premises, this General Introduction and the Essay on Sources.

Book One, *Remembering Pinochet's Chile: On the Eve of London 1998*, is a short introductory volume written especially for general readers and students. It uses select human stories to present key themes and memory frameworks, historical background crossing the 1973 divide, and conceptual tools helpful for analyzing memory as a historical process. Its main purpose, however, is to put human faces on the major frameworks of memory—including those friendly to military rule—that came to be influential in Chile, while also providing a feel for memory lore and experiences silenced or marginalized by such frameworks. The "ethnographic present" of the book, the most "literary" and experimental of the three, is the profoundly divided Chile of 1996–97, when memory impasse seemed both powerful and insuperable. Pinochet's 1998 London arrest, the partial unraveling of memory impasse and immunity from justice in 1998–2001—these would have seemed fantasies beyond the realm of the possible.

Subsequent volumes undertake the historical analysis proper of memory struggles as they unfolded in time. Book Two, *Battling for Hearts and Minds: Memory Struggles in Pinochet's Chile, 1973–1988*, traces the memory drama under dictatorship. It shows how official and counterofficial memory frameworks emerged in the 1970s, and expressed not only raw power but also brave moral struggle—remarkable precisely because power was so concentrated—centered on the question of human rights. It proceeds to show how dissident memory, at first the realm of beleaguered "voices in the wilderness," turned into mass experience and symbols that energized protest in the 1980s and set the stage for Pinochet's defeat in a plebiscite to ratify his rule in October 1988.

Pinochet's 1988 defeat did not lead to a one-sided redrawing of power but rather to a volatile transitional environment—tense blends of desire, initiative, constraint, and imposition. The most explosive fuel in this combustible mix was precisely the politics of memory, truth, and justice. Book Three, *Reckoning with Pinochet: The Memory Question in Democratic Chile, 1989–2006*, explores the memory-related initiatives and retreats, the tensions and saber rattling, the impasse of power versus desire, that shaped the new democracy and its coming to terms with "Pinochet's Chile." For readers of the entire trilogy, Book Three completes the circle by bringing us back to the point of frustrating impasse, now traced as historical process, that served as an "ethnographic present" in Book One. But Book Three also spirals out from there—by taking us into the realm of accelerated and unexpected unravelings of impasse and taboo after 1998, and into historical conclusions about memory and the times of radical evil that are, paradoxically, both hopeful and sobering.

An unusual feature of these books' organization of chapters requires comment. Each main chapter of a book is followed by an Afterword, intended as a complement that enriches, extends, or unsettles the analysis in the main chapter. At the extreme, an "unsettling" Afterword questions—draws limits on the validity of—a main chapter. Each book's numbering system links main chapters and corresponding Afterwords explicitly (the chapter sequence is *not* 1, 2, 3 ... but rather 1, Afterword, 2, Afterword, 3, Afterword ...). In an age of Internet reading, such lateral links may not seem unfamiliar. But my purpose here has little to do with the Internet or postmodern tastes. On the one hand, I have searched for an aesthetic—moving forward in the argument while taking some glances back—that seems well suited to the theme of memory. On the other hand, the Afterword method also draws out useful substantive points. At some stages, it sharpens awareness of contradiction and fissure by creating counterpoint—for example, between a lens focused on changes in the adult world of memory politics and culture, and one trained on the memory world of youth.

Above all, I am aware that in books about remembrance, which pervades human consciousness and belongs to everyone, something important is lost in the analytical selectivity that necessarily governs chapters about main national patterns or trends. The Afterwords allow the revealing offbeat story, rumor, or joke that circulates underground; the incident or bit of memory folklore that is pertinent yet poor of fit with a grander scheme; the provincial setting overwhelmed by a national story centered in Santiago, to step to the fore and influence overall texture and interpretation more forcefully. They are a way of saying that in cultures of repression and impasse, it is the apparently marginal or insignificant that sometimes captures the deeper meaning of a shocking experience.

A history of memory struggles is a quest, always exploratory and unfinished, to understand the subjectivity of a society over time. At bottom, this trilogy is a quest to find *Chile profundo*—or better, the various Chiles profundos—that experienced a searing and violent upheaval. Sometimes we find "deep Chile" in a chapter about the nation's main story. Sometimes, Chile profundo exists at the edges of the main story.

Introduction to
Book Three

※

Reckoning with Pinochet

Between 1989 and 2006, Chileans reckoned with the legacy of state terror and atrocity while setting out on an uncertain journey of democratic transition, repair, and rebuilding. General Augusto Pinochet had lost a plebiscite, in October 1988, originally meant to ratify his continuing rule, but the building of a democracy would take place under conditions of constraint. The interim of pretransition jockeying to chart the future was substantial. A civilian president would not even be inaugurated—in other words, the military government's legislative and administrative powers would not formally close—until March 1990. Under the rules of transition, moreover, Pinochet held the right to continue as army commander in chief until March 1998, and the civilian president did not have the legal right to dismiss him. The social climate and structure of power in the immediate postplebiscite period created a democratic opening, not a fast track to vigorous democracy.

The most contentious issue was the memory question. How to record and remember the crisis that yielded a military coup on 11 September 1973, how to record and remember the reality and violence of military rule, how to reckon with the legacy of atrocity—to build social repair and peace, to respond to hungers for truth and justice and prevention—and how to do all this without throwing a fragile democracy into a death spiral of conflicts leading to economic and political failure, these divisive yet inescapable issues constituted a strategic challenge, politically and morally. To address them successfully might establish moral contrast and legitimacy for the new democracy, and perhaps the resilience to wear down constraints and promote a culture of human rights. To evade them or address them in a manner that set up failure, on the other hand, would poison democratic legitimacy and staying power. If a sense of continuity with the might-is-right culture of dictatorship triumphed, or if political and economic failure induced nostalgia for authoritarian order, hopes for truth and justice after atrocity, let alone a culture of human rights and prevention, would also crash.

In many ways, the memory question confronting democratic Chileans was personalized in the figure of Pinochet. He had headed the military government continuously since 1973. He had turned into an icon of dirty war and attendant memory struggles, both inside Chile and internationally. During the transition, he carried on as army commander and ultimate guardian of the military regime's legacy, including its commitment to shield soldiers from criminal trial for human rights violations. The reckoning with memory after 1988—the subject of this book—was also a reckoning with Pinochet.

Three dramas unfolded, and this book attends to each of them. The first was loud and obvious—memory clashes over human rights that included heated public debates, scandalous events in media and courtrooms and streets, military saber rattling, and tough standoffs. In a society of divided memory, the structure of impasse on truth-and-justice issues seemed to emerge repeatedly—as conflict between majority sentiment and outsized minority power, as tension between the "soft" power of civilians and the "hard" power of soldiers, as juxtaposition of the desire for justice and the impossibility of achieving it, as culture of avoidance prompted by the intractability of memory issues, as performance by one or another memory camp, whether to reimpose standoff backed by de facto power when earlier constraints seemed to soften, or to reassert moral urgency when de facto power seemed to push human rights into a marginal corner. These dynamics produced a theater of frustration, as well as hard-won limited achievements, in the battle over memory and human rights in the 1990s.

The second drama was more interior and subtle. Given the structure of power and desire that bred impasse and frustration, the additional debilitating effects of revisiting memories of horror, and the climate of social demobilization and elite political engineering that attended the transition and was at first reinforced by fears of instability, what also unfolded were deeply human stories of ambivalence about the memory question. These were smaller, sometimes intimate dramas: the personal weariness of the victim-activist or activist, followed by a return to insistence; the frictional synergies among state and civil society partners united in a particular truth-telling project, but divided by distinct logics of politicocultural action; the retreat of political elites into indifference or complacency, interrupted by an event that reawakened moral appeal and pressure; the swings people lived between the imperative of prudence and the urgency of memory. Such experiences ended up crisscrossing with the louder politicocultural dramas, and also drove the refusal to accept closure that kept the memory question alive. When political elites retreated from the memory question, or when the overall tone of cultural life suggested the time had come to leave the past behind, the retreat and indifference proved illusory. Even if the burden of initiative shifted to civil society, there were social actors in the wings who regathered their efforts, responded to or created scandalous events, and pushed to reawaken in others the urgency they might have preferred to leave behind. The importance of these smaller dramas and their impact on the public culture became increasingly evident in the late 1990s and early 2000s, when larger events—including Pinochet's retirement as army commander and his arrest in London, both in 1998—opened up more cultural space to insist on new memory initiatives.

The third drama was that of cumulative achievement against the odds. When considering the 1989–2006 period as a whole, a certain paradox comes into view. In the heat of the memory struggle at a given moment, what proved apparent to human rights activists and sympathizers was sharp constraint—the deep insufficiency of any advance on truth or justice issues, and the impulse of many political elites, including those aligned with the human rights camp, to convert particular achievements into a formula for closure. In the perspective of time, however, the snapshot sensation was misleading. A given advance on truth or justice turned out not to be the end of the story, but a wedge to crack apart resistance or impunity, to galvanize a new cultural effort, to set a new legal or political precedent, to lay groundwork for a demand to address that which had been excluded in the earlier step. The sensation of slow progress in the moment or, even worse, of getting "stuck" in the impasse of the moment was based in a hard reality, but coexisted with determination and eventual capacity to build cumulatively in the medium run. Put another way, former perpetrators of atrocity had good reason to fear—and resist fiercely—the phenomenon of the "slippery slope."

A central goal of this book, therefore, is to understand the combined experience and effect of these dramas: the tensions, consequences, and paradox of living in a world of slowly "rolling" impasse on memory matters. From a human rights perspective, hard-won limited achievements happened and might provide building blocks for future gains, but they entangled with dynamics of blockage and frustration that also proved strong and rendered the future uncertain, even bleak. From a historical perspective, the resilient structure of power produced standoffs unfriendly to human rights, yet proved unable to block a shifting center of gravity—the redefining of the specific issue in contention, and with it the boundaries of truth-and-justice politics and containment. Eventually, the combined dynamics of blockage and movement set the stage for an unraveling of impasse itself.

How did such a paradoxical process happen? What social actors or forces pushed it along and kept memory reckoning alive for another day, for the moment of shift in the balance of power and possibility? Although this book does not dwell on theory or method as such, its working method is to trace the formation and social impact of "memory knots"—that is, the specific human groups and leaders, the specific events in time including anniversaries and commemorations, and the specific physical remains or places that *demanded* attention to memory. Elsewhere (in Book One of this trilogy), I have provided a theoretical discussion of the role of specific sites of humanity, time, and space as "memory knots on the social body" that unsettle the complacency or "unthinking habits" of everyday life, and stir up polemics about memory in the public imagination.[1] Informed by that theoretical approach, this book focuses on social actors and human networks seeking to find and shape meanings of the traumatic past-within-the-present, that is, to push the memory-truths they considered urgent into the public domain. It focuses too on the role of "unforgettable" times and places—a calendar of sacred events (some predictable and some unpredictable) and anniversary commemorations on the one hand, a geography of sacred remains, sites, and material symbols on the other. These compelling knots in time and space galvanized appeals for moral or political awareness, drew people into identifying with one or another framework of memory-truth, and inspired some to join the social actors who "performed" memory work and identification in public spaces.

The memory question was strategic precisely because it had turned into the key battleground for politicocultural legitimacy under the dictatorship. To understand the reckoning of the 1990s and beyond—its inexorability and difficulties, what was achieved and not achieved—it is helpful to review briefly the earlier history, and how it culminated in distinct memory camps with distinct power bases at the point of transition. During the dictatorship years, Chileans built four contending memory frameworks whose influence would endure into the 1990s. (These frameworks are traced historically, with attention to shifts of nuance and social reach between 1973 and 1988, in Book Two of this trilogy, and are presented ethnographically, within a 1990s life history context, in Book One. These volumes provide the basis for the summary descriptions below.) Partisans of junta rule remembered military intervention in 1973 as the salvation of a society in ruins and on the edge of a violent bloodbath. This was the official framework favored by the military regime. Already in the 1970s, victims, critics, human rights activists, and persons of conscience built up counterofficial frameworks—while struggling against fear, repression, and misinformation—to document the brutal new reality of life under military rule. Relatives of those who vanished remembered military rule as an astonishingly cruel and unending rupture of life—an open wound that cannot heal—through massive executions and "disappearances" of people after abduction by state agents. Cruelty and torment were compounded by the state's continuous denial of knowledge or responsibility. A third and closely related framework remembered the past-within-the-present as an experience of persecution and awakening. Solidarity and religious activists who supported victims and their families and who pushed human rights concerns into the public domain bore witness to the junta's multifaceted and layered repression—not only deaths and disappearances but also torture, imprisonment, exile, employment purges, and intimidation, organized by a secret-police state and accompanied by a general dismantling of socioeconomic rights and organizing rights. This memory camp also bore witness to the repression's antithesis: the moral awakening of conscience.

As controversy over memory and human rights sharpened and coincided with other causes of political split and crisis in the late 1970s, regime leaders and supporters developed a fourth framework—memory as mindful forgetting, a closing of the box on the times of "dirty" war and excess that were now thankfully superseded, even as they had laid a foundation for future progress. It would do no good to society to revisit the wounds and excesses of those times.

These four memory frameworks—memory as salvation, as cruel rupture, as persecution and awakening, as a closed box—did not arise all at once or smoothly. Nor did their meanings, justifications, and implications remain flatly uniform over time. People forged them in a process of trial and error and struggle, in an era at once traumatic and frightening and confusing, in the 1970s. It was only by the late 1970s and early 1980s, and as a consequence of such struggles, that the idea of "memory" itself crystallized into a major cultural code word in its own right.

By then, what proved increasingly clear to a wide range of social actors was the strategic role of remembrance in politicocultural legitimacy. How to record and remember the crisis of 1973, and the violence and reality of military rule, had shaped the "battle for hearts and minds" since the coup. Indeed, a memory battle over the denouement had already begun in the final crisis months of democracy. The strategic aspect grew even more obvious in the 1980s, when the politics of memory ended up merging with tumultuous mass struggles for control that rocked the regime. Dissident memory voices of the 1970s, although they included morally influential people and received important backing by high Catholic Church officials, were in a sense "voices in the wilderness." The military regime managed to control most of the public domain most of the time, that is, to weather crises and come out stronger. By 1980–81, it seemed resilient and hegemonic—to have institutionalized itself successfully, despite earlier moments of crisis sparked in part by memory struggles related to human rights. In the 1980s, however, struggles for control broke apart earlier boundaries of containment and turned into mass experience—through repeated street protests and rallies despite fierce repression, through media muckraking that broke taboos and self-censorship, and through explicit revival of politics despite official suspension of politics. One result was that dissident memory focusing on the reality of human rights atrocities underwent rapid and turbulent expansion, and fed into wider struggles to defeat the regime. Memory of military rule as a story of rupture, persecution, and awakening turned into a kind of common sense, acquiring new layers of meaning and symbolism. The idea that memory mattered—that it brought forth fundamental issues of truth, justice, and morality—also turned into a cultural common sense.

The process of memory making—the turning of the dissident memory camp into society's majority memory camp—unfolded not smoothly, but in relation to fierce contests for control and in the face of state suppression and violence. Nor were memory struggles free of divisive internal dynamics within one or another memory camp. Nonetheless, the turbulent process of mass memory struggle *did* create a majority common sense, and set the stage for a plebiscite vote (55 percent "No" vs. 43 percent "Yes") that backfired against the regime.

The memory struggles of the 1980s yielded a deep structural strain at the outset of transition, in 1989–90, and beyond. All the major memory frameworks continued evoking strong and even passionate adherents. In combination, they played out as a stubborn and explosive cultural tension. The reality of majority sentiment clashed with the reality of minority power, yielding not only opposed memory camps but also gray zones of ambivalence and uncertainty. On the one hand, Pinochet had lost cultural control of the public domain and lost the instruments of "soft" political control. He had lost the hearts and minds of the Chilean majority, which had come to see in military rule a deeply troubling narrative of human rights violations—memory as wounding ruptures of life, memory as persecutions whose witness also inspires an awakening into new values. Some sort of reckoning with atrocity was morally necessary and urgent. The majority social base included significant middle-class sectors, as well as workers and urban poor. On the other hand, Pinochet had not lost the instruments of "hard" political control. He retained a substantial minority social base that included strategic social sectors—the investor class and a cohesive army under his command. That base was deeply loyal, in part because it remembered military rule as salvation of a country in ruins. For some, loyalty also meant counting on Pinochet to continue enforcing legal amnesty, that is, closure of the memory box of "dirty war" events that could produce cultural humiliation and legal risk through charges of human rights violations.

In sum, the memory question, particularly its intersections with culture and power dynamics, produced a tough double reality at the outset of transition. It undermined Pinochet and the regime, thereby making a reckoning unavoidable. It built powerful social loyalties to Pinochet and the regime, thereby making a reckoning dangerous. Small wonder that the memory question soon produced a third reality: ambivalence, even among persons aligned with the human rights memory camp.

Four features of this book require special comment: the role of top-down and bottom-up social actors, and the related emphasis on synergistic social dynamics; the irony of the memory-reckoning story, given the rise of privatized cultural sensibilities; the transnational dimension, brought to the fore analytically in the conclusion; and the ambiguity of the title's reference to "democratic Chile."

Like its predecessor volumes in the trilogy, this book adopts an integrative approach to top-down and bottom-up social dynamics, and their mediations.[2] It does so in a manner adapted to the specific historical conditions that shaped the democratic transition. The social climate and power dynamics of early transition favored top-down engineering by political elites seeking to achieve accords and steer a fragile course, not bottom-up social movement organizing oriented toward massive street mobilization in support of or resistant to social projects, political parties, or governments. At a deeper level, older models of social movement mobilization, influential in the competitive multiparty democracy of pre-1973 Chile, and in a distinct way during the culture of protest against dictatorship in the 1980s, proved somewhat obsolete or ineffectual in the 1990s. As we shall see in this book, this situation did not imply a pure absence of street protests, especially on the 11 September anniversaries, nor did it imply an absence of direct action events such as hunger strikes, assassinations, and noisy "outings" of torturers. Such events continued to matter. Also, mass mobilization and direct action events eventually returned to a more prominent role in politicocultural life, especially toward the end of the period under consideration.

What the circumstances of transition *did* do, however, was foster distinct dynamics of exerting bottom-up moral and political pressure and of seeking effective political mediation within a constrained democracy. The premium placed on elite political engineering, the difficulty of articulating traditional social movement organizing to influential political parties and effective results, the governance of an elected Center-Left coalition whose legitimacy and social base rested on a human rights contrast with dictatorship, these factors closed some doors to grassroots organizing and influence while opening others. Put another way, the overall climate of demobilization did not mean that moral and political pushiness from below vanished. The relevant arena, however, shifted notably. Conflictive synergies between civil society actors and select state or political actors who worked on particular truth-telling or justice projects defined a sometimes subtle terrain of moral collaboration, protest, and pressure. The partners united to work on projects in common, to build or sustain politicocultural legitimacy, and to exert mutual influence within a collaboration needed by all. But their logics of politicocultural action, and visions of the ultimate goal, could also divide them and yield dynamics of tension and frustration. As we shall see, the importance of frictional synergy was already evident in the first major memory initiative of the transition—a truth commission established to document the reality of killings and disappearances under military rule.

To achieve a holistic account that attends to dynamics from the top down and bottom up, while also attending to the specific circumstances and mediations of democratic transition, this book adopts a double strategy: narrative and conceptual. In narrative terms, its early chapters play close attention to the top-down dynamics critical in setting the climate of the early 1990s, while leaving room for readers to "see" the more subtle synergistic dynamics —including their deterioration—and the moments of protest and direct action that unfolded within a climate of relative demobilization. As the book proceeds, the narrative balance between the space devoted to top-down versus bottom-up dynamics shifts and slowly gives more prominence to the latter, so that the book incorporates historical change "on the ground" into its aesthetic style, albeit without losing sight of top-down dynamics. Conceptually, the book builds a historicized analysis of frictional synergies among civil society and state actors aligned (at least ostensibly) with human rights memory—the ups and downs and limits of collaboration, the deteriorations that moved tension among partners from the "frictional" to the openly "conflictive," the exclusions and limitations that fed into sensibilities of frustration and disappointment, the shifting map of social actors as judges, youths, and prisoner-survivors took on distinct roles in the reckonings of the late 1990s and early 2000s. The conclusion builds on the narrative analysis to provide, as well, a more theorized reflection on conflictive synergy and its implications for memory struggles and transitional democracies.

The second of the four aspects that require comment is an irony that accompanies the memory-reckoning story recounted here and its connection to historicity. Precisely because memory struggle about times of atrocity cannot be disentangled from an account of wider political, economic, and cultural contexts—even as it offers a useful lens on them—this study attends to a cultural transformation that reframed the relation of society and the individual by the late 1990s. In a word, the privatization of culture grew more powerful and tipped the balance toward the individual as self-actualizing agent and consumer, away from the individual as citizen whose actualization occurs *through* relationships of mutual claims with state, society, and community. The transformation, which began before the 1990s, can be overstated through a reductionism that fails to see countervailing currents— not just the more extreme individualism but also creations of moral claim and community through family, religious or social associations, and civic issues such as environmentalism and human rights itself. A sense of limits and crosscurrents will emerge in the narrative. Nonetheless, the shift of cultural sensibilities about the individual-society relation was real, and it imparts an ironic underside evident by the second half of this book. Even as human rights memory gained cultural and ideological traction, the overall pull of "community responsibility" politics and values diminished, or at least rested on shifting cultural ground. The irony: advances on specific truth-and-justice objectives and in overall sensitization to human rights emerged within a wider cultural transformation that put the strategic weight of memory work at risk in the future.[3]

The historicity of memory also implies a conceptual irony. In tracing the making and consequences of memory frameworks and struggles, in this volume and previous trilogy volumes, I relied on two key theoretical tools. The first is the idea, mentioned earlier, that we can trace the making of influential memory frameworks and sensibilities by focusing on "memory knots" in society, time, and place. Strongly motivated human groups, symbolically powerful events and anniversary commemoration dates, haunting remains and places—these galvanize struggles to shape and project into the public cultural domain ways of remembering that capture an essential truth.

The other conceptual tool is the idea of "emblematic memory" and its unfolding interaction with the lore of "loose memory." Here the relation of historicity to theorization grows more complicated. Elsewhere (in trilogy Book One), I have provided a fuller theoretical discussion of the selective and reciprocal interplay between emblematic memory, a socially influential framework of meaning drawn from experience; and loose memory, a realm of personal knowledge that can remain rather private—socially unanchored —unless people see in it a compelling wider meaning. Emblematic memory frameworks—memory as salvation, as cruel rupture, as persecution and awakening, as a closed box of dirty war—draw out the great truths of a traumatic social experience, while loose memory provides a rich lore of raw material, the authenticity of stories and symbols grounded in particular lives and useful for the making of emblematic memory. I have also observed the undersides of memory making and struggles: the emergence of *some* memory lore that circulates and seems to capture an important truth, yet escapes enclosure within major frameworks; and the ways the selective making of memory is simultaneously a making of "silence."[4]

This book applies that theoretical discussion, without dwelling on theory as such, but a certain irony also unfolds on a conceptual level. What makes a memory "emblematic" and thereby feeds into struggles over legitimacy? Memory is the meaning we attach to experience, not simply the recall of the events and emotions of experience. What makes a memory framework influential—what makes it resonate culturally—is precisely its emblematic aspect. Memory struggles about traumatic times that affected or mobilized large numbers of people create a symbolic process that blurs the line between the social and the personal—creating a two-way street of influence and testimony. When the cultural echo effect happens, the mysterious vanishing of "my" son is no longer a story of personal misfortune or accident that floats loosely, disconnected from a larger meaning. It is the story of Chile: the reality of a state terror that inflicted devastating rupture on thousands of families transformed into subhuman enemies. The question asked when I bear the photo of my son at a demonstration is phrased in the plural. Where are they? ¿Dónde están? My personal experience has acquired value as a cultural symbol or emblem, but conversely, what matters most when remembering my son is shaped by a wider social struggle about memory.

The privatization of culture and the heightened value placed on the self-actualizing individual, however, eventually weakened the force of such effects. The reciprocal dynamics of "emblematic" and "loose" memory making did not cease. They remained significant throughout the period under study, especially on human rights matters. But the cultural value of meta-narrative—and the conceit of the imagined national family—declined. Put more positively, the value of the fragment as a story in its own right, rather than testimonial symbol of the national reality, gained some ground.

The final two aspects—the transnational dimension, and the ambiguity of "democratic Chile"—require only brief comment. A rounded account of the Chilean memory-reckoning story requires attention to transnational as well as domestic dynamics. The London arrest of Pinochet in 1998 is only the most obvious example. The truth-and-justice drama of Chile also raises questions that spill outside the space-time boundaries of conventional case study analysis. In a world littered with postatrocity transitions, in South America and elsewhere, how did the Chilean case compare with others? In a Chile whose historical experience included earlier moments of rupture and violence, and whose memory struggles about the Pinochet dictatorship preceded democratic transition, what happens analytically if one sets this case study within a longer time perspective? Does the long view require a look at shifts in international culture—norms, practice, expectation, influence— that added up to a transnational regime of human rights? The narrative chapters of this book incorporate transnational aspects when relevant, but do not dwell on them as such. The principal focus is the Chilean reckoning. The conclusion, however, steps back to enlarge the space-time perspective.

It considers analytically the comparative perspective that cuts the discourse of Chilean exceptionalism down to size, without losing sight of the unique; the intersections of nation-state and transnational dynamics that illuminate what happened inside Chile, as well as its influence within an evolving world culture and regime of human rights; and the ways the long view recasts one's vision of the adversity, as well as achievements and limits, of democratic memory reckoning.

The reference to "democratic Chile" in the title is ambiguous, a wordplay by design. Does the phrase mean that soon into the transition Chile and its polity indeed turned into a democracy? Or does it refer to a subgroup, the democratically inclined sectors of a nation still struggling, with only partial success, to come out from under authoritarian dynamics, legacies, and institutions? On the one hand, I have avoided the temptation to create an asterisk effect by resorting consistently to an adjectival diminutive such as "constrained" or "weak" democracy (or by substituting a technical term such as "polyarchy") when describing the polity.[5] The main reason is not that such adjectives are inappropriate—they are part of the debate among Chilean critics and intellectuals themselves—but rather humility. Other "really existing" democracies fall short, and the democratic dynamics in the society of my own citizenship, the United States, arguably became notoriously weak during the same period. Under the circumstances, and given that I am a historian rather than a political scientist, I consider it less useful to create an asterisk effect—and perhaps fall into the trap of an accusatory exceptionalism—than to offer substantive analysis that makes clear the limitations of the Chilean version of "democracy." On the other hand, what matters most in the long run are the social actors—and their world of dreams, possibilities, conflicts, achievements, and failures. As we shall see, the memory question of democratic Chile involved and implicated everyone. But as we shall also see, the people who pushed for memory initiatives saw themselves as democratically minded actors seeking to overcome a confining, unjust, and still present legacy of the dictatorial past.

Chapter 1

✳

The Perils of Truth:
Opening the Memory Box, 1989–1990

Street sellers are a normal feature of life in Latin America's large cities. In downtown Santiago, book vendors spread their titles on the ground, wait politely for a pedestrian to pause and look, then speak and hope to make a sale. Late in 1989, the street culture of books turned loud. On the pedestrian mall streets Paseo Ahumada and Paseo Huérfanos, vendors kept shouting "Los zarpazos, Los zarpazos" to a public eager to find a new book. When the author of the book being sold, journalist Patricia Verdugo, walked downtown and heard the sellers, "I did not know if I had written a book or manufactured a cookie . . . every ten meters there was a seller." Vendors would bring piles of the book but sell out anyway.[1]

Published in September, *Los zarpazos del puma* (The Swipes of the Puma) caused a sensation. It reconstructed, through testimony by former military officers, the history of the "Caravan of Death" of October 1973. A team led by the army general Sergio Arellano Stark hopped by Puma helicopter from province to province, backed by an authorization document from General Pinochet as commander in chief and president of the Junta. The declared mission: to regularize military justice proceedings. The Arellano group set aside the army's normal chain of command and military justice procedures to achieve a rapid execution of political prisoners. In the cases studied by Verdugo—Cauquenes, La Serena, Copiapó, Antofagasta, Calama—the massacres claimed seventy-two victims, their bodies often mutilated by multiple gunshots and brutal hacking. Their imprisonment had been public knowledge. Most victims were local functionaries of Allende's Unidad Popular government or state enterprises, or they were elected officials. Many prisoners had actually turned themselves in. Lack of resistance had created an atmosphere of gentlemanly repression. Local army generals and colonels saw the rather orderly, tranquil transition in their provinces as an achievement, worthy of professional pride.

The Arellano visits shocked officers and soldiers by inventing a war. Appearances of social peace were deceptive. Commanders who organized a soft, rule-bound repression were incompetent or even dangerous. Chile had barely escaped a bloodbath conspiracy by the Left ("Plan Z") and now faced a war emergency. To prosecute the war, special officer teams from Santiago could override normal army jurisdiction and law. The cover stories that explained the sudden deaths or disappearances of prisoners mainly resorted to alleged escape attempts, a narrative consistent with the idea of an ongoing threat of war. Late in 1973 and early in 1974, such massacres served multiple purposes. They imposed a hardened war atmosphere on military officers and troops as well as civilians; they served notice of the superior power of secret police and intelligence groups; they spread fear and complicity and normlessness within the armed forces. They also consolidated Pinochet's personal power and his ability to marginalize potential army rivals—including Arellano, his hands dirtied by the mission. His Caravan of Death colleagues were part of the nascent DINA group loyal to Pinochet and Lieutenant Colonel Manuel Contreras, head of the DINA.[2]

(The DINA, Dirección de Inteligencia Nacional, or National Intelligence Directorate, was the original secret police organized under military rule in 1973–74. It was replaced by a new secret police organization known as the CNI, Centro Nacional de Informaciones, or National Center of Information, in 1977.)

The stunning victory of the "No" vote in the October 1988 plebiscite on continuation of rule by Pinochet, and the expected victory in December 1989 by Patricio Aylwin, the presidential candidate of the Center-Left Concertación coalition that had urged a No vote, created a new cultural environment. The time was arriving when the memory box of political violence by the state could no longer be kept closed, not even for constituencies of the Right or Center-Right. The new government would have to respond, somehow, to the history of human rights violations. As elections and the March 1990 transition to democratic government approached, hunger for truth about the hidden past—and anxiety about adjusting to the human rights revelations of a new political era—intensified.

Verdugo's book, compellingly written and superbly researched, connected to the hunger and anxiety of the cultural moment. Its revelation of an invented war waged with cold-blooded brutality against unarmed prisoners, and its testimony by retired military officers that Arellano's team violated professional and civilized norms of command and punishment, provided a "wake-up" to the memory-truth that Chileans now had to face. For persons inclined toward opposition to military rule or who saw themselves as democratic, to read *Los zarpazos* was to confront the depths of barbarism to which Chile had sunk—and to continue building bridges between personal experience and "emblematic" memory frameworks of rupture, persecution, and awakening built up during the struggles of the dictatorship years. Luz M., a middle-class youngster who slowly awakened to Chile's human rights drama as a university student in the 1980s, had witnessed the wounding and beating of various student protesters. In 1989, she began reading *Los zarpazos* and similar books with her mother. The books helped her connect personal witness and experience to a wider frame, the systematic and war-inventing project of state terror that ruptured life and spread fear of persecution.[3]

For persons whose trajectory had been more officialist, or whose fear or passive conformity had encouraged them to close the memory box ("look the other way") on matters of state violence, the book could prove compelling in a different way. A reader who had not before "known"—or could not believe—the ugly truth could begin to navigate a complex path of discovery and adjustment. A review in *El Mercurio*, Chile's conservative and influential newspaper of record, illustrated the adjustment process that led to a more regime-friendly sort of "awakening." It praised the book as "moving" and lauded the author's unimpeachable knowledge of the facts. The qualm was not about the facts but their explanation. To understand the "why" of the atrocities and the army's internal crisis, the author would have had to analyze the "political climate that made possible such madness."[4]

Book sales constituted one barometer of the new memory environment. In its first year Verdugo's book sold over 100,000 copies (excluding at least 25,000 pirate copies), an extraordinarily high figure in the Chilean market. On a per capita basis, the equivalent figure in the United States would have exceeded 2 million. The bestseller lists during the 1989–90 transition were dominated by books on hidden aspects of collective memory. Consider early April of 1990, as the Aylwin administration completed its first month in office. The themes of the top six books: the Caravan of Death slaughter; the reality of torture, as told by a former judge; a history of human rights violations and the struggle by the Vicariate of Solidarity and others to expose and stop them; an interview-book with the controversial Socialist Carlos Altamirano, considered by many the key "ultra" on the Left who undermined a political exit from the 1973 crisis; a warm and humanizing memoir and defense of Allende by a close associate; the "inside story" of military rule by investigative journalists. Such books had staying power. Four titles were mainstays (14 to 23 weeks on the bestseller list), while the other two were recently published.[5]

The key memory question that faced Chileans was how the Aylwin government and society more generally would reckon with the hunger for truth, and related demands for justice and social repair, bequeathed by an era of state terror and violence. The answer would not be simple, because the stability of the new government and the rules shaping the transition were not simple.

PROLOGUE TO A NEW CONVIVENCIA?
PROSPECTS FOR TRUTH, JUSTICE, AND ADVERSITY IN 1989

The fundamental objective of Patricio Aylwin's administration was to build a new *convivencia*—a living together in peace—after a period of immense violence, fear, and polarization, and thereby achieve an irreversible recovery of democracy.[6] In this view, military rule had been a time when a war mentality prevailed and converted critics into "enemies." To recuperate Chile's best traditions and build a democracy required a society premised on reencounter with the whole of Chile, a unity founded in the ability to accept differences of viewpoint and experience as a normal part of life. Convivencia meant seeing the political adversary as interlocutor, not as enemy to be liquidated. It would yield a certain reconciliation, that is, peaceful coexistence and mutual acceptance within the once divided and wounded "national family."

Convivencia was not simply a value in its own right. The key objectives of the new government depended on it. Politically, the government needed to demonstrate the viability and stability of democracy by returning the military to a professional role subordinate to civilian control. It also needed to chart an ethical basis for legitimate governance, in fundamental contrast with the norms of dictatorship, by recognizing a history of human rights violations and the attendant thirst for truth and justice. It needed to promote democratization reforms of an undemocratic constitution. Success on these fronts would also presumably hold together the Center-Left coalition and its electoral base.

Economically and socially, convivencia would foster the stability the government needed to reconcile the logic of economic growth with that of equity. In this vision, strong and sustained growth would reduce poverty and provide political and economic underwriting to sustain equity-oriented reforms: tax reform to generate revenues to address the cumulative "social debt" of dictatorship, through increased spending on health, education, and housing; upward adjustment of minimal wage and pension levels; moderate reform of a labor code that lacked protection against firing without cause and placed a miniscule cap (a five-month wage formula) on indemnifications to dismissed workers. To achieve high growth, the state had to build investor confidence, despite initial hostility and skepticism, that it accepted the basic outlines of Chile's neoliberal revolution—privatization of many enterprises and functions once run by the state; policy emphasis on market competitiveness, export-driven growth, and efficient modernization, through an aggressively "open" strategy within the international economy; and technical credibility with multilateral economic agencies and foreign investors, through fiscal discipline and overall coherence.

In the minds of Aylwin and his most important advisors, such goals required broad social backing—not only a wide base of political support, but also an atmosphere of convivencia that convinced at least some skeptics and critics that the government acted in good faith and considered the needs of all. To the degree that the government could build accords with leaders of Renovación Nacional—the party that defined itself as a "flexible" and democratic Right, in contrast to the ethos of Pinochetista loyalism that suffused UDI (Unión Democrática Independiente), the other major party of the Right —it would solidify convivencia and render its policies sustainable. Leaders of the key parties of the Center-Left Concertación—particularly the Christian Democracy and Radical Party in its centrist wing, and the Socialist Party and Party for Democracy in its leftist wing—would also constitute major players, but they would be expected to understand and support presidential leadership. In this vision, it was better to proceed toward the objective by steps, through negotiated understandings among political elites and accompanied by public acknowledgment of constraints, than to insist on one's goal so rigidly that the stability of the transition process itself would come into jeopardy. Nor should one, according to backers of Aylwin's vision, encourage street mobilization to create political pressures from below and a climate of conflict that might block or undermine accords among political elites. Precisely because Chile was coming out of a period of dictatorship that transformed dissidents into "enemies" and covered truth with misinformation, convivencia was not a habit. Aylwin concluded his victory speech in December 1989 with a call on Chileans to learn democratic habits of dialogue and mutual respect, to keep maximalist politics in check, and to remember what was at stake. "For the higher well being of the nation, I ask of everyone prudence and collaboration. What is at stake at this hour is constructing a stable democracy that can guarantee liberty and progress for all. . . . The challenge is beautiful."[7]

Truth and political adversity, these were the rub. As we shall see, the difficulties emerged forcefully during the long prologue to democratic governance—the interim between the plebiscite of October 1988 that rejected continuing military rule, and the actual inauguration of an elected civilian president in March 1990. Looking back in 1997, Aylwin likened the task of his government of transition to that of building a new "common sense," based on truth. The legacy of human rights violations and false cover stories required a response. Truth was important not merely because the human rights legacy was important within the culture of the Concertación coalition and its voting base. The issue went deeper. Truth was an ethical imperative and a prerequisite for convivencia. During the 1989 presidential campaign, Aylwin had not yet figured out specific policies on truth and justice. But he considered truth about human rights indispensable.

> We considered the theme of human rights a vital matter to reestablish *confianza* [confidence, good faith] among Chileans. . . . I always said . . . that truth is the basis of collective convivencia, that where truth is lacking one loses confianza, [whether] in the heart of a marriage, in the heart of the family, among parents and children, among neighbors, among citizens. In political life it is the same. We either trust [in good faith] or do not trust and to trust one has to start with respect for truth.[8]

Truth about political violence by the state, however, posed a paradox. It was essential to build convivencia, but it could also explode convivencia. It constituted the most controversial legacy of military rule—the focal point of struggles over competing frameworks of collective memory and ultimately, the legitimacy of the dictatorship. Truth also posed a volatile corollary: justice. The election program of the 1989 Concertación coalition called not only for truth about human rights, but also for penal sanction of perpetrators and revocation or annulment of the junta's 1978 Amnesty Law. Translating such calls into effective policy, however, was another matter. In 1989 Pinochet bluntly drew his line in the sand. In June: "If they want to go to the homes of officers looking to jail them, submit them to trial, one can also put an end to Rule of Law." In October: "The day they touch one of my men, the Rule of Law is over!"[9]

During 1989, the Concertación's advisory commission on human rights and justice pondered the dilemma.[10] José Zalaquett, a key human rights lawyer-activist expelled in 1976, had returned to Chile. He offered acute analysis in comparative perspective—the intellectual architecture for a new government's truth-and-justice policy. Zalaquett's exile had sparked years of work with Amnesty International (he eventually became its president) and similar groups, fellowships to facilitate analysis and reflection, and service on Amnesty International missions to transitional regimes facing a legacy of atrocities in Argentina, Uruguay, the Philippines, and Uganda.

These experiences enabled Zalaquett to clarify Chile's specific dilemma by building a theory of the ethical, legal, and political dimensions of truth and justice in democratic regimes emerging from a period of massive human rights atrocities. The emergent democracies had to undertake fundamental objectives: the prevention of atrocities in the future, through societal rejection at large and through deterrence of potential perpetrators; and the repair of social harm to victims and their families. Zalaquett's probing analysis focused on two tensions. First, how should a new government coordinate or reconcile the ethical and political logics in play? Only in a few instances—Germany and Japan after the Second World War, Nicaragua after 1979—did a new regime achieve a decisive military victory that cleared away political constraint to trials and punishment. Constraint loomed larger in most cases—for example, militaries that "have lost legitimacy but retain control of armed power," as in Greece and Argentina in 1974 and 1983, respectively; or militaries pressured or motivated to negotiate a way out of rule, yet still in control of force and retaining strong cohesion and morale about past action, as in Uruguay in 1984.

The cases of Argentina and Uruguay were sobering. In the former, the military's loss of the Malvinas / Falklands war in 1982 undermined its legitimacy and internal unity, and enabled the democratic government of Raúl Alfonsín to place high generals on trial. This audacious move garnered wide attention and promoted human rights values. But the military's monopoly of force, its internal unity about the legitimacy of its "dirty war" to rid Argentina of subversion, and its destabilizing acts of 1985–87 (mystery bomb attacks and military revolts in Buenos Aires and Córdoba) forced the government to retreat from justice-oriented policies by passing "final stop" and "due obedience" laws. The reversals undermined the government's legitimacy, hindered exposure of truth about the past, and more or less ratified impunity. The Uruguayan scenario was even worse, and its circumstances of military negotiation of an exit path more closely resembled the Chilean situation. During 1984–89 military officials disobeyed judicial orders to testify in human rights cases, refused to admit they had practiced torture, and even secured an amnesty ratified by democratic vote. The military and its sympathizers succeeded in playing on fear of conflict to defeat opponents of the amnesty in a referendum on its legitimacy.

The second tension analyzed by Zalaquett was that between the goals of truth and justice. In his view, the lesson of other transitions—reinforced by a Chilean judiciary historically complicit with the dictatorship—was that if one granted truth and justice equal priority within an immediate time frame, one might end up with neither. If justice proceedings had to carry the burden of ferreting out truth, they would spur a closing of the ranks among the military, and a fragmentary and inefficient process of truth investigation. Such a process would *undermine* the inscribing of collective truth about the past in society's public record and consciousness. The passage of time, moreover, would favor those who sought to hide truths and thereby reinforce their impunity.

The implication of Zalaquett's analysis was that the new government had to chart a way to coordinate irrenunciable ethical objectives with the likely political consequences of its actions. Otherwise, even the most well-intentioned policy would undermine the presumed goal. The theoretical foundation was Max Weber's distinction between "the ethics of conviction," founded on the highest ends that define moral imperatives; and "the ethics of responsibility," analysis of likely consequences as crucial for ethical decision making. One conclusion was that although the specific policies to achieve ends could vary from case to case in light of constraints and context, certain principles remained irrenunciable. These included goals of prevention and social repair, and respect for international norms of human rights law that nullify statutory limitations and amnesties for profoundly offensive crimes (genocide, torture, war crimes, crimes against humanity) while observing due process protection for perpetrators.

The irrenunciable also included truth. Without publicly and officially recognized truth about atrocities, a rigorous punishment policy would seem arbitrary or vengeful, a clemency-oriented policy would amount to mere impunity, and the social repair and prevention that begins with recognizing the harm could not begin. In a society where massive disappearances of people had taken place, moreover, the secrecy of the original repression "perpetuates its pernicious effects as long as truth remains hidden." Zalaquett's second conclusion was that if truth and justice could not be effectively pursued with equal immediate priority, establishing the truth would constitute a first priority. The state could exercise more discretion and a longer time horizon in designing policies of justice, understood as both the negative justice of criminal prosecution and the positive justice of reparation.

Zalaquett's thinking proved influential. In December 1989, the Concertación's Human Rights and Justice Commission voted (10 to 2) to recommend granting higher priority to truth over criminal justice. His analysis also resonated strongly with the thinking of President-elect Aylwin. As Aylwin approached the March 1990 inauguration, it was clear that annulling or revoking the 1978 amnesty had become a moot point. The December elections had left the Concertación short of a Senate majority. In addition, Aylwin considered the justice branch of government itself a major problem. "The courts had in practice become engaged with the dictatorship and had neither the will nor the capacity to clarify things." Many political leaders in the world of the Concertación coalition had not really thought out the issue. "It was thought they would initiate trials and that we would reform the courts and that this would be aired out in the courts, and for me it was clear that we were not going that way."[11]

Truth, the foundation for convivencia and the irrenunciable ethic of a new democracy aimed at breaking the normlessness and violence of dictatorship, presented a paradox. Truth was indispensable, yet it was also an explosive that could shatter a stable and effective transition. For the large minority (including an economically powerful investor or business class) wedded to memory of military rule as the salvation of Chile from ruin and bloodbath, the memory-truth that framed military rule as cruel rupture and persecution in violation of human rights constituted a slanderous accusation against those who rescued and modernized the country. It transformed the occasional excesses of a few soldiers who had been forced to fight a war to save Chile into broad moral and political accusation against patriots. For the military, especially high army officers and former secret police agents, the politics of human rights truth meant not only unjustified slander, but also the beginning of the slippery slope. Next would come the dishonor of required appearances in justice proceedings, the wrecking of amnesty, and possibly, sentences and imprisonment.

Pinochet himself, mindful of the trial of junta head General Leopoldo Galtieri in Argentina, was obsessed with keeping the door shut on possible prosecutions. For him, too, the airing of human rights memory meant a climate of pressure—conflict, harassment, ingratitude, and illegitimacy that could eventuate in prosecutions. He had hoped to have the junta pass a second Amnesty Law in 1989 to close the loophole left by the end date of the 1978 Amnesty Law, and to reinforce the principle of immunity. The massive political blowback such a move would spark, and internal junta opposition, especially by air force general Fernando Matthei, rendered the idea unfeasible. As we shall see below, Pinochet and the junta and their allies would rely on a more multifaceted strategy to protect and institutionalize the legacy of the regime, and to block vulnerability to prosecution.[12]

The memory question, understood as "truth," was inherently paradoxical—both indispensable and dangerous. Political adversity in a more general sense constituted a second major challenge to building convivencia, let alone a vibrant democracy. From the victory of the "No" campaign in October 1988 to the inauguration of Aylwin in March 1990, the Pinochet regime had nearly a year and a half to organize an exit path in keeping with its vision of "protected democracy." The point was to restrict the next government to a narrow range of constitutional, legal, and political maneuvers—to tie down its options—and to consolidate a high level of military autonomy. Aylwin and Concertación leaders had to decide, as they bargained over the precise terms of transition, how hard to push a junta that still held power and that swore loyalty to a Constitution enshrining the military's permanent tutelary role and Pinochet's right to remain army commander in chief until 1998. Aylwin and Concertación leaders sought to find common ground about the terms of transition with Renovación Nacional—to isolate Pinochet and the loyalist UDI politically, to drive Pinochet and the regime to make concessions, and to build bases for an additional round of reforms after taking office.[13]

The difficult conditions of transition proved apparent in three areas: constitutional rules, election results, and last-minute law and adaptations. The 1980 Constitution had been designed to achieve a simulacrum of democracy on the assumption that Pinochet would win the 1988 plebiscite and rule as president until 1997. It created a "protected democracy" with strong restrictions. Article 8 prohibited political parties whose doctrines offended the family or favored violence, class conflict, or totalitarianism. The provision was so broad and vague it might be interpreted to apply to all leftist parties, and even centrist ones if they advocated, for example, legalization of divorce. Further provisions secured the military's permanent tutelary role by denying the president the power to remove the four commanders in chief of the armed forces and the *carabineros*, and by creating a National Security Council as a watchful higher organ of the state. Consisting of a military-police majority (the four commanders in chief, along with the president of the Republic, the president of the Senate, and the president of the Supreme Court), it would have the power to represent to any government authority events, acts, or themes it considered threatening to institutional order or national security. The legal status of the communication implied obligation to take some sort of corrective action. Further restriction would derive from the partly appointed character of the Senate: nine designated senators would be selected by the outgoing regime, and twenty-six senators would be elected. Terms of the nine designees would lapse in 1998, but appointment procedures—four selections by the National Security Council from among former military and carabinero commanders, three selections by the Supreme Court, and ascension of Pinochet as former president to designated Senator status—would expand the designated bloc to ten and guarantee its conservative-military character. In addition, and as we shall see, a binomial election system guaranteed overrepresentation of the Right in the elected Congressional seats.

The constitutional engineering guaranteed a strong military voice, supported by a powerful Right, in the making of state policy and law, and in the inside-game of state administration. It also guaranteed great difficulty to achieve the quorum and the vote thresholds required for democratizing amendments to lift the restrictive features of the Constitution.[14]

In the first half of 1989, a complex negotiation unfolded between leaders of the Concertación, Renovación Nacional, and the Pinochet regime (the latter represented by a new interior minister, Carlos Cáceres). The victory of the No in the October 1988 plebiscite and Renovación's stance in favor of constitutional reform generated pressure on Pinochet and the regime (and to an extent UDI, as the most loyalist political party) to accede to partial reform. Two additional factors intervened. The original design was hyper-presidentialist, on the assumption that Pinochet would win the plebiscite. The elected president, now assumed to be Aylwin, would hold office eight years and would have the power to dissolve the lower legislative house and call for new elections. Even worse, a technical blunder in the 1980 Constitution lowered the quorum needed to amend its article governing constitutional amendments. A resounding Concertación victory in the December 1989 elections might open the door to constitutional reform by simple legislative majority. The Aylwin-led wing of the Concertación, for its part, feared that if it did not achieve constitutional reform via assent by Renovación Nacional and a broad voting majority in 1989, it would ruin the first years of its presidency—and sideline its other priorities—in a debilitating struggle to achieve constitutional reform and legitimacy through a Constituent Assembly. The struggle might fail, moreover, and the environment of conflict might undermine the project of building convivencia. The socialist sector of the Concertación voiced skepticism about a negotiated pact and pressed for tougher stances, but ultimately adjusted to the inexorability of a negotiated package. For Renovación Nacional, fruitful negotiation could assure it a strategic role and enhanced political prospects as shaper of a successful, moderate transition. In sum, despite vast differences of perspective, political elite players had reason to negotiate.

The result of the bruising negotiations was a compromise that satisfied no one—but for which almost everyone voted. Article 8's prohibitions on political ideas were repealed, and replaced by proscription on promoting violent acts against the state. The president still could not remove commanders in chief, but the military's tutelage power eroded. The National Security Council would have four civilians among eight members, and weaker authority to intervene in governance. It could no longer direct concerns to all holders of government office, but only to the president, National Congress, and Constitutional Tribunal. As important, its communications fell to the legal status of advisory opinion, not obligation-creating opinion. The designated senator system was retained but diluted by expansion of elected senators from twenty-six to thirty-eight. The president lost power to dissolve the House of Representatives and call for new elections, and the first civilian president would have only a four-year term, but the constitutional reform process (a two-thirds congressional vote rule for strategic articles) was somewhat eased by eliminating the requirement of passage by two consecutive congresses. And so on. The package of fifty-four reforms was submitted to a plebiscite on 30 July and secured a huge (85.7 percent) majority.[15]

Election results added to the adversity. For Aylwin and his close political advisor and conegotiator, Edgardo Boeninger, the failure to eliminate the designated Senator system was difficult to swallow. But they thought they had a firm oral agreement with Renovación Nacional to unite with the Concertación to abolish the designated Senator system after the new government took office. Also, Concertación leaders hoped momentum from the October 1988 plebiscite would generate a huge victory in the December 1989 elections—a two-thirds majority of seats in the lower house, and a Senate majority strong enough to exert pressure on Renovación to make good on its commitment. The main obstacle was the binomial election system, established to create overrepresentation of the Right. Each Senate or Representative electoral district had two seats, and the winning coalition slate would have to beat the closest competing list by a 2-to-1 ratio to gain both seats. In practice, this meant exclusion from Congress of the Communist Party and other parties unaligned with one of the two coalition slates, and necessity for the Concertación alliance to win a huge two-thirds majority against the Right's coalition (Democracia y Progreso, mainly comprised of Renovación Nacional and the UDI) if it were to capture both seats in a given district. Put another way: in congressional races, the strategic goal of the outgoing regime and its sympathizers was to win a third of the vote, not a majority.[16]

Aylwin and the Concertación won a resounding victory yet fell short. In the presidential race, Aylwin won a solid majority (55.2 percent) but failed to enlarge on the 1988 No vote. The regime candidate, Hernán Büchi, the finance minister who led Chile's economic turnaround in the late 1980s, garnered only three-tenths (29.4 percent); the conservative populist Francisco Javier Errázuriz, a wealthy businessman of modest origin who merged nationalism, anti-Communism, and criticism of neoliberal economics, took a sixth (15.4 percent). The congressional elections yielded a tough scenario. The Concertación picked up three-fifths (60.0 percent) of lower house seats *despite* the binomial system. But institutional engineering served its purpose well in the Senate, where the Concertación picked up twenty-two of the thirty-eight elected seats—two short of a majority, given the outgoing regime's appointment of nine designated senators. Also, the binomial system led to the stunning defeat of Ricardo Lagos, leader of the Concertación's Left wing, and the equally stunning victory of Jaime Guzmán, the military regime's most visible intellectual leader and also leader of the loyalist UDI. Lagos outpaced Guzmán hugely in the popular vote (30.6 percent to 17.2 percent), but to no avail (see table 1).[17]

Last-minute law and adaptations by the outgoing regime constituted a third source of adversity. The junta used its remaining months to write and

TABLE. Senate Election, District 7, Western Metropolitan Santiago, 1989

Coalition Candidate and Election Rules	Votes	Percent of Vote
Concertación: Andrés Zaldívar	408,227	31.3
Concertación: Ricardo Lagos	399,721	30.6
Democracia y Progreso: Jaime Guzmán	224,396	17.2
Democracia y Progreso: Miguel Otero	199,856	15.3
Minor candidates	73,269	5.6
Concertación coalition's total: Zaldívar and Lagos	807,948	61.9
Democracia y Progreso coalition's total: Guzmán and Otero	424,252	32.5
Binomial rules: To elect both senators in this district, the Concertación slate would have had to win 65.0 percent of the vote (twice the Democracia y Progreso total of 32.5 percent).		
Elected senators under binomial rules: Concertación: Andrés Zaldívar		31.3
Democracia y Progreso: Jaime Guzmán		17.2

Source: Adapted from Peter M. Siavelis, *The President and Congress in Postauthoritarian Chile: Institutional Constraints to Democratic Consolidation* (University Park: Pennsylvania State University Press, 2000), 35.

pass "organic law" of the armed forces. Organic law held a constitutional rank higher than "ordinary law," and therefore required more than simple legislative majorities for change. The organic law secured a high level of military autonomy: protection against presidential dismissal of commanders and high officers, against civilian intrusion on the officer promotion-and-retirement system, and against pressure through reduction of budgets. The military forces would receive, independent of the politically driven budget process, 10 percent of gross sales revenue from the state copper corporation, CODELCO; its proceeds could not fall below a floor of US$200 million. Last-minute law also enabled Pinochet to prolong his base in the Supreme Court, by offering large bonuses to elderly justices (over seventy-five years old) to retire early. Several refused, but Pinochet still managed to appoint a renovated Pinochetista majority by March 1990.

Late adaptations included an accelerating final round of privatization of public enterprise, underway in earnest since 1987, in lucrative sectors such as energy and utilities, mines, and forestry. In part, the final round of privatizations had an ideological purpose, in addition to reflecting policy beliefs. By targeting "natural monopolies" such as energy and utilities, and establishing a program to create some worker-owned shares in companies, the new phase took a last step toward inscribing the neoliberal idea that private property and market-driven decisions by investors and consumers constituted the key to good economic management in *every* sector of life. The privatizations also served to expand material interest in and political protection for the new economic order and the Pinochet legacy. They rewarded regime allies with wealth and market opportunities, enhanced by bargain prices or technical subsidies, such as debt-and-share swaps that transferred US$500 million of foreign debt from the giant electric generating company ENDESA and its subsidiaries to the state. Economic favor and opportunity went not only to traditional private investors, such as the powerful and regime-friendly Cruzat-Larraín clan, but also to former high officials and their relatives and friends. Consider but a few examples. Between 1987 and 1990, the former minister of economics and minister of finance Sergio de Castro emerged as director of Soquimich, the newly privatized nitrate-iodine-lithium company; the former minister of labor and minister of mining José Piñera Echeñique turned up as president of Chilmetro and president of the Directorate of Chilectra, the privatized electric utility companies; the former executive secretary of the National Commission on Energy Bruno Philippi Yrarrázaval took over as president of the electric generating company Chilgener (also known as Gener). Meanwhile, Richard Büchi, brother of the former minister of finance and 1989 presidential candidate Hernán Büchi, took on the general manager position in Chilquinta, another privatized utility company, and Julio Ponce Lerou, at the time the son-in-law of Pinochet and very well connected to military circles, emerged as president of Soquimich.

The point of late-regime adaptations and law was to create pillars of loyalty and continuity far into the future. Pinochet would be the army commander in chief with a loyal officer corps, a stable budget, and a Constitution and organic law that would be difficult to amend. The judiciary would be restocked with loyalists at the highest level. A newly rewarded business class would have an even deeper stake in the regime's property laws and final transitional arrangements, and would be infused, as well, with regime allies and loyalists.

Other laws and adaptations sought to protect silences and shape a favorable media environment for coming struggles over truth, justice, and memory. In January 1989, Law 18,771 went into effect. It exempted the Ministry of Defense and its dependencies, and the military, police, and security forces from the legal requirement to turn over their documents, after normal statutory delay (usually five years), to the National Archive. The exempted agencies could also destroy archives in accord with their own internal institutional rules. Translation: internal records of secret police and military intelligence operations would be legally off limits, withheld from a new government's truth-telling or justice-related initiatives. In October, Pinochet acceded to pressure to dissolve the secret police (the CNI, Centro Nacional de Informaciones, the successor organism to the original secret police known as DINA, Dirección de Inteligencia Nacional). But he reassigned its several thousand agents to the army, under his command and protection far into the future. Translation: keeping secret police agents in the military tent would protect the code of silence about dangerous knowledge.

Other silencing operations took place discreetly. Effacing harmful physical as well as documentary evidence became a focus of preparation. We now know that such efforts, like those that followed discovery of human remains at the abandoned lime ovens of Lonquén in 1978, included operations to remove or obliterate human remains at secret grave sites. Projects to reward friends and to destroy troublesome "memory knots" sometimes came together. The DINA's most important torture-and-disappearance compound, Villa Grimaldi, was transferred to an investment group including relatives of the outgoing CNI director, General Hugo Salas Wenzel. The new owners planned to replace the ruins of memory with a housing complex.[18]

In the last desperate year of military rule, efforts to secure a favorable media environment complemented silencing operations. Favorable financial transactions (assisted by political blessing) relieved the alarming debt structure of Chile's two largest and officialist-oriented media companies and their flagship newspapers, *El Mercurio* and *La Tercera*. The print media aligned with the opposition's memory camp would be left to struggle precariously, in a marketplace dominated by the financially healthy giants. The immense popularity of Radio Cooperativa and its news programming immunized it from commercial pressure, but state-owned Televisión Nacional (TVN) was another matter. Renovation of the Council of TVN coincided with severe depletion of its assets and an exploding debt structure. In constant December 1989 pesos, assets between 1986 and 1989 plummeted 74 percent, from 3,500 million pesos to 900 million. Meanwhile debt soared 100 percent, from 3,700 million pesos, roughly equal to 1986 assets, to 7,400

1. The awkward moment of transition: Aylwin (left) and Pinochet smile amidst tension. *Credit: Jesús Inostroza, Secretaría de la Presidencia.*

million—more than eight times the 1989 assets. The outgoing regime could no longer control directly TVN, but economic crisis and a loyalist council would presumably create pressure to privatize the "white elephant" and to avoid controversy by its news department. Patricia Verdugo and others could write bestselling books that documented memory as wounding rupture and persecution. The most important television channel could not be allowed to follow that path.[19]

Adversity, of course, was not the whole story. Aylwin and the Concertación won a clear popular majority in December 1989, despite media harassment during the campaign.[20] He appeared able to reach workable agreements on key questions of democracy with Renovación's Sergio Onofre Jarpa and Andrés Allamand. He projected a sense of calm, stability, and competence that would reinforce the benefit of the doubt expected in a honeymoon period. Nonetheless, the hunger for truth and the explosiveness of truth, the military's continuing coherence and near-autonomy under Pinochet's continuing command, the reality of a two-fifths national minority aligned with the outgoing regime and including a powerful business sector, the political restrictions built by constitutional engineering, the electoral system, and last-minute operations of law, silencing, and reward: all spelled a difficult road to convivencia.

SHAPING A NEW CONVIVENCIA (1): DEMOCRACY AS ACKNOWLEDGMENT, EXPRESSION, AND DILEMMA

The first nine months of Aylwin's government brought into bold relief three aspects of the new democracy: state acknowledgment of harm, as acts of repair and legitimation of heretofore stigmatized memory-truths and social actors; social expression of ideas and needs, as normal and legitimate features of life; dilemma and tension related to stable governance in a society still sharply conflicted by the legacy and memory of military rule. The most obvious dilemma was that of the true boundaries of civilian and military power, especially on truth-and-justice matters. A more subtle dilemma related to the conflictive synergy—mutually sympathetic and dependent, yet also beset by friction and frustration—that shaped relations between political elites of the Center-Left Concertación on the one hand, and social activists and grassroots groups on the other.

Each aspect of democratic Chile—acknowledgment, expression, dilemma— came through in the first major event of the new government: a televised inaugural celebration and speech before a crowd of 70,000 at the National Stadium, on 12 March 1990.[21] Giant banners—*Así me gusta Chile,* "This is the Chile I like"—proclaimed the joy of returning to the real Chile, the suppressed Chile that was also a collective longing. "This is Chile," began Aylwin. "The Chile we yearned for . . . The Chile free, just, democratic." He quickly moved toward acknowledgment by evoking memory of the National Stadium itself as a giant prisoner camp immediately after the 1973 coup. "From this site, that in sad days of blind hate, of force dominating over reason, was for many compatriots a place of prison and torture, we say . . . Never again! Never again tramplings of human dignity! Never again fratricidal hate!"

After seventeen years of dictatorship, words such as these from an elected president were powerful. Only three years had passed since *pobladores* (residents of shantytown neighborhoods of the urban poor and working class) had caused shock and scandal—and a quick cutaway by Televisión Nacional —by speaking bluntly to Pope John Paul II on live television about violence and dictatorship, during his 1987 visit to Chile.[22]

The natural complement of acknowledgment was a wider arena of legitimate social expression, symbolized in the choreography of the inaugural celebration. The most poignant symbolic expressions related to memory: Roberto Bravo's piano interpretation of "Te recuerdo Amanda," the tender song of working-class love, politics, and loss by Víctor Jara, the beloved artist killed at another soccer stadium after the coup; the dignity of fifteen women as they marched on the field holding photo-posters of their disappeared relatives, while a giant screen scrolled hundreds of names, and as they danced their "Cueca Alone," an adaptation of Chile's national dance of couples to the reality of life with a disappeared partner.

In Aylwin's conception, acknowledgment of truth and the pledge of prevention ("never again"), like social repair and expression, was to lay the basis for convivencia. Convivencia was goal and starting point for the work ahead; he knew he would need to wield moral authority as a democratic and frank president to foster a new civic culture and common sense. As he spoke to establish the centrality of convivencia, however, democracy as dilemma and tension also came to the fore. Aylwin departed from the text to reassert the moral authority of frank talk.[23]

> The task we have ahead: to reestablish a climate of respect and confidence in convivencia among Chileans, whatever might be their beliefs, ideas, activities or social condition, whether civilians or soldiers—[Whistles begin breaking out from the public. Aylwin breaks from the text to impose moral authority and underscore convivencia.]
>
> —Yes, señores! Yes, compatriots! Civilians and soldiers. Chile is one only! The guilt of individual persons cannot apply to everyone! We have to be capable of rebuilding the unity of the Chilean family!
>
> [The improvised remarks have their effect. The whistles end; Aylwin returns to the prepared text about convivencia among all sectors.]
>
> —whether workers or business people, laborers or intellectuals.

The intense expectations and emotions released upon transition from a long, violent dictatorship elevated the politicocultural importance of the event. This was no routine rite of inauguration in a well-established democracy. What would be said and symbolized mattered greatly, and involved consultations and negotiations with organizations such as the Comisión Chilena de Derechos Humanos (Chilean Human Rights Commission).[24] Aylwin's frank style signaled a government of antidemagoguery in the face of adversity and pent-up frustration. So many tasks lay ahead, so many necessities had been postponed, yet Chile belonged to the "developing world," nations with limited resources and a strong need for economic growth to leave poverty behind. Chileans had to be patient; the government had to set priorities and focus special attention on the poor; the attainment of legitimate goals would take time. Chileans needed to reckon with the dilemma and tensions of a democracy shadowed by the constraints engineered by the outgoing regime, and by the path taken to achieve transition. Chilean democrats, for lack of a better alternative and to avoid risking new suffering and new loss of life, had chosen "the path of defeating authoritarianism on its own court. It is what we have done, with the benefits and costs that it entails." He thought the path taken was the best available and he believed the new Congress (subtext: the Concertación and Renovación Nacional) would eliminate most of the shackles.

What did such dilemmas imply for the explosive question of truth and justice? Truth was absolutely fundamental. "It is legitimate and just that after such a long period of absolute and mysterious power, in which so many people have suffered so much and in which public matters were secret . . . , [the people] want to know the truth of what happened." Even more, "the moral conscience of the nation demands clarifying the truth about disappearances of people, about horrendous crimes and other grave violations of human rights."

As one moved from truth to justice, however, one needed to consider the difficult balance between desire and constraint, and to envision a process playing out over time. "We must approach this delicate matter reconciling the virtue of justice with the virtue of prudence and once the corresponding personal responsibilities are established, the hour of pardon will come." Aylwin agreed with Zalaquett's analysis. His careful language was a somewhat cryptic foreshadowing of what would come—presidential insistence that the courts should undertake formal proceedings to identify the legal facts and the criminal responsibility of individuals, especially in disappearance cases, before allowing application of the 1978 Amnesty Law to close cases. But he also had a phrase that circulated readily and summed up the approach: "truth, and justice to the extent possible." He did not elaborate on whether the point was to live within the boundaries of the possible, or to change them. On this point, he exercised his own form of prudence.[25]

Six weeks later, on 24 April, Aylwin announced a truth initiative on television. "A deep yearning for peace and understanding prevails in the heart of

Chileans," but convivencia cannot be achieved without truth. Human rights violations and other violence "constitute a still open wound in the national soul, that cannot be ignored or healed up by any attempt to forget it. . . . Closing eyes on what happened . . . as if nothing happened, would be to prolong indefinitely a constant source of pain, of divisions, hatreds and violence." The justice of establishing criminal responsibility in specific cases was a matter to be resolved in the courts, but the prolonged and individually focused nature of such proceedings would not enable the nation to achieve a wider truth—"a global knowledge of the truth of what happened"—within a reasonable time frame. Moreover, delay in clarifying the truth was itself "a factor disrupting collective convivencia and conspires against the yearning for peaceful re-encounter." Accordingly, he had decided, without prejudice to the criminal jurisdiction of the courts in specific cases, to enable Chilean society to achieve "a serious and well documented [fundado] collective concept of the truth of what happened in this transcendent matter."

The path was formation of a National Truth and Reconciliation Commission. It would have to report quickly, within six to nine months. Its fundamental mandate would be to establish "the most complete picture possible" of the gravest human rights violations committed between 11 September 1973 and 11 March 1990. It should identify the individual victims and their fates, recommend measures of repair and revindication, and propose policies of prevention. It should steer clear of usurping the jurisdiction of courts. It could not name publicly the individuals it considered responsible for specific crimes, but would confidentially convey such evidence to the courts. Its report to the president would be public.

Behind the scenes, Aylwin had moved forward despite skepticism by his advisors including his top political managers, Edgardo Boeninger (secretary general of the presidency) and Enrique Correa (secretary general of government). The Truth Commission was of limited scope—it would focus only on violations leading to death or disappearance, it would lack subpoena powers, it would not name perpetrators, it would steer clear of criminal justice functions. Nonetheless, the inner circle counseled against it. As they considered the paradox of truth—indispensable yet explosive—they concluded a commission would be too hot to handle. It could jeopardize a successful transition and presidency. The Truth Commission initiative represented a personal strategic decision by the president, with an ensuing obligation of support from an initially reluctant team.

Aylwin's announcement of the initiative was solemn, a mix of the educational and the nearly sacramental. Peace, he observed, could not mean mere defense of existing order, "which is usually disorder filled with violence and incompatible with peace." Truth was the indispensable foundation of moral society. "As the old Christian wisdom teaches, peace is a work of justice and can only be built on foundations of truth." To Aylwin's left sat the eight members of the Commission. Persons of strong and long public reputation—"of great moral character and prestige"—they were known not to be easily manipulated.

A subtext of solemn civic duty higher than normal politics came into play as Aylwin introduced the Commission members. By naming eight persons equally divided between those who leaned toward the Center-Left Concertación and those who leaned Right, Aylwin signified a refusal to predetermine the outcome of the report. In effect, he put the Commission under pressure to avoid a split—majority and minority reports based largely on political ideology or inclination. The chair, the elderly Raúl Rettig, had built his career with the centrist Radical Party—he was not identified with the Concertación's dominant players, whether the Christian Democrats or the socialist wing (Socialists, and Party for Democracy). The members included not only Jaime Castillo and José Zalaquett, persons with a forceful trajectory as human rights advocates, but also conservatives with pasts sensitive to human rights issues yet connected with the junta. Ricardo Martin, a former Supreme Court justice, was a designated senator and had served on the junta's human rights commission to analyze exile cases in the mid-1980s. Gonzalo Vial, a prominent historian, had served as minister of education until conflicts with Manuel Contreras and differences over educational policy rendered his ministry untenable. The point was civic duty, not political party or inclination.[26]

The Truth and Reconciliation Commission formed the cultural centerpiece of democracy as acknowledgment and social repair. At the same time, the Commission was part of a wider package of initiatives to serve a similar function. On the one hand, there was the "social debt" question, a reference to those harmed or postponed under dictatorship. By the end of July the government passed—via negotiations with Renovación Nacional, business, and labor—a major tax reform that raised us$600 million for social spending, and labor and pension reforms to adjust wage scales and raise indemnifications to dismissed workers. On these projects the administration expended political capital, showcased its ability to rule through broad accords among political elites, and sought to demonstrate that its "growth with equity" idea could harmonize neoliberal economic principles with social need and responsibility. (Neoliberalism granted primacy to international and national market incentives, private property, and economic growth as principles of economic and social policy. Two key corollaries, also points of principle, followed: the necessity to turn the state away from activism in social welfare and economic life, toward a more austere economic and social presence; and the usefulness of conceptualizing citizens as citizen-consumers, when framing social policy and incentives. The Concertación did not contest market incentives and state austerity as basic principles of economic policy. In discursive terms, however, a certain debate unfolded and the neoliberal label became something of a sore point. Proponents of "growth with equity" considered the increased state revenues and social spending—the latter rose 20.5 percent in 1990–91 and continued to increase thereafter—to have constituted, along with declining poverty rates, a softening of inequities and a corrective to neoliberalism. In this vision, such correctives would prove sustainable and cumulative over time precisely because of care to attend to market incentives that would assure macroeconomic stability and growth. Critics saw the corrections as modest in impact, noted the persistence of extreme maldistribution of income, and considered overall policy "the usual neo-liberal soup." In the first year of transition, this debate was relatively muted. As we shall see in chapter 4, it would gain more importance over time and lead to politicocultural wear and tear in Concertación support by the late 1990s.) The Right had its own motives to consent to tax and labor reform, and an increase of social spending. The economic Right came around to accepting compromise as a moderate price to pay for stability, protection of privatized property including the last-minute transfers of the outgoing military regime, and ratification of neoliberalism. Politically, Renovación Nacional hoped such reform would consolidate its strategic, statesmanlike role as "the keys of the transition," that is, as the responsible Right that could be trusted to govern wisely in the future.[27]

On the other hand, acknowledgment and social repair also meant dealing with the social and legal justice needs of the heirs of political persecution: particularly the exiles who lived abroad and might wish to return, the political prisoners who still languished in jail, and the victim-survivor families who sought an end to impunity blocking penal sanction of human rights crimes. As we shall see (chapter 3), the impunity issue could not be disentangled from a larger multifaceted project to reform and modernize the judiciary, and to press for a particular interpretation of the 1978 Amnesty Law. The exile and prisoner issues received more specific focus.

The exile waves, at first exclusively political and later a mix of the political and the economic, had been massive: well-informed estimates range from 200,000 to 400,000. The same evening he announced formation of a truth commission, Aylwin also declared that he had sent Congress legislation to establish an Oficina Nacional de Retorno (National Office of Return) to study, promote, and facilitate the return of exiles and their reintegration into society. In practical terms, the Oficina Nacional did not prove commensurate with need. Its duration was transitory (1991–94), its allocation of personnel and state funds modest, its operation marred by inefficiency and corruption. It functioned largely as an informational and referral office, and as an agency that channeled international grants—the bulk of its budget— from other governments and NGOS (nongovernmental organizations).

The social acceptance and psychological well-being of returnees to a dramatically transformed society proved difficult for other reasons too. In a sense, returnees were the human carriers of unwelcome memory and unwelcome conscience. They were representatives of times and values that failed, observer-critics of a culture more egotistical and individualistic than the Chile they remembered and idealized. Many adult returnees suffered a sense of ostracism, misplaced expectation, and out-of-placeness, compounded by the anguish of children wrenched from the lives they had known abroad. Some retreated into a social world of returnees and succumbed to a "'nostalgia for nostalgias' . . . the yearning for country and people and life ways as lived in exile." Despite such problems and insufficient state effort, the symbolism of acknowledgment and repair by the state was culturally significant, and some 52,500 Chilean adults and children did return with some assistance from the Oficina Nacional.[28]

Aylwin inherited some 400 political prisoners, held on charges ranging from illicit association, to illegal possession of arms, to terrorism and endangerment of the internal security of the state. Detained without due process guarantees, most had suffered torture. Some had received long sentences, but most had not—they twisted in the wind of interminably slow judicial proceedings, a de facto prison sentence without a timeline. Aylwin pardoned forty-five prisoners of conscience held on lesser charges upon taking office, but lacked authority in the other cases. Given the vacuum of legal rights and the torture suffered by the prisoners, the distinction between resisting a violent dictatorship and resisting a democracy, the Center-

Left character of the Concertación, the prisoner protests including a hunger strike, and the solidarity protests by relatives and human rights groups, Aylwin had strong political and ethical reasons to review the cases and bring an end to the imprisonments. He and the justice minister, Francisco Cumplido, prepared a package of laws to achieve the goal, but on matters of justice the politics of consensus broke down.

On the prisoner matter, Chile's memory struggles over the meaning and legitimacy of military rule proved particularly intense. The volatility was heightened by the fact that the prisoners included those who had killed Pinochet's bodyguards in an attempted assassination in 1986—and by a fresh attack. Just ten days into the new democracy, an assassination team of the Frente Patriótico Manuel Rodríguez, the same armed resistance group that had tried to kill Pinochet in 1986, broke into the office of (retired) air force general Gustavo Leigh. The assailants shot Leigh, a member of the original 1973 junta, and another general. Both survived, but the wounds were severe and Leigh lost an eye. For military regime sympathizers, release of political prisoners meant freeing the violent enemy to act again. The arguments that the prisoners had already suffered horrific punishments outside the rule of law, that many had not committed violence, that cases would undergo individual review rather than resolution en masse, that failure to acknowledge and resolve the prisoners' fate would create a climate of *increased* risk of vengeance attacks—these seemed more like excuses.

Finally, early in 1991, after Cumplido gave excruciating public testimony before Congress on three torture cases, and threatened to continue recounting histories of prisoners and their torments, case by case, Renovación Nacional offered a formula. It would back a transitory presidential pardon-commutation power for acts before 11 March 1990, and coordinated with an antiterrorism law for acts after democratic transition. In other words, the president would resolve the problem but also take the heat if former prisoners committed violence after release, or if Pinochet overreacted. Case reviews began and pardons released some 300 prisoners by the end of 1992. Aylwin reserved the most volatile cases—Pinochet's fourteen assailants—to the very end. On 10 March 1994, his last day in office, he closed the circle. With cooperation from Belgium, he commuted forty years of imprisonment into exile.[29]

Aylwin understood the symbolism of social acknowledgment after times of dictatorship. Some initiatives related to memory in the diffuse sense of "social debt" or inclusion of the once excluded. In May 1990, for example, Aylwin announced formation of a Special Commission on Indigenous Peoples, half of its members elected by indigenous organizations, to develop proposed legislation on lands, waters, community rights, language, and education, through a new indigenous law under the auspices of a new agency of indigenous affairs, CONADI (Corporación Nacional de Desarrollo Indígena). He also announced a legislative project to create SERNAM (Servicio Nacional de la Mujer), a high-level government agency to advocate women's equal rights and opportunities in policy formation and in society. The project responded to a demand of the women's movement, which had played a major role in grassroots mobilization for democracy and human rights as well as women's rights in the 1980s.[30]

Other forms of symbolic acknowledgment related more directly to memories of persecution. When stigmatized symbols of the past were honored, the line between acknowledgment and repair dissolved. A charged symbolic moment came during the first September, Chile's season of divided memory, under the new government. The September memory season, which actually began in late August, concentrated key commemorations of the nation—the birthday of the independence liberator and army general Bernardo O'Higgins (20 August), the traditional pre-1973 presidential election day (4 September), the anniversary of the 1973 military coup that brought down Allende (11 September), the two-day Patriotic Holidays of Independence Day and Army Day (18–19 September). In the early years of military rule, the season turned into a time to *perform* "memory as salvation." The ceremonies featured not only official speeches and symbols, such as the lighting of an "Eternal Flame of Liberty" in 1975, but also huge crowds to celebrate the 11 September anniversary as a heroic intervention to save the Chilean people from the crisis—chaos, scarcities, tyranny, and a near-bloodbath—they experienced under rule by Salvador Allende. In the memory-truth promoted by the military regime, Allende was the most vilified example of an even bigger problem—rule in the twentieth century by demagogic politicians who stoked democratic excess and thereby created the need for a strong saving hand. The commemorations associated the "second independence" of 1973 with the original independence of 1810, a point underscored by the proximity of the O'Higgins birthday and the independence and army day holidays.

In the 1980s, struggles to define the true reality of military rule turned the memory season and its 11 September anniversary into a "memory knot" that concentrated competing memories and galvanized conflict. Language changed. *El once* (the eleventh), which once meant celebration, came to signify dispute—street protest to define the memory and meaning of military rule. In the dissident version of the season, the date of 4 September also gained some attention as a memory knot in its own right. The day marked the presidential election day of the destroyed democracy, and as such, the election of Salvador Allende as president.[31]

In 1990, the memory season took a new twist—restoration of Salvador Allende to the national community of the honorable. Allende's widow, Hortensia Bussi, and a surviving daughter, Isabel Allende Bussi, had returned to Chile. The family and the government organized a dignified official funeral. In 1973, Allende's body had been shunted off to Viña del Mar for discreet burial after troops assaulted and took the presidential palace of La Moneda. Now, a funeral procession would take Allende from Viña del Mar to the Cathedral in Santiago for a *responso* (prayer for the dead), a gesture by Archbishop Carlos Oviedo that called implicitly to memory Allende's fulfillment of a promise to respect the Catholic Church. From the cathedral facing Santiago's massive central plaza, the body would then proceed to the entrance of Santiago's General Cemetery for a public ceremony to honor his life and memory, and finally inside for a more intimate burial. The procession and funeral would take place on 4 September, the twentieth anniversary of Allende's election as president.

As symbolic acknowledgment simultaneously from above and below—from the state and the grass roots—the event was powerful. Humble folk accompanied Allende on his last journey through roads and public spaces, beginning with those who clustered along the highway from Viña del Mar to Santiago to wave, climaxing with massive crowds in Santiago. They sang, applauded, and felt the tears well up. Admirers shouted cheers of loyalty. They bore signs that declared "Hasta siempre, Compañero Presidente" (Until Forever, Compañero President), and broke into a well-known rhythmic chant. "Allende, Allende, Allende está presente" (Allende, Allende, Allende's here with us). People tossed red carnations at the casket as it passed. Televisión Nacional broadcast the funeral, pulling a wider audience into the swirl of emotion and memory and implicitly underscoring the importance and dignity of the event. Most galling for the military, and most important as a symbol of legitimation, Aylwin—despite resistance to the idea from some in his own party—attended the cathedral service and spoke at the public ceremony.

2. Allende's second funeral: Above, as Allende's coffin leaves the cathedral for loading and transfer to the Santiago Cemetery, crowds jam the giant Plaza de Armas. *Credit: Helen Hughes.*

3. Below, crowds cheer, weep, sing, and clap for Allende as his casket passes. *Credit: Helen Hughes.*

4. At the cemetery: Above, Aylwin steps forward and prepares to speak. *Credit: Helen Hughes.*

5. Below, after the burial people visit Allende's tomb day after day and may now buy a picture. *Credit: Helen Hughes.*

Aylwin connected the occasion to the project of building convivencia. "We are repairing the unjust error that put off for so long the funeral rites that every human community offers its dead, especially those who . . . stood out among their peers." Salvador Allende had a long and outstanding trajectory in national life. "Representative, senator, minister of State, president of the Senate . . . and, finally, President of the Republic of Chile, he came to be the most representative leader of the Chilean Left." He embodied dreams of change and justice held "by vast sectors of our pueblo," and for which he "fought . . . with courage and gave his life out of loyalty to his convictions." Whatever his virtues and defects, or the passions he aroused, Allende was a part of Chilean history.

Aylwin drove home the idea of convivencia. The day marked "a reencounter of Chileans who, upon rendering posthumous homage together to the leader of whom some were followers and others of us adversaries, we recognize our common national identity." Allende was a democrat, he declared, even in an explosive crisis. Their political conflict "prevented neither him nor me from dialogue in search of formulas of agreement to try to save democracy." The dramatic breakdown of those times would not return, because "the horrors and sufferings . . . lived by Chile have taught us that those circumstances ought not and cannot repeat themselves." The project of never-again was the "task of all Chileans."

Aylwin's speech was more than a gesture to the left wing of his coalition. He put forth a presidential civics lesson, laced by a certain moral courage in view of memories of Aylwin's own past. In the Allende years, Aylwin played a prominent political role, in alignment with the dominant wing of the Christian Democratic Party led by former president Eduardo Frei Montalva. The Frei wing initially supported the coup as unfortunate but legitimate (although it later turned toward critique and the memory camp that framed military rule as rupture, persecution, and awakening). Some in the crowd began to jeer and whistle when Aylwin mentioned plainly his political conflict with Allende, and that he would return to an adversarial role if the same circumstances were to be repeated. He faced down the resistance by declaring truth the basis for convivencia: "To those who are whistling I say . . . the only language in which we can understand each other is the language of truth! I am here to give a testimony of truth." He had been Allende's adversary but he could also respect him, recognize his merits, sometimes agree with him. The interplay of disagreement with respect, dialogue, and partial agreement was "the essence of democratic life." Chileans were learning from past errors and accepting their own measures of responsibility for the crisis of 1973.

Aylwin went on to connect Allende's delayed funeral to the larger framework of memory as rupture and persecution—and to the awakening of conscience and effort memory required. "We Chileans still have other debts with compatriots from diverse places in the country who still do not rest in peace." To say a dignified goodbye to Salvador Allende was also a way to "remember all the fallen, committing ourselves to banish forever violence and intolerance."[32]

SHAPING A NEW CONVIVENCIA (II): DEMOCRACY AS DILEMMA

Democracy as acknowledgment and expression could not be disentangled from democracy as dilemma. Perhaps the most subtle dilemma was the conflictive synergy—especially on matters of memory—that marked relationships between political elites of the Center-Left Concertación, and their natural base of supporters and social activists. A collaboration of mutual sympathy and necessity unfolded, but also went hand in hand with friction and frustration. To an extent the new government needed expression, collaboration, and even a measure of pressure from below, and it needed exposures of hidden truth in a freer media environment, to stake out and sustain values and policies for a postdictatorial era. In this sense, participation from below built legitimacy and underscored a vital contrast between democracy and dictatorship. But the government also feared that if citizen-activists crossed the line between prudent participation and aggressive pressure, they might intensify conflict and shatter convivencia. In practice, government and Concertación leaders discouraged independent social mobilization, struck notes of caution about expectations, and underscored the value of moderate accords achieved by elites steering a delicate transition.

At stake in this tension were the boundaries of the possible, the shape of citizen participation, and ultimately the quality and values of the new democracy itself. The tension went beyond the intentionality of individual leaders and activists, and beyond the normal disappointments that attend the compromises of politics and state-society relations in a democracy. The tension went to the heart of cherished core values—the very struggles over memory, truth, and justice that galvanized society and mass experience in the 1980s and that finally brought down a dictatorship in the 1988 plebiscite.[33] As important, the tension was built into the very structure of politics and culture in the new democracy. The adversity, pacts, and last-minute arrangements that shaped and restricted the transition from military to civilian rule could not but breed ambivalence—deep uncertainty about the feasibility of legitimate goals, about the consequences of too much pressure on the military. The ambivalence could affect political leaders and social activists alike.

The symbolic heart of memory of military rule as cruel rupture were the disappeared and the relatives, mainly women, who had organized themselves to find loved ones kidnapped by state agents. Their heart-wrenching quest exemplified why forgetting was morally outrageous. The persistent women of the Agrupación de Familiares de Detenidos-Desaparecidos (Association of Relatives of the Detained and Disappeared, hereinafter Agrupación) embodied the metaphor of the "open wound"—for years they had searched for the truth of the detention and fate of their loved ones; for years they had met with state denial and misinformation that rubbed salt in the wound. It did not take long, in relations between Agrupación activists and leaders of a new democratic government, for a subtle mix of synergy and friction to emerge. Both needed one another to accomplish key objectives: a public reckoning with the reality of disappearance as state policy, a promotion of human rights as a fundamental value and contrast between democracy and dictatorship. But conceptions of how best to advance and to sort out the relationship between truth and justice differed. In the first eight months of the new government, in addition to their cultural and street activities to raise awareness, the women met repeatedly with high officials—Minister of Justice Cumplido in April and August, Interior Minister Enrique Krauss in July, President Patricio Aylwin in November. One aspect of such meetings was the practical work of collaboration—for example, how best to handle human remains newly discovered in April at an army firing range, both to secure proper forensic evidence and to arrange a dignified burial. Another aspect was to communicate and press the other party toward one's understanding of the best path toward mutual objectives—for example, exchanges on how to handle justice and the 1978 Amnesty Law. Some sore points emerged—for example, Agrupación activists lobbied media for full coverage of human rights news, including the graphic and the shocking, and resented occasional calls by Cabinet ministers, particularly Krauss, for a restraint that lessened cultural consternation.

On Aylwin's central memory initiative, the National Truth and Reconciliation Commission, the Agrupación responded with sentiments of appreciation and collaboration—and a push for more that also yielded irritation and critique. Upon the initial announcement in April, the Agrupación declared, "We value and recognize as an act of moral constancy [*consecuencia*] and moral honesty this decision by the President of the Republic." The Agrupación would adopt a stance of "active collaboration" with the Commission, and it called on other parties to do the same. The Agrupación did not criticize Aylwin, but announced it would continue to demand that the judicial branch fulfill its "essential mission which is to do justice." The complexity of frictional synergy emerged more forcefully in August, when the Supreme Court ruled that the 1978 Amnesty Law was valid and applicable to disappearance cases, and implied that the amnesty obviated the necessity of criminal investigation to establish facts and responsibilities. The Agrupación continued to focus the bulk of its moral pressure on the judicial branch —it called on the justices to resign because of grave abandonment of duty— but it also ran into stiff resistance, in the administration and Congress, to launching an impeachment process. (The reluctance derived from the fact that the process would have been politically contentious and likely to end with failure and a weaker capacity to negotiate accords with Renovación and military actors.) The Agrupación could not secure the minimum number of ten cosponsors in Congress for a constitutional accusation. Despite a sense of deception about the political will of their presumed allies, the Agrupación continued to blend moral sympathy and moral pressure in its treatment of the two key leaders of truth-and-justice policy: Minister of Justice Cumplido and President Aylwin. When Cumplido met with criticism from the Right for frank comments on the Supreme Court's ruling, the Agrupación sent him a letter of solidarity and expressed understanding of the "many obstacles" the government faced on human rights, while adding pointedly that "now is the time to take decisions to reform the Judicial Power."

A similar blend—appreciation of genuine obstacles and of advances toward truth, insistence and partial discrepancy on justice and amnesty— marked relations with Aylwin. At bottom, leader-activists of the Agrupación and of the counterpart Association of Relatives of Executed Political Prisoners (Agrupación de Familiares de Ejecutados Políticos) feared that unless they pushed the point hard, the government's truth-oriented strategy would culminate in a de facto acceptance of legal impunity for perpetrators. Even before the March inauguration, Agrupación leaders had pressed for a "truth and justice" commission. When Aylwin announced in April a "truth and reconciliation" commission, recalled Sola Sierra, the late president of the Agrupación, "the first frustration occurred, because it is the word justice that they erased and we felt that something was lacking."[34]

The frictional synergy that shaped relations between political elites and human rights activists was part of a larger dynamic and dilemma. Many grassroots groups and activists committed to social justice for the lower classes and the excluded had cut their teeth in the confrontational political culture of the 1980s, when street mobilization, direct action, and media muckraking raised awareness and undercut the authority of a dictatorial regime. Others had come of age even earlier, in the pre-1973 democracy that blended social mobilization with electoral competition. Now, in 1990, a government elected with the support of such grassroots groups steered a transition amidst great constraint and adversity, and adopted a stance of caution that encouraged trust in negotiated accords among elites, and discouraged pressure or even support through strong mobilization. Under the circumstances, activists and citizens who constituted part of the "social debt" bequeathed by dictatorship felt displaced and unsettled. They found themselves pulled toward a new kind of "participation" that put a premium on accommodating the delicate circumstances of transitional democracy, and on providing social services that supplemented the limited efforts and resources of government.

Consider, for example, the health promotion group Llareta in the southern shantytown of La Bandera in metropolitan Santiago. In 1990, an outbreak of meningitis required immediate effective action. When leaders of the group met with officials of the Health Ministry, they received a welcome distinct from the contempt that greeted them when seven children died in a similar outbreak under military rule, in 1985. This time a doctor received Llareta and other health groups warmly and praised them for their good work in distributing educational material to improve pubic health. But the answer to a request for tangible resources was that the government had no additional funds. When Llareta activists stated they would launch a street demonstration to protest government neglect, the response was not repression but reproach—a warning not to betray their government or to place at risk the stability of democratic transition. Significantly, the ambivalence and uncertainty built into the structure of transition was not confined to government administrators and political elites alone. Health activists went forward with a downtown march, but fewer people turned out to support the protest than in 1985. The network of grassroots health groups was itself divided on the wisdom of the march.[35]

In the new democracy, was the point of citizen participation by a grassroots health group to supplement the government effort by providing services such as health education, vaccinations, and environmental cleanups? Or was the point also to make social needs known and to demand, if necessary by protest, a better state response? Over time, a grant application system would emerge and privilege the former, through a solidarity and social investment fund (FOSIS) that considered community development and microenterprise proposals. Such an approach did not sweep away the frictional synergies that shaped relations between community groups and political elites. On the contrary. In both city and countryside, an emerging model of muted citizen participation—and awareness of the adversity of transition—channeled discontent toward more subtle forms of government-citizen engagement and tension, and away from open social protest and mobilization. The latter did not disappear but began to seem more anachronistic. As Mapuche activist Don Heriberto Ailío put it, when considering his community's long history of land struggles, "Before struggle was about taking over a road, writing up a list of demands. Now struggle is about writing grants."[36]

The most explosive dilemma of the new democracy, and the root of much of the frustration that marred relations between government leaders and social activists, was the elusive boundary between military and civilian control —and the impact of the memory question on military power and legitimacy. The new cultural environment placed the military on the defensive. The hunger to open the memory box of Pinochet's rule and find hidden truths did not only shape the market of bestselling books. It affected the mirror of the nation put forth in mass media. Disturbing events and images—memory knots that demanded attention—burst into the news despite the best efforts of the outgoing regime to limit the economic prospects and audience reach of unfriendly media.

Particularly important was television. The new government envisioned Televisión Nacional in the mold of an independent public service, such as the BBC (British Broadcasting Corporation). Led by Jorge Navarrete (the new director), Bernardo de la Maza (the news director), and journalists such as Patricia Politzer (who would become the news director in 1991), the news group would be responsible for building professional credibility and an audience. Meanwhile the government promoted a reform to alleviate the crushing debt structure left by the military regime and to create a more independent directorship. The result: Already in 1990, hard-hitting news and expression found a forum on television, not just in print media and radio.[37]

The most explosive memory-truths came quickly. People began discovering hidden human bodies. On 21 March—only ten days into the new administration—construction workers discovered three cadavers on former army property near Colina (about thirty-five kilometers north of Santiago). "Someone is lying," proclaimed the influential magazine *Hoy* in its cover story. The most dramatic discovery took place in June in Pisagua, the legendary site of political banishment and rumored death in the desert North. Attempts to find people in Pisagua had gotten under way since the 1980s. Relatives and friends of the executed and the disappeared, and former political prisoners, led the effort. Their work had yielded information, held at the Vicariate of Solidarity of the Catholic Church, about one probable location. A search, begun on 31 May, turned up nineteen bodies within a week.

The cultural impact of the find was huge. The dry climate had preserved not only the cruel bodily mutilations inflicted on the victims, but also the look of shrieking agony. The discovery occurred only six weeks after Aylwin had announced formation of a National Truth and Reconciliation Commission, and the Commission sent members to inspect the site. Renovación Nacional had rejected participation by its militants on the Commission. Now it was thoroughly shaken, and the Truth Commission's necessity legitimized further. As the Renovación representative Evelyn Matthei (also the daughter of the air force general and former junta member Fernando Matthei) put it, "We are beginning to face up to the truth of what has happened during all these years."[38]

The explosion came on a nightly news program of Televisión Nacional. On 11 June the program featured an eleven-minute interview by Politzer of (retired) General Horacio Toro, now a key official as *director de investigaciones*, head of the police office of intelligence and crime research. Toro's background as a coauthor of the junta's 1974 Declaration of Principles placed him squarely in the camp of those who had once believed in the junta's takeover as the salvation of Chile. The politicocultural shock of Pisagua was the subtext as the discussion moved from charges of police corruption and prisoner abuse that signified a debilitated moral ethos, toward the now dissolved secret police (CNI) and the legitimate methods for achieving security and intelligence in a democracy. Finally, Toro and Politzer reached the danger zone: military honor and the army role in human rights violations. Toro asserted that military honor had been damaged under junta rule, and that at first, when he served on the presidential advisory staff, he had not known about human rights violations. Politzer asked if "it could be" that Augusto Pinochet also did not know.[39]

> [TORO:] There is an old principle among soldiers that says that the Commander . . . is responsible for what his unit does and does not do, so that from the point of view of military principle, General Pinochet, even if he were unaware or ignorant of the facts, is morally responsible for them.
> [POLITZER:] From this point of view and in your judgment and considering military honor, should he resign from the institution?
> [TORO:] In my opinion, yes.

Precisely when Chile was reeling from the shock of Pisagua, Toro and Politzer had pushed the ultimate hot button—Pinochet's accountability for cruel and dehumanizing state violence inflicted on defenseless prisoners, and as such, his betrayal of the right to honorable command.

The military response followed the well-worn path of legal ensnarement in a military tribunal—charges against Toro and News Director de la Maza (permitted by the 1980 Constitution) for defamation of high officials and pressure on Politzer to divulge the raw interview footage for comparison with the edited version. For Politzer, the worst pressure came from within the government, some of whose officials blamed her for creating problems and suggested tendentious editing. She was confident about her editorial judgment—she had won fame for interview-books in the 1980s and had never before faced accusations of distortion—but she refused to turn over raw footage to the court on grounds of professional principle. Here, too, a certain frictional synergy was at work.[40]

The news section of Televisión Nacional stood its ground. On 25 October, its magazine program of investigative journalism, *Informe Especial*, focused on the detained-and-disappeared. The program directed attention to the Pisagua saga: the twenty-one cadavers discovered at midyear, the process of excavation, the secret 1970s footage of Pisagua's prisoners by German journalists, the memorial mass in the cathedral of Iquique, the interviews with witnesses—former political prisoners, and mothers and wives—who humanized the victims and their values. The editorial message was that the country could not advance unless it faced "the truth"—that many victims were worthy people loved by their relatives, that they died at the margin of law, that official lying had shrouded the reality of their torment and executions, that Pisagua was not an exceptional event. The most moving moment came when Lidia Saluzzi, widow of Juan Ruz, a Socialist executed at Pisagua but still disappeared, explained why she thanked God.[41]

> Thanks to God, my children do not feel hatred, and for that I thank God, because that was what my husband asked me the most when alive. In his last words that he had someone tell me, when he now realized they are going to shoot him—"Lidia, I ask you a favor," he tells me. "Please, do not raise our children with hatred, let them know the truth when they are old enough to understand it, but that [the children] should forgive [the executors] because they do not know what they are doing."

The Pisagua and Televisión Nacional affairs were the tip of the proverbial iceberg. For junta partisans and sympathizers, and for the army and Pinochet in particular, the new memory environment meant harassment, ingratitude, loss of prestige, and ultimately pressure for Pinochet to resign in disgrace. The memory put forth by the human rights camp amounted to a campaign waged against the people who had saved the country and built prosperity. If the campaign were not resisted, it would finally breach the wall of protection against dishonor and trials.

In this framework, and for persons whose background inclined them to see Televisión Nacional as an instrument of state propaganda, Aylwin himself seemed to stoke the campaign. As president-elect in 1989, Aylwin met with Pinochet and asked him to resign in the best interests of the country, even as he acknowledged Pinochet's legal right to remain army commander under the 1980 Constitution. As president, Aylwin avoided asking for a resignation, in part because to ask and be refused would undercut presidential authority. He continued to recognize formally, too, that Pinochet had a legal right to continue. But Aylwin's words and acts also exerted moral pressure that cut the other way. On 20 August 1990, he spoke at a ceremony in Chillán to honor the birthday of Bernardo O'Higgins, Chile's Independence hero and first president. In 1822, when O'Higgins no longer enjoyed wide support and opposition threatened to spark internal military clashes, he had resigned and left for exile. The act of ultimate sacrifice for the country he loved entered the national lore. Aylwin praised the patriotism of O'Higgins, who "never brandishes his weapon nor his condition of soldier against the will of his people." Upon realizing his presence stood in the way of Chile's tranquility and progress, O'Higgins "accepts, resigned to ostracism." The allusion was obvious. It questioned the symbolic core of memory as salvation, Pinochet's patriotism. Adding to the blow was the fact that it came at the outset of "Army Month." The September memory season that began with the O'Higgins birthday and that culminated with the military parades on 19 September was both an army memory season and a national memory season; the overlap conflated national well-being and army heroism. Two weeks after the O'Higgins address, Aylwin seemed to add insult to injury when he honored Allende's memory at the funeral held on 4 September.[42]

In the weave of presidential discourse and gesture, Aylwin balanced such blows with the theme of a convivencia that included respect for the military. In tone and political strategy, his administration placed high value on "prudence," on achieving workable accords among political elites including the Center-Right, and on the symbolic courtesies consistent with dialogue and convivencia, all to be accompanied with defense of basic principles and with frankness about constraints. Aylwin greeted Pinochet with civility—a shrug, a smile, a handshake—during the awkward transition act of 11 March. He rejected the aggressive political honeymoon strategy, favored by Lagos and some sectors in the Concertación, of pushing harder for deep constitutional reform at the risk of jeopardizing relationships and tax and labor accords with Renovación. The administration much preferred the gentleman politics of negotiation and consensus building among elites, to the unpredictable politics of street pressure and mobilization. The political memory that influenced the moderate approach was that leaders and activists of the 1960s and early 1970s—in Left, Center, and Right, each representing only about a third of Chileans—had become so doctrinaire and bent on achieving the whole loaf, that they destroyed politics as the art of the possible through dialogue, compromise, and pacts. The balancing act—keen awareness of constraint and keen interest in accords, alongside affirmation of principle—sometimes yielded strained defensive language. "This is a prudent government, but not a cowardly one," insisted Enrique Correa, the secretary general of government, in May 1990.[43]

Aylwin therefore complemented acts of pressure and civilian moral authority that placed Pinochet on the spot with acts that reaffirmed civilian-military convivencia, and respect for the rules of transition. On 18 September, just a month after the address on O'Higgins, he saluted the army and declared that Chile had always had confidence in its armed forces to defend national sovereignty, territory, and rule of law. He again underscored the necessity of frank truth for convivencia. The "political abnormality" that prevailed in Chile over sixteen years had left "grave wounds on national convivencia. It would be blind to ignore that this situation especially affects relations between civilians and military." But he was "President of all Chileans" and he stood by his National Stadium declaration that convivencia should include civilians and soldiers alike. The political objective of restoring presidential power to remove high military officials did not imply disrespect, nor lack of clarity about the legal institutionality the new government inherited.[44]

THE POLITICS OF TRUTH: WAR BY OTHER MEANS?

For Pinochet, his Army loyalists, and his political advisory committee, headed by army general Jorge Ballerino, such comments were hardly reassuring. They understood themselves to be caught in a struggle that inverted Clausewitz: politics as war by other means.

A serious struggle to define lines of authority and control had taken hold during the crucial first year of transition, and it could not be disentangled from the memory question. Despite the pointed allusion to retirement in the O'Higgins address, Aylwin was *not* obsessed with securing a resignation from Pinochet—even less so with securing it at any cost. His top priority was to achieve a successful democratic transition. A successful transition was understood as the impossibility of return to military rule, built on a foundation of moral values, political support, and climate of convivencia that would legitimize the new democracy and render it sustainable. In this conception, a successful transition would increase the likelihood of achieving additional democratizing reforms over time.

Aylwin's stance on Pinochet as army commander in chief was, therefore, subtle and fraught with ambivalence. On the one hand, to keep Pinochet in the army commander role was to tie him down to the same institutional-legal rules of transition that hampered the Aylwin administration. The irony: Pinochet would have an interest in respecting rather than wrecking the laws of transition, even if politics, culture, and institutional rules moved in an adverse direction, and over time lessened his authority and ability to shield officers from accountability. Continuity of leadership and coherence in the army also provided a certain insurance against rogue colonels and soldiers—a Chilean version of the Argentine *carapintadas* (painted faces) whose rebellions wrecked the success of the Alfonsín presidency. Also, to ask for a resignation without having the power to force it would invite rebuffs that would undermine rather than consolidate presidential authority. On the other hand, for Pinochet to continue as army commander only made sense if the process of transition actually corralled him, and ended up producing a more democratic society and polity. The process would have to erode Pinochet's moral and practical ability to act in the style of a dictator or supreme authority. It would have to yield a society of distinct values, common sense, and social outcomes, despite the major economic and institutional continuities with the military era. Pinochet would have to be made to learn new habits: submission to presidential and ministerial authority, even though the president could not fire him; acceptance of a digging into the past that yielded stinging critiques and calls for truth and justice, as a fact of life to be tolerated even if he considered himself a hero; lack of control over the inner workings of government including the Defense Ministry and Justice Ministry, even if some officials were "enemies."

The bottom line followed. Pinochet's resignation was less important to Aylwin than the terms under which it might happen, and the consequences for the success of transition. For the same reason, it mattered to keep asserting moral pressure that built legitimacy and hemmed in Pinochet—to voice forcefully the value of human rights as well as convivencia, to reckon openly with the truth of morally indefensible acts under military rule. In this perspective, the work of the Truth and Reconciliation Commission was both an ethical necessity and a political necessity.[45]

Neither Pinochet nor Aylwin escaped the paradox that bound and divided them. Aylwin held most of the "soft power" of moral legitimacy and elected position; Pinochet held most of the "hard power" of military control and a loyal investor class. For both, the pacts of the transition were real and constraining, but they did not seal once and for all the lines of authority and power. Rather, they set terms for an ongoing struggle over its boundaries. A part of such struggle took the form of "inside game" jockeying to set contours for everyday government. Before the inauguration, the outgoing defense minister sought in vain to clip presidential appointment power by asserting a right of the military to form the short list of suitable nominees for subsecretary positions in the Defense Ministry. In the early months after transition, Pinochet sought in vain to convince Aylwin that presidential protection by the carabineros was deficient, and that the army should handle presidential security.[46] A key part of the struggle, however, would unfold in the public opinion arena. It would continue the quest for "hearts and minds" that had proved so important during the dictatorship years. In this effort, the memory question—how to define the true reality and meaning of military rule, especially the crisis of 1973 and the state violence unleashed on citizens—was strategic. It galvanized Chileans powerfully. How the memory question played out, moreover, might shift the boundaries of "justice to the extent possible," Aylwin's famous and often demeaned phrase of constraint. The new political game was about control. Each side saw the question of Pinochet's continuity of office in this context.

For Pinochet and Ballerino, his chief political strategist, dangerous memory talk did not stop with Pisagua and human rights. The most dangerous talk homed in on corruption. Such talk belied the image of selfless patriotic sacrifice. It could corrode *from within* the memory camp that remembered military rule as Chile's salvation—by placing at risk the loyalty of the political Right, by compromising protection and promotion of allies and clients within the military, and by rendering Pinochet and his family vulnerable to legal sanction. In September, publicity about military corruption turned serious. The evidence involved not only army and secret police officers who had benefited from an illegal financial laundering company (nicknamed "la Cutufa"), but the Pinochet family itself. The previous month the government had secretly received photocopies of three army checks totaling some 972 million pesos (about us$3 million), written in January 1989 to complete a sales transaction of Valmoval, a manufacturer that supplied the army light arms of dubious value. The beneficiary of the checks was none other than Pinochet's son, Augusto Pinochet Hiriart. Chilean slang did the rest of the damage. The checks were dubbed "Pinocheques."

Pinochet and the army seemed to be returning to the turbulent 1980s, when muckraking articles in *Cauce, Hoy,* and other magazines homed in on corruption in order to destroy the myth of patriotic salvation. Copies of the checks were leaked to the press. On 6 September, Concertación representatives in Congress initiated a request for official investigation. For Ballerino, Pinochet, and high army officers, the first half-year of civilian government had brought a litany of bad events. The announcement of a truth commission in April, the Pisagua affair and the Televisión Nacional interview of Toro in June, the presidential contrast between the patriotism of O'Higgins and Pinochet in August, the "Cutufa" and "Pinocheques" corruption revelations in September, these were not isolated events. Nor could persons accustomed to an institutional culture of strict control from the top easily see some such events as markers of a hunger for truth that exceeded a capacity for top-down coordination and control. No, the events must have formed part of a strategy, pushed along by enemies such as the hostile defense minister Patricio Rojas, to break down army prerogative and protection by humiliating Pinochet and forcing a resignation. The "truth" preached by Aylwin and the Concertación was dangerous. It would not only open up the memory box of human rights violations, but also paint military rule as opportunistic self-enrichment. Unless stopped, it could create pressure so fierce and varied—from Renovación Nacional, sectors of the military and the economic Right, and public opinion—that the rules of the game and Pinochet's role as ultimate guardian would finally unravel.[47]

What rendered the pressure even more galling, for Pinochet and his base of supporters, was their own firm belief in memory as salvation. Pinochet and the military had rescued Chile from an awful fate including imminent war, and they stood as guarantors of its future progress. Indeed, memory as salvation had begun to acquire a new layer of meaning in 1990. In February, during his last weeks as president, Pinochet undertook a tour of the country to rally the two-fifths minority that voted for him in 1988, and the officials and functionaries who assisted him over the years. The tour also served to remind everyone that he would continue on as guardian in the new order: "I will look, I will listen, and I will continue working." The slogan of the tour: "Thanks General. Mission Accomplished." The day before the transition, Pinochet personally distributed a special medallion to high officials and many low-level functionaries. The words on the medal proclaimed pride and a sense of control: "Mission Accomplished."[48]

The new layer of meaning brushed lightly over the original idea of the pro-Pinochet campaign in the 1988 plebiscite. The "Yes" had campaigned to project Pinochet's rule far into the future precisely to avoid the ruin of a successful society, and the return to Allende's Unidad Popular. The new discourse adjusted to defeat by turning it into intention and accomplishment. The military had achieved its fundamental objectives of stopping civil war and a violent Marxist dictatorship, stabilizing and modernizing the country and its economy, and building a protected democracy under a new Constitution. Pinochet and the junta had—after arduous work to tackle problems at the root—*chosen* to give the country back to civilians, in excellent working order. They had waited until their work was finished and the country and its civilians were ready for the return. The new approach was underscored in the book launch of Pinochet's memoirs *Camino recorrido*

(Path Taken) in September 1990. By the mid-1990s, the new layer of meaning—"Mission Accomplished"—had congealed strongly in the minds of proponents of memory as salvation.[49]

In the seesaw struggle of "politics as war by other means," symbols of authority and the control of career paths mattered. At the army parade of 19 September, army general Carlos Parera, former head of the DINA's Department of External Operations, capped the symbolism of discontent by violating the formal protocol of presidential authority. Parera neglected to ask the president "permission" to begin the parade. Earlier, jeers greeted Aylwin as he entered the stands at O'Higgins Park. The government had suspected the ceremony would go poorly, since Parera had provided its director of civilian organizations only 800 of the 5,000 tickets for the reviewing stands. Aylwin, sensitive to the symbolism of authority and aware that Parera's actions were "part of the game," would exact his price later. He used the incident to shrink military control over career paths.

After the September memory season, pressure on Pinochet's authority among his own tightened. He found it more difficult to protect the careers of his own loyalists. In October, the "Cutufa" affair forced out sixteen high officers, among them four generals including the former CNI director Hugo Salas Wenzel. At the end of the month, Pinochet completed an institutionally strategic function, formation of the promotion list of generals for presidential approval. He ran into a roadblock. Aylwin vetoed two Pinochet loyalists recommended for promotion from brigadier general to major general—Parera, who had violated the protocol of submission to presidential authority, and Ramón Castro Ivanovic. Castro Ivanovic had a DINA past and also had served as the go-between for Pinochet in a financial transfer scheme. State funds were used to purchase and resell property in a manner that enabled Pinochet to acquire, at undermarket prices, a huge complex of valuable properties known as El Melocotón. The scheme had first come to light during the media muckraking of the 1980s. Pinochet and Ballerino fought the vetoes. Their argument: the president was legally obligated to sign the nomination list before sending it on to the comptroller general of the republic for the last step (final review that documents and procedure are legally proper). In short, the president's function was mere transmittal of an autonomous military decision. He could not treat the promotions as a proposal to approve or disapprove. Ballerino and Pinochet found themselves ensnared and lost the argument. On 5 November, Aylwin offered a television interview to

Patricia Politzer, and declared that Pinochet was not accustomed to his subordinate role, since he had ruled for so many years "as absolute master of the country." Four days later, the comptroller general backed the documents submitted by the administration. It fell to army vice-commander Jorge Lúcar to negotiate some face-saving arrangements—Parera and Castro would move into military attaché positions abroad, and Parera would retire in a year.

The new bottom line was clear. Military commanders would have to negotiate the promotion lists with the civilian administration. They could not necessarily protect high officers they wished to reward from vetoes that blocked or ended careers, nor could they protect those whose history of human rights violations made them unacceptable. In 1993, Ballerino himself ran aground. He found his path blocked to the vice-commander position and ended up retiring.[50]

THE DENOUEMENT

Democracy as dilemma came to a head on 19 December. That afternoon, sensitive negotiations for a possible early resignation of Pinochet, conducted by Ballerino as head of Pinochet's advisory committee and Rojas as Minister of Defense, reached impasse. Could the government wind down investigation and publicity about the "Pinocheques" case, and the rhetorical pressure on Pinochet, in exchange for a promise of early resignation? The Pinocheques case was a sword of Damocles. Although it was the son of Pinochet whose name appeared on the checks, theoretically the investigation might uncover evidence implicating Pinochet directly. (At the time, the scale and the direct involvement of Pinochet in corruption was a murky area, despite some earlier scandals such as El Melocotón. As we shall see in chapter 6, not until the Riggs Bank revelations of 2004 did the scale of Pinochet's self-enrichment take hold as a firm cultural truth.) Investigation of the Pinocheques case by a congressional committee and by the Council of Defense of the State (the legal arm of the executive branch) had continued, and the congressional committee had yet to issue a report.

The prologue to the discussion had its subtleties. It was unclear how seriously Pinochet or Aylwin took the idea. As we have seen, Aylwin saw some advantages in Pinochet's continuation, and also wanted to avoid undermining presidential authority by asking for a resignation—or appearing too interested. Pinochet, despite the pressures of 1990, had a strong sense of honor and equated his personal well-being with that of the army and the nation. It would be difficult to relinquish his role as the ultimate guardian of the army and the rules of transition. Under the circumstances, any exploration would be cautious—inseparable from efforts to define the political forces that would govern transition, justice, and the military legacy well into the future, and also difficult to separate from a laying of traps. Was a retirement offer by Pinochet "real," or was it bait? Was an interest by the administration in providing Pinochet a dignified way out "real," or would it be a hard shove down the slippery slope of military vulnerability?

On 18 December—the day before events turned explosive—Pinochet and Aylwin met in Aylwin's home. The presumable purpose of the meeting, relayed by Senator Sergio Onofre Jarpa of Renovación Nacional as intermediary, was that Pinochet wanted to resign. The matter never came up. Aylwin followed his policy by which he avoided either asking or appearing too interested. Pinochet was too ambivalent and proud to bring the matter up unless Aylwin provided the opening. After all, it had been Pinochet's political advisor, Ballerino, who suggested that a resignation offer might provide a path to relieve political pressure and protect the legacy of military rule. After the fruitless meeting, Ballerino conveyed continuing interest. Aylwin directed that discussions to improve civilian-military relations would take place with Minister of Defense Rojas. In effect, Rojas could explore the resignation issue as the civilian Cabinet member charged with oversight of the military, while enabling the skeptical Aylwin to draw some distance. Rojas as interlocutor would also assure that the administration had a tough negotiator.

The next day Rojas and Ballerino met twice. The discussions went poorly, and the laying of traps was evident. Ballerino wanted conditions that would protect the current institutional scheme and Pinochet's role as dignified guardian—and buy time for rules of transition and army autonomy far into the future. Pinochet would resign after a decent interval, perhaps at the end of Aylwin's term in 1994, perhaps earlier. As important, Pinochet wanted to name the new army commander. Rojas wanted specific commitment to an early resignation, before 15 April. An early resignation, roughly coinciding with release of the Truth and Reconciliation Commission report, would maximize the political, institutional, and cultural impact. At the second meeting, Rojas reaffirmed the necessity of a quick exit date, 15 April. Rojas miscalculated. He apparently thought he had Pinochet cornered, and could produce a spectacular realignment of political forces. Ballerino thought he heard an ultimatum.

The public pressure also failed to let up. The Pinocheques inquiry in Congress continued on—and mobilized witness testimony from a general. Rumors of possible resignation reached the press. On the day of the Ballerino-Rojas talks, when Pinochet left a ceremonial luncheon with Aylwin and high officers at La Moneda, reporters asked him if the rumors were fact.

That same Wednesday evening, Pinochet played his trump card. At six o'clock he ordered a Grade One *acuartelamiento*, that is, an emergency alert ordering army troops to report to their units within two hours. Within an hour the alert had been executed in Santiago and many provinces. News of the alert began to appear on the radio. Aylwin continued with the symbolism of civilian control by ordering Rojas, as Pinochet's immediate superior, to call Pinochet on his private line. Rojas warned him that there were constitutional means to make his discontent known. Pinochet cut to the core as he saw it. "Yes, sir, I know it very well. But you are blackmailing me." As rumors and alarm spread, Aylwin went to his home to manage the crisis with senior advisors. Rojas contacted the navy and air force command; they had not issued parallel alerts. The government and the army both wanted to step back from the brink. The point had been to demonstrate that if pushed too hard, Pinochet and the army could destroy political stability and authority, even without organizing a coup.

By midnight both sides had found a language of polite fiction that restored normalcy. The pressure to resign, interpreted by Ballerino as an ultimatum, had been a misunderstanding—not an ultimatum. The official government position had always recognized Pinochet's right to continue as commander in chief. The Grade One alert, which violated procedure under the 1980 Constitution, was not really an acuartelamiento. It was a lower-grade and legally permissible readiness exercise (ejercicio de alistamiento y enlace). The government and Concertación representatives lowered the political profile and judicial reach of the "Pinocheques" affair, and of similar investigations involving Pinochet's daughter Lucía and her husband, Julio Ponce Lerou. Pinochet would not be called to testify before Congress; the investigative reports were filed with the comptroller without direct reference to possible individual responsibility by Pinochet and without corresponding judicial action or participation by the legal arm of the Executive, the Council of Defense of the State. The understandings were in keeping with a painful Weberian "ethic of responsibility." They were also in keeping with an older aspect of Chilean political culture, reaching a political "arrangement" of problems by elites who forged a language of normalcy.[51]

Democracy as dilemma had turned into a real-life drama, not an abstraction. It was also reviving, within the Concertación and among political elites more generally, a familiar Chilean cultural device—the keeping of multiple knowledge registers. Everyone knows what happened; no one acknowledges what happened. "No pasó nada" (nothing happened) becomes the cultural code phrase for saying "Let's pretend nothing happened—we've gotten over it."

The adaptation was understandable, but it was also ambivalent and temporary. The hunger to expose and reckon with volatile truths long hidden or denied did not go away. The memory question had turned Patricia Verdugo's book on the "Caravan of Death" into a best seller. It had driven people to find bodies hidden in the Pisagua desert. As Chile's president and citizens recovered from the shock of troop alert, the Truth and Reconciliation Commission entered its final feverish phase of research and writing.

✵

"My Dear President"

When Señora Hortensia Bussi de Allende spoke at the reburial of her husband in Santiago on 4 September 1990, she evoked the memory of his special connection with many ordinary Chileans. "Salvador Allende is now alongside the pueblo. Nobody will be able to block the pueblo now from coming to his mausoleum in search of consolation, inspiration, or company."[1]

She was right. For days upon days, crowds of people streamed to the tomb to pay their respects, leave a flower, open the mind's memory box, perhaps buy a picture. After the initial crowds and attention subsided, something more subtle happened. Of course, there continued to be symbolic dates—Allende's birthday, the 4 September anniversary, human rights anniversaries—that drew visits by the family, foreign dignitaries or activists, delegations from the Socialist Party and human rights groups, especially the Agrupación of relatives of the detained and disappeared. Foreign dignitaries sometimes left wreaths, and women of the Agrupación sometimes left ribbons bearing the names and dates of disappearance of their loved ones.

Beyond the commemorative visits and delegations, however, another phenomenon unfolded. For years, a trickle of ordinary people kept coming. Some kept thoughts to themselves or spoke quietly with relatives or friends. Some, especially in the first two years, felt compelled to write a note or a letter.[2]

Consolation, inspiration, company. All were evident in notes and letters to a president alive in mind and memory. Also evident was a desire to say "thank you," "I won't forget you."

Good morning
My dear president, the present card is to greet you and give you thanks for

living. Yes, because like you said, you will continue alongside us. In my heart will continue to live your beautiful words of love, justice and equality. . . . Thank you for having fought for all of us, thank you for having given your life for us. You will all days be in my Heart and my children and children will know you eternally.

Some thank-you notes were from youngsters, who could only have known Salvador Allende as legend. Allende's death at La Moneda Palace—he refused to surrender or seek exile despite the bombing of the palace—had an epic quality, reinforced by his eloquent last radio address for History. In that address he calmly accepted his fate and framed it as loyalty. He had decided to remain true to democratic constitutionalism, to the ordinary people who placed their faith in him, to the dream of a just society. The memory struggles that unfolded in Chile and turned into mass street experience in the 1980s reproduced and fortified the symbolic power of Allende's sacrifice.[3] The circumstances of constraint and pragmatism that defined the transition, which some youth viewed as near-capitulation, also lent mythical power to a president willing to die for his principles. One young man wrote simply, "you / I Remember Always With / great Affection and appreciation / A grateful youth. H. M. Q." One young woman elaborated. She was an infant in 1973 and rarely saw the two *tíos* (two uncles, or an aunt and uncle) forced to flee Chile. She bore no hatred: "There is no hate in me but anguish, yes." She confessed that she held only limited historical knowledge of Allende. But she knew enough to feel inspired: "but you fought! and that gives me strength also to fight for the true and the unmentionable. I admire you. and I ask of you strength for my struggle to live, to overcome, to exist and to accept. . . . [signature] Thanks."

Some youths noted their admiration of Allende's *consecuencia*, the consistency of behavior and professed values symbolized in the last day of his presidency, even as they drew some critical or political distance. "I did not know you and less / will I mystify you / I admire your consecuencia / and love of truth / constancy and / believing in / man."

Two themes kept recurring in the memory notes. First, people kept mentioning consecuencia, or closely related ideas such as honor, courage of conviction, loyalty to one's people and values. Allende's last gesture to history was, in this sense, expressive of his entire political career or project. Second, people frequently used a language of affection (*cariño*) and familiarity (the *tú* form of address in Spanish) to express the personal sense of connection, remembrance, and "thank you."

The orthography of some such letters also exposed modest social background.

> Dear compañero Salvador Allende i write these simple lines to express to you all my thanks and [that] of my family for your devotion [*entrega*] for all of us the Chilean poor ones and workers. . . . for us you always will bi our compañero, friend and president that we always yurned for; forgive my writing and my spelling defects, but I tell you with all affection and sencirity that these my words come from the deepst of my feelings, because it is a lot the affection we feel for you and it is a lot the pain of not having you alive alongside all of us . . . a compañero a compa[ñ]era and their two little children [the names follow]

The hard circumstances of Chile's transition occasionally translated into notes of desperation. One woman addressed a note to Señora Hortensia about her son's mental and emotional troubles, which she saw as a legacy of abuse under the dictatorship, made worse by the anger and threats of a husband who was a former military man. She left a name and address. Other notes asked Salvador Allende, as if he were family, for spiritual help and fortitude. In June 1992, one anguished woman left a note for her *viejito lindo*, a term of endearment roughly similar to "my darling Pops." (In Spanish, the diminutive ending of *viejo*, a word like "Pops" or "my old man," accentuates the affection.)

> For you
> Salvador
> Viejito, Lindo
> Help me
> in this long walk
> of life. Give me the strength
> that I need to continue in this
> hard walk of life.
> to continu [*sic*] instilling good
> principles to my children
> Believe me . . . I feel, now
> without strength to continu [*sic*] . . .
> Help me viejito
> lindo

A compañ era of
the heart
A. V. S. 21.06.92

Most people did not leave notes. Flowers, especially carnations, were the most common artifacts of affection and remembrance. The impulse to leave a memory note diminished markedly by 1993–94. But visiting by ordinary folk, beyond the politically symbolic dates and visits by elites or activists or dignitaries, continued. On 1 November 1996, the Day of the Dead, when Chileans remember and visit the graves of their loved ones, my family and I went to Santiago's General Cemetery. For hours a small stream of people stopped by Allende's mausoleum to read the engraved excerpt from his last radio address, to sit on a bench to reflect, to leave a flower or shed a tear, to explain softly to their children why they were visiting. Allende was now accessible. He passed the day "alongside the pueblo."

Chapter 2

✿

Toward Memory Impasse?
The Truth Commission Moment, 1990–1991

On 13 August 1990, Ester Barría testified before Chile's Truth and Reconciliation Commission about her disappeared brother, Arturo Barría Araneda.[1] A music teacher at the school Liceo Darío Salas in Santiago, Arturo Barría was also a Communist. He was arrested on 28 August 1974 with two other teachers and a student. The act that drew ire had happened two days earlier; people sang the "International" and chanted some slogans at the funeral of a student. At the time of arrest, Arturo Barría was thirty-eight years old.

Pinochet himself authorized the arrests. During 1974, he and the DINA (secret police) had worried about knots of critique and resistance by the Left and Christian Democrats in schools and universities. On 28 August, the day of the arrests, Pinochet sent the minister of education, Admiral Hugo Castro, an authorization memo. He instructed Castro to act in light of DINA and other intelligence that Communists were working underground to organize a resistance network including the Center and Left. Castro and his ministry should identify Communists, separate them from their posts if caught in political activity, and entrust coercive measures to the Defense Ministry.[2]

Ester Barría wanted the Commission to understand Arturo Barría's human qualities—not simply administrative data such as age, occupation, political affiliation, and arrest date. "For me," she explained, "my brother was a guide, a support. . . . He had an immense value, an enormous capacity to give affection. He also taught me to raise my children. That loss was irreplaceable. He was the life of the party. He would give away chocolate to children so that they would learn to play piano."

Testimony by surviving political prisoners, part of the judicial trail organized by Barría's relatives and the Vicaría de la Solidaridad (Vicariate of Solidarity, hereinafter Vicaría) of the Santiago Catholic Church, confirmed Barría's rather remarkable personality. He was generous, warm, musical, and joyous. He somehow remained true to himself despite the descent into horror. In September, the DINA held him at its Cuatro Alamos holding camp. He was taken away at least twice to torture centers—including the infamous Villa Grimaldi—for brutal interrogations. Despite his ordeal, Barría also focused on the needs of others. Prisoners remembered that he sought to lift the spirit of the student who had been arrested. They remembered that he organized a prisoner chorus and put on shows with permission of the guards. Once, the chorus went to the female section to serenade the prisoners. Arturo Barría sang "Ave María" for the women.[3]

Now that the time for officially recognized truth telling had arrived, what did Ester Barría want? "I want his name cleared and his memory revindicated, that he be recognized for what he was, he was an excellent teacher, a joyous human being who was the center of the family." She also wanted to know the hidden truth of the repression. Her brother's name had appeared on the cruel 1975 list of "119 MIRistas" allegedly killed in fratricidal killings abroad, and the family had suffered from constant lies and denials.[4] "I want to know the truth, there cannot be reconciliation without first knowing with whom we are reconciling." She wanted justice, an accountability she distinguished from vengeance. "We want justice. We do not want vengeance, despite having been vilified, treated as crazy women looking for 'presumed detained-disappeared ones,' as they would say."

When considering violence and human rights, Chileans on all sides of memory conflicts did not readily separate truth from justice. For Pinochet, military officers, and their supporters, truth telling about human rights under military rule was not just unfair. It could push officers onto the slippery slope leading to trials, a de facto if not de jure voiding of the 1978 Amnesty Law. For Aylwin and leaders of the Concertación, the decision to make truth the first priority and pursue justice "to the extent possible" did not imply absence of a strategy to promote some sort of justice proceedings. For many victim-survivors and their relatives, and for human rights activists, official discovery and recognition of truth was important, but the pursuit of justice was its natural corollary. In the case of the disappeared, moreover, pursuit of justice was needed to round out or "complete" the truth—to establish the details of individual imprisonment, repressive violence, and final fate of the prisoner. Accountability was also a moral necessity for building a democratic society.

The Chilean populace as a whole made such connections. A culture of legalism had long roots in Chilean history. Talk of democracy as return to the rule of law, and the experience of supine justice under military rule, could only fortify justice as an ideal. A national poll in 1989 illustrated the truth-justice connection. Chileans did not blame the military or police as a whole for human rights violations. On a prestige scale of 1 to 7 (from "very bad" to "very good," respectively), the military and police forces secured respectable ratings (4.6 to 5.0, with the army at 4.6). Most Chileans, however, refused to reduce human rights violations to a problem of occasional excess by rogue soldiers. Asked about the magnitude of violations under Pinochet's rule, a majority (54.2 percent) perceived them as many (6–7, on a 7-point scale). Asked to choose between justice proceedings or amnesty for those responsible, two of three Chileans (67.5 percent) chose justice. Less than one in four (22.9 percent) favored amnesty. As important, only one in ten (9.5 percent) thought military tribunals should be entrusted to judge human rights cases.[5]

In sum, the values and assumptions of organized social actors and elites, and of the citizenry at large, entangled questions of truth with those of justice. The work of the National Truth and Reconciliation Commission (hereinafter called by its ubiquitous nickname, the Rettig Commission, after its chairman, Raúl Rettig) would be important, but it could not constitute an end point. During the Aylwin government (1990–94), Chileans began a long walk down the road of polemical and entangled policy issues—from truth to justice, justice to force, and back again to truth and justice. Genuine accomplishments were made along the way. Nonetheless, the walk could also resemble movement in a grand circle leading back to the same frustrating places. In their civic life, Chileans were beginning to walk the circle of memory impasse. The next two chapters examine the journey; the first homes in on the "moment of truth" during 1990–91, the second steps back to consider the circle of truth, justice, and force that shaped the longer journey to 1994.

INSIDE THE RETTIG COMMISSION (1): CONFRONTING TRUTHS THAT CRUSH

The Rettig Commission faced a daunting task as it began work in May 1990. At the time, few useful examples of truth commissions existed for transitions from the violent dictatorships that had spread across most of South America by the mid-1970s. Argentina had a notable truth commission experience, but its circumstances of transition—the military's legitimacy was in tatters after the 1982 Malvinas-Falklands war with Britain—were quite different. Also, Argentina's military rebellions in the late 1980s and its subsequent retreat to "due obedience" and "final stop" laws had undermined the first democratic government's truth-and-justice policy. Argentina seemed more a warning than an inspiration.[6]

Aylwin had limited the Rettig Commission's mandate. It was to focus on maximal cases—death, disappearance, and torture leading to death by agents of the state or persons in their hire, and deaths by private persons acting from political motive. (Strictly speaking, the former corresponded to international human rights law, which focused on violations of the state's basic duty to protect the lives and integrity of its citizens. The latter corresponded to international humanitarian law, which established minimal norms of conduct by anyone, even in war. Including the latter allowed the Commission to take cognizance of and define as violation acts of armed resistance leading to deaths of soldiers or police.) Despite the bounded mandate, the scope and multiple layers of political violence by the state added pressure. At the time, the Vicaría already had specific knowledge of 2,354 individual cases of death or disappearance under military rule. Its count of specifically known political arrests was also huge: 82,429. Even this figure was far less than the real number; a good conservative estimate of political imprisonment under military rule is 150,000 to 200,000. The combined political and economic exile flow had also been massive—200,000 at the lower-end estimates, 400,000 by one Vicaría estimate.[7]

Torture—applying severe bodily pain and mental terror to break down the prisoner's integrity as a human being—was difficult to quantify yet clearly massive. Only a small fraction of torture cases had led to formal legal denunciation under military rule. Problems of evidence compounded the usual problems of fear and unresponsive courts. In most torture cases, physical evidence on the survivor such as maiming, scars, and organ damage faded or disappeared over time and became more difficult to establish in the absence of confirming witnesses. For many victim-survivors, the most lasting and debilitating effects of torture were on mental and emotional health. Despite these problems and a weak rate of legal denunciation, the Vicaría knew of 2,741 specific cases. Translated into estimates, informed by knowledge of the pervasiveness of torture and the numerical scale of arrests, even José Zalaquett—a human rights professional inclined toward conservative methodology in the interests of credibility—thought torture cases would number in the dozens of thousands. The scale of the Commission's work would change drastically if it sought to investigate torture systematically, on a case-by-case basis.[8]

In sum, the number of individual cases to be investigated under the Commission's bounded mandate was large, and the number of persons for whom its report would matter directly, regardless of the Commission's technical scope, was even larger. In 1989, a sixth of the national citizenry (16.6 percent) believed they or a family member had been the direct victim of a human rights violation.[9]

The political ambience and limited powers of the Commission added to pressure and skepticism. On the Right, the decision to form a commission met with criticism—not only by the military, its core supporters, and the hard-Right UDI (Unión Democrática Independiente), but also by Renovación Nacional. In practice, Renovación proved a more reliable partner when negotiating labor, tax, or social spending accords with Aylwin and the Concertación than on truth-and-justice policy. Renovación argued the Commission would not advance reconciliation and might infringe on the 1978 amnesty. It objected to individual case history research and to limiting analysis to the period of military rule. It sought to keep party militants off the Commission and its staff. Although Aylwin succeeded in recruiting four of the eight Commission members from the Right, he tried but failed to persuade two Renovación leaders, Francisco Bulnes and Ricardo Rivadeneira, to join the Commission.[10]

Allies from the world of the Center-Left also had doubts. As we have seen, Aylwin's top advisors had been dubious. They thought a truth commission on such a volatile issue would turn into a political boomerang. Within the human rights community, the composition of Commission members and the rules governing its work provoked worry. Among the eight, only Castillo and Zalaquett had a proven background of expertise and activism in human rights. The Commission's mandate carefully stripped away any attributes that might be seen as a usurpation of judicial function. The Commission lacked subpoena powers and it lacked authority to name perpetrators of crimes, although it could forward evidence confidentially to the courts. The stripping had its rationale—it protected the legality of the Commission, respected due process, bowed to political realism. But it also fed anxiety. What could a Commission of such heterogeneous composition and such limited powers and mandate really accomplish?[11]

Inside the Rettig Commission, some concerns dissipated as the work itself took over. It took about two months for the Commission and its energetic and skilled executive secretary, Jorge Correa Sutil, to lay the foundation—to organize ground rules and procedures; to consult with and officially request collaboration from relevant entities (from domestic human rights groups, such as the Vicaría; to international religious and human rights organizations, such as Amnesty International and the World Council of Churches; to political parties decimated by the repression; to the various military and police forces; to the state's Medical-Legal Institute, for forensic evidence); to organize the information received from collaborating offices; to arrange appointments for relatives and other relevant witnesses to provide their testimony and documentation; to determine the universe of cases; to hire and orient a staff. The Commission received nearly 3,900 denunciations. Eliminating cases of victim names with no additional information, and cases that fell outside its mandate, still left a universe of 2,920 cases for thorough investigation. The appointment requests numbered 3,173, about equally divided between Santiago and the provinces.

Between July and November, as the focus turned to hearings with relatives and other witnesses and rigorous analysis of documentation, the workload turned crushing. One aspect of the crush was quantitative. Compared to the net case load of about 3,000, the staff to assist the 8 Commission members and the executive secretary was modest: 59 persons, comprised of 17 lawyers, 18 legal assistants (law students or recent graduates), 6 social workers, 8 documentary and program analysis specialists, and 10 secretaries and office assistants. The dominance of the lawyers and legal assistants reflected the core obligation of each staff team: to produce for each case a precise executive summary, usually several pages, reporting verifiable facts and enabling members of the Commission to decide either that the evidence established that a person died or disappeared as a consequence of state action (or by private persons acting under a political rationale), or that the evidence was insufficient to reach a definitive conclusion. Each lawyer would need to produce about 170 such summaries (and about 30 summaries of cases eliminated on technical grounds). In practice, many files included a thick foundation of documents provided by human rights organizations, particularly the Vicaría. The memory struggles that unfolded during the dictatorship years now proved crucial: they yielded copious documentation, including witness testimonies collected when the initial events of repression were fresh. The job of the lawyers was, in their executive summaries, to analyze meticulously this information and its veracity, as well as complementary information obtained from hearings with relatives or surviving witnesses or from data such as forensic reports.[12]

Another aspect of the crush, however, was qualitative.[13] The realities finally narrated and uncovered were intense and sometimes shocking, even to the experienced. They cut to the core of the human condition—the amazing lows of brutality, violence, and duplicity to which human beings can descend; the ennobling aspect when people act with dignity or ethical clarity amidst extreme fear and degradation; the ultimate issues of mortality, love, and loss that render other issues small. Often it was the oral testimonies by relatives that brought such issues to life.

The presence of social workers on the staff reflected the fact that the hearings with relatives were fundamental to the truth process—not only for fact finding, but also to start the long overdue process of social repair. Most detentions leading to death or disappearance took place before 1977. In other words, most relatives had endured *at least fourteen years* of state hostility and denial of responsibility. Building *convivencia*, and a culture of democracy and human rights, meant recognizing officially that which had gone unrecognized. For the first time in many years, relatives would find a state that would "listen" respectfully to the torment and humiliations they had endured. As the first step of social repair of unjust harm, as the climax of a long struggle to find truth, as the moment of reckoning with the possible death of a disappeared relative, the hearings were potentially cathartic events. Even the making of an appointment was emotionally powerful. Señora Herminda Morales, a veteran of struggle who had searched seventeen years and had joined a hunger strike to find her two disappeared sons, nearly fainted as she made her appointment.[14]

One task of the social workers was precisely to sensitize lawyers and Commission members to the symbolism and social repair aspects of the hearings. Indeed, one mandate of the Commission was to provide recommendations on social reparation, an objective facilitated if staff invited relatives to narrate not only the facts of repression but also its impact on their families. The professional training of staff lawyers, their lack of experience in human rights work, their core obligation to analyze whether the evidence clearly established a case as a violation leading to death or disappearance, all prepared them poorly for such considerations. Paula Serrano, a psychologist hired as a social worker, recalled that for the lawyers, "a concept they found very difficult to understand . . . was that reparation began with the first hearings, that the hearing was not just a collection of information like it was for [the lawyers], that it had a symbolic meaning." The huge number of requests for hearings reinforced the lawyers' tendency to focus on efficient fact collecting and cross-examination, rather than first "listening" and only then moving on to assessment, questioning, and verification of key facts. When Serrano insisted that the relatives needed to be given ample time to relate their own experiences, some staff lawyers panicked. "They would say no, we do not have time, there are 900 or so . . . Let them send it by fax!"

The result of such discussions was the working out of symbols and practices to facilitate truth telling in its double sense. On the one hand, truth telling was a narrative of facts of repression whose veracity and implications would need to be assessed and compared with the rest of the documentary record. On the other hand, truth telling was a narrative of family *experience* to be recognized and respected as such by the state. The hearing offices had to be made into a dignified and welcoming environment, despite Spartan physical facilities in Santiago, and despite fearful memory associations of the Intendancy offices in the provinces. Symbols mattered. A Chilean flag at every hearings desk signified that the listening process was official. The presence of a Commission member, not simply staff members, during a substantial portion of testimony underscored that the relatives' experiences mattered. To offer coffee and cookies, a modest act of cultural hospitality, recognized the dignity of persons after a long period of stigma and cruelty. A few open-ended questions ("Tell us about . . .") served to legitimize the full range of themes relevant to relatives—not only the facts of the repression but also the search for truth and justice; the personality, ideas, or work of the victim; the impact of the experience on families. Sessions with relatives generally lasted about an hour, but some went on much longer.[15] Lawyers listened as families told their stories on their own terms, then moved on to specific questions, corrections, comparisons, or follow-up interviews to establish the facts that might affect the merits of a case.

Such circumstances turned many hearings into emotionally intense experiences for family members—and Commission staff and members. Relatives who for years needed to avoid showing weakness before a hostile state could finally expose the deeper meanings of their saga: the treasured "goodness story" that restored the good name of the person killed or disappeared; the humiliation and despair endured when quests for truth met with cruel misinformation and denial; the economic and health toll on relatives, including young children. Since the late 1970s relatives often used a bodily metaphor—the wound that remains open, unallowed to heal—to express memory of military rule as endless rupture.

The metaphor was apt, the health effects physical, mental, and emotional. In the experience of relatives, the line between psychological and somatic afflictions sometimes dissolved. Consider the testimony of the sister of a disappeared person. "My mother succumbed to a gastric cancer as a result of her excessive nervousness, caused without a doubt by the detention and subsequent disappearance of my sister [name]. One of my nephews, who witnessed the arrest of my sister, is in these moments in a psychiatric hospital, specifically [name of hospital]." She believed that "his dementia owes to his having witnessed the detention of his aunt, something that seriously marked his state of mind and emotion."[16] Verbalizing such experiences produced a powerful impact on listeners as well as speakers.

The cathartic aspects of testimony also came through in more unexpected ways. The Commission was considering human behavior and experience at the outer limits of the imaginable. Not all members of a family reacted similarly to such events, not only for the obvious reasons of fear, politics, or personality but also for reasons more profound. The experience itself crossed over into human impossibility. As philosophers, artists, and survivor-witnesses have recognized, situations of "radical evil"—what we call today "crimes against humanity"—test and break the very premises we use to define order, rationality, and ethics. Under the circumstances people invent responses in a world without the usual normative guideposts. They may become deeply confused or ashamed in their own minds. Some of the most powerful truth-telling moments emerged when relatives exposed to each other their own deception or their own regret about the choices made in an impossible context. A staff lawyer could never forget the moment when a woman's appearance coincided with that of her children and their grandparents. To carry on the search for her disappeared husband, she had decided to leave the children to be raised by their grandparents. Without renouncing the search for her husband, she was also overcome by a sense of having abandoned her children. Experientially, she had lost them, too. She asked for and received their forgiveness. The lawyer wept along with everyone present.

Some such moments defied resolution. A staff social worker remembered two children who discovered the truth about their father. After his detention, the family experienced stigma and danger. The young mother—she loved her husband but also wanted to shield her children—moved to another city to live with her parents. She invented a cover story to explain the missing father. He had abandoned them, she said. The children grew up hating their father. Now, in 1990, the children's grandmother—their father's mother—decided that the time had come for the truth. "And she said, 'You are going to accompany me to bear witness for the life of your father,' and she told them . . . who their father had been and took them to the Commission." The youths had to switch from imagining the negligent father to imagining the caring father torn away from them, and then subjected to torture and death. The emotional turmoil of the children and the bitter family conflicts cut in several directions. Such matters would take years to "work through," if they could be worked through at all.

For the staff and members of the Rettig Commission, the sessions with relatives were especially important in building their own bonds of confidence, good faith, and mission. The hearings provided direct exposure to a reality more momentous than politics in the narrow or partisan sense. A strong sense of civic duty (politics in the larger sense) had driven them to work on the Commission in the first place. For conservatives whose political instincts ran against the government, such considerations had been especially important. Gastón Gómez, a staff lawyer aligned with Renovación Nacional, did not consider himself "represented" by a government led by Christian Democrats. Andrés Allamand and Sergio Onofre Jarpa of Renovación tried to dissuade him from joining the staff, arguing he would be manipulated. Gómez joined anyway, "as a personal matter." Why? "Seriously—I think this will seem ridiculous to you—I felt it was what had to be done." The human rights legacy was grave and strategic for Chile, "regardless of the political question, and that is why I considered it an honor to participate. . . . One had to face up [to it]." Such ideas might be abstract at the point of joining. Once the hearings with relatives got under way, the momentousness of the task and the human issues that transcended politics turned real and vivid. Years later, staff members recalled work on the Commission as the most important undertaking of their lives.

An important consequence of intense encounter with the factual and emotional truths hidden under military rule quickly emerged. Political pairing on specific work teams (one leaning Right, one leaning Left) lost relevancy. Gonzalo Vial and Laura Novoa, both conservative, could be sent as the Commission delegation on a field visit. Personal distances shortened, also in ways that cut across political background. On Right and Left, respectively, Commission members Vial and Zalaquett, and staff members Gómez and Serrano, developed an obvious mutual regard and capacity to work closely. When differences of inclination arose, they did not necessarily line up with politics. When Commission members worked on specific cases before reaching a vote, it was Laura Novoa, a distinguished conservative lawyer and a former head legal advisor to the state copper company (CODELCO) under military rule, who placed great weight on testimony by relatives even if corroborating evidence was soft. Zalaquett, on the other hand, pushed for a standard that guaranteed that no finding of a human rights violation would be reversed at a later point.[17]

INSIDE THE RETTIG COMMISSION (II): UNITY AND TENSION

The Rettig Commission lacked subpoena powers to crack codes of silence. The army and the carabineros, the two forces massively implicated in human rights violations and most strategic for truth inquiries, resisted offering useful documents or witnesses. A few retired military officers, especially those affected by the October 1973 "Caravan of Death" scandal, provided useful testimony. A few anonymous testimonies, including some by former conscripts acting out of conscience, also proved helpful. The bulk of useful witness testimony came from relatives and their organizations, especially the Agrupación de Familiares de Detenidos-Desaparecidos (Association of Relatives of the Detained and Disappeared) and the parallel Agrupación de Familiares de Ejecutados Políticos (Association of Relatives of Executed Political Prisoners).[18]

Aside from the relatives and their organizations, there was a small but very strategic group of witnesses—surviving political prisoners. Some lived abroad and provided notarized testimony in Chilean consulates.[19] Others had returned to Chile in the late 1980s. Once the moment of official reckoning with truth arrived, they realized they held critical information: memories of specific persons seen in specific prisons at specific times.

Erika Hennings returned from France in 1989. In high school in the late 1960s, she and her boyfriend, Alfonso Chanfreau, had joined the Young

Communists. By 1970, Chanfreau had joined the MIR (Movimiento de Izquierda Revolucionaria, or Revolutionary Left Movement), the party that preached direct action and preparation for armed guerrilla struggle as a path more revolutionary and effective than the institutional-electoral politics of Allende. As a college student in the early 1970s, Hennings remained with the Young Communists another couple of years but slowly gravitated toward the MIR. Participation in Chile's political and social organizing, from the late 1960s through the Allende presidential campaign and the early years of the Unidad Popular, evoked in her "a great passion and much emotionalism, with great love . . . truly believing that it would mean change favorable for the pueblo, for the poor, for the youths." The time was also one of youthful love. She married Chanfreau in 1972. They had an infant daughter, Natalia, when the coup struck in September 1973.

Personal disaster followed the political disaster. On 30 July 1974 DINA agents seized Alfonso Chanfreau and took him to a DINA torture house, "Londres 38." The next day they seized Erika Hennings. Chanfreau and Hennings were together thirteen harrowing days at Londres 38. Like other prisoners, they endured torture-and-interrogation sessions in small upstairs rooms, then were left bunched together in a large room—blindfolded but able to feel the scurrying rodents, to hear the moans and screams of the tortured, to talk with each other. After his time at Londres 38, Chanfreau was seen by survivors at Villa Grimaldi, where he was also tortured. The DINA subsequently disappeared him. Erika Hennings was transferred to the Tres Alamos prison camp several months before her expulsion to France.[20]

By 1990, people such as Erika Hennings had grown into a small but significant critical mass in Chile. Many former political prisoners had suffered torture: the shattering of the captive's integrity (the world and identity as one knows it) by application of extreme pain and powerlessness, through bodily, mental, and sexual degradation, and by terror of imminent pain and death. Many also developed that sense of responsibility to bear witness that can attach to survivors of a great collective trauma. The memory of prisoners who disappeared or died—whether relatives, friends or comrades, or persons first met in prison—represented a sacred trust. Many were also women. The sexism of the 1960s and 1970s meant that leftist women were treated as less important within the culture of secret police extermination. The layered and ad hoc aspects of repression and the assumptions about gender translated into distinct destinies for DINA prisoners. Some women were killed or disappeared, but some were eventually released. A few succumbed to unrelenting pressure—torture, sexual degradation, threats to children—to accept a role as collaborators.[21]

When Erika Hennings returned to Chile in 1989, she and other former prisoners, especially the women, began to see one another. The meetings were informal, a space for sociability and affection among those who shared an extreme experience incomprehensible to others. They would let loose and "just get together, affectively, . . . drinking a bit of tea, talking of exile. 'Do you remember Londres [38], [Villa] Grimaldi, such-and-such prisoner?' " Over time, they realized their memories mattered in a larger sense. "Then we realized that we are talking and remembering and remembering, and we remembered this prisoner. So, suddenly it occurs to us that why jeez [*pucha*], well why don't we give meaning to these memories?" Hennings, Viviana Uribe, and other former prisoners began to give the meetings a new orientation, and the group expanded to include more men. Aylwin's appointment of the Rettig Commission in April 1990 reinforced the urgency of giving meaning to personal memories.

The "Grupo de Testigos Sobrevivientes" (Group of Survivor-Witnesses) began to research their memories systematically. They set up witness work groups, torture house by torture house, to develop a precise record of information: specific dates, prisoner names, names or nicknames of torturers, and events. To facilitate the work, they organized group visits to former torture houses and cross-checked testimonies to detect and correct errors. The group reached critical mass, an activist core of sixty to seventy former prisoners and a wider network of about a hundred participants. To reactivate memories of terror deliberately was no simple act. One returned, physically and mentally, to the house of torment and death. But the work also lent meaning to suffering. As the Rettig Commission staff compared and cross-linked evidence, the survivors proved crucial. They could provide inside corroboration of key points, especially the identities of people secretly held by the state. The work of the survivor-witnesses also produced some unexpected poignant moments. When a group of women returned to the torture house in Santiago known as "Venda Sexy," the occupant did not know the prior history of the property. They wept together.[22]

The survivor-witnesses had their own values and agendas. Their collaboration with the Rettig Commission is an example of the frictional synergy that shaped relationships between the Aylwin government and human rights activists. The survivor-witnesses threw themselves into supporting the Rettig Commission's work of documenting denied truth. Yet survivor-witnesses, who themselves were victims of a horrifying repression, also tended to see justice as a goal of equal priority with truth, and to critique the scope, policy direction, and discursive emphasis on reconciliation that bound the Commission. The Commission group, for its part, valued the strategic role and dedication of the survivors, and appreciated the toll exacted by their own life histories of torment. Yet the Commission worked within a scope defined from above and could reach decisions on sensitive points—including how to handle the issue of torture—that upset the sensibilities and goals of survivor-witnesses. As in relations between the Agrupación of Relatives of the Detained and Disappeared and the Aylwin administration (see chapter 1), each group needed and valued the other to achieve a larger goal and social good: the building of an irrefutable documentary foundation for memory as a narrative of rupture and persecution that could spark moral awakening and a healthier nation. A certain mutual sympathy could also arise, given the life-and-death quality of the issues and awareness of the adverse conditions of democratic transition. Nonetheless, each group followed a distinctive logic. Their synergy also carried them to points of tension, frustration, and disappointment.

The story of collaboration between the Rettig Commission and the survivor-witnesses, however, does not exhaust the problem of tension and unity among those working to reconstruct the long-denied truth. *Inside* the Rettig Commission and *inside* the groups organizing in civil society, not everyone saw eye to eye. Among former political prisoners, a tiny but crucial subset produced tension late in 1990. Most former prisoners could only piece together the fragments of their own firsthand experiences, which were in turn limited by conditions of imprisonment, including the wearing of blindfolds at the torture centers. A prisoner could not normally acquire the wide range of knowledge about specific prisoners, torturers, practices, dates, and places that accrued to a true insider of the DINA. Two women tortured to the breaking point and transformed into collaborators did, however, have such knowledge: Luz Arce, a former Socialist, and Marcia Alejandro Merino, a former MIRista. They had the institutional memory that comes with continuity and strategic activity. Both were entangled with the secret police web for years, both went out on street operations to identify people for detention, both performed secretarial and documentary analysis functions. In other words, they had entered Primo Levi's "gray zone," where once clear categories of victim and perpetrator bleed into one another. They served as organic parts of the machinery of imprisonment and torture.[23]

Arce's trajectory was especially controversial. Her combined secretarial and street functions, her analytical capacity, the mask of rationality she put on to hide her terror and to revive some forcefulness of personality, her sexual history with DINA officers, these rendered ambiguous the lines between victim, collaborator under duress, and traitor. Some former prisoners could only see a collaborator-traitor. The reaction is understandable, not only because of the traumas they experienced, but also because Arce's collaboration sometimes took on a proactive aspect at odds with neat victim imagery. A female survivor recalled Arce volunteering false and damning information during the street ride that initiated her detention, and in a torture house session afterward. The prisoner, Arce claimed, supported popular militias before the coup and served later as a clandestine radio contact for the underground resistance. The accusations increased pressure on the new prisoner to provide information about "Marcos," a Socialist the DINA was eager to find and seize. Merino also evoked bitterness, but at least her body language and the resulting memory folklore harmonized more readily with victim images. In car trips by the DINA to identify and arrest MIRistas, Merino shook uncontrollably whenever she recognized someone.[24]

In 1990 both women engaged in a wrenching coming to terms with their own pasts of suffering, broken identity, and complicity. The new politico-cultural environment and truth commission, of course, favored reflection by anyone who experienced a remorseful tug of conscience. So did the sensitivity to human rights that had developed within the Catholic Church during the dictatorship years. For both women, religious self-examination and support proved vital to the process of facing and accepting truth—and rebuilding spiritually. Arce began her spiritual journey in 1987, and started writing manuscripts about her past in December 1989. Merino began her journey toward renewal and truth telling later and more tepidly, in 1990. Both, however, provided testimony to the Rettig Commission. Correa and the staff lawyers knew the strategic value of their information, and they also related to the women in a respectful manner, sensitive to the fact that the women had suffered torment. Arce recalled Correa and lawyers Carlos Fresno and Gastón Gómez as "the first, aside from my Dominican friends, who considered me as a victim." When their questions turned to sexual liaisons within the DINA, it was obvious that the point was information to establish truth, not degradation, voyeurism, or manipulation.[25]

Former political prisoners wanted justice as well as truth, but the question of building a relationship of mutual acceptance with Arce and Merino divided them. Late in 1990 Erika Hennings and the Chanfreau family had managed to reopen the court case to find her disappeared husband. Like her friend Viviana Uribe, Hennings had decided—with the Chanfreau court case in mind—that she could indeed reach out to the two women. Arce sensed an acceptance and a desire for justice that set recrimination aside, and she developed an admiration and affection for Hennings and Uribe. Arce and Merino became witnesses in the Chanfreau case, and received support from Hennings, Uribe, and some other survivors. Many former prisoners could not make the same leap. To consider former DINA collaborators not as traitors, but as victims whose torture had robbed them of the capacity for moral integrity, this remained a sore point for years.[26]

The achievement of the survivor-witness group in 1990 was not like-mindedness on every aspect of truth, justice, and memory work. What defined their achievement was the determination, despite disagreement on searing issues, to organize precise information that could pull the dead and the missing from oblivion.

The Rettig Commission process, too, produced a dynamic of internal debate accompanied by a will to unity on fundamental points. Beyond the initial frictions as social workers and lawyers worked out the purposes and protocols of family hearings, other points of strain arose. Aylwin's mandate kept judicial functions off limits; the Commission would not name suspects even when it had preponderant evidence. But how should one *interpret* the nonnaming policy? When narrating a particular act of repression, should the description provide suggestive information, such as the name of the commanding officer of the relevant military, carabinero, or secret police unit? Would this kind of naming add moral pressure for thorough court investigation and witness testimony? Or would it usurp judicial function, violate rights of the accused, even open the door to vengeance assassinations? The issue generated diverse reactions before the Commission decided on a strict anonymity standard—and consulted the government to confirm agreement on the point.

How to apply the mandate on torture also sparked contention. The Commission was to identify cases of death under torture, not undertake systematic investigation of torture. Investigating torture in its own right would have raised issues of scale and evidence difficult to reconcile with the time frame and the objective of irrefutable truth conceived by the architects of the Commission. (One could accept this argument but still believe—as I do—that a second commission with a mandate to investigate torture should have followed soon after the Rettig Commission report. Twelve years would pass before a second commission finally undertook the task; see chapter 6.) The principle might be clear, but how to apply it was a volatile point, given the pervasiveness and moral significance of torture. Torture weighed heavily not only on its survivors, but also on relatives of the executed and disappeared. Most feared their loved ones had suffered torture. If Commission members knew enough to think it certain a victim died as a result of torture, but lacked medical-forensic evidence to confirm the point, were they speculating or were they providing truth to the nation? Beyond documenting individual cases of death under torture, did there exist a moral imperative to delineate in detail the systematic and pervasive use of torture, perhaps in a special annex? The Commission applied an extremely conservative standard to the individual cases, and it eschewed a special annex. But it was blunt in its short descriptions of the pervasiveness, techniques, and effects of torture.[27]

The existence of these and other debates during the course of the work brings into sharp relief the building of good faith within the Commission, almost as if the intense experience of the work produced its own subculture of understanding. The Commission members and staff could air their sometimes sharp disagreements, but these did not necessarily line up politically and they did not foreclose being convinced or reaching a conclusion. Two aspects of the work process are especially revealing. First, in deciding whether individual cases constituted a human rights violation, the Commission settled on a conservative standard of proof and ended up with unanimous votes in most cases. In other words, Laura Novoa could see José Zalaquett's point that opening the door to error and disproof of individual cases would play into the hands of regime loyalists determined to undermine the report's legitimacy, while Zalaquett could reverse his initial judgment of a case when Novoa questioned a flaw of reasoning or evidence. The discussion process was rigorous. Vial, Zalaquett, and Novoa read every executive summary report—a pace too crushing for elderly members of the Commission, but one that assured that at least half the persons present had specific prior knowledge of each case as it was discussed and decided.

Second, some of the most strategic sections of the narrative were drafted by conservatives. The report's stinging descriptions of law and the judiciary's failure—in civilian as well as military courts, at the Supreme Court level as well as lower levels—came from the likes of Ricardo Martin, a former Supreme Court justice, and José Luis Cea, a constitutional scholar.

In some ways, the conservatives were more scandalized and shocked than human rights veterans such as Castillo and Zalaquett, who had for years read many cases and experienced steady denial of habeas corpus petitions in matters of life and death.[28]

The historical section on events leading to the crisis of 1973 was one of the most delicate tasks. Given the memory struggles unfolding since the 1970s and their centrality to politics, such discussions brought to the fore divisions within the Commission and society at large. Two major memory frameworks built up under military rule—memory as salvation, memory as a closed box—rested on the idea that Chile had reached the point of utter ruin and imminent civil war by September 1973. The corollary was not simply justification of military takeover, but also the idea that an embryonic potential for war and occasional armed outbreaks to ignite it continued after 1973 and required a "dirty war" of strong suppression. Memory frameworks that emphasized rupture and persecution, on the other hand, rested on the notion that the dictatorship used a *myth* of war to justify the unjustifiable and to encourage indifference to atrocity. The myth of war served as an excuse to seize, disappear, and exterminate prisoners; to hide truth in a shroud of secrecy and misinformation; and to terrorize people more generally. By restricting the case mandate of the Commission to the period of military rule, Aylwin implicitly rejected the idea that the crisis of 1973 justified resorting to massive human rights violations under the junta. But the making of the 1973 crisis had to be addressed somehow. Otherwise the report would depict a Chile that suddenly entered a period of craziness and barbarism, for no discernible reasons. This would do little to lend the report credibility, let alone serve one of its mandates—to consider how to prevent a new cycle of human rights violations in the future.

As with all sections of the report, the Commission discussed and debated key points and principles that would define a draft, and followed up with critiques as drafts were refined into a final version. It entrusted the conservative historian Gonzalo Vial to draft the narrative of the 1973 crisis. Two key points framed the account. First, at the level of historical probabilities, the crisis that culminated in 1973 was relevant, and responsibility for it did not fall on one small sector alone. The Commission would sidestep a deep analysis of socioeconomic and long-term causes of the crisis, considered a task for historical interpretation and debate. It would focus the historical analysis more narrowly, on political and ideological dynamics that created an atmosphere conducive to overthrowing democracy and to characterizing the political adversary as an "enemy" unfit for rights. The latter was especially relevant as a tipping point against human rights.

At this level of analysis, the Commission provided a brief account of sharpening polarization and demonization. It inserted Chile's drama in a double frame, as an aspect of international Cold War and as bitter internal conflict. The polarization process rendered resort to force, tramplings of law, and expectation of armed confrontation more real and thinkable to wider sectors of society. The Commission saw responsibilities on both Left and Right during the Allende years—among those who preached the necessity of armed struggle, and those who equated opposition with making society ungovernable. " 'Armed path' and 'ungovernability' came to be . . . signs of [mutually] exclusive concepts of society, neither of which could be imposed over the other democratically" and whose adherents "could not accept giving in to the adversary, thereby opening a peaceful way out." But it was not only acts at the ideological extremes of political movements, nor only those of a state that tolerated property invasions and stretched legal technicality to the limit, that created an atmosphere of crisis, demonization, and unrule of law. In the press, on all sides of the conflicts, "the destruction of the moral person of adversaries reached incredible boundaries." It took few steps to go from the heated casting of the "political enemy as despicable" to the idea that "his physical annihilation seemed justified." By the last weeks before military rule, each violent incident—sabotage, street confrontation leading to injury, outright assassination—served to intensify the climate of civil war and to "banalize violence and death. That broke the moral dikes of society."

A second key point, however, drew a sharp line between historical probability and historical justification. Probability was not inevitability; some rights were inalienable. A crisis of institutionality and bitter social division did not grant a right to organize a campaign of extermination. The legal and ethical norms relevant to the cases under review had an "absolute character." Fundamental rights of life and physical integrity could not be renounced or excused by historical circumstance. Even in cases of war, ethical and legal norms placed certain behaviors out of bounds. In addition, arguments about exigencies of war did not line up with the facts. "In the great majority of [the cases considered] the events did not occur in the heat of an armed clash, nor immediately after. On the contrary, it was a matter of attacks against unarmed or detained persons."[29]

As the Rettig Commission raced toward its completion deadline of 8

February 1991, debate did not prove incompatible with unity. The members and staff were exploring, classifying, ordering, and explaining the most volatile memory issues bequeathed by military rule. They understood the task as high civic duty. Precisely for that reason, as well as the insistence on investigating individual cases with their inevitable idiosyncrasies, discrepancies mattered and embraced a wide range of issues—even secondary points of language, technical classification, evidence, context. Jaime Castillo and Gonzalo Vial agreed in separate interviews that each, if writing individually, would have worded the historical section differently. As often as not, however, differences fed into teamwork and heightened confidence in the group's characterization of individual cases, and overall descriptions and conclusions. The Commission delivered a unanimous report.

TRUTH, PRESIDENT, AND NATION

The tone of the report was sober rather than indignant, descriptive rather than argumentative. The facts described were dramatic enough. The Commission found that 2,115 individual cases of death or disappearance qualified as human rights violations, and that an additional 164 persons died as a result of political violence situations (mainly street protests, but also some armed clashes). For another 641 cases, the Commission could not reach a definitive conclusion by its deadline but thought the evidence warranted further investigation. Among the 2,115 confirmed cases of human rights violations leading to death or disappearance, state agents or persons in their hire were responsible for nearly all cases (2,025 cases, or 95.7 percent). The balance (90 cases) comprised deaths by private persons acting under political pretext, as in an ambush or an indiscriminate terrorist act. From a technical point of view, the Commission mandate collapsed classic "human rights law," which focused on illegitimate action by state agents, and "international humanitarian law" on rules of war and armed engagement. It also sidestepped ethical doctrine on conditions creating a right of armed rebellion.[30] From practical and political points of view, however, the mandate made sense. It deferred to sensibilities of the military and the Right, and it recognized that technical distinctions regarding the transcendent value of life would not register with the larger Chilean public. In other words, the inclusions built legitimacy. They defined a truth investigation conducted in good faith.

The inclusions also made sense for the factual truths they uncovered. The extreme one-sidedness of the statistics meshed with recurring qualitative discovery of the falseness of an internal war thesis, and of the reality of systematic violence to exterminate an unarmed "enemy" after detention. *Qualitatively*: The military rapidly took control; in region after region, armed resistance was either nonexistent or pathetic and easily isolated; many victims voluntarily complied with arrest lists. *Quantitatively*: Over 2,000 cases were death or disappearance by state agents or persons in their hire, while the number of military and police killed amounted to 132 (including 26 in the first days of takeover, 11–15 September 1973). The large mass of established cases of persons who were detained and disappeared by the state (957) also confirmed the reality of organized secrecy, misinformation, and cruelty, especially by the DINA, after the initial deaths of 1973. Disappearance could not be dismissed as a problem of occasional excess by rogue agents of the state.

The machinery of death reached widely. It targeted leaders and activists of three political parties—MIRistas, Socialists, and Communists accounted for half (50.1 percent) the dead and disappeared. But significantly, it gathered up and destroyed nearly as many people with no known militancy (46.0 percent), that is, either unaligned or inconsequential in party politics. Many sympathized with the Left in the broader sense or were grassroots activists, such as trade unionists or peasant leaders, but others were simply unlucky —victims of social "cleansing" of common criminals, targets of local vengeance, or persons in the wrong place at the wrong time. The social class composition of targets was heterogeneous. Middle-class sectors such as professionals, white-collar workers, and university students accounted for about a third (29.7 percent); workers and peasants amounted to about a third (30.1 percent); small independent producers constituted another seventh (13.8 percent). The figures slightly underestimated the social class profiles since housewives, the unemployed, and the retired were consigned to a miscellaneous category (9.9 percent).[31]

The picture of Chilean society and its recent history was dispiriting. The memory framework that saw military rule as a time of cruel and ceaseless rupture indeed had a solid foundation in truth. A killing violence at the margin of basic law and ethics had indeed been organized by the state. As discouraging, with the notable exception of the Catholic Church, social and institutional responses were weak or late. The judiciary failed miserably.

Aylwin received the report, its typescript bound in six volumes, at a brief televised ceremony in Santiago. He promised to devote the rest of February to read and reflect, then address the nation and release the report. He put the volumes in a suitcase, left Santiago, and enclosed himself in the rural summer home of a friend. For two weeks he read and studied the report. The reading was, he told me, "quite bitter."[32]

On the evening of 4 March, the president was ready and the nation was glued to television.[33] "Compatriots," he began, "tonight I address you to deal with a painful theme that still divides Chileans: that of violations of human rights." He invoked the familiar bodily metaphor of memory as a brutal and unending rupture. "This is an open wound in the national soul, that we can only heal if we try to reconcile with one another on the bases of truth and justice."

Aylwin provided a sober summary of the statistical and qualitative facts. Significantly, he quoted the Commission's biting conclusion on the judiciary's failure: "The Judicial Power did not react with sufficient energy." The result, even if unintended, was "a worsening of the process of systematic violations of human rights, not only in the immediate sense of not offering protection to arrested persons in the cases denounced, but also because it offered repressive agents increased certainty of impunity for their criminal actions."

But how should Chileans respond to the hard truth documented by the Commission? As Aylwin turned from factual summation toward issues such as reparations, prevention, and personal reflection, the tone changed subtly—not consistently nor at the level of formal narrative, but at the level of voice and body language. The emotional charge of the truths at stake—the sense of a president recognizing and taking in a tragedy of families that could never be fully repaired—began to come through. The scene was not theatrical sentimentality. It was emotion insinuating itself, that is, the sight of a composed speaker asserting control over a great sorrow swelling within. As he described Commission recommendations on reparations and prevention, Aylwin's eyes began to blink more rapidly. He looked at the paper text more often. He swallowed to clear his throat.

A surge returned as Aylwin presented his own reflections. He reiterated the importance of recognizing truth, regardless of one's views on politics or on the legitimacy of military takeover on 11 September 1973, as the foundation for convivencia. He linked the Commission's finding on the absence of a state of war with common sense. "We all know—and the Report establishes it—that the Armed Forces [and Carabineros] took total control of the country very rapidly, in few days at most." "War also has its laws," he reminded citizens. "Nothing justifies torturing and executing prisoners, nor making their remains disappear." Chileans wanted mutual understanding and reconciliation, not deepening conflict and recrimination, but one could not get there by artificially looking away from the past. A time for pardon or reconciliation might arrive, but first one had to arrive at a recognition of truth—to know who was offended and who in need of pardon. The process was personal and deep. "I cannot pardon for someone else. Pardon is not imposed by decree." It required a meeting ground between remorse on one side, generosity on the other.

It was at this juncture that Aylwin defined a responsibility that was public and collective, in addition to those that were personal. And it was at this juncture that the surge of emotion broke through. Even as he maintained a presidential dignity and composure, Aylwin's voice thickened and his eyes glistened.

> When it was agents of the State who caused so much suffering, and the pertinent organs of the State could not or knew not to avoid it and punish it, and there also was not the necessary social response to stop it, the State and the whole society are responsible, whether by action or by omission. It is Chilean society that is in debt to the victims of violations of human rights.
>
> That is why the suggestions for moral and material reparation that the Report formulates are shared by all sectors.
>
> [Voice turns emotional, eyes fill with tears.]
>
> That is why I venture, in my condition as President of the Republic, to assume representation of the entire nation in order, in its name, to apologize [*pedir perdón*] to the relatives of the victims.

It was Aylwin's finest hour as president.

How did Chileans respond to the moment of truth? Aylwin invited all to read the report and help build a culture of healing and respect for human rights. *La Nación* published a newspaper edition of the report; by May a book edition appeared.[34] Beyond the call for everyone to build a culture of "Never Again," Aylwin laid out specific tasks of recognition, repair, and justice by specific state sectors. After his own moment of sorrowful recognition, he "solemnly" asked the armed forces, carabineros, and any others involved in human rights violations "to make gestures of recognition of the pain caused and to collaborate to lessen it." Posing justice as the antithesis of vengeance—the rule of law and reason was the alternative to criminal vindictiveness—he called upon the courts to conduct individual case investigations based on evidence given to them by the Rettig Commission. They should establish the full truth about the final destination of the disappeared and deliver the human remains to relatives; they should also establish the individual responsibilities of perpetrators. He put forth what came to be known as the "Aylwin doctrine": the 1978 Amnesty Law did not relieve the courts of a legal duty first to investigate and establish the facts and the individual criminal responsibilities of a case, *before* they could apply an amnesty. He also announced reparation proposals to Congress.

Aylwin's speech and the officially documented truth of massive state violence had a strong impact. Years later people remembered watching and reacting to the address, especially the climactic moment when Aylwin emotionally assumed the mantle of responsibility by state and society. The speech resonated. It condensed into a peak moment of recognition the agony of the memory struggles waged by survivor-victims, relatives, human rights activists, and persons of conscience since the 1970s. It resurrected the cultural appeal of early Christian Democracy, a fusion of the best communal values of Catholicism with a call for sociopolitical justice. Its core facts revealed a horrifying truth and punctured myths cherished by some. Most subtly, its mention of acts of omission as well as commission drew a wider range of people into the moral net of responsibility and complicity— and into the cathartic moment of recognition and remorse. In this sense, it restored the idea of a "national" community of shared bonds and responsibility after a period of lawlessness. The nation could begin to be imagined again as a kind of "family," reunited after losing its way. The touching of so many cultural chords at once was effective because it lacked an obvious guile. The speech expressed Aylwin's own values and instincts. He had bypassed speech writers when composing it.[35]

The resonance of the speech and the inscribing of the report as factual truth in public consciousness proved evident in several ways. First, even skeptics found themselves moved, sometimes to their own surprise. In human rights and victim-survivor circles, persons who dissented from the limits placed on the Commission and human rights policy remembered the emotional impact of state recognition of the truth of harm inflicted. As we have seen (chapter 1), Sola Sierra, leader of the Agrupación of Relatives of the Detained and Disappeared, had her share of frustrations with Aylwin and the Concertación, even in the early days of frictional synergy between government and activists. Nonetheless, she conceded, "When President Aylwin delivers the Report to the country and apologizes . . . for us it was very powerful because it officialized the truth that we had been saying during many years." Three-fifths of the nation "had not suffered the problems" and now faced a truth that was for them "still incredible." Erika Hennings watched Aylwin's speech with about ten witness-survivors. Their mood was solemn but turned complex as the speech unfolded. "There was joy, excitement, because it was the first time there was a recognition." As with Sierra, such reaction did not preclude sharp disagreement. Hennings turned angry, for example, when she learned later in the speech that the Commission and Aylwin proposed a procedure to allow for a legal declaration of death of disappeared persons.[36]

Not all skeptics, of course, could suspend experiences that rendered them wary. To a degree, however, even persons leaning Left whose political memories of the Allende era rendered them uneasy about Aylwin, and persons leaning Right whose loyalty to the junta inclined them to dismiss violations as sporadic excess by rogue subordinates, found themselves drawn into the moment.[37]

Additional aspects of the report's inscription as truth unfolded over time. The Commission's conservative standard of proof—its choice to err on the side of caution when concluding that a case constituted death or disappearance by state agents—worked. Not one such case was later disproved, despite strong interest by the military in disproof and despite the media custom of publishing alleged disproof stories during the years of military rule.[38] The terms of cultural debate inscribed the core factual findings of the report as irrefutable truth. This was an important accomplishment, and a building block for future struggles over memory, truth, and justice. As we shall see (chapter 3), the achievement would also exact an important price. By the mid-1990s, the terms of cultural discussion tended to reduce a massive and layered history of violent repression to an irrefutable core of maximal victims: the 2,279 victims of death or disappearance established by the Rettig Commission, or the modified total of 3,197 victims in the report of a follow-up agency in May 1996.[39]

The Rettig Commission report and attendant presidential speech solidified an emerging majority culture of collective memory. This majority culture, which crystallized in the 1988 plebiscite but remained fragile in view of the constraints and continuities of Chile's transition in 1989–91, broke decisively with the myth of salvation. It did so despite ambivalence about distinct legacies of military rule. Polls between 1989 and mid-March 1991 asked Chileans to evaluate Pinochet's years of rule. When asked to consider both "the good" and "the bad," a large majority (57.9 percent) continued to affirm a mixed legacy ("in part good and in part bad") in March 1991. But when asked to rate Pinochet's government as a whole, the die-hard loyalists who remembered the regime as "good" or "very good" shrank to only one in five Chileans (from 30.3 percent in August 1989 to 20.0 percent in March 1991). Strong critics defining the regime as "bad" or "very bad," on the other hand, increased to two in five (from 25.6 percent to 40.5 percent). A tipping point had been crossed, and with it a memory transition among some who once resisted it: from dismissal of state violence as an occasional excess by rogue subordinates in the heat of war, to the idea of state violence as planned, systemic, and indefensible.[40]

Over time, the effect of the report, the lack of contradiction of cases, and additional memory-related struggles and publicity consolidated a cultural majority that framed military rule as an era of rupture and persecution. In 1993, after the twenty-year anniversary of 11 September, a carefully worded survey asked Chileans about the deeper meaning of the date. Chileans held different points of view about 11 September 1973. Which of two common viewpoints "on what happened on that date" was closer to that of the respondent? The choice: memory as salvation ("on 11 September of 73 Chile was liberated from Marxism"), versus memory as rupture and persecution ("on 11 September of 73 democracy was destroyed and a military dictatorship was begun"). Less than a third (30.0 percent) chose memory as salvation, while a majority (53.9 percent) affirmed destruction and dictatorship. A sixth (16.1 percent) still felt too torn to choose. The social class profile was also revealing. The middle-class and lower-class segments opted decisively for memory as destructive dictatorship (53.6 percent and 59.0 percent, respectively). The upper-class segment found such a stance much more difficult. A majority (53.3 percent) still adhered to memory as salvation, another fourth (25.0 percent) proved too torn to choose.[41]

The early years of democracy and truth telling sealed memory as rupture and persecution for a cultural majority. Within a divided and ambivalent society, however, persons of high influence and wealth still tended to see matters differently. The memory that counted was salvation—or was at least too mixed for words like *destruction* and *dictatorship*.

WINNERS AND LOSERS?
THE RETTIG REPORT ON EMBATTLED TERRAIN

The sectors of influence most directly implicated by the findings of the Rettig Commission were the judiciary, and the military and police. We shall consider the judiciary's response later. The air force quickly issued its relatively moderate statement. On 8 March, it affirmed loyalty both to the ideals of 11 September 1973 and to reconciliation. Chile's "grave crisis" before September 1973 was necessary to contextualize and understand the report properly; also, military rule had modernized Chile and brought it to "a greatness that opens up brilliant prospects." The air force lamented loss of life on all sides, "with the painful consequences to which it gives rise." The statement implicitly adhered to the internal war thesis and was something less than the gesture of acknowledgment and regret for which Aylwin appealed. But it was also less than fierce in defending memory as salvation, and included an acknowledgment of sorts.[42]

But what of the other branches? The practical reality was that army and carabinero forces were those most implicated by the deaths and disappearances. The army, navy, and carabineros deliberated longer and did not release responses for over three weeks, after a meeting of the Council of National Security on 27 March to air military and police reactions to Aylwin and other council members. The carabineros observed that it was the police who suffered the most casualties in the disorder before and after 1973, and considered themselves most at risk of private vengeance in the climate generated by the report.[43]

All three branches shared a key criticism. They believed in the internal war thesis and saw the period *before* 11 September 1973 as crucial. The memory that mattered displaced responsibility for violence under military rule onto leftist extremists considered to have brought Chile to a state of crisis and imminent war. In other words, they rejected the Commission's separation between historical probability and historical justification.

The army's rejection was the most militant: The Rettig Report, it contended, "does not recognize the legitimate use of force" once political consensus is exhausted. The Unidad Popular "considered civil war as a resource to reach total power." With Cuban help, it armed and trained a clandestine army of "thousands of extremists." Military action on 11 September suffocated "the revolutionary civil war . . . in its latent stage [*fase larvada*], without it exploding in all its dimensions." But the initial pounce did not suffice. The "subversive war" continued and "to exorcise definitively the state of war, a long task of neutralizing the possible preparation capacity of the paramilitary extremist groups was necessary." To apologize was out of the question. The army could not accept "being placed before the citizenry in the dock of the accused, for having saved the liberty and sovereignty of the fatherland." Pinochet reinforced internal cohesion by reading the declaration to 1,500 officers at a ceremony in the Escuela Militar.[44]

Pinochet held to the war thesis in private, too. Aylwin repeatedly sought—ten times, he estimated—to convince Pinochet personally that a gesture recognizing the pain inflicted would serve the country. Even in war, Aylwin argued, one does not kill or torture prisoners. Pinochet's reply was always the same: " 'But they were going to kill us all! President, there were 15,000 armed men,' and from that I never pulled him away." At times Aylwin invited Pinochet to his home to talk unencumbered by aides and formality, but, he explained, "every time that we got to this theme, the armor [comes out], 'they were going to kill us all.' "[45]

The army response, if not its belligerent tone, set the pattern for sectors of the Right and the socially privileged seeking damage control. The war thesis —and the persons who brought Chile to the point of imminent war—defined the real meaning of the Rettig Report. *El Mercurio*, the daily that served a conservative educational function for elites, professionals, and middle-class readers, presented the most sophisticated version of damage control. On Monday morning 4 March, before Aylwin's evening truth speech, it pondered "Truth and Reconciliation." Two points dominated. First, the prehistory to military rule was crucial and pinned responsibility on the Left. The country had rightfully feared the civil war whose imminence and bloody consequences were proclaimed by the Left. The offenders were those who "subscribed to the thesis of class struggle and the necessity of sharpening the social confrontation," in contrast to people who "sought to calm down spirits" and defend rule of law. Second, the social cost of saving the country proved modest. Some critics had wildly claimed the repression "cost the country nearly 100,000 dead," but the Rettig Commission documented "the true dimension of the facts." To be sure, "in the persecution of the terrorist groups tragic abuses occurred" and "excesses" merited repair. In short, the war thesis was true, and the salvation operation well done.

This approach enabled sophisticated defenders of the military regime in the 1990s to acknowledge a core of now irrefutable truth—the factual reality of human rights violations they had denied in earlier years—while contextualizing causation safely. It also enabled them to align themselves safely with the call for reconciliation. Culturally and politically, it accepted the narrow factual findings of the Rettig Commission but contravened its fundamental memory-truth and its fundamental ethical principle. To assert the war thesis as if it negated the finding of an absence of war, as if it negated the point of impermissible behavior against unarmed prisoners even in war, and as if it negated the finding that state agents regularly crossed into the impermissible zone, was to dissolve the line between historical probability and historical justification.[46]

It took few steps to walk from contextualizing causes within a framework asserting salvation marred by occasional excess, to suggesting that closing the memory box on dirty aspects of the past was the wisest policy after all. After rejectionist declarations by the army, navy, and carabineros, the spectrum of conservative thinking fell into place. Alberto Espina of Renovación Nacional, many of whose members had been stunned and moved by the Rettig Report, responded moderately. People differed in their visions of the past. While the search for a shared core truth was valid, he believed "in the historical framework that the Army points out." Sergio Fernández, the former interior minister and hard-line U D I leader, declared that "the Army and the Navy have put things in their place." *El Mercurio* editorialized that it was time to reconsider the merits of amnesty and *olvido*, a tradition "that to the extent it has been abandoned appears ever wiser."[47]

By the end of March, the military and the Right had adjusted to the documented factual truth of memory as rupture. The war thesis was fundamental. It explained unfortunate events, it displaced responsibilities, and it justified looking away.

The problems that beset the Rettig Report and its memory-truths did not come exclusively from the military and the Right. The Aylwin administration saw mass publication and dissemination of the report, assisted by relatives of the disappeared and other human rights groups and by a program of public speeches and fora including high-profile officials, as a follow-up phase to build a culture of human rights. The idea of the campaign also reflected some prodding by activists—part of the frictional synergy that defined their relationship with the Aylwin administration—and a desire to diminish the force of criticism of the limited scope of the Rettig

Commission. In some sectors of the Left and the human rights community, such critiques resonated. The "no-naming" policy on perpetrators of human rights violations stung, even if one understood arguments of due process and political realism. It raised the specter of impunity. How much could one expect from the courts, given their Pinochetismo and historical abdication of duty, in the absence of public naming and pressure by the Commission? In March a small grassroots monthly, *El Popular*, published "123 identified torturers" based on a document the Vicaría presumably supplied the Rettig Commission.[48]

The larger issues underlying the publicity campaign and no-name controversy were twofold. First, the memory work of the Rettig Commission put into play the tension between "formula" and "wedge" in truth-and-justice policy. Was the point of a Rettig Commission to define the scope of painful memory narrowly, provide some acknowledgment and repair, and then declare the problem resolved as society turned to other priorities and tasks? To settle on the truth commission as "formula" would be to create a politico-cultural irony: memory followed by silence. Or was the point of a Rettig Commission to begin with a forceful cracking of the wall of denial and impunity, then widen the cracks to bring down the wall, and finally build a culture of democratic respect and accountability for human rights? To treat the Truth Commission as "wedge" was to see it as an indispensable yet insufficient first step in a longer process. During the 1990s and as we shall see (chapters 4–5), events that turned into a "memory knot" which galvanized struggles over the meaning of Chile's trauma *also* concentrated the tension between formula and wedge. Was a given truth-and-justice struggle or a given advance a formula to settle the matter, or another wedge in an unfinished struggle? Over time, the frictional synergies between government and activists would end up defining tendencies. Ambivalence and constraint created a certain pendulum effect that defies simple reductionism. Nonetheless, by the mid-to-late 1990s many political elites would align with a formulaic approach, while many human rights activists put forth a vision of unfinished struggle.[49]

In the short run, it was a second underlying issue that proved decisive. The nature of the transition pushed some groups outside its rules of the game—but their reactions might nonetheless influence the climate of cultural follow-up to the Rettig Report. The electoral rules translated into exclusion from representation for some organized and influential groups. As serious, some guerrilla groups believed that vengeance was legitimate justice. Their premise: the absence of institutional justice under the rules of transition.

The Communist Party occupied an ambiguous place in such considerations. It did not back vengeance, but it had little faith in the Concertación's interest in a wedge effect and bore a complex relationship with the Frente Patriótico Manuel Rodríguez, the guerrilla group that tried to assassinate Pinochet in 1986. The Communist Party's political marginalization derived from many causes: deep differences between the Party and renovated Left parties in the Concertación, and historical distrust with Christian Democrats; cultural revulsion after the failed ambush of Pinochet in 1986; binomial electoral rules that suffocated parties unaligned with large coalitions; internal strains about strategy after 1986, and intensified by Chile's transition and the collapse of the Soviet Union during 1989–91. Such factors, a mix of the self-inflicted and the imposed, built a formidable barrier to effective participation. In the early 1990s the Party's electoral base plunged by historical standards: from the 15–20 percent level that made it a major player in the pre-1973 electoral system and Congress, to about 5 percent and nil Congressional representation. The same factors, however, *also* made the Party a reliable voice for critique of Chile's constrained transition and a reliable home for the politics of grassroots mobilization and protest, in contrast to the politics of elite negotiation.

As a result, the Communist Party was politically marginal in the narrow sense of electoral success and representation, but not as marginal in the larger political culture and debate. The democracy of the 1990s in any event bore greater disconnection between the "social movement" and "electoral competition" aspects of politics than the democracy of the 1960s. Notwithstanding its electoral impotence, the Party became a significant grassroots force in select settings, including university student federations, some trade unions, and specific shantytowns or regions where it had a prior history of influence. Some Chileans could function with distinct political registers. A person might vote for a moderate Concertación or Renovación candidate for Congress, yet back a Communist rally or candidate in a trade union or other grassroots context. Such organizational presence, and ongoing publication of the newspaper *El Siglo*, meant that voices of sharp dissent and exclusion from the rules of the game—and sympathy with those who refused to play by the rules—could find a degree of cultural echo and circulation.[50]

It was the guerrilla groups, especially the Frente Patriótico and the Mapu-Lautaro, that defied the rules most openly. The Frente was the most well organized. Since its inception in 1983, its relation with the Communist Party oscillated from close but unacknowledged, to strained and semi-independent. Internal tension also split the Frente into "Party" and "Autonomous" factions, but the bottom line was clear. A core of guerrilla activists and sympathizers, rooted in the 1980s struggle against military dictatorship, saw Chile's constrained transition as a fraud justifying select vengeance. The rules of transition constituted a betrayal of justice and of the earlier struggle. The Frente's dramatic 1990 attack on Gustavo Leigh made the point—and clarified a challenge for Aylwin's administration. It would have to mount a police capacity to sniff out and stop street justice, yet avoid accepting the "help" offered by Pinochet and avoid relying on his former agents and methods. The broader prevention strategy was the project of building a democratic convivencia, through works of truth and social repair that could lessen or isolate the impulse to vengeance. Looking back in 1997, Aylwin told me he expected more vengeance attacks during his government. In this perspective, the project of convivencia worked.[51]

But not on 1 April 1991. In the late afternoon, Jaime Guzmán—the controversial political advisor of the junta and leader of the UDI, and a senator under the binomial election system—taught his law class at Catholic University. When he left, a team from the Frente Patriótico gunned him down at a red light. His driver rushed Guzmán to the Hospital Militar. Pinochet visited—and announced that Guzmán had died. Outraged demonstrators gathered. Some called for a resurrected DINA to stop terrorism.[52]

Guzmán was a major figure and symbol in Chile's memory struggles. Aside from his behind-the-scenes work as a political architect and speech writer, he had thrown himself into polemical public moments. In 1976, it was he who appeared on Televisión Nacional to denounce as unpatriotic the five jurists who asked the Organization of American States to investigate Chile's hidden human rights reality. In 1991, it was he who took the Senate floor to thunder against the accord between Aylwin, the Concertación, and Renovación Nacional to achieve a presidential pardon power for political prisoners. Some aspects of Guzmán's trajectory were more nuanced and discreet. He came into conflict with the DINA head, Manuel Contreras, and apparently sought to save one or more detained individuals. During the ups and downs of his long association with Pinochet and the regime, three constants proved symbolic. Guzmán was a devout Catholic; he provided a cogent intellectual anchor at political turning points; and he passionately defended the military regime against critics. As leader and symbol, Guzmán embodied the traditionalist morality, intellectual rationality, and patriotic fervor that junta defenders wished to associate with the salvation of Chile. The passions of admiration and revulsion Guzmán aroused were almost as strong as those surrounding Pinochet and Contreras. Small wonder that Televisión Nacional provided live coverage of the funeral.[53]

The murder of such a potent symbol changed the politicocultural environment. Subliminally and emotionally, if not factually and intellectually, it lent credence to the war thesis. Each side waged war; each lost victims. Earlier, critics of the Rettig Commission and Aylwin relied on the idea of war to diminish the devastating findings and the ethic of unacceptability in the report. Now Guzmán's murder made the idea of war vivid and raw. The new psychology: each side of Chile's divided past lost human beings it treasured to the violence of the other side. Stopping terror was the state's urgent task. To dwell on the violence of the past was irresponsible; it invited more vengeance.

Fundamental politicocultural objectives had not changed. For the Aylwin administration, human rights activists, and citizens sensitized by the Rettig Report and climactic presidential speech, or by activist-victim testimonies and media stories, the work of building a culture of human rights remained important. But an aggressive publicity offensive—barnstorming the country by a high-level commission conducting forums in tandem with relatives of victims—was now out of the question. Could a campaign backfire by provoking resistance or counterorganizing? The old instincts of prudence pushed back stronger. From the start, a certain cautiousness marked Aylwin's initiatives on human rights memory. He spoke frankly about constraints and he fostered awareness that certain lines could or would not be crossed. Even at his boldest, when he created the Rettig Commission against advice of key counselors, care in weighing practical consequences and limits was evident. Aylwin's speech on the Rettig Report also drew lines that would not be crossed. He summarized but declined to endorse one of its potentially explosive recommendations: to criminalize the cover-up of information relevant to locating the disappeared and the missing cadavers of the executed. (The recommendation also offered the carrot of protection against self-incrimination.) To endorse the recommendation would have committed him to pursue a very strong "wedge" effect in the face of uproar and resistance. In its remaining years, the Aylwin administration evinced more caution about high-profile initiatives or publicity related to human rights.[54]

Instincts by veteran human rights activists provided a measure of the difficulty. The change of climate was so drastic and harmful to human rights discussion that Jaime Castillo, aware of Manuel Contreras's enmity with Guzmán and his interest in shutting down the discussion, initially wondered if Contreras had ordered the murder.[55]

Notwithstanding the difficulties and taken on their own terms, the Rettig Commission and presidential report to the nation were successful. They established a memory-truth that stood the test of time. They stirred Chileans who did not expect to be moved. They strengthened the documentary foundation for subsequent truth-and-justice struggles. In the long run, they contributed, along with activist efforts, to a public culture more sensitized to human rights issues. But the birth took place on embattled ground. Release of the report did not coincide with an early resignation by Pinochet, the politicocultural scenario that tantalized Rojas and perhaps others in December 1990. Nor did it feed into cultural barnstorming by activists and officials, the intriguing possibility of March 1991. Hard bends kept appearing on the road of memory work. They exposed the limits of accomplishment and suggested costs of social exclusion, awareness, and accountability yet to pay. Would bends in the road turn the journey from truth to justice into a circle?

The Futility of History?

Some violent human happenings take people so beyond the realm of the normal and the possible, they defy our ability to comprehend. They also defy our ability to represent. How does one portray the reality of what we desperately wish to be impossible?

Projects of genocidal destruction—annihilation of a group through massive killing of its individuals and dismantling of its understandings of life—inexorably raise such issues. Projects of mass atrocity—for example, the humiliation and ripping apart of human identity that is the heart of torture—pose similar challenges. What moral philosophers call "radical evil," what jurists call "crimes against humanity," cross boundaries so fundamental they destroy faith in our ability to comprehend, portray, and thereby domesticate. What happened seems so grossly incommensurate with any human response or capacity, including the capacities of punishment and forgiveness. The ordinary quality of many of the individuals who carry out such projects deepens the paradox, the outrage, the bewilderment.

Not surprisingly, the Holocaust has raised such issues in especially acute form among scholars, survivors, philosophers, and artists. Lawrence Langer's brilliant *Holocaust Testimonies*, a study of oral video testimony, sensitively and relentlessly strips away any illusion of finding an adequate narrative, let alone a redemptive one, to remember and describe survivor experiences. In the end, language proves inadequate. The problem of adequacy surfaces repeatedly—not only amongst scholars, but also in the public culture of memorialization. In Germany, it eventually inspired an aesthetic of antimemory in a younger generation of artists and architects. Hannah Arendt's 1958 formulation of the way radical evil upends normal powers to understand and act in human society remains, a half-century later, among the most trenchant. "Men are unable to forgive what they cannot punish and . . . unable to punish what has turned out to be unforgivable. That is the true hallmark of those offenses which, since Kant, we call 'radical evil.' " In other words, the sheer outsized quality of the offense—it is larger than life, fundamentally incommensurable, an assault on the very idea of the human —shatters the possibility of restoring order and balance to life on earth. This is what makes the deed not simply a wrongful act, but an evil that offends humanity. Acts of radical evil seem to "transcend the realm of human affairs and the potentialities of human power, both of which they radically destroy wherever they make their appearance."

Several years later, the trial of Adolf Eichmann in Jerusalem led Arendt to wrestle famously with the "banality" of perpetrators of monstrous evil. She never fully reconciled the paradox of ordinary and "thoughtless" people as handmaidens of extraordinarily radical, willful, and humanity-defying evil.[1]

And yet . . . Even for the most extreme cases of atrocity, it goes too far to renounce historical analysis and contextualization. A scholar who studies the history of genocides—whether a microscale event such as the massacre of the Jews of Jedwabne, Poland, by their Gentile neighbors in 1941, or a macroscale event such as the slaughter of European Jewry in World War Two or of Tutsis in Rwanda in 1994—can offer a multifaceted analysis that helps us "understand" or "explain" the event. As a historian, I believe the European and Rwandan genocides can be analyzed as a converging of several forces: (1) a murderous political project by elites who have taken control of one or more states; (2) opportunism by various actors—often at local levels such as the province or municipality, not merely at national or international levels—who gain property, influence, or other advantage by blowing with the winds of persecution; (3) an unleashing of grassroots resentments and prejudice, some of which may have long cultural and historical roots, but are now stoked into a virulent frenzy of demonization and purging that also builds a new community; and (4) the terror that induces passive complicity—conformity—even among those who experience some qualms about the direction of events. A deep social crisis does not guarantee or determine such an outcome, but it may foster a climate for such convergence by throwing into turmoil the basic assumptions, adaptations, privileges, and expectations people use to order their lives.[2]

Such reflections have a point. They are vital if we are not to mystify what has happened and turn it into an "act of God or Nature," such as a massive earthquake. Mystification of this sort is dangerous; it can take us into a zone beyond human responsibility and prevention. But however vital the task of historical analysis, in cases of radical evil it also runs up against a sense of limits or futility. Arno J. Mayer summed up the point in the ironic title of his book on the Holocaust, *Why Did the Heavens Not Darken?* The text relentlessly sought to limit mystification by placing the "Judeocide" within a wider historical context, as a horrifying consequence and social dynamic of the general crisis of twentieth-century Europe that climaxed in a "war-cum-crusade" between Fascism and Bolshevism. The counterpoint of text and title is echoed even more strongly in the confession that concludes the preface: "at bottom the Judeocide remains as incomprehensible to me today as five years ago, when I set out to study and rethink it."[3]

Similar problems of representation and comprehension hover over the memory of Chile's violent past. Every historical project of violent destruction of demonized groups, of course, has unique aspects. The specific historical contexts and dynamics differ. In the Chilean case, the scale of violent annihilation was far smaller than the extermination campaigns of Nazi Germany and Hutu Power Rwanda. In Chile, the main targets for systematic destruction were defined as political beings, not ethnically or racially. (If one looks closely, some ambiguities blur the contrast a bit. In German Europe, Communists were systematically persecuted and Jews were vilified as Communist schemers. In Rwanda, Tutsis were depicted as the aristocrats favored under colonialism.) In addition, the concept of "genocide," now part of world vocabulary, bears an uneasy connection to the state violence in Chile. The concept emerged in the 1940s—prodded by the horrors of Nazi slaughter during World War II, the seminal 1944 book by Raphael Lemkin making a case for the term and new international law, and the political debate leading in 1948 to United Nations approval of the Universal Declaration of Human Rights, and the Convention on the Prevention and Punishment of the Crime of Genocide. The interests and fears of politically repressive states, and the overwhelmingly racial and religious character of the Nazi project of destruction, assured exclusion of political groups from the list defining potential victims of genocide.

The classic definition of genocide adopted in the 1940s referred to destruction of national, ethnic, racial, or religious groups. Interestingly, in 1933, when Lemkin first began formulating the case for new crimes of extermination based on group hatred (at the time he called them "barbarity"), he included any "social collectivity"—political, as well as racial or religious—among the potential targets of the crime.[4]

If one moves away from a lawyerly discussion of historical taxonomy, however, one can see a family of similar historical phenomena. In Chile the project of policide—annihilating the Left and more broadly, Center and Left cultural understandings of politics as a process of popular mobilization, via massive killing and abduction of real and alleged Left activists, complemented by additional layers of persecution and fright heaped on dissidents of any political stripe—yielded issues of comprehensibility and representation similar to those in classic cases of genocide. From this point of view, "policide" is shorthand for political genocide. From this point of view, too, the project of policide committed the state to mass atrocities—murder, disappearance, torture—that raise the "radical evil" problem of moral philosophy regardless of whether one accepts the nomenclature of "genocide."[5]

It was inside Chile's Rettig Commission that the paradox of analyzing and representing the unrepresentable turned into a human experience. The Commission members and staff were charged with documenting the truth of the past, as rigorously and irrefutably as possible. The process, however, yielded encounters with family experiences, documents, and forensic evidence so powerful they outstripped powers of narration or representation. The rather restrained and juridical tone of the report, justifiable as a narrative strategy creating irrefutable factual truth about a controversial issue, underscored the paradox. In a world of experiences beyond normal limits, that which was inspiring and that which was horrifying were difficult to convey in words.

Not all the work was depressing, horrifying, or unpleasant. On the contrary. The worst of human affairs can also draw out the best and the inspiring. "I'm a somewhat cold person," conservative historian Gonzalo Vial told me in 1997. Nonetheless, he found himself inspired and struggled to explain why. Researching the vengeance acts of *carabineros* and landowners late in 1973, and the subsequent "monstrous thing" organized by the DINA (secret police), produced "a terrible impression of fright."

> But also—listen to this—the impression of people's dignity . . . like the concentration camps, in those places where the last thing that one loses is dignity, moral dignity. One loses all physical dignity, you're a piece of furniture, a rag, an animal, something to laugh at, but inside you're still a man. . . . That was what was new for me, you see, the dignity of the people, the dignity of their family, the women, the women of the victims.[6]

The relatives of the dead and the disappeared called themselves "victims" of human rights violations. But they put forth their stories and demands in ways that made them something more than pitiful victims. Subjected to dehumanizing degradation and vilification, they responded not with the snarls or whimpering of animals but with demeanors and discourses asserting values of civilization. As human beings, they had the right to have rights, they wanted to give the dead a proper burial, and they valued justice over vengeance. The parallel inside the prisons were the stories of persons who asserted a small dignity beyond the imposed degradation—the prisoner organizing a song of hope, the guard daring to provide a cigarette or a word of encouragement.[7]

For young staff members of the Rettig Commission, encounters with the relatives were profoundly formative experiences. They unsettled much and taught much. The family listening sessions pushed by social workers exposed the lawyer Gastón Gómez to "something wonderfully human, real." The juxtaposition of "the suffering and the generative capacity of life" was powerful. In a majority of the cases, "people carried on, so they had this thing that was very strong, they bore a load, but also a certain pride." Cruel and brutal rupture did not cancel determination to build life; determination to rebuild lives did not cancel commitment to achieving truth. Gómez was prodded to think about the human condition. Our capacities for greatness and smallness, goodness and evil, resilience and disintegration, seemed distilled in the experiences of the families. "I matured a lot there."[8]

Some aspects of encounter with atrocity and political genocide, however, shatter faith in representation, analysis, and drawing of lessons. The devices we use to comprehend, navigate, and somehow tame experience turn inadequate. A document haunted Gómez as we spoke. He remembered a letter from a youth, a "boy" (*niño*) in Chilean cultural vocabulary. Henry Francisco Torres Flores, only sixteen years old, was held at the Pisagua prisoner camp in July 1974 and then permanently disappeared. He had no known party militancy. In other words, whatever his political sympathies may have been, he either was not a party member or was so inconsequential that no such background could be traced. In this respect, he resembled nearly half the persons the Commission ended up classifying as proved victims.

There was something more. The letter transformed the official image of the subversive demon—so monstrous and irredeemable that only torture, execution, or disappearance were suitable responses—into a humble, respectful, and frightened youngster. Of working-class origin, Henry Torres worked as a trucker's loading assistant (*peoneta*). At the Rettig Commission his mother, Rogelia Flores Mejías, testified she knew he would have gotten in touch if released. Her son Henry was attentive to his family, his personality neither one of "a street guy nor an adventurous type." Here is how he addressed his mother in a letter from Pisagua on 23 July 1974.

> My dear and remembered Mamita [the affectionate diminutive for Momma], I hope that when you get this letter I hope you'll find yourself in very good health, and likewise my brothers and sisters, I'm so-so [*regular*] in health . . . Momma, this for you, it is very sad if my Dad has not written you to let you know that I find myself under arrest in Pisagua.

Only after easing his mother into the news of his imprisonment did he proceed to ask for supplies—first a writing block and pencil (presumably for letters), then personal items such as cookies and cigarettes, finally a plea for a little money through family pooling with his sisters, "to buy bread." He wanted to know if his sister Uberlinda and her baby were well, and he hoped his relatives would write. He apologized for having to send sad news— "feeling very sorry about the bitter news I say goodbye to you, Momma . . . and may God watch over you."[9]

Even to a historian familiar with the political violence and project of the state, the disappearance of Henry Francisco Torres Flores staggers analytical balance and confidence. Can we truly comprehend how a youngster of this personality was transformed into a monster to be disappeared from humanity?

When deep comprehension is difficult, artists may supply an answer—or a representation—unavailable to historians. But here too, historical reality may stagger us. William Styron's brilliant novel *Sophie's Choice* draws us into the memory and meaning of the Holocaust by exposing us to the torment of a mother who survived. Sophie's "choice" was to give up one child to save the other. But what are we to do if the facts of history outstrip the imagination of the novelist? The staff social worker Paula Serrano could never forget when a mother told of the disaster that befell her family. Secret police agents forced her to turn over one of her children to spare the lives of the others. Like Styron's Sophie, she was destroyed by the "choice." But in the real-life version of the novel, there was also something more. The mother kept the secret from the surviving children—but they learned anyway, through their connection and good works with the solidarity community that assisted victims. They lived with a torment so devastating that our standard words, "survivors' guilt," seem grossly inadequate. Any representation seems a caricature.[10]

Encounters with the reality of the impossible do not really render historical analysis, or a drawing of lessons, beside the point. The staff worker Serrano confronted another moment of horror when bodies discovered in the North turned out to be people hacked to death. The victims had not even been shot. The youth of the conscript soldiers who mutilated the victims also disturbed her. Could young people be manipulated or driven by fear into acts of blinding hatred, regardless of their professed values? Encounters with the human realities of violence, including that suffered by military families, proved troubling, confusing, and instructive. As Serrano came face to face with a time of "historical madness," she found herself pulled into profound self-questioning about the weight of one's political words, the responsibility of political parties, the dangers of sectarianism, the sources of violence. Eventually, the experience proved a maturing one, and she drew lessons from it. "I became transformed into a democrat, genuinely, of the heart."[11]

Working on the Truth and Reconciliation Commission pulled its staff and members into a paradox. Even as they undertook the vital work of documenting, analyzing, and representing a memory-truth of utmost importance, they were also exposed to experiences beyond normal powers to document, analyze and represent. An aspect of what was important about the remembered past would always remain elusive. It was a paradox known to relatives of the disappeared and the executed, when they tried to communicate to others an experience beyond analogy or description. It is a paradox that troubles and humbles the author of this book.

Chapter 3

The Circle of Truth, Justice, and Force, 1990–1994

Justice and accountability posed the knottiest dilemma as Chileans reckoned with the Pinochet legacy. For Pinochetistas and officers of "dirty war," justice was the nightmare at the end of the slippery slope. For Pinochet, the accountability issue also included questionable financial transactions involving his family. After all, it was investigation of the "Pinocheques" case that had precipitated his troop alert in December 1990 and that could bring down, as well, his ability to act as shield for other soldiers.

For the human rights memory camp and a majority of Chileans, the memory-truth built by the Rettig Commission could not be disentangled from the question of justice. Once one understood the truth of what happened, how should society respond? To fail to respond would ratify as a basic value not a democracy of citizens with basic rights and dignity, but rather a Hobbesian world—rule by violence and might. It would fail to serve the cause of prevention embodied in the "never again" slogan, let alone the cause of social repair. It could render hollow rather than legitimate the idea that Chile was rebuilding a democracy. For these very reasons, the Rettig Report itself addressed the issue of justice in its several senses.

This chapter explores how Chileans walked the road from truth to justice to force after the March 1991 Rettig Report. Its conclusion, which draws on chapters 1–3 of this book, steps back to assess the dynamics and social consequences of memory struggles during the entire 1990–94 period. As we shall see, the memory question yielded continuous making and breaking and remaking of impasse, and with it an irony. One experienced the sensation of a "stuck" transition, with no movement beyond a circular march back to the same place. Yet the specific points concentrating the contention slowly shifted. The reckoning with Pinochet and the memory question did not really remain in the same place.

The ideas of justice in cultural play included both repair and prevention, and did not reduce to penal justice alone. Justice as social repair meant positive measures, symbolic and material, to recognize officially the truth of harm inflicted, to restore the good name of once stigmatized victims and families, and to provide tangible assistance to victim-survivors. Such assistance was at once an act to provide partial relief for a harm beyond full measure and repair, and to assert a public responsibility to reckon with the impact of state terror on citizens. Justice as prevention required additional positive measures, particularly educational work (including a revised school curriculum) to build a culture of respect for human rights, and institutional reform in the judiciary and the military. Justice as prevention also implied, however, the negative task of enforcing criminal justice. To reestablish "rule of law" rather than impunity by right of power required holding individuals accountable for unacceptable behavior.

Looked at closely, of course, the dichotomy of repair versus prevention blurs. For example, to establish the irrefutable truth of violent state terror was a work of social repair. It recognized that which had been cruelly denied or trivialized. To a degree, however, it also yielded negative sanction: cultural repulsion, disintegration of honorable facades, uncertainty in the minds of perpetrators that a new climate of documents, witnesses, and legal doctrine might wear down impunity. Conversely, criminal justice served prevention by penalizing those who used state power to trample human rights. But in reviving the rule-of-law idea, it also served moral and normative repair, and contributed to social repair by filling in truth gaps in the stories of victims.[1]

Among the varied forms of justice, material social repair offered the path of least resistance. During 1991–92, the Aylwin administration could rely on broad support as it established—without much publicity, fanfare, or controversy—a program of economic pensions, medical attention (including mental health), educational scholarships, and exemption of youth from mandatory military service for relatives of the dead and the disappeared. Also important was the creation in 1992 of a follow-up organism to the Rettig Commission, the Corporación Nacional de Reparación y Reconciliación (National Corporation of Repair and Reconciliation, hereinafter Repair Corporation). Its mandate included resolving the status of cases left pending by the Rettig Commission. Its work also included implementing social and legal assistance for families of victims, sending relevant information to courts for criminal proceedings, organizing the Truth Commission archive it inherited (and to which it also contributed new material), and promoting a culture of human rights. It was this organism that revised the confirmed death-and-disappearance figures upward in its 1996 report, from 2,279 to 3,197.

Such measures were consistent with a wider range of repair initiatives to redress partially the effects of repression on particular segments of society. Some initiatives began early, as in the 1990 creation of an "Office of Return" to reintegrate former exiles. Social repair initiatives continued on past the creation of the Rettig Commission and the Repair Corporation, as in the 1993 law on pensions of "exonerados políticos," employees dismissed in political purges. When material repair programs sparked dissent, the objection normally focused not on the principle of repair as an aspect of justice, but on implementation. The details of pension rights, legal formulations, sectors still excluded from benefits (e.g., victims of torture, officers and soldiers purged from the military), and budgetary allocation sparked disagreements.

The main exception to agreement in principle occurred when a material repair measure could not be disentangled from the charged symbolism of collective memory. In some instances, entanglement of the material and the symbolic created poignant private dilemmas. Most relatives of victims accepted economic compensation, but many also experienced ambivalence. The economic privation caused by state repression and the symbolism of official recognition of harm pulled one way; the sense that accepting aid might betray the memory of a loved one, if construed as canceling the loss, pulled in the other direction.[2]

Justice as material repair sparked mild politicocultural resistance, but justice as symbolic repair was different. It pulled Chileans onto a more challenging, deeply conflictive terrain. Here initiatives ran into tougher shifting balances of politicocultural acceptance and resistance, and the tension included points of principle. As we have seen, even within the culture of the Concertación, Aylwin's early symbolic politics—his 1990 decisions to organize a truth commission and to honor Allende's memory at an official funeral—placed him out front of some political allies and advisors. The responses to his March 1991 speech on the Rettig Commission again illustrated the complex mix of acceptance and resistance to symbolic repair. On the one hand, the factual memory-truth he summarized and the peak moment of recognizing remorsefully the responsibility of state and society resonated with a large majority of Chileans. The political opposition accepted the core factual truth of the report and acknowledged its gravity. The quasi-sacramental clearing of names also went unchallenged in television commentary and interviews following the speech. "I publicly and solemnly revindicate the personal dignity of the victims in consideration of their having been denigrated by accusations of crimes that were never proved and of which they never had opportunity . . . to defend themselves." On the other hand, the call for military and police forces to offer their own gestures of acknowledgment of the pain inflicted went unheeded. By the end of March, critics of the Rettig Report revindicated the war thesis and memory as salvation, shifting responsibility for state terror onto victims and their sympathizers.[3]

Politically and culturally, symbolic justice was complicated precisely because Chilean society remained so deeply divided about the meaning of the violent era. Those who passionately believed that military rule saved Chile from disaster and framed violence as a modest social cost were a minority. But they turned into a majority or near-majority toward the upper end of the class structure, and were led by powerful people with great disruptive potential—generals in command of troops and former secret police agents, business-oriented clans and opinion makers vital to the climate of economic growth and investment, senators with powers of legislative gridlock.[4]

The blend of the feasible and the complicated was especially evident in struggles over memorials and monuments. Aylwin acted with great alacrity on symbolic initiatives such as the Rettig Commission and the Allende funeral, considered foundational acts for building *convivencia* in which the passage of time mattered greatly. These initiatives had their complications, as we have seen, but were feasible as acts of presidential authority. The politics of memorials and monuments, however, required navigating more complex presidential, legislative, and grassroots currents. The complications showed up in delayed timing. On 9 September 1990, five days after the Allende funeral, high officials—Interior Minister Enrique Krauss, Secretary General of Government Enrique Correa, Education Minister Ricardo Lagos—returned to Santiago's General Cemetery. There they joined the organizations (*agrupaciones*) of relatives of the detained-disappeared and of the politically executed, and well-known solidarity figures such as Father Cristián Precht of the Vicaría (Vicariate of Solidarity), to lay the first stone for a mausoleum. A giant wall would inscribe the names of the victims with verse evoking a love attached to Chile's rocks, sea, and mountains. The wall would sit atop immense silent boulders that gathered persons in to live the verse. On and among the giant rocks, they could sit, contemplate, and remember loved ones by leaving flowers, or a message, or a small shrine. Facing the wall would be a ceremonial gathering area, and to its side would stretch funeral crypts for recovered bodies. Completion of the memorial, however, kept getting delayed. The formal inauguration did not occur until February 1994, nearly two years behind schedule.[5]

Subtleties of language and urban geography also exposed the political delicacy of symbolic justice and memory. Grassroots activists distinguished between a "memorial" and a "monument." A memorial was the site at a cemetery to bury, remember, and honor one's dead. It was a set of crypts, a wall of names, a place to remember one's loved one, friend, or comrade. A monument was a civic site to honor the values and ideals of the fallen. Its location should be a central communal place, and it should be comple- mented by a wider range of civic initiatives, including a major park whose trees would bear memory plaques. The politicocultural obstacles to a promi- nent monument, which required legislative approval, were formidable. The project sputtered. Political leaders unattuned to the language of relatives and grassroots activists began using *memorial* and *monument* as inter- changeable descriptors of the cemetery site.[6]

Memorializing Salvador Allende in civic spaces was an especially charged issue. Already in 1990, Allende loyalists and other leftist activists cam- paigned to honor his memory as a democrat by authorizing a statue on the Plaza of the Constitution facing La Moneda Palace. In May 1991 a group of representatives introduced legislation to authorize Allende memorial stat- ues in Santiago, Valparaíso, and Punta Arenas through funds raised by voluntary donation. The left wing of the Concertación coalition (Socialist Party and Party for Democracy) found itself in an uphill struggle. The proj- ect sparked too much resistance and controversy. Military and conservative figures denounced Allende as "the most terrible" of all Chilean presidents. Absences during votes by Renovación Nacional and by some in the Concer- tación undermined a quorum in the House of Deputies in 1992. All but one designated senator stood fast against the idea to the bitter end. When Senate approval finally came in June 1994, it did so by pulling the Right into an act of reconciliation, not agreement on the appropriateness of honored remem- brance, that gave everyone a piece of the memorial pie. The statues of presidents to be memorialized would include Jorge Alessandri, Eduardo Frei, and Salvador Allende, respective pre-1973 leaders of the Right, Center,

6. Memorial to the disappeared and executed: Above, a family gathers on the giant boulders. Behind them is the massive wall of names of known victims. *Credit: Helen Hughes.*

7. Below, a funeral in October 1994. Note the empty crypts for those whose remains have not been found. *Credit: Helen Hughes.*

8. Shrines at the Memorial to the disappeared and executed: Above, tucked inside the boulders, flowers and a picture.
Credit: Florencia Mallon.

9. Below, a youngster has left a drawing and message for her loved one, and flowers in a soda can.
Credit: Florencia Mallon.

and Left. The Socialist senators pulled in three votes from the UDI (Unión Democrática Independiente) by agreeing to vote to authorize a memorial for Jaime Guzmán.[7]

The civic geography of Allende's memorialization captured well the tensions of symbolic justice, and underscored the nature of Allende's social base. The transition to democracy inspired neighborhoods and provinces whose political pasts and mythologies linked them to Allende—with support by some municipal officials, political leaders, and Socialist Party groups—to float projects to name streets and plazas (and occasionally, schools) in Allende's memory. Most such initiatives did not crystallize until 1994 or 1995. They ended up yielding a geography that reaffirmed Allende's history as a leader of the marginalized. It was in the provinces and in poor and working-class neighborhoods, distant from the major downtown civic cores, that a few streets and plazas would bear his name. Proposals to rename portions of major avenues running toward the downtown of large cities—Avenida Santa Rosa in Santiago, Avenida Alemania in Temuco—simply proved unfeasible.[8]

PENAL JUSTICE:
WALKING THE CIRCLE OF IMPASSE, 1991–94

The justice that sparked the fiercest politicocultural resistance was penal justice. The problem was not just the Amnesty Law of 1978, but the judiciary inherited from dictatorship. As we have seen, the Rettig Commission bluntly observed that its failure as guardian of law had compounded Chile's human rights failure.

On 4 March 1991, before his evening speech to the nation, Aylwin sent an advance copy of the Rettig Report to the Supreme Court with a letter. He urged it to activate pending criminal cases, based on evidence sent by the Commission. The 1978 Amnesty Law "should not nor cannot be [an] obstacle to carrying out judicial investigation and determining the corresponding responsibilities." The Aylwin doctrine, as it came to be called, held that courts first had a duty to establish the nature, details, and timing of the crime, and any individual culpabilities, and only then could apply the amnesty if relevant. At a press conference, Aylwin was blunt about the judiciary's shameful past. Some judges had lacked "moral courage" on human rights.[9]

The findings of the Rettig Commission, and Aylwin's comments and amnesty doctrine, cut hard. The judiciary's treasured self-mythology and source of legitimacy was the idea that it stood as an independent government branch and protector of law. The idea had fallen into considerable cultural disrepute under military rule, but now the challenge was stronger. Highly credible figures took frank public aim at the Court's frayed mystique. The analysis of judicial failure by the Rettig Commission was all the more biting because written and signed by conservative jurists. Aylwin was a lawyer with a sharp judicial mind and the son of Justice Miguel Aylwin, president of the Supreme Court in the 1950s and a judge of strong moral reputation.

The judiciary experienced pressure as an institutional problem child from the start of the transition. On 30 March 1990, the new president addressed the Convention of Judicial Magistrates. Aylwin recalled his father's rigorous grading system based on quality of judicial reasoning, not friendships or personal deferences, in promotion decisions. The tribute contrasted implicitly with the widespread cronyism of contemporary judicial careers and promotion. The central message—shocking because expressed so openly—held that Chilean justice "is experiencing a grave crisis." Evidence abounded: ratings in public opinion polls, inadequate funding and inefficient institutional practice, lack of effective access by citizens, a perception of docility and lazy routine. "The citizenry holds the view that the judiciary does not act as a truly independent Power of State. Rather it sees it as a mere public service that 'administers justice' in more or less routine manner, too attached to the letter of the law and often docile to the influences of power." Lack of independence and commitment to real-world justice and rule of law had become painfully evident in Chile's recent human rights drama. Aylwin proposed institutional reform, overseen by a National Council of Justice, to promote analytical rigor in judges' training, promotion, and justification of sentences, whereby the judiciary could become an independent and effective branch of government. He softened the shock by declaring that many judges were well-prepared persons of integrity who served justice as best they could under adverse circumstances, and who shared the desire for renovation.[10]

This and other frontal reform proposals failed. To detail the struggles for judicial reform would take us far afield. The crisis was multifaceted. It involved not only docility to power and Pinochetismo, and use of "letter of the law" to justify substantive avoidance of human rights, but also the poisonous small corruptions of power. Promotions based on personal deference and political loyalties; a collegial ethos so extreme it tolerated corruption, alcoholism, diminished capacity, and sexual exploitation of the young;

institutional silences that left the legal rationales of sentences unexplained and inconsistent reasoning unreconciled—the closer one looked, the more the judiciary turned into a swamp. Some individual judges met high standards of integrity and legal reasoning, but they did not shape institutional ethos. Over time pressure for reform derived not only from the human rights camp, but also from the Right and economic concerns. The civil law's unpredictability—the lack of tight judicial reasoning, the time it might take to achieve resolution—dampened the enthusiasm of foreign investors for complex projects. The Frente Patriótico's April 1991 assassination of Jaime Guzmán and its September 1991 kidnapping of Cristián Edwards, son of the El Mercurio magnate Agustín Edwards, also sparked elite concern about crime. Poorly funded and slow, hampered by the double role of magistrates as investigator and judge, resistant to technical efficiency and computerization, how could such a judiciary serve modern life? The Pinochet regime's modernization reforms had not touched the judiciary.[11]

The pressures on the judiciary did not lead to reforms in the short run. The changing politicocultural environment exerted a more subtle effect—a softening-up process that prompted judges to reactivate cases under the Aylwin doctrine or in light of new information, that prodded them to display integrity as they proceeded, and that complicated the disciplining of lower-court judges who pursued human rights cases seriously. Rhetorically, the Supreme Court aggressively defended its honor. On 13 May 1991 it issued a vehement response to the Rettig Report. The Commission exceeded its scope, infringed on the courts, and allowed passion "to place the judges on a plane of responsibility almost equal with the actual authors of abuses against human rights." Like the person whose vehemence tells more than the words spoken, the Court said much by its angry tendentiousness. Chile's memory-truths proved potent. Strain was seeping into the tribunal halls.[12]

The pressures reflected synergies of state and civil society. The problem was not only political elites in the Executive and Congress, but also relatives of the victims, former political prisoners who had turned into survivor-witnesses, human rights lawyers and activists, and cultural activity and media events related to human rights. Relatives and survivors proved particularly committed to a combined quest for truth and justice. In June 1990, the Santiago Court of Appeals agreed to reopen the Chanfreau case and appointed Judge Gloria Olivares to preside. Olivares took the case seriously. Meanwhile, the Rettig Commission process prompted survivor-witnesses—

not only Erika Hennings as widow and ex-prisoner, but also Luz Arce as former DINA collaborator—to ready themselves to provide testimony. By 1992 the Chanfreau case turned into a dramatic test of the implications of the Aylwin doctrine. After providing her testimony to the Rettig Commission, Arce had left for Germany to assure her physical security and calm her fright. She returned in 1992 to testify in the Chanfreau and other cases. Her controversial life history guaranteed publicity. As important, Judge Olivares ordered legal testimony by any relevant people—even military and police personnel on active duty.

The court process yielded unprecedented spectacle: torturers confronted by victims, untouchable people forced into court. On 9 March Luz Arce, Erika Hennings, and Miguel Angel Rebolledo, another torture survivor, testified and endured cross-witness confrontation (*careo*) with the carabinero major Gerardo Godoy. Godoy, head of the DINA's "Tucán" group, led the Chanfreau arrest team and worked at the Londres 38 torture house. In July Judge Olivares ordered the arrest of Osvaldo Romo Mena, a notorious DINA torturer then living in Brazil. The Aylwin government requested extradition; relatives of the disappeared flew to Brazil to file petitions and build pressure. Romo was expelled in October. Olivares ordered other former DINA officers into court. They included the army colonel Miguel Krassnoff Martchenko. Remembered as a particularly sadistic torturer, virulently anti-Semitic and anti-Marxist, he had headed the DINA's "Halcón 1" group. Krassnoff was still on active duty, on the command staff of the Army Fourth Division in Valdivia. In October he faced Luz Arce and others in court.[13]

Such confrontations posed tremendous challenges to former victims. When Luz Arce calmed herself by looking up at Judge Olivares, who seemed so composed and dignified, she suddenly realized what had happened. Seeing Krassnoff had returned Arce to the "quasi fetal position, leaning forward, looking for a bit of warmth to relieve the physical and psychic pain." She had always bent her body into that position after torture.[14]

For Pinochet and former officers of "dirty war," the Chanfreau and similar cases exemplified the slippery slope. It explained why even a truth commission of limited scope was dangerous. After Olivares ordered Romo's arrest, the army petitioned to transfer the Chanfreau case to military justice. Everyone knew this would mean invoking the 1978 amnesty to dismiss the case without judicial investigation. Romo's expulsion and Krassnoff's court appearance in October turned the inside game frenetic. On 30 October the

Third Chamber of the Supreme Court voted four to two to approve the transfer. The majority: justices inherited from the Pinochet regime including army auditor general Fernando Torres Silva. The minority: justices appointed under Aylwin.[15]

Stopping one court case could not really stanch the cultural, legal, and political bleeding. At the level of culture and media, damaging memory images continued on past the Pisagua affair and the Televisión Nacional controversy of 1990. To conspiratorial minds on the defensive and accustomed to top-down control of media and courts, the sequence of negative events looked like a concerted campaign. Aylwin's March 1991 speech on the Rettig Report; new bodies discovered in Patio 29 of Santiago's General Cemetery during the 1991 memory season; the drumbeat of cultural activity, street demonstrations and press interviews by relatives of the disappeared in 1991–92—these set up the logical climax: court appearances by patriotic soldiers now cast as criminals. They were besieged by reporters and relatives of victims on their way in and out of tribunals.[16]

The hard work of human rights activists and the influence of the Aylwin doctrine began—slowly and unevenly, against the odds and subject to reversal—to pry open the box of judicial *olvido*. By mid-1993, reactivated human rights cases had snowballed to 184 and dragged some 50 active duty officers into court. Temporarily dismissed cases that might yet be reactivated amounted to another 600. Also new was an unusual Supreme Court ruling in December 1992. Notwithstanding a certain zigzag of Court decisions and a tendency to confine jurisprudential implications to the particular case at hand, the overall pattern of 1990–92 was clear. The Court openly rejected the Aylwin doctrine in August 1990, followed up with rulings that allowed use of the 1978 amnesty to shut down cases without full investigation, and imposed discipline on lower court and appellate court judges who pushed too hard on human rights cases or who backed the Aylwin doctrine. Judges Carlos Cerda Fernández, Nelson Muñoz, and Gloria Olivares were censured. Muñoz resigned to sidestep dismissal. Cerda, who had laid the jurisprudential groundwork for the Aylwin doctrine (and endured temporary suspension from duty) in a 1986 case, was ousted but reinstated upon application. Now, in a new case that converged with the heated politicocultural climate aroused by the Chanfreau ruling—controversy about Court legitimacy, and constitutional accusation against four justices—the Court retreated. It not only backed the Aylwin doctrine, but interpreted disappearance as a kidnapping crime. Unless the facts of the case were judicially investigated and established the date of the prisoner's death or release, the kidnap crime continued into the present. In other words, the 1978 amnesty was not pertinent until proved pertinent. Judges activated cases, and the disappeared loomed large. By mid-1993, they accounted for 103 of the 184 reactivated human rights cases, and for 377 cases susceptible to reactivation.[17]

The broader political terrain also looked threatening to those who saw themselves as Chile's saviors. Aylwin's economic policy was yielding strong growth—6.0 percent in 1991, an astounding 10.4 percent in 1992. In the early transition years, disillusion with the economic model's continuities with neoliberalism and its intense income inequality had not yet taken a political toll. On the contrary. By January 1993, robust economic performance, increased social spending, declining poverty rates, and an image of level-headed effectiveness yielded strong presidential approval ratings (55.7 percent approval, only 17.4 percent disapproval). Could political conditions undermine the institutional safeguards Pinochet thought he had left in place? For the memory question, the crucial shield was impunity. Protection from prosecution gave all soldiers of "dirty war" reason to adhere to a code of silence, not save the self by accusing comrades. To impede new revelations, in turn, stemmed erosion of the social base of memory as salvation.[18] Early in 1993, the possibility that political conditions would erode safeguards turned real, not theoretical. In December 1992, Concertación representatives infuriated by the ruling that aborted the Chanfreau case launched a constitutional accusation for grave neglect of duty against the justices who voted to transfer the case to military court. When the Senate voted on 20 January 1993, three narrowly escaped removal, but Justice Hernán Cereceda lost his post.

It did not matter much that Cereceda survived the specific count on the Chanfreau affair. Technically, he lost on a count of gross negligence on a different case; substantively, information on corruption was what convinced three Renovación Nacional senators to vote against him. For Pinochet and his loyalists, such details were beside the point. Pressure on the Supreme Court had crossed the danger threshold: destitution. Interpretation that corroded the 1978 Amnesty Law—the Aylwin doctrine, the disappearance-as-kidnap doctrine—would find a more receptive judicial environment after destitution. Also, Aylwin was meeting with Justice Marcos Aburto, the new Supreme Court president, and Senator Sergio Diez of Renovación to negotiate a judicial reform that would expand the Supreme Court, that is, increase presidential nominations and leverage. With Cereceda's replacement in April, Aylwin had already named six of seventeen justices.[19]

Aylwin's famous phrase, "justice to the extent possible," turned out not to constitute a guarantee against prosecution. It implied something more subtle: a struggle to define and shift the boundaries of the possible while proclaiming the necessity to live within the possible. The struggle was waged by civil society activists and some political elites, in a dance of conflictive synergy that continued beyond 1990. For Pinochet and his closest allies, the struggle had taken an ominous turn. The reliability of the Supreme Court as guardian of impunity was slowly softening.

The explosion came on Friday, 28 May 1993. Aylwin was in Copenhagen, on a European tour to promote Chile's transition as a success story, to encourage new foreign investment, and to thank the Scandinavian countries for their solidarity. In Santiago, an elite "black beret" army battalion—dressed in combat gear—burst into the heart of downtown. Their mission: protect the Armed Forces Building, located across the street at the rear of La Moneda Palace, while Pinochet presided over a meeting of discontent with army generals and placed troops on alert. The maneuver, nicknamed the *boinazo* (from the *boinas*, or berets), dramatized the army's power to revive panic and upset the climate of political stability. The saber rattling—troop alert, generals in battle uniform—continued for five long days. Rumors abounded. Would the generals arrest some Cabinet ministers? Occupy La Moneda? The crisis pressured Interior Minister Enrique Krauss (as acting head of government) and Secretary General of Government Enrique Correa to negotiate an end to army discontent with Pinochet and his close advisor, General Jorge Ballerino—or at least to defuse the crisis until Aylwin's return.

As in the December 1990 crisis, the precipitating cause and ultimate bottom line was personal—the threat posed to Pinochet and family, and to his image as the austere patriotic savior, by fraudulent commercial transactions. The "Pinocheques" affair had entered legal limbo for reasons of state (see chapter 1), but the case could be reactivated. New shady transactions discovered in 1992 involved Pinochet's son, Augusto Pinochet Hiriart, and a company sold to the army. In April 1993, the Council for the Defense of the State (the agency for pursuing legal interests of the state) sought court reactivation of the trail of corrupt finance. Given the high stakes and delicacy of the case, Guillermo Piedrabuena, president of the Council, had consulted Aylwin, who told him to proceed in accord with law. Judge Alejandro Solís ordered testimony by high officials. On 28 May the headline of *La Nación* announced the reopening of the case and court citation of eight generals. To Pinochet, a "BBC explanation" of the headline was not credible. The state was majority owner of *La Nación*, and La Moneda aimed to undermine him—and the army. As in 1990, Pinochet had no reason to distinguish between his personal or familial well-being and that of the Army. His clout depended on fusing personal interest with army interest; as commander in chief, he served as the army's guarantor against enemies. Even before the headline, army generals had been meeting to review their discontents and to decide how to rearrange the political balance.[20]

TAKING BACK THE TRANSITION?

The details of negotiations after 28 May 1993 matter less than the larger political effect—return, on matters of memory, to the state of impasse in December 1990. All the actors seemed to be trying to "take back" a transition stolen from them. The army and Pinochet wanted the transition of honor and amnesty, now at risk of dissolving. Aylwin and his allies wanted the transition of political stability and ethical clarity, now yanked into a zone of saber rattling in defense of impunity. Memory activists and victim-survivors in the human rights camp wanted the transition with justice they had imagined and fought for since the 1970s.

The army used the boinazo to air a wide range of discontents. Three core objectives related directly to memory struggles about the legacy of the Pinochet regime, and how to reckon with its legacy during times of transition. Pinochet and the army wanted agreement to defuse the Pinocheques case; to create a new amnesty or a technical equivalent to stop damning justice proceedings and publicity; and to drop a new effort to reform the organic law of the armed forces. Negotiated with sectors of the Right, the new initiative would include presidential power to remove high command officers for cause. Aylwin maintained a presidential posture by refusing to cut short his European trip, even as Krauss and Correa negotiated to defuse the crisis. On 6 June, he returned and began a round of intense consultations with Pinochet and military officers, political elites, and jurists and human rights lawyers. The process dragged on two months and had an astute political effect. It rendered earlier negotiations moot and put the initiative back in the presidency.[21]

The boinazo succeeded in two objectives. The Pinocheques affair was again shelved, and the reform to assert civilian control over top military command undermined. It failed, though, to achieve the third objective, a new amnesty or its technical equivalent through a "full stop" (*punto final*) law to draw an endpoint to criminal justice related to human rights. This objective was the knottiest. For the Aylwin government to give way on amnesty or its equivalent would undermine its strategy of memory politics, subject its Center-Left coalition to deep internal strain, and raise profoundly troubling ethical questions. Yet a certain ambivalence also prevailed. The Aylwin administration held an interest in bringing to a halt contentious political struggle over human rights memory, even as it held an interest in reaffirming its ethical principles and its rejection of a full stop equivalent of amnesty.

Politically, the Aylwin government's memory strategy had not envisioned an endless responsibility to focus on the past as a top priority for building a democratic present and future. The goal was a bounded healing process, followed by a period of focus on new political priorities. The idea of a second phase took on greater urgency in mid-1991, when the strategic intellectual advisors who met weekly with Boeninger argued that the government risked erosion of support and loss of initiative if its agenda remained stuck on the divisive themes of an earlier phase. (The argument reflected nervousness about the memory question present from the start. Let us recall, from chapter 1, that strategic advisors including Boeninger were at first skeptical about Aylwin's decision to form a truth commission.) The memory question —truth and justice related to human rights, the new contours of civilian-military relations—had been an essential force shaping the early transition. Notwithstanding the success of the Rettig Commission, the hazards and the sense of memory impasse were by now clear enough. The troop alert of December 1990 and the toughened cultural climate for memory work after the April 1991 assassination of Guzmán were strong warnings. The new agenda would push the "growth with equity" idea, understood as the building of a more developed, just, and modern society with a higher standard of living. On the one hand, the state would accelerate work on the institutional infrastructure (from an improved network of roads and ports, to expanded access to export markets and foreign investment, to modernization of state operations and property rights) conducive to high economic growth. This vision of Chile saw its emergence as a highly competitive nation in the international capitalist market. On the other hand, the state would address equity by increasing public investment in education, health, and housing, and in basic infrastructure such as potable water and electricity. This vision of

Chile promoted an idea of citizenry in which all gained dignity and collaborated, notwithstanding great socioeconomic inequality. Sectors of modest means would escape extreme poverty, gain access to goods and services that improved quality of life, and join in state-society partnerships to improve social development and opportunity via grants to grassroots groups.

In this conception of "transition," the point was to define its boundaries tightly—impossibility of reversion to military rule, fostered by a climate of democratic convivencia—and to declare success. Success allowed the government to place the accent on a new agenda, and to interpret reform of remaining undemocratic features as tasks of improvement and "consolidation" of the transition. In August 1991, Aylwin declared the transition "is already done" and announced a major National Infrastructure Program.[22]

This political strategy did not imply a simple embrace of memory as a closed box—the framework of mindful forgetting of the dangerous past—nor an endorsement of amnesty. Politically and ethically, the government could not renounce basic principles of truth and justice. The main responsibility and protagonism, however, would shift to other state actors and social actors as memory work turned toward the "hot potato" question of justice. Thus Aylwin embraced an initial phase of memory work. To establish public truth and acknowledgment of massive human rights violations, and to launch social repair policies, was both an ethical duty and a top political priority to achieve democratic transition and a new convivencia. Success in this phase would also consolidate the Center-Left Concertación as the coalition of human rights and democracy. A second phase of memory work—to complete truths and establish culpabilities in individual cases—was a responsibility properly transferred to courts. Justice in its penal sense implied longtime horizons before resolution, and conflicts that would prove debilitating if allowed to shape the political agenda. Insulation of penal justice from politics was in any event the goal of a society of "rule of law." In this conception, the political and ethical obligation of government was to create an environment of institutional reform, legal doctrine, and judicial promotions that would enable the judicial power finally to own up to its responsibilities.[23]

In sum, in the tension between memory work as "formula" and memory work as "wedge," Aylwin leaned toward an ambiguous splitting of the difference: Envision the Rettig Commission process as part of a longer saga and struggle that would include judicial reform and a reactivation of cases under the Aylwin doctrine, but slowly transfer increasing portions of the initiative to other actors of state and society. Also, avoid pushing for policies, such as criminalization of cover-up, that would increase the scope of potential judicial action. Some political elites and advisors in the world of the Concertación, of course, proved less subtle. They had found the formula, and it enabled them to find some common ground with the Right. Turn away from the past—now that it has been acknowledged! Meanwhile, grassroots human rights activists pushed for a strong wedge effect. For them, the Rettig Commission process was profoundly unsatisfactory unless it fed into a larger process of memory work leading to full truth and justice. For the military and the Right, the net result of these crosscurrents was that a wedge effect had become real and dangerous by 1993.

The boinazo undermined the lines that had been drawn. It prompted a retraction of Aylwin's announcement that the transition had been completed. He now had to revisit the memory question and fashion a new initiative. Aylwin rejected Pinochet's insistence in their July meetings on direct fortification of amnesty. The general wanted either a new Amnesty Law, or interpretive laws to nullify the Aylwin doctrine, to accept as judicially valid an army conclusion that a prisoner had died, and to convert temporary case dismissals into permanent closure. Aylwin turned toward finding an approach that might, as he understood it, address the demand for justice without falling into ethical fraud on one side, perpetual destabilizing conflicts with the military on the other.[24]

On 3 August, Aylwin announced a new initiative. The "Aylwin Law," as the proposal came to be known, would presumably render judicial investigation more agile yet preserve the discretion prized by the military. It stipulated appointment of fifteen special judges to focus on human rights cases, and allowed secret provision of information to enable them to establish the fate of the disappeared while protecting informants from publicity. It provided a two-year horizon for the specialized judge to establish the fate of a disappeared person and apply the Amnesty Law, if relevant. Otherwise, the case would revert back to the regular tribunals. "This idea," as Aylwin put it to me, "ended up not being liked by anybody." Pinochet, the military, and the Right wanted a full stop—an end to judicial cases and media vulnerability—even when a special judge could not reach a definitive conclusion. Human rights activists saw the secrecy provision as another cover-up. It would encourage and ratify the misinformation practices habitual under military rule and would violate truth as a public right. Whatever the nomenclature, the law would reinforce impunity and bring justice to a "full stop."

Activists—notably the Agrupación de Familiares de Detenidos-Desaparecidos (Association of Relatives of the Detained and Disappeared, hereinafter Agrupación) and Communists—quickly assembled to demonstrate against "Full Stop" in front of La Moneda. Within a few days, the Agrupación and the human rights group CODEPU (Comité de Defensa de los Derechos del Pueblo, Committee for Defense of the Rights of the People) also placed newspaper ads excoriating the project. The Agrupación declared that the proposal "validates and legitimizes" the military's self-amnesty decree, that is, "the institutional negation of truth and justice." Only a week after Aylwin's speech, the Agrupación launched a rotating hunger strike. The frictional synergy of earlier times had now broken down into open conflict. Among political elites, figures in the Left of the Concertación coalition especially criticized the project, but skepticism also emerged in the Center. In a notable interview, Andrés Aylwin, the president's brother and a Christian Democrat in Congress, warmly admired the values and intentions of his brother but doubted that the project could achieve its purpose.

On 2 September, only a month after the original announcement, Aylwin retired the initiative (technically, he removed its "urgent" legislative status). Social actors on distinct sides of Chile's memory struggles had mobilized, and the impasse could not be broken. A piecemeal path to penal justice would resume, in an environment less propitious for the Aylwin doctrine. Individual cases would make their way through the courts. Doctrine and practical results would at best resume a zigzag path, influenced by the politicocultural environment, the quality and integrity of the individual judges, and, eventually, Supreme Court recomposition through presidential selection of candidates from the internal promotion process leading to five-person slates.[25]

The impasse restored by the boinazo ran deep. No one managed to "take back" the transition, that is, to put the memory question to rest or on a path to one's liking. Aylwin had wagered his considerable moral authority but could not produce a miracle. He entered the roughest period of his presidency. The "Aylwin Law" sparked tensions within his own political camp and brought tension with relatives of the disappeared to a peak. It catalyzed painful spectacles—carabineros beating women demonstrating for justice, and a hunger strike by women still searching for justice. Soon thereafter came another 11 September anniversary. It too produced painful images—clashes between protesters and carabineros. Such scenes, a kind of eerie replay of memory clashes in military times, exposed the limits of convivencia. They seemed to question how much had really changed.

The deterioration in relations between the government and human rights activists and victim-survivor families also showed up as absence. A lost symbolic opportunity occurred in February 1994. Only two weeks before the end of his term as president, neither Aylwin nor Cabinet-level officials attended the inauguration of the memorial wall for the disappeared and the executed at Santiago's General Cemetery. Grievance was too raw. The symbolism of shared sorrow and commemoration would not have worked.[26]

CONCLUSION: MAKING AND BREAKING
MEMORY IMPASSE, 1990–94

Chile walked a circle of impasse on the memory question between 1990 and 1994, but impasse was not the whole story. What memory struggles generated was not impasse in the static sense—a deadlock that freezes time, since the issue in play remains unresolved and the contending social forces prove unable to win, compromise, or cede ground. Instead, the memory question yielded a slowly shifting center of gravity in an ongoing struggle, and return to deadlock on a new focal point in contention. This was a society of rolling impasse, a making and breaking and remaking of standoff as Chileans reckoned with the legacy of Pinochet and the military regime.

A society of slowly rolling impasse yields a peculiar experience: the repeated sensation of "frozen" or deadlocked transition, even as social change unfolds and points of deadlock shift. For many Chileans on all sides in the early 1990s, the memory question was heartfelt and strategic. It was at once a moral, political, and even existential question. For democratic Chileans sensitized to human rights and for victim-survivors of atrocity, the circular march of forward steps followed by bends in the truth-and-justice road under threat of force could spell agony, not simply stalemate.

To understand the memory question and the society of rolling impasse in the 1990–94 period requires assessment of three themes: the adversity that bred impasse, the accomplishments in spite of impasse and including the costs and limits of such achievement, and the cultural psychology of agony.

For democratic Chileans, adversity ran deep. Two hard realities could not be wished away. First, the strategy for achieving a democracy against the will of a dictator imposed sharp constraint. Win a plebiscite in 1988, negotiate terms of law and transition with a still powerful outgoing regime in 1989, chart a coexistence in the 1990s between an elected democratic president and a former dictator in command of the army—these constituted both a path of release from military rule and a path of binding. For better or worse, civilians and soldiers had agreed to abide by rules of the game that hemmed in the play of democratic action. The second hard reality was one of deep social division about the meaning—and the legitimate policy consequences —of a great and violent trauma. By the late 1980s, a cultural majority had "awakened" into remembering military rule as an era of violent rupture and persecution, and saw pursuit of justice as a logical and necessary comple- ment to truth seeking. About two in five Chileans, however, remembered military rule in heroic terms, and that large minority turned into a majority in socially powerful sectors, particularly the military and the business class. The judiciary failed to serve as a meaningful counterweight to the socially powerful.

In a sense, the strategic rules of transition and the deep divisions over memory constituted a recipe for impasse. Democratic leaders of the Center- Left held much of the "soft power" of public opinion and election votes; Pinochet and his sympathizers held much of the "hard power" of institu- tions, force, and investment. Victory of the No in the 1988 plebiscite on continuation of Pinochet's rule in 1988 created not a democracy, but a democratic opening. The structure of transition almost guaranteed a ten- sion between "formula" and "wedge" among those who identified them- selves as sympathizers of memory work on human rights violations. Once Aylwin established a truth commission, should it constitute the mechanism to settle a difficult problem and move on, or the strategic point of entry in a widening struggle for a culture of human rights and rule of law?

Given Chile's deep memory divide, its constrained structure of transition, and the constant threat of impasse, the accomplishments of "memory work" in the first years of transition were real and important.[27] At the level of Aylwin and state actors, the fundamental achievement was the Rettig

Commission and its politicocultural consequences. After the Rettig Report, the truth behind memory as rupture—massive lethal harm by agents of the military state, cruelly compounded by state denial, too large and well organized to be written off as anomaly or occasional excess—was inscribed as factually real and proved in the public domain. The definitive factual basis of memory as rupture became a new common sense that had to be acknowledged to achieve a new convivencia. It clinched the idea that work of repair and prevention was necessary, and it shifted the terms of memory debate. In the public domain, at least, those inclined to heroic remembrance of military rule shifted from denying the state's killing violence or pretending it was insignificant, to emphasizing and debating how far one should go when connecting Chile's pre-1973 history to subsequent state violence. The exculpatory stance—the war thesis that shifted responsibility toward victims, and sidestepped the point that unarmed prisoners had been victims of torture and execution—was now placed, however, on the cultural defensive. Over time, the net result was a culture more sensitized to human rights as a core value, and a climate of public leadership that turned proclaimed indifference to human rights into a taboo. If one was indifferent to human rights, one had better express it privately.

The major exception was Pinochet himself, whose apparent lack of self-control translated into occasional public comments of disdain. In September 1991, annoyed by media questions about the bunching together of newly exhumed bodies at an anonymous grave at Patio 29 of Santiago's General Cemetery, he remarked, "What great economizing!" Such comments did not undo the cultural shift. They provoked scandal—they embarrassed supporters of heroic memory, and turned into a "memory knot" that reactivated cultural revulsion and human rights sensibilities.[28]

A related achievement was the creation of a new agenda of debate on justice and amnesty. The frontal critique of judicial failure by Aylwin and the Rettig Commission, the pushing for judicial reform by a president-jurist with substantial moral authority, the creation of the "Aylwin doctrine," on obligation of judges to investigate and to establish culpability in human rights cases before a decision on applicability of amnesty—these shifted the politicocultural ground of memory struggles. Before 1990, the justice-amnesty problem constituted a zero-sum game—one either passed legislation and won constitutional tests to nullify or revoke the amnesty, or one failed to do so. Failure implied application of the amnesty to shut down justice cases before they could gain traction. In other words, justice proceedings would not produce additional information relevant to truth, nor findings that created cultural accountability. Given the de facto balance of power in the judiciary and Congress, and in state and society at large, the zero-sum game constituted a formula for impasse and impunity. Putting forth forcefully that the judiciary badly needed reform, that close legal *interpretation* could undermine the once presumed effects of an Amnesty Law, and that judges fell under an obligation to consider rigorously the evidence turned over by the Rettig Commission, these factors cut away at the Gordian knot of the zero-sum game. The new climate of legal doctrine and debate generated pressure on judges to perform, openings for some justice cases to proceed, obligations that compelled reluctant soldiers to testify and confront accusation in court. Precisely for this reason, one objective of the 1993 boinazo was to bring such developments to a "full stop"—or at least remake impasse.

The Aylwin administration failed to institute judicial reform, could not block judicial rollback after the boinazo, and could not split the difference between formula and wedge via the Aylwin Law proposal. What it did accomplish was to create a new agenda of debate about judicial failure and legal doctrine. The debate was set back in 1993, but it would reemerge in subsequent years.

To focus on Aylwin and state actors alone, however, is too narrow. Grassroots social actors aligned with the memory camp that emphasized rupture and persecution under military rule also proved fundamental. Two achievements of activists and their supporters were critical. First, their conflictive synergy with state actors proved indispensable—notwithstanding the ups and downs of conflict and collaboration—to the shaping and fate of state-led initiatives on truth and justice. As we have seen, the knowledge and organization of former political prisoners, as well as relatives of the executed and the disappeared, provided critical contributions for the truth-gathering project of the Rettig Commission. Behind such success also lay the human rights activist networks that supported victim-survivors and their families, and that built a historical record of witness and documentation turned over to the Rettig Commission by the Vicaría (Vicariate of Solidarity) and similar organizations.

As important, it was the environment of moral, cultural, and political pressure created by determined activists that prodded state actors to respond—and that gave wider cultural resonance and necessity to memory work initiatives. It was the determination of activists such as Erika Hennings, who insisted on pursuing the justice case for her disappeared husband, Alfonso Chanfreau, that set the stage for congressional outrage and impeachment proceedings against negligent Supreme Court justices. It was the pressure of Sola Sierra and Agrupación activists for justice, and for more detailed truth, that set the stage for interpretive legal doctrine to undercut traditional use of amnesty to shut down cases before they could get started. Protests by political prisoners built a climate for congressional approval of a presidential pardon power. Revelations about Pisagua by journalists working with survivors, relatives, and human rights activists boosted powerfully the climate of receptivity and necessity for the Rettig Commission. And so on.

A second major achievement by the human rights community of activists and sympathizers related to the tension between formula and wedge in memory work. Put simply, the human rights community blocked political elites from being able to settle on a formulaic closing down of memory work. Put positively, they kept culturally and politically alive the tension of formula versus wedge, within society at large and within the world of the Concertación and political elites in particular. Grassroots activists thereby guaranteed that despite hard setbacks and returns to impasse, the reckoning with human rights and the Pinochet legacy could not really be bound up in a neat package and subsequently set aside.

To keep the memory question open, as an unfinished moral and political and legal agenda, was an achievement precisely because so many forces pulled in the other direction. Many political elites were tempted, after the Rettig Commission Report and the Guzmán assassination, to see in the report a formula that ironically granted permission to close the memory box and move on. Aylwin himself, although sensitive to the human as well as political and ethical aspects of the memory question, wrestled cautiously with the problem of unintended consequences. He proved inclined to split the difference between formula and wedge. He declined to endorse the Rettig Commission's recommendation to criminalize cover-up, yet also pushed for a more responsible judiciary and for more innovative legal doctrine. He also held a certain interest in defining the memory question in a bounded manner that would enable him to resolve it successfully as his historical legacy.

Above all, it was the structure of de facto forces in Chilean life that made it an accomplishment to keep the memory question open, as a wedge for building a democratic culture of human rights and accountability. The contradiction between "soft" and "hard" power that shaped the transition, the return to impasse and saber rattling when the memory question turned too explosive, these bred temptation—whatever one's moral inclinations—to close the memory box. If one could not solve the memory question and if it always turned back, as if in a circle, to nerve-wracking threats of force that could wreck a successful transition, why not find a formula to settle the problem once and for all?

The boinazo brought the structure of adversity and temptation back into sharp focus. (This was the case even though, let us recall, it was the personal and familial legal problems of Pinochet that constituted his precipitating cause and minimal bottom line for resolution.) Its aftermath was revealing. The hunger among political elites to find a definitive solution, the fear by human rights activists that the "Aylwin Law" proposal amounted to a formula for a full-stop to justice, the fear by Pinochetistas and military officers that the same proposal would open the door to trials without an endpoint— these made clear the temptations of formula and the impossibility of formula. Here, too, Chileans walked a circle. As we shall see (chapter 4), the temptation *and* impossibility of formula bred moral ambivalence and renewed temptation to find a formula—or in its absence, to look away and finally close the memory box.

Accomplishment in the face of adversity was real, but exacted a cost. Democratic Chileans—their vehicle was a frictional synergy, with ups and downs, among state actors and grassroots actors—built an undeniable foundation of truth for memory as rupture. After March 1991 no one could credibly deny in public the reality of the massive "open wound" on the social body, nor that the wound was an inheritance of organized state action under military rule. Democratic Chileans also built a political and cultural foundation for the work of social repair, a new agenda of debate and pressure about justice and legal doctrine related to amnesty, and a perhaps unexpected reality. Memory work would carry on—it was a fact of life that could not be stopped, whatever the military threats or returns to impasse.

The reality of an open-ended process was in part a cultural inheritance and achievement from earlier times. It drew on a depth of sensibility and commitment forged in the social organizing and memory struggles of the dictatorship years, not simply in the early transition years. The reality was also in part political in the immediate sense. Human rights victims and activists and their sympathizers formed an irrenunciable base within the Center-Left Concertación. In the Left parties of the Concertación, especially, political elites included persons who had themselves suffered repression or had friends and comrades among the killed and disappeared. In this sense, the social worlds and sensibilities of "political elites" and "activists" sometimes overlapped. Their networks, values, and experiences could bleed into one another.[29]

Yet the costs were also substantial. Two stand out. First, the bounded scope of the Rettig Commission's mandate narrowed down the symbolic circle of those who suffered rupture and persecution to its maximal victims —the executed and the disappeared. Over time, the multilayered nature of the repression, particularly the tens of thousands tortured, and regardless of care by the Commission to take cognizance of distinct forms of repression, could fall off the cultural radar screen. (As we have seen, the Rettig Commission did analyze torture succinctly and debated how to present it, but its case studies were limited to instances where torture culminated in death of the prisoner.) Over time, too, the role of proven individual cases of persons executed and disappeared as the minimal "floor" on the estimate of lethal repression could fall away.

In short, what had been a multilayered repression whose direct victims numbered in hundreds of thousands and their families, could become symbolically reduced to a horrifying repression of two or three thousand people and their families. During the 1980s, when dissident memory expanded explosively and turned into mass experience, the lines blurred between memory as a cruel rupture inflicted on maximal victims, and memory as a multifaceted persecution experienced or witnessed by vast social sectors who "awakened" into defense of life, human rights, and democracy. The disappeared and their female relatives continued as a potent memory knot, but the symbolic circle of victims of dictatorship also widened rapidly. It included not only the killed and the disappeared, but also prisoners subjected to torture, dissidents condemned to exile or relegation (internal exile to isolated places in the provinces), shantytown women and youths whose protests against poverty and repression subjected them to more repression, street priests and middle-class women who turned into targets because they defended "life," and so on. In a sense, a social majority had turned into "victims of dictatorship" to some degree; memory as rupture, persecution, and awakening had merged into a single (albeit heterogeneous) memory camp.[30]

The narrowing of the symbolic circle to several thousand maximal victims was not an inevitable cultural consequence of the bounded Rettig Commission mandate. One needs to distinguish between cause, effect, and symptom. The narrowing derived most fundamentally from the balance of social forces that shaped the uses and nonuses of the Rettig Commission achievement. A follow-up commission to focus on torture, a criminalization of cover-up to crack codes of silence, a stronger "wedge effect" in general after the Rettig Commission—these all might have produced a widening circle. What determined their feasibility and likelihood was not the language of the Rettig mandate, but the conflicts and adversities of the transition itself. Nonetheless, the narrowing of the circle took hold and solidified, especially by the mid-1990s, and it exacted a cost in social exclusion and social awareness.

The second major cost was the deterioration in the frictional synergy that connected state actors on the one hand, and human rights victims and activists on the other. The most creative and subtle synergies unfolded in the early years, in relation to the launch of a new democracy whose sensitivity to memory and human rights would underscore a contrast with the Hobbesian world of military dictatorship and thereby promote a new convivencia. The inaugural at National Stadium, the backing of Televisión Nacional as an independent entity when it engaged in human rights journalism, the funeral of Allende: these, and especially the Rettig Commission process, promoted collaboration and a sense of inclusion despite strains and disappointments that also arose. Yet precisely because memory work sparked fears of a slippery slope in the military and among partisans of Pinochet and his regime, advances also sparked blowback—dramatic moments of saber rattling. The dialectic of advance and blowback reinforced caution and a leaning toward the formulaic by state actors, and induced estrangement and suspicion of betrayal among victim-activists. By the late phase of the Aylwin presidency, particularly after the boinazo, the synergies had more or less worn out. The impasse problem on the memory question was not only one of relations between civilian government and military officers. Impasse had also begun to afflict relations between government and grassroots human rights activists. It remained to be seen whether a new Concertación government could revive the old synergies.

In the early 1990s, Chileans embarked on a circular journey: the making and breaking and remaking of impasse on the memory question. The journey was tough. For democratic Chileans and the human rights camp, it yielded quarter-loaf or at best half-loaf achievements. The memory question, moreover, was the most heartfelt and strategic issue to achieve a successful transition—a democracy viewed by most citizens as morally legitimate and politically effective, that is, as a sustainable and welcome new order of values and policy in contrast to dictatorship. The flip side of the coin was to achieve a democracy viewed by most of its detractors as too resilient, credible, and effective to upend the rules of the game, some of them unanticipated.

What, then, of the cultural psychology of agony? The experience of quarter-loaf achievements, on matters of deep moral import, can be dangerous and embittering. In the heat of the struggle, it stokes frustration and cynicism. Aylwin himself was a kind of barometer. He was a highly successful president in terms of his central goals—achievement of an irreversible transition and a new convivencia—based on moral engagement of the memory question, a strong economic track record, and a start on paying down the social equity debt inherited from the military regime. He maintained majority approval ratings and consolidated the electoral base of the Concertación. In the presidential election of December 1993, Eduardo Frei Ruíz-Tagle, the Concertación candidate and son of the former president Eduardo Frei Montalva, won 58.0 percent of the vote for a six-year term beginning in March. Given the Center-Left composition of the coalition, the electoral dominance guaranteed that a politics of olvido or "full stop" on human rights justice, although tempting to the Right and some Concertación leaders, was not likely to become a workable policy option.[31]

Yet as a president who staked his legacy on the human rights issue, Aylwin also understood that the moral line between pursuing justice while recognizing constraint, and abdicating the pursuit of justice in the name of constraint, was a thin one. One had to defend it; one had to bolster confidence in it. The boinazo and related political stumbles of 1993—at bottom, the revitalized memory impasse—harmed the moral foundation and confidence he had sought to build. They also turned his hope to bring "closure" to political contention over human rights—to have a strong court system take control and insulate the political world from volatile human rights conflict during the next administration—into an ever receding mirage. All along, the human rights question had been a major priority that drew personal attention. On matters of economics, Aylwin could set a basic course, follow the advice of Treasury Minister Alejandro Foxley, and leave the details to technocrats. Matters of truth and justice, however, were central to the project of convivencia and sparked serious crises. They also spoke to Aylwin's own values, family history, and professional background. José Zalaquett recalled that when he supplied memos and drafts on truth-and-justice matters to the administration, it was the president's handwriting that appeared all over the returned documents.[32]

Perhaps for these reasons—part of that awareness of history that settles on outgoing leaders—in his last months in office, Aylwin sought to reset the moral compass of democratic transition. Early in 1994 he spoke clearly and energetically again about values—decrying the tendency in his own Christian Democracy party to lapse into a culture of political patronage rather than ethical responsibility, declaring that the market had its purposes but that its logic of advantage and competition harmed social justice and ethical balance. On his last day of office, he released the last group of inherited political prisoners—the ones who tried to assassinate Pinochet in 1986—by commuting their sentences to exile in Belgium.[33]

For Sola Sierra, the activist-leader of the Agrupación, the moral compass was not readily redeemed. She experienced a bitter agony after the May 1993 boinazo. She met with Aylwin, and he assured her that he would not cede to military demand for a final-stop law. She took heart from his determination to send a legislative proposal to Congress if soldiers did not provide information on the disappeared: "I leave from La Moneda contented." In August the psychological pendulum went the other way. The secrecy provision of the Aylwin Law proposal seemed a trap. The military forces had not really collaborated with the Rettig Commission, despite a promise of anonymity. They would surely use the new law to tell lies to friendly specialized judges, who would in turn ratify lies about death dates and permanent disappearance of bodies tossed into the ocean, using the lies to close down justice cases permanently. She appreciated the impact of the truth documented by the Rettig Commission and put forth forcefully by Aylwin. But she had had different truth-and-justice expectations when struggling for a democratic transition. She and veteran Agrupación activists had expected little from military rulers. Looking back, she concluded in 1997, "our frustration begins from the time of this transition to democracy."[34]

In the world of quarter-loaf or half-loaf achievement and slowly rolling impasse, frustration is not the only phenomenon. The achievements of the early years included the dignified clearing of names, one of the goals sought by Ester Barría, sister of the gifted and joyful music teacher Arturo Barría Araneda, when she testified before the Rettig Commission (see chapter 2). Some name clearing focused on the dead or the disappeared; some focused on the larger community of human rights memory and solidarity. Consider the case of the Vicaría, which since the 1970s had organized to assist and never forget the victims of military rule and which itself endured considerable stigma during the dictatorship. On the eighteenth anniversary of the founding of its predecessor organization, the Comité Pro-Paz (Pro-Peace Committee), Patricio Aylwin spoke at the invitation of the Santiago Archbishopric. "I come, as President of the Republic, to offer a heartfelt tribute of recognition to those who have dedicated so much effort and generosity." They had suffered "misunderstandings and criticisms; some, jail and exile; many, persecution and harassment, and even . . . the violent death of [Vicaría activist] José Manuel Parada." The time had arrived to say "thank you" for laying the foundation of moral dialogue and testimonial truth needed for democratic convivencia. A year later the Vicaría was closing down as an active vicariate and converting itself into an archive and documentation center, in a different building, with ongoing research, judicial support, and educational functions. Human rights and victim groups launched their own events of commemoration. At the old site, in the heart of downtown Santiago, they placed a memory plaque to honor the Vicaría. "In time of selfishness and fear, love and solidarity dwelled in this house."[35]

But what of Arturo Barría Araneda? On 28 August 1990, the anniversary of his 1974 abduction and disappearance by the DINA, teachers and students of his school, Liceo Darío Salas, could finally join relatives of the disappeared and activists to honor and remember him. Barría's remarkable qualities and inspirational legacy no longer belonged to the family alone. The music teacher belonged again to the school. In the auditorium, a plaque of remembrance bore his name.[36]

※

The Sound of Tick-Tock

The one murder case exempted from the military regime's self-amnesty law in 1978 was the assassination, via a car bomb that exploded on 21 September 1976, of Orlando Letelier and Ronni Moffitt. The murder took place in Washington, D.C., some fifteen blocks from the White House.[1]

Letelier, a moderate Socialist with background in Washington as Allende's ambassador, had in exile become a formidable adversary of the Pinochet regime. He worked at the Institute for Policy Studies, a Washington think tank influential in liberal-Left circles. Ronni Moffitt, his colleague at the institute, was a U.S. citizen. From his institute base, the exiled Chilean gained a reputation as an urbane nonsectarian voice of influence—with Senator Edward Kennedy, progressive Democrats, and advisors of presidential candidate Jimmy Carter. Letelier also built influence at the United Nations and in Western Europe, especially Holland. In 1976 he lobbied the Dutch to boycott the Pinochet regime and to resist World Bank loans to Chile. The campaign began to show fruit when a Dutch investment company, Stevin Groep, cancelled a mining project that would have invested 62.5 million U.S. dollars. In Western Europe, trade unions, social democrats, and labor parties were at the time politically important forces. Pinochet was for many an icon of the brutal dictatorships that swept over South America with United States support to suppress the social justice aspirations of laborers, peasants, and the poor.

Pinochet and the DINA, the secret police headed by Colonel Manuel Contreras, had begun in 1974 to track and kill prominent leaders in exile. They also promoted transnational South American secret police operations against leftist activists in exile, institutionalized in the program known as Operation Condor in 1975. From 1974 to 1976, each September memory season witnessed a high-profile assault on foreign soil. The targets were Chileans in exile whose prestige or activities made them formidable foes, in reality or potentially. In Buenos Aires in 1974, the DINA used a car bomb in

Buenos Aires to kill the army general Carlos Prats and his wife, Sofía Cuthbert. Prats had been the Chilean army commander and a firm constitutionalist—a problem for pro-coup forces—until pushed out by officer pressure and opposition pressure in August 1973. Just before the murder, he completed the manuscript for a memoir that framed the military takeover as a study of Chile's betrayal, not its salvation.

In Rome in 1975, the DINA organized the shooting of Bernardo Leighton and his wife, Anita Fresno. They were badly wounded but survived. Leighton, a distinguished Christian Democrat and former vice-president aligned with the Left-leaning branch of the party, immediately denounced the coup in September 1973. In 1974, with other Chileans in exile, he launched in Rome the discussion group and journal both known as "Chile-America." The group promoted Center-Left dialogue and a community of socially progressive Christians seeking a reborn and renovated democracy. Leighton, the group's most prestigious leader, was adept at fostering dialogue across political and ideological lines. The DINA tracked the group and saw it as the dangerous enemy abroad. In November 1974, it informed the junta that Rome was the "most important Marxist center in Europe and from which is led all action against Chile."[2]

The 1976 murder of Orlando Letelier fit the pattern of audacious state terror on foreign soil during the September memory seasons. The difference was that the murder took place in the political capital of the United States and that it took the life of a U.S. citizen, Ronni Moffitt. Also, it occurred shortly before the election of a U.S. president inclined to chart a different policy course on human rights, and from a political party with leaders who valued Letelier and his work in defense of human rights.

The U.S. attorney general and the FBI (Federal Bureau of Investigation) launched a criminal investigation. The judicial drama heated up in 1978. By March, Eugene Propper, the assistant U.S. attorney prosecuting the case, had arrived in Chile on a very public visit to interview witnesses and press the case. Domestic conflicts over the human rights question also surged in the public domain. Indeed, the Letelier scandal and tensions served as a memory knot galvanizing publicity and struggle over the wider meaning and reality of military rule. By May relatives of the disappeared launched a long and dramatic hunger strike. Meanwhile, Propper proceeded to secure the expulsion of DINA agent Michael Townley, a U.S. citizen married to a Chilean and long residing in Chile. Townley was the DINA's key operator in the conspiracy, and planted the car bomb that killed Letelier and Moffitt. Propper also launched extradition proceedings, which ultimately failed, against Manuel Contreras. The extradition request also extended to two additional DINA agents including Contreras's second-in-command and chief of operations, Pedro Espinoza. Contreras no longer headed the secret police. In August 1977, an earlier moment of pressure and damage control had led to replacement of the DINA by a new secret police organization, the CNI (Centro Nacional de Informaciones, National Center of Information). Contreras served as CNI director only for an interim. In 1978, General Contreras (he had been promoted in partial compensation for his diminished power) had again become a liability. In March he resigned from the army. By August he was under indictment in Washington and preventive arrest in Chile, pending resolution of an extradition request.

The 1978 Amnesty Law was an initiative meant to lessen the sharpening crisis. The international and internal pressures of 1978 were interrelated and fierce. They included not only the transnational and domestic memory conflicts embodied in the Letelier-Moffitt case and in the protests and hunger strike of relatives of the disappeared. Also heating up were a border crisis with Argentina, and internal junta tensions culminating in the July destitution of General Gustavo Leigh, the air force commander. It was against this backdrop of tension that Pinochet reshuffled his Cabinet and had the new interior minister, Sergio Fernández, push a new idea. The junta had completed the rough first phase of its work. Now the task was "institutionalization" and the making of a modern and prosperous society, and eventually a protected democracy. This was the launch of memory as a "closed box"—a mindful closing of memories of the past. The ugly times of dirty war had been superseded, but they were contentious. If revisited, they would undermine national unity, institutionalization, and forward movement.[3]

The 1978 Amnesty Decree, announced on 19 April and covering acts from 11 September 1973 through 10 March 1978, was the legal instrument of mindful erasure of the past. It was a crisis measure, and it emerged at a time of surging tensions between the United States and Chile over the Letelier matter. Perhaps not surprisingly, the amnesty had a loophole that deferred to U.S. pressure and its bottom line. It excluded criminal acts in the Letelier-Moffitt case. At the same time, the Pinochet regime pursued its own bottom lines. It secured an understanding on boundaries of the case that shielded Pinochet from personal ensnarement in United States criminal court proceedings, and it secured from the Supreme Court president and judge Israel Bórquez a denial, issued in 1979, of the extradition of Contreras and company. Pinochet's interest in isolating himself from the case was not theoretical. The U.S. ambassador to Paraguay, George Landau, reported to the State Department in August 1976 that Pinochet had telephoned President Alfredo Stroessner directly to ask, as an "urgent favor," that he provide Paraguayan passports to two Chilean army officers who needed to go to the United States on a special mission. The fake passports would presumably enable them to secure visas more easily. The incident mattered because the two officers, "Juan Williams" and "Alejandro Romeral," were in reality DINA agents Michael Townley and Armando Fernández, and their mission was the Letelier assassination. In addition, the CIA reported in August 1978 that Contreras "has warned Pinochet that if he takes the fall he will bring Pinochet down with him."[4]

During the 1980s, the great struggle for the Letelier and Moffitt families and the human rights community was to block permanent closure of the case by military judges. Fabiola Letelier, the sister of Orlando Letelier and a lawyer and human rights activist, and Jaime Castillo, a prominent Christian Democrat and also a lawyer and human rights activist, waged a tenacious battle to appeal closure rulings. They directed appeals to the Chilean Supreme Court and made use of findings and legal steps in the evolving U.S. court case and FBI investigation. If Letelier and Castillo could not win a reopening of the case, their arguments could at least suffice to convert the case to "temporary" dismissal status—achieved in 1982 and again in 1987— and to block reversion to permanent dismissal. The net result, when Aylwin became president in 1990, was that the Letelier case was not quite dead. It was temporarily closed. At least theoretically, new evidence or circumstances could revive it.[5]

In 1990, the Letelier case was like a time bomb whose clock had been deactivated—but could be restarted.[6] In 1991 the combined efforts of Fabiola Letelier and allied human rights lawyers, the Aylwin government, and the United States finally reactivated the clock. They also managed to strip the case from the military courts. The method was the Aylwin administration's appeal to the Supreme Court for a special judge, under a new law for cases that affected Chile's relationship with another state. The presiding judge in the reopened case was the Supreme Court justice Adolfo Bañados, a conservative jurist known for his prickly independence and his forthright handling of the 1979 case of disappeared peasants whose bodies were found in an

abandoned lime oven in Lonquén. Passed over during military rule, Bañados was finally appointed to the Supreme Court under Aylwin but maintained an independent posture. He avoided the court culture of patronage
and friendship as a corrupting influence, and he joined the court in its
angry self-defense against the Rettig Commission.[7]

As August 1993 approached, informed persons believed Bañados was
ready to issue his ruling. The ruling would be subject to appeal, but its
politicocultural symbolism would be enormous—all the more so since the
boinazo had placed other justice proceedings in such doubt. A guilty sentence might impose jail on the once untouchable top two members of the
DINA, General Contreras and General Espinoza.

The dance of frictional synergy, on strategic memory issues, did not simply shape relations between government officials and grassroots activists. It
also affected relations with journalists committed to deep human rights
reporting. Already in 1990, the issue had arisen in the case of the press
group at Televisión Nacional. On the one hand, coverage on the remains of
brutalized prisoners discovered at Pisagua and the interview of General
Horacio Toro about Pinochet's duty to resign pressed the memory question
—poignantly and forcefully. In this sense they provided cultural traction for
the new Rettig Commission initiative. On the other hand, government officials also feared *too* strong and graphic a reporting style on explosive issues,
and Interior Minister Krauss called for greater restraint.[8]

Now, in the first days of August 1993, the press group of Televisión
Nacional prepared a spectacular two-hour version of its television magazine
program, *Informe Especial*, to coincide with the approaching sentence of
Judge Bañados.[9] The timing would also coincide with a new delicate stage of
fallout from the boinazo. On 3 August, Aylwin announced his ill-fated legislative proposal to channel human rights cases to special judges working on
a finite clock, and who could secretly receive witness information on the fate
of the disappeared.

Televisión Nacional had worked on the program for two years. It tracked
down and interviewed Michael Townley, the DINA agent who planted the car
bomb and lived under protection in the United States. It planned to air the
interview on 5 August—just two days after Aylwin announced his initiative
to calm a nervous country and presumably map a path to justice without
ethical fraud or political destabilization. The program had little new hard
information for specialists, but it would be a powerful cultural event. The
advance publicity and interest guaranteed a large viewing audience. Town-

ley spoke with chilling coldbloodedness. He invoked the war thesis. He had not regretted killing Orlando Letelier, an enemy soldier in the struggle, although he felt differently about Ronni Moffitt. He spoke with authority about DINA international operations to kill Letelier, Carlos Prats, Bernardo Leighton, and Socialist leader Carlos Altamirano—and to spy on Patricio Aylwin during a European trip. He exposed lies. The Spanish diplomat Carmelo Soria had not committed suicide in 1976, as the official story went. The DINA's "Brigada Mulchen" unit had brought Soria to Townley's own house for torture and execution.

Townley undermined the idea of human rights violations as excess by rogue subordinates, unknown to superiors. He issued a macho challenge.

> There are certain señores, among them Manolo Contreras, who have equated their own honor, their own ego, their own vanity with that of the country. . . . They use the name of the institution of the country to hide their guilt, their responsibilities, so that they never have been manly enough to stand up and say, "Yes, I did this. The country is not responsible for these events. I am the one who did it."

The implication: The leaders of "dirty war" were cowards. Like DINA officers who testified in court that they were mere analysts of information, the dirty war leaders lied about their knowledge, commands, and participation. To save their own skins, they heaped dishonor on Chile.

Townley did not implicate Pinochet directly in the murder. But the program came close when it showed a 1975 memorandum from Contreras to Pinochet. The memo documented their agreement on a special fund for international operations, including "neutralization of the main adversaries" in other countries. The country list included the United States—where the most important enemy was Orlando Letelier. Left discreetly unstated was an obvious question. Would a breakdown, under pressure, of Contreras's loyalty to Pinochet produce information even more damning?

The contents and timing of the program were explosive. Director Jorge Navarrete shared an advance copy, probably as a precaution, with his friend Subsecretary of War Jorge Burgos. It did not take long for the news to filter up to Aylwin, who requested postponement of the program. One reliable inside account states that Aylwin's worry was not the fate of his legislative initiative, but that Judge Bañados would construe the program as political pressure, then reassert his independence by modifying his ruling on Contreras and Espinoza. The two hypotheses are not mutually exclusive. Televisión Nacional complied with the request—it did not air the program until 16 August. As expected, the Townley program won a high rating (33, or one-third of television viewers). Its postponement, however, also sparked a minor scandal and softened the "B B C" model of independent public media.[10]

Perhaps to reinforce its professional and cultural identity as a site of serious journalism and truth telling, Televisión Nacional went ahead with another striking memory program. *Informe Especial* prepared a retrospective on the coup timed for its twenty-year anniversary. The program reported that Allende planned to call a plebiscite on 11 September to resolve the 1973 crisis. In other words, force had been unnecessary. It also broadcast his eloquent farewell radio address on the final day, and aired footage—sidelined from television for twenty years—of bodies floating in the Mapocho River.[11]

The boinazo aimed to mute justice and "take back" the transition. For a time, and for almost all the relevant justice cases, the saber rattling worked. Between 1990 and 1993 Chileans walked the circle from impasse to truth to justice to force—and back to impasse. But the sounds of a television program and a court case, both widely publicized, suggested other dynamics also at work. Memory knots continued to form on the social body and to scream for attention—in courts, media, and popular culture. The memory question had even placed the former head of the secret police in jeopardy. In November, Judge Bañados found Contreras and Espinoza guilty of homicide and sentenced them to seven and six years, respectively. Televisión Nacional aired another program on the Letelier case. The interviewees included Orlando Letelier's sister, Fabiola, and son, Juan Pablo; Ronni Moffitt's husband, Michael; and Carlos Prats's and Sofía Cuthbert's daughter, Sofía.[12] The appeal process would postpone final resolution until 1995. When the final reckoning arrived, what would happen? How would Augusto Pinochet and Manuel Contreras respond? Anyone who bothered to listen could hear the sound: tick-tock, tick-tock, tick-tock. . . .

Chapter 4

※

Between Prudence and Convulsion:
Memory, Triumphalism, and Disenchantment, 1994–1997

Since the late 1980s, supermarkets became a quotidian mirror of Chile's "silent revolution"—transformation of a state-oriented society, comprising political citizens whose electoral and social mobilization pressed the state to serve as an engine of social fairness and economic development, into a market-oriented society, comprising consumers and sellers whose purchasing preferences and competitive talents drove social and economic opportunities. By the mid-to-late 1990s, a majority bought food in supermarkets. The traditional corner store, the indoor market stall, the open-air market day, these moved toward a supplementary role in urban food culture. Like the giant new shopping malls dotting the urban scene, supermarkets were a cultural symbol, not simply a commercial arena. They embodied the plenty and pleasures of prosperous efficiency. Evoking the new Chile—modern, tranquil, efficient, transactional—were hygienic climate control and food wrapping, abundant product choices, use of price scanners and automated information to track demand, pleasant background music, and polite verbal exchanges at point of purchase. For sympathizers of the military regime, economic transformation was a success story and the supermarket one of its early symbols. In the influential 1987 book, *Chile: Revolución silenciosa*, in which Joaquín Lavín coined the "silent revolution" idea, the supermarket figured as metaphor for a choice-filled, successful society.[1]

In middle- and upper middle-class neighborhoods in the mid-1990s, the exit path in a supermarket might offer the citizen-consumer a chance to supplement food and wine with culture. A book corner run by a young person enabled customers to pause to buy a romantic novel, a best seller, or a literary work by celebrated authors such as Isabel Allende, José Donoso, Gabriel García Márquez, or Marcela Serrano. In 1996, Alicia M. sold books in one such supermarket. Dressed respectably, dark of skin by Chilean standards, and blessed with a winning smile, she was unfailingly polite. She spoke only if the customer stopped to look at her display table. Otherwise, she passed the time reading books.

One day the culture of polite calm fell apart. Alicia M. was reading a revised edition of Patricia Verdugo's 1989 best seller *Los zarpazos del puma*, on the "Caravan of Death" of October 1973. As we saw (chapter 1), the book had caused a sensation. It appeared just as Chileans began their transition from dictatorship to democracy, when hunger for a reckoning with truth was strong. It exposed the mythology of a supposed war—and the reality of an unnecessary and murderous brutality. An army team authorized by Pinochet to regularize military justice intervened to kill and disappear dozens of political prisoners held by regular army officers, in provinces where order and calm had prevailed. In 1991 the book sparked a lawsuit by General Sergio Arellano Stark, the commander of the traveling team who insisted he did not order the executions and that Verdugo injured his honor. The supermarket clientele where Alicia M. ran her book corner included people who believed in memory as salvation—as a tale of soldier-patriots who in 1973 rescued the nation from economic ruin, social chaos, and a likely bloodbath, and went on to build a successful nation. Some clients were from military officers' families.

On the day when calm fell apart, a middle-aged man exiting the store saw Alicia M. reading Verdugo's book. He was her social superior—an older man, also whiter and more prosperous. The book is not true, he scolded her, and she should not read it! He had military relatives and knew the truth. Alicia M. replied that he no doubt knew some things, but she was, as she put it, searching for "my truth." He turned angry, but heated words and superior social rank failed to break the standoff. Finally he left. The culture of polite calm and silence amidst marketplace transactions resumed.[2]

The sudden switch from polite calm to angry standoff distilled in microcosm a wider cultural dynamic. The 1993 *boinazo* yielded a memory impasse tougher than that of the army "readiness exercise" of 1990. The sense of intractability had hardened. One might formulate the problem as the tension between "cultural hegemony" and "political hegemony." Each memory camp in Chile sought not only to mold public policy, but also to persuade—to shape the language of politicocultural understanding and debate. Each sought to "hegemonize" politics and values in the Gramscian sense of seeking not only to impose, but to educate.[3]

The problem was that dynamics of cultural and political hegemony did not move in tandem. Cultural hegemony—what people believed, the dominant common sense about violence under military rule—pointed toward memory as rupture. Even if the tightly drawn mandate of the Rettig Report and its subsequent cultural uses tended to reduce "memory" to the documented maximal cases of repression, few could challenge the truth of the "open wound" created by thousands of executions and disappearances— and by state cover-up. A majority of the populace had awakened to the reality of massive state violence, and believed that such a truth ideally required justice, including punitive sanction. Even the minority that held fast to memory as salvation no longer contested the core factual truth documented in the Rettig Report. On the other hand, political hegemony pointed toward closing the box tightly on the past. For powerful sectors of society, the memory-truth that mattered most contextualized human rights violations as a necessary social cost. Chile had been saved by patriots from a disastrous fate including a far worse violence, and the junta went on to build a modern and effective society. Given the volatility of the memory question, and the de facto powers of disruption held by those who viewed Pinochet and the military legacy favorably, even those who remembered the military regime as tyranny could fear that insisting on the point would destroy Chile's future.

The memory question exposed a profound strain between "soft" and "hard" power. The cultural majority aligned with memory as rupture meant an electoral majority for the Concertación. The internal dynamics and electoral base of the Center-Left government meant it could not renounce the objectives of truth and justice on human rights, regardless of the intentions of individual leaders. But the political power built on elections and majority opinion was soft, compared to the hard power anchored in a watchful army still commanded by Pinochet and in investor clans who remembered military rule gratefully. As we have seen (chapter 1), such power was amplified by institutional binding, especially via the 1980 Constitution and the binomial election system, that boosted the role of the Right and military loyalists within the state. In short, the design of the system set limits to that which could be effectively determined through the electoral realm, particularly on memory matters. By 1993 even sectors of the Right used slang—"fact-of-life powers" (*poderes fácticos*)—to describe this "hard" version of power.[4]

The contradiction between soft power and hard power, the standoff between dynamics of cultural hegemony and political hegemony, these did not simply produce a sensation of impasse, as one walked the circle from truth to justice to force. The structure of the situation bred a memory culture of ambivalence—swings from extreme prudence to momentary convulsion, from apparent calm to expressive outburst. The memories people held about the 1973 crisis and the violence of military rule mattered to them. The Chile of 1994–97 was a country of intimate memory impasse. Its middle-aged and elder citizens wielded cultural authority, and many had *experienced* 1973 as a decisive moment of "before" and "after," when personal life history merged with the collective life history of society. Many younger adults had come of age during the 1980s, when memory struggles for and against the regime turned into mass experience and violent repression again turned fierce.

Divisive yet deeply felt, the memory question bred a dialectic of passion and temptation. Memory mattered, but forgetting was a great temptation. On the one hand, Chile was a society filled with people and generations who took the memory question personally and passionately, as an intensively lived and searing and formative experience. The middle-aged and elderly included many people like Doña Elena F., a middle-class woman of high family background horrified by a world upside down between 1964 and 1973, and who remembered 11 September 1973 as the happiest day of her life. They also included many like her social opposite, Señora Herminda Morales, a working-class mother who remembered the same day as the start of her family's suffering and unending search for two disappeared sons. They included persons like Violeta E., a middle-class woman whose awakening to the reality of multifaceted persecution and to the Catholic call to solidarity brought her to embrace human rights and memory as new values. Such persons not only understood their personal stories emblematically, as symbols in dialogue with wider memory struggles and frameworks that unfolded during military rule. They also had family and friendship circles to some degree aware, sympathetic, or sensitized to the intimacy and passion of such memories. On the other hand, everyone was also aware that the politics of memory produced division and dangerous flash points. Prudence had a point. The country had plenty of people like Colonel Juan F., who professed indifference to the memory question while believing passionately that the stance was vital for the future. Mindful forgetting was the solution for a dangerously divisive problem without solution. In addition to cultural and political logics, there were also individually driven logics of ambivalence. Who could fault a torture victim who might swing from outrage at social neglect, to desire to rebuild a tolerable life by leaving behind memory of extreme pain and humiliation?[5]

Intimate impasse produced a culture of contradiction, nearly schizophrenic in its moral tone. Because the memory impasse was so intractable and debilitating, it seemed to dictate prudence, a sophisticated calm and indifference lest one cross into a zone of destructive passion and conflict. Why place at risk a stable and successful transition, and a strong economic growth record? But because memory mattered so much—existentially and morally, not just politically—it took little to set off "irruptions," as Alex Wilde has put it. Events suddenly destroyed the facade of calm and set off media frenzy, street demonstrations, or angry political exchanges including military maneuvers. Such convulsions were more transitory than permanent. They were "memory knots" that demanded attention but gave way to calm—until the next episode. Chile in the mid-to-late 1990s was less a culture of forgetting than a culture of stalemate and ambivalence. Expressive repression alternated with expressive outburst.[6]

Caught between prudence and convulsion while also passing through major socioeconomic and cultural changes, by the mid-1990s Chileans built an ambivalent culture. It was a culture susceptible both to triumphalism and disenchantment. There was a culture of self-satisfaction that could convert constraint into success, vice into virtue. Why not see the prudent caution and constraints of Chile's democratic transition as the secret to its success—the stability and resilience of the new democracy, the astounding economic growth sure to produce a new standard of living? These signs of mastery and cumulative progress marked Chile as a "model" society in the era of democratic transition and economic globalization. In contrast, there was also a culture of upset, the creeping disenchantment that sets in when stalemate on important matters recurs and some social sectors find themselves excluded from the promised land. Triumphalism and disenchantment turned out to be opposite sides of the same cultural coin. The memory question was not alone the motor of this ambivalence, but it figured significantly as cause and effect. This chapter seeks to understand how memory struggles generated swings between prudence and convulsion between 1994 and 1997, and fed into the culture of triumphalism and disenchantment.

WHO'S IN CHARGE?
FROM AVOIDANCE TO SHOWDOWN, 1994–95

Some memory convulsions took place on a personal scale. A sudden flaring of temper as in Alicia M.'s supermarket incident, an abrupt insistence that you hear the story of someone swept away by the repression, such episodes were strictly microlevel events. The wider cultural environment might frame such talk as abnormal or as outburst, but the episode was without wider effect.[7]

Other convulsions, however, erupted in the public domain and connected more clearly to the wider political context. After the 1993 boinazo, Chile's memory impasse hardened not only because of the tension between "soft" and "hard" power described above. It also hardened because political leadership of the Concertación shifted and the capacity for creative state initiative seemed exhausted. Aylwin's fundamental project was to rebuild *convivencia* and to establish the moral compass and legitimacy of a stable democracy. He undertook the task with skill and despite adversity, but he also had some advantages. He could count on a measure of citizen goodwill and patience, a honeymoon effect blended with awareness of the fragility of transition. He had personal assets as a leader. His background in law, his formation in the founding generation of Christian Democrats who emphasized moral community, his expressive range and ability to project the image of the "good father," such skills and experiences served him well. They lent moral force and coherence to memory initiatives large and small—from the Rettig Commission project and the Aylwin doctrine on court investigation before amnesty, to the funeral honoring Salvador Allende as a historical leader, to pointed allusion to Bernardo O'Higgins as a patriot who knew when to resign. Even so, Aylwin saw his key memory initiatives as work of a "transition" period he sought to bring to early closure, not as an endless political priority of the Executive, and hoped the courts would bear a greater share of state responsibility in future memory work.

The new president, Eduardo Frei Ruíz-Tagle, came into office in March 1994 with different priorities and leadership skills, and under distinct circumstances. The patience, hopes, and state-citizen synergies that marked the 1990 beginnings of transition had receded; the Aylwin project of convivencia had been more or less accomplished; the hardness of the post-boinazo impasse was obvious. Although Eduardo Frei was the son of a president (Eduardo Frei Montalva), he had built a career as an engineer and businessman. Until 1986, it was his sister, Carmen Frei, who acted as the family's new political voice. Eduardo Frei shifted career paths as Chile moved toward transition, but he was not a "natural" politician—adept at tuning in to the yearnings of one's public and adjusting accordingly, or at bringing an audience around to an inspired vision. He came of political age late, to an extent at odds with older Christian Democrat circles emphasizing moral community. His personal style was laconic, his instincts technocratic.

Frei's background and skills meshed well with the cornerstone project of his administration: modernization. The idea was that if Chile could consolidate a sustained spectacular record of economic growth, complemented by higher social spending to equalize citizen opportunities, it could within two generations establish a truly unprecedented standard of living, superior to that of most developing countries. Accelerated modernization—infrastructure investment in energy, highways, ports, and telecommunications; reform of education and the judiciary as institutions whose outdated practices were unfair and harmed competitiveness; deeper integration of Chilean business with world business—would feed the engine of change. The fundamental motor was private market incentive, superior competitiveness, and global reach. New privatizations would modernize anachronistic sectors such as coal mines and the port system. Chilean diplomats would aggressively integrate a competitive economy into the *multiple* market blocs of a globalizing world—the APEC (Asia-Pacific Economic Cooperative) group of the Pacific, NAFTA and Mercosur in the Americas, the European Union—whether as a full bloc partner or as a player with favorable associative rights.[8]

Frei's priorities did not imply abandonment of human rights or memory work. Formally and sometimes substantively, the government defended human rights interests. Its general policy stances on many issues—economic growth, social spending, human rights—resembled those under Aylwin. The internal politics and social base of the governing Center-Left coalition, not to mention the constraints of the transition, limited possibilities for sharp change. On a key objective of the human rights memory camp—reform of the judiciary—Frei eventually had more success than Aylwin (see chapter 5).

The debilitating changes were more nuanced. First, the government became more reactive than proactive on human rights issues. Avoidance displaced strategy, and symbolic presidential gesture toward memory also dwindled. Second, the tone of official discourse suggested that the time to close the box on the dirty past had arrived. The idea of memory as a drag on the future, an obsession by those stuck in a time warp, began to crystallize as government sensibility. To be fair and as we shall see in this chapter, in its reactive moments the government had its hands full. The memory showdown of 1995 was fierce and raised the question of how many more such episodes Chile could really withstand. But even in its earliest moments, the administration signaled little interest in the moral line drawn by the Aylwin government. On 23 May 1994, Edmundo Pérez Yoma, defense minister and one of Frei's closest advisors, affirmed that "nobody has moral superiority for judging the governments of the last 30 years." The statement was unimaginable under Aylwin. Times had changed.[9]

The desire to leave memory behind did not, however, imply an absence of swings between prudence and convulsion. "Memory knots"—volatile events and anniversaries, sacred places, motivated human groups—continued to demand attention to the past as a force within the present. Pérez Yoma's comment itself sparked a minor scandal and political damage control. In 1994 and 1995, moreover, the government found itself in a cat-and-mouse game directly related to memory. The focal point was Rodolfo Stange, the *carabinero* director general and a former junta member. On 31 March 1994, Judge Milton Juica ruled on the notorious 1985 murder case of "the three professionals." The victims, kidnapped and killed by throat slash, included José Manuel Parada, the well-known veteran human rights activist of the Vicaría de la Solidaridad. Juica found sixteen persons, including fifteen carabineros, guilty, and recommended Stange's prosecution for obstruction of justice. The government pressed for a voluntary resignation—it lacked power to dismiss a commander in chief—but found itself mired in a standoff, with government weakness compounded by a not-guilty ruling (in military court) on the obstruction-of-justice charge. Stange did not finally retire until October 1995.[10]

Who was in charge? Stange's resistance was a prelude to a bigger drama. Early in 1995, the media, political elites, military leaders, and the human rights world began to brace themselves for a showdown. All knew the Supreme Court would soon rule on the appeal of the 1993 conviction of Generals Manuel Contreras (retired) and Pedro Espinoza (active), the DINA'S former head and chief of operations respectively, for the 1976 double murder of Orlando Letelier and Ronni Moffitt. Contreras's position as the top architect of "dirty war" made the case crucial for the culture of memory struggle. His defiance added to the drama. Already in 1993, he warned he would release compromising information against those who betrayed the DINA and added, "I will not pass a day in jail." In January 1995, government negotiation with Renovación Nacional and some arm-twisting within the Concertación produced authorization to build a special high-security prison in Punta Peuco, some forty kilometers north of Santiago, for officials convicted of human rights crimes. Still, no one really knew how hard Contreras might resist serving sentence, nor whether the army would back him. On 30 May 1995, the Supreme Court upheld the sentences—seven and six years of jail for Contreras and Espinoza, respectively.[11]

The ruling sparked months of convulsion, a soap opera played out in media and street as well as the political back room. To appreciate the tension and high stakes, one must sample some of the flow of event and surprise—the sudden twist, the backdoor maneuver, the theatrical assertion, the rumor that feeds suspense. Consider just a few highlights.[12]

Late May: Tension mounts. On 22 May, forty-five army generals meet with the deputy commander in chief, General Guillermo Garín, to consider the approaching sentence. On 25 May, a bomb scare takes place at the Supreme Court. On 30 May, thousands converge on the Supreme Court to hear and cheer the sentence; street disturbances break out. Frei appears on television to affirm the value of rule of law and to ask Chileans not to let divisions over the past undermine an opportunity to achieve development in two generations. From his landed estate "Viejo Roble" in the south, Contreras grants television interviews. The sentence is the work of Marxists and intimidated officials; the CIA (U.S. Central Intelligence Agency) killed Letelier. His army friends will help him. "I am not going to any jail . . ." On 31 May, the follow-ups begin. Relatives of victims, political leaders, and human rights activists organize a *romería* (pilgrimage) to Orlando Letelier's grave. Santiago Sinclair, former army deputy commander in chief, now a designated senator, declares "the Army is wounded."

Early June: Rumor mounts. What agreements are being reached in behind-the-scenes negotiations between the government and the military? Can the government really force Contreras and Espinoza to serve time in a jail under civilian authority and under custody of gendarmes, the normal prison guards? Does Contreras intend to resist arrest by all means, including a shoot-out at his estate? What does it mean when Pinochet says on television that the law will be respected but also affirms that Contreras is innocent? Meanwhile, on 8 June Judge Adolfo Bañados issues an order to implement the sentence.

Mid-to-late June: The four-month saga of hide-and-seek begins. It is melodrama and media spectacle, punctuated by sudden surprises, mystery health news, demonstrations—and anxiety about rule of law. On 12 June, Contreras takes refuge in a military base, then returns to his estate. On 13 June, with army and navy assistance he again escapes civilian control, by helicopter to the Talcahuano Naval Hospital. (Secretly, the operation had the consent of Defense Minister Pérez Yoma, who wanted to buy time to negotiate an accord.) On 16 June, the acting hospital director says that to allow arrest of Contreras, who has diabetes and high blood pressure, would compromise his metabolic and cardiovascular health. On 18–19 June, Espinoza takes refuge in a military base and says he will not serve time. But he is second fiddle—the army retires him, and he is delivered to the Punta Peuco jail. On 27–29 June, Contreras has a medical exam to diagnose possible cancer; doctors announce he has a hernia and needs an operation. Judge Bañados orders gendarmes to take custody of Contreras as guards in his Naval Hospital room. They comply.

July: The standoff hardens. Gendarmes examine Contreras and find him medically fit for transfer to Punta Peuco; the conservative jurist José Luis Cea says Contreras's health would justify serving sentence in his home; the congressman Juan Pablo Letelier (son of Orlando Letelier) says confidence in rule of law is reaching the breaking point. Demonstrations add pressure. On 6 July, several hundred persons gather at the armed forces building in downtown Santiago to support Pinochet and denounce those who ruined the country before military rescue in 1973. On 22 July, officers and their wives join other military families on a "picnic" of about a thousand people at Punta Peuco, to show disgust at the course of events and support for Espinoza and Contreras. On 30 July, some seventy human rights activists counter with theater. They stage a mock imprisonment of Contreras near Punta Peuco.

August to October: Spectacle and standoff continue. The twists and turns include conflicting medical reports on Contreras by naval doctors and other state doctors; a hernia operation conducted without prior legal authorization; more medical disputes, about a possible second operation; symbolic acts and demonstrations during the September memory season; a hunger strike by Espinoza. Finally, on 21 October, the endgame is achieved and formal rule of law reaffirmed. Contreras enters the Punta Peuco prison, under joint custody of gendarmes and military guards.

The stakes were serious. The occasional reassuring words of an official were like the unconvincing comfort message a doctor delivers to a gravely ill patient. The words coincide with knowledge that cuts otherwise, and the conflict can only feed the anxiety. In July, for example, after the military "picnic" at Punta Peuco the secretary general of government, José Joaquín Brunner, took care to deny that the army was pressuring the Executive.

Meanwhile, rumors abounded about an army petition to pardon Contreras, and Alejandro Foxley, the president of the Christian Democrats, warned that people would lose faith in rule of law if Contreras did not go to Punta Peuco. Earlier, an anonymous high government official bluntly told a *New York Times* reporter that cat-and-mouse with Contreras amounted to "a technical coup." Behind the scenes, according to Camilo Escalona (at the time president of the Socialist Party), Minister Pérez Yoma warned "that socialists were 'crazy' if they thought Manuel Contreras was going to go to jail." A general "very close to Pinochet" made sure to reinforce the point directly to Escalona. The army could not accept the jailing of a general and chief of intelligence.[13]

A July poll illustrated the risks at the level of political culture. If Contreras ended up serving sentence in a military site or under house detention, would Chileans see the result as "rule of law" or fraud? If the latter, would the legitimacy of Chilean democracy suffer fatal erosion? Only half the population (49 percent) thought Contreras would serve time in Punta Peuco. Yet two-thirds (66 percent) thought he received a fair trial, and nearly as many (62 percent) *wanted* trials to clarify truth and to sentence offenders in at least the worst cases of human rights violations. Two in five (43 percent) favored trial and sentencing in *all* cases, not just the most serious ones.[14]

Pinochet and the Frei administration both had reason to pull back from the brink. Neither could afford a failed transition. Whatever his sympathies, Pinochet proved willing to sacrifice Contreras—if he could convert that step into assurance of an end to the slippery slope of trials against other soldiers. A scenario of escalating conflict climaxing in overt refusal to comply with the Supreme Court would shatter the gradualist and institutionally restricted design of the democratic transition, its economic prosperity and rules of the game, and the role of the armed forces as the guarantors of institutionality. Beyond a certain point, a logic of escalation would destroy not only the transition, but also Pinochet's legacy and politics of memory—his stance as Chile's savior and modernizer. Better would be to bargain hard to protect the army from future human rights cases, to bring a final end to his own vulnerability in the "Pinocheques" matter, and to preserve army unity and command by convincing Contreras and officers that the former DINA director was making a last patriotic sacrifice for the good of Chile and its soldiers.[15]

In the political hardball of July and August, Frei signified his will to reach an accommodation. He successfully pressed the Council of Defense of the State (the body that represents legal interests of the state) to drop its appeal of court closure of the "Pinocheques" fraud case implicating Pinochet's relatives. The case had been leitmotiv and bottom line in the military-civilian crises of the 1990s (see chapters 1, 3). Frei's private appeal to the head of the council was blunt: "What is at stake is the rule of law." The administration also put forth an initiative to accelerate and bring to closure judicial investigation in human rights cases, especially those related to the disappeared. Similar to the "Aylwin Law" floated after the 1993 boinazo, the Frei legislative proposal envisioned special judges working on a two-year clock and using confidential testimony from informants who would not need fear prosecution.

The Frei proposal, although useful to prepare the way for the jailing of Contreras and to reassert some presidential initiative, proved no more viable than its predecessor. The memory question sparked passionate conflicts that eluded a meeting of the minds. In November, negotiations between Carlos Figueroa, interior minister, and Miguel Otero, Renovación Nacional senator, produced an agreement, but with such backtracking that it outraged many members of the human rights community. The modified proposal restricted the judges' focus to establishing the fate of the disappeared (not responsibility for the disappearance), and allowed judges to declare permanent closure of a case if convinced the victim had died, even in the absence of definitive information about the victim's fate and remains. In other words, the original proposal had deteriorated into an obvious "Full Stop." The tension between memory initiative as "formula" for closure or as "wedge" for continuing advance had been lost. The modified proposal was a clear formula for closure.

Once again, Chileans seemed to be walking a circle of impasse, even as impasse in the simple sense was not the entire story. The Figueroa-Otero proposal catalyzed street and political opposition, ending up in the legislative dustbin by April 1996. By then, the Pinocheques case was also firmly closed, and the Supreme Court had swung back to applying the 1978 Amnesty Law without prior investigation of facts and responsibilities. But memory impasse was a dynamic social phenomenon, a standoff that slowly "rolled" to a new center of gravity. The specific points that concentrated the contention shifted over time. The legacy of a previous conflict altered the culture of the thinkable and the possible—even as the structure of power and memory division that generated standoffs remained. In 1996 impasse reemerged, but the thinkable had also changed. Contreras and Espinoza, the architects of secret police terror whose sentencing produced a crisis, were in jail at Punta Peuco. Thirteen others including two (retired) army officers were now also serving time at Punta Peuco. Two new precedents had been set: the jailing of persons once considered untouchable, and the decision by the army to sacrifice some officers in the name of a higher good. Meanwhile, a closure proposal had failed. Human rights cases would be decided one by one—by individual judges whose legal interpretations varied and might shift over time, not by grand political accord or centralized jurisprudence.[16]

WHEN VOLATILE MEMORY MEETS STUDIED INDIFFERENCE, 1996–97

The Contreras affair constituted an extreme instance of the oscillation between prudence and convulsion. After 1995, the most significant outbursts of expression, spectacle, or mobilization evoking memory fell in a middle range—less than a national soap opera about a general, more than an isolated scolding of a book seller. Some involved political elites and therefore elicited media coverage despite general retreat from memory and human rights as newsworthy events. The swings imparted a schizophrenic tone to cultural life. Chileans could seem like a circle of persons at a group therapy session who keep insisting they are calm and unbothered by life's small irritations, yet prove so thin-skinned that almost any remark sets off a fight.

After 1995, precisely because the politicocultural imperative to turn away from the past was so strong, it channeled the memory question toward the status of "unexpected outburst" rather than necessary social reckoning. This was especially true in the world of political elites. The perils of the Contreras affair and the Frei administration's own priorities heightened desire, within Concertación sectors as well as the opposition, to close the memory box of Pinochet's Chile. Prudence dictated polite indifference to emotion and its flip side was fear of politicocultural conflict, stoked not only by older memories of the 1973 crisis of democracy and the dictatorship years, but also by outbursts of military discontent in 1990, 1993, and 1995. Could conflict and unbridled expressiveness unhinge Chile's transition? The culture of elite prudence, a kind of self-censorship within democracy, took especially sophisticated form in Concertación circles—not crude renunciation of human rights concerns as legitimate, but perpetual postpone-ments of meetings with members of the Agrupación of Relatives of the Detained and Disappeared, formulaic calls for maturity and realism, sug-gestions to look to the future and more pressing issues, hyperpride in economic dynamism. Looking away from the past, Chileans might arrive at the promised land.

On the other hand, even for political elites, confrontational memory out-bursts were unavoidable. The temptation to shut the memory box was am-bivalent and politically unworkable. Memory as rupture and persecution had played a galvanizing role in Center-Left rapprochement and widening popular insistence on democracy in the 1980s, and as a point of moral contrast for the Concertación coalition and its social base in the 1990s. Human rights memory had also played a significant role in the formation of mavericks on the Right, especially in Renovación Nacional. The memory question connected, as well, to personal experiences of persecution and loss by many political elites in the Left and Center. The same political leader who at one moment called on Chileans to look to the future and avoid divisive-ness could, at another, become aroused by or mired in a new memory conflict. In sum, memory matters proved morally and existentially irrenun-ciable, and politically irrenunciable, even if one's personal inclination was to settle for silence in the face of impasse. What was stubborn and unavoidable about memory for political elites was even more true for many grassroots families and activists. Personal weariness and temptation to move on hap-pened—the memory impasse was debilitating—but such sentiment com-peted with the sense that indifference was morally indefensible. The mem-ory struggles of the past and the experience of repression had left a deeply felt legacy, even among people who were not relatives of a disappeared or executed victim.[17]

Two consequences followed. First, Chilean politicocultural life yielded the classic tension between "snapshot" and "moving picture" perspectives. At a given point in time, politicocultural life could seem eerily calm, engineered, and restrained, its tone set by elites successfully seeking out compromise and consensus. But a month could hardly pass before an unwelcome mem-ory knot appeared on the social body—an event, a place, a social actor to interrupt the silence and demand attention to the past within the present. Suddenly cultural discourse turned volatile and exploded the placid facade.

Second, the balance between state actors and civil society actors shifted. As political elites retreated from memory initiatives, grassroots actors took on a greater share of the role as protagonists of memory politics. More than ever, grassroots actors were the keepers of the flame. If they sometimes built creative conflictive synergies with state actors, they needed to do so at lower layers of the state—against the wind that blew down from high. For the same reason, grassroots activists and their sympathizers experienced a deepening sense of political frustration and isolation.

Some memory convulsions were reasonably predictable. By the mid-1990s, the Chilean year was littered with contentious memory knots—the September memory season, anniversaries of deaths and disappearances and cover-ups, commemorations of general memory-truths such as the homage to the disappeared on 30 August and the Rettig Report on 4 March, the assassination dates of persons aligned with memory as salvation, including Jaime Guzmán, soldiers, and police. Court proceedings, such as the Supreme Court's application of amnesty in August 1996 to the assassins of Carmelo Soria, a Spanish citizen who worked with the United Nations in Chile, also yielded some predictable attention.[18]

Just as important, some convulsions erupted "out of nowhere." They entangled unexpected social actors, occurred at a distance from the September memory season, testified to the rawness of traumatic memory associations. Consider three outbursts within just two weeks in mid-1996. U.S. ambassador Gabriel Guerra-Mondragón mentioned at a 22 July press conference—the context was possible sale of F-16 jets to Chile—that complete military subordination to civilian authority had not yet been achieved. Chilean presidents could not remove commanders in chief. At a diplomatic level, the tiff was quickly resolved by wordplay. Guerra-Mondragón said reporters took his words out of context, and that the military was constitutionally subordinate although it operated with a high level of autonomy. He told Chileans what they wanted to hear: their nation "has been a model of transition to democracy in the region." At a domestic level, however, the range of reaction testified to the stubborn presence and conflictive nature of the past. Some political elites flatly denied the truth of Guerra-Mondragón's words or denounced foreign interventionism. For others, the infraction had to do with discretion. He had a point, but "reminding us something we know" was out of line. Some professed surprise. Why react with shocked indignation when Guerra-Mondragón told the truth?[19]

A week later, another incident of sudden memory association broke out. Christian Democrats criticized Renovación Nacional for its "clean hands" slogan in the municipal elections campaign. Renovación used the slogan to symbolize its anticorruption stance, but the Christian Democratic leader Foxley claimed it evoked the sinister past. The Aylwin presidential campaign of 1989 had used "clean hands" to signify a break with violence trampling human rights. Renovación was reactivating bad experiences. "To people there inevitably arises in their memory scenes in which there were people taken away from home by unidentified people at midnight." Foxley was claiming moral ownership of the words—and also reminding voters which sectors led Chile away from its dirty past. Renovación's Alberto Espina retorted that Foxley's reaction was "hysterical" and put forth his own memory politics. What truly worried Christian Democrats was that they had allowed Ricardo Lagos, leader of the Concertación's left wing, to become a symbol in the municipal campaign. Once again, Christian Democrats were "paving the way for a socialist government."[20]

Scarcely two days had passed, when, on 1 August, the menacing past again erupted. The intelligence chief of the carabineros, General Raúl Olivares Góngora, resigned at the behest of Director General Fernando Cordero, who had replaced Stange. Why? Police intelligence personnel had been investigating the subsecretary of the carabineros, Luciano Fouillioux—their own civilian superior. The political fallout and convulsion related to this affair would not be as quickly resolved as those of the other two.[21]

The September memory season was a time of especially acute tension between snapshot calm and moving picture drama. The social actors at the heart of earlier memory struggles could not let the season pass in silence; moments of convulsion alternated with appeals for transcendence. The run-up to 11 September always included honorary lunches for Pinochet by business groups such as the Rotary Club, and also the anniversary of the 1986 assassination attempt that killed five of his military escorts. At the lunches Pinochet often improvised memory remarks. In 1996, for example, he joked about the military's tutelary role and the dangers of a Socialist candidate (Lagos) in the next presidential election. "Watch out," he teased, "let's not repeat history." A serious moment came as he recalled his fallen guards and complained that convicted assassins had been let off the hook. "And then, on top of it all [como gracia], they pardoned the five señores. . . . And the five are strolling around, some in Europe." No such mercy, he added, was available for Manuel Contreras.[22]

The remarks catalyzed a ministorm—and appeals to ignore its roar. The Socialist Party denounced them as an unconstitutional interference in politics by a military commander; the UDI (Unión Democrática Independiente) retorted it was the duty of the military to prepare for any eventuality. Aylwin corrected Pinochet's distortion of history. The prisoners released in 1994 had already been punished by passing years in prison, subjected to torture and incommunicado status; even so, their release was tied to exile, itself a serious punishment. Impunity resided elsewhere. "It is to the good that the country remember that most of the material and intellectual authors of over three thousand homicides and disappearances . . . were left unpunishable [*impunes*] because of the amnesty . . . not only free in streets abroad, but also in Chile." Meanwhile, government leaders asked Chileans not to pay attention. Secretary General of Government Brunner wrote off Pinochet's commemorative lunches as "a ritual" unworthy of comment; Foxley echoed they were the "folklore" of September. Interior Minister Figueroa appealed to lay memory to rest. "Let September be the month of patriotic joy . . . not memory of events about which there are very distinct visions. . . . It does no good to reproduce them."[23]

Temptations to close the memory box did not translate into practical reality. Chilean culture continued to swing between studied prudence and sudden convulsion. The root of the problem was the contentiousness of a memory culture deeply felt, yet prone to standoffs. Part of the problem, moreover, resided in powers to discipline speech that continued on during the 1990s transition. Such powers encouraged self-censorship, but also had the potential to provoke scandal and renewed memory conflict.

During the Tuesday morning rush hour of 29 October 1996, police suddenly intercepted the car of Gladys Marín, Communist Party secretary general. Her crime: words injurious to the commander in chief of the army. Under the Law of State Security, inherited from the 1980 Constitution, words injurious to military commanders or high state officials constituted a crime. In other words, journalists and public figures who (unlike members of Congress) lacked immunity from prosecution tread onto vulnerable terrain if they criticized Pinochet *too* harshly. Marín had spoken at the 11 September protest march in Santiago to remember Allende and the victims of dictatorship. Some 10,000 people marched from downtown to the giant memorial wall to the executed and disappeared at the General Cemetery. There one of the most compelling speakers was Marín. Her dynamic history as a leader-activist included her election to Congress in 1964, when she was only twenty-three years old; her exile and the disappearance of her husband,

Jorge Muñoz, after 1973; and her secret return to Chile to organize underground resistance to dictatorship. In the 1990s, Marín had a social following that transcended Communist Party loyalty as such, and a voter appeal that would have easily won her a seat in Congress in a proportional rather than binomial electoral system. Marín galvanized the crowd at the cemetery. She bluntly called Pinochet the architect of state terrorism who continued to intervene in political life, and a cowardly traitor who hid behind threats and the army to evade his responsibility. Then came the dramatic memory gesture. Pointing to the great memorial wall with its thousands of names, she proclaimed it "the great work of Pinochet."

Seven weeks later came the sudden arrest. The next day—amidst street demonstrations by Communist Party activists and relatives of the disappeared, among others—the criminal chamber of the Supreme Court ruled by a three-to-two vote that the arrest was legally valid. Marín refused to retract her words. "I am not any criminal. I am the president of a political party and I have exercised my right to criticism and political judgments." The presidents of the Concertación parties (notwithstanding her stinging critique of the Concertación in the same speech) offered solidarity by visiting Marín in jail and declaring the arrest antidemocratic. The army soon withdrew its criminal complaint by request of Defense Minister Pérez Yoma, for reasons of state and humanitarianism. A key subtext in press reports and government statements was Chile's international image. The arrest sparked denunciation by Amnesty International, concern in the European Economic Community; it might sully the Sixth Ibero-American Summit, scheduled to open on 10 November with Chile as the host country.

Prudence had been restored, but significantly, the impulse to self-censorship continued even as the memory flap ventilated. Journalists reported the controversy but avoided quoting or summarizing the offending words—an act that would render them and their editors liable to criminal complaint. What Chileans learned was that *something* offensive had been said. A common reaction among political elites who criticized the arrest was that it violated the ethos of prudence. The arrest was "inconvenient" or "exaggerated." It inflated Marín beyond her true importance. Chileans—at least those in the *other* memory camp—needed to thicken their skins and return to a culture of studied calm.[24]

The cool turning away from the past was a mantra easier to preach than live. Sudden swings from calm to acrimony, from the ahistorical present to the contentious past within the present, continued to pepper politicocultural life in 1997. Even Pinochet and Pinochetistas, the memory group most inclined to argue for the virtues of mindful forgetting (*olvido*) in the heat of human rights controversy, were ambivalent. During the Contreras showdown, Pinochet promoted mindful silence as a positive good, the road to reconciliation. "The only way to solve the problems is olvido," he declared in a television interview in September 1995. "If day after day we are always returning to the same point, we will continue fighting. Forget it, do not talk more about the issue, then you will forget and I will forget." At bottom, however, memory conflicts pitted one kind of "meaning of the past" against another. The struggle was not flat opposition of remembrance against olvido, but an effort to define what was important to remember and why—and what to set aside as a distraction or a lie that undermined the important. All memory frameworks were in this sense selective, and all protagonists sometimes denounced olvido. In June 1997, when Pinochet appeared on a popular television program to regain momentum in the ongoing memory struggle, he *complained* about olvido. "Nobody remembers," he insisted, just how bad things were in 1973 and what had been accomplished. Communists had inserted 15,000 foreign guerrillas and weapons for 45,000 fighters, to train Chileans to kill Chileans. Nor did people remember the catastrophic state of the economy. "There are many things that have been forgotten."[25]

Pinochetistas therefore had their own reasons, personal and political, to organize themselves into memory knots demanding attention to the divisive past. During 1996, the "war thesis"—central to remembrance of military rule as salvation from disaster—received a cultural boost from extensive news coverage of judicial twists and turns in the case of the murder of Jaime Guzmán. Subliminally, the Guzmán story legitimized the idea of the past as a war struggle between two bands, one of them terrorists willing to break any civilized norm. The Guzmán case received more television news attention in the second half of 1996 than any other story including national municipal elections. Two days before the new year, a spectacular event brought the story and war thesis back to life again. Members of the Frente Patriótico Manuel Rodríguez used a hovering helicopter to pull out four prisoners—two were convicted assassins of Guzmán—from the interior patio of a high-security prison. The great escape rocked government credibility on security and crime, and guaranteed sharp polemics about how to combat terrorism, the menacing past within the present.[26]

The impossibility of "letting go" consistently, even for those inclined toward a politics of olvido, would not take long to reemerge. On 31 March Chilean media reported on a Mexican newspaper interview with Patricio Aylwin. Aylwin stated that Pinochet would be judged responsible by History for the crimes under his watch, even if trials were another matter. Pressed to consider his own role as a hard-line opponent of Allende during the crisis leading to the coup and repressive horror, Aylwin stated he had acted in conscience based on what he understood at the time—but yes, he had been mistaken. "We all have responsibilities for what happened beginning in 1973. The thing is that we had a mistaken vision of what the Chilean military [forces] were!" He misjudged when he thought the armed forces would adhere to the democratic tradition of the army commanders René Schneider and Carlos Prats. Aylwin's account of his mistake and awakening was framed as a memory both personal and emblematic. "I feel the tragedy that occurred in Chile as my own, but I fought the dictatorship fiercely. And just as I made a mistake, many of us were mistaken." His remarks ignited a storm—and organizing of countermemory. Army generals met and declared the remarks "highly offensive to the Army of Chile and its Commander in Chief." Fifty-one former ministers under the junta released a letter of rejoinder. The military government rescued a people in trouble, and built a successful and prosperous nation. When Pinochet appeared on television in June 1997 to combat olvido, the point was to regain the initiative in the cultural memory war.[27]

CONSEQUENCES: STATE AND CIVIL SOCIETY (I)

One consequence of the hardening memory impasse of 1996–97 was a shifting balance in the source of meaningful initiatives. Within the state, protagonism and initiative shifted from the executive branch to the judiciary. Within the nation, the balance of new initiative shifted from state toward civil society.

A simple dichotomy of state and civil society overlooks the synergies that build "everyday forms of state formation."[28] As we have seen, in the early 1990s the conflictive synergies of state and society yielded some creative results. Nongovernmental organizations (NGOS) such as the Vicaría and the Chilean Human Rights Commission, activist groups such as the agrupaciones of the relatives of the disappeared and of the politically executed, new groups such as the survivor-witness network consisting of former prisoners, all proved important in the Aylwin administration's most important memory initiative, the Rettig Commission. Grassroots actors also generated some acts of pressure—hunger strikes by political prisoners, street demonstrations and cultural forums that mobilized the human rights community and awareness, justice proceedings by aggrieved relatives pulling military officers into court—that shaped the social environment of state policy making. Organized groups in civil society sought allies within the state, especially in Congress and the Executive. Congressional representatives such as Juan Pablo Letelier, the son of Orlando Letelier, and Isabel Allende, the daughter of Salvador Allende, had a double role as legislators and as family victims in search of truth and justice. Such synergies were crucial. Nonetheless, and as we have also seen, even in Aylwin's presidency, creative conflictive synergy on the memory question deteriorated over time and reached a low after the May 1993 boinazo.

Under Frei, the low priority of memory matters and the sobering effect of the Contreras affair sealed the collapse. Synergy—collaborative action inspired by mutual dependence and sympathy, in which the parties know they need one another to achieve a larger good and social effect than they can accomplish alone, even if their collaboration does not exclude tension over goals, strategies, or tactics—seemed a distant memory by 1996. Protagonists of memory as rupture were more or less on their own. Connection with the state, especially its upper leadership layers, declined to the role of an "interest group" with little leverage, not a "partner" in a shared but sometimes contentious relationship. Significantly (see chapter 5), the key exception to the rule of withdrawal of executive branch initiative involved "inside game" work, not cultural expressiveness. The generational renovation of judicial and military leadership, through retirements and promotions and judicial reform, would presumably create an environment more favorable to human rights work.

In 1996–97, then, the burden of new memory initiatives shifted decisively toward grassroots activists, professionals and artists, and NGOS associated with the human rights camp of civil society. The task for memory activists was to create new cultural and judicial "facts" that might erode impasse. At the least, they needed to keep the memory question alive, and hopefully lay a foundation for stronger politicocultural pressure and state action in the future.

The task was easier said than done. Simply to repeat the same symbolic acts or demonstrations by the same social actors, although loyal to the memory of victims, would be to walk the well-known circle of impasse. Repetitiveness without advance was a recipe for stagnation—lack of "news-worthiness," lack of widening audience, lack of generational renovation. Such a situation would do little to erode the 1978 amnesty, let alone build a culture of human rights memory. It would invite even sympathizers to dismiss human rights activists and victims as persons stuck in the past.[29]

One response was to seek out new judicial paths, especially in the international arena. Prosecuting assassinations that had taken place on foreign soil already constituted one such instrument. The Letelier-Moffitt murder in Washington, D.C., had undermined the impunity of Contreras and Espinoza. By mid-1996 the court case on the murders in Buenos Aires of General Carlos Prats and his wife, Sofía Cuthbert, was heating up. On 30 July, Argentine judge María Servini de Cubría sent a letter rogatory requesting testimony by Chilean witnesses. A second judicial initiative was to press for universal jurisdiction in crimes against humanity, genocide, or acts of terrorism proscribed by international law and treaties, if the crimes could not otherwise be tried effectively. On 30 July, Spain's Audiencia Nacional (the body charged with special cases such as terrorism) accepted a criminal complaint by the Progressive Union of Prosecuting Attorneys against Augusto Pinochet and other junta members for crimes against humanity. The cases included the execution, disappearance, and torture of Spanish citizens in Chile. On 5 August, Sola Sierra and other leaders of the Agrupación of Relatives of the Detained and Disappeared joined the case. Precedent had been set in June, when Judge Baltazar Garzón accepted jurisdiction in a similar case involving Argentina.[30]

A third judicial initiative was to press for altogether new legal instruments to address impunity, that is, immunity from prosecution for human rights crimes. Impunity, whether derived from de facto rules of power or from self-amnesty laws by outgoing rulers, was a problem common in South American and other societies in transition from times of state terror. In December 1996, three human rights groups—CODEPU, FASIC, and SERPAJ—organized a major symposium on the issue in Santiago. (The acronyms stood, respectively, for Comité de Defensa de los Derechos del Pueblo, or Committee for Defense of the Rights of the People; Fundación de Ayuda Social de las Iglesias Cristianas, or Social Assistance Foundation of the Christian Churches; Servicio de Paz y Justicia, or Peace and Justice Service.

All were well known and active since the times of dictatorship.) The conference drew nearly two hundred participants from twenty-three countries. Chilean attendees included relatives of the disappeared, relatives of the politically executed, and prisoner-survivors, among others. The organizers considered impunity not only an obstacle to democratic transition, but itself a violation of human rights. The Nobel Peace Prize winner Adolfo Pérez Esquivel spoke of the spread of a "complex and confusing" political transition in Argentina and beyond. The era of state terrorism had ended, he stated, but new elected governments "have generated mechanisms of impunity that affect the life of persons and compromise the future of peoples." The idea of "memory" as a cultural struggle against olvido and inseparable from truth and justice, permeated the proceedings. As the organizers put it, a movement against impunity required a network of groups "that firmly oppose olvido, the absence of truth and justice." One needed "to build Memory" as one strove to achieve repair, truth, and justice.[31]

But how might one get to the promised land of memory and justice? Conference participants endorsed an international convention on impunity, and an international high court for crimes against humanity. The idea crystallizing in Santiago was part of a new emphasis in world culture, not simply in Chile. It resonated with activist and diplomatic efforts at other levels, including a projected United Nations conference in Rome to create an international criminal tribunal. Diplomats negotiated the Rome treaty in 1998. After ratification by seventy-four countries, the International Criminal Court—presumably a replacement for ad hoc tribunals created to address war crimes, crimes against humanity, and genocide—formally opened in July 2002 amidst intense diplomatic pressure and objections by the United States.[32]

A second response to impasse was to create *cultural* facts of life—initiatives to promote awareness and education. The stream of activities to keep memory alive and encourage involvement by the young came from diverse quarters. The Vicaría de la Solidaridad's successor entity, a documentation center organizing Chile's most important human rights archive and library, began awarding annual student thesis scholarships and prizes. Women of the disappeared continued an intense pace of cultural activity in 1996–97: launch of a photo-history book to mark twenty years of memory struggles, visitations to university and theater forums, organization of concerts, and the annual round of nine permanent commemorations including cultural forums and protest marches. The commemorations marked specifically Chilean anniversaries such as the Rettig Report on 4 March, the false DINA cover story of 119 persons whose disappearance was explained as death by fratricidal shootout on 22–24 July, and the coup anniversary on 11 September; and also transnational dates of meaning, such as Women's Day on 8 March, International Day of the Disappeared on 30 August, and the U.N. Universal Declaration of Human Rights on 10 December. Testimonial initiatives also came from other quarters. A network of 62 authors assisted by a student team produced a book to remember the 70 journalists killed or disappeared under military rule and the 21 more who died indirectly from health consequences. The book launch in March 1997, before a standing room crowd of some 500 journalists and others squeezed into a room at the National Library, turned into an event of living memory to honor the qualities and values of persons lost to repression. Daughter remembered father, friend remembered friend, idealist remembered idealist.[33]

Cinema also offered a path to memory awareness. In May 1997, the Goethe Institute of Chile organized a "First International Festival of Documentary Cinema." For two weeks, multigenerational audiences (300–500 persons, in the larger events) kept crowding the halls to catch one of the eighty screenings of documentary films, some of them supplemented by panel discussions. Many focused on Chile, and some were first public screenings in the country.

Among the most celebrated films were those by the exiled cinema artist Patricio Guzmán. His new documentary, *Chile: Obstinate Memory*, brilliantly explored the generational meanings of memory and silence. On the one hand, Guzmán's film homed in on middle-aged and elderly survivors of the Unidad Popular era—Allende's bodyguards and a secretary; an activist who had appeared in the young Guzmán's *Battle of Chile* trilogy in the 1970s; an aged refugee from Hitler's Europe, who suffered the disappearance of his son under Pinochet; pedestrians reacting with shock, irritation, or delight to a sound experiment. The camera observed responses in downtown Santiago when a young musical band marched and played "Venceremos" (We Will Win), the optimistic and catchy theme song of the Unidad Popular that had turned into a cultural taboo. The words, body language, and emotions of some of Guzmán's survivors gave a new twist to memory as unresolved rupture, by turning the Unidad Popular experience itself into something *treasured*. More than a prologue to disaster, it was a heartfelt memory of the right to have dreams and ideals. On the other hand, Guzmán's film also explored memory as generational void—by recording the intense and varied reactions of youths when for the first time they saw *The Battle of Chile*, Guzmán's once-prohibited trilogy. The rawness of *Battle* — words, images, emotion, and propaganda in the heat of an epic struggle— evoked the Chile of the 1970s they could not know directly. By putting on display the tears, debate, identifications, and bewilderment of youths when they first viewed the earlier film trilogy, *Obstinate Memory* gave ingenious form to silence as an overpowering and present absence. The young knew that the Unidad Popular era and 1973 crisis were foundational, yet had come to know it mainly as void and negation. The festival reproduced the film experience by drawing overwhelmingly young crowds to screenings of *The Battle of Chile*.[34]

Some efforts to preserve cultural memory facts were anchored in specific community identities. In Iquique, in the desert north of Chile, ex-prisoners and their relatives and friends organized an annual march to Pisagua to remember their disappeared and executed. In Concepción, the southern city whose history was linked to the University of Concepción and the MIR (Movimiento de Izquierda Revolucionaria, or Revolutionary Left Movement), the military had organized a ferocious repression. Activists painted giant memory murals on the walls surrounding the main university plaza and cultural forum. In 1996, they marked International Day of the Disappeared by painting a huge Chilean flag gripped by fists, its red section transformed into the blood of repression falling on a field of crosses. After twenty-three years, the words proclaimed, "we have not forgotten anything." Another mural remembered Miguel Enríquez, the famed leader of the MIR.[35]

In some of the historically "combative" shantytowns of Santiago, *pobladores* remembered people and events that embodied community histories of struggle and repression. In La Victoria, a *población* with a strong sense of history and struggle, police had sprayed bullets at the local parish house during the protest day of 4 September 1984. Fathers Pierre DuBois and André Jarlan had become a part of the community. They blended social service and protection functions with spiritual guidance; the parish house served as an emergency clinic for the injured on protest days. One of the bullets took the life of the beloved André Jarlan while he was praying in his upstairs room. Jarlan had worked with youths to steer them from drug addiction and self-destructive behavior, and to find nonviolent paths to social improvement. The killing of Jarlan quickly turned into a memory knot of national importance during the 1980s struggles against the dictatorship.

10. Memory murals at Concepción.
Above, "we have not forgotten anything." *Credit: Florencia Mallon.*

11. Below, Miguel Enríquez and Che Guevara. *Credit: Florencia Mallon.*

But it also became an important marker of *community* memory and identity. Even after the Jarlan anniversary faded as a national memory knot in the 1990s, community residents continued their annual commemorations. Jarlan's life symbolized the community's history of struggle and suffering and its socially oriented, liberationist Catholicism. His upstairs room at the parish house became a memory shrine; it preserved photos of his final moment, when his head rested on a bloodstained Bible. A week of cultural activity—from memory pictures and slogans in murals, banners, and chalk drawings, to street processions and candle vigils, to climactic masses and speeches remembering Jarlan and the community's history—culminated on the 4 September anniversary.[36]

La Victoria was unusual in the depth of its local memory tradition. But in two respects it was not unique. First, other communities and activists organized to keep local memory alive, as part of a struggle against olvido or sanitized official memories. In Villa Francia, another "combative" población, people organized a celebration and mass in October 1996 to remember and honor fifty years of service by Father Roberto Bolton. Bolton, like Jarlan, was a street priest who cast his lot with pobladores who suffered severe repression as well as poverty. He lived in a shack in the población. To remember him was inevitably to remember the youths with whom he had worked and who had fallen victim. Bolton had been particularly close with Rafael Vergara, killed in an alleged shootout in 1985 and a symbol of the persecution that came down hard on local families. Second, the activist-promoters of memory understood their work as struggle "against the current." The prevailing trend pointed toward olvido. State actors, especially at the higher levels, were hostile or uninterested.[37]

RECLAIMING VILLA GRIMALDI:
STATE AND CIVIL SOCIETY (II)

The most ambitious effort to create new cultural facts of life was the transformation of the infamous torture-and-disappearance compound "Villa Grimaldi" into a memory site, the Villa Grimaldi Peace Park (Parque por la Paz Villa Grimaldi). Late in 1973, the nascent DINA had taken over the property, once an aristocratic villa attractively located near the Andean foothills east of Santiago. Under its code name, "Cuartel Terranova," Villa Grimaldi turned into the DINA's largest torture center—some 4,500 prisoners were sent there for torture during 1974–76. The toll of executions and disappearances was also important—cases documented amounted to 223 by 1996, and almost all (205) were disappearances. In the late 1980s (see chapter 1), when the outgoing junta sought ways to suppress future exposures of atrocity, one memory erasure project transferred Villa Grimaldi to an investment group including relatives of Hugo Salas Wenzel, director general of the secret police (CNI). The commercial project would demolish the old structures and construct new housing.

Expunging Villa Grimaldi's past did not prove so simple. The sounds and lore of the site had affected neighborhood residents. Over the years, some had covered windows facing Villa Grimaldi to protect themselves from the malevolence. Even so, some persons saw or sensed spirits—tortured prisoners unable to rest. In August 1990, a tip by a concerned neighbor led to media discovery of the construction project and its corrupt inside connection. Human rights activists including prisoner-survivors of Villa Grimaldi and priests launched a campaign of demonstrations, neighborhood forums, and legal work to block the construction project. They secured key allies within the state—at the Cabinet level the minister of education, Ricardo Lagos, and the subsecretary of interior, Belisario Velasco; in Congress, the nationally prominent deputy Andrés Aylwin and local District 24 representative Laura Rodríguez; at the local levels of La Reina and Peñalolén, all the 1992 municipal election candidates from Right to Left and La Reina's newly elected mayor, Fernando Castillo Velasco. By December 1992 the umbrella group of organizers, the Permanent Assembly for Human Rights in District 24, secured agreement by the Ministry of Housing to expropriate the property and to finance partially its conversion into the Peace Park. Too late to reverse the demolition, the activists were nonetheless turning an erasure site and its residual wreckage into a memory knot. A mural on an external wall proclaimed, "THESE WALLS THAT HID DEATH AND TORTURE WILL NOW HAVE SIGNS OF LIFE."

As the Peace Park project took shape, it also bore witness to the shifting balance between state and civil society on memory matters. At each step activists sought and built constructive synergies with state actors. Such links were politically, legally, and financially indispensable. The long struggle to block the intended oblivion project and build a meaningful memory site in its place coincided, however, with the turn toward greater wariness, at presidential and top ministerial levels, about expressive memory politics. The energy, pressure, research, and persistence would have to come from grassroots activists, somewhat against the prevailing political currents. The order to expropriate the property was not finally issued until January 1994. Three more years passed before the Peace Park could be opened.[38]

The inauguration on 22 March 1997 demonstrated the dual legacy of synergy and tension. Some 1,000–2,000 people accepted invitations and crowded into the small park. They included not only surviving Villa Grimaldi prisoners, relatives and friends of the victims, including the executed and disappeared, and human rights activists. Also present were leading figures of the Concertación. Cabinet ministers included Ricardo Lagos (Public Works), Soledad Alvear (Justice), and Edmundo Hermosilla (Housing). Senator Sergio Bitar, leader of the Party for Democracy and a former Cabinet minister under Allende, also attended. But there was also a symbolic absence. President Frei declined to attend and speak, despite rumor and expectation to the contrary. His inner circle—the powerful troika of Interior Minister Figueroa, Defense Minister Pérez Yoma, and Secretary General of Government Brunner—was also conspicuously absent.

The speakers evinced both the reality of synergy and its deterioration over time. Minister Hermosilla delivered the park key to the Corporación Parque por la Paz Villa Grimaldi, the NGO created to run the site. He spoke sensitively about the temptation to forget what was painful, the healthiness of learning to live with memories both sad and joyful, and the value of social repair and preventive lessons, so that past suffering will not have occurred in vain. Tension came out into the open when grassroots activists spoke. Carlos Gho, the Corporación president, expressed joy and hope upon receiving the park, and underscored the urgency of memory—"oblivion is like death." But he *also* criticized the climate of forgetting and impunity that had taken hold of Chilean society. María Isabel Ortega, a former prisoner and the wife of a disappeared person, declared bluntly that the country had "thrown into oblivion" earlier efforts such as the Rettig Commission. Immediately after the inauguration, Justice Minister Alvear felt compelled to respond. She disagreed. Significant works of truth, social repair, and criminal justice had taken place.[39]

The inauguration also displayed the enormous power of Villa Grimaldi as a "memory knot." Tears flowed and melted tensions, at least temporarily. Significantly, what rendered the inauguration moving and powerful was not an aesthetic of literalism. It was the living memories of mind and heart, catalyzed through human contact and performance on sacred ground where desecration once took place. The symbolism proved potent. It was the chil-

12. Before the inauguration of the Villa Grimaldi Peace Park: Above, grassroots activists led the effort. Pedro Matta, a former prisoner of Villa Grimaldi, sits on the grounds with a research notebook. *Credit: Helen Hughes.*

13. Below, the buildings and structures had been demolished, but some of the barbed wire remained. *Credit: Helen Hughes.*

dren of prisoners who locked the old black entry doors and gave the key for safekeeping to Father José Aldunate, so that human beings would never again suffer the fate of their parents. It was a Mapuche woman and a Catholic priest, twin anchors of Chilean faith and culture, who performed dual rites of purification to transform loss into life. It was moral witness through accompaniment that reminded all what was at stake, when crowd members joined with grieving relatives as they lay flowers for dead and disappeared victims inscribed on a wall of remembrance.

Artistic performance, too, drew out the call of memory on sacred ground. Over the central patio, precisely where prisoners were once beaten and where some had legs crushed by rolling trucks, dancers evoked the deeper memory-truth in a ballet of pain and solidarity. Complementing their own living faces and bodies with stick masks of pain and fragile tissue mesh, they glided into the webs of human connection and solidarity, only to fall away into death and isolation, in and out of the contrasts that evoked the doubled legacy of prisoners. They were both victims and social actors with dreams. They presented a doubled invitation to the living to take meaning from memory. Remember their suffering and loss; remember, too, their idealism and solidarity.[40]

The saving of Villa Grimaldi for collective memory was a major accomplishment. It created a new cultural fact of life. Villa Grimaldi was not only the most important torture center in Chile; it was also the first such center converted into a human rights memory site in Latin America. Others had succumbed to erasure.

But the Villa Grimaldi Peace Park was also a symptom of the shifting balance between state and civil society in memory work. State assistance was modest and left the Peace Park in a gray zone of semimarginality after the inauguration. The aesthetic design of the Peace Park did not emphasize physical reconstruction of the cells and implements of horror. Rescued or reconstructed physical artifacts were few—the black doors through which trucks entered to dump blindfolded prisoners, some barbed wire salvaged from the ruins and set atop the western wall. The aesthetic focused on symbolism, a series of plaques and artistic representations that required active exercises of memory, imagination, and human contact to come alive. The symbolism was minimalist and inexpensive, almost low-key. Small memory plaques were abundant, new artistic creations scarce. The aesthetic reflected in part the outcome of internal debate among activists about the

14. The inaugural ceremony, Villa Grimaldi Peace Park:
Above, the dance of pain and solidarity.
Credit: Helen Hughes.

15. Below, relatives lay flowers for their loved ones at the wall of
remembrance. *Credit: Helen Hughes.*

balance of symbolism versus literalism as a strategy to promote reflection, visitation, and a culture of human rights. In part, it reflected adversity—the tough overall climate for memory work, the difficulty of securing state support even for inexpensive projects.

Consider, for example, "La Torre." A site of extreme terror within the compound, the Tower included a ground floor level for electric shock and bodily suspension tortures, a watch post at the top level, and on two levels in between, prisoner holding closets. The closet cells were tiny—about 28 by 28 inches and too short for standing on the third level, about 39 inches by 39 inches on the second level. Short doors that slid up from the ground into the closet wall required that prisoners crawl low into the closets—or that guards shove them in, if the preceding torture session left prisoners too exhausted. Stuffed into the closet, sometimes with another victim or even two or three in the second-floor cells, prisoners would pass several days searching for ways to lean or crouch that diminished pain and might allow a bit of rest or sleep. The torment was not only physical. The prisoners knew that those sent to isolation closets in the Tower almost never returned alive.

For the visitor in the 1990s, remembrance would not be evoked by a physically reconstructed Tower, nor by invitation to crawl into a closet cell. The catalyst of memory and imagination would be more subtle: accompaniment to the spot by a survivor. A former prisoner such as Pedro Matta movingly told the story of the Tower and Villa Grimaldi by drawing on personal experience and research. In general, the symbolic plaques and the artistic representations of the Peace Park lost their opaqueness only through human accompaniment and storytelling. It was through human contact that one might come to understand the symbolism of the painted stone "flames" of memory that reached up from the ground, precisely at the spot where entering trucks dumped blindfolded prisoners who touched stones on the ground to sense the surroundings.

The long-term plan for the Peace Park followed a similar strategy: remembrance into reflection, horror into peace, through direct human dialogue and witness. A documentation center and symposium facilities would presumably enhance dialogue, research, and reflection. There was a catch, however. In the absence of state funding sufficient for regular hours of business, for training and employment of former prisoners to conduct memory tours, and for a professional staff to promote educational visits to build a culture of human rights, the Peace Park entered a kind of cultural limbo in the late 1990s. A network of dedicated activists kept the site going.

They encouraged memory tours by Chilean and foreign students, organized commemorative events to draw people, invited newsworthy dignitaries to visit and raise awareness, and built electronic and social-academic outreach. They also assessed effectiveness and planned improvements. After 2000, private fundraising finally enabled the Peace Park Corporation to build a reconstructed Tower and its interior closets in two phases over a five-year period. But such accomplishments were very much the product of the activists' own initiative and persistence. After the 1997 inauguration, the Peace Park activists waged much of their struggle as political orphans, despite the state-society synergies they sought and built in earlier years. They had learned to use moral capital as the survivor-keepers of a sacred memory-truth to push for responsiveness by a reluctant state, yet also learned not to expect too much. The Peace Park activists rescued Villa Grimaldi from oblivion. Their dedication established Villa Grimaldi as a memory knot, a site that demanded remembrance and reflection. But they lacked support to turn the Peace Park into a more dynamic and frequently visited site.[41]

THE AMBIVALENT CULTURE:
TRIUMPHALISM AND DISENCHANTMENT

By the mid-to-late 1990s, Chileans had built a profoundly ambivalent culture of democratic transition. The contradictory, fluctuating sensibilities about the kind of society and values under creation were evident not only in swings between prudence and convulsion on the memory question, or in retreat from initiative by state and Concertación leaders while remaining formally committed to human rights memory as a moral matter. The mixed sensibilities also related to a wider change—the accelerated modernization that took hold in the 1990s, transformed Chile economically and culturally, and built a more privatized relation of society and the individual. A new model of the successful society had gained traction and produced spectacular socioeconomic results including unprecedented prosperity. But cultural sensibilities that attended the new society were contradictory. One side of the cultural coin was triumphalism and the cult of success (*exitismo*). Chile and Chileans were exceptionally effective. Their stable political transition and their economic competitiveness were a model. The other side of the coin was disenchantment and unease (*malestar*). The new Chile exalted the egotistical and forgot about community. It created social exclusions while evading them with euphemism.

By 1996–97, politicocultural disenchantment thickened notably. More currency attached to the idea that whatever their stated principles, political elites of the Concertación were not very willing or able to serve the causes and social sectors they theoretically supported. As we shall see in this chapter, it goes too far to reduce the disenchantment to the debilitating effects of memory conflict and impasse. But as we shall also see, it also goes too far not to notice how Chile's divided reckoning with the past figured as cause and effect. For some, disenchantment put a new memory question on the cultural table. What went wrong with our transition?

Triumphalism had its logic. Economically, Chileans had plenty to crow about. Despite initial nervousness about likely economic performance and business responses under democratic rule, Chile embarked on a spectacular economic growth trajectory. The GDP grew at a 7.7 percent annual rate during 1990 to 1997. The sustainability testified to outstanding strategy and technical management. Indeed, democrats achieved high growth despite bringing inflation down from 27 percent in 1990 to 6 percent in 1997. (The junta had primed the pump for the 1988 plebiscite and 1989 elections.) Exports, a key component of overall strategy, grew at about 10 percent a year. They included nontraditional items, such as wine and aqua-farmed salmon, and venerable products, such as copper and wood. The strategy of aggressive international commercial integration yielded regional and bilateral trade agreements in the Americas, Europe, and Pacific Asia—and a diversified export geography that diminished dependence. By 1998, Latin America, the European Union, and Pacific Asia each accounted for 24–28 percent of the value of Chilean exports, while the United States, Canada, and other countries accounted for 20 percent. Meanwhile, the investment motor hummed. The internal savings rate ran at 20–25 percent of GDP. Foreign direct investment—encouraged by Chile's reputation of high growth, sound technical management, and democratic political stability—soared to 7.1 percent of GDP by 1996–97. The sustained growth added about 70 percent to GDP by 1998. After 1998, the ripple effects of the financial crisis in the Asian Pacific brought an end to the high-growth era. Before the "Asian flu," however, Chile's growth engine kept pushing up purchasing power and augured a per capita GDP of about US$6,000 (about US$10,000 in purchasing power parity) by the turn of the century. Such numbers translated into a high standard of living in Third World contexts—and a vision of moving beyond the status of a "not-yet-developed" nation within a couple of generations.[42]

As Chile turned into a "tiger"—the lexicon equated it with star economies of East Asia—its business class also became significant as investors in adjoining countries. Direct investment abroad reached 1.7 percent of GDP by 1996 and turned Chilean capitalists into "players" with billions of dollars of ownership in sensitive sectors—energy, telecommunications, supermarkets, transportation—in Argentina, Bolivia, and Peru. Such exploits bolstered self-images of competitive success. It was Chilean entrepreneurs who responded superbly to challenge and opportunity in a market open to competition. The more the state retreated from distorting the market by ownership or regulation or taxation, the better. As Sergio de Castro, a private-sector player in the 1990s and an architect of junta economic policy in the 1970s, put it in 1996, "We are tigers in the private sector and house cats in the state." A businessman who bumped up against a cap on duty-free purchases after sealing a deal in Argentina asserted pride with a swagger. "It's easier for a Chilean to buy a company in Argentina than it is to buy duty free."[43]

The social consequences of sustained high growth were also notable in lower social strata. During 1990–97, unemployment dropped from 7.8 percent 1990 to 6.1 percent, while average real wages in the formal sector rose about a third (31.8 percent). High sustained growth meant social spending could rise substantially without eating into a fast growing pie for investors. From 1990 to 1996, per capita social spending increased 51.0 percent (at a higher rate for education, health, and housing), but the share of GDP devoted to social spending remained fairly stable (12.2 percent and 13.2 percent in 1990 and 1996, respectively). Meanwhile, poverty declined at an annual rate (about 2.5 percent) among the world's highest. The standard international measure of poverty in the developing world uses a "food basket" methodology. Total annual income for all expenses, if inferior to the cost of two adequate annual food baskets, amounts to poverty. Extreme poverty, or "indigence," occurs if total income is inferior to the cost of one food basket. By this modest definition, the military regime bequeathed an enormous poverty legacy. Two of five Chileans (38.6 percent), some 5 million persons, lived in poverty in 1990. By 1996, the poor population had dropped to some 3.3 million persons, or about one in four persons (23.2 percent). Indigence shrank even faster, from about one in eight people (12.9

percent) to about one in seventeen (5.8 percent). Economic growth did not alone account for the velocity of poverty reduction. Technical analysis attributes about two-fifths of the decline to changes in social policy and spending. Given the magnitude of the inherited poverty problem, its fast reduction was indeed a high priority and achievement.[44]

The economic success story was related to a political success story. The Concertación governments achieved a reputation as able guardians of a stable political transition (notwithstanding the saber-rattling moments of 1990, 1993, and 1995), and as elites whose understanding of "governability" meant they would not succumb to populist temptations that might upset the economic rules of the game. Chile offered investors not only the attractions of an economy favorable to their interests and open to the international market. It also offered political reliability over time—a stable investment climate, credibility when negotiating commercial accords. When Guerra-Mondragón calmed the diplomatic waters by calling Chile a "model of transition to democracy," he spoke to elites who understood the intertwining of political reputation with economic reputation. They understood themselves to have built, within the Latin American context, an exceptionally successful society and transition.[45]

The rub was that not everyone believed the success was real—or if real, that its consequences were welcome and socially inclusive. Was the success of Chile a story of good "marketing" and public relations that hid a less benign underside? If real, had it created the kind of society whose values, expectations, and loss of identity were to be embraced?

Significantly, unease did not arise only among those marginal to a culture of abundance within global capitalism. An accelerated coming into prosperity and international integration can produce a variety of sociocultural anxieties, even for beneficiaries. One may sense a loss of authenticity and identity, the cultural anchors that define social place and expectation. The naked self-regard and ostentatious wealth displays of some upper-class Chileans, particularly the nouveau riche, departed from familiar cultural tropes and self-images. Educated Chileans once regarded Argentines (or *porteños* of Buenos Aires) as the epitome of persons too brash, narcissistic, and self-impressed. Chileans were more humble or at least discreet, and inclined to serve community. A Chilean hero could be a "loser" such as Arturo Prat, the nineteenth-century naval officer who gave up his life to inspire compatriots to take a Peruvian ship in a lost-cause battle. Ironically, as *exitismo* rendered values of good taste anachronistic, conservative Chilean elites themselves warned of the perils of arrogance and hyperidentification with success. Beware, noted an influential politician, of turning ourselves into "the Argentines of the twenty-first century." Watch out, warned a television campaign by an energy company, your expectation of easy success can give way to the embarrassing fall. Our myths of self-pride, cautioned *El Mercurio*—"the most beautiful women, the best wine . . . we are the tigers of Latin America"—do not really hold up.[46]

Chile's economic transformation was entangled with cultural transformation, a privatization not only of economic life but also the social actor and the cultural quest. The worker-citizen was a core cultural icon and the pursuit of a just community a key political value in popular culture of the late 1950s to early 1970s. The consumer and the quest for individual self-actualization emerged as the influential icon and value of the 1990s. The shift was both symbolic and material. The closing of the famous Lota coal mines in April 1997, notwithstanding the historical combativeness of the miners and official reassurances after conflicts including a hunger strike in 1996, signaled the end of an era. It marked the demise of a celebrated worker tradition and its state-run energy company (Enacar) and the rise of privatized energy (Chilgener) whose investors owned and imported cheap coal from Colombia. Consumption served, above all, as the nexus joining economic and cultural trends. During the high-growth 1990s, the pursuit of individual self-actualization as such seemed more within reach for more people. The credit card revolution, for example, took hold in mass society. Credit cards numbered only hundreds of thousands in the 1980s, but by 1998 soared to some 6.3 million—in a nation of less than 16 million people. Similarly, great malls transcending specific neighborhoods turned popular as centers drawing people for shopping, socializing, and entertainment. By 1998, fifteen great malls ("regional" or "supraregional") had opened and drew an annual flow of 124 million visitors. The public plaza was ceding some ground as the arena of sociability.[47]

The problem was not only that the new culture of consumption might sometimes seem too "empty" of meaning, or too encouraging of drift from authentic values or community. People could seek to balance such effects, at least in part, by devotion to family or religious community. Other problems might not be ameliorated as readily. On the one hand, not everyone benefited equally or smoothly. The culture of convenient consumption brought strains as well as opportunities, especially for lower middle-class and middle-class persons. By

1996–98 Chileans carried an average credit card debt of us$220–240, roughly half the per capita monthly G D P. Sectorial analysis of total consumer debt showed that payment burdens of middle-income strata (from upper middle to lower middle) exceeded optimal carrying load. Only at the poles— the very wealthy and the poor—were debt and carrying load in alignment. Human development surveys at the turn of the twenty-first century confirmed a socially differentiated map of participation in the individualism, fulfillments, and insecurities of modern consumer culture. A quarter of Chileans (26 percent) were "model consumers" who bought high-quality goods and felt fulfilled. Other strata evinced more strain or at least ambivalence. A third (32 percent) were either "existential" middle-class consumers for whom purchases symbolized worth, but who could not afford the best-quality goods or meet their standard of self-comparison with others; or they were "well-being" consumers, often lower middle class, who improved the life of the family by buying an appliance, such as a refrigerator, but had little left over for individual consumption. Two-fifths (42 percent) felt excluded altogether from the culture of pleasurable consumption. They at best had enough for necessities.[48]

On the other hand, even for the relatively well off, consumer culture and its high-growth engine could bring some downsides, among them a softening of social exclusivity. We already noted tension between values of understated good taste and the brash ostentatiousness associated with nouveau riche. Other erosions of social geography occurred. In a mall compared to a plaza, people performed social roles differently, as comparable individuals whose gawking and purchasing defined the fashionable. Widened access to "the good life" brought other complications. Cheap cars and more income and credit enabled more people to own the road—but worsened traffic congestion and pollution. The rise of tourism as mass entertainment, recreation, and adventure sparked more subtle unease. People of distinct social classes had always taken vacations, of course. In the "old" Chile, trade unions organized facilities to enable families to afford a nice summer vacation, perhaps at the beach. But the culture of tourism—access to rest, countryside getaway, and travel—had also evinced a social geography of respectability and exclusivity. The old geography wobbled in the 1990s. The national stock of tourist hotels tripled, from about 900 to 2,700. Chilean tourism adventures abroad jumped from 770,000 departures a year to 1.8 million. The values of "cool" tourism also shifted, in part as a function of transnational trends and the simultaneous rise of foreign tourism visits to Chile. Adventure discovery of the "less known" and the ecologically pristine gained ground, in addition to such stalwarts as the restful getaway, the beach, and the museum. Either way, a certain invasion of "masses" violated exclusivity. More people and kinds of people crowded the lakes, beaches, parks, and mountains where one was once special. The truly rich could always find exclusive and beautiful ground. But others found that who and what counted in Chilean society were not quite so clear anymore.[49]

One aspect of disenchantment with the Chilean success story was ambivalence by those who participated and embraced some of its benefits, while also finding some elements wanting. Another aspect was more embittered—the sensation of being excluded or the conclusion that the story was a myth.

The Chilean economy grew rapidly and the poverty rate fell, but maldistribution remained extreme. The top fifth of households consistently captured nearly three-fifths of national income (56–58 percent) in the 1990s, and the bottom fifth less than a twentieth (4–4.5 percent). Even if one imputed the value of social spending targeted at the poor, the concentration remained extreme (54–56 percent for the top fifth, 6–6.5 percent for the bottom). The lion's share was concentrated not simply in the top fifth, but among the very rich. In 1997 the top tenth of the population enjoyed *triple* the income of the next tenth. It was this hyperconcentration that ranked Chile's Gini coefficient of income inequality (0.57) among the world's worst. Excluding the top tenth produced a low coefficient (0.27), one of the world's best for bottom nine-tenth distributions.[50]

Such figures translated into strong potential for disillusion. For the two-fifths of the nation that lived in poverty or eked out a lower middle-class existence modestly removed from it, the persistent precariousness of life, alongside amazing opulence and declarations of economic success at the top, could become more difficult to accept. Ostentatious success was flaunted everywhere, in castle homes and upscale malls and office towers, in advertising images of the prosperous consumer, in the street swagger of early cell phone users, in news reports that Chilean business conquered new export markets or acquired foreign holdings. In the early 1990s, the honeymoon effect of a long-awaited return to democracy, the sense of a fragile transition whose president faced limitations but sought benefits for all, and the reality of new social spending and material improvement generated a certain patience and good faith. By the mid-to-late 1990s, patience wore thin and sentiment tipped toward disappointment. Workers in varied industries—

textiles, metallurgicals, copper, export fruit, seafood, timber—did not see the benefits they had expected in the new democracy, even as they saw a tiny minority prosper fabulously. The high-growth economy was not a "miracle" for them nor for families in poblaciones where youth alienation, crime, gangs, drug addiction, and dead-end lives were serious problems. More subtly, the new prosperity alongside social insecurities relativized the cultural definition of poverty. The old minimalist standard grew more obsolete in a society of middle-class consumer culture and high-growth statistics.[51]

Disillusion materialized as a gap in public opinion surveys in 1995–97—during the golden economic years, *before* the Asian financial crisis hit—between "objective" economic trends and their "subjective" perception. People rating the country's current economic condition "good" or "very good" dropped precipitously, from a 35–37 percent range in 1993–94 to a 16–20 percent range. (The drop was less steep for ratings of personal and family economy, but the trend was similar.) Parallel drops about the country's *future* economic situation, and majority skepticism about whether most poor Chileans could climb out of poverty, were also evident. Most telling was the shift in the perceived beneficiaries of economic development. Surveys allowed Chileans to select more than one beneficiary—the respondent, all Chileans, the rich, and the poor. Only "the rich" improved upon the 1993 rating (76 percent). All others dropped sharply in 1995–97. "All Chileans" sagged from 43 percent to 22 percent, "the poor" from 25 percent to 11 percent. People did not believe or perceive what the statistics said about poverty. In 1996, seven of ten (69 percent) thought poverty remained the same (42 percent) or even worsened (27 percent) during the previous five years.[52]

As skepticism about economic inequality and sharing of benefits widened, it posed a delicate political question. How deeply committed or effective was the Concertación, after all, about the equity side of the growth-with-equity formula? Did development include everyone? Again, the issues were both symbolic and material. In the 1997 winter rainy season, flooding plagued small homes constructed in the 1990s by the company Copeva. The company had been contracted by the Housing Ministry to fulfill the government's ambitious social agenda, access to decent homes and affordable mortgages to families of modest means. But construction was poor and walls failed to withstand the rains. Some people had to abandon the homes altogether. Was the scandal the result of bad luck, negligent oversight, or company cheating? Was it a sign of trying to do decent social policy "on the cheap"? The equity policies of the Concertación governments had followed a double logic: (a) reduce poverty and improve life fast by high growth and employment, supplemented by social spending; and (b) promote equal opportunity in the future by socially targeted programs to improve education, health, and housing. The corollary was to keep social policy within bounds that would not upset the rules of the market-driven economic game, particularly the investment and export motors that assured high growth and a satisfied business sector. People sensed that the balance of effort among these competing goals was not even. For those who felt excluded or marginalized, it was as if two Chiles existed, each with its own imaginary. As one pobladora put it, the idea that democracy would bring improvement, social justice, and a climb out of poverty lost credibility. "There is a side of Chile that is for sure into that, that is the tiger. But the other side of Chile, the other Chile of we the poor, continues almost the same."[53]

MEMORY IN THE MAKING OF TRIUMPHALISM AND DISENCHANTMENT

To reduce sensibilities of disenchantment *only* to the politics of memory would lose sight of the wider context. Chilean society experienced rapid social change—a modernization that further privatized economic and cultural life while integrating the country aggressively into global economy and culture, that created a consumer culture and its image of the self-actualizing individual while boosting purchasing power, that concentrated income within the top tenth of society while also reducing poverty. The new Chile reconfigured relations between society and the individual, sparking some new anxieties and values. Like any society where "hurtling" into an ever more updated, uncertain, and self-transforming future becomes a strong sensibility, the new Chile bore a more fragile sense of connection to the past.[54]

Yet it also goes too far to ignore how the memory question fed into and reflected triumphalism and disenchantment—and for some, moral drift. Triumphalism found ardent partisans in the camp of those who remembered military rule as the salvation of Chile from ruin and imminent civil war in 1973. When Sergio de Castro praised private-sector businessmen as the true "tigers," the context was a memory interview. The military junta saved the country from the suffocating statism that once drove public policy, set up the successes of the 1990s, and provided a history lesson for the future: keep scaling back state interference with market-driven success. Like de Castro, many players in the dynamic business class of the 1990s experienced the military period as formative. It was the era when they went into public service, developed an ethos of aggressive market competitiveness, and turned themselves into capitalist pioneers by taking over and modernizing newly privatized sectors of the economy. Sensibilities of triumph resonated with those of gratitude and loyalty, a remembering of Chile's salvation that was at once personal and emblematic.[55]

As we have seen (chapter 1), Pinochet's defeat in the 1988 plebiscite and adjustment to civilian rule sparked a new layer in the evolving memory framework of salvation: the idea of "mission accomplished." The idea glossed over the reluctance of transition to civilian rule—as if turning over the country to democrats in 1990 had been the plan of Pinochet and his associates all along. Within this adapted framework of memory as salvation, the strong economic achievements of the 1990s owed not to the policies or skills of Concertación governments, but to the course set under military rule and continued into the 1990s. For the Pinochetistas, triumphalism and memory were inseparable. *They* created the successful democracy and prosperity of the 1990s.[56]

Some Concertacionistas put their own stamp on triumphalism—a glow of pride, complacency, or partisanship about accomplishments in the 1990s. Such sentiments were also not distant from the memory question. Memory was the foundation for assessing what had been accomplished since 1990. Our opposition to military tyranny and violence, went such thinking, culminated in a sustainable rebirth of democracy against the odds, a new respect for liberty and rule of law, and improved quality of life for those condemned to poverty and persecution under dictatorship. Defects and imperfections remain, but such problems will recede over time. As we shall see, within the culture of Concertación elites and their social base, there was also plenty of ambivalence and criticism by 1996–97. This reality tempered triumphalist discourse by elites. We have improved but not enough, we have more work ahead, went the more restrained narrative of success. Ironically, the most fervent triumphalism came from the opposition and the business sector.[57]

Memory also proved important in the culture of disenchantment. For poor and lower middle-class groups, disappointment with the results of democratic rule was not far removed from the idea of a "social debt," created in the times of dictatorship and not yet fully paid. In focus group sessions with pobladores in 1996–97, the sense of being the "poor relations" of democracy connected to an idea of disinheritance. Memories of rupture, persecution, and awakening during the 1980s—the era of mass mobilization against dictatorship—implied a right to higher expectations within democracy. Since 1990, moreover, pobladores found themselves asked to participate supportively in the new democracy, by administering social spending and volunteer programs (often via NGOs) in health, housing, and microenterprise formation, and by bearing in mind the need for democratic stability rather than resorting to disruptive street protest when discontented. But the resources provided seemed too stingy compared to social needs, and the dialogues with state representatives less than democratic. Such situations generated grassroots irritation, at first contained by a sense of progress, democratic fragility, and moral good faith—a "marketing," as Julia Paley has shrewdly observed, of the new democracy. By the mid-to-late 1990s, as Chile turned into a vaunted economic tiger with a flush upper class while problems of poverty, crime, and youth alienation persisted, and as government at the presidential level retreated from expressive concern about social justice, such irritations hardened into a discourse of disenchanted memory.

Pobladores complained they had been forgotten, despite the hardship and persecution endured under dictatorship, and the activism and protests by which they helped end military rule. At stake was the quality and depth of effort by leaders of the new democracy—and the ways memory drove fear as well as expectation. Female grassroots leaders were among the most vociferous critics. The opportunities for new job skills, microenterprises, and education promoted by the state did not match up to people's real aspirations: "They bury us there [in the poblaciones], that's all," as one pobladora put it. The government seeks "to make us women content," said another, with low aims and modest advances, out of fear of military-civilian tensions and a return to the past.[58]

The most volatile entanglements of memory and disillusion occurred among networks of activists, victims, and sympathizers in the human rights community. Here were concentrated the social actors who had turned themselves into memory knots on the social body and demanded attention to that which the dictatorship denied. They had helped spark a new moral conscience for the nation and a democratic transition. Here too was concentrated the sense that moral drift and complacency had set in since the early 1990s.

Consider the 1997 observations of Sola Sierra, the late president of the Agrupación of Relatives of the Detained and Disappeared. Significantly, she had since 1990 criticized the memory politics of democratic governments as too cautious in the fight against oblivion. But her critique also bore witness to change over time. I asked if the Rettig Commission's achievement of an officially investigated truth that undermined earlier state lies changed the meaning of olvido. Did "oblivion" now refer mainly to impunity or to lack of additional information about the fate of individual disappeared persons? "Today olvido is more than that. In the year that Aylwin delivers the [Rettig] Report . . . they tried not to create problems for the Armed Forces, not to make names [of perpetrators] known, but it was recognized that the Armed Forces had committed violations of human rights. But today this olvido has the objective of improving the image of the terrible tragedy our country lived." Recognition of the damage done was being lost, and the war framework revived. The new climate converted Pinochet back into a savior and taught future generations that state violence and cover-up of crime "had its justification." Building a culture of prevention was harder.[59]

The convergence of memory and disillusion came through vividly when a "common and ordinary" Chilean spoke out at a forum in June 1997. Convened by the Agrupación of Relatives of the Detained and Disappeared to address ways to overcome the 1978 Amnesty Law and impunity, the event began with a panel of experts. Everyone present was aware that the memory question often ended up in impasse and, worse, that the current climate sapped cultural interest and political initiative. In the forum after the panel, one of the persons who asked to speak was a middle-aged man. Handsome, with high cheek bones and thick graying hair, dark of skin by Chilean standards, bearing old scars near the right eye and ear, wearing a frayed cloth jacket, his appearance and diction marked him as a working-class man of the "old" Chile. He began quietly and with somewhat shaky voice, but turned louder and more passionate as he spoke. What people needed to understand was "the cruelty of this moment." The reality of the terrible repression under military rule no longer received the necessary cultural diffusion. It had fallen prey to "the denial, the ignorance, that comfort habit [comodidad] of the Chilean, always in lukewarm waters." But the hurt, he explained, had not really gone away for us. "Those of us who were kidnapped, tortured, scourged—and to this day we still are!—that's clear, those of us who were inside are still scourged, one way or another we continue tortured." One needed to remember what really happened. The disappeared were not just disappeared—they also had been kidnapped and tortured, before finally assassinated. His political trajectory summed up his disillusion. "I *was* Socialist," he declared emphatically. For thirty-four years he had been a Socialist—Senator Jaime Gazmuri, who spoke at the panel, listened intently—but no longer. The Socialist politicians, he said, "turned their backs" on human rights.[60]

The intimacy of the memory question, the frustration of impasse, the sense of moral abandonment, all could hardly have been more apparent.

When considering the thickening sense of disillusion, it does well to ask precisely what had changed since the early 1990s. What shifted was not a politics of prudence, but prudence balanced by moral counterweight. Aylwin understood the need to establish a moral line of clear distinction between the military past and the democratic present—both as a political underpinning of the Center-Left coalition, and as lifeblood for a new convivencia. The moral line built legitimacy for democratic transition, a task all the more vital *because* the transition unfolded within a structure of constraint and continuity, and because social memory of military rule was so divided. Oscillations between prudence and convulsion occurred throughout the 1990s, and Aylwin himself promoted the virtue of prudence and realism in his 1990 inaugural address. At another level, however, Aylwin's emphasis on truth as the foundation of social peace, his memory-related initiatives and symbolism (notably, the truth commission, social repair programs, the "Aylwin doctrine," the critique of judicial inadequacy, the Allende funeral), his penchant for moral discourse when sensing a fade into cynicism, his moments of dramatic tension with Pinochet and the army—these facets of his presidency provided a certain complement and moral credibility to the politics of prudence.

In the early Concertación, therefore, prudence did not imply a formulaic excuse to avoid pursuing truth or justice. It implied searching for balance between competing objectives (the goals of democratic stability, and truth with justice). It implied that even a leader who took memory work seriously had to take into account the reality of constraint, while also pressing to change the boundaries of constraint. To be sure, the unfolding of policy and declaration was not always linear. After the murder of Jaime Guzmán in April 1991, Aylwin retreated from expressiveness on memory issues and prematurely declared the transition over. In the tension between use of the Rettig Commission as a "formula" for closure of the past, or as a "wedge" to begin a fuller reckoning with the past, he fell in between and sometimes edged close to formula. Nonetheless, in the flow of presidential pronouncements, programs, gestures, and responses to critiques, Aylwin evinced a "Shakespearian tension," as Ascanio Cavallo perceptively put it, between the imperatives of power and those of conscience. He restored moral contrast and promoted interpretive doctrine that did not foreclose justice proceedings. As we saw, the path of moral counterweight was not smooth. Impasse hardened in the post-boinazo atmosphere. The gap between "soft" and "hard" hegemony grew more intractable; state-society synergies deteriorated further; citizen patience faded. Nonetheless, Aylwin retained moral capital and knew to reinforce it, even in the last months of his presidency.[61]

The sense of moral counterweight dissipated after 1994. Frei's disinterest in a "bully pulpit" role, his administration's ethos of economic modernization as the supreme value, and a public relations tone more one-dimensional —technocracy without a complement—fed the sense of drift and indifference on matters of memory and social justice. Fairly or unfairly, presumptions of good-faith effort by high political leaders eroded, even among grassroots activists and clienteles in the poblaciones who continued collaborating with government officials and programs. Significantly, the broad outlines of economic and social policy, and truth-and-justice policy, had not shifted notably. It was the Frei administration, after all, that put Manuel Contreras in jail and that continued to increase social spending. People perceived in the administration and the political class, however, a shifting balance among priorities and a decline of moral leadership. The political values that mattered were economic growth and investment opportunities—and an opportunistic getting along among elites that kept the engine of social advantage and social injustice humming. A hint of nostalgia began to inflect some conversations of disappointment: under dictatorship "we were better" at valuing moral solidarity; at least Aylwin showed remorse and genuine interest in social repair.[62]

COMING HOME TO ROOST

The chickens came home to roost. We have already seen the decline of good faith during 1995–97 that economic development really benefited everyone. Public opinion surveys on other themes pointed in a similar direction.

For example, people continued at about the same rate (73–78 percent) to consider democracy the most legitimate political system, but the perceived effectiveness of democracy at solving problems sagged from 67 percent in 1993 to only 52 percent in 1997.[63] Other signs of unease materialized: book culture, the 11 September anniversaries, election results.

At the level of elite and middle-class culture, new kinds of books became best sellers. In 1989–91 the hot works of nonfiction were those that exposed the ruptures and persecutions of military rule (see chapter 1). Such books contributed to a culture of democratic awakening about the past. In 1997–98 celebrated nonfiction books also focused on the past—but now the point was to question the transition. The most influential was the sociologist Tomás Moulian's 1997 best seller, *Chile Actual: Anatomía de un mito* (Chile Today: Anatomy of a Myth). Demand generated nearly a printing a month for two years. Moulian argued that the new Chile of the 1990s, a rupture with the old Chile, had been created by military rule and state terror; that notions of transition, change, and democracy constituted a myth that masked continuity with the military past and its neoliberal revolution; that such forgetting was the premise of political culture in the new Chile. Today's Chile was marked by "compulsion to forget." The obsession with consensus by political elites was anchored in amnesia. "Consensus is the higher stage of oblivion."[64]

Moulian's book, as he admitted, was an interpretive essay rebelling against the sterility of academic convention. Considered as a historical study, the book—despite its brilliance—had weaknesses. As research, it offered little new investigation or findings. As interpretive analysis, it left aside crosscurrents that nuanced, contradicted, or placed limits on its main arguments. These aspects paled, however, next to its resonance with the cultural moment. Its cutting critique of the new society of malls and the "citizen credit-card" tapped into anxiety about the kind of society consolidated in the 1990s. The historical argument that turned the transition into a cosmetic fraud tapped into the theme that gnawed away within the memory camp once focused on military rule. What had gone wrong and why, in the late 1980s and early 1990s?[65]

As a cultural phenomenon, Moulian's book and other works of disenchantment—notably, two celebrated books by the historian Alfredo Jocelyn-Holt in 1997–98 (*El peso de la noche*, *El Chile perplejo*)—yielded an important irony. Read as historical documents rather than as works of history, their success signaled disquiet and self-doubt seeping into middle-class and elite culture, including the culture of Concertación elites. Strictly speaking, what

Moulian's book demonstrated was not a dominant culture of oblivion, but a contradictory culture of impasse and disenchantment.[66]

The 11 September anniversaries also took a new turn. Keeping public order grew more difficult and polemical. In 1994, the new administration overruled the intendant of Santiago, Fernando Castillo Velasco, by prohibiting a permit, customary since 1990, to allow marchers to deposit flowers at Morandé 80, site of the disappeared door to La Moneda Palace used by Salvador Allende and his visitors. The door and address had been erased during repair and refurbishing of the bombed presidential palace, reopened in 1981. Its absent presence became a symbol of democracy and the struggle against memory erasure. The prohibition—and Frei's quick acceptance of Castillo's resignation—sparked anger and speculation that fear of street disturbances had been a pretext for removing an official of moral stature and independence. During 1994–96, street conflicts related to 11 September protest marches from downtown Santiago to the General Cemetery indeed turned more intense. Masked youths established a stronger presence on the fringes of crowds, and they sought to provoke carabineros. Nervous carabineros complied. They moved quickly to launch tear gas and disperse crowds, sometimes before disturbances broke out. The 1996 toll—224 arrested, 38 wounded—suggested a hardening deterioration. (In 1994 and 1995 the respective numbers were 171 and 169 arrested, 3 and 4 wounded.) The deeper concern was whether intensified public order problems on 11 September signified tougher youth alienation, not as a leftover from military rule but in reaction to life conditions within a restricted democracy and grossly unequal economic order.[67]

The concern was not misplaced. For youth who came of age as "children of dictatorship" in the 1980s or during the constrained democracy in the 1990s, the thinning line of moral contrast fed skepticism and alienation. The culture of military rule and the political failures of elders had long fostered antipolitical sensibilities. Youth of the 1980s had been the most difficult segment to mobilize for the 1988 plebiscite. In the mid-to-late 1990s, a government unable to project a larger social vision—beyond economic growth and modernization—and plagued by a gap between statistics of economic success and perception of social success could not combat a resurgence of disgust with politics as a kind of fiction. Energies were best concentrated elsewhere, on getting ahead in the predatory world, or finding expressive liberty and identification as soccer fans (*barra brava*), or drawing deeper meaning by devotion to a religious community, a cultural group, or one's family. Institutional politics was a world apart. If memory mattered, it mattered as disillusion or betrayal. Hopes and promises of the late 1980s had turned into a mirage.[68]

The new climate of skepticism and alienation came to the fore dramatically in the congressional elections of December 1997. The most important sign was not erosion of the Concertación vote, which declined to a very slender majority (50.5 percent, about 5 percent and 8 percent less than the congressional and presidential votes, respectively, in 1993). Nor was it the ups and downs of particular parties in the two major electoral coalitions. The Christian Democrats slipped (from 27.0 percent to 22.9 percent), and the right-wing UDI enjoyed a bounce (from 12.1 percent to 14.4 percent). More revealing was the "protest voting." Votes for the Communist Party jumped to 6.7 percent (from just shy of 5 percent in 1993). The party leader, Gladys Marín, secured the eighth-highest vote total among Senate candidates—higher than those of sixteen elected Senators. (Under the binomial electoral rules, however, her 15.7 percent share remained insufficient to win a seat in District 7 of western Santiago.) The slates of other candidates without a chance to win seats (the "La Izquierda" and "Humanista" lists) garnered a tenth (10.4 percent).[69]

The most severe extrainstitutional stances—pure protest votes, abstentions by the registered, noninscription by potential registered voters—shot up sharply. Null and blank ballots, some scrawled with insults, slogans, or drawings, amounted to over a sixth (17.8 percent) of the votes cast! Abstentions (despite the legal obligation to vote) raised the total disaffected share to nearly one in three registered voters (31.5 percent), compared to about one in six (17.4 percent) in 1993. Also, over a million young persons who reached voting age between 1993 and 1997 declined to register altogether. Such figures did not translate into a redistribution of seats held by the contending coalitions in the new Congress, compared to the previous one. But they said something large about sensibilities: we feel forgotten, excluded from a social model in which we want a more just inclusion. Or, for the more embittered: we self-exclude from a system that is a fraud. It has little to do with our reality.[70]

The culture of prudence and convulsion produced sensations of being "stuck" in a dynamic leading back to the same place. In the mid-to-late 1990s Chileans continued walking a circle of impasse. Tension between desire and constraint had long brewed and bred ambivalence. From the start in 1989–91, this was a transition caught between awareness of the deeply conflictive nature of the memory question, and awareness that reckoning with the past would prove strategic to launch and legitimize a reborn democracy. Throughout the 1990s, democratic Chileans contended with a breach between the politics of "soft" hegemony—where desire for truth, justice, and socioeconomic equity proved strong—and the politics of "hard" hegemony—where cooperative coexistence with the powerful shaped sustainability and constrained rules of the economic game and the memory game. As long as social sectors aligned with the world of "soft" hegemony—essentially the social base of the Concertación, including critics—perceived tangible progress and determination by leaders to pursue larger objectives that served all, the frustrations and ambivalences built into the transition did not necessarily destroy legitimacy or good faith. Over time, however, the sense of balanced tension between moral centeredness, necessary compromise, and political will eroded. By 1996–97, sensibilities of moral drift and disenchantment thickened.

The unease derived in part from a larger transformation including the accelerated modernization and privatization of economic and cultural life, but it also reflected the legacy and conflictiveness of memory struggles. Triumphalists saw in Chile's spectacular statistics of economic growth and declining poverty a revindication, whether of military rule or the transition. The alienated saw in the hyperconcentration of income and the retreat from memory work a culture of willful forgetting of the victimized and the excluded. For activists, victims, and sympathizers of the human rights memory camp, Chile's inability to escape memory impasse was especially demoralizing. The memory question was intimate—moral and existential and personal, not simply political. One could not walk away from it.

The paradoxical reality was that on memory matters Chile was both "stuck and unstuck." On the one hand, by 1996–97 the debilitated memory climate—returns to impasse or silence after a passing outburst, retreat from moral leadership and interest by high state leaders and influential media—shifted the culture of memory discussion in troubling ways that rendered future advances more difficult. The new climate consolidated the already existing tendency to reduce memory of repression to its narrowest possible terms—the maximal cases, deaths and disappearances definitively documented by the Rettig Commission (and in follow-up work by the Repair and Reconciliation Corporation). These cases served not as a minimal baseline and a wedge to open up a wider reckoning with the multifaceted repression that affected other families, too, but as a cultural endpoint. The reductionism included even those sympathetic to human rights memory. On the Day of the Dead in 1996, when a million persons visited Santiago's General Cemetery to pay respect to loved ones, a man took his teenage children to the giant memorial wall of the disappeared and executed. Here they would learn that lethal repression by the military state was real and affected many. As they reflected in stunned silence, he tried to soften the blow. "They were 3,000 people. Let's see, less than 1 percent of the national population, right?"[71]

Such reductionism was not unusual, and it amounted to a major change in the politics and culture of memory since the beginnings of transition. During the 1980s, when the human rights memory camp underwent explosive expansion, two complementary frameworks—memory as a narrative of rupture, and as a story of persecution and awakening—shaped the democratic memory camp. The reality and meaning of military rule was that of cruel and ceaseless rupture of life, an open wound that never healed for families who lost people to the state's disappearances and executions, a hurt compounded by disinformation and denial. The remembered meaning of military rule was *also* a more multifaceted struggle and response—the bearing of witness to many kinds of persecution, and the social awakenings prompted by such experiences. State punishment included not only execution and disappearance of people after abduction but also the violence and degradation of torture, the roundups of young males and the spraying of bullets to quell protests in the poblaciones, the exile of Chileans abroad or to isolated provincial towns, the purging of schools and universities and labor unions, the behind-the-scene intimidations that also contributed to fear and self-censorship, the condemnation of almost half the society to dead-end lives of poverty. To experience or bear witness to such events also prompted awakenings—the rousing of moral conscience, new appreciations of solidarity, human rights, democracy, religious faith; the awakening-into-anger of youths, pobladores, and workers afflicted by repression and poverty; the self-discovery of women as social actors asserting a voice as persons with rights and as advocates for democracy. By the time of the 1988 plebiscite, memory as rupture, persecution, and awakening had merged into a mass experience—and an umbrella of meaning for a wide variety of specific experiences of repression.[72]

The reductionism of the mid-to-late 1990s stripped away the heterogeneity of that which was culturally recognized as important. The emblematic memory framework of rupture, symbolized by women relatives of maximal victims and especially the disappeared, still resonated, despite the frustrating environment of impasse and state retreat. Memory as persecution and awakening, a more multilayered framework of acknowledgment and call to solidarity, had fallen on even tougher times. People had individual memories of a variety of persecutions, but such memories were no longer so "emblematic" of a larger experience or call to solidarity.

Indeed, the second major effect of the debilitated memory climate of 1996–97 was that entrenched impasse had brought the struggle for primacy among emblematic memory frameworks to a point of exhaustion. Created in the times of dictatorship, the four major emblematic frameworks —in one camp, memory as salvation and as a closed box on the dirty past, in the other, memory as rupture and as persecution and awakening—emerged originally as a struggle for "hearts and minds." They served either to legitimize military rule, or to expose the unjustifiable brutality that required its end and a rebirth of democracy. It was this struggle, too, that crystallized "memory" as a code word and sacred value by the early 1980s. In the early years of transition, the framing of memory as emblematic—symbolic of a larger tragedy and reality, in need of repair to build a healthy present— continued to be recognized as strategic. Now, however, the cultural struggle for primacy risked becoming futile or obsolete. Repeated returns to impasse meant that no one could hegemonize the meaning of the military past. Retreat from leadership and symbolism from above also meant that memories of repression found less "echo" from the state and media. All memory of repression and the military era was at greater risk of becoming "loose"— the personal experience of individuals—rather than emblematic of a collective experience. In this sense, memory culture was not immune from the larger privatization of culture and economy unfolding in Chile.[73]

On the other hand, being "stuck" in a circle of return to impasse was not the whole story during 1994–97. The specific points of contention and standoff shifted. One did not return to precisely the same place. Memory struggle continued to be a world of slowly rolling impasse. Over time, in part because of grassroots initiatives and pressure against closure, the terms of memory debate evinced an "unstuck" dynamic, even as the structure of power reproduced the experience of getting stuck in a standoff.

Despite moral drift and memory convulsions leading to nowhere, key advances—for those historically aligned with memory as rupture, persecution, and awakening—took place during 1994–97. First, military and police officials were not so untouchable any more. New precedents, especially culturally and politically, were taking place. The 1985 murder of the "three professionals" led to jail sentences for sixteen perpetrators, and to a cover-up struggle that eventually pushed the carabinero director, Rodolfo Stange, to resign. Most important, the former DINA director, Manuel Contreras, and his associate Pedro Espinoza succumbed—not without a prolonged struggle of very high stakes, in the case of Contreras—to guilty verdicts and jail at Punta Peuco. Notwithstanding the status of the Letelier-Moffitt murder as a legal exception to the 1978 Amnesty Law, the jailing broke a *cultural* barrier. Jailing a high officer was thinkable, not only in society but also the military.

Second, human rights activists and their political allies blocked outright closure of justice prospects despite enormous pressure to achieve it. Contreras swallowed his jailing, and the army went along, on the premise that he sacrificed himself to bring an end to criminal proceedings affecting other soldiers. Contreras would heroically stop the "slippery slope" effect. This vision and the Figueroa-Otero accord that might have implemented it, however, failed.

Third, even as the memory climate grew bleaker and state interest receded, memory activists and artists and intellectuals created new politico-cultural and legal facts of life. In so doing, they kept the memory question alive for a better day, reframed debates about the past within the present, and revived the idea that legal *interpretation* might undermine impunity, even if the 1978 Amnesty Law were not formally revoked. The rescue of Villa Grimaldi from oblivion placed a new memory knot—the place of torture, the people who can tell about it—on the social body. The cultural interventions by the filmmaker Guzmán and the authors Moulian and Jocelyn-Holt opened up a new debate: what went wrong with our transition and how does it relate to our historical memory? The fora organized to address the impunity issue announced a new legal path. What would happen to impunity if international law and justice were more actively utilized and promoted?

A fourth shift was institutional, the "inside-game" story that points in a new direction. The Frei administration retreated from expressive symbolism and initiative related to human rights memory, but it also followed the broad outlines of Concertación policy, proved adept at generational renovation of key institutions, and had to respond to the same political pressures that shaped the Aylwin administration. Memory knots—judicial cases linked to notorious murders, circles of activists and politicians who mobilized both visibly and discreetly—kept up pressure for partial purging and renewal of military leadership. In November 1997, Frei vetoed the promotion of Brigadier General Jaime Lepe, whose background linked him to the DINA, the 1976 assassination of Carmelo Soria, and judicial proceedings in Spain on the Soria case. Defense Minister Pérez Yoma put final touches on his plan to promote General Ricardo Izurieta as army commander in chief upon Pinochet's retirement in 1998. The operation required passing over five more senior officers—a retirement was needed simply to nudge Izurieta into the "top five" of eligible candidates. Izurieta was the officer least associated with military rule (his only political office was as subsecretary of war in 1989). His promotion meant the push for generational and leadership renewal, and greater civilian influence at the top, was serious.[74]

New developments also affected the institutional inside-game of justice. One aspect was transnational. In 1997 the case in Spain against Pinochet began to mobilize testimony and documents, assisted not only by Chileans but also by agreement of the Bill Clinton administration to provide access to relevant documents from the United States. In Chile, new Supreme Court appointments affected the jurisprudence of amnesty. The Court moved toward the Aylwin doctrine when it included 112 disappearance cases within a criminal investigation of "Colonia Dignidad," the notorious German immigrant colony that collaborated with the DINA; and when it reversed a military court's amnesty ruling in the case of the disappeared Socialists Rodolfo Espejo and Gregorio López. (Early in 1998 it also rattled impunity by shifting the "Caso Albania," the 1987 execution of twelve Frente Patriótico members by the secret police, to civilian court.) In September, the military public ministry office complained to the Supreme Court that amnesty was still not being correctly applied. About 100 cases had been opened or reopened in the last fifteen months; about 400 soldiers and carabineros, some on active duty, had been ordered to give testimony. About 640 more cases constituted a sword of Damocles, if amnesty were "incorrectly" applied, since their technical status was that of "temporarily" dismissed. Contreras had failed to eliminate the slippery slope.[75]

On the eve of 1998, Chileans lived a culture of ambivalence and impasse, not a culture of forgetting. The overall climate of public life was marked by declining moral leadership and increasing coldness to memory by top leaders of government. The appeal: close the conflictive memory box; turn away from the past; look to the modernized future for the good of Chile. Yet both in politics and civil society, matters were not really so simple. On the memory question, Chileans were both prudent and convulsive. Such swings affected the same individuals or memory camps at distinct moments in time; they did not simply amount to the pitting of one camp against another. Caught between the temptation and the impossibility of forgetting, Chileans alternated between avoiding the conflictive memory question and stoking it.

Small wonder that triumphalism and disenchantment were two sides of the same cultural coin. Did identification with success have a compensatory aspect, as if one needed to bluster one's way past the claims of original sin? Perhaps it was no coincidence that one of Chile's most acute cultural observers, the playwright Marco Antonio de la Parra, was also a psychiatrist. Late in 1996, he received the José Nuez Martín Prize for *The Little History of Chile* (La pequeña historia de Chile), a tragicomic drama on the end of national identity and history. He observed that writing had become more difficult than ever. Asked by a reporter what he meant, he explained that the artistic challenge was to figure out what was happening to the country "in this time of such change, such triumphalism." He had seen a tremendous impulse of exitismo, hyperpride in Chilean success and superiority, whether exploits in export markets and economic growth, or feats of the sport stars Chino Ríos (tennis) and Iván Zamorano (soccer), or fame in the celebrity pageant that launched the beauty queen Cecilia Bolocco. What drove this cultural impulse? He ventured an idea. "If you allow me a psychotherapeutic phrase, *exitismo* has to do with a kind of manic repair of the sorrow of Chile. . . . The past political experience is extraordinarily painful. . . . It is like a necessity for us to have reached a kind of heaven, paradise. The exitismo is the equivalent of saying 'all that we suffered had a meaning. We are good exporters, we are the best in something, we win.' "[76]

De la Parra went too far, if one takes him literally rather than metaphorically. One cannot leap from analysis of an individual to that of society so easily. Also, one aspect of exitismo was pride by those who identified with the memory of military rule as a tale of rescue and who had shown no remorse. But de la Parra was no fool. His audience was the well-educated and well-intentioned upper middle and middle class, a public that could understand and perhaps identify with the point. Somehow, the great successes of Chilean modernization seemed to be sitting on a foundation of unease—a terrain where memory and sorrow and demands for social inclusion cried out for attention.

The Joys of "Not Too Much"

In a sense, Chile in the 1990s was the land of "not too much." From the start, Aylwin put forth a strong discourse of memory and moral contrast with dictatorship, but he also took care to remind Chileans of the constraints of democratic transition. The military saber rattling of December 1990 and May 1993 reinforced the point. So did memories of the Unidad Popular. Renovations in the Center-Left under military rule fed readings of the Unidad Popular, and more generally the 1964–73 period of presidents Frei Montalva and Allende, as a prologue to disaster driven in part by maximalist politics. In this reading, the hyperideological spirit of the 1960s and early 1970s favored purity over pragmatism, desire over realism. In the 1990s, on themes of memory and human rights, and social equity and economic redistribution, Chileans had to remember not to ask for too much, or too much too soon, lest they jeopardize the stability and success of transition. Yet, a key legacy of dictatorship was precisely the enormous pent-up demand for redress of harm, both the harm of political persecution and that of economic suffering.

By the mid-to-late 1990s, as disenchantment thickened, a second aspect of Chile as the land of "not too much" became notable. Among social bases important to the 1988 plebiscite victory and the Center-Left transition— *pobladores* (especially women) and workers and youths, whose mobilizations for an end to dictatorship had been intense; middle-class sectors aligned with ideas of social solidarity or human rights, including intellectuals and professionals; activists in Christian lay communities, human rights circles, and NGOS—a nagging question gained wider influence. How much did political leaders really care about key issues they theoretically supported, whether those of social repair or those of social equity? To skeptics, the formal beliefs of Concertación leaders in truth, repair, and justice did not seem to matter too much. On memory matters, leaders did not seem so eager to wage political battle to put principles into practice. On matters of social equity, leaders either did not care so much, or accepted as a positive good a model of economic growth and poverty reduction whose results for families of modest means were too austere.

The memory culture of prudence and convulsion reflected the frustrations of living in the world of not too much. Do not ask for too much too soon; do not expect too much of leaders who say the right things. The modern future—market driven, efficient, prosperous—is arriving and will eventually provide opportunities for all and erase dissatisfactions. Meanwhile, the social needs and memory passions bequeathed by the past remained serious.[1]

Not all was bleak, not even for the critics. As we have seen, real accomplishments did take place, not only in the realm of economic growth but also in memory matters and social policy. Even when memory impasse hardened in the mid-to-late 1990s, it is more analytically precise to conceptualize it as a rolling impasse: hard-won advance on specific issues concentrating the contentiousness, even as the structure of power and constraint reproduced standoff on other memory issues. Also, for enthusiasts and skeptics alike, there was the balm of humor and entertainment. One aspect of entertainment culture was escapism, the suspending of normal time and frustration by entering, for example, the world of spectacle and vicarious identification in televised sports, soap operas, and humor shows.[2] Another aspect, however, was the entertainment that turns memory itself into pleasurable self-recognition—a way to acknowledge yet somehow transcend memory as a narrative of conflict, sorrow, or loss of the past. As we shall see, there was also humor that pokes fun at the absurd. In talented hands, life in the land of "not too much" provided comic material.

From 1988 to 1998, *La Negra Ester* (Black Esther), a theater show styled in the traveling circus-tent tradition, enjoyed an amazing run.[3] Its success included an international component. From time to time the company left for tours in Canada, England, France, Germany, Ireland, Italy, Mexico, Sweden, and Switzerland. More important, its appeal extended to all layers of Chilean society—the shows took place not only in the major theater and exposition sites of downtown Santiago and drew not only middle-class and elite theatergoing publics. It also had a "popular sector" appeal and brought theater directly into the *poblaciones* and the provinces. *La Negra Ester* opened in December 1988 in the población Puente Alto, on the southern fringe of metropolitan Santiago. Three months later the company was performing in a gymnasium in Magallanes, the cold and windy province near Antarctica. As sometimes happens in the arts, the show "took off." Its appeal and staying power surpassed expectations.

La Negra Ester was a love story crisscrossed by betrayal and forgiveness. Its central personalities were Ester, the prostitute of a port town, and Roberto, the man who repeatedly abandons her only to return again. He leaves when his fortunes turn up and he wants to take advantage of agricultural conditions in another province; he leaves when he decides Ester is socially beneath him; he returns when his own relatives push him to admit he loves her. Ester and her women friends are strong personalities—survivors in a tough world, unsparing when they castigate Roberto. As Esperanza puts it, "Jerk who do you think you are / doing this to Negra Ester" (Güevón qué te hai creído / hacerle esto a la Negra Ester"). But times of forgiveness and reunion are also a pretext for food and partying. The conclusion and epilogue are classic romantic melodrama and male paternalism. Roberto rescues Ester from an abusive client-lover; Ester is getting too old for the life of the prostitute but has an offer from a good widower; Roberto sacrifices his desire for the good of Ester, who would be better off with the widower. Later, in his old age, he realizes he needs to see her again but learns she has died. He can only experience the sweet sadness of nostalgia.

What explained the appeal and staying power of *La Negra Ester*? One cannot reduce the resonance of art to one dimension. The artistic quality—the directing of Andrés Pérez, the text of Roberto Parra, the acting of Rosa Ramírez and Boris Quercia—was truly superb. The musical component and verbal fire were well-executed fun. The story line was romantic and classic and struck chords. As the actress and theater scholar Violeta Espinoza has observed, the show itself became a fiesta—a fun happening, like a holiday, that gave range to emotions from tears to laughter, that invited people to party and eat at intermission.

The timing of the takeoff was also perfect. Much like the October 1988 plebiscite, its characters celebrated the return of the stigmatized and the marginal—of popular culture—to a Chile hungry for joy and democratic inclusion. In a sense, one may read *La Negra Ester* as a continuation into the 1990s of the best of the culture of the plebiscite. Fun, yearnings, and popular culture literally retook center stage.

All these aspects mattered, yet there was also something more. *La Negra Ester* was a time-travel experience. It evoked the lost pre-1973 Chile, more "authentic" yet erased by vacuous modernity and its shopping mall society.

The itinerant street theater style, complete with exaggerated makeup, fan-fare, emotion, and clowning, invited people to *reexperience* the times when tent theater was a spectacle that connected to people directly in their com-munities and neighborhoods. The musical components brought back the sounds of mid-century and tradition, from Chilean *cuecas* to cross-national mambos and tangos. The language deployed the accents, slang, and prov-erbs—and sarcastic dressing downs—of the pueblo. When Ester first meets Roberto, she scoffs at the worthless pretenses of yet another musician: "You pure good for nothing bastard / the stick t' be feather duster / is all you're lacking" (Soh un puro huachuchero / el palo pa' ser plumero / es lo que te está faltando). The language unfolded in verse, the poetry prized as a Chil-ean gift of cultural expression. Consider the opening, as Roberto conjures up the irresistible image of Ester in her reddish makeup. ("Negra Ester" is pronounced NEH-grah ehs-TEHR.)

Conocí a la Negra Ester	I met Negra Ester
aquí en casa e' Oña	Berta here at Ma'am Berta's house
esta casa llena de puertah	this house full o' door
. . . .	. . . .
Un día por la mañana	One day in the morn
anteh que rayara el sol	b'fore sun brightens sky
máh linda que un arrebol	prettier than red cloud
fresquita como manzana	delish as fresh apple
muy alegre muy ufana	so happy so proud
venía la Negra Ester.	here came Negra Ester.

There were also more subtle memory currents. *La Negra Ester* evoked something of the political spirit of culture that once flourished. It reenacted the idea of culture as preferential option for the poor and the stigmatized, through its humble touring sites and social atmosphere, even while updat-ing the concept via fundraising, for example, for AIDS prevention and edu-cation. Its spirit of bringing theater to the pueblo, and its fusion of folk tradition and quality artistry, evoked the idealism and innovations of theater, music, and art in the 1960s and early 1970s. At this level, *La Negra Ester* celebrated not only the joyful triumph of popular culture over Pinochet, but also a return to the authentic Chile where cultural and political expressive-ness blended.

And yet this was not all. Art that resonates draws people into its multiple layers of meaning. It amounts to an invitation to find and reconstruct the meanings of text and performance. Over time, the process can shift the meaning of what one sees or can see. The undercurrent of betrayal and elusive reconciliation was a leitmotif never far from the surface in *La Negra Ester*. It was an authentic part of popular culture and experience, and dealing with betrayal was also a part of what made women strong and assertive. Did the dance of betrayal and elusive reconciliation in *La Negra Ester* resonate in new ways by the mid-to-late 1990s? Remembrance in Chile had long mingled with notions of treason, betrayal, disappointment—not merely on the Right, which accused the Center and Left of betraying the country during the Frei-Allende era, but also in the Center-Left. The early 1970s versions of treason: Pinochet and the military betrayed Allende and the 1925 Constitution; Leftist leaders took refuge in embassies after bringing their followers to slaughter; Christian Democrats betrayed democracy and the 1925 Constitution. The 1970s and 1980s versions: Pinochet and the military betrayed, through state terror and economic restructuring and rule without end, the original purposes of the 1973 salvation of Chile; Pinochet was not an austere and benevolent patriot, but the head of a corrupt family looting the country like other rich clans; the moderate opposition promoted a political strategy playing into the hands of the regime; the extreme opposition promoted a political strategy playing into the hands of the regime. The 1990s versions: the leaders of the transition are duplicitous; they have not lived up to their promises; they have violated our expectations.[4]

The artistic genius of *La Negra Ester* was that it invited its various publics to experience time travel without resentment. One could enjoy the sheer pleasure of reencountering an authentic Chile—the sorrowful and the delightful, the raucous and the problematic. One could experience the loss of something meaningful and treasured, even something political that had been lost, yet one could also transcend the loss in the joy of an old-style theater party. One was free to notice or set aside darker undercurrents. Memory was no longer only a frustrating experience—a tale of suffering, conflict, and loss, trapped inside Chile's eternal swings between prudence and convulsion. Memory was also pleasurable.

Humor sometimes took direct aim at frustrations or conflicts linked to memory—sensations of history and identity dissolved by the market and the temptations of oblivion, sensations of duplicity and self-censorship imposed by living in a land of "not too much."

In 1996, a brilliant play by Marco Antonio de la Parra, *La pequeña historia de Chile* (The Little History of Chile), presented the impossibility of History in the new Chile.[5] Traumatized by its past and enthralled by its modernization, Chile was ripe for a marketing of life and identity that dissolved the past. The impossibility of History is distilled in the absurd plight of its carriers—the teachers of history at a public school in the provinces. Ghostlike, they might be dead, or alive, or perhaps they are trapped in the purgatory of teaching the irrelevant. The illusionary nature of history teaching—and contemporary life—is immediately evident. In the opening scene, teacher Sanhueza, on top of a sea of student chairs and wrapped in a Chilean flag, seeks to escape persecution. Police sirens wail. The principal tries to restore order and convince Sanhueza to step down. Sanhueza refuses. He will not submit to brainwashing. History teaching cannot compete. "Do you know what these kids get as information? As image of the world?" He will not submit again to playing guard in a juvenile reformatory, nor to teaching what no longer exists. The principal threatens execution and begins the countdown, but Sanhueza remains obstinate. Chile isn't real. History isn't real. The rifles go off; the funeral march begins—but Sanhueza is unaffected. "Even death is a fraud." What can a disillusioned history teacher do? Shrug the flag listlessly and repeat the old slogan, "Viva Chile."

As the play unfolds, the impossibility of History becomes the dilemma of all the teachers, regardless of age or temperament. The map of Chile, the starting point for history teaching, is lost. The teachers act out fantasies and scenes from a violent history at odds with the myths everyone learned and wanted to believe. Since they have lost the flag, they also cannot perform the civic rituals that forge identity in school. The principal dies, and they need to organize some kind of civic act. The solution: an act to revive History. Law will join State and Education in sacred matrimony. After the traditional wedding march, the coupling begins.

> MUÑOZ: Mr. State, do you accept Education as agent of nationality and creator of patriotic consciousness, the future of the country and the riches of wisdom and knowledge as trampoline of progress?
> FREDES: Yes, I accept.
> MUÑOZ: And you, Señora Education, do you accept State as wise and disinterested guide of your principles, without ever renouncing an interest that embraces all of society, complete, just and integrated?
> LOUREIRO: Yes, I accept.

As the poorly paid Sanhueza returns from an unpleasant appointment with a financial services company, Muñoz seals the union. "I unite you in matrimony and I create the Nation of Chile. Sign here, please." State and Education now copulate joyfully, he proclaims, over the land of Chile.

Sanhueza punctures the illusion. He reminds the trio they are not alone. Have they forgotten him, the Market? "I will destroy you both as expensive and inefficient. I will not spend another peso on you. I will tear you apart." Young Fredes announces his manly readiness for combat, "with rectitude and nobility." Sanhueza the Market scoffs, "I will corrupt you with better pay. Credits and debts. . . . Contests. You will give in, you'll see." As they join in combat, a mysterious force overcomes Fredes. He does not understand it.

FREDES: Something has got hold of me, I cannot go on.
SANHUEZA: It is my invisible hand . . . Hallelujah!

In the end, it will be Sanhueza, whose mind always races when he gets in debt, who discovers the solution. "Maybe the problem is our history . . . Maybe we should resist another way." Since the country has no history, why not invent and market a better one? Let Chile become the center of Western civilization, from the Egyptian Pyramids to the French Revolution, from Bach to jazz. And how about a more dignified name? "United States of France."

In the mid-to-late 1990s, indigenous Mapuche communities of the south, concentrated especially in Chile's Ninth Region, became a focal point of conflicts symbolizing a gross imbalance between the social equity aspect of democratic transition, and the drive for economic growth that deferred to investor interests. Tensions between Mapuche groups seeking to claim or reclaim land rights, and a government promoting timber exports and hydroelectric projects, heated up and grew stark in 1996–98. They brought into focus the difficulty of harmonizing distinct logics of the transition—and the fear that the mature Concertación, regardless of its internal political diversity or declared values of specific leaders, now gave primacy to investor projects above all else.

Tension between logics of public policy in the South had long been present, and bore a connection to memory themes. On the one hand, official government policy in the early 1990s inscribed the idea of democratic respect for Mapuche rights, including land restitution and protection of the environment and sacred sites. This approach responded to the reality of pressure from below—a strong Mapuche movement had emerged under military rule and needed to be incorporated into the project of *convivencia*. The policy and pressure from below were also related to the idea of a "social debt" inherited from the dictatorship, and compounded by a longer history of injustice to indigenous peoples since Spanish arrival in the Americas. During the dictatorship, losses of Mapuche lands, division of communities into smaller units, continuing educational neglect, persecutions including deaths and disappearances in activist areas, these constituted a new cycle of injustice—and sparked the indigenous social movement of the 1980s. Now, when conflict arose between investors and indigenous peoples, the public organism CONADI (Corporación Nacional de Desarrollo Indígena, or National Corporation of Indigenous Development), created in the 1990s to promote indigenous rights through grassroots consultation and involvement, was to negotiate property exchanges with assent by the affected families and communities. This logic of social policy was anchored in principles enunciated when Aylwin established a Special Commission of Indigenous Peoples in 1990 to lay a consultative foundation to create a new Indigenous Law, which would be passed in 1993.

On the other hand, political effort and economic favor in the South tilted toward the powerful, and the quality of state effort in support of Mapuches proved dubious. The degree of economic support available to indigenous peoples in the 1990s was modest, the problem compounded by administrative negligence: poor attentiveness to indigenous petitions and to the eligibility of recipients as intended beneficiaries of the law, poor follow-up, and the like. When communities or families did manage to receive lands, whether as restitution or as exchange, the "devil in the details" was lack of effective support via credits, technology, or other assistance to render the lands productive, compounded by slack attention to ecological aspects of community production and land use. In cases of land exchange agreements, grassroots tensions between investors and Mapuches, and among Mapuche families and community factions over acceptance of specific exchange transactions, sometimes turned very strong. Reaching agreement was difficult, even as pressure to assent to investment plans dictated from above was enormous. Meanwhile, the contending parties tried to create de facto realities. Companies advanced projects before final legal rulings; Mapuche activists occupied lands and some seized and burned lumber trucks.

Such circumstances made achieving practical solutions through democratic negotiation and consultation exceptionally difficult. Hydroelectric projects also set several principles against each other: the principle that a minority of holdout families did not have an absolute right of property blocking the public interest of a wider collectivity; the principle that indigenous peoples did have irrenunciable rights to lands they considered sacred or tied to ancestors; the principle that investment projects with major environmental impacts required a calculus of benefit and cost beyond private market measures biased toward private investor interest. Hydroelectric projects gained new urgency after energy shortages in the Chilean summer of 1996–97, even as they also sparked opposition by some Mapuche families who resisted land permutation to compensate for inundation, and by ecology activists. Perhaps no solution-by-agreement could have been found, even had the state mediated skillfully with an even hand and credibility among all parties.

Whatever the case, in 1997–98 the clumsy handling of the massive Ralco hydroelectric project on the upper Bío-Bío River amounted to a declaration by central government that the time had ended for negotiation with Mapuche Pehuenche families, mediated and ratified by CONADI. Fourteen of ninety-eight families still held out against inundation, and the director of CONADI, Mauricio Huenchulaf, a Mapuche of activist background, stated that CONADI was unlikely to approve the project because it had ethnocidal implications. Early in 1997 the administration sacked Huenchulaf. The incoming director, Domingo Namuncura, had a background of human rights activism and was close to Lagos and the Left, but he was appointed without grassroots consultations and considered too compliant with the government by local activists. Yet by 1998 he too had moved toward skepticism on Ralco. In July, Endesa, the Spanish-owned company promoting the Ralco project, sought to create a de facto reality by pressing ahead with site work despite lack of legally necessary approval by CONADI. Early in August, CONADI filed a lawsuit and Namuncura requested a meeting with President Frei to explain his views. The reply: a request for resignation.[6]

For the disenchanted, the Ralco affair fit with sharpening tension about what to believe and remember about the nature of the transition, what to believe about soothing words versus political will at top layers of government. The early Concertación culture had stressed balancing acts. The government presumably sought to balance and blend the logic of achieving democratic stability with that of truth and justice, and the logic of achieving high economic growth with that of social equity. It linked such balancing

16. The joys of "not too much": Minister Lagos: " . . . and so to conclude, dear Pehuenches . . . WE ARE WITH YOU! WE ARE WITH YOU! . . . but not too much. Many thanks." *Credit: Guillo (Guillermo Bastías).*

acts to the goal of convivencia and mounted strong moral defense of stances taken. The mature Concertación, despite increased social spending and continuing decline of poverty, was more haunted by a sense of debilitating impasse and retreat from moral leadership. Credibility and good faith assumptions weakened. The taint could touch any leader. One's words or political location within the Concertación did not matter too much. Chile's brilliant satirist, Guillo, captured the relation of the Ralco affair to euphemism in the land of "not too much." Minister of Public Works Ricardo Lagos, the leader of the Left within the Concertación, addresses a community of Mapuche Pehuenche peoples. The play of mixed letter sizes (in the cartoon bubble) captured the play of mixed messages. " . . . and so to conclude, dear Pehuenches . . . We are with you! We are with you! . . . but not too much. Many thanks."

The impasse of Chile—the structure of constraint and frustration produced by tension between "soft" and "hard" hegemonies—was easier to denounce than to resolve. At bottom, the problem was more than a matter of individual intentions or presidential leadership styles. All kinds of Chileans, at varied points in the political spectrum, experienced tensions between the logic of democratic rule and desire and the logic of inherited constraint. The memory question generated quests for truth and justice that brought the contradiction into sharp focus. The temptation to forget in view of debilitating constraint was strong, but the necessity to remember also proved strong.

For the affliction of memory impasse, lived as continual swings between prudence and convulsion, there was some relief. Entertainment and humor —time travel to a place authentic or nostalgic, laughter at the absurdity of life and the running away from history, the hurling of barbs at the constrained transition—allowed for a more energizing play of identities, self-recognition, critique. In 1996 *Hoy* magazine asked political elites, entrepreneurs, and professionals and artists what they wished for the country's future. Most offered solemn answers. The poet Nicanor Parra offered some imprudent fun. "How would I like to see Chile? / In democracy . . . / I'd like to see it in democracy / I just love asking the impossible." He also reassured readers that whatever else might happen in the next century, something would remain of Chile. The country would be what it had always been: "a house of poets."[7]

Chapter 5

✿

The Turn:
Consequences of 1998

The years 1998–2001 marked a turn in Chilean life—the start of a major unraveling of memory impasse. To understand the turn, an analogy borrowed from the historian and philosopher of science Thomas Kuhn is useful.[1] When a bend on the highway takes the traveler in a new direction, one may see the curve as culmination of movement in an old direction, or as start of movement in a new one. What one sees depends on standpoint. At the point of transition, both views are valid. The leader of a scientific revolution or paradigm shift may have conceded more to the old thinking than meets the eye, especially if controversy about the new thinking kicks up dust. The converse may also hold. A great curve in politicocultural life may generate events that reaffirm the old ways, even as it begins to steer energies in a new direction.

Something of this paradox occurred in 1998 and continued into the new century. The culture of swings between prudence and convulsion was more forcefully present than ever; yet, the events sparking convulsion marked a profoundly changing environment of possibility. A quarter-century of memory struggles had culminated in impasse—more precisely, a climate of impossibility in view of repeated returns to standoff rooted in the gap between soft and hard forms of power, and retreat from the memory question at upper levels of politics and media. The rise of a privatized culture of consumers reinforced the sense of impossibility. If impasse had once "rolled" from one point of contention and standoff to another, by 1997 the old language and terms of memory struggle seemed more futile than ever, more at risk of "freezing" impasse into a ritualistic repetition leading nowhere. The cycle of memory struggles launched in 1973 had yielded a large impact. It had not only created a language of debate about the past within the present, but also shaped politicocultural values and legitimacy. It had galvanized both an enduring base of support for military rule and its legacy, and an opposition that expanded into majority demand for democratic rule. It had ultimately built, notwithstanding great adversity, a culture more sensitized to human rights as an irrenunciable value, and to moral obligation to reckon publicly with the truth of state atrocity. Now, however, that memory cycle was exhausted, giving way to something else. The structural gap between hard and soft forms of power, the ability of high political actors to avoid new public initiatives on the memory question, the language and terms of memory struggle and self-censorship, all began shifting decisively—even as old habits and assumptions also failed to disappear.

THE OLD AND THE NEW, 1998

The great convulsions came in March and October. On 11 March, after retiring as army commander on the last day permitted under his 1980 Constitution, Pinochet took up his post as lifetime senator. Pinochet's ascent to the Senate seemed to reaffirm the rules of the power game and his central role in them. He would continue to hold great de facto political stature, reinforced by protection from prosecution under the 1978 amnesty and Senatorial immunity, by army loyalty and other military-police loyalties, and by a Right economically strong and politically fortified through the quota of nonelected Senate seats and the binomial electoral system. As senator, he retained a platform as a commanding figure in public life. In short, he would continue as the ultimate guarantor of the rules of transition and, if necessary to stop a slippery slope effect on justice matters: impasse.

Not surprisingly, Pinochet's oath-of-office ceremony produced the familiar swing between official calls for prudence and calm, and memory convulsion. Several thousand people—Christian Democratic and Left youth, human rights activists, and ordinary citizens aroused by rage or disgust—converged on Congress in Valparaíso to shout their rejection of Pinochet, remembrance of the executed and the disappeared, and support for a constitutional accusation to strip Pinochet of legal right to join the Senate. Inside, a group of deputies and senators with posters bearing faces of the disappeared and executed suddenly appeared, pushed their way past guards, sang the national anthem, and pointed fingers accusingly. Deputy Isabel Allende bore the picture of her father, Salvador Allende. (The famous writer of the same name was Allende's niece.) Some conservative senators walked over to Pinochet to offer support, and a fistfight broke out. Outside the tensions also mounted. Carabineros used clubs to beat demonstrators who sought to go inside—Sola Sierra, president of the relatives of the disappeared, suffered head wounds. Farther from the entrance, some youths tried to push past police barricades with rocks and sticks. Carabineros used water cannons and tear gas to drive crowds away, while protesters set fire to barricades along Pedro Montt Avenue, the street in front of Congress. To *La Epoca*, the major pro-Concertación newspaper, the fires, tear gas, and sirens created a "battle atmosphere"—a 1980s street protest scene brought back to life. Santiago was similarly convulsive. A month later, however, prudence prevailed. The lower house rejected—by secret vote—the constitutional accusation against Pinochet for illegitimate political intervention during the 1990s. His prominence and immunity as senator remained intact.[2]

In October, memory again galvanized a convulsion, with Pinochet once more the central figure. The unthinkable happened on 16 October. Scotland Yard police arrested Pinochet at the London Clinic, where he was recovering from herniated disc surgery. Pinochet had gone to England in September for business (consulting on arms manufacture and sales) and a bit of tourism. He liked London and hoped to visit Napoleon's tomb in France. Now eighty-two years old, he also sought medical advice for his ailing back. He was aware of the judicial cases in Spain, where Judges Baltazar Garzón and Manuel García Castellón investigated charges against the former military juntas of Argentina and Chile, respectively, for genocide, international terrorism, torture, and disappearance of persons. But the cases seemed a mere irritant. As a former head of state and as a senator with a diplomatic passport, he did not take universal jurisdiction seriously. In truth, Chilean activists who pressed for the doctrine in 1996–97 had held only limited hope for success. By 13 October, news of Pinochet's presence and imminent departure leaked and sparked a flurry of activity to persuade Tony Blair's Labor government to consider Pinochet accountable, under British and international law, to justice proceedings in Spain. Judge García Castellón sought permission to take a statement; Amnesty International and other human rights groups, and some members of Parliament, pushed for arrest. The decisive technical step came on 15 October, when Judge Garzón requested, through Interpol, Pinochet's arrest as a suspect in crimes of genocide and terrorism including murder of Spaniards, and to testify on Operation Condor, the transnational scheme of South American dictatorships to detain, disappear, and kill people targeted by the secret police of their home countries.[3]

In Chile, the arrest provoked shock, convulsion—and pleas for restraint.

On 17 October, several hundred pro-Pinochet supporters converged on the Spanish and British Embassies to sing the national anthem, shout protests, and throw eggs, fruit, and rocks. Some broke windows at the Spanish Embassy. The next day some 3,000 protesters converged on the homes of the British and Spanish ambassadors. Over the next week, tension continued to build, with pro-Pinochet and anti-Pinochet demonstrations. Pinochet's fate dominated television news, radio talk shows, and print media. Rumors of intra-army tension and a possible military alert were squelched. Political recriminations broke out. Pinochetistas claimed that Chilean Socialists had masterminded an international conspiracy against Chile. Center-Left voices accused Pinochetista politicians and demonstrators of overreacting and polarizing the country, making governability and a civilized solution more difficult. A few leftist political leaders and Carmen Soria, daughter of the murdered Spanish diplomat Carmelo Soria, received anonymous death threats. Symbolic politics took hold. Street theater activists taunted an imprisoned Pinochet, dressed in prison stripes and pleading for mercy. Conservative municipal officials suspended garbage pickup at the British and Spanish Embassies. Chilean volunteers organized teams to haul away the garbage.

Meanwhile, pleas for calm were accompanied by declarations that Chile's legal rights and rules of transition, peculiar and therefore subject to world misunderstanding, would be explained, defended, and restored. The Chilean ambassador to Great Britain, Mario Artaza, argued that the British mistakenly interpreted international law, violated the sovereignty of Chilean law and diplomatic immunity for legislators, and "opened old wounds" that could bring harm to a "young democracy." Top officials joined in. President Frei stated he expected a solution from Britain "shortly." Foreign Minister (and prominent Socialist) José Miguel Insulza said the government would consider pushing not only legal arguments, but also a return of Pinochet for "humanitarian reasons." (Pinochet had diabetes and used a pacemaker.) Interior Minister Raúl Troncoso reminded citizens that "this is not the time for passions." The new army commander in chief, General Ricardo Izurieta, met with officers and declared army concern for Pinochet but also sought to tamp down rumors of irregular military alerts. The army welcomed the government's diplomatic activity and stance and would use proper means— "the government's channels for collaborating and cooperating"—to bring Pinochet back to Chile.[4]

On 22 October, Frei went on television to ask Chileans to think of the big picture. He contended with a situation both ironic and difficult. He was the head of a Center-Left government whose base included opponents and victims of Pinochet, yet whose diplomatic stance pressed for an end to detention. His government argued that Chilean courts were the proper vehicle to pursue justice, yet their historical track record had been Pinochet-ismo and at best inconsistent resolve and jurisprudence. Against this back-drop, he sought to frame context and draw distinctions that explained the government's priorities, diplomatic stance, and call for calm. As president he had to protect "a future of civilized convivencia." His government "defends principles, not given persons." At stake were two precepts of law: "diplomatic immunity and the sovereignty of our courts to judge crimes committed in our country." The high emotions of the moment were "natural and understandable," but people should also remember the value of calm. Violent conduct, hateful sentiment, and aggressive actions against friendly nations were counterproductive. "We need, especially at this hour, the respect of the international community," through "honorable action" in the proper legal and diplomatic channels. Chile's democratic transition was not perfect, but one ought not throw away what had been achieved through "much effort and sacrifices."[5]

Only six days later, government insistence on calm defense of sovereignty seemed to have paid off. The London High Court ruled the arrest warrant and the extradition request invalid. Pinochet had been head of state at the time of the alleged crimes, wrote Law Chief Justice Lord Bingham, and "is entitled to immunity as a former sovereign from British criminal and civil process." Even the legal charter for the 1945 Nuremberg War Crimes Tribunal had not overturned the principle that one state "will not impugn another in relation to its sovereign acts." The ruling would be stayed, pending possible appeal by the Crown Prosecution Service to the Law Lords, a higher panel drawn from the House of Lords. As Chileans reacted with protest and celebration, Interior Minister Troncoso appealed for calm and said he expected a speedy resolution.[6]

The convulsions of March and October were on one level the latest incidents in a familiar story—tension and quick swings between prudence and convulsion, understandable as a product of deep division and "intimate impasse" over memory. On another level, however, they marked and pushed along the exhaustion of the old scheme. Even before the Pinochet detention, the sustainability of memory impasse was weakening notably. One strategic aspect was institutional. The military and the judiciary had served in the early

1990s to set legal and de facto limits—barricades—against the expansion of truth-and-justice work. By 1998, however, generational reform and renovation of both institutions had become unavoidable. Pinochet's ascension to the Senate was *also* his stepping down from command of the army, and the stepping up of a new commander. General Ricardo Izurieta's climb was a political operation premised on a new profile for the armed forces, based on a revised sense of its corporate interest. Pinochet's and the elder officers' personal interests and legacy would not be equated quite so readily with institutional interests. Modernization and professionalization of the armed forces would become the overriding priority. A new public relations stance would emphasize harmonious collaboration with civilian government superiors and cast aside the albatross of a polemical past. The grip of the elder military generation and its memory problem had to fade, if the armed forces were to recover prestige and advance technology and training.[7]

Under the skilled leadership of the minister of justice, Soledad Alvear, major judicial reform also began in 1998. It drew broad backing in Congress and among business groups. Alvear framed the larger purpose as modernization. To remake a judiciary notorious for lentitude and lack of transparency, inconsistent and mediocre jurisprudence, and a culture of clientelism harmful to meritorious promotion and to external access ungreased by personal influence or corruption, reform in alignment with international standards was necessary. Without it, Chile could not deepen investor confidence or continue strong socioeconomic development and competitiveness. A modernized judiciary would presumably improve ordinary citizen satisfaction and expectation, too. Alvear eventually won support from much of the judiciary, by wooing judges as allies within a beneficial project of upgrading—and by making clear that reform was the price judges had to pay to receive an infusion of state funding their branch sorely needed. In sum, the driving discourse and strategy were no longer the confrontation with Pinochetismo and judicial doctrine on human rights that marked the early 1990s. Such confrontations had not produced a reform, although they softened up sectors of the judiciary for accommodation to a democratic era and fostered experiment with new interpretive doctrine. An important and welcome byproduct of the Frei-Alvear reform, however, was precisely the demise of the judiciary as a bulwark of Pinochetismo and impunity. For the Supreme Court, the reforms included mandatory retirement—without a "grandfather clause"—at age seventy-five, expansion of seats from seventeen to twenty-one, and a quota of five seats to distinguished external jurists who had not come up through the judiciary's promotion system. The short-term practical effects were strong: ten new Supreme Court jurists in 1998, definitive disintegration of Pinochetista hegemony within the Court, new openings in Appellate Court posts vacated by promotion to the Supreme Court, declining deference to military tribunals and to the 1978 amnesty as justification for early closure of cases.[8]

The weakening of the two institutional bulwarks—military and judicial—facilitated a new strategy by victims and human rights lawyers that also took hold in 1998. They took direct aim at Pinochet in criminal complaints in Chilean court. In effect, they tested his power as lame-duck commander and as ex-commander to count on judicial prudence or indifference. Gladys Marín and the Communist Party began the trend in January with a complaint on charges of genocide, homicide, and kidnapping, among other crimes. After Pinochet stepped down as army commander in chief, criminal complaints accelerated—at least fourteen were filed by the end of the year, most *before* the London arrest. The plaintiffs came from varied directions: leftist political parties (Socialist and Communist), organized associations of relatives of victims (the disappeared and the executed), professional associations and trade unions (teachers, nurses, metal workers, journalists), relatives of victims who came together specifically for the complaint. On 20 January, Judge Juan Guzmán allowed Marín's case to proceed, under a doctrine that undermined the practical effect of the 1978 amnesty. Legally, disappearance cases amounted to an act of kidnapping whose unresolved character—no established date of death or release—meant the crime continued permanently, with effects into the present. For Pinochet, this was a new slippery slope and the old formula, troop alerts to reimpose impasse, was out of reach.[9]

Politically, too, the old scheme and premises of transition were reaching a point of exhaustion. The debacle of the 1997 congressional elections (see chapter 4) was compounded by an unfavorable economic horizon, and awareness of an approaching presidential election in December 1999. The ripple effect of financial crisis in East Asia brought an end to the Concertación's spectacular high-growth cycle. In 1998, for the first time since 1990, economic growth dipped below 5 percent. The sharp second-half slide pushed unemployment up—to 7.2 percent by October 1998, and at its peak, 11.5 percent in June 1999. The likely presidential candidates also unsettled earlier premises. The most probable conservative candidate was Joaquín Lavín, from the UDI (Unión Democrática Independiente). Lavín, the youngish dynamic mayor of Las Condes (an upscale municipality in greater Santiago), had a can-do reputation and complemented it with the symbolic distance he drew from Pinochetismo. Lavín met with relatives of the disappeared to understand their travail, visited *pobladores* and slept in their homes, and declared the military period a matter that belonged to the past. As an attractive voice of a pragmatic, effective, and compassionate Right, Lavín was well positioned to capitalize on the disillusion evident in the 1997 elections. The most probable Concertación candidate was Ricardo Lagos. The leader of the Left pole of the coalition, Lagos had an obvious interest in projecting a break with debilitating sensations of impasse and complacency that had begun to haunt the Concertación. The prospect of a Lavín candidacy with a real chance to win—and a Socialist as the alternative—fed interest by the Right in ending a reputation for obstructionism on human rights. Why push away voters who might otherwise be tempted to abandon the Concertación?[10]

Significantly, signs of politicocultural searching for a fresh way out of memory impasse emerged even before Pinochet's detention in October. As the September memory season approached, political elites embarked on a theater of *gestos*—gestures declaring the time to retreat from efforts to hegemonize collective memory. Chileans needed to accept that differences in visions of the past were normal, that persons had reasons for the truths they perceived, that they need not flaunt their own memory-truths in the face of others. By accepting a more privatized culture of plural memories—everyone held an experience of the tragedy of 1973 and its aftermath, no one need push a collective meaning into the public culture—Chileans could find a larger unity. The most dramatic moment came on 19 August, when agreement between Pinochet and the Christian Democratic Senate president, Andrés Zaldívar, led to unanimous approval of a law to abolish the 11 September anniversary as a national holiday after 1998. A new "Day of National Unity" would be celebrated on first Mondays of September. Pinochet's last-minute agreement enabled him to pose as the political star and king maker —and as statesman who sacrificed his deep attachment to *el once*, for him the day of Chile's second independence, to help the nation overcome its violent memory division. The message between the lines was that he would continue to shape key turns in national life and perhaps boost Zaldívar as a presidential alternative to the leftist Lagos and the disloyal Lavín. The reality, however, was that his power and ability to sustain impasse were weakening.

The proposal to abolish the 11 September holiday had led to repeated tie votes. The technical rules meant that one more tie vote would put the matter into a congressional conference committee and on track for approval. Pinochet's late maneuver aimed to salvage appearances and political capital.[11]

A dance of gestures followed. The air force, navy, and carabineros announced they would abandon immediately public commemorative acts to mark the 11 September anniversary. General Izurieta declared the army would simply hold a private mass to pray for all who fell on the eleventh. The older practice was to invite civilian guests and journalists to ceremonies and masses that recalled thankfully the salvation of Chile. Surviving members of the personal bodyguard of Allende (known as GAP, or Grupo de Amigos Personales) announced they wished to talk with Izurieta and other army officers. They hoped to clarify the fate of GAP comrades, to meet with families of soldiers who fell under GAP fire and explain their obligation to defend an elected president, and to propose an act honoring young soldiers who had fallen.[12]

The dance of memory gestures was an effort to find a way out of familiar dynamics and sterile repetitive standoff, but it could not excise tough issues at the core of memory conflict. On 3 September Pinochet complained on Radio Cooperativa that his unity gesture had gone unreciprocated by the Left. "We have already done a gesture: we erased the Eleventh . . . But they have not made any gesture." Concertación and Left leaders responded that Pinochet's appeal for a gesture was disingenuous. It ignored enormous efforts made to reconcile the country, including acceptance of a disliked Constitution. It sidestepped a true gesture of reconciliation: information on the fate and remains of the disappeared.[13]

On 8 September, Santiago's archbishop, Francisco Javier Errázuriz, put a religious stamp on the new atmosphere. Before political and military dignitaries assembled for a mass of reconciliation and unity making, he made the observation: various leaders "intuit that we face signs and challenges that we ought not let pass, because they invite us to advance on the path of unity, solidarity, and peace." The task was to view recent history not at the surface level of politics, facts, and responsibilities, but in its deep human dimension. Chileans exhibited a paradox. A generous people, they valued "respect and concord" and could show great solidarity with those in need. But they also tended "to affirm ideas and plans forcefully as something absolute . . . Suddenly there is no truth other than one's own, nor solutions to conflicts other than one's own." Taken to an extreme, the tendency "can poison consciousness and convivencia" and this was what happened before and after 11 September 1973. Its consequences "filled with suffering and mourning entire families, vast sectors of society, and [eventually] the entire national community." Criminal acts of torture, killing, and elimination, he said, had claimed "our brothers," some of them members of military or police forces but most often political or grassroots leaders. They were "without any justification." The time had come for "new initiatives" to find the remains of the disappeared, and to pray for those who "in hours of blind rage and inhuman passion vented themselves against their brothers and sisters." The press reported that Archbishop Errázuriz thought a new initiative, perhaps with Church assistance, could yield information on the whereabouts of the disappeared.[14]

The difficulty of moving past memory impasse was obvious in the absences. Frei and Izurieta attended along with other high political and military figures, but to avoid a walkout Pinochet was uninvited. To avoid a possible walkout by Socialists, Lagos was also absent (presumably with a cold or flu). Some relatives of victims attended as individuals, but human rights groups, including the Agrupación de Familiares de Detenidos-Desaparecidos (Association of Relatives of the Detained and Disappeared, hereinafter Agrupación), declined to attend officially. Skeptical activists who organized a "Movement for National Dignity" feared that the new climate of elite gestures would turn into a trap—ratification of judicial impunity in exchange for unreliable information. When 11 September arrived, serious street violence broke out in Santiago amidst controversy about aggressive repression, with water cannon trucks, tear gas, and an overhead helicopter, of a crowd assembling to march by the disappeared door (Morandé 80) of La Moneda. The toll: 2 dead, 77 wounded, 327 arrested. Meanwhile, at the Military Academy a group of young Pinochetista demonstrators chanted loyalty to their hero and whistled disapproval of General Izurieta when he arrived for the private army mass.[15]

What was unmistakable in the atmosphere of September 1998 was the sense that even for elites, memory impasse had to give way to something new. One aspect of the new climate was an opening—under pressure by a culture of disenchantment, by the approach of a new presidential election, by generational renovation in the judiciary and the military—to float new initiatives to transcend the familiar dialogue of the deaf. At this level the most specific ideas came in newspaper editorials by two leading intellectuals of the Rettig Commission: Gonzalo Vial and José Zalaquett. Zalaquett argued that "gestures" would not suffice if two pending tasks were not addressed. First, maximum effort to discover the remains of the disappeared, he affirmed, "is an inescapable moral duty for a nation that wants to call itself civilized." Like Vial, he believed the time had arrived to revisit an earlier Rettig Commission proposal—criminalization of cover-up, with practical incentives to do the right thing. Covering up the crime of disappearance by failing to provide knowledge should be a crime, while offering information should bestow on the witness a guarantee of anonymity. The recent experience of the South African truth commission, in which 7,000 perpetrators provided information on political crimes in exchange for amnesty, suggested that incentives could work. Second, it was still necessary that the military "recognize what happened and reaffirm healthy military doctrine." The armed forces need not apologize for the coup itself, whose inevitability or necessity remained a point of debate, but they needed to recognize and reject the systematic practice of killing defenseless prisoners. The practice "is not morally debatable, but rather absolutely violates law, morality and military honor." Continued institutional silence "is equivalent to tacitly accepting the perverse doctrine that [killing defenseless prisoners] is permissible." Failing to acknowledge and reject the practice would damage the military and the country "because we are going through a foundational historical phase." Acts of commission and omission in this period would shape the moral code of the future.[16]

The shifting judicial environment also fed the pressure for new initiatives. On 4 September, the Supreme Court reversed the dismissal by a military court of a case against seven former CNI (secret police) agents for murder of three MIRistas in 1984. The evidence called into question the shootout narrative accepted at face value by military judges. On 10 September, in the case of Pedro Poblete Córdova, a MIRista detained and disappeared by the DINA in 1974, the Court cited Chile's ratification of the Third Geneva Convention of 1949—technically applicable because the junta's Decree No. 5 declared a state of internal war—to overturn the amnesty earlier prescribed by a military court. Like Judge Guzmán when he equated disappearance with permanent kidnapping, the Court was moving toward doctrine that undermined the practical effect of the 1978 amnesty. Only a day later, Foreign Minister Insulza underscored the relevance of international law at a ceremony in Rome. Chile signed on to the treaty to create an International Criminal Court for crimes of war and crimes against humanity.[17]

Another aspect of the new atmosphere, more subtle than elite gesture and initiative, involved cultural expressions of desire to break away from old schemes. At this level, too, September 1998 mixed the old and the new. On the one hand, the quarter-century anniversary of the coup sparked a flurry of familiar memory season activities. In La Victoria, pobladores remembered their beloved priest André Jarlan with a mass and other cultural activities. In Arica, Valparaíso, Viña del Mar, Concepción, Temuco, and Valdivia, as well as Santiago and other cities, persons gathered to remember with candle lightings (*velatones*), marches, and masses. The quarter-century moment also sparked a boom in memory books, both favorable and critical, about the 1973 crisis, Allende, and the military past.[18]

On the other hand, not all expressions of remembrance lined up with the frameworks of salvation, rupture, or persecution that had dominated memory struggles in the past. On 4 September, Chile's customary presidential election day before 1973, some 60,000 people—the majority young, especially in the cheaper seats—streamed into the National Stadium for a musical festival to celebrate the memory of Salvador Allende. The notable aspect of the atmosphere was the determination *not* to concentrate mainly on loss, nostalgia, or persecution, but to be joyous: to delight in the mystique of a pre-1973 time, when people believed they had a right to dream, to be happy, and to have hope. In memory frameworks aligned with opposition to military rule, the pre-1973 years had long been a delicate matter. They played the role of prologue to disaster. They inspired not only sentiments of learning from one's mistakes, but also shame and discretion—the latter to avoid reactivating discord within the Center-Left, and to avoid playing into the hands of those who used the pre-1973 years to justify salvation of a Chile in ruins. Now, the point was to find in the Chile of Allende some values and experiences worth remembering and treasuring, above all in times of disenchantment and frustration. Celebrated musical groups such as Inti-Illimani, Congreso, and Sol y Lluvia, and individual artists such as Patricio Manns, León Gieco, Joan Manuel Serrat, and Isabel and Angel Parra, pulled protest memory toward the celebratory.[19]

A NEW MEMORY ENVIRONMENT, 1998–2000 (I): MEDIA AND EXPRESSION

Mass media exemplified the paradoxical element—uncertain interplay of old and new, suffocating inhibition and groundbreaking initiative—of the turn in memory culture initiated in 1998. On the one hand, a freer expressive climate did take hold and stoked a new memory environment, and media developments were a part of this story. On the other hand, concentration of ownership, ideological conformity, and habits of self-censorship fostered journalistic timidity, especially in the most influential and accessible media. Mass media reacted to new "memory knots" that remade the cultural landscape, and thereby contributed to the shifting expressive climate, but—with notable exceptions—did not play a lead role as initiator or investigator.

The retreat of government from the memory question during the mid-to-late 1990s was matched by erosion of diversity and boldness in news media. In the print media market, commercial advertising flowed heavily to just two ownership groups—the *El Mercurio* chain secured some 70 percent of newspaper advertising revenue in 1997–98, while the COPESA (Consorcio Periodístico de Chile, S.A.) group and its flagship newspaper, *La Tercera*, secured some 16 percent. Government policy (with the exception of the official newspaper, *La Nación*) avoided indirect subsidies, such as placement of government notices or public service ads to bolster weaker media in the interest of greater pluralism. For media that once played a bold muckraking and investigatory role in opposing military rule and pushing memory-truths for a new democracy, the deepest dilemma was not simply market share and hostility of the business class, but also the cultural transformation of Chile and its malaise of halfway sensibilities. In a culture of ambivalence—caught between desire and constraint on the memory question, between embrace and disillusion on the high-growth modernization model—what constituted a new and imaginative editorial strategy to grow one's audience and secure a viable market niche? The government was no longer tyrannical. It was an undertaking of partial achievement and partial failure, within a context of real and perhaps imagined constraint. Editorial impulses mixed desire to criticize and to support. Habits of self-censorship made a comeback, fostered by fears of political instability, legal harassment, or lost advertising. Ironically, the main newspapers and magazines that diversified and rattled the public domain in the 1980s had trouble surviving in democracy. By 1995, *Análisis, Apsi, Cauce,* and *Fortín Mapocho* had all closed. *La Epoca* and *Hoy* finally succumbed in 1998.[20]

Debilitation in broadcast media markets was more subtle. Radio Cooperativa, the radio station with the most dynamic news tradition, still ranked high in 1996–98. But between 1990 and 1996, its share fell back (13.3 to 4.9) toward the levels of other leading stations. The television market changed substantially with the international cable revolution. But investment and dynamism were channeled to entertainment, not news. Among free network channels, Televisión Nacional had the strongest news tradition, in terms of human experience and national audience reach. Its news programming was solid but also stolid, no longer driven by the aggressive, groundbreaking style of the Aylwin years. A certain cautiousness had set in. The reality of a politically negotiated directorate and greater accommodation to the politicocultural climate was brought home by a reshuffling of internal leadership after 1993—Jorge Navarrete and Patricia Politzer were pushed out. In December 1997 Patricio Guzmán complained he had run into boundaries of the permissible. His new documentary, *Chile: Obstinate Memory*, had won first prize at the Florence Film Festival and aired on French and German television. But Chilean media were afraid to broadcast it, and Televisión Nacional's executives had spoken bluntly. "They told me that the time is not right . . . that I should have no illusion about it."[21]

Yet despite the ways major media reflected the state of memory impasse to which Chile had arrived by 1997, they did not escape the stirrings and convulsions of 1998. As we have seen, expressions of new desire and necessity to break away from memory impasse were crystallizing on a number of fronts by September—and included newsworthy events by elites. It goes too far to reduce all changes in memory politics and culture after 1998 to Pinochet's detention in October. Nonetheless, the detention became a huge factor in its own right, like an exceptionally powerful catalyst that speeds up an agonizingly slow chemical reaction. For news media, the detention created an irresistible memory knot—an obligation to report and an eager audience.

The catalyst did not quickly disappear. The 28 October ruling that granted Pinochet sovereign immunity by the London High Court turned out to be a mirage. A drama of uncertain twists and turns unfolded. Consider a few highlights. On 25 November 1998 the Law Lords reversed the sovereign immunity ruling. Crimes against humanity could not constitute a legitimate sovereign function. On 17 December they decided to reconsider all over again, because of links between Amnesty International and a member of the November panel. On 24 March 1999 they rejected sovereign immunity—but narrowed the technical basis to torture acts committed after 29 September 1988, the date Britain incorporated into national law the United Nations Anti-Torture Convention. On and on the legal case went. Meanwhile, Pino-

17. Pinochet in London before the arrest. The respectable gentle-
man poses for an article that will appear in the *New Yorker*.
Credit: Steve Pyke/Contour by Getty Images/Courtesy of
The New Yorker.

chet lived under house arrest in a mansion at Virginia Water, near London,
and Chilean exiles and human rights sympathizers mobilized periodic noisy
demonstrations on site to shout out his criminality and their disgust. The
British phase of the drama kept going nearly seventeen months. Finally, on 2
March 2000, Home Secretary Jack Straw ruled Pinochet could return to
Chile—not because extradition lacked merit but because his deteriorating
health, especially ministrokes in 1999, presumably rendered him mentally
unfit for trial.[22]

18. After the arrest. The notorious criminal is taunted by demonstrators who go to his temporary living site in a Virginia Water mansion. *Credit: Florencia Mallon.*

The transformation of Pinochet from an untouchable political star into a criminal suspect in the eyes of the "civilized world" and its law exerted a profound effect inside Chile. It accelerated and brought to a head the sluggish tendencies, of uncertain effect, evident before October 1998. Pinochet returned to a Chile with a substantially altered memory environment. In this different Chile, he was a diminished politicocultural figure, unable to dominate public life or to enforce memory impasse as a protective shield. Something important had unraveled, and media reaction was a part of the new state of play.

Pinochet's detention was a classic "memory knot" on the social body. For months it fed an outpouring of memory—not only in street protests and demonstrations, but also in media and websites. The Pinochet case dominated television, radio, and print news continuously into early 1999. Only slowly did the case and related memory themes turn into a more intermittent story.[23]

The reawakening of memory converged with the take off of Internet technology. Telecommunications deregulation in 1995 sparked competition, falling telephone rates, and an explosion of Internet hosts and users. To be sure, important obstacles—price, market size, institutional factors—had hampered the growth rate in 1996–97, and maldistribution of income created a gap between the minority of Internet "haves" and the "have-nots." Nonetheless, vehicles of news and memory communication were beginning to change in the culturally influential world of universities, media, and middle-class information. Between 1994 and 1997, Internet servers rose from 1,703 to 19,218, computer stock from 369,000 to 653,000. By mid-1998, the Internet edition of *La Tercera*—its market strategy now included replacing the defunct *La Epoca* as the leading newspaper for human rights stories and online communication—was receiving 60,000 daily hits. By 1999, a quarter of homes with telephones in Santiago had at least one person connected to the Internet at home, school, or work.[24]

When the Pinochet detention story broke, *La Tercera*'s online edition quickly developed a link to track the case, and a comment forum. A transnational memory flood ensued. In three months readers sent over 1,600 letters—a majority were exile voices, a third domestic Chilean voices. Two-thirds were anti-Pinochetista, a fourth Pinochetista, a tenth ambiguous. A minority (7.0 percent) took an extra step: they wrote *testimonio*, personal memory stories to tell a larger memory-truth. "I can't stop remembering the times [of the Unidad Popular] and the long lines with my 11-month-old son at 10 at night to buy 1 kilo of meat." The signature: "from someone grateful to Pinochet." A survivor held in the National Stadium in 1973, when it was turned into a giant prison camp, remembered not only the brutality of junta rule, but poignant solidarity among prisoners. "One cold September night, Mario, a worker accused of hiding explosives, would be carted off for the third time for interrogation . . . Teacher, he said to me, take your blanket, I don't need it anymore; tonight they are taking me to the Cerros de Chena, from which no one returns."

As authors built bridges between "loose" personal experiences and "emblematic" turning of the particular into a symbol of a larger memory-truth, they spoke bluntly about the situation in England. Concluded the former prisoner, "For the 7,000 prisoners, we who were in the National Stadium and never shouted 'goal,' let me celebrate this 'CHILEAN GOAL' of the English."[25]

The reactivating of memory was like a relentless storm—hurling wind, rain, and objects against the wall of silence. A dramatic example occurred in April 1999, when tensions between Pinochetistas and former DINA head Manuel Contreras broke out into the open. Was the code of loyal mutual silence falling apart? Press reports held that loyalists close to Pinochet thought Contreras sought to diminish his legal jeopardy by sending documents to Judge Garzón implicating Pinochet in Operation Condor. Contreras's son, Manuel Contreras Valdebenito, declared on television that claims of ignorance by Pinochet and current army leaders about their "war" and its victims were absurd. "My father had breakfast every day with General Pinochet during four years. . . . I cannot understand that General Pinochet could say today 'I have no idea.'"[26]

The Chile Declassification Project approved by the Bill Clinton administration contributed to the buzz of revelations. A few declassified documents offered truly new findings. Others clarified the basis for earlier U.S. congressional findings in 1975 on intervention in Chilean politics up to 1973. The project, announced in December 1998, was itself a symptom of new pressure to expand globalization beyond economic relations—to include memory and justice reckonings. Diplomatic need on the part of the United States to avoid flat obstructionism stemmed not only from the Pinochet affair and associated legal requests in Spain and Britain, but also from war crime and genocide issues in the Balkans and Rwanda, the rhetoric of opposition to international terrorism, and the 1998 Rome treaty to create a war crimes tribunal. Domestic pressure also emerged, from human rights activists including Joyce Horman and Elizabeth Horman—widow and mother, respectively, of Charles Horman, a U.S. citizen and victim of the junta—and from the legacy of Pinochet and his regime as an icon in world culture. There were sympathetic officials in Congress and the administration (as well as Britain) who had come of age politically in the 1960s–1970s. Among the domestic network of NGOs advocating human rights, moreover, the National Security Archive was very adept with the Freedom of Information Act and very committed to the inside history of Chile and the United States.[27]

The documents, released in stages between February 1999 and November 2000, included sensitive disclosures about events *after* the 1973 coup. The complex dance of collaboration, information exchange, conflict, and duplicity between the DINA's Contreras and the CIA yielded an astonishing moment. In mid-1975 Contreras was placed on the CIA payroll as an informant. He received one payment—before a countermanding order, more sensitive to official policy and possible political embarrassment, took effect. Revelations were not limited to the 1970s. In December 1989 a CIA report held that the CNI chief operating officer, Major Alvaro Corbalán, was exploring with "friends" of the Pinochet family the possibility of blocking the transition. How? They would assassinate President-elect Aylwin.[28]

The barrage of memory knots—events demanding attention to the past within the present—had their impact on media culture. Televisión Nacional focused a special edition of its news magazine program, *Informe Especial*, on the United States documents. The main theme was intervention by the United States in Chilean politics between 1964 and 1973, but the hooks were the utterly new and grotesque memory facts—Contreras on the CIA payroll in 1975, a plot to kill Aylwin in 1989, Contreras agents infiltrating the Frente Patriótico sector that killed Jaime Guzmán in 1991.[29]

Electronic vehicles of expression broadened the kinds of relevant memory information available. In 1998 human rights and Pinochetista websites began to appear. By 1999 they had multiplied, not only as an added feature of established print media, but as a strategy for groups seeking to project their memory voice. In July 1999, the Villa Grimaldi Peace Park organizers launched "a true interactive book" to recuperate the full humanity of disappeared persons. In addition to the admirable values that turned them into targets of repression, the victims would be remembered as "guitarists, dancers, painters, boyfriends and girlfriends [*novios*], teachers, cyclists, soccer players, musicians, fathers and mothers." Documents would include moving artifacts, such as the teenage diary of the prisoner María Cristina López Stewart. In October "Derechos Chile," a human rights site established with Ford Foundation assistance in 1998, supplemented its own "map of memory" with nineteen human rights "links of interest" in Chile and internationally, and eleven more on the Pinochet detention. Meanwhile, the Augusto Pinochet Foundation offered its own electronic memory map. The tour of Chile's salvation included a link to "unpublished photos of the thousand black days of the Allende government."[30]

By 2000 the most dynamic newspaper in Chile was not a print medium, but the online publication "El Mostrador." Its reporters' ability to ferret out sensitive documents and its avoidance of a paid subscription strategy (until late in 2001) gave it importance beyond direct circulation. Its memory scoops and breaking of taboo meant newsworthiness—secondhand reporting by other media, and broadening lines of cultural inquiry and judicial risk. On 11 October 2000, for example, Senator Carmen Frei announced her family had reason to wonder if secret police agents had introduced a bacterium causing the death in 1982 of her father, the former president Eduardo Frei Montalva. Only a week later "El Mostrador" published secret intelligence documents in the 1990s on the mysterious death in Uruguay of the DINA expert on biological poisoning—the agent Eugenio Berríos—and asked why the Concertación government failed to follow up aggressively on its own information.[31]

The emerging online culture of news, comment, and documentary links was not the only sign of a freer expressive climate. The spate of memory books included notable new *testimonios*. The Socialist leader Camilo Escalona, aroused, he said, by "shame for my country" when he saw government defense of Pinochet in London, published a blunt self-critique of the transition. The writer Adolfo Cozzi Figueroa shared a youth story—his 1973 imprisonment at the National Stadium, when he was nineteen years old. The celebrated human rights journalist Patricia Verdugo finally told her own story—the struggle to find the truth about the arrest and assassination of her father, Sergio Verdugo Herrera, a Christian Democratic trade unionist. Video rental culture countered the television blockage of Patricio Guzmán's documentary *Chile: Obstinate Memory*. The film became a popular item in youth culture and arts festivals, and aired in commercial theaters in October 2000.[32]

In 1999, an irreverent bimonthly newspaper began to appear at kiosks. Its title—*The Clinic*—alluded brilliantly to the event that liberated cultural expression. Its editorial style and success demonstrated a new market: journalistic absurdism for the age of ridiculous news. Parodies of mainstream media, sarcastic headlines, and mock stories told the politicocultural truth by laughing at it. A feature on "the 100 least influential figures in Chile" spoofed media obsession with the rich and famous. Number 5 on the list: Lucía González. Twelve years of begging for coins outside churches had garnered her a spot right at the Cathedral, and the expertise to opine "about priests, religion, the faithful and . . . her Catholic-Satanic past." A front-page headline said more about the memory question than a solemn treatise. Controversy had surrounded Pinochet's medical exams and alleged feeble health in London. His vigor upon returning to Chile in March 2000—he stood up and raised his cane high to salute supporters—added fuel to the fire. *The Clinic* distilled controversy and memory of dictatorship into a head-line: "PINOCHET DONATES ARMORED WHEELCHAIR AND 45-CALIBER CRUTCHES." Mockery mingled with straight coverage, such as documents on torture and essays by relatives on the personalities, habits, and values of disappeared individuals.[33]

Not all changed, and not all that changed did so right away. Media (notwith-standing a few exceptions) tended to follow rather than initiate the broaden-ing of cultural expression and awareness, remaining a sphere of highly concentrated ownership. During the turn, moreover, the Law of State Se-curity continued to give high state officials the right to lodge criminal com-plaints against persons they considered to have offended their honor and to seek confiscation of offending books. Indeed, a notorious case of censorship exploded in April 1999—one day before the launch of a book by the journal-ist Alejandra Matus. Her inside account of the judiciary, *The Black Book of Chilean Justice*, homed in on clientelism and negligence in the performance of public duty and on their corrupting impact on the institutional culture. An extreme case was the Supreme Court justice Servando Jordán, who earlier in the 1990s sometimes worked in an inebriated state, his pants wet from urine. Jordán, like Pinochet against Marín in 1996, used the anti-democratic weapons at hand to fight back. He had the extant books rounded up and publication prohibited. Cited to face criminal complaint, Matus fled to Miami, where she won political asylum. On one level, the Matus case showed how much had not changed. The rules of prudence, self-censor-ship, and legal harassment still carried weight. The Frei administration proved lackluster and ineffectual in pressing for repeal of the authoritarian provisions.

On another level, however, the Matus scandal exposed just how anach-ronistic the old rules of cultural and media expression were becoming. During 1998–2000 the government argued on a world stage that Pinochet should be considered accountable to Chilean courts. The Matus case was notorious and cut in the opposite direction. Meanwhile, Human Rights Watch used Matus's plight to push strongly against antidemocratic restric-tions on speech. The technology of photocopying and electronic communi-cation meant the contents of *Black Book* circulated anyway, and the Chilean press supported Matus. The scandal did not fade away; it became a point of extreme embarrassment, especially in international contexts. In April 2001 —a month after Ricardo Lagos assumed the presidency—Congress voted overwhelmingly, with support by most of the Right, to revoke the offending articles of the Law of State Security.[34]

A NEW MEMORY ENVIRONMENT, 1998–2000 (II):
OUTING TORTURERS

The most audacious sign of a freer atmosphere on memory matters was a new street happening. Young people organized noisy "outings" (*funas*) of torturers. The idea crystallized as an activity specific to the children generation, "Hijos," of families of the disappeared and the executed and their allies. (The formal group name was Acción Verdad y Justicia Hijos-Chile, or Chilean Children for Truth and Justice Action, and a vanguard "Hijos" group had already formed in Argentina.) First, however, from February to May 1999, Hijos organized Saturday street exhibits in Santiago's shantytowns and its downtown pedestrian street Paseo Ahumada. The point was to build personalized memory awareness—not statistics, but the stories of individual victims and perpetrators.[35]

The catalyzing effect of Pinochet's London arrest was important. The group formed after the detention, as surprise gave way to a sense that "the word justice was not abstract." Patricia Lobos recalled that impunity and impasse in the 1990s had turned her *away* from political activism, toward a conventional home-oriented life. News of the arrest galvanized her and other young adults. "It is like going back to having hope and saying, 'This cannot happen again . . . never again and something has to be done.'" Once the early convulsions and rumors of instability passed, cultural fear diminished. Pinochet's detention dragged on and on—yet failed to produce institutional disaster in Chile. The boundaries of "the possible" were in flux. Alejandra López recalled that ordinary people came to the Saturday street exhibits finally to share their stories. "We [were] amazed listening to the stories. . . . There was an incredible need for people to tell their story, 'Look, this is what happened to me.'" Torture produced especially strong reactions in the conversation circles: "It was super strong because it was super unknown to people . . . It was like us facing up to something that really is not talked about in this country." Another sign of loosened inhibition proved critical. Older people, "señoras some 50 years old," returned flyers with notes written on the back. As the señoras walked away briskly, the youths discovered they had been given leads—names of torturers, sometimes with an address or a phone number. The storytelling and the notes lent weight to an encounter with a member of Argentina's "Hijos" about *escraches* (the Argentine word for outings) they had undertaken.

Such experiences fed a sense of generational need to lay claim to memory —to break impasse, and to go beyond forms of struggle charted by elders. Even children of the disappeared, many of them powerfully bonded with older relatives, could feel a need to place their own stamp on memory. "The issue of human rights is not only the detained-disappeared ones [but also] a generational thing. It's like one as a youth feels the theme is much bigger, that it touched the society in a much wider way." New actions were needed to break down walls—the social distance between distinct kinds of maximal victims (relatives of the disappeared versus those of the executed); the politicocultural tendency to reduce a multilayered history of repression to one set of maximal victims; the assumption by perpetrators of torture including civilians that they could live free of accountability. Deciding to chart a new course led by the young was complicated by affect and by desire not to undermine the *viejas* ("elder women," inflected with respect and affection). The idea of an autonomous Hijos group, a counterpart to that in Argentina, had been brewing since 1996–97 but spurred ambivalence. Some, notably the older thirty-something "children" long supportive of the Agrupación, felt the main task was to continue accompanying the elder women in their struggle—perhaps form a youth branch of the Agrupación, but not autonomous memory identity and actions. The post-1998 atmosphere and street exhibit experience tipped the balance, without erasing complex questions of intergenerational affect and loyalty.

As the September 1999 memory season approached, activists decided to take the plunge—direct action to out torturers and break assumptions of impunity. An organizing group of about twenty youths, mainly children of the disappeared and the executed, obtained research help from former political prisoners. On 1 October, some sixty to eighty youths suddenly converged on the clinic of Dr. Alejandro Forero Alvarez. A smaller group went inside to distribute flyers to patients and staff. Forero's picture appeared on one side, a summary of his past as a torturer on the back. It cited a 1986 court case, when Judge Carlos Cerda's tenacious investigation of disappearances led to an arrest order against Forero, implicated by witness testimony of medical work on tortured prisoners of the "Comando Conjunto" intelligence group. The charges included injecting victims with drugs before helicopter flights to toss them into the ocean. Forero claimed in 1986 and again in a 1991–92 court case that the problem was mistaken identity—"bad information with some type of basis," as he put it to me. On 10 September 1986 the Santiago Court of Appeals cited the 1978 amnesty to overturn the arrest order. Forero resumed a normal life. The funa brought back the taint—Forero hid in the bathroom while staff and patients talked inside and noisy protest continued outside.[36]

Between October 1999 and December 2000, funas continued at a pace of nearly one a month. The activists had embarked on a learning process. Their first outing was tense and smallish. The idea of funas was controversial—but it caught the imagination, especially in university student settings. Three hundred people assembled for the second funa. By December 1999 activists formed a new organizing committee (Comisión FUNA) for the widening participant networks: children of the disappeared and executed, other youths interested in human rights, a sprinkle of older people including former political prisoners. A performance aesthetic had also emerged—an accent on youth identity and the carnivalesque. Outings featured a raucous outpouring of joy and anger—a musical racket (*batucada*) of drums, cymbals, guitars, wind instruments, whistles, and chants trumpeted the confrontation with truth.

The joy of cathartic release was tied up with the value of a cleansing openness, in a society where too much secrecy still prevailed. A principle of funa action was that the demonstrators would not hide their identities. "We do it with unmasked faces and so we say, cleanly . . . we feel anger and hostility at the guy . . . but it is happiness [too] to be facing him and tell him, 'You were an assassin, you were a torturer.' And all that goes accompanied by *batucada*, by whistle blowing . . . like another way of repudiating him and [remembering] our elders." Anger and happiness went together. "It is difficult to explain . . . because sure, there is anger but likewise it is super pleasurable for us to go happy, to know that . . . your neighbors are finding out that you are an assassin, they are going to look at you ugly . . . at least for some months."

Over time, what some elders initially dismissed as silliness or a cultural blip turned into something more serious. The central slogan posed a genuine problem: how to achieve cultural justice if legal justice was beyond reach. "If there is no justice, there is funa!" (Si no hay justicia, ¡hay funa!). The determination to expand the language and impact of human rights memory was evident not only in torture as a theme in its own right, but also in the diversity and social respectability of targets. Persons outed between

October 1999 and November 2000 (eleven in Santiago, one in Valparaíso-Viña del Mar, one in Arica) included two doctors, a journalist, a university professor, and a wealthy businessman, in addition to standard DINA and military figures. Sometimes the sting was dramatic. Dr. Werner Zanghellini, for example, denounced as part of a medical team in a DINA clinic, suspended his practice. Research, moreover, backed up the selection of targets. Activists selected persons about whom they could provide credible evidence—witness testimony, legal documents—if challenged.[37]

Funa activity did not fizzle out quickly, and sometimes produced public consternation. On 31 May 2000, a crowd of 700 to 1,000 persons converged at the Hotel Militar, on a major traffic artery in Santiago's respectable Providencia neighborhood. The hotel catered to military guests and its manager was General (retired) Miguel Krassnoff Martchenko, a leading DINA officer who stood out in memory lore as a particularly sadistic torturer. The traffic jams and sheer notoriety of the target made the action a major media event. Similar commotion followed in October, when at least 500 persons gathered at Elecmetal, one of the companies of business magnate Ricardo Claro Valdés. In street theater to reenact the crime, the protesters declared that Claro had handed six trade union leaders at Elecmetal—later found dead, with marks of torture—to the police after the 1973 coup. They also denounced the use of ships from another Claro company, Sudamericana Vapores, to hold prisoners tortured and disappeared in 1973. The swelling crowd—perhaps 2,000—then marched to Claro's Megavisión television station to underscore media control by persons with an interest in hiding the past.[38]

Significantly, during fifteen months of funas, *none* of the targets sued for injury or defamation. A lawsuit was a double-edged sword. Pinochet and military officers had objected to court appearances and digging in the 1990s as an unfair disgrace visited upon patriots who saved the nation. Under the pressure of court investigation and comparative witness testimony, moreover, alibis could fray. Consider my telephone interviews with Manuel Rivas Díaz, a former DINA agent targeted in a funa. He was notorious among survivors for electric shock torture on metal cots (*la parrilla*) and for sexual assault at the house known as "La Venda Sexy." In a first conversation, he stated vigorously, "I am totally innocent and it is easily provable." As a carabinero, he had been busy in a course on interrogations in 1975; he claimed that Pedro Valdivia, a prefect at Carabinero Investigations, could corroborate his activities. When I spoke with Valdivia, he confirmed that Rivas worked in Carabinero Investigations and added that he then became

19. Outing torturers. Above, funa demonstrators publicize names and do not hide their own identities. *Credit: Claudio Barrientos.*

20. Below, the festive aspect of funas, even amidst rain. *Credit: Claudio Barrientos.*

an analyst with the CNI in the late 1970s. I pressed for information on 1974, the year that mattered in the memory of prisoners. Yes, Valdivia conceded, Rivas worked for the DINA as an agent on loan (*agregado*). The DINA people "did the dirty war." They were ill trained in interrogation and "got out of hand." He did not know what Rivas did with the DINA but could say that as a carabinero, he had been properly trained not to commit excesses.

I followed up with Rivas and summarized Valdivia's remarks. Yes, he admitted, he worked at Londres 38 and Venda Sexy in 1974—but it was *others* who killed people during electric torture. His role was simply to take the declarations of prisoners. When I asked whether, while taking declarations, he saw other agents torture the prisoners, his response was "That I do not say." In a court case mobilizing multiple witnesses and documents—including Rivas's own 1993 judicial declaration on pervasive torture of prisoners—the pressure on a fraying alibi would have been far more severe. Small wonder that Rivas told me he was uninterested in a lawsuit against the funa activists. "I prefer to swallow it [*comérmela*]. . . . Let it sit in oblivion."[39]

The funas were controversial—not only among partisans of the military past, but also within the human rights camp. The Agrupación did not endorse the concept. At first the women worried that the outings were a counterproductive adventure of the young. Tension later declined, and a few individuals in the Agrupación even participated.

The funas were a classic memory knot—they had powers to convene that demanded attention—and they did not fade quickly. In August 2000, a flurry of media stories appeared. The most sensational effort to put the genie back in the bottle, while reporting on it, appeared in the major afternoon paper of the "El Mercurio" group, *La Segunda*. It gave front-page status to the "ASSASSINS OF IMAGE" and relied on metaphors of violence. The *funadores* made a point of their nonviolence and open self-identification, even holding cultural events to raise funds. But appearances were deceiving, according to the coverage. "All a pseudocultural activity . . . more deadly than a bullet."

The newspaper ran commentary, mainly hostile, by prominent persons. The subsecretary of the interior, Jorge Burgos, denounced the activity as an inclination to take justice into one's own hands, "an antidemocratic and very totalitarian behavior." Legal justice was the only legitimate way to establish criminal responsibilities. The human rights veteran Jaime Castillo added a touch of paternalism: "There are other, more serious procedures."

The most subtle comment came from the historian Sol Serrano. The point was not whether one liked or disliked the funas, "but rather if [the participants] have the right to demonstrate." The "interesting question" was the line between one person's right to demonstrate and another's right to defend honor if falsely accused. Pressed to moralize simply—to say if such activities "contribute or not"—she did not take the bait. "It matters much more to me that civil society can organize itself and express itself . . . whether because the relatives of victims are getting themselves together or because the supposed perpetrators defend their stance of not being such. The strength of society is in exercising rights."[40]

A NEW MEMORY ENVIRONMENT, 1998–2000 (III):
ELITE INITIATIVES

The shifting memory environment included elite initiatives. The street passions produced by Pinochet's detention added force to the calls for a new memory initiative in September 1998. The reactions, Patricio Aylwin declared, "cause me great concern and pain. I believed that reconciliation had really advanced much more." Those pushing for Pinochet's release on humanitarian grounds, he added, would benefit if Pinochet or his loyalists offered "a human gesture of recognizing responsibilities." In November José Zalaquett reiterated the idea that the time had come for "a new great effort . . . to achieve a genuine act of acknowledgment." The opposed memory camps still could not find a meeting ground for recognizing what mattered to the other side. The Right wanted the Left to accept that Allende's government "brought the country to dissolution of the rule of law and confrontation among Chileans." Meanwhile, "the persistent denial of the grave crimes of the dictatorship by the Right is incomprehensible" to those who opposed military rule. The truth was for years denied, then conceded after the Rettig Commission, but without recognizing leadership from above —"that Pinochet might have had some responsibility."[41]

Such discussions buzzed in Chile's "political class" in 1999. Discreet explorations of an initiative embraced the Right, including the UDI, the Concertación, military officers, and figures important in human rights policy under Aylwin. The new climate of 1999—above all and as we shall see later in the chapter, increased judicial pressure on the military, but also the ongoing Pinochet problem in London, the less predictable expressive climate, and the awareness of presidential elections in December—increased incentives to reassert some sort of control. A sense of Pinochet-as-albatross piqued interest by a new generation of military leaders. Might a new settlement leave the past to the past? In August 1999 Defense Minister Edmundo Pérez Yoma announced he would launch a "Dialogue Table" (Mesa de Diálogo) to take up the unfinished legacy of human rights violations. A core agenda quickly emerged: clarify the fate and return the remains of the disappeared, with military-police cooperation; and review the past more mutually, in a manner that respected distinct visions yet recognized historical responsibilities.[42]

The most significant aspect of the Dialogue Table was its composition. The twenty-two members included sectors whose memory frameworks clashed sharply—human rights lawyers and high military-police officers, in addition to government officials, moral-religious leaders, and civil society professionals, including two historians and a psychologist. The difficulty was immediately obvious in the opening ceremony on 21 August. Pamela Pereira, a human rights lawyer and the daughter of the disappeared industrialist and Radical Party member Andrés Pereira Salzberg, explained that she could not yet shake hands with the military officers. She remembered her father, who disappeared "for believing in the word of a military man who went to get him."[43]

The human drama of face-to-face talk between members of opposed memory camps deepened in the first weeks, as participants presented reflections on the task before them. Human rights activists had to sit and listen as army general Juan Carlos Salgado told them his memory-truth. The truth meant not only a search for the disappeared, but acceptance of why Chile lost consensus in the first place, with violent consequences that produced victims "in all sectors and strata of Chilean society." A week later, on 7 September, they listened again as Rear Admiral Alex Waghorn told them the group had to confront "the whole truth." For the navy the full truth meant a narrative of salvation that inverted human rights chronology and denied state terror under military rule. State agents fomented institutionalized violation of human rights against persons and property *before* 11 September 1973. Afterward, a new state had to bring social peace to "a society in upheaval, violent, faced with armed conflict with terrorist factions." Violations of human rights happened, but not as state policy. They were problems of individual excess and vengeance—provoked by violence, danger, and loss of comrades.[44]

The discomfort of direct talk went the other way, too. On 31 August, the day of General Salgado's presentation, Pamela Pereira stated that the point of the military coup was not simply to solve a crisis but to impose a new model of society "by blood and fire." The repression was systematic, institutional-ized—and massive. It directly affected hundreds of thousands of persons. The secret disappearance of thousands obeyed a larger, multifaceted logic of terror. Two weeks later military officers listened as the psychologist Elizabeth Lira personalized the history of repression by discussing Marta Ugarte, a woman who was tortured at Villa Grimaldi and whose cadaver the ocean tossed onto a beach in 1976; and seven more women, each disappeared and each pregnant when detained. Had their children been born? If so, where were they?[45]

Such exchanges occurred against the backdrop of a memory struggle sharp-ened by Pinochet's detention and including historians as protagonists. In December 1998, Pinochet sent a public "Letter to Chileans" and stated his case for History. He never sought power and turned it over "loyally" as required by his Constitution. In 1973 he had waited "until the last moment" to act, hoping for an alternative solution to misrule and disaster under the Popular Unity government, even as "citizen clamor was knocking at the doors of the barracks asking us to intervene." In the end, he said, "we men of arms acted as the moral reserve of a disintegrating country, in the hands of those who wanted to submit it to the Soviet orbit." The soldiers defended the country's Christian and Western values of civilization and human dignity— against materialism, atheism, and tyranny—and built a greater nation. Pi-nochet's enemies never forgave his defeat of Communism. Now trapped by their conspiracy, he was, he insisted, "absolutely innocent of all the crimes and acts irrationally imputed to me." Both sides lost people in the war, but "especially great is the suffering of those who did not provoke the clash . . . and ended up being its innocent victims." He felt "sincere pain" for all the fallen, and asked God for understanding and humility "to accept this cross" and have it serve the nation. "If with my suffering an end can be put to the hate sowed in our country," he would accept the sacrifice.[46]

This was memory as salvation at its most grandiloquent, with a revived war thesis pointing the finger of blame at victims of repression. The conservative newspaper *La Segunda* fed the fire with supplements by historian Gonzalo Vial on the crisis of Chilean society during 1964–73. The chief causes of crisis were the projects of total social transformation that took ideological hold in the Left and Center in the 1960s; their conjunction with an ethos of necessary violence (*guevarismo*) inspired by Che Guevara; and the resulting polarization that spread hate, violence, and total conflict in a variety of sectors. More by omission than commission, and notwithstanding Vial's condemnation of human rights violations when he served on the Rettig Commission, the articles supported the sense of justification held by sympathizers of Pinochet and the war thesis. In January, eleven historians—alarmed by Pinochet's letter, the Vial supplements, and government protest of Pinochet's detention as an affront to the nation—issued a "Manifesto of Historians," circulated in newspapers and online and later endorsed by at least seventy-three Chilean scholars and thirty-six North Americans. The authors included scholars with intimate knowledge of state terror. Among them were Gabriel Salazar, arguably the leading senior scholar of modern social history in Chile and also a survivor of torture at Villa Grimaldi; and Mario Garcés, a pioneer of grassroots community workshops to document and recover popular memory. In the 1980s, a forum of Garcés and colleagues with workers in Concepción had led to a harrowing siege by carabineros who considered worker meetings about history subversive. The vicar of the Workers Pastorate finally persuaded the police to relent.

The authors challenged Vial's reduction of the 1973 crisis to a short-term political narrative of polarization instigated by social actors of the Left and Center. One needed to set the era within a long-term analysis to understand the structural crisis of Chilean society by the 1960s. The interplay of oligarchical and neooligarchical rule on the one hand, and sociopolitical movements to democratize social benefits and opportunities but contending with repression on the other, had framed Chilean history and its recurrent episodes of violent repression since the early 1900s, if not earlier. The model of state leadership and social inclusion charted since the 1930s yielded multiple moments of oligarchical resistance and popular frustration, and had come to a point of exhaustion and redefinition by the 1960s and early 1970s. It was this larger history that helped one understand why projects of total transformation took on such appeal by the 1960s, the multiple sources of radicalization and violence, and the determination to destroy the Left and Center as political forces during the "war" waged after 1973. The authors faulted Vial for manipulation with partisan effect: "a silencing of structural historical processes and the corresponding cumulative oligarchical responsibility" in the making of a crisis, and a framing of the coup as "the unavoidable and moralizing armed intervention of soldiers" while steering clear of the atrocities of military rule. A bitter debate ensued.[47]

The controversy put on the cultural stage the gap between understandings of historical truth held by historians, and by other actors. This mattered, because—as the remarks of Salgado and Waghorn at the Dialogue Table showed—military partisans of memory as salvation hoped that agreement on basic historical facts and causes would diminish the sense of culpability otherwise attached to soldiers as perpetrators. The historians' controversy was early notice that the idea of an agreement to reduce causes and responsibility for the crisis of 1973 to a shared factual narrative of political decisions during 1964–73 was naive. The world of historiography considered and debated long-term and structural causes, as well as short-term and episodic causes, of great upheavals. The point was to reach not unanimity of opinion, but new insight through ongoing debate and research that built a solid foundation of significant—historically consequential—facts. Also, historical research often saw contingency and probability, not inevitability. Historians would not establish that a coup, however probable and backed by some social forces, "had" to happen to resolve the crisis of 1973, nor that its natural consequence had to be "war." In the expressive climate after 1998, moreover, the historians' debates and objections would have greater force.

Part of the work of the Dialogue Table, therefore, was to create awareness about what historical analysis could *not* do—to strip History of its imagined role as a security blanket. This was the point of the historian Sol Serrano, in her opening remarks as a member of the Dialogue Table. "I do not think our task . . . is to try to construct an interpretation of our history we all share." An official history was not only undemocratic, but self-defeating. It failed to see that history is the play of multiple interpretations, framed by questions put to the past by each generation and historical moment. "It is not a text of consensual history that we want, but rather sources for history, for reflection about the past." That past included both a history of human rights violations and a preceding crisis of democracy. Intellectually serious reflection required considering the structural depth of the crisis that, she said, "led us to build a society so weighed down by exclusions," as well as cumulative disaffection with democracy that perhaps reached back to the 1930s but clearly intensified into a total polarization by 1973. In this sense everyone had a hand in the making of a crisis of democracy. Yet historical explanation of how a military regime came to pass did not justify what happened once in power. And, one came up against a crucial point in the Chilean tragedy—the lethal violence, and indifference to it—where historical causation alone no longer sufficed. One came to see the value of a more searching interior reflection— "consciousness that the horror of the violence is within our own nature and that repair also comes through grieving together about having built a society where that was possible." This kind of recognition, a reflection coming to terms with the past rather than agreeing to an official history of it, could build "new sources for history" and a culture of "never again."[48]

Coming from distinct perspectives, the authors of the Manifesto and Serrano arrived at a key point in common. An authoritative short-term political narrative could not provide a safe harbor of justification when reckoning with the atrocities of the past. Social acknowledgment and repair would be more effective if the past catalyzed not a search for the mitigating explanation, but a process of moral reflection and a taking of responsibility.

The Dialogue Table was an uncertain venture onto new ground. To forge an accord out of such conflicting memories and interests would not be easy. The experiment sparked strains among allies within established memory camps, not simply tense dialogue between opposed camps. From a human rights perspective, was the Dialogue Table a worthwhile experiment that might finally pull the military into recognizing the truth of harm inflicted, and cooperating in a search for disappeared persons? Or, was it a trap that would pull people into a pact ratifying impunity in exchange for questionable information? The Agrupación led a street demonstration against the initiative on the ceremonial opening day. Some veteran human rights groups, notably the Left-leaning group CODEPU, denounced the initiative. Others, notably the ecumenical religious group FASIC, offered cautious support. The historical layers within informal networks of relatives of the disappeared started to become more relevant. Some elderly parents of disappeared MIRistas (a "Founding Line" group split off from the Agrupación) seemed open to hoping that the Dialogue Table might help them find their children. Wives and mothers of disappeared Communists, who first came of age in the moderate Left world of Communist subculture before 1973, then led struggles of the Agrupación after 1976, evinced more fear of a trap.[49]

Such distinctions mattered, but only somewhat. To reduce the strains to a crude sociology of generation, political leanings, and factions would miss a crucial aspect. Within the human rights and victim communities, the pressures and ambivalences were pervasive and personal, even existential. The memory question—not only loss of cherished people turned into victims, but also the long struggle to document the loss and to appeal to moral values against a regime of misinformation and denial—raised powerful issues of human loyalty and betrayal. This was why Pereira, conscious of her father, could not at first shake the hands of military officers at the Dialogue Table. During his opening statement to the Dialogue Table, the lawyer Roberto Garretón, a tenacious defender of human rights, rigorously rebutted the misuses of "historical context" to explain away human rights violations while narrating a memory of salvation. First, however, he felt compelled to express his inner conflict. "I want to confess here that the decision to participate in this table has been, without doubt, the most difficult of my life, even more than that taken in September 1973 to dedicate all my professional activity to defending victims of the dictatorship, taking on the personal and familial risks."[50]

The military-police officers had their own fears of a trap, and their own loyalty issues. Two sticking points proved crucial. First, the former Rettig Commission members at the Dialogue Table—Jaime Castillo, Gonzalo Vial, José Zalaquett—pressed the idea that hiding information on the fate of the disappeared should itself become a crime. Without incentives, those who had information were unlikely to come forward. The negative incentive would be the criminalization of cover-up; the positive one would be protection against self-incrimination including confidentiality. For obvious reasons, the military and police would find criminalization of cover-up hard to swallow. It amounted to the principle of "wedge" in a widening truth-and-justice process, not "formula" producing closure. Would it be a hard shove down the slippery slope? If codes of silence broke, even if the guarantee against self-incrimination by informants held up, who else might get caught in the snare as a result of their testimony?

The second sticking point was Pinochet. His detention cut both ways. It added to the urgency of a new initiative, but it also produced facts of life that rendered agreement more difficult. Recognition of the moral-historical responsibility of the military state for systematic violations of human rights, by a panel including the armed forces, might be construed as validating Pinochet's legal culpability in pending criminal cases. Pinochet's own actions, like the public "Letter to Chileans," also affected the cultural climate and made loyalty a delicate theme. The most dramatic example came when a tentative draft agreement fell apart in March 2000. Ricardo Lagos of the Concertación had narrowly beaten Joaquín Lavín of the UDI and the Right in the runoff round of the presidential elections in January 2000. The Dialogue Table participants raced to reach agreement before the transition to a new administration on 11 March. By 3 March, the draft—not yet approved, with a few gaps still unresolved—included recognition of historical responsibilities *and* a clause to criminalize cover-up. But Pinochet's return to Chile that day scrambled the work. The rationale for the return: Home Secretary Straw's decision that failing health rendered Pinochet unfit for trial. The televised airport event: Pinochet stood up from his wheelchair, walked, and smiled triumphantly as he lifted his cane for the crowd. The dramatic gesture played to his crowd of admirers, and brought back bitter memories of how he had always relied on misinformation to outfox opponents and get through a crisis. The presence of the military and police commanders in chief at the ceremony, with music and greetings fit for a returning hero, also provoked ire. At the Dialogue Table, good-faith assumptions that had slowly built up—among others, that Pinochet would not resume a dominating presence in public life—wobbled. Suspicion and recrimination intensified. Human rights lawyers pressed for new concessions; military officers backed away from understandings.[51]

The Lagos administration continued the Dialogue Table under Defense Minister Mario Fernández. The road to agreement, however, had become rockier. When the agreement finally came on 12 June, the provision to criminalize the hiding of information on the disappeared had been dropped —a retreat Gonzalo Vial protested by not signing. The key mechanism would be a fact-finding effort led by the armed forces and carabineros, with collaboration by civic groups and moral-religious leaders, and a guarantee of secrecy to informants. Within six months the military and carabineros would report the results to the president; the Supreme Court would presumably appoint special judges to follow up. The president would evaluate the quality of the report. If necessary, he could extend the effort another six months and propose "complementary measures" previously "analyzed, although not agreed to"—in other words, propose to criminalize cover-up.

The weakened agreement did not imply lack of innovation. For the first time, military and police agreed to acknowledge—and presumably document—the truth of disappearances. For the first time, they acceded to a reflection on historical responsibilities that went beyond demonization of the Left or politicians, did not use pre-1973 history and the war thesis as justification for post-1973 violence, and declared agents of the state responsible for horrors under military rule. The Dialogue Table saw the agents of a sociopolitical crisis reaching back into the 1960s in broad terms, including acts of commission and omission. Chile experienced "a spiral of political violence, that the actors of the time provoked or did not know to avoid." Advocacy of violence as a "method of political action" was a particularly grave aspect, but the allusion did not point exclusively at the Left. The Dialogue Table considered the events of 11 September 1973 a culmination of prior history, and a point of legitimate interpretive disagreement among Chileans. But it also considered that responsibilities for the making of a crisis did not diminish—nor justify—the violence of military rule. Chileans had an obligation to condemn and never again allow "the grave violations of human rights, which agents of organizations of the State incurred during military government." The same applied to political violence "by some opponents."

In effect, the Dialogue Table floated a new framework for collective memory —memory as a shared tragedy. By acknowledging and taking responsibility for a history of violent rupture across the memory camps and including the military, Chileans could come to terms with the past. They could do so without imposing a hegemonic or official version of history on major interpretive issues, such as the causes of crisis or the necessity of a military coup, and without reviving acrimony based on denial. The point of the declaration was "to accept and take on [asumir] our past. We understand that it is unjust to pass on to the young the conflicts and divisions that have hurt the country."[52]

A NEW MEMORY ENVIRONMENT, 1998–2000 (IV): JUSTICE

The nexus of courts, elites, and society was also an arena of initiative—a crucial factor in the new memory climate and in the pressures that drove the Dialogue Table. As we have seen, in 1998 judicial reform and generational renovation produced a new phase in the wearing down of Pinochetismo and impunity doctrine in the courts. Here, too, the Pinochet detention had a certain catalytic effect. Public opinion surveys and elite discourses shifted the context of judicial decision making. The ongoing London detention, alongside an absence of institutional disaster, encouraged the idea that "untouchables" could be touched—Manuel Contreras and Pedro Espinoza need not be exceptions. Surveys in 1999 showed that seven of ten Chileans (72 percent) thought it best to submit Pinochet to justice, whether by keeping him in London (31 percent) or returning him to Chile to be tried in court (41 percent). A vast majority (68–69 percent) also considered him responsible for the human rights violations under his rule, and by July, eight in ten (78 percent) believed the future of Chile did *not* depend on the outcome of the Pinochet case. In other words, Pinochet was much diminished as a potential threat to stability. Meanwhile, Chilean government arguments to secure Pinochet's release placed more accent on Chilean justice. The sovereignty argument of late 1998 (and its implicit corollary, that Pinochet's impunity was important for democratic stability) failed to produce Pinochet's release. In 1999, the government began emphasizing that Chilean justice was vigorous and independent—perfectly capable of judging Pinochet, suitable for a first claim over other jurisdictions. It also announced that the Council for Defense of the State, the legal arm of the state, would become a co-plaintiff in lawsuits filed in Chile against Pinochet.[53]

Judicial renovation and the postdetention climate yielded dramatic court actions in 1999. One need not resort to a crude conspiracy theory. Renovation yielded judges less inclined to the old ways, and the climate of public opinion and elite politics put a higher premium on judicial integrity. Impunity weakened as doctrine and practice. On 20 July the Supreme Court's Second Criminal Chamber undermined the 1978 amnesty by ruling unanimously that for legal purposes, disappearance cases were kidnappings. The crime continued indefinitely until a court resolved the fate—the date of release or death—of the person abducted and disappeared. A document prepared for the Dialogue Table listed seventy-one agents or former agents of the military state arrested in 1999 for human rights cases. As alarming, from a military perspective, if the new Supreme Court ruling were applied consistently, some 200 additional court cases could be reopened. Meanwhile, informal walls of untouchability crumbled. By November court investigation or reactivation of key cases—the Caravan of Death expedition of 1973, the Tucapel Jiménez murder of 1982, the "Operation Albania" murders of 1987—led to arrests of top architects of "dirty war." Among them were the retired generals Sergio Arellano Stark, commander of the Caravan of Death group whose helicopter visits led to prisoner massacres and disappearances, and Humberto Gordon and Hugo Salas Wenzel, the last two directors of the secret police (CNI).[54]

Equally telling, arrests disturbing to the army exposed a new inability to create a standoff with de facto power. The September arrest of the ailing Gordon provoked military upset. Gordon had reached the rank of lieutenant general, equal to that of the army commander Izurieta, and he was the army's junta member in the 1980s. Some eighty retired generals visited him at the Hospital Militar to express solidarity—but they could not do more. The age of military alerts to enforce impunity had passed. Indeed, the case that snared Gordon—the Tucapel Jiménez assassination—led to the first indictment of a general on active duty, the army brigadier general Hernán Ramírez Hald, in November 2000. Again, colleagues could offer solidarity, but little more. To spare the army, Ramírez asked for early retirement.[55]

Pinochet occupied a central place in the new nexus of courts, elites, and society. His status as a legal hostage in London gave pause—rogue military alerts to flex muscle against new judicial doctrine and court proceedings could backfire. Nor could Pinochet enforce his own immunity from legal troubles inside Chile. As we saw, early in 1998 Pinochet's retirement as army commander and ascension to lifetime senator stimulated criminal complaints. Judge Juan Guzmán of the Santiago Court of Appeals received assignment of the Pinochet cases, and related Caravan of Death cases against Arellano and other officers. Pinochet had lost the power—even before the London arrest—to abort the process. He would risk rupture with the new army leadership, and a constitutional accusation removing him from the senate and its legal protections. The London detention accelerated the legal cascade inside Chile, and reinforced the impossibility of stopping it. In ten months through October 1998, plaintiffs presented about one case a month to Judge Guzmán (twelve cases); during the next ten months the pace doubled, to about two a month (twenty-three new cases); in the final four months of 1999, it doubled again, to four a month (sixteen new cases). By December 1999, Guzmán's docket of Pinochet cases reached fifty-one—with no end in sight to the spiral.[56]

In the shifting memory environment of 1998–2000, Guzmán took on the role of "star judge," a jurist of conservative background determined to apply the law without regard to the status of the accused or the surrounding political pressures. In 1999, he issued arrest orders against five retired generals and colonels as coauthors of permanent kidnappings in the Caravan of Death case. In October, he sent a letter rogatory to London—questions for Pinochet as an accused person under investigation. Pinochet declined to answer, on grounds of legal vulnerability in London. Guzmán pointedly observed he would press on with his investigation and consider petitioning to strip Pinochet of parliamentary immunity. Under Chilean law, the request would ultimately go to the Supreme Court, which would consider whether the evidence in the Caravan of Death investigation justified an indictment of Pinochet. On 7 March 2000—Pinochet had returned to Chile only four days earlier—Guzmán filed the request. On 8 August, the Supreme Court voted (14–6) to approve the stripping of immunity. The ruling authorized Guzmán not only to apply the doctrine that disappearances amounted to unresolved kidnapping, but also to consider (per the Aylwin doctrine) Pinochet's responsibility for homicides. Meanwhile, the Pinochet docket had soared to 158 criminal complaints.[57]

Pinochet's loss of legislative immunity was the most dramatic symbol that *lo posible* had changed, even on matters of justice. Memory impasse had long led to standoffs that drew boundaries on the possible. Such standoffs reminded all of the contradictory structure of power, that is, the tense coexistence between the "soft" hegemony of an electoral and public opinion majority inclined toward the human rights memory camp, and the "hard" hegemony of an institutionally and socioeconomically powerful minority, inclined toward remembering military rule gratefully while seeking permanent closure of the memory question. For democratic Chileans committed to headway on the memory question, the structure of power meant that one fought to achieve an advance on a specific truth-and-justice issue of importance, then hoped to build cumulatively on such gains to achieve a new advance in the future. Impasse could "roll" to a new center of gravity, even if its structural underpinning remained intact and reproduced moments of severe standoff. By 1996–97, the rolling effect appeared to have slowed to a halt, at least in terms of state initiative and policy. The balance of initiative shifted to civil society actors, more or less on their own. Indeed, until January 1999, Frei had declined repeated requests to meet with the Agrupación.[58]

During the turn of 1998 and years immediately following, the deep rules of impasse—its structural undergirding, especially Pinochet's role as guardian of power—frayed significantly, albeit partially. In September 1998, the structure of power still provided Pinochet a strong foundation to defend his honor before History. He could present himself to the nation—at least a large minority—as the legislator-statesman who agreed to suppress his cherished 11 September holiday, as one more act of self-sacrifice for the good of Chile. He could defend the idea, to Chileans and foreigners alike, that subordinates were the culprits of any human rights problem. He was a patriot and statesman who saved Chile and avoided becoming a true dictator, he told the *New Yorker* writer John Lee Anderson. While he could not supervise the detailed actions of subordinates, when he learned of human rights problems, he sent the information to the courts. A similar pride, albeit wounded, was still evident in his December 1998 "Letter to Chileans." By September 2000, Pinochet's diminished politicocultural standing undermined his aggressive defense before History. He had escaped interna-

21. Play of memory: The satirist Guillo brilliantly recalls his equation of Pinochet with Louis XIV (and the requisition of *Apsi* in 1987). The unraveling of impasse and immunity is the unraveling of Louis XIV's wig. *Credit: Guillo (Guillermo Bastías).*

tional trial not by legal innocence, but for reasons of health. A Chilean judge had connected him criminally to the Caravan of Death—an operation to execute and disappear unarmed prisoners in the provinces, and to install a war thesis justifying unlimited powers of violence. A new book by the journalist Patricia Verdugo, *La caravana de la muerte*, analyzed key documents studied by Guzmán to put the evidence that stripped Pinochet of legislative immunity "before the eyes" of the public.[59]

Perhaps most revealing were the changing terms of defense by natural loyalists. The courts had moved into a new phase of human rights trials and doctrine. The army no longer responded with the crisis alerts nor the cat-and-mouse chase (in the Contreras affair) that rocked civilian authority in 1990, 1993, and 1995. Now the response was frown-and-negotiate, by officers eager to put the Pinochet legacy behind, in part via the Dialogue Table. The old equation of Pinochet's personal well-being with institutional well-being no longer held such sway. On the cultural and legal fronts, too, belligerence softened in 2000–2001. Pinochet and his family, lawyers, and political allies began letting go—ambivalently, incompletely, under pressure—of the instinct to mount a vehement defense of historical honor and legal innocence. They moved toward a language of reconciliation over self-defense, evident in the mollifying tone of Pinochet's September 2000 letter to Chileans. They edged toward uncomfortable legal strategies—try to escape on technical grounds; do not bet on a finding of legal innocence.[60]

The slide worsened. On 1 December 2000, Judge Guzmán indicted Pinochet and ordered house arrest for fifty-seven murders and eighteen kidnappings in the Caravan of Death operation. The Santiago Court of Appeals stayed the order to allow for wrangling on technical points—the status of the 1999 letter rogatory to London, the timing of medical examination, the criteria to assess medical fitness for trial, the controls over appointment of doctors, and the like. Meanwhile, politicocultural defense of Pinochet as innocent had taken a body blow. More was yet to come. On 25 January 2001, General Joaquín Lagos Osorio, commander of the Army First Division in Antofagasta in 1973, appeared on Televisión Nacional. He had a document originally delivered to Pinochet. It divided prisoners into two lists: those executed under regular army trial procedures, and those summarily executed by the intervening team headed by Arellano as "representative of the Commander in Chief of the Army." Pinochet's handwriting was on the document. He instructed Lagos to unify the lists and to strike allusions to Arellano and Pinochet—that is, to alter it in accord with the idea that illegitimate acts were excesses by subordinates, unknown to superiors. The program was culturally devastating. By then, Guzmán had already interrogated Pinochet and decided on his next step. On 29 January, he again indicted Pinochet and ordered house arrest.[61]

CROSSROADS: THE IRONY OF 2001

The great turn of 1998–2001 opened up fresh possibilities, but did not eliminate tension between the old and the new. It was as if Chileans traveled the bend in the highway only to arrive, in 2001, at a crossroads. The culture of memory argument was notably different, but one path clearly pointed toward a wedge principle that opened truth and justice work wider, while another toward a formula that might lay such work to rest. In addition, the new openings in memory work rested on an irony: a privatized culture in which the old referents of memory struggle faded and seemed less strategic, and in which metanarratives translating the personal into the emblematic held less appeal. Even as democratic Chileans broke down old barriers, they approached an era where living memory might truly become "loose," the residual domain of the personal within a public world of *olvido* and indifference.

The new memory environment unfolding after 1998 broke barriers in three ways. First, state actors and branches that had retreated from the memory question turned active, even strategic. Whatever their inclinations before 1998, political elites—from the Frei administration and Center-Left Concertación, to the Right, including the UDI—found themselves compelled to chart a memory initiative and seek some sort of breakthrough. The Dialogue Table embodied the new dynamic. So did its effort to build a new framework of meaning: memory as a shared national tragedy, recognized and mourned by soldiers as well as civilians. The judiciary and judges also took on a more decisive role, as actors pushing rather than sidelining the memory question. Before 1998, especially at the Supreme Court level, Pinochetismo and inclination to use the 1978 amnesty to shut down cases gave way, slowly and under pressure, to inconsistency. A jurisprudence of zigzag meant at best applying the Aylwin doctrine to open cases for serious investigation, at worst closing cases without serious inquiry and disciplining lower judges who pressed otherwise. During 1998–2001, the Court shifted decisively toward opening cases and to supporting both the Aylwin doctrine and permanent kidnapping doctrine. It still issued warnings—notably to Juan Guzmán—to restrain judges considered too aggressive, but overall jurisprudence was now more supportive of pursuing rather than evading justice.[62]

Second, immunity shields cracked, both discursively and in practice. Discursively, the military and police forces—the branch of the state most recalcitrant and fearful on memory matters—formally acknowledged the truth of massive violent persecution perpetrated by state agents under military rule. Denial that human rights violations were systematic, and use of pre-1973 context to deflect responsibility, could no longer serve as official military memory. The practical shift was the heightened vulnerability of Pinochet and other former military or police officers to criminal justice, and greater acceptance of the new reality by the military. It could offer some solidarity to an officer in trouble, and some hope that behind-the-scenes maneuvers or the Dialogue Table experiment might lessen vulnerability. But the military was now willing to sacrifice some comrades as justice took its course, rather than equate each person's fate with institutional well-being. The earlier synergy of justice and the military as recalcitrant branches of the state had fallen apart.

Third, a more open climate of memory expression took hold. It felled taboos, drew out new information, and pushed to the fore the uncomfortable memory-truth of torture. As we saw, the more open climate was paradoxical, since ownership of mass media was highly concentrated, and since the magazines and newspapers that played pioneering roles in human rights memory under dictatorship all folded by 1998. The dominant media players were more "followers" than "leaders" in the widening climate of memory expression and investigation. Nonetheless, new media and street expression emerged; old barriers and silences fell. The historians' controversy meant that a short-term narrative of political polarization to explain the crisis of 1973 would run into ferocious public resistance by intellectuals, and lose authoritative luster. The funa activists turned torture, a theme formally acknowledged but substantively marginalized during most of the 1990s, into a memory knot—a demand for acknowledgment, a break with the culture of polite anonymity, a scream that would not fade away.

Politicocultural change is rarely linear. It results from the messy push and pull of contradictory forces, and these were especially intense during the bend of 1998–2001. If memory impasse unraveled substantially, the future of memory struggles was still far from clear. Several aspects of life in 2001 seemed to revive the status quo ante. Habits of impasse, the creation of standoff rooted in de facto power, remained formidable.

On 5 January the armed forces and carabineros delivered to President Lagos their Dialogue Table report on the fate of disappeared persons. Collecting such information constituted the act by which they solemnly recognized the core truth of human rights memory, and institutional responsibility to address and relieve suffering caused by those in their ranks. Lagos went on television two days later. The information, he warned citizens, was "harsh and painful." It referred to "death . . . clandestine burials, bodies thrown to the sea, to the lakes and rivers." The follow-up investigations by judges should help clarify the fate of some 180 disappeared persons, most of them thrown into the ocean or other waters, and 20 people in a clandestine burial site.

Lagos highlighted the qualitative significance of the report as an act of recognition. (The quantitative results were meager; unresolved disappearance cases numbered about 1,000.) "More than the number, what is transcendent is the recognition by the high commands of the armed forces, who have accepted that Chile cannot look to the future without clearing the debts of the past." They agreed political violence should never happen again, and shared "the pain that said acts caused." The new stance marked a generational shift. "Those in uniform today have had to respond for those of yesterday, thereby recovering . . . the deep sense of honor inherent in the military profession." Chile had finally arrived to the point of memory as a shared tragedy, while accepting the pluralism of social experiences and memories, and distinct types of mourning. Some relatives of the disappeared would grieve while finally providing dignified burials to loved ones; others would mourn for relatives lost forever, tossed by helicopters into the ocean. The armed forces would "engage in the sorrow that comes with daring to look at the truth, recognizing the horrors committed by members of their ranks." There would also be "a mourning as country" by looking squarely at the immensity of the tragedy, "without comforting subterfuges and euphemisms."[63]

The problem was that the report's credibility fell apart. From the start, the Dialogue Table had evoked skepticism among many relatives of the disappeared, and divided responses in the human rights community. Fresh doubts soon surfaced. Some relatives of the disappeared noted that information limited to a victim's name and an approximate date of death or toss into the ocean was too vague to constitute credible truth, especially if it did not line up with other information relatives had obtained over the years. Some victims on the list corresponded to judicial cases against architects of dirty war. Was the report a subterfuge to prompt closure of these cases? Silences also spoke loudly. The report included a majority of the cases attributed to army agents (soldiers not reassigned to the DINA), but only a few attributed to DINA agents or carabineros. Verification proved problematic. Excavation to find six bodies reported with reasonably precise coordinates at Cuesta Barriga (some twenty-five kilometers west of Greater Santiago) produced no results. The frustrated presiding judge, Héctor Carreño, called off the work.[64]

Such doubts were like jabs that take a toll without knocking out the boxer.

The devastating blow came in April. At Fuerte Arteaga (near Colina, north of Santiago), remains of a disappeared person had been discovered in March. The Legal Medical Service identified him as Juan Luis Rivera Matus, a Communist electrician and trade unionist detained in November 1975. The shock: Rivera was on the Dialogue Table list as a person tossed into the ocean near San Antonio. The cruelty: In January, Rivera's family, including four exiled children and their families who flew in from France, had gathered to mourn and honor him at a symbolic funeral on the coast. In addition to suffering emotional fraud, the French-Chilean branch of the family had gone into debt. President Lagos called the family to acknowledge the mistake and express sympathy, and to offer state purchase of air fares to gather the family diaspora for a new funeral. In May sixteen relatives, including four sons and seven grandchildren, flew again to Chile to lay their elder member to rest.[65]

Rivera's identification constituted the first hard proof of false information in the report. The contrast with the 1991 Rettig Commission report, whose individual case findings had stood ten years without a single counterexample, was notable. More cases of disproof followed in April and May, making apparent that the cooperating military and police officials lacked the means (or the will) to submit the evidence gathered from informants to rigorous analysis separating wheat from chaff. Operations during the dictatorship to prevent discovery of bodies—exhuming bodies for relocation, churning the earth in old sites—meant that even information provided in good faith could be out of date. The absence of analytical procedure and incentives with teeth now hit hard. It revived the specter that old rules of impasse and cover-up still secretly operated.[66]

For many, the denouement of the Pinochet case pointed in the same direction. On 9 July 2001, the Santiago Court of Appeals panel ruled 2 to 1 to suspend prosecution of the case (technically narrowed in March to cover-up crimes, not coauthorship of murder and kidnapping) because Pinochet was mentally unfit to defend himself. A report by the Legal Medical Service found "moderate subcortical vascular dementia." The diagnosis was not the lay concept of dementia, but a technical term for modest loss of mental agility (less complex problem-solving ability, less sharpness of memory), caused by ministrokes and diminished blood circulation. The diagnosis proved controversial, in part because the official report modified, without consulting the full panel of doctors, the degree of vascular dementia attributed in the original draft: "slight to moderate." Days before the ruling,

Pinochet's dramatic admission to a hospital and rumors of imminent death fed suspicion. Did the ruling amount to protection of valid legal rights in a democracy? Or the product of secret pressures and pacts?[67]

Behind the scenes, Guzmán had reason to suspect the latter. Pressures on him had included visits by Concertación congressmen who offered friendly advice. He had done a great good by breaking impunity with a new legal precedent, but it would help social peace if a thorough medical exam allowed an escape for humanitarian reasons. They wanted a formula, not a wedge.[68]

Meanwhile, partisans of memory as salvation remained active and sought to revitalize the war thesis: the Left was responsible for the violence unfairly denounced as human rights violations under military rule, and had brought Chile to the brink of war by September 1973. The post-1998 climate sparked some intellectually serious efforts to explore aspects of pre-1973 Left history —political strategy debates, agrarian reform conflicts, presidential security practice—that fed war sensibilities. More spectacular and chilling were propaganda initiatives by architects of "dirty war." In September 2000, Manuel Contreras had published the first massive tome of his memory project, entitled "The Historical Truth." The statistics and documents—contemporary political elites appeared on the lists of subversives—conveyed a clear double message. Contreras controlled DINA archives with damaging information or misinformation: Beware of crossing him! And, he could purport to document a "war" dating back to 1967: the guerrilla army drawing on 30,000 foreigners in addition to Chileans; the trampling of human rights through assaults on persons and property supported by the Unidad Popular government and yielding 1,198 casualties, among them 919 "wounded"; the relative evenness of casualties on both sides of "subversive war," if one began tracking the count in 1967. The reasoning was specious—the "wounded" were counted as casualties of only one side. The veracity of the data was questionable, even to conservative media such as *El Mercurio*.[69]

Nonetheless, the propaganda initiatives mattered. For hard-core loyalists of military rule, they added fuel to the fire of memory as salvation. For critics of military rule, they suggested that the world of blackmail, disinformation, and impunity had not been superseded. In July 2001 Contreras launched an Internet site that alleged collaboration between judges and Marxists. In August, Interior Minister Insulza announced that former CNI agents had created a website with "extrajudicial declarations," the alleged confessions of prisoners subject to torture under military rule. The grotesque news coincided with the sudden—and enigmatic—withdrawal of the Senate candidacy of Sebastián Piñera, a moderate conservative and the president of Renovación Nacional, in favor of UDI candidate Admiral (retired) Jorge Arancibia. Piñera had endured mystery stalkings during the campaign. The incident brought back memories of a 1993 covert operation by former intelligence agents against the "disloyal" Piñera.[70]

The denouement of the Dialogue Table and Pinochet cases, the memory initiatives of dirty war architects, the shadowy mystery events of politics—the Chile of impasse was alive and fighting back. How much had the environment of lo posible changed?

Sensations of impasse, understandable in the heat of politicocultural battle and disappointment, were misleading. On memory matters, Chilean society had arrived at a situation more complex: a crossroads, one of whose paths offered a wedge into the unknown and unprecedented. That prospect inspired resistance—a push to take the road of finding a formula to bring closure or at least restore prudence. Either way, however, the terms of memory struggle and the underlying balance of de facto power were shifting. Barriers fell. As we saw, a new state activism that included the judiciary and judges as major players, a cracking of impunity that included military acceptance that saber rattling to defend an earlier generation of officers was obsolete, a bolder expressive climate that pushed aside taboos and confronted the torture question, all took hold during 1998–2001.

For every event or pattern suggesting a revival of impasse in 2001, therefore, there was another event showing the impossibility of rolling back the clock. Consider two core aspects of 1990s-style memory impasse—justice, military defiance—in relation to Pinochet, the most intense embodiment of the impunity problem. *Justice*: In July, even as publicity focused on the suspension of the Pinochet case, Judge Guzmán ruled that the DINA had constituted an "illicit association," a finding that expanded the scope of relevant investigation and subjected its high leadership, including Contreras and Krassnoff, to ongoing judicial jeopardy. Also, since in theory Pinochet's health could improve and the dismissed case could be reopened, Guzmán had ground to expand his investigation into the Caravan of Death. *Military defiance*: Under Izurieta, the army charted an ethos of renewed professionalism, a modernization whose political foundation rested on shedding the taint of human rights controversy—and avoiding defiance of civilian authority, if former officers got into trouble. The strategy of using the promotion-and-retirement process to shape a new military leadership had finally borne fruit. On 5 January 2001, Izurieta went to Pinochet's estate "Los Boldos" to tell him the tough news. If Pinochet resisted the judicial steps coming in the next few days—a mental and neurological exam he considered humiliating, a new interrogation by Guzmán, a potential arrest if he defied the court—the army would not back him. "Do not pay attention to everything your friends tell you," Izurieta warned. "You came here to ruin my afternoon," Pinochet replied.[71]

At a cultural level, the most important development was insistence on torture as central to the memory question. We have already seen that as fear and self-restraint diminished, torture inspired new memory knots: funas by young people determined to "out" torturers with forgotten pasts. More subtle was a microlevel phenomenon: the swelling of individual torture victims who began confronting their own pasts, by discarding an implicit hierarchy of victimization, by seeking therapy and group meetings with other survivors, by actions of redress and public truth telling. The boundaries of memory as rupture and persecution had narrowed by the mid-to-late 1990s to maximal victims, some 3,000 proved cases of persons disappeared or executed under military rule. Now, as torture turned into another "open wound" that could not be shunned, another testament of cruel and unresolved rupture of life, the circle of potential victims—and perpetrators—widened. By 2000–2001, serious estimates of torture victims ranged from tens of thousands to hundreds of thousands. The Chilean College of Medicine cited 200,000.[72]

The reemergence of torture further eroded the power balances breeding memory impasse. In February 2001, General Hernán Gabrielli, the second in command of the air force, suddenly faced a reckoning with the past. In November 2000, the newly discovered remains of Eugenio Ruíz-Tagle gave graphic testimony of what it meant to be a victim of the Caravan of Death. Ruíz-Tagle had been a civil engineer and state enterprise administrator in Antofagasta. His social background upped the ante. Well remembered and liked within the small world of Chilean elite families, Ruíz-Tagle was a distant cousin of the former president Frei Ruíz-Tagle. His class background and appealing personality made him a prime example of an idealistic young person converted into a dehumanized enemy. His broken back and missing ears (and other evidence) vividly brought home the ordeal of torture, beating, and mutilation. A "Captain Gabrielli" had stood out in survivor memory as an especially eager, opportunistic, and brutal torturer of

Ruíz-Tagle and others. In February, four witnesses made the link between current general and former captain. They were socially respectable and credible: an accountant, a university vice-rector, a philosophy professor and administrator at the Ministry of Education, a former soldier who had become a doctor. Their accounts circulated on television and in other media, in part because reform in the aftermath of the Matus scandal undermined Gabrielli's ability to use the Law of Internal Security against journalists. Gabrielli claimed he was a victim of image assassination and tried to use the Law of Internal Security against witnesses, but lost in court. His military career also crashed—Lagos vetoed his promotion in October. A new accountability boundary had been crossed. Gabrielli had once been on track to become the air force commander.[73]

Because the torture question affected so many people, the decline of cultural inhibition prompted worries about memory spinning out of control. In February and March 2001, Interior Minister Insulza and former president Aylwin warned about the effects of a potential avalanche of judicial accusations. The right to make a criminal complaint was to be respected, Insulza stated, but beating, abuse, and torture of prisoners had been pervasive under military rule. To pursue all cases of abuse or to conflate all agents of abuse with systematic torturers could lead to unending strains and could damage social peace. Aylwin supported Insulza and added a note of caution for victims. To prove a torture case after many years and without corroborating witnesses was difficult. Victims pursuing criminal lawsuits risked a new frustration.[74]

An avalanche did not materialize but as with Ruíz-Tagle, a specific revelation could prompt shock, soul searching, and demand for accountability. The academic world was shaken in 2001 when the press reported that Felipe Agüero, a Chilean political science professor at the University of Miami imprisoned at the National Stadium in 1973, had seen his torturer. In February Agüero wrote the director of the Institute of Political Science at the Catholic University about Professor Emilio Meneses, also a political scientist. The news leaked. The dean of the Faculty of History, Geography, and Political Sciences suspended Meneses with pay—presumably to give him time to clear his name. Meanwhile, university officials considered what to do, while academics debated rights of due process, the substance of the charges, and proper institutional response. The whole episode bore witness to the new post-1998 atmosphere of truth telling—and to the horrifying legacy of torture for victims. Agüero and Meneses were political scientists who specialized on military and defense matters. They had bumped into each other at occasional conferences and symposia since 1988. The encounters had left Agüero ashamed, shaken—and unable to do much. As the Ruíz-Tagle affair unfolded, Agüero began to experience a new resolve. He believed he had a responsibility to let colleagues at Catholic University know the truth, in order not to be a "silent accomplice."[75]

By 2000–2001, the political-electoral foundations of memory impasse had also eroded. The issue was not simply the election to the presidency of Ricardo Lagos, leader of the Left pole of the Concertación. The electoral calculus had shifted. The Center-Left coalition had to compete harder; it could ill afford to alienate its own base by shunning the memory question. The Right had a real chance to win; to hold too tightly to its old politics of memory could wreck the chance. Since 1997, the electoral majority of the Concertación had declined from a solid claim to leadership—at its peak a three-fifths majority—to a bare advantage. Lagos failed to secure a majority in the December 1999 presidential election, then squeaked out victory against Joaquín Lavín in a runoff round in January. Congressional elections in December 2001 also yielded a rather evenly divided vote (47.9 percent to 44.3 percent for Concertación and Alianza por Chile, respectively). Fairly or not, the ruling coalition had become more vulnerable to charges of complacency and distance from everyday issues such as employment and crime. Meanwhile, the Right, especially the UDI, built a dynamic cross-class voting base, fostered by grassroots organizing and by Lavín's image as the can-do problem solver.[76]

Part of the new dynamism of the Right rested on a will to leave behind its Pinochetista image and legacy. Lavín hitched his star to the wagon of pragmatic modernity, a conservatism that refused to be cornered into self-defeating gestures of Pinochetista loyalty and obsession with memory as salvation. In January 2001, when General Izurieta told Pinochet that the army would not back him if he defied the courts, what added force was Pinochet's bitter knowledge that the Right had begun to draw distance. The icon of memory as salvation had lost his magic, and signs of the ebbing loyalty had multiplied since late 1999. Financial backers who helped with living and legal expenses in England grew less generous; political leaders took care to state their loyalty was not "unconditional"; Lavín almost won the presidency. On 1 April 2001, the ten-year anniversary of Jaime Guzmán's assassination, the UDI president, Pablo Longueira, spoke in the language of memory as a shared tragedy: "we were all responsible" for the problem of political violence.[77]

In sum, the de facto powers of the military and the Right no longer played out as memory impasse—the will and ability to protect the leaders of a dirty salvation. When Pinochet escaped legal jeopardy in July 2001, he had already paid a price: marginalization as a public figure, even by erstwhile allies.

The turn of 1998–2001 opened up a freer (if uncertain) memory climate and a crossing of barriers, but it also yielded irony. Even as old constraints fell, the culture of memory argument that once galvanized democratic Chileans faded and turned less strategic.

The privatization of culture—the making of a nation comprised of individual consumers, not political citizens—rendered all metanarratives less persuasive and relevant. The interplay of "loose" memory and "emblematic" memory, the turning of personal experience into testimonial symbol of national experience, had inspired memory struggles during the dictatorship and early years of democratic transition. Such struggles had sought to hegemonize the meaning of a traumatic experience: on one side, to create an official memory of salvation under military rule, and eventually, a memory that justified mindful forgetting of the times of dirty war; on the other, to counter with testimonies of rupture, persecution, and awakening that exposed the true reality of military rule and the necessity to remember it. For victim-survivors, human rights activists, and democratic Chileans more generally, memory struggles to persuade and hegemonize had been strategic. During the dictatorship, they amounted to a life-and-death imperative in the face of repression and misinformation, as well as an effort to build moral values and achieve a democracy. During the early 1990s, they amounted to an effort to refound and legitimize a democracy on moral ground sharply contrasted with dictatorship, and to achieve the long-postponed reckonings with truth, justice, and social repair. But in a world of cultural individualism and privatized action, translating the personal into the emblematic was out of step. Ironically (and notwithstanding social discontent and disillusion), the very success of the economic growth model and cultural transformation of the 1990s had drawn wider sectors of society into a "structure of common sense" that privileged the individual over the social. Put another way, Chileans had made the *cultural* transit to globalization, an arena of identity and action that weakened *lo nacional*.[78]

The struggle to persuade and hegemonize gave way—slowly and incompletely, not smoothly or without struggle—to a contending common sense. Memory was a plural domain of recollections and meanings. No one's framework of memory and meaning could stand for the collective experience. Everyone's "little memories" had worth, and it was perhaps the personal and the intimate that mattered most. Moreover, and as we have seen, it was not only the privatization of culture that rendered older styles of memory struggle less persuasive. The subjectivity of memory impasse—the experience of repeated returns to standoff—also generated a sense of politico-cultural exhaustion by the late 1990s.[79]

The accent on the personal over the social (rather than the personal as symbol of the social) and the retreat from hegemonizing thus reflected a double phenomenon: deep cultural transformation of civil society, and political restlessness to find a way out of frustration in the public domain. An early marker of the emerging cultural sensibilities came in the memory season of 1997, when seventeen individuals—poets, writers, journalists, academics—published the book *What Was I Doing on 11 September 1973?* The problem, noted the editors, was that the public domain discourse about 11 September took the form of "a painful dialogue of the deaf" or, if debate ensued, "grave accusations of political misconduct and treachery." An advantage of "little history" was that personal experiences "do not refute one another." There was room to accept the plurality and instability of memory —one person remembered the drizzle of 11 September and the giant Unidad Popular banner, now soaked and ruined, at a downtown construction project. "The Third Year On the Move" (El Tercer Año Va), it had proclaimed. Others did not remember drizzle or the sign. The emerging political sensibilities about memory and history were evident not only in the Dialogue Table experiment, but in President Frei's state-of-the-nation address in May 1999. Upon reviewing Pinochet's detention in London and the intense divided sentiments it provoked, he asked what had been learned. His answer: "That there are pending problems, that there are distinct visions of our recent history. Let us accept this reality and give up the desire to impose our points of view about the past."[80]

The passage of time and generations also contributed to exhaustion of the older terms and referents of memory struggle. The most tangible marker was mortality. The leaders of memory as salvation, rupture, and persecution with roots in the 1970s—the founding era of emblematic memory making— aged visibly. Icons passed into "history." During 1996 to 1999, death claimed Pinochet's original junta colleagues: the admiral José Toribio Medina, the carabinero general César Mendoza Durán, the air force general Gustavo Leigh Guzmán. In 1999 death also claimed his two most formidable memory adversaries: Cardinal Raúl Silva Henríquez, of the Santiago Catholic Church; and Sola Sierra, the president-activist of the Agrupación. Both had legendary qualities of moral determination. Their passing sparked impressive outpourings of street affection—memory knots that again demanded attention to the past within the present. But their deaths were also a reminder: "living memory" could not last forever.[81]

The mortality of veteran leaders was but one sign of a larger shift. At the turn of the century three of ten Chileans (28.5 percent) were under fifteen years old—that is, people coming of age in a world of constrained democracy, individual consumerism, and highly skewed incomes, and without conscious personal memories of violent dictatorship before the 1988 plebiscite. Another one in six (16.3 percent) were under twenty-five. Their conscious personal memories might reach back to the 1980s era of mass protest and mobilization under dictatorship, but not to the founding traumas and memory struggles of the 1970s. In sum, at least four in nine Chileans (44.7 percent) could not personally remember the Unidad Popular and early junta years. Those times were history, not life experience. For young adults coming of age in a new era and century, the building of bridges between loose personal memory and emblematic collective memory of military rule —the dynamic crucial to politicocultural struggles under Pinochet and in the initial democratic transition—was becoming more elusive than resonant. It was a cultural habit of one's elders, not a common-sense experience of one's own.[82]

The decline of "living memory" did not imply linear descent into olvido. It did imply changing terms of memory struggle and heightened risk of a new kind of olvido. Every generation finds and constructs its own memory-truths and its own forgetfulness. At the turn of the century, the mixed messages of youth action and youth cynicism signaled both the continuing moral pull of memory, and the profound temptation of forgetting. On one hand, youths played roles as agents of conscience who energized memory initiatives for a postimpasse era—from the funa actions of 1999–2000 to joyfully expose torturers, to symbolic reenactment of the Caravan of Death across various provinces during its anniversary month of October 2001. On the other, a survey of Chileans between the ages of fifteen and twenty-nine demonstrated weariness with human rights struggles. (In the Chilean cultural context, we should remember, "youth" includes not only adolescents but "young adults" under thirty years of age.) Such views expressed disillusion with political squabbling whose results failed to meet everyday needs, not lack of awareness about injustices of Chilean society. Among middle- and lower-class youths, for example, three-fifths thought Chile "discriminatory" and "classist," but also expressed a desire to forget the human rights controversies of the past. The new risk of olvido: Younger Chileans might equate the memory question with the particular problems of particular elders and interest groups, not with a strategic moral reckoning for society. Put another way, memory would become the domain of "loose" personal recollections, not an effective call to a larger memory-truth or moral value.[83]

The irony of the turn in memory culture was that precisely as constraints on justice and expression fell, and as the structure of power undergirding impasse eroded, the memory question lost much of its cultural and strategic grip. The terms of memory argument forged by democratic Chileans and human rights activists in the 1990s lost resonance. The older cycle of memory struggle—its contending meaning frameworks, its social referents and voices—had reached a point of exhaustion. The connection of the individual and society had shifted, with tamped-down interplays of the personal and the emblematic. Memory struggles had not ended, but an uncertain search for a new style of memory politics and a new way of framing meaning was underway. In the world of elite politics and initiatives, especially, a new framework had emerged: memory as a shared national tragedy. In the arenas of grassroots action against torture and for judicial ensnarement of perpetrators, a new framework was also beginning to emerge: memory as unfinished work. Could the two approaches blend? Could either gain traction? The answers were not clear in 2001.

✕

Covering History with History?
The Making of Silence

As Chile entered the twenty-first century, its civic geography began bearing witness to the erosion of memory impasse. By then, of course, the Chilean landscape had already accumulated plaques marking people and events important to distinct memory camps: the Vicaría (Vicariate of Solidarity) and its legacy of moral support and awakening during times of state terror; the schoolteacher Arturo Barría Araneda, whose gifts of music, joy, and caring rendered his disappearance all the more cruel and poignant; the military escorts who died under fire as they sought to save Pinochet, the presumed savior of the nation, during a 1986 assassination attempt. By then, too, Chile's civic landscape included larger memorials for rescuing the denied and stigmatized past from secrecy and oblivion—the giant rocks, wall of names, and (largely empty) crypts for remembering the disappeared and the executed at the General Cemetery of Santiago; the Villa Grimaldi Peace Park for recovering the DINA's largest torture center from a commercial construction project. By then, too, the spread of the Internet fostered a cybergeography of memory on all sides.

What was new by 2000–2002, however, was a memorialization process that began to crack boundaries of containment—a certain discretion or self-censorship—in the formal civic geography of Chile. The nation's capital city began to sprout a new geography of remembrance. Two downtown plazas constitute Santiago's civic heart. On the western side of the Plaza de Armas stood the cathedral—and in 2000, where the central pedestrian street Paseo Ahumada emptied into the Plaza de Armas, a statue to remember Cardinal Raúl Silva Henríquez, the recently deceased giant of the Catholic Church who pushed values of solidarity and human rights during the terrifying 1970s.

On the opposite side, toward the northeast, stood the National History Museum. The historical exhibits once ratified silence through an elite-oriented vision that emphasized colonial roots and the patriotic glories of the nineteenth century—and stopped abruptly in the 1930s. The exhibit strategy ratified the military regime's vision of heroic memory and its silences: the nineteenth century was a time of patriotic national heroism, presumably recaptured and modernized after 1973; the twentieth-century era of mass politics and social conflict was a time of hatefulness and manipulative declension. Its politicians ruined Chile, and its legacy required erasure, not acceptance or reflection.

By 2002, however, a ten-year project to end the erasure and build a more realistic—inclusive and accepting, provocative and sobering—portrait of the past finally bore fruit. The new permanent exhibits included a section inviting reflection on the paradox of the twentieth century in Chilean and world history: on one hand, a century filled with cruelty, violence, injustice, conflict; on the other, a century of advances in such areas as material life, public health, and extension of rights to once-excluded groups, such as women. Against this backdrop, while the interpretive thrust found nothing to mark as positive within the Allende presidency, it also avoided easy moralizing and reductionism. History was more than the work of great-versus-evil individuals. Struggles for social justice and inclusion, ideas of class conflict, the passions and conflicts of the Allende era did not mysteriously drop out of the sky; nor were they the product of a handful of manipulative opportunists and schemers. The depiction of Allende could include a human touch. Powerful artifacts—Allende's cracked glasses, a photo of La Moneda bombarded by air—invited the visitor to imagine and consider the sheer violence of the coup.[1]

Changing civic geography was even more dramatic in the other key downtown plaza, the flag-lined Plaza de la Constitución, which stands before the entrance to La Moneda Palace. The redesign of La Moneda Palace and the Plaza of the Constitution during 1980–81—part of the military regime's institutionalization project and celebration of a new Constitution—gave symbolic expression to official memory and its silences. The one memorial anchor on the plaza was a statue of Diego Portales, the nineteenth-century lawgiver lauded as the hero, parallel, and inspiration of Pinochet's regime. At the presidential palace, the doorway at Morandé 80 used by Allende and his predecessors no longer existed. Portales and the missing door anchored the aesthetic of nineteenth-century continuity and twentieth-century erasure. In 1994 difficult congressional debates finally culminated in a new memory aesthetic: mutual acceptance of the historical reality—and therefore, a measure of social legitimacy—of several streams of twentieth-century experience. The Plaza of the Constitution facing La Moneda could now include statues, to be financed through private fundraising, of Jorge Alessandri, Eduardo Frei, and Salvador Allende, the presidents and leaders of the Right, Center, and Left, respectively, before 1973. Obviously, a congressional vote to authorize remembrance of the three presidents at La Moneda Palace did not imply endorsement of any one of them. It *did* imply rejection of aesthetic erasure, founded in stigma.[2]

On 26 June 2000, inauguration of Allende's statue completed the troika of twentieth-century remembrance. President Ricardo Lagos and Representative Isabel Allende, among other dignitaries, spoke at the inaugural ceremony. The date coincided with Salvador Allende's birthday. The ceremony did not go smoothly—memory remained a contentious terrain, the past within the present, and also a dispute over ownership of the Allende legacy. Perhaps a thousand demonstrators gathered to demand justice in the Pinochet case, and some threw coins and eggs. Communists who felt excluded from recognition and invitation despite their historic support of Allende protested, even as they also sparked a moving moment: the singing of "Venceremos" (We Will Win), the theme song of the Unidad Popular, when Lagos and Hortensia Bussi de Allende unveiled the statue. Lagos spoke of Allende's fitting return to the spot where he had acted heroically amidst a great political tragedy and of his legacy as a democrat, while also emphasizing that times had changed. Chileans had learned to place "the rights of man" in the center of their political values.[3]

The new aesthetic design did not erase Portales; instead, it turned him into a starting point, rather than an endpoint. At the far northern end of the giant plaza, still the symbolic Giver of Law, Portales faced the entrance of La Moneda Palace. Closer to the palace and the diagonals of flags that extended from its front corners toward the plaza center, the trio of new presidential statues bore witness to the competing projects and social bases of politics and constitutionalism during the twentieth century. Frei's statue, aesthetically the most attractive, had the pueblo at his side. Workers and peasants provided him a foundation as his uplifted arm called forth a following. Allende stood closest to the palace, symbolically wrapped by democratic constitutionalism—his presidential sash and a giant flag—and by his declaration of faith in Chile's future during the eloquent final radio address.[4]

It was not simply in Santiago that civic memorialization began to crack taboos. The Villa Grimaldi Peace Park, inaugurated in 1997, also constituted

22. Detail from the Temuco Peace Park: A sacred *canelo* tree bursts through the heavy concrete of repression. *Credit: Florencia Mallon.*

a starting point. In Temuco, the (sometimes tense) synergy of local grass-roots and state actors, and the freer memory environment, finally produced in 2001 a regional Peace Park. It invited remembrance and reflection on the southern regions that experienced a ferocious repressive violence, in part vengeance in the aftermath of agrarian reform struggles. The Temuco Peace Park included, in addition to its wall of persons disappeared and executed in the south, a striking metaphor of memory as the life-giving force. A *canelo* tree, a sacred symbol of vitality and renewal among indigenous Mapuche peoples, burst through the heavy concrete of repression.[5]

The making of memory, however, is neither a linear process of triumph nor an ever-growing recovery of the totality of the past. It is a social process pushed and pulled by social conflicts. It is a selective process of finding meaning. It is a process that makes silences even as it makes memories. At times, the selectivity and the contentiousness of memory yield not simply a problem of flat denial of historical facts or truths but, more subtly, the use of some slices of history to cover up others.[6]

Civic geography bore witness to both dynamics. On the one hand, plaques, statues, museum exhibits, and peace parks marked particular struggles to remember the flatly denied and stigmatized. They marked particular advances against an aesthetic of erasure. On the other hand, civic geography also bore witness to the ways memory impasse and division yielded subtle silences: discretion. The most striking cases came from the uses of Chile's hero of Independence, Bernardo O'Higgins, to provide cover for contentious symbols of the recent past.

At the century's turn, homage to the memory of Bernardo O'Higgins provided a protective mantle for two of the most controversial symbols of opposed memory camps. Across the street and facing the southern back side of La Moneda Palace stood the Eternal Flame of Liberty, inaugurated at the 11 September anniversary commemoration of 1975. Of all the material symbols of heroic Pinochetista memory—military rule as salvation from the violent dictatorship planned by the Left—the Eternal Flame of Liberty was arguably the most important and contentious. Its location shifted twice; groups of oppositional youth sought to douse it during the memory wars of the 1980s. In 2000, the Eternal Flame remained a sacred symbol of salvation—for those loyal and grateful to the military past—in the civic heart of Santiago. But the discretions of memory impasse also prevailed. The Flame was unmarked, its meaning subsumed. It sat near the top stairs of the "Altar to the Fatherland," which honored the memory of Bernardo O'Higgins and nineteenth-century patriotism. A valiant statue of O'Higgins the Liberator stood atop the monument, and over the buried remains of the independence hero. If one personally *knew* the history of the Eternal Flame, one understood privately that the old equation of 1810 with 1973—the idea that toppling Allende constituted another Independence, again a release from tyranny—was discreetly symbolized in the altar. The public civic geography and markings, however, managed to fold the meaning of the Flame under the Liberator's mantle of glory.[7]

A half-dozen blocks to the east of O'Higgins and the unmarked Flame lay the beautiful district of Barrio París-Londres. The cobblestone streets; the human scale and tasteful stone-and-stucco aesthetic of homes, shops, institutes, and cafés; the relative quiet—they amounted to an oasis of peace and charm within a downtown of noisy streets and large undistinguished buildings.

Inside the oasis, however, stood one of the most searing symbols of memory as rupture. During the first year of military rule the DINA took over Londres 38, an elegant two-story house used as an office of the Socialist Party, converting it into a torture house. Londres 38 corresponded to the early history of lethal repression, when the nascent DINA had only begun to build itself into a more complex organization with a more well-defined infrastructure of routines, personnel, functions, and detention centers. The house was large but tremendously crowded with prisoners; it lacked capacity to separate them and block communication. Its tortures had a certain ad hoc and even jumbled aspect, more like pervasive torments at all hours than select ("scientific") application within a carefully staged process of intimidation, degradation, and questioning. Alongside the focused abuses such as electric shock, sexual violation, bodily hanging, and beatings when prisoners were taken upstairs for torture and interrogation, there were the interminable general ones downstairs—the nude and blindfolded sitting while tied to chairs, the intense hunger and thirst, the loud noise and music to prevent sleep. The ordeal of prisoners included not only their own electric "grilling" (*parrilla*), which was very common at Londres 38, but also the bearing of witness: torture and sexual violation of others, including relatives.

The ad hoc aspect of Londres 38 led to heterogeneous results. Some disappeared prisoners were last seen in Londres 38; some transferred to Villa Grimaldi for additional torture and eventual disappearance; some later released or exiled, or converted into collaborators. In short, Londres 38 loomed large in memory as a cruel and unresolved rupture of life. Its history crisscrossed with the history of the disappeared and the history of Villa Grimaldi. Its history yielded survivors who later participated in memory and human rights struggles such as the Rettig Commission process, court cases, and street demonstrations. Like Villa Grimaldi, Londres 38 was a sacred memory knot that aroused efforts to preserve it from oblivion. Unlike Villa Grimaldi, it was located downtown, near the civic heart of Santiago, only a short walk from a subway stop. Also unlike Villa Grimaldi, activists had not succeeded in rolling back an erasure project.[8]

Londres 38 disappeared—within a mantle of glory provided by the mem-

23. The disappeared Londres 38, renamed Londres 40 and dedicated to the study and remembrance of Bernardo O'Higgins, in the year 2000. *Credit: Author.*

ory of Bernardo O'Higgins. Sometime during military rule it acquired a new address, Londres 40. No "Londres 38" existed on the block. By 1988 the military regime had fixed up the home and arranged its transfer to the O'Higgins Institute of Chile (El Instituto O'Higginiano de Chile), founded in 1953 to study and remember the history and patriotic legacy of the great liberator. A close informal connection to the army remained. In 2000, the president of the institute's directorate was the retired General Washington Carrasco. In 1973, he was the army general in command during the extra-legal executions of activist-leaders from the Lota coal mines, near Concepción. As with the Eternal Flame of Liberty, historical remembrance of O'Higgins served to subsume and deflect acknowledgment of a sacred—and sharply divisive—memory symbol. As one stepped into the archway of Londres 40 to visit the O'Higgins Library or to attend a talk, it was the bust of the Independence Liberator that marked the meaning of the site.[9]

The world of the 1990s—competing emblematic memories, skewed power, politicocultural impasse—was a structure that breeds constraint. Such a world also breeds irony. Some symbols become exceptionally hot to handle. Under the circumstances, History and Memory may provide the soothing balm. Remembering History serves to cover history. Monument serves to cover experience. The making of Memory discreetly serves the making of silence.

Chapter 6

✳

Memory as Unfinished Work:
New Reckonings, 2002–2006

On 1 July 2002, the Supreme Court let Pinochet off the criminal hook. A year had passed since the controversial 2001 ruling by the Santiago Court of Appeals (chapter 5) to suspend prosecution in the Caravan of Death case, on grounds that moderate subcortical vascular dementia compromised his mental fitness for trial. Now the Court's Criminal Chamber went further: Pinochet's mental health defect was incurable and justified permanent closure. A few days later, Pinochet retired from his post as lifetime senator. The decision protected him from a dangerous contradiction—fit to legislate, not fit to stand trial—while qualifying him for a presidential pension. The events ratified the formula of 2001: release from criminal jeopardy, marginalization from active public life.[1]

The formula revived sensations of impasse and elite deals that plagued memory politics in the 1990s but in truth, and as we have seen, Chile had changed dramatically since 1998. Old constraints and styles of memory politics had cracked. During 2002–06, the idea of memory as unfinished work gained traction, leading to new reckonings with the past. The most dramatic was the confrontation with torture as a massive reality and memory-truth. Even Pinochet's release from legal jeopardy proved illusory. Until his death in 2006, fresh revelations about the past and additional legal cases kept ensnaring him. This chapter and the next explore the new memory culture that emerged, and the twin sensibilities—ongoing unfinished work, shared national tragedy—that came to define it. This chapter focuses on reckonings related to military rule and the pre-1973 Chile that culminated in crisis. The next attends to the conflictive reframing of democratic transition and mobilization, and its paradoxical consequences—unprecedented advancement, declining strategic weight—for the politics of human rights memory.

Three pressures reshaped the memory climate by 2003. In political society, the institutions that once signified sharp constraint—the judiciary and the military, and the UDI (Unión Democrática Independiente) as party of the hard-core Right—found themselves crossing a point of no return on truth and justice. Second, in civil society, grassroots demands to address pending memory issues—torture of political prisoners, sexual assault as central to violent degradation, the role of civilians in abuse—continued to build. Third, the thirty-year anniversary of the 11 September coup—after two years of eclipse by the shocking 2001 suicide-jet attacks by Al Qaeda on the World Trade Center in New York—turned into a major memory knot. The approaching memory season gathered up the cultural impulse to address the past as still troubled and unfinished. In all these ways, barriers broke and the idea of memory work as a vehicle to achieve closure turned into an anachronism. Pressures for a major governmental initiative built up during 2002—03.

Judges continued their emergence as forceful actors. The contrast with an earlier moment of judicial opening is revealing. In 1993 (see chapter 3), the Aylwin doctrine and the impeachment of the Supreme Court justice Hernán Cereceda yielded a snowball effect. Open (or reopened) human rights cases mounted and compelled officers to appear in court and account for their pasts. Saber rattling—the *boinazo*—drastically altered the climate. Ten years later, the balance of power had shifted. Saber rattling was not an option, and the careers of high judges were less tied to Pinochetismo. Influential judicial interpretation included not only the Aylwin doctrine but also equation of disappearance with an ongoing crime of kidnapping, until proved otherwise. The Dialogue Table initiative, although a failure from the point of view of reliable new information on the disappeared, also had consequences that expanded judicial inquiry. The accord called on the Supreme Court to appoint specialized judges to follow up on information about the disappeared provided by the military and police reports. In June 2001, the Court designated nine "exclusive judges" to work full-time on some four dozen cases, and fifty-one "preferential" magistrates to give priority treatment to other such cases. Meanwhile, the new human rights program of the Interior Ministry of the Lagos administration provided re-sources—economic, logistical, legal—to promote and expand specialized judicial investigation of human rights crimes.[2]

The result was a new snowball effect—not just more judicial cases but fresh legal precedents and truth revelations. The doctrine of permanent kid-napping, which eviscerated the 1978 Amnesty Law unless proof of the pris-oner's death or release fell within its applicable dates, took hold among some specialized judges in addition to Juan Guzmán. In November 2002, Judge Jaime Salas sentenced a retired army general and a retired army colonel in the 1973 kidnap-disappearance of Pedro Segundo Espinoza Barrientos. In April 2003, Judge Alejandro Solís found five former DINA officers guilty in the 1975 kidnap-disappearance of Miguel Angel Sandoval Rodríguez. The longer sentences went to the notorious and once untouchable leaders: Man-uel Contreras (fifteen years), Marcelo Moren Brito (fifteen years), Miguel Krassnoff Martchenko (ten years). In January 2004, the Santiago Court of Appeals confirmed the sentence, ratified the doctrine of permanent kidnap-ping, and added another line of legal reasoning—the superiority of interna-tional law and treaties to national law, on amnesty or time-lapse of human rights crimes, by virtue of a provision in the Chilean Constitution. Such reasoning opened up yet another road to evisceration of the 1978 self-amnesty. Meanwhile, open human rights cases under criminal investigation mounted to over three hundred cases, with some two hundred accused individuals by mid-2003. The cadre of specialized judges, the failure of the military-police branches to impose a stop, the interpretive doctrines under-mining amnesty, the widening net of accused officers—for soldiers of "dirty war," the imagined slippery slope had turned real.[3]

This was not all. The specialized judges uncovered new crimes and memory-truths. The irony of the Dialogue Table was that the unreliability of the infor-mation it generated *also* justified new investigations to which the military and carabineros forces had, in effect, signed on. Magistrates searched directly on military property to find remains and corroborate evidence. The 2002 inves-tigation of Judge Amanda Valdovinos led, in 2003, to indictment of five former soldiers by Judge Juan Carlos Urrutia for illegal exhumation of remains—a crime ineligible for amnesty under any interpretation. In December 1978, the discovery of human remains of fifteen peasants in abandoned lime ovens at Lonquén, in central Chile, had provided the first forensic proof that relatives had spoken the truth when asserting that state agents abducted and disap-peared their loved ones. For the military regime, Lonquén turned into a dangerous memory knot, galvanizing people and belief in counterofficial truth. Shortly after the discovery (and again when facing democratic transition), military and secret police personnel carried out orders to neutralize the danger by mapping, exhuming, and erasing traces of disappeared bodies. The result—a second disposal of bodies, to make up for imperfect first disposals—left behind evidence and witnesses of unlawful exhumations *after* the 10 March 1978 closure date of the amnesty decree. The operation also left behind gruesome archaeology and stories—body bits broken in the churning of earth, body bags taken away for reburial or incineration or a toss by helicopter into the ocean.[4]

The irony was also evident in a cover-up scandal in 2002–03. General (retired) Patricio Campos, the designee for the air force section of the report on the disappeared mandated by the Dialogue Table, went on trial for obstruction of justice. He had held back information. The Santiago Court of Appeals ruled the prosecution valid in May 2003. Meanwhile, the cover-up had forced the resignation (under implied threat of criminal prosecution) of the air force commander in chief, Patricio Ríos.[5]

Judge Guzmán himself remained an active and highly visible force until his retirement in April 2005. Notwithstanding redistribution of some cases to other judges and warnings by the Supreme Court to cut a lower profile, he tenaciously pursued his cases. In 2002, he organized witness testimony and reenactment of the 1973 transformation of National Stadium into a site of mass detention, torture, and execution. The international aspects of his inquiry—the executions of U.S. citizens Charles Horman and Frank Teruggi, the role of U.S. government complicity, the conflicting testimonies by U.S. citizen and prisoner-survivor Adam Schesch and former U.S. consul general Frederick Purdy, the arrival of famed filmmaker Costa-Gavras, whose 1981 movie *Missing* focused on the Horman case—added to the media attention. A year later Guzmán brought another chilling memory-truth to light. Inquiry into the kidnapping-death of Marta Ugarte, whose body washed up on a beach in 1976, spun into a larger investigation of other disappeared prisoners and Villa Grimaldi. The discovery: the DINA used helicopter flights to disappear many prisoners held in the Santiago Metropolitan Region. The actors—and potential witnesses—included pilots and mechanics, not just secret police agents. From 1974 to 1978, the army's Aviation Command flew at least forty times to toss prisoners—their bodies tied to rails to assure they would sink—into the Pacific Ocean. The Puma helicopters carried 8–15 bodies per flight, and threw out some 400–500 people. Guzmán indicted not only four pilots and the head of the helicopter command, but also the top organizers: DINA chief Manuel Contreras, and General (retired) Carlos López Tapia, who ran operations at Villa Grimaldi.[6]

Culturally and politically, what lent greater force to the judges' work was knowledge that the military, particularly the army, would not and could not resort to the crude tactics of the past. We have already seen (chapter 5) that the London arrest of Pinochet and the renovation of military leadership under a new commander in chief, Ricardo Izurieta, complicated the army's inclination to hold fast to the traditional vehement defense of Pinochet and his legacy—even as the ups and downs of the Pinochet case and ongoing Pinochetista loyalties among current and retired officers pressured against too open a break. The Dialogue Table talks formalized and pushed along the evolution toward a new public stance. The promotion of General Juan Emilio Cheyre to army commander in chief in 2002, and the final marginalization of Pinochet as an active public figure, consolidated the new line. Under Cheyre, the army's overriding priority would be to establish itself as a professional force with a strong budget and modernized equipment and training—liberated from the controversies of an earlier military generation. On the memory question, Cheyre charted a path consistent with the Dialogue Table's stance on the unacceptability of human rights violations regardless of historical circumstances, and consistent with the Lagos administration's line of letting justices do their work as independent state actors. In the new era of military-civilian collaboration, the army joined in the sensibility of shared national tragedy. The point of army lobbying was not defense of the Pinochet legacy as such, nor a veto on the reach of justice into high officer strata, but a more subtle form of damage control. Could the new emphasis on harmony and respect for law help persuade key actors to agree, finally, on a political solution to speed up justice cases, neutralize permanent-kidnap doctrine, and create a firm timeline on trials?

The result was nuance: a mixed message. Cheyre and the army would collaborate with civilian institutions and judges as they went about their work—even when justice pointed at retired or current officers, even in a case where Cheyre had to account for his past as a lieutenant in 1973. At the same time, Cheyre would establish points of concern about open-ended justice that could go on interminably. In January 2003, Cheyre formalized his stance in a widely publicized editorial column and army communiqué. The army recognized the imperative of social repair and, through the Dialogue Table accord, the reality of the abuse inflicted on citizens. He point-edly rejected historical context as a mitigating excuse: "Said violations of human rights have no justification." Social peace required "accepting the sentences of the justice tribunals" and respecting the accused by avoiding public pressure. Most dramatically, Cheyre parted company with memory politics that once equated army identity with the Pinochet regime and its legacy. The army was not "heir of a given regime of government. Its de-fense, if such were needed, corresponds to other people or entities." The mission of the army was to consolidate itself as a professional force, whose respect rested not on might but "the legitimacy of its contribution—its military function."[7]

The mixed aspect came through more forcefully in June, as pressure mounted on the Lagos administration to define a new human rights initia-tive. Cheyre proclaimed his belief in "never again," interpreted the vow to apply also to civilians complicit in the 1973 crisis and supportive of military rule, and asked for a political solution "so that the Army does not continue as prisoner of the past." He voiced sympathy with relatives of the disap-peared but also frustration with permanent-kidnap doctrine: "How can someone be kidnapped for thirty years!"[8]

Lagos had reinforced the symbolism of military subordination to civilian authority in 2002, when he appointed Michelle Bachelet as minister of defense. The political and gender symbols of military hierarchy under Pino-chet were now reversed. Cheyre reported to a talented woman who emerged from the military tradition (constitutionalism) and the political camp (the Left) repressed in 1973. Bachelet, a Socialist and former prisoner at Villa Grimaldi, was also the daughter of the air force general Alberto Bachelet, a Constitutionalist who died in jail in 1974. Known to suffer from a serious coronary condition, he endured ill treatment and torture, including simu-lated executions; he succumbed to a heart attack.[9]

Justice had turned into an engine with its own momentum by 2002–03. The politicocultural climate facilitated the emergence of more forceful judges with the legal doctrine, resources, and will to press on. The dialectic of judicial and military actors had shifted, compared to the early 1990s. Judge Guzmán was still a pioneer, but not so alone.

Judges and generals were not the only relevant actors. The post-1998 decline of inhibition yielded grassroots pressure to take on memory work once left aside—and new synergies with select state actors. After all, justice could not proceed far without a web of collaborating witnesses. Powerful moments of human connection and unburdening emerged between survivor-victims on the one hand, and human rights judges on the other, as they worked to establish facts and culpabilities. Together they reactivated a time at the outer edge of the human and imaginable. The intimate and existential aspect of such memory could create a pressure of its own. As survivors told their histories of deep rupture—violent degradation, sexual humiliation—sometimes Guzmán and the witnesses could not hold back their tears. "So I would ask the witness to go to the bathroom to wash her [or his] face."[10]

Pressure also took the form of critique. Human rights and victim groups forcefully assailed the flaws and subterfuges of elite initiatives. The paradoxical consequences of the Dialogue Table—cruel omission and misinformation in the military-police reports on disappeared persons, but also a discourse of shared tragedy that drew the military into accepting expanded justice investigations—could yield tough debate. From time to time, Lagos or government leaders sought to accent the positive—the creation of specialized judges—while activists such as Lorena Pizarro, president of the Agrupación of Relatives of the Detained and Disappeared, denounced such talk as sham. What the Dialogue Table really produced, she observed acidly, was "false information that caused new pain for relatives."[11]

The most innovative pressure—given the earlier narrowing of memory as rupture and persecution to a subset of maximal victims, some 3,000 persons definitively confirmed as executed or disappeared—focused on torture and former political prisoners. As we have seen (chapter 5), the politico-cultural turn of 1998–2001 put the torture issue into the public domain. Young activists organized *funas* to "out" perpetrators. The stories of Eugenio Ruíz-Tagle and Felipe Agüero resonated. They were dramas not of numbers but individuals—likeable victims subjected to terrible torments by named perpetrators. The role of torture in the British ruling that Pinochet's extradition was legally valid, and a cultural climate more conducive to decisions by torture survivors to seek therapy and to network to come to terms with their life histories, also laid a groundwork. In 1999, when Pinochet's legal fate in London was unresolved and government authorities argued justice could be served in Chile, victims began organizing evidence and domestic criminal cases against him for torture, not just for disappearances and executions. Associations of former political prisoners began to grow in number, visibility, and coordination. By November 2000, prisoner-survivors from eleven detention sites scattered across the country—including famous ones such as Pisagua in the north, National Stadium in the center, Dawson Island in the south—formed a coordinating group. The Association of Former Concentration Camp Prisoners (Agrupación de ex Prisioneros de Campos de Concentración) decided not only to press for truth and criminal justice, but also to sue the state for damages.[12]

Such initiatives did not wither. The push to address torture as a fundamental memory-truth—a ripping apart of the humanity of prisoners, central to the project of state terror, inflicted on *both* those who survived and those who did not—turned more insistent. In the post-1998 environment, each new revelation could feed the sensibility of having to reckon, finally, with a pending ethical imperative. The Felipe Agüero example in February 2001 is instructive. He had wrestled with silent agony for years. How should he respond to the fact that Emilio Meneses was a political scientist in the same subfield at Chile's most prestigious university? It was the case of Eugenio Ruíz-Tagle that inspired Agüero to take the plunge—to decide he had a *duty* to end a personal silence he now viewed as complicity. Once news broke that Agüero had recognized his torturer and written the head of Catholic University's Institute of Political Science, faculty and students embarked on their own reckoning. What were *their* ethical duties? Did they also need to examine the broader history of complicity and repression at their university? By August, the institute's academic council declared its loss of confidence in Meneses as a professor. By January 2002, Meneses—also under pressure of a conflict-of-interest investigation of his consulting business on arms sales —resigned. In December, Agüero saw his truth confirmed in court: Meneses lost a slander suit.[13]

The sense of reckoning spilled beyond an academic community tied to a specific case. The shock of the February 2001 revelations about Meneses and Gabrielli created a climate favorable to launch a coalition of human rights groups determined to move torture into the center of public debate—as unfinished and morally urgent memory work. By mid-year, the Ethical Commission Against Torture (Comisión Etica Contra la Tortura) had written an initial report and met with President Lagos. It estimated the number of people imprisoned for political reason under the dictatorship in the hundreds of thousands, and those subjected to extended detention at over 100,000. For two years it kept pushing, via informational reports, petition drives and demonstrations, and meetings with political elites and allies. In June 2003, Mireya García—her double role as spokeswoman for the Ethical Commission and as vice-president of the Agrupación of Relatives of the Detained and Disappeared symbolized an end to back-seat status for prisoner-survivors—reported that the latest meeting with Lagos had met with a positive response. "The Government understands that it has to create the commission [on torture] as a basic means to recognize the kind of violation of human right that has not until now been socially, politically, or judicially recognized."[14]

Grassroots work was slowly turning torture victims into the symbolic sibling of maximal victims—the surviving sister, as it were, whose suffering showed what also happened to the disappeared or executed brother. As former political prisoners organized to press their demands, they launched civil suits in addition to criminal complaints. By December 2002, some class action suits against the state grouped hundreds of victims into fiscally significant claims—tens of billions of pesos (equivalent to tens of millions of U.S. dollars). The sense of having to push hard against state reluctance was strong. As the activist Víctor Rosas put it, "We are obligated to continuing suing the State in the face of indifference by the Administration." Damage suits for human rights violations (including those related to the disappeared and executed) swelled to some 160 by 2003, and one byproduct was a certain schizophrenia. In criminal cases, the Council for Defense of the State argued *for* the prosecution of perpetrators; in civil cases, it argued *against* the award of damages.[15]

As struggle to recognize the harm of torture and political imprisonment mounted, women broke an additional barrier. Despite the intimacy and humiliation of the topic, and the fear of shame so powerful in respectable Chilean culture, former prisoners began to speak about sexual violence. In July 2003, Odette Alegría, a victim-activist of the association of former political prisoners in Linares (in the Seventh Region, some fifty kilometers south of Talca), accused Nelson Mery of violating her in November 1973. During the day, political prisoners were taken for torture and interrogation to the army's Artillery School of Linares, where Mery was stationed as police liaison. "Maybe it is a bit crude to say it," Alegría explained on television. At the Artillery School, where she was made to witness tortures, "[Mery] would often go from his office to the bathroom and . . . come out with his fly open and penis out, he would shake it in my face and put it in my mouth." What made her testimony audacious was not only its public telling, but that Mery was a powerful person whose career since 1990 cut the other way. Under the Concertación, he had risen to become national director of the Investigations Police (the civilian detective force of the executive branch). As such, he had built a credible human rights record, brought prominent perpetrators including Manuel Contreras to justice, faced down army officers and intelligence agents, and gained respect in the Center-Left including some Socialist Party circles. Mery launched a criminal complaint for slander without foundation, and a classic war of gendered credibility and innuendo—she said versus he said—ensued. Was Mery an opportunist who blew with the political winds, whether dictatorial or democratic? Was he a man wrongly accused? Was he a person who had redeemed his sins—if only he would admit them? Some of Alegría's skeptics suggested her manipulation by the Right to undermine the Concertación's credibility. Others asked why she waited thirty years to make the accusation. It soon emerged, however, that Alegría told another woman prisoner about groping and oral rape in 1973, that she again shared her plight with a human rights psychiatrist in 1990 at the start of democratic transition, and that she suffered a mental health setback in 1992, upon learning of Mery's promotion to the directorship.[16]

As significant, other women and men broke the taboo on sexualized torture. As Alegría prepared for court, fifty-eight women once detained at the Artillery School of Linares worked with the local association of former political prisoners to compile pertinent information. The National Association of Former Political Prisoners (Agrupación Nacional de Ex Presos Políticos) also had relevant documents from 1999, when Alegría shared her ordeal with the activist Pedro Matta. On 23 July, forty-two women who had been political prisoners issued a declaration. What had come out thus far, it said, "is only a sample of what we lived. To disqualify and insult the women who dare denounce these facts inhibits other declarations, when what is now needed is to open welcoming spaces." The women's decision to speak out about their experiences had been difficult. "It has an individual and collective cost for us, but we think it crucial to inform the public . . . that sexual violence as torture included anal, vaginal, and oral violation; by persons, [and] with objects or animals." In addition to penetration, they had contended with nudity, sexualized insult, forced witness of rape, and threats of rape, all aimed at "destroying us as women." The signers included women such as Mireya García and Erika Hennings, well-known activists who once put their own torment as political prisoners on the back seat while seeking truth and justice for disappeared relatives. Now, they pressed both issues and cast aside gendered rules of discretion. Mery resigned his post in September, although he later had more success in court. In 2004, a judge ruled against Alegría on the grounds that corroborating testimonies were insufficient to reach a definite conclusion. Meanwhile, however, sexual torture had cracked into the public cultural arena as another important but postponed reckoning.[17]

The approach of the thirty-year anniversary of the 1973 coup added to the buildup of tension and expectation. The old boundaries of memory politics no longer held up very well, and political elites had an interest in *charting* the path for unfinished memory work. Grassroots actors and judges were creating new realities and claims, even as memory remained divisive yet relevant for politicocultural legitimacy. In July 2003, one of three Chileans still remembered the coup as liberation from Marxism (34 percent), and nearly as many thought the Pinochet years "good" or "very good" (29 percent). A majority, however, wanted to establish truth and to sanction those responsible for human rights violations (52 percent in at least the worst cases, 41 percent in all cases). A majority also disagreed with the idea that passage of time meant "one should not insist" anymore (53 percent). The 11 September date still constituted a potent memory knot, notwithstanding its 1998 suppression as a national holiday. The arrival of a major round-number anniversary seemed to set a deadline for a new advance on the memory question.[18]

Given the conflictiveness and violence that historically surrounded the date, and the renewed tensions about trials, torture, and the Dialogue Table since 2001, could the political elite afford to fail to present a path? As we have seen (chapter 5), the freer memory climate, and the eroded structure of impasse had brought Chile to a crossroads by 2001. Would a wider acknowledgment of human rights violations, and of memory as unfinished urgent work, translate into an ever stronger "wedge" principle? If so, truth-and-justice work might continue far into the future and ensnare a widening range of actors. Or, could such acknowledgment translate into a new "formula" that drew clear temporal and social boundaries on memory work?

Such considerations were not far from the surface as elite actors readied themselves for 2003 as a defining year. Cheyre understood the point when he dramatically renounced, in January, an army role as heir and defender of the Pinochet legacy. To sustain a professional force less drained by memory conflicts—because it would not defend perpetrators in criminal cases, but also had some sort of endpoint in sight—he had to nudge the political world into a proactive stance. He was not coy about the timing. "This year will mark three decades since the situation that culminated with the events of 11 September 1973," he began, and he hoped reflection on values would build a new kind of anniversary "of the day when we found ourselves involved in a most grave civic enmity." Nor was Interior Minister Insulza coy when he promised—in June, under pressure of numerous proposals by political parties and activist groups—that the government would complete its work on a major human rights initiative before 11 September.[19]

The thirty-year commemoration did indeed break boundaries. Even before September, television and print media prepared for a big memory year. Television programs injected a "lost world" aspect—authenticity through attention to the human and the nostalgic, such as the music, sports, and social scenes and fashions that defined the era, in addition to the standard focus on political crisis and violence of 1973. It was as if the trends of recent years—the retreat from earlier struggles to hegemonize memory, the emphasis on shared tragedy still unfinished and festering, the breakdown of old taboos and silences, the cultural transformation that placed the foundational moment of "today" within a truly different yesterday world—readied many Chileans to return with fresh eyes to 1973. On the eleventh, television and radio competed to recapture the sights, sounds, and secrets of the historic day in documentaries, and in "minute-by-minute" re-creations including radio-theater. The memory programs captured a willing audience. Six of ten Chileans (62 percent) said in a September survey that they had seen a program or read a report about the coup, most of them (73 percent) with considerable or much interest. But it was not just mainstream media that sought a fresh look or injected the sense of an authentic but lost world. *The Clinic* criticized the superficiality that cleansed the Unidad Popular into a reassuring story line. The Popular Unity was above all "impure"—chaotic, exasperating, transgressive. It was a time when "the wretched could for a while feel themselves to be persons, as much as their millionaire bosses."[20]

The most striking new aspect was the heightened mythical power and civic rehabilitation of Salvador Allende. Allende had long been a figure important in memory struggles, and Aylwin's decision to honor him at a second funeral in 1990 had initiated a process of dignified civic acceptance. But now a new surge of interest and homage prevailed, drew in a wider range of political elites, and reshaped the interior civic geography of the presidential palace itself. About 80,000 people, most of them young, turned out for "The Dream Exists," a concert festival (5–6 September) at National Stadium to celebrate Allende and a dream worth having. The anniversary inspired Angel Parra to write a rap and talk to the fallen president. "You were the hope / for a world of justice / without hate or vengeance" and you went down fighting, rifle in hand. "You were right." To be sure, the cultural celebrations and commemorations in *poblaciones*, universities, trade union centers, civic plazas, and memory sites such as torture houses also remembered and honored other social actors.

In addition to Allende's presence in varied grassroots and media happenings, and the mingling of his memory with that of other social actors, the Lagos administration embraced him as a democrat and leader true to his vision. The day before the anniversary, Allende returned as forebear to La Moneda Palace. Interior Minister Insulza honored Allende and others who fell at the palace "for a just cause," and placed plaques and paintings of Allende that anchored his presence inside the building. On the eleventh, President Lagos circled the presidential palace with invitees, including participants in the Unidad Popular government, and reopened the once-disappeared side door at Morandé 80. The door—next to a pedestrian side-walk, less pretentious than a grand front entrance, often used by democratic presidents and their visitors until 1973—vanished when the military regime remodeled and reopened the palace in 1981. In the 1980s and 1990s, the absent door turned into another memory knot, a sacred invisible place that registered loss and to which protesters sought to march and leave flowers.[21]

The reinstallation of the Morandé 80 door completed an effort, since the election of Lagos in 2000, to symbolize the return of a more democratic and citizen-friendly palace—open to visitors and museum exhibits, repainted white to brighten the somber facade, its tradition of democracy symbolized by statues of the last three elected pre-1973 presidents on Constitution Plaza (which faced the main entrance), and now, with Allende's memory as president honored inside. A permit also allowed a gathering of some 12,000 persons on Constitution Plaza for evening homage and song to honor Allende and the revered musical artist Víctor Jara.[22]

The symbolism summed up the reality that the memory question had again become potent. What it could not do was strip away its contentiousness. Much of the embrace of Allende by political elites sidestepped his revolutionary project as he and others in 1973 might have understood it. The welcome focused especially on other aspects of his legacy—Allende the democrat, Allende the leader true to his ideals. During the week of the eleventh, memory conflict among those who honored Allende also took place. Six women of the disappeared held a rotating protest fast. They worried about "some signs" that despite assurances, the Lagos government's human rights proposal would shut down criminal cases and reinforce impunity.[23]

CONFRONTING TORTURE:
THE VALECH COMMISSION, 2003–04

Memory as unfinished work turned into a politically inescapable idea by 2003. Lagos responded with a human rights initiative in August. An important consequence was a truth commission to reckon with the legacy of torture and political imprisonment.

Upon taking office in March 2000, the Lagos administration did not evince an especially innovative strategy for a politics of memory, nor a commitment to examining the torture question. Its human rights policies tended toward reactive problem solving as urgencies arose—the ups and downs of the Dialogue Table process, the pressures of the Pinochet case, the endgame when memory placed Generals Gabrielli and Ríos under the microscope. An important exception was the Interior Ministry's proactive support program for specialized judges, in tandem with rhetorical emphasis on letting justice do its work. The administration's main strategic priorities, however, lay elsewhere—with recovery of economic dynamism after the dip of 1998–99, a task challenged by the softening world economy (and Argentine meltdown) in 2001–02. Chile's average annual rate of economic growth amounted to only 3.2 percent during 2001–03, in a society whose 1990s culture had rendered sharp inequality more palatable by creating expectations of 7 percent annual growth—and as corollaries, poverty reduction and increases in jobs and social spending. Only during 2004–05 did Chile return to sustained high growth (5.9 percent), and only in 2006 did unemployment drop below 8 percent. Early stumbles also sapped political focus. Lagos finished his presidency strong in March 2006—with high presidential approval ratings, a return to dynamic economic performance and poverty reduction, and reputation as an effective statesman. But political storm clouds had gathered in 2002, when charges that some Concertación officials and lawmakers accepted bribes and channeled public concessions to clients had not yet cleared. It was only in 2003 that the political turnaround began.[24]

Under the circumstances—human rights as a lesser priority, a government reactive and fighting to gain political traction—those pressing for a major new initiative on the divisive memory question found themselves frustrated. They did not know where the government stood. Repeatedly, during 2001–03, human rights groups, such as the Ethical Commission Against Torture, the Agrupación of Relatives of the Detained and Disappeared, and organizations of former political prisoners presented proposals to the administration, but did not receive answers. A sense of strategic indecision also occurred as an inside-game, notwithstanding efforts by capable figures such as the undersecretary of interior, Jorge Correa Sutil, who was also the former executive secretary of the Rettig Commission. The most dramatic case was that of Luciano Fouillioux, director of the Human Rights Program at the Ministry. Asked by Correa to produce a policy document on political prisoners and torture, he submitted a proposal for review by Lagos and Interior Minister Insulza in January 2003. But he could not get a reply. The administration seemed too distracted or divided. Fouillioux resigned in March.[25]

Into the vacuum stepped the UDI, the party traditionally associated with loyal Pinochetismo. In May it announced that it had worked with relatives of the disappeared and the executed in Pisagua to devise a human rights initiative to resolve pending issues and establish social peace. The UDI's loyalist sensibilities had been tempered by new developments after 1998—the knowledge that Joaquín Lavín came close to winning the presidency in 1999, the discourse of shared tragedy built at the Dialogue Table and accepted by the army since 2000, the breakdown of boundaries and inhibition that brought memory culture to a new crossroads. The memory box of Pinochet's Chile would not close. Criminal and civil actions in the courts had proliferated; the memory actors demanding recognition had branched out; the number of accused facing legal or reputational jeopardy had risen. The UDI had come to its own political crossroads. One could devise a formula to deal with pending issues while drawing clear boundaries on the future of the memory question—and building credibility on human rights with centrist voters. Or one could risk an uncontrolled "wedge" effect, as each new gain by the human rights memory camp galvanized more demands and ensnared more persons in a justice spiral. The UDI initiative proposed to increase the pension formulas for relatives of the disappeared and the executed, to create a path of negotiated indemnity payments to the relatives in lieu of civil suits, and to bring an end to permanent-kidnap doctrine. It would accomplish the latter by allowing judges to use plea bargaining and lessened culpability as inducements to gain confidential information about disappeared persons but also by obligating them to conclude, after a finite period, either that the kidnapping continued or that the person had died. The UDI also proposed to clear the record of persons once judged guilty of treason by military tribunals.

The UDI shock was the great catalyst. It produced concentration of mind and will among the political elite. Lagos convened a high-level working group, including Correa and Insulza, to devise an initiative. Alternative proposals streamed in from political parties and human rights groups. Human rights and labor activists, including relatives of the disappeared, protested the UDI proposal as manipulative or evasive. Notably missing was grievance redress for prisoner-survivors of torture. Notably worrying were the exchange of confidential information for plea bargaining or lessened culpability, and the requirement that judges declare after a finite period that the person had died or that the kidnapping continued. Skepticism about plea bargaining was reinforced by the misinformation episodes after the Dialogue Table accord, and the compulsory time-bound conclusion by judges sounded like a "full stop" law. To critics, the proposal amounted to impunity and a formula for closure.[26]

What the UDI proposal *did* accomplish was a shift in political climate at top levels of the elite. It made a new initiative unavoidable and widened its basis. For the Right, too, memory was a shared tragedy that could not be wished away, and it was unfinished work whose neglect would lead to irresponsible consequences.

In August, Lagos announced his initiative, "There Is No Tomorrow Without Yesterday." On one level, the proposal dealt with well-known issues and sparked predictable debates. It included a major raise (50 percent) in the reparation pension formula for relatives of the disappeared and the executed, a clearing of the criminal record of those persecuted for political reasons, and a witness incentive strategy—plea bargaining, lessened culpability, immunity from self-incrimination—to facilitate judges' work on the disappeared. The incentives would apply to the accomplices of action or cover-up and to those compelled by their own risk to obey, but not to the lead actors who planned, ordered, or put into practice human rights crimes. Not surprisingly, it was the plea bargaining and related incentives, and the fear that in practice they would amount to a full-stop ratifying impunity, that prompted the strongest resistance by human rights groups, relatives of the disappeared, and the Socialist wing of the Concertación. Lorena Pizarro blasted the proposal as offering "impunity to criminals." The witness incentive system would not survive the political and legislative polemics.

On another level, the tone and content of the Lagos proposal marked some new departures. The framing tossed aside the idea, common in the formulaic impulse of elite political culture in the 1990s, that a human rights initiative could bring closure of the memory question. Memory work—truth, justice, repair, prevention—was a cumulative and continuing process, not a transition with a natural endpoint. Chileans had embarked on a long moral journey, initiated with democratic recovery and the Rettig Commission, sustained over time, and in need of continuing improvement. They now agreed, in ways they could not before, to reject any contextual justification of human rights atrocities. They now accepted that the pursuit of truth and justice in the courts was necessary "to repair, even if only partially," the suffering of relatives of the disappeared. The state had spent over 400 billion pesos (over US$578 million) for various social repair programs related to human rights. Such achievements constituted not an endpoint, but a context and foundation for next steps. Among them, Lagos proposed, would be a National Institute of Human Rights and Public Liberties—a public agency that would audit, promote, and provide advice on human rights and that would receive deposit of germane archives such as that of the Rettig Commission. Lagos held out the promise of a bright and unified "tomorrow," though one built "not on the deceiving and fragile base of olvido, but on . . . incorporating lessons of pain and rupture into our historical memory."

The new steps included the long-awaited reckoning with torture and political imprisonment. The pain of the prisoner-survivors, Lagos declared, "cannot be repaired except minimally." But he would create a presidential commission to document a list of persons subjected to the ordeal and whose recognition would include the right to "an austere and symbolic indemnity." By November, the National Commission on Political Prison and Torture, known informally as the Valech Commission, was ready to begin its work. Most of the eight commissioners had a background in human rights work. Two persons—the political leader Miguel Luis Amunátegui and jurist Lucas Sierra—were anchored in an "enlightened Right" trajectory. The president, the retired bishop Monsignor Sergio Valech, had served as the last head of the Vicaría de la Solidaridad and as a member of the Dialogue Table. The trajectory of its executive vice-president, María Luisa Sepúlveda, included two key groups, the Vicaría and FASIC (Social Assistance Foundation of the Christian Churches), as well as human rights affairs at the Interior Ministry. The most ironic appointment: Luciano Fouillioux, who had resigned in March as director of the Human Rights Program of the Interior Ministry.[27]

The Valech Commission's mandate was to identify persons who suffered imprisonment and torture for political reasons under military rule, and to make recommendations for social repair. Its broader mission was awareness: the truth of torture, irrefutably documented and recognized by the state. Conceptually, the Valech Commission relied on international law of human rights since the 1940s, especially the United Nations Convention against Torture and the Organization of American States Convention to Prevent and Sanction Torture, both promulgated (ironically) in Chile in 1988. Its working definition of torture focused on intentional acts by state agents or their proxies to inflict extreme physical or mental pain, in order to gain information or produce a confession, to punish or intimidate or discriminate, or to destroy the victim's integrity as a person, in other words "to annul her personality."[28]

Destroying personhood resonated with the scholarship of torture, as well as international law and witness testimony. The infliction of unbearable mental and physical pain, under circumstances of utter isolation and defenselessness, breaks down the integrity of the person—the identity, values, and social world that make us ourselves and human. You face the excruciating death-agony alone, stripped from a world turned into unreality, only to be drawn back from the brink for a while by the omnipotent force degrading you. The process humiliates the person, rendering return to human society problematic. As a former prisoner put it to me, after torture one reenters society as a kind of "zombie," frightening to others and in need of rebuilding a human identity.[29]

The technical mandate excluded the short hold-and-release detentions that came down indiscriminately on men and boys during massive search raids (*allanamientos*) of poor and working-class homes in the poblaciones, and which were accompanied by verbal and physical maltreatment. Only individuals subsequently separated from the roundup group for continued detention qualified as political prisoners. Also excluded were persons who died as a consequence of torture and were therefore included in the Rettig Commission's mandate.[30]

Despite these and other exclusions, the scope of cases to consider was huge. By 31 May 2004, when the half-year period for interviewing expired, 35,868 people had signed up to tell their stories. Metropolitan Santiago accounted for the largest share (37 percent), but the other regions accounted for over half (54 percent) and the diasporic aspect—Chileans abroad who delivered evidence to consulates—was also significant (9 percent). Even the follow-ups with victims to clarify pending aspects were massive—about 14,000 second-stage queries by personal or telephone interview or by e-mail. The Executive Vice President Sepúlveda assembled staff teams, largely lawyers, for the frontline work of interviews, information gathering and analysis, and preparation of preliminary recommendations. These summarized the state of the evidence—the testimonies and documents of victims; the cross-checks for consistency with documents from human rights groups, victim associations, and state organisms, and with testimony by other witnesses. After a week to consider a case list and its evidence summations, and to review raw data and documents if needed for clarification, Valech Commission members met to present, discuss, and vote on a case-by-case basis whether the evidence sufficed for "moral conviction" that the person was a victim of prison and/or torture for political reasons. A majority vote could qualify a case, but usually a consensus emerged.

The Valech Commission concluded that 27,255 persons qualified. Their average confinement had lasted a half-year (180.1 days). Significantly, among the 8,613 not certified, the commission concluded that most (6,845) *might* do so if given more time to present evidence. (In April 2005, a reconsideration period qualified another 1,201 persons, with total certification rising to 28,456.) Another group (1,330) suffered other sorts of human rights violations, not within the scope of the commission.[31]

The bottom-line criterion for inclusion on the confirmed victim list was proof of political imprisonment, not proof of the specific acts of torture inflicted on a person. The latter could be difficult to establish definitively for each individual case. Decades had transpired; medical ailments could arguably have had other contributing causes. Most disturbing, a consequence of torture was precisely the silence, social isolation, and medical negligence that could compound the problem of definitive evidence, lead to arbitrary (false negative) results, and rub salt in the wound. In any event, the political imprisonments themselves violated human rights. Meanwhile, the Valech

Commission collected testimony and evidence on torture for each case, and used a cross-check methodology—comparison across testimonies and across genres of sources—to analyze pattern and convergence at the 1,132 detention sites that came to its attention.[32]

As a result, the Valech Commission established a *pervasiveness* of torture so powerful that in practice and for most cases, the conceptual distinction from political imprisonment proved moot. Nineteen of every twenty persons (94 percent) certified as victims of political imprisonment also provided testimony of torture, and comparison across the testimonies yielded consistency and credibility on key points—the specific torture methods and daily routines that shaped prisoner life at particular locations; the specific military, police, or intelligence units and perpetrators at a given location. The variety of torture techniques, like the astounding number of detention sites and the slang, constituted a monument to pervasiveness. Techniques of torment included extreme physical pain via beatings, body hangings, asphyxiations, prolonged forced positions, and electric shock, and mental ordeals such as mock executions, Russian roulette, witness of others' torment, and eating of excrement. Many broad categories actually referenced a variety of more specific torments. A simple category—"beatings," for example—could refer to the inner ear shock technique known as "telephone"— open hand blows against both outer ears simultaneously—or to gauntlet line ordeals of kicking and punching, or to repetitive excruciating blows to testicles. The mental aspect was often as important as the physical, and difficult to disentangle from it. After all, the point was to break down the person. When a prisoner suffered repeated sexual violation, or "wet submarine" asphyxiation in fouled waters, or waited alone nude and tied for the next "interrogation," was the assault physical or mental?[33]

The Valech Commission found that torture was massive—of "deliberate institutional character," in view of the personnel, resources, logistical support, and interagency collaboration mobilized to make use of it. Torture and political imprisonment were "a policy of State . . . defined and promoted by the political authorities of the era," not a series of unsupervised or anomalous practices. The overwhelming and immediate character of the repression after the 11 September coup—an effort to spread fear and intimidation rapidly in a highly mobilized society—came through clearly. More than 20,000 of the 33,221 political detentions certified by the commission occurred in 1973, that is, in less than four months. (The number of certified detentions was higher than that of the 27,255 certified prisoners because some persons were imprisoned more than once.) In this stage, the established security forces predominated: the carabineros and the army accounted for three-quarters (73 percent) of the arrests. Over time, the secret police (especially the DINA, and after 1977 the CNI) took on a greater role and refined the targeting. The certified detentions dropped to less than 7,000 in 1974–75, and to hundreds annually thereafter.[34]

Documenting the massive scale and institutionalization of torture was important. It turned torture into an undeniable memory-truth, the facts of state policy that came down on dozens of thousands of families, not stories of occasional excess by rogue subordinates. The scale of torture also drew out a painful moral complicity problem—in media and civil society, not just military and police sectors and courts. With so many victims dragged into the web of horror and then released, the moral issues included not only direct participation in the machinery of torture, but indirect consent through denial—looking away despite so much evidence in plain sight.[35]

Did the Valech Commission uncover additional memory-truths? Did it offer a surprise or a new insight, even in social circles sensitive to human rights? After all, Chile had long witnessed memory struggles to document the denied realities of military rule, and to build a culture more sensitized to human rights.

The Valech Commission broke ground in two additional ways. First, it offered a new lens on silence. Silence was not reducible *only* to the politico-cultural struggle between "memory" and "forgetting" (or more precisely, between different frameworks of selective remembrance). Nor was it only a function of fear. There was also another aspect, intimate and personal. For many survivors, the humiliation of torture—its shamefulness and defenselessness—served up a profoundly challenging legacy. Reconstructing the basics of identity and dignity, not to mention a degree of trust and acceptance within a social web, was complicated. For some, rebuilding an affective and sexual life within families proved a mirage. Most had been released during an ongoing dictatorship—times of fear, stigma, and joblessness that compounded the indignity and narrowed access to therapy. Coming to terms with survival was not simple. Why did I blurt out names? How do I live after rape? Whom did I place at risk? Who will shun me if the worst is known? "I have never told this truth that I bear painfully," confessed one victim, "because of what I did. I gave names. I feel ashamed and fear rejection." To make a conscious choice to remember—beyond the moment when a nightmare or sudden sound or anniversary or surprise encounter forced it—was to reactivate the degradation. "I will not narrate all the details and aspects of the torture and outrages . . . committed there," stated another survivor, "because in my personal case I ended up too badly . . . [It is] an agony . . . to go back to remembering those sad and bitter moments."[36]

Not all persons were permanently broken. Some rebuilt lives and demonstrated a remarkable resilience. But the rebuilding did not necessarily do away with the wound. The survivors of the unspeakable live a double life: the "deep memory" life so indescribable and terrifying yet foundational, the everyday normal life that is somehow superficial yet necessary to carry on and find strength.[37]

Under such circumstances, how and with whom could one verbalize the trauma? Precisely what should one remember and why? To be sure, some former prisoners courageously organized their experience of horror in the service of human rights values and memory struggles, with increasing visibility and insistence after 1998. But many remained on the sidelines, and even memory activists might tread carefully around some aspects of their imprisonment. Staff on the Valech Commission had come of age in a Chile culturally attuned to the idea of memory as struggle against the silence imposed by perpetrators. It was "the silence of the victims . . . that surprised us." The surprise was not naiveté. It was not that former prisoners had difficulty verbalizing their experience, nor that they could share it only in a tiny circle of trust. It was that the difficulty ran *so* deep that many could not bring themselves to share the experience with *anyone*—not even spouses or close relatives, not even decades later. It was precisely for this reason that a formal truth-telling exercise that recognized the fact of the horror and its moral illegitimacy, while respecting the dignity of the victim, proved important as an act of repair. Even so and despite the promise of confidentiality (beyond identification as a former political prisoner), the decision to testify was tough to reach. Many former prisoners could not bring themselves to testify at all. One important implication was that the torture had been even more massive than the documented cases. The historian Anne Perotín-Dumon, following a cautious methodology, considers 60,000 torture victims a "very prudent" estimate. This is a helpful conservative baseline. The real number may be higher.[38]

The cultural implication was subtle: an imperative of dignity entangled with a grave social hurt, an understandable silence but a necessity to break it.

"It is one thing to present oneself to the family after prison," the commission argued. "It is not hard to claim innocence and up to a point pride for having suffered an injustice or suffering for a cause one considers noble. But it is also human to want to hold oneself high and not humiliated." Under the circumstances, "to pull back the veil of torture, of humiliation, of physical and psychological violation, is something very difficult to do. Even to one's own spouse." Silence was an act of "elemental dignity," but the privacy of unacknowledged suffering could also deepen the wound. Torture was a past-within-the-present that required recognition, reencounter, and repair.[39]

The Valech Commission also broke new ground by focusing specifically on women and on sexualized torture. The overall sociology of the political prisoners was not surprising. The repression dragged in people of all ages, but the young figured prominently; nearly three of five (57.9 percent) prisoners were under thirty years old when detained. The repression took special aim at leftists. Party militants and unaligned leftist sympathizers accounted for two-thirds (64.7 percent) of the prisoners; Socialists and Communists alone accounted for over two-fifths (43.1 percent). The repressed, however, were mainly the small fish in the political sea. Nearly a third of victims (31.2 percent) declared no political affiliation or leaning; only one of five party militants (18.4 percent) held local or supralocal leadership posts. Among activists in grassroots organizations—such as trade unions, student unions, church groups, and block associations—only one of four (23.7 percent) held leadership posts. The class composition of targets emphasized the working class, but middle-class sectors were not immune. Skilled and unskilled workers composed half (51.0 percent) the victims, but professionals and students nearly a third (30.4 percent). In sum, the machinery of repression spread its wrath widely. The repression emphasized leftist and activist leaders as a strategic priority, but more often than not dragged into the inferno ordinary base-level activists and persons on the fringes of social activism.

But what about women as political prisoners? Here, the issues were more subtle. Overall, the certified women prisoners numbered 3,399, a small but significant minority (12.5 percent). This result is hardly surprising. The sexist assumptions of the early 1970s defined men as more dangerous, and pushed activist women toward support roles in political parties. Significantly, however, the *relative* presence of women grew swiftly—from only one in ten (9.7 percent) in 1973, to one in six (17.6 percent) during the heyday of the DINA in 1974–77, and one in five (19.3 percent) thereafter. In other words, it was precisely when the "dirty war" grew more sophisticated in its targeting and techniques, and more organized by secret police forces, that women victims figured more prominently in the culture of torment.[40]

Women's imprisonment brought to the fore another truth—sexualized torture. The design of the interviews and data forms did not seek information about sexual violence. Nonetheless, almost all the women brought up the topic without prompting, even as they *also* indicated how impossible it proved to speak about it, and how grave and enduring the consequences. "Many persons who came to this Commission indicated that they had never before dared to tell these experiences." The "sexual aggressions and violence" included not only vaginal, oral, and anal rape, but also sexualized insults, simulations of rape and forced witness of it, stripping and groping, forced sex with prisoners and relatives, and penetration by trained dogs, and rats and insects. Sexual violence and humiliation provided no shield from other torments. One woman at Tejas Verdes, site of the nascent DINA in 1973, was stripped and tied to a stretcher with a hood over her head, subjected to a burning light while men laughed, then endured a man striking her with his penis while taunting her about the size she might like—while another wrote graffiti on her body with a ballpoint pen. She also endured electric shock rituals. "They ordered current to the breasts, vagina, and knees. . . . Later, the shocks stopped for a while . . . Then they restarted the interrogation, this time saying they had connected me to the truth machine." The machine blew a whistle—signal of a supposed lie, time for another shock—"and the whistle . . . turned into a hell."[41]

The ambivalence and difficulty of speech did not really disappear in the commission. Although nearly all the women victims spoke without prompting about sexualized violence and humiliation, those who stated they were personally raped amounted to about 1 in 10 (316 of the 3,399 women). Given the inhibitions, and the gap between so few who admitted personal rape and so many who saw it in so many places, the commission concluded that it had gained individualized knowledge of only a fraction of the cases.[42]

The reckoning with sexualized violence showed the great complexity— weighed down by shame and invisibility—of the legacy of torture. Silence was a defense of dignity, but it also fed the social grievance of invisibility: nonrecognition of harm. The issue was not limited only to women. Men testified less often than women about sexualized violence. But enough did so to make clear that the climate for them, too, included sexual humiliation and assault. One man held prisoner at an air base in the Ninth Region reported that while he was nude and blindfolded, "they would beat my testicles with a kind of ruler, which caused me unbearable pains." The beating was a prelude to sodomy. For both men and women, electric shock torture targeted genitalia among other sensitive body parts. There was also the matter of children. More than 200 women had been pregnant when detained. Not all aborted, and some child-survivors later contended with their own sense of violation. Also, some raped women became pregnant, and not all of them aborted. What did this mean if the child sensed or learned the truth? One woman, twenty-nine years old when she gave her testimony, said she sensed her mother's rage and at first tried to support her. Eventually, though, she had to contend with her own rage—and invisibility. Her mother might at least go to the Vicaría for moral support. But until she appeared at the Valech Commission, the child-survivor had nowhere to go. "I prefer for my situation to exist, that it be recognized . . . It took me many years to be able to tell this, keeping it secret made me anxious . . . With this I get the certificate of being a person, I am this which happened to me, I [can] ask for help, that people understand me." The point, she explained, is that "before I did not feel like a person."[43]

SEEING WITH NEW EYES, 2004–06 (I):
THE COLLAPSE OF MEMORY AS SALVATION

By 2004–06, memory culture passed a tipping point—into the era of new reckonings and less self-restraint. The fears and saber rattling of the 1990s became less thinkable and less intuitively understandable, as if from a distant time. Chileans began to see the past-within-the-present with new eyes, able to take in legacies once pushed to the edge of a narrower visual field. The reality, massiveness, and indefensibility of human rights violations turned more irrefutable. The contentious aspect of memory turned more subtle, less driven by a confrontational struggle to hegemonize truth in the face of outright denial and mutually exclusive frameworks. The crude dynamics of "dialogue of the deaf"—memory as salvation *versus* memory as rupture—ceded ground to the nuanced tensions of "accept and contain"— memory as shared tragedy *and* as unfinished work, with differences of emphasis and implication. Was memory mainly about a tragedy shared and made by all? Was it mainly about completing a truth-and-justice agenda to shatter impunity? Shared acknowledgment of the human rights catastrophe and of pending work of repair and prevention did not imply agreement on the solution, let alone the balance between "formula" and "wedge" in any proposed solution.

The "new eyes" for viewing the past within the present were evident in all three domains of contested memory: military rule under Pinochet during 1973–90, the pre-1973 era, the democratic transition since 1990. We shall consider the first two in this chapter, and turn to the third in the next.

Memory as salvation, particularly its heroic association with Pinochet, fell apart. Defense of Pinochet and military rule as the patriotic saving of a nation—a great rescue mission—turned excruciatingly difficult, even for the Right. Positive readings had to rely more than ever on a mixed, postheroic defense. Yes, the human rights record was indefensible and subjected tens of thousands of families to atrocity. Yes, Pinochet may have turned out to be a corrupt power seeker for whom no outrage was too much. But, the economic and social modernization legacy of military rule was positive, and separable from the legacy of human rights and the person of Pinochet, and the crisis of 1973 was real. To assert the positive accomplishments of military rule required recognizing the horrific and stripping away the epic.[44]

Two developments proved decisive in the final crumbling of heroic memory of salvation. First, the Valech Commission report, presented in a presidential speech to the nation on 28 November 2004, widened dramatically the scale of unspeakable atrocity—from some 3,000 cases definitively documented by the Rettig Commission (and a follow-up agency), to dozens of thousands. We shall postpone for later (chapter 7) discussion of politico-cultural debate surrounding the Valech Report—on institutional versus personal responsibility, the scope of its mandate, justice and accountability, and reparations. For now, what matters is the widespread acceptance of a new historical fact: horrific torture of political prisoners took place on a huge scale and as institutionalized practice, and it left a massive legacy of ruptured lives and families. Few voices contested the substantive truth of the report, or used historical context arguments to undermine the moral gravity of its findings. The army commander, Cheyre, was typically proactive. Early in November he announced the army "took the hard, but irreversible decision to accept the responsibilities that correspond to it as an institution in all the punishable and morally unacceptable acts of the past." The veracity of the Valech Report would not be in dispute: "We will accept its content and conclusions."[45]

The conservative *El Mercurio* joined in the framing of memory as a shared tragedy. Whatever the disputes about historical origins, it editorialized, the new facts coming to light "reveal situations completely unacceptable in the civilized world." The paper also ran testimonies by torture victims including a moving account by Mireya García, vice-president of relatives of the disappeared. The physical blows were painful, "but the pain of the hit, the bruise, passes. Other pains remain forever." She did not shrink from discussing consequences that remained forever. "And you did not need for a torturer, a psychopath, a crazy one to consummate the sexual act to feel violated. You were violated from the moment they tell you 'take off your clothes,' when they touch you, when they go about intending to abuse you and when they rape you." She could not bring herself to have children. "I felt incapable of giving life to a person in a world where there was no assurance that she could be respected as such."[46]

The logic of "accept and contain" did not preclude dispute, as we shall see, over the implications of memory for future truth-and-justice projects. But it recognized that which could no longer be avoided or euphemized. Tens of thousands of Chileans had testified—and their compatriots believed them. As a December "Manifesto of Historians" pointed out, the Valech Report constituted more than a state exercise or a call for legal justice. It was "citizen testimony" and a call for "historical and political justice." A December poll revealed that three of four Chileans (74 percent) approved the Valech Report and six of seven (86 percent) thought the testimonies truthful.[47]

A second development that undermined heroic memory was revelation about Pinochet—on the one hand, corruption and money laundering, on the other, criminal findings by judges. Corruption hit hard because it turned Pinochet into a mafioso: the gang boss who lines his pockets, not the selfless leader who serves a patriotic cause as he understood it, however crudely and controversially. In July 2004, the U.S. Senate Permanent Subcommittee on Investigations found, while examining financial aspects of terrorism, that executives of the Riggs Bank in Washington, D.C., failed to report suspicious transactions—and that Pinochet held up to $8 million dollars in disguised accounts. News of secret sums far beyond public salary earnings created a sensation. It exploded the image of Pinochet as austere patriot, and destroyed the last shreds of unconditional loyalty in the public culture of the Right. The Santiago Court of Appeals appointed Judge Sergio Muñoz to investigate the offshore accounts and related issues such as tax payments. Muñoz, known for legal rigor, moved quickly to interrogate Pinochet's wife, Lucía Hiriart, and his five children.[48]

Meanwhile, the once reliable Pinochet sympathizers cautiously drew distance. The rule of law applies to all, we need to let the judge do the work and draw the conclusions, went the most common defense. Some figures on the Right went further. Senator Hernán Larraín, of the UDI, stated he "would not put hands in the fire" to defend Pinochet. Congressman Alberto Cardemil, of Renovación Nacional, voiced the sense of having been used. "Many of us who put ourselves on the line . . . civilians and military working selflessly for a work of common good, even leaving personal interests aside, today we have a sensation of discomfort, worry, and pain." Even the retired high officer corps could not unite. Reporting on "the week when Pinochetismo fell apart," *El Mercurio* learned that at a meeting of eighty retired army generals on 5 August, the younger retirees argued against the instincts of the elders. Let justice take its course and do not leap blindly to Pinochet's defense, they insisted.[49]

On economic crime, Pinochet kept going downhill. In January 2005 Judge Muñoz seized key files and computers. In November, Pinochet was arrested for tax evasion and passport forgery. By this point, the minimum estimate by Muñoz for the offshore fortune had risen to US$27 million; informed speculation ran as high as $100 million; new secret accounts had been discovered and funds in Florida impounded; and his wife, Lucía Hiriart, and son Marcos Antonio had been indicted. When another wave of family indictments came down in January 2006, Pinochet's daughter Inés fled the country. A new image of Pinochet now competed with the old ones of the benevolent savior and the violent dictator: the outlaw who duped some loyalists, robbed the public purse, and evaded civic responsibilities. The fiercest partisans of memory as salvation had learned to cope with the stain of human rights with arguments about historical context, modest social cost, and anomalous excess by subordinates. As we have seen, such arguments met with resistance throughout the democratic transition and turned more difficult to sustain in the post-1998 public culture. But the stain of corruption was in some ways tougher; it corroded assumptions of good faith among the remaining Pinochetistas. Small wonder that Pinochet resorted to saber rattling to keep the money issue at bay when he commanded the army in the early 1990s.[50]

Pinochet's return to the criminal hot seat included human rights cases. The 2001–02 rulings that spared him in the Caravan of Death case for reasons of diminished mental capacity did not set a binding precedent, and Pinochet blundered by indulging his desire to set the memory question straight. In November 2003, he granted an interview to Spanish-language television (WDLP-22) in Miami. He offered a reasonably coherent self-defense, called himself an "angel" who had welcomed the 1988 plebiscite and acted to serve "democratic principles," and appealed for posterity to remember him properly. The result was not only scandal, but new evidence on mental capacity— for judges inclined to review it. The Riggs Bank case added another blow by serving up an image of Pinochet as the mentally fit fox—duplicitous as he rigged his accounts. The new climate and the lack of binding precedent led in 2004–06 to rulings by the Santiago Court of Appeals and the Supreme Court to strip Pinochet of immunity as ex-president, and enabled judges to reconsider mental capacity on a case-by-case basis. Judge Juan Guzmán provided the first breakthrough in December 2004. His investigation docket included Operation Condor, the Chilean-led transnational program of South American secret police forces to track, detain, disappear, and kill dissidents beyond their home country borders. He ruled Pinochet mentally competent, in part based on evidence from the Miami interview and the Riggs case, and ordered his arrest for nine Operation Condor kidnaps (disappearances) and a murder, in Argentina, Paraguay, Bolivia, and Chile. Relatives of the disappeared and human rights lawyers hailed a "historic" ruling that could open the door to justice in other pending cases.[51]

In January 2005, when the Supreme Court rejected appeal of Guzmán's ruling, the retired admiral Jorge Martínez Busch, former commander in chief of the navy and a loyalist to the end, lamented that "all of Chile has abandoned General Pinochet." He had a point. The other side of the coin, however, was that Pinochet had shamed loyalists into abandoning him. Also, an approaching presidential election increased the stakes. Until his death in December 2006, Pinochet rode a legal roller coaster, with multiple judges ruling there was well-founded evidence to indict him for human rights crimes, with defense lawyers uncertain when a medical argument might stop a particular case, with natural political sympathizers reluctant to step out on a limb. Medical arguments, reinforced by incidents such as hospitalization after a fainting spell, brought some relief in specific cases—but not from the roller coaster ride. In mid-2005, for example, Pinochet won a halt to the Operation Condor case from one chamber of the Santiago Court of Appeals, but another chamber of the court considered him fit for trial in the disappearance of two brothers in southern Chile. The Court of Appeals also allowed the financial fraud case to continue. Key blows included Pinochet's arrest in November 2005, by order of the investigative Judge Víctor Montiglio, for the "Operation Colombo" cover-up of 119 disappearances; his loss of immunity in January 2006, by order of the Santiago Appeals Court, in Judge Alejandro Solís's investigation of torture and murder at Villa Grimaldi; and the reopening of the Caravan of Death case, by order of the Supreme Court in July 2006, and followed by arrest in November. The Operation Colombo case brought forth testimony by the former DINA head Manuel Contreras that he reported daily to Pinochet, and the Villa Grimaldi case testimony by former DINA agent Ricardo Lawrence that Pinochet personally questioned some prisoners and requested updates. The Caravan of Death reversal coincided with testimony by the helicopter pilot Chino Campos (in a parallel case) that his superior told him Pinochet gave the order to toss five poisoned captives into the ocean. In a legalistic culture, such rulings and testimonies were devastating.[52]

By 2006, positive memory of military rule had made its postheroic turn. Pinochet, the most important symbol, was an albatross. In September 2003, one of four Chileans (25 percent) still affirmed he would be remembered by History as "one of the greatest rulers" in twentieth-century Chile, not as "a dictator." By August 2006, the Riggs Bank revelations of fraud, the Valech Report on torture, and the indictments for human rights crimes had worn down the loyalist core to only one of eight Chileans (12 percent). Viewed in a longer horizon, Pinochetismo had fallen hard from the two-fifths social base at the advent of democratic transition. Four of five Chileans (82 percent) now saw "a dictator" instead of a great ruler, and they included a solid majority (60 percent) on the Right.[53]

Equally revealing was the cultural response to the high-profile accusation, in August 2006, that assassination explained the 1982 death of the former president Eduardo Frei Montalva. An investigation by Judge Alejandro Madrid, under way since 2002, was expected to wrap up in 2007. Two hypotheses contended. The first: Frei, after surgery by Dr. Augusto Larraín to correct gastrointestinal reflux late in 1981, died of medical complications compounded by negligence or incompetence. Before succumbing in January, Frei suffered a litany of crises—septic shock, two more surgeries, and finally, virulent infection of internal organs. The second hypothesis: The secret police had a chemical or biological toxin introduced into the body to induce a fatal crisis. On 23 August, Televisión Nacional's investigative magazine, *Informe Especial*, aired the dramatic first chapter of a two-part program on Frei's death. To a large audience (535,000 viewers), it bluntly argued for a murder conspiracy: "This is the history of a crime." The point was to eliminate the most potent opposition leader. The program used witness testimonies and circumstantial evidence to build a powerful case: secret police surveillance of Frei and conversion of his chauffer into an informant; access to Frei at Clínica Santa María by medical personnel serving the secret police; technical capacity and use of toxic agents against others by the secret police; anomalies of record keeping and body handling, including a secret autopsy without family permission. The trouble, aside from the implication that Pinochet approved the murder, was that some evidence also pointed to medical blunder. Critics jumped on the point and Televisión Nacional backed away from claiming definitive proof in the second broadcast.[54]

From a politicocultural standpoint, what did *not* happen proved most significant. No respected voice emerged to say that the murder hypothesis was unthinkable, an outrageous slander. No one argued that if true, the murder conspiracy was surely the work of rogue subordinates, not a project approved by Pinochet. No one contested the idea of unfinished business— the necessity to find out the truth, no matter how unsettling. The defense of Pinochet and the regime, such as it was, amounted to the idea that the evidence was contradictory and only a judge could arrive at a conclusion. As *El Mercurio* put it, Televisión Nacional's case "was far from amounting to a body of proof" established by "an impartial court." The wheels of justice turned slowly, but did not diminish the cultural plausibility of murder by toxin. In July 2007, Judge Madrid indicted four doctors and two nurses of the DINA in the 1977 murder of the DINA agent Manuel Leyton, whose silence in disappearance cases was considered unreliable. The Leyton murder was germane because sarin gas served as the weapon, and because one of the doctors, Pedro Valdivia Soto, saw Frei and ordered an operation when he was rehospitalized. On Frei's death itself, however, Madrid did not in 2007 reach a conclusion.[55]

SEEING WITH NEW EYES, 2004–06 (II):
THE NEW CHILE AND THE OLD

The memory question was a cultural argument not only about military rule, but also about what came before and after. What was the relationship of the new turn-of-century Chile with its founding moment, the crisis of the old

Chile of the 1960s and 1970s? During 2004–06, cultural defensiveness about touchy topics lessened. Memory as a shared tragedy translated into a disposition to revisit the old Chile somewhat less encumbered by polemics of disaster.

In earlier cycles of memory struggle, during the dictatorship and into the 1990s, the Chile of pre-1973 played a star role in the framework of salvation. The old Chile and its demagogic politicians culminated in madness: the upheavals of the Frei-Allende era of 1964–73, especially under the Unidad Popular during 1970–73. In this framework, the crisis provoked by Allende and the Popular Unity—the economic chaos, the war climate, the imminent bloodbath, all so palpable by August 1973—explained how military takeover in September saved ordinary Chileans just in time from catastrophe, and the far-reaching nature of the social, economic, and political accomplishments under military rule. The pre-1973 Chile also offered an exculpatory context for controversy over human rights. What happened in the 1970s was a "war" destined to produce some "excesses" by subordinates—and false propaganda by the enemy. Most alleged human rights violations did not really happen. Those that did happen were a regrettable byproduct of war and amounted to a modest social cost within the great work of national rescue. The crisis of the old Chile and its politics of mobilization, especially the strife of the Unidad Popular era, constituted the trump card of justification—and denial—by proponents of military rule.[56]

Given the perverse manipulation of pre-1973 history into excused atrocity, and given the urgency of saving lives in the present, for the emerging human rights camp the Unidad Popular era came to constitute a semitaboo, an area of relative silence in public memory struggles to win over the national imaginary in the 1970s. Activists who sought to document the truth of massive state violence and persecution tried to avoid the trap of entangling the human rights issue in diversionary polemics about the Unidad Popular. Within the Center and the Left, moreover, the catastrophe of 1973 and the attendant critiques and self-critiques were painful and divisive. Here was another reason for touchiness about the Unidad Popular and the wider Frei-Allende period. Within the oppositional memory camp under military rule, a processing of the period and its political failure *did* take place. But deep readings of pre-1973 history tended to remain confined to "sect" memories, more an activity of reflection and dialogue within political party and intellectual circles or other communities of trust, rather than a theme to pursue aggressively in national memory struggles. Even in the 1980s, at the level of the national imaginary what was most important to promote was the sense of having learned from the pre-1973 failure—of having awakened into a new appreciation of democracy and human rights, as values to be treasured and won. During the democratic transition of the 1990s, when memory struggle remained polarized and vulnerable to impasse, and when partisans of memory as salvation and Pinochetismo remained strong, revisiting the Unidad Popular era was still haunted by the specter of catastrophe and rejection. Such revisiting devolved into claims by a specific memory camp—the partisans of salvation claiming pride of achievement in military rule, the victims of repression rendering homage to ideals and dreams worth having and that motivated their loved ones.[57]

The sensibility of shared tragedy opened wider the door of cultural curiosity. It softened the defensiveness that shuts down interest and blinds the eye. Was there a story in the Chile of pre-1973 beyond the familiar run-up to catastrophe? Already in 2003, the thirty-year anniversary of the coup seemed to call forth a certain hunger for a fresh look at the lost world of 1973.

In August 2004, on the eve of the September memory season, the brilliant film *Machuca*, directed and cowritten by Andrés Wood, spoke to the yearning. It broke the box office record for a Chilean film release (59,520 viewers during the first Thursday–Sunday cycle) and began a run highly successful for the Chilean market (over 650,000 cinema viewers, before release of the DVD edition). Two years later, the film still held a strong place in the cultural imagination. Viewers of the interactive television program *Chile Elige* (Chile Elects) cast 2 million votes to select, among thirty nominees, the all-time best Chilean film. *Machuca* won with a fourth (24.6 percent) of the vote.[58]

The ingeniousness of *Machuca* was that it blended the honesty of a child's viewpoint with an undeniable authenticity. It thereby escaped political didactics while achieving insight into the tragedy and dreams of an era. We see the tumultuous Chilean world of 1973 through the eyes of Gonzalo Infante, a boy eleven years old at a prestigious private school in Santiago known as Colegio Saint Patrick. The school's rector, Father McEnroe, embodies the experimental idealism of the times by promoting a social integration project. Poor children are brought into the school and exempted from tuition payment. A farm worked and managed by students will presumably pay for the tuition scholarships. Gonzalo befriends Pedro Machuca, a student from a nearby shantytown to whom he gives bike rides. They also hang out with Silvana, a feisty girl who helps her father sell miniature flags at demonstrations for and against the Popular Unity government and who teaches the boys how to kiss.[59]

The children carry the film, and they enable viewers to shed defensiveness. The screenplay casts aside predetermined political readings by reproducing the fragmentary understandings of a child coming of age. It spends time with the trials and quests of early adolescence—friendship, taunting, games, parties, fantasy, romance—while providing glimpses of sociopolitical menace. The wall sign rejecting civil war, the street weapon brandished by a sister's boyfriend, the sudden violence at a demonstration, the school meeting where parents argue heatedly about social integration, from time to time the menace intrudes, at first lightly, then with more force, until the climactic scenes burn away any remaining innocence. The casting aside of a heroic political reading is also enhanced because the adult world is so mediocre in Gonzalo's eyes, especially in the socially respectable circles he knows best. Inadequate to the larger needs of the moment, most adults simply adapt as best they can. Gonzalo Infante's mother sleeps with a well-connected, wealthy lover who supplies her black-market goods. His father aligns with the socialist political winds, but he is no hero—he is eager to leave the country. Pedro Machuca's mother is dynamic and appealing, but his father is a drunk who knows life will not improve for those at the bottom. In his view, the toilet cleaners of society will always be toilet cleaners. Salvador Allende is seen in a less-than-glorious moment—on television with Leonid Brezhnev, during a frustrating visit to Moscow seeking aid.[60]

When the coup happens and Gonzalo loses his last bit of innocence, he is also not a hero. Gonzalo has arrived on his bike and witnesses the brutal repression in Pedro Machuca's community—the homes are violently raided and subversive material set afire; soldiers rough up the residents and treat them like criminals while pushing them up against walls; arguments and chaos break out. Silvana screams and hurls herself on her father the flag seller, to protect him during a ferocious kicking as he lies on the ground. Soldiers had discovered the miniature Communist flags he sold at leftist demonstrations. The soldiers try to continue the beating, but they cannot stop her screaming and her flinging body. One suddenly shoots her dead to bring the bedlam to an end. Amidst the shocked silence, a soldier grabs Gonzalo and orders him to move to an area where residents are being held. Terrified, Gonzalo escapes by invoking his class privilege. "Look at me," he tells the dark-skinned soldier. The soldier stares at the fair skinned and freckled boy, looks down to see the Adidas tennis shoes unaffordable to any poor person, and stares at Gonzalo again. The soldier realizes the kid does not belong in this place, and sends him off on his bike. Gonzalo weeps as he rides away. Is he grieving—before forgetting—in ways the adult country cannot?

What added power to the film was authenticity. Wood reproduced the visual details that brought a lost world alive—from the cans of condensed milk so prized and sweet in a culture of scarcity and social class discrimination, to the *linchacos* (hitting batons tied by leather) used as street weapons, to the *allanamiento* (house raid) scene reenacted by real pobladores and depicting soldiers in real Chilean uniforms. The social integration experiment at Saint Patrick was based on the true story of one of Chile's most famous and dynamic schools, Colegio Saint George. Father McEnroe, the rector whose rocky experiment ended with military intervention of the school, was really Father Gerardo Whelan, to whose memory the film was dedicated. In the 1960s and 1970s, before the junta implemented a project of social class segregation that expelled poor people to distant neighborhoods, there had indeed sprung up zones of mixed social geography. Particularly in the Las Condes area of eastern metropolitan Santiago, prosperous families lived within blocks of migrants and squatter communities. Boys of different social classes sometimes played soccer together in the plazas. In several progressive Catholic schools, not just Saint George, there had been true "Machucas"—the new slang for lower-class children who integrated schools of the privileged. The film inspired *La Tercera* to track down "Machucas" and tell their fates. Some had experienced difficulties, did not complete a university education, and held rather modest social positions, such as working in a supermarket or running a precarious microenterprise. One, Amante Eledín Parraguez, had gone on to advanced studies, published poetry and a memoir, and taught at Saint George. The melding of art and life came through when the memoir quoted Father Whelan's standard response—paralleled in a dramatic moment in the film—to objections by some parents and students to his experiments. "And we all are free to choose the school we like the most; if someone does not like what we are doing, let them go!"[61]

Machuca was a cultural phenomenon. What stood out was not simply the box office appeal but that so many sectors embraced it as a moving and insightful story—evocative of something important belonging to everyone.

24. Unforgettable people from the film *Machuca*. Above, Gonzalo Infante, Silvana, and Pedro Machuca (holding flag) jump with the crowd as they sell flags at a demonstration. *Credit: Andrés Wood, Wood Producciones.*

25. Below, the iconic image of the film—the two boys share a ride on Gonzalo's bicycle. *Credit: Andrés Wood, Wood Producciones.*

26. Father McEnroe teaches Pedro Machuca that he must speak up—
make himself heard—to take his rightful place.
Credit: Andrés Wood, Wood Producciones.

The embrace occurred notwithstanding its understated yet clear sympathy with the egalitarian ideals of the era, its unflattering view of socially privileged families, and its depiction of the violent brutality of the coup—aspects that in the 1990s would have produced resounding controversy and rejection by the Right and Pinochetistas. When the military intervenes in the school and Father McEnroe loses his post, the children discover they value him more than they might have realized. At a tense moment in an interrupted religious service, they follow Pedro Machuca's lead by rising to say "Goodbye, Father McEnroe." Earlier, when parents heatedly argue about the social integration experiment, Pedro Machuca's mother, with an eloquence of expression evocative of 1973, states the injustice reproduced by the debate. The subtext poses a challenge to the legacy of social inequality still powerful in the present.

> When I was a girl, I lived on a landed estate over by San Nicolás. My father was one of the *inquilinos* [peasant tenants] who cared for the cattle. When something happened to an animal, they deducted it from the provisions they gave us at the end of the month. Why the loss happened did not matter. The guilty one was always my father. I came to Santiago at fifteen because I

did not want my children to be the guilty ones all the time. But it seems that things are the same here in the city. The guilty ones, we're always the same. So that's the way it has to be. . . . I just ask myself, when will things be done differently?

The wide embrace of the film also occurred notwithstanding the indeterminate and postheroic political messaging, and the unsparing depiction of failure, that left room for conservative viewers to reinforce their outlook. The film's social sympathies did not translate into political preaching or identification. Even if conservatives gained a new appreciation of the era's tragedy and dreams, they could still conclude that a military coup was necessary and that an experiment of social class integration was foolish. In an earlier time, such aspects might have pushed the Left or the human rights community into public polemic or critique.[62]

Machuca turned into a memory knot on the social body—a compelling call to see with fresh eyes the past-within-the-present, now in the context of a "shared tragedy" sensibility while still attracting distinct readings of the legacy. Conservative newspapers (and their columnists, not all of them conservative) joined in hailing the film as a must-see achievement, while printing a few letters to the editor objecting to political manipulation. Criticism of an open-endedness that might reinforce conservative social prejudices was muted. Critiques tended toward the minor quibble that recognizes a towering achievement, or a bit of doubt about implications of some artistic choices. Did the movie mislead about some details of what really happened at Colegio Saint George? Did it veer too close to a stereotype of the "bad" upper classes? Did Pedro Machuca's continuous use of a torn sweater, not a school uniform, strip the poor of their dignity or did it constitute useful artistic license? In the end, such objections proved a minor current. The artistic decision to sense through a child's eyes the era—its climate of social barriers simultaneously tumbling and reasserted, with showdown looming —defanged political objections. It allowed the magic of the story to work. Significantly, youths who had not lived through the era proved intensely interested. The film served as a generational memory bridge of sorts. Many sent e-mail messages to Wood and declared the film helped them understand their parents better.[63]

Perhaps most important, the pobladores and extras who worked on the film found themselves moved, sometimes to tears. The depiction of an allanamiento of a *población* with significant realism—a scene largely absent from audiovisual media during the democratic transition—proved especially powerful. As with the Valech Commission, it was as if something precious and silenced had finally come out into the open, as citizen testimony and recognition. "Many people cried," recalled the director, Andrés Wood, who had not anticipated the emotive aspect of the filmmaking and learned its meaning as he went. He found himself sensing "We were doing something important for people," experiencing "a sensation that we are touching sensitive spots [*fibras*] that had not been touched before."

Timing mattered. Aside from its undeniable artistic value, *Machuca* caught the cultural moment—and strengthened it. It connected to a sentiment of desire, a certain yearning to fill the void that cut across memory camp lines. In 2001, when Wood first began working on the idea of a film about the Saint George experiment, he had "zero expectations" about its mass appeal, despite hoping to reach a wider public: "When I told people that I was doing this, [they would say], 'Why are you going to go back and get involved in this? People are not interested in looking back.'" He thought the film would end up with a niche market—those who lived through and found meaning in the social experiments of the old Chile, in schools such as Saint George—not a crossover market of mass appeal. Even after a strong premier run in Spain raised expectations, Wood remained cautious. The Chile of 2004, however, was culturally more open than that of 2001. Sensibilities of memory as shared tragedy and unfinished business had grown more influential. The Valech Commission process and the Riggs Bank revelations unlocked the mind to new reckonings. More Chileans were willing to return to the society that had exploded in 1973—and to find something of value in it.[64]

Machuca embodied and consolidated the new sensibility, but it did not create it. As we have seen, the constraints of memory culture in the 1990s had begun eroding after 1998, and the thirty-year anniversary of the coup brought to the fore that yearning for the authentic that finds in a lost social world something appealing and fundamental. The Chile of the 1960s and early 1970s exploded in a terrible calamity, but it was also more than the precursor to calamity. It was also a world whose musical creativity, technological promise, sports heroes, youth culture, religious stirrings, and sociopolitical experiments and mobilization infused life with a sensation of unprecedented possibility. People could make history and culture anew, and the once humble or excluded could sit at the table of possibility. Book culture, like *Machuca*, captured something of the new interest in returning to pre-1973 Chile with more than demonization or defense-against-demonization as the principal point. During 2002–06, historians produced books, sometimes in collaboration with grassroots communities, that rendered vivid a lost world of possibility without sidestepping the internal divisions and sociopolitical dynamics that ended in catastrophe. The "little history" of daily life and culture in 1973, the audacity of proposing a uniquely Chilean and democratic path toward socialist revolution, the making of shantytown dwellers into key social actors in addition to workers, the agrarian reform that for a time blew away hunger in Mapuche Indian communities, the strategies for incorporating military forces into alliance with a democratic-national project, the culture of internationalism that turned local experiment into a sense of continental solidarity and possibility—such topics recaptured the creativity and the "fiesta" aspect of the era without marginalizing the more familiar history of menace and catastrophe.[65]

CONCLUSION: THE CULTURE OF
UNFINISHED MEMORY WORK

Chileans created a culture of unfinished memory work—inflected by a sense of shared tragedy and by struggles over practical consequences—during 2002–06. Aspects of the past-within-the-present postponed, deflected, sidelined, or hidden by memory conflict and impasse in the 1990s turned into fair game. The new reckonings were several: the truths of torture and sexual violation, and their legacies of personal and social silence; the justice of invigorated magistrates, who turned a more specialized eye on human rights crimes, deployed national and transnational legal doctrines to undermine amnesty, and refused hasty dismissal or conclusion; the recognition of responsibility from the top down, by an army accepting of its institutional legacy and by judges willing to ensnare high officers; the exposure of Pinochet as a mafioso leader, responsible not only for human rights crimes but also secret self-enrichment.

These achievements derived in large part from a revival of creative conflictive synergies between civil society actors committed to human rights memory, and select state actors. After the early 1990s (as we saw in chapters 3–4), such synergies dissipated and deteriorated into estrangement. By the mid-to-late 1990s, state actors and political elites had largely pulled back into a reactive stance; memory activists found themselves in the wilderness of political constraint without much moral counterweight from above. In part because pressure and initiative by civil society actors reopened the door, and in part as a consequence of national and international developments that eroded constraints since 1998 (see chapter 5), spaces for creative synergy between state and civil society reemerged. The state was not uniform, of course. Most notable were the synergies of citizens with judges who came on stream as "exclusive" or "preferential" human rights magistrates after 2001, and with Valech Commission members and staff. Relations with the high executive branch—top officials of the Lagos administration—were more problematic and tilted toward conflict. But here, too, a certain frictional synergy was evident, especially in 2003–04. After all, it was the Lagos administration that created a program of support for specialized judges, appointed a truth commission to investigate political imprisonment and torture, and had to respond to insistent pressure by civil society actors. Their claims resonated with sectors of the ruling Center-Left political coalition and with the administration's own sense of values and politicocultural legitimacy.

The culture of the unfinished also meant a freer climate of curiosity about a semitaboo topic: pre-1973 Chile. Was there something more than a run-up to disaster in the story of the late 1960s and early 1970s? Could memory travel to the Frei-Allende era take one into a world of authenticity and loss? Was there anything appealing about the era? The cultural response to *Machuca* marked new sensibilities of curiosity, authenticity, and loss. Here, as with the uncovering of torture under military rule, the new climate favored a "coming out" of that which had been silenced—but remained intimate and close to the heart.

New reckonings with military rule, new synergies of state and society, new curiosities about the old pre-1973 Chile: these shaped the culture and conflicts of unfinished memory and shared tragedy. Yet the unfinished aspect also suggested flaws and injustices—and struggles over how to remedy them. The question that remains is, To what extent did the contentiousness reframe memory of democratic transition itself? By 2006, did flaw, failure, or frustration testify more to the legacy of military rule, or to that of democratic transition? As we shall see in the next chapter, the reshaping of the memory question yielded a surprising juxtaposition: unprecedented advance of human rights memory, alongside sharper risk of marginalization.

Unsettled Monuments: The Struggle for Londres 38

The irony of memorials and monuments is false fixity. They materialize and affix memory to a spot, but they emerge within the dimension of time, as products of human struggle to assert the meaning of the past. New memorials come on stream, as memory projects backed by a social base; others lose their publics and fall into neglect, as contending social forces shift or as living memory gives way to oblivion; others get a new look, as social actors revitalize or update their memory projects. The actors in play vary. The state and dominant social actors may wish to promote an official memory and its heroes or to reconcile contending memories; other social and political actors may wish to promote counterofficial memories or to honor fallen victim-heroes who might otherwise be forgotten or stigmatized. In cases of contentious and traumatic "living memory," the physical places where searing events took place can turn into sacred memory knots. They have powers to convene highly motivated human actors and to mobilize conflicting memory-truths. The struggle to take ownership of memory—and to create social awareness—bears down on key places, as well as key dates on the annual calendar. As Hugo Achugar has observed, the memory site is not simply a geographical place; it is also a "place from which one speaks." The memory site affixes the past to a place and creates an illusion of permanence, but the struggle for moral ownership and awareness that created the site is historical. The origins and future destiny of a monument, memorial, or memory museum are anything but fixed or static.[1]

An additional irony of monuments, and related memory sites such as memorials and museums, is their capacity to materialize silence. Monumentalizing some slices of history in a given place can serve to cover over the wounding past that took place on the same spot. As we saw (Afterword to chapter 5), this is precisely what happened in the case of the O'Higgins

Institute, dedicated to the memory of Chile's Independence hero and "founding father," Bernardo O'Higgins. Located in a beautiful house once owned by the Socialist Party, in a quiet but convenient downtown location in Santiago, the house was seized and transformed in the summer of 1973–74 into the DINA's key secret torture site in the capital city. It continued operating during most of 1974, although Villa Grimaldi displaced it as the new strategic site by year's end. Retired army generals ran the O'Higgins Institute. The address and colloquial name of the torture house, Londres 38, disappeared. The new address was Londres 40.

One aspect of the era of new memory reckonings—when sensibilities of shared tragedy and unfinished work took hold—was increased state support of memorials for victims of the dictatorship. Notwithstanding inauguration of the major memorial to the disappeared and executed in the Santiago Cemetery in 1993, and the opening of the Peace Park at the former Villa Grimaldi torture center in 1997, state policy on memorial construction was rather ad hoc in the 1990s. Civil society actors made demands, sought and occasionally won support from state actors, and contended with a climate of increasing state reluctance after the early 1990s. In 2003, the year of pressure for a human rights initiative in time for the thirty-year anniversary of the coup, the Lagos administration and the Human Rights Program of the Interior Ministry established a more systematic policy. The administration signed an accord with associations of relatives of the disappeared and the executed to build works of symbolic repair in sites across the country. Lagos assigned a modest budget (450 million pesos, about US$0.65 million in 2003) to support such projects, whose civil society initiators would presumably raise additional funds from other state agencies, including municipalities, as well as private sources. The result was a notable acceleration. Between 2002 and 2006, twenty-three memorial projects (a few were additions or improvements at older sites), organized by civil society actors with partial support by the Human Rights Program, sprang up across the country to honor the memory of persons executed or disappeared in specific locales or to recall specific aspects of repression, such as the use of rails to weigh down bodies tossed by helicopter into the ocean. Seventeen projects were completed by the end of 2006, and a half-dozen continued into 2007. At any given moment, about a half-dozen artistic competitions for sculptures or other memorial designs were also under way.[2]

Among the twenty-three projects, only a half-dozen were located in Metropolitan Santiago. The aesthetic designs of the memorials reflected the varied natural and cultural landscapes of repression, as well as distinct artistic styles. The stark cross and low-lying memory wall in Pisagua, at the spot in the northern Atacama desert where remains of twenty-two of twenty-nine executed prisoners were buried and finally discovered, graphically captured their end—betrayal and abandonment in the middle of nowhere. The promise of peace at La Serena—a town whose ambience, architecture, and Catholic cultural tradition stretches back to the colonial past—is evoked in the gentle embrace of seventy victims by outstretched hands. In rugged Punta Arenas, whose icy winds remind one that Antarctica lies nearby, indomitable permanence—the memory wall rising up from the earth below, flanked by taller stellae of remembrance—stands up to the forces of nature and disappearance.

The new memorialization, pushed along by grassroots insistence and initiative but also drawing on state support, was an important accomplishment. It created an enlarged civic geography of remembrance—places for relatives and friends to honor and mingle with those whom they had lost, and places for souls and spirits to rest. It diversified the geography of memory knots where activists could go to press for a culture of human rights. It contributed to a sensibility of memory as ongoing unfinished work, not a matter subject to completion in a short time frame and then cast aside.

Equally significant was what the new memorialization did *not* do. It provided a place of rest to victims, and a place of dignified reencounter with their relatives and comrades, but it did not resolve what to do about the houses of horror—the places where prisoners were maltreated and tortured and where some ended up disappeared or executed. Nor did it resolve knotty questions of ownership and awareness. Was the point of a memory site to provide symbolic repair for victims—a place to grieve and to regather energy —or was it to stimulate awareness and visits by the rest of society? Both mattered, but arguably the memorials accomplished the former more than the latter. Promoting wider social awareness was a more conflictive task in a culture of divided memory, and it posed questions still without answers. What should be done with the sites of horror, particularly the most famous ones? What sort of museum work or other public history work should be promoted to build a civic culture of human rights? Should the state undertake such tasks as its exclusive domain, or in collaboration with civil society actors including victim-survivors? Much memory work remained pending

The spread of
memorials, and
their varied
geography and
aesthetics.
*Credit: Ministerio
del Interior.*

27. Pisagua,
inaugurated 2006.

28. La Serena,
inaugurated 2003.

29. Punta Arenas,
inaugurated 2006.

in 2006 and beyond. In this sense, Chile was very much a world of "unsettled monuments."[3]

The saga of Londres 38 bore witness to the unsettledness of memory—to advances in the boundaries of the possible compared to 2000, to the struggle required of civil society actors to achieve advances, to the conflicts in the "ownership" of memory that could turn apparent advance back toward a state of limbo.

The struggle for Londres 38 was not the only effort to monumentalize iconic places of repression. In August 2003, for example, the Council of National Monuments declared the National Stadium a historical monument, and approved a plan for commemorative work including plaques, recordings, and sculpture. As Katherine Hite has observed, civil society actors had pushed for the declaration. Initiatives included the notable documentary film by Carmen Luz Parot entitled *Estadio Nacional*, released in 2001. Parot used survivor testimonies effectively. Stories of prisoner solidarity and moments of humor built an aesthetic of counterpoint that rendered maltreatment and torture all the more horrifying, without having to depict the cruelty graphically. The film thereby invited viewers to connect with the human story, rather than succumb to repulsion. One consequence of the 2004 Valech Report, moreover, was awareness of the huge number of locations where detention and torture had taken place and a renewed push by former political prisoners to reclaim at least some such sites for memory. Among former torture houses (and as we have seen), only Villa Grimaldi had been rescued in the 1990s from oblivion by blocking a commercial construction project to erase the past.[4]

In the post-2004 climate of struggle to document and monumentalize once invisible torture sites, the struggle for Londres 38 was strategic. Its location in downtown Santiago, near subway and bus lines, meant that the potential for visits and civic education was large. Its history gave the house potency—not simply as one among many memory anchors but as a foundational site. It concentrated "first-time" events. Londres 38 was the DINA's first house of secret torture, execution, and disappearance in Metropolitan Santiago, before a systematized larger operation at Villa Grimaldi eclipsed it later in 1974. Londres 38 also served as a holding-and-torture site for prisoners transported to the coast-side camp of Tejas Verdes. Tejas Verdes was the other key early site of torture and disappearance organized by Manuel Contreras in central Chile. Hundreds of prisoners suffered in the Londres

38 house at one point or another, and at least ninety-four were disappeared. The memory of most of the disappeared prisoners was further violated when they showed up as subjects of Operation Colombo, the first DINA misinformation campaign exposed as a fraud by the solidarity community inside Chile. Operation Colombo was a cruel cover-up story in July 1975 that sought to explain away the disappearances of 119 persons, by fake news stories from Argentina and Brazil documenting their end as fanatics responsible for their own deaths—supposedly killed in fratricidal leftist conflicts and in shootouts with Argentine security forces. The alarming implication, once the story unraveled, was that the state had killed the 119 missing prisoners—and would not hesitate to use lies and stigma to hide secret killing of other disappeared people. The first-time aspects of Londres 38 made it a powerful symbol of dirty war atrocity and struggles for truth.[5]

In the post-2004 environment, where torture had moved into center stage of public culture and where heroic versions of memory as salvation disintegrated, the cover-up of Londres 38 in the form of a reinvented address and an institute to render homage to the national founding father, Bernardo O'Higgins, constituted an outrage increasingly difficult to ignore or tolerate. The decree that turned over the property to the O'Higgins Institute dated back to 1978—the year of the Amnesty Law and of a systematic effort to "close" the memory box of dirty war. The director of the Institute was the army general (retired) Washington Carrasco, who as commander of the army's Third Division headed the ferocious repression that came down in Concepción and Lota in 1973. His directorship added to the sense that de facto powers still remained important and still promoted erasure of the past. In 2005, upset turned into alarm when victim-survivors and their relatives discovered that the O'Higgins Institute planned to demolish the house in August. With support by influential political figures, including the Socialist senator Carlos Ominami and the education minister, Sergio Bitar, the activists blocked the plans and secured a declaration of the site as a national monument in October 2005. The declaration protected the house from demolition but did not legally require a transfer of ownership. News reports intimated, however, that the institute would move to a new site.[6]

The vision of activist-leaders such as Gloria Elgueta, sister of the disappeared MIR prisoner Martín Elgueta, went further than symbolic recognition and pushing out the institute. "Beyond affixing a plaque or elements people can see, the point is to achieve conversational connection [*una interlocución*] with people so that the history is known and everyone takes up responsibility as a citizen today." As a foundational house of crimes against humanity, Londres 38 required more than passive memorialization. It had to anchor interactive civic education.[7]

Did the O'Higgins Institute really intend to leave? If so, what would happen to the property? Were Carrasco and the board of directors playing for time, while searching for an outcome other than a human rights museum reclaimed by victim-survivors? The reality of the house's future destiny, and of understandings to help tamp down conflict, proved murky indeed. The government had sought since March 2005 to reach an exchange-of-property agreement with the institute, but to no avail. In February 2006, the institute put the property on the market to private bidders but backed down in the face of grassroots protest, political tension, and an adverse technical ruling by the Council of National Monuments. Carrasco agreed to accept a government offer to exchange properties, and he implied that the institute would be out within six months, if not sooner. Follow-up negotiations, however, failed to produce a solution. Was the initial agreement a mirage? In August, Romy Schmidt, a new minister of National Properties aligned with the Left of the Concertación, spoke of the difficulties. In principle, the institute wanted to sell or exchange the property, and the government, interested in memorializing sites where crimes against humanity took place, wanted to acquire it. In practice, achieving a meeting of the minds proved tough. In addition to issues of sale price and market value, as Schmidt put it, "one has to understand that the majority of [the members of the Institute Directorate] . . . are military men strongly tied to the Pinochet regime and they have a logic different from those of civilians, which makes the conversation more awkward."[8]

The uncertain destiny of Londres 38 did not simply reflect difficulties of conversation or market price. Londres 38 was a memory knot that seared. Its destiny sparked protest demonstrations by victim-activists, resistance to memorialization by former army officers, tension between human rights activists and the state. The street aspect peaked in July 2006, the anniversary of the infamous Operation Colombo, with a round of educational events and street pressure to reclaim the building. A month later, the house and the street of Londres, just off the main downtown traffic artery known as Avenida O'Higgins, still looked like an urban archaeology site—filled with the material traces of street struggle. As one turned from Avenida O'Higgins toward Londres street at the Church of Saint Francis, the church wall included a prominent painted sign with a large arrow to guide people to the torture house: ⇒ Londres 38. Upon entry into the cobblestone street of

Londres, the remnants of protest—the remains of flyers and posters stuck to walls, street, sidewalks—had not all been scraped away. One poster, still in relatively good condition, bore the photographs of the 119 disappeared persons declared killed by their own armed actions in Operation Colombo. For the activist group known as the Colectivo de Familiares y Amigos de los 119 (Collective of Relatives and Friends of the 119), as well as the group known as Colectivo Londres 38, the anniversary of Operation Colombo was a memory knot. Time and place merged. The July anniversary was a powerful moment that demanded remembrance, galvanized moral conscience and support, and fed into the struggle to recuperate its associated memory place, Londres 38. The groups had come together a year earlier, in order to be ready in time for the thirty-year anniversary of Operation Colombo to push the struggle to recuperate the house. A similar poster, showing the house with its original address and the photos of the 119 victims of the cover-up story, also remained in relatively good condition at distinct points on the street. It proclaimed the objective clearly: "RESCUE LONDRES 38 AS A HOUSE OF MEMORY!!" Did some posters remain because municipal workers could not bring themselves to scrape away the memory faces? Did the address and arrow on the church wall remain visible for similar reason?

Aesthetically, the house no longer exuded the charming faded elegance of the O'Higgins Institute in 2000. The deterioration loudly declared its limbo status. The address number "40" was broken, with the "4" removed. The wooden entrance doors were scarred with remnants of memory posters imperfectly scraped off, instead of refinished and restored. The little window on the entry doorway was boarded up and the large street windows shuttered, to prevent breakage. The walls and shutters were pocked with poster remnants, without repainting or refinishing. In short, the will to invest in keeping up external appearances had vanished. Inside, the house continued to function and remained untouched, but outside what remained were the ruins of struggle. If one looked closely, one could see the wax bits left everywhere by the candles lit to commemorate the prisoners, the bits of red paint still not scraped off the window shutters. After the large mobilization in July, weekly protests and candle vigils continued into the summer of 2006–07 to try to hasten the departure of the O'Higgins Institute.[9]

Political and judicial pressure also heated up, albeit more ambiguously. In August, news reports on criminal cases implicating Pinochet reminded readers of Carrasco's involvement in the execution of the former Socialist intendant Germán Castro, of Talca, in 1973 and in the wider history of regional repression. Colonel Efraín Jaña, removed from his command at Talca for insubordination less than three weeks after the coup and subsequently imprisoned, had testified that "General Washington Carrasco told me one or two days before the execution [of Castro] . . . to kill everyone detained in Castro's group." Pinochet had sought to shore up his own defense by stating that Carrasco acted on his own authority in the region under his command, and by linking such divisions of military labor with a code of silence. "Each person stores things for himself and these things are not commented on." A judge dismissed the Castro case on the grounds that a military tribunal had officially sentenced him. But it was perhaps not the final irreversible word on criminal responsibility, given the overall judicial trend by 2006 and potential vulnerability in other cases. The climate of street action and political-judicial tension deepened the institute's troubles and undermined Carrasco. He left the directorship. The new director, Pedro Aguirre Charlin, was a civilian and the son of the original institute founder. He would presumably focus on the needs of the institute rather than those of Pinochetistas, and would presumably prove amenable to a property exchange that would pave the way for a memory museum. In fact, the O'Higgins Institute did find a new home on the same street by 2008.[10]

The fixity of the preserved house—mobilization and pressure since 2005 meant it could not be destroyed; nor could its recovery be blocked—continued to mislead. In 2007, victim-survivors worked on their own ideas for a memory house or museum, but soon contended with a shot across the bow. In August, Minister Schmidt announced that with approval by President Bachelet, the state would dedicate the house to the new Institute of Human Rights called for by the Valech Commission. The institute would not be a public history institution such as a museum or a memory park, but a state organism. It would become the new center of state programs and promotion of human rights, and the custodian of relevant archives and documents —the institutional heir of the Human Rights Program of the Interior Ministry. Its specific functions, jurisdictions, and memorialization politics were still unsettled and contested. How would this use of the site square with the memory house, dedicated in large part to the specific history and meaning of Londres 38, envisioned by victim-survivors? The former prisoner Erika Hennings voiced disquiet. "We were working on a project to define the future of that house which we think must be [dedicated to] memory, but I think that many more opinions had to be gathered. The idea of the institute is great, but to install it here seems to me premature. It is a very delicate subject." Within a month, the Londres 38 Collective organized a petition drive against the proposed location of the Human Rights Institute. "Bearing in mind [differences of] scale, it is as if Auschwitz, the symbolic space of crimes against humanity, were converted into the offices of the Human Rights Council of the United Nations."[11]

In times of living memory, the spot where the unbelievable and the unacceptable really happened can indeed turn into a "place from which one speaks." For this very reason, ownership of the memory site is contested. The monument is unsettled and unsettling—unless amnesia has truly set in.

Chapter 7

※

Reframing Democratic Transition:
Toward the Memory Paradox of Bachelet's Chile

Memory is about the meaning of the past within the present. Did sensibilities of shared tragedy and unfinished work recast memory of the democratic transition itself? Did the developments of 2004–06 *conclude* the politico-institutional transition, but not its reckonings with contentious memory? Did they move the focus of contention toward the meaning of post-1990 society? Did they widen the issues in play when reckoning with the past?

Such questions are misleading if taken to suggest resolution, or a hegemonic memory of democratic transition, by 2006. They are also misleading if taken to imply that memory of the transition during 2004–06 turned into a matter as searing and strategic as memory of military rule during 1990–92. What *did* unfold, however, was a new phase in ongoing contention about the transition: on one hand, lesser defensiveness by political elites about *some* pending tasks long recognized, but stalemated since the 1990s; on the other, greater pressure on elites to address "other" legacies of military rule, largely sidelined from the public agenda in the 1990s.

To be sure, such characterizations are tentative. When analyzing very recent events, distinctions between fleeting and enduring effects are more difficult to discern. The short arc of retrospective time casts evidence in a suggestive rather than definitive light. Also, memory of the transition and its limits was an issue interwoven with the launch of a new presidency by Michelle Bachelet in 2006, and with civil society pressures and rocky political fortunes early in her term. Nevertheless, by allowing ourselves to peer somewhat beyond the formal closure date of this study, we may stretch the arc of time to see more clearly whether an incipient reshaping of the memory question by 2006—what I term the memory paradox of Bachelet's Chile —truly took root.

This chapter therefore serves as both culmination and epilogue to our story.

In a deep sense, the answer to whether and how the transition and its memory reckoning were concluded or enlarged in 2004–06—and with what social consequences—was still being written by contending social actors in 2007.

Three politicocultural dynamics that affected memory of democratic transition are clear: reemergence of the familiar tension between "formula" and "wedge" on truth-and-justice issues; declining patience with limitations of the 1990s transition that now seemed anachronistic; and a shifting agenda of public issues. The latter bore a contradictory connection to memory. Some rendered the memory question as traditionally understood less strategic, but others focused urgency on legacies once sidelined from mainstream understandings and conflicts.

The result was the memory paradox of Bachelet's Chile: a capacity for unprecedented advance went hand in hand with greater risk of marginalization. This chapter explores the politicocultural dynamics that reshaped memory of transition and set up such a paradoxical twist to the politics of memory.

RESPONSES TO THE VALECH REPORT: FORMULA VERSUS WEDGE

Responses to the Valech Report were revealing. Beyond the wide acceptance of its veracity and its importance as a reckoning whose time had come, the report drew out tensions between using a memory initiative to draw firm boundaries—as a new formula to acknowledge yet contain the past—or to boost ongoing struggle—as a new wedge to keep cracking apart walls of impunity and *olvido*.

President Ricardo Lagos presented the report to the nation in an evening television address—brief, solemn, blunt—on 28 November 2004. The Valech Commission, he said, brought the nation to see the "inescapable reality: Political imprisonment and torture constituted an institutional practice of State that is absolutely unacceptable." The shattering testimonies—almost all the prisoners tortured, almost all the women sexually assaulted—raised questions about human conduct that defied explanation. The silence of thirty-one years "could not be allowed to turn into olvido." Although motivated in part by desire to protect dignity, it was also a veil of denial covering over the broken lives, destroyed families, and continuing pain. The immensity and cruelty of the suffering required recognition and response. "I express publicly my solidarity, warmth, regard, and affection to all the victims and their families." He supported three paths of repair: a National Institute of Human Rights to promote human rights awareness and education, and to protect the archival patrimony dating from the 1970s documents of the Vicaría (Vicariate of Solidarity) through the Valech Commission; symbolic and collective acts by society and the state, to recognize the victims and to prevent future atrocities; and recompense to individual victims, including a judicial clearing of names, a modest monthly pension, and preferential access to health, educational, and housing programs to alleviate damage and lost opportunities. The point of repair was to overcome wounds and build civic unity, not rancor: "In order never again to live it, never again to deny it." Within a month, Lagos secured legislative approval of his social repair proposals—unanimously in the lower chamber, with only two dissenting votes in the Senate.

Lagos called the Valech Commission "an unprecedented experience in the world," a sign of national maturity. After thirty-one years of denial, the country could look squarely into the inferno of torture. The road to accepting truth and responsibility had been hard, and the Valech Report was the last step in a cumulative story of moral progress. "As a society, we have been opening our eyes to the reality of our compatriots, the disappeared, the executed, the exiled, the purged. Now . . . to those who suffered political imprisonment and torture." With this step and the attendant measures of repair, "we complete a chapter through which we had to pass. But we finish it to look to the future, not to scrutinize the past eternally."[1]

Lagos had a point when observing the groundbreaking aspect. In a world-historical moment when truth commissions had multiplied as a vehicle for coming to terms with mass atrocity, the Valech Commission represented the first to attempt to address torture as such, individual victim by individual victim, and to propose remedies. Its report came at a time, moreover, of danger and setback in the international culture of human rights—in the same year that the Bush administration in the United States, faced with the Abu Ghraib scandal and its gruesome photographs, resorted to familiar Pinochetista-like denials. The atrocities inflicted on Iraqi prisoners were acts of rogue subordinates, not the result of policy or consent from above.[2]

But was the Valech Commission an exercise to bring the memory question to a conclusion, or was the point to open a new chapter? Here Lagos was on softer ground. The answers were more ambiguous and contested, the knottiest aspects related precisely to closure and justice. As we have seen (chapter 6), General Cheyre got out front by announcing three weeks before release of the report the army's acceptance of institutional responsibility. He hoped his strategy of conciliation would rid the army of a generational albatross and improve prospects for legislation to speed an end to pending criminal justice cases. Other military figures, especially the navy and *carabinero* leadership and retired high officers including army generals, held to the line that responsibility for abuses could only be individual (even as they lauded Cheyre's conciliatory spirit). They feared that admitting institutional responsibility would encourage, not dampen, the wedge effect. Would admission provide a lever for human rights lawyers to pull new documents into the purview of judges? Also a pressure point to force new actors to admit responsibilities? If so, the concession would exacerbate individual vulnerabilities, not generalize into a responsibility so diffuse that no one bore criminal blame, nor speed up judicial resolution. For his part, Interior Minister Insulza pointedly noted that collective moral responsibility did not cancel out individual criminal responsibility. Amidst the cacophony, one bottom line stood out. The government would *not* actively promote expanded judicial action based on the Valech process, although it would not oppose the right of individual torture victims to initiate criminal complaints. Like the Rettig Commission, the Valech Commission did not name perpetrators. Unlike the Rettig Commission process, there would be no turning over of truth commission material to the courts. Lagos secured legislation to seal the testimonies—on grounds of witness confidentiality—for fifty years.[3]

Times had changed. In 1991, Aylwin used the Rettig Report to challenge a Pinochetista court culture to do its duty. Now the judiciary was more responsive and criminal inquiries had snowballed, partly because of the administration's support for specialized judges. To add torture to the judicial mix, however, would change the scale of open cases and add strains to relations with the military (in addition to raising vexed evidentiary issues). Lagos aimed to be the president who completed the transition and its political reckoning with memory, and who consolidated the role of judges as independent state actors—not the one who launched an interminable spiral.[4]

Not surprisingly, the lines of containment met with resistance, especially in the human rights community and the non-Concertación Left, and disquiet in some sectors of the Concertación. The ironic effect of a successful truth commission experience was soon evident. A truth commission sparks a drawing of new political boundaries on the memory question, but it can *also* create a social space for new initiatives including critique of that which has been excluded. Within days of the report's release, lawyers initiated torture complaints against Pinochet, the former interior minister (and sitting senator) Sergio Fernández, and other former high officials, based in part on the institutional responsibility recognized by the Valech Commission and Cheyre. The no-name policy, combined with recognition of the massive and institutional character of torture, raised questions of civilian and press complicity. Early in December, the reporter Ana Verónica Peña published in *La Nación* a controversial top-ten list, "the civilian face of torture." Among the accused: private-sector tycoons Agustín Edwards, whose *El Mercurio* media empire published misinformation to shield the junta from human rights critiques, and Ricardo Claro, whose shipping business provided the junta floating jails for prisoners tortured in 1973. Also in December, a new "Manifesto of Historians" underscored the value of the Valech Commission as citizen-testimony, and a major prisoner-survivor group, the Coordinadora de Ex-Presas y Ex-Presos Políticos de Santiago (Organizing Committee of Women and Men Ex-Prisoners of Santiago), published and delivered to the Supreme Court a testimonial document. The prisoner-survivors listed 1,958 people as organizers, agents, and collaborators of torture. They protested the anonymity of perpetrators and wanted them brought to justice.[5]

Other issues also sparked critique. The monthly pensions were very modest supplements to quality of life—a baseline of some 112,000 pesos (us$196), rising by age-step to about 125,000 pesos (us$224) for persons over seventy-five years old. Collectively, the estimated payments and programs amounted to some us$70 million annually, but critics and victims slammed the small size in relation to the immensity of suffering and potential indemnity claims, and objected to rules that eliminated a fourth of potential beneficiaries on grounds that they already received recompense under other human rights programs.[6]

But it was the push-pull between impulses to narrow versus enlarge the memory question that drew the most persistent and creative attention. Perhaps the most innovative grassroots experiment came from the Collective of Historical Memory (the full name was Colectivo de Memoria Histórica Corporación José Domingo Cañas). Formed in 2003, the Collective documented the history and consequences of violent mass repression in the *poblaciones* of Santiago under military rule. Its report, published in 2005, made the case for considering the *allanamientos* a form of torture and political imprisonment, distinct from the classic case of individuals brutalized in isolation from their social world. These were victims indiscriminately rounded up within the occupied neighborhoods, whose public spaces were for a day or two converted into holding pens—and sites of physical and mental cruelty. The point of the raids was political, but the target was an entire community treated as subversive. These were precisely the operations excluded from the mandate of the Valech Commission, but important in the repressive violence of the 1980s, as well as the early junta years. The interdisciplinary group of professionals and activists—drawn from fields such as anthropology, history, law, psychology, and psychiatry—researched press sources and human rights archives, conducted fieldwork in 12 communities, and drew into its universe 359 allanamientos in 113 poblaciones. The estimated victim population was huge—in just 16 poblaciones where all males over 15 years old were violently rounded up and held for a day or two, and for which reliable 1982 census data were available, the directly affected group numbered about 98,000.

Significantly, the collective reflected a return of creative conflictive synergy between civil society actors and the state. At first, the Collective sought to stimulate participation in the Valech Commission process. Some pobladores hesitated, but others provided testimony to the Commission in vain. Once it became clear that the criteria for qualification excluded many pobladores who suffered brutal repression, the collective moved toward analysis of allanamientos in their own right, within an enlarged concept of torture it characterized as complementary to the Valech Commission's work. Whether the Collective made a persuasive case for a more elastic nomenclature and conceptualization of torture, rather than documenting cruel and degrading treatment also prohibited under international human rights law, was perhaps beside the point. (This author was more persuaded of the latter than the former.) What emerged clearly was that the Valech Commission experience stimulated anew the tensions of formula versus wedge, that the additional histories of cruel repressive violence directly affected hundreds of thousands —and that what pobladores wanted was recognition of their suffering. "The interviewed pobladores at no time referred to a monetary indemnity, but rather their wish that the State acknowledge the 'dignity of persons' and that 'the truth be known.'" The colectivo had tapped into the hunger for truth telling that moved pobladores when, as acting extras, they performed an allanamiento scene for *Machuca*.[7]

DECLINING PATIENCE WITH CONSTRAINT:
THE 1990S AS ANACHRONISM?

The climate of 2004–06 stimulated a sense of anachronism about three limits of the 1990s transition: the antidemocratic constitutional restrictions, the impulse (reinforced by memory impasse) to seek a clear finishing point to criminal justice, and the formal validity of the 1978 Amnesty Law. The approach of a highly competitive presidential election in December 2005 and the disintegration of heroic versions of memory as salvation (see chapter 6) blew new winds into the politics of constitutional reform. In 2005, Lagos successfully pushed through two reforms that had eluded his predecessors: presidential authority to fire military commanders in chief, and an end to designated Senator and lifetime Senator seats. Leaders on the Right, conceding these had outlived their usefulness, concentrated their efforts on a strategic prize: blocking a disadvantageous reform of the binomial election system.[8]

The new climate also widened acceptance of justice as an open-ended process, with no clear finishing point—although such acceptance did not come without a struggle. The push-pull between intents to enlarge and to narrow the scope of criminal justice continued. Particularly controversial was the shot across the bow by the Supreme Court on 25 January 2005. After reviewing the slow progress of human rights cases assigned to special judges—of 356 cases, only 8 had come to conclusion and sentencing—it ordered the judges to complete their investigations in six months. By 25 July, they either had to proceed to trial or to close cases if evidence remained insufficient. (Technically, the mechanism would be temporary dismissal, subject to reopening if justified by new evidence. Substantively, judges would no longer actively investigate, and reopening cases would prove difficult.) The order applied to 315 cases. Ostensibly, the point was to streamline justice and assure a reasonably speedy trial, in tandem with a larger modernization of criminal procedure in the Santiago Metropolitan Region. Human rights advocates, however, pointed out that lack of cooperation by perpetrators who had key knowledge or evidence affected investigatory progress and that the short finish line added incentive to dilatory tactics.

The order coincided with other strains—and met with suspicion that its real purpose was to achieve a settlement with de facto power. On 17 January, the army colonel (retired) Germán Barriga Muñoz, a former DINA agent on trial for disappearances whose initial abductions occurred in 1976, leaped from a tall building in an upscale neighborhood of Greater Santiago to protest persecution and ruin. His suicide intensified the call for an end to prolonged judicial limbo of former officers—a point long pushed by General Cheyre—and sparked polemics about the perversity of inverting the roles of perpetrator and victim. The suicide added to the climate of pressure on the Supreme Court. Two days later its president, Justice Marcos Libedinsky, declared the tribunal "permanently worried" about slow progress in human rights cases. Within a week, the Court issued its six-month rule.

The rule stoked resistance and failed to stick. Mireya García, vice-president of the Agrupación de Familiares de Detenidos-Desaparecidos (Association of Relatives of the Detained and Disappeared), denounced President Lagos's warm initial reaction. "Every day we realize that we were mistaken when placing our hopes in this government, which has advanced on other aspects. ... When it comes to justice, what is sought is to inhibit." Even more striking, *judges* protested. In February, the Metropolitan Region Branch of the National Association of Magistrates, representing about 150 judges, declared that the order "lacks legal foundation" and violated the independence of investigatory judges necessary for "the concept of due process." In effect, the lower-level judges served notice that the Supreme Court had placed institutional cohesion at risk. The upsurge of human rights cases in recent years had not only sensitized many judges and drawn them into synergies with civil society actors. The judges also wished to block a precedent that could enable the Supreme Court to undermine, by administrative decree, professional autonomy in all kinds of cases. Resistance mounted. By April, the Socialist Party stated the Supreme Court had "surpassed constitutional limits," and the human rights community announced it would appeal the legality of the order to the Inter-American Human Rights Court. Interior Minister Insulza announced a formula to exclude human rights cases from legislation to guide the transit to a new criminal justice system. By May, the specter of a constitutional accusation in Congress came not only from the Left but also from the Christian Democratic Senator Carmen Frei, daughter of the former president Eduardo Frei Montalva. His death under suspicious circumstances in 1982 (see chapter 6) and the difficulty of establishing judicial truth about it taught the perils of dilatory tactics and premature closure. On 6 May, Libedinsky and the Supreme Court threw in the towel—but not completely. The Court suspended the six-month rule, but redistributed some 200 cases and ended the specialized judge system.[9]

Soon after the struggle over accelerated closure exposed its impossibility, the gutting of the 1978 Amnesty Law by jurisprudence—not by legislation— entered its final stage. The journey of doctrinal interpretation had begun in the 1990s with the Aylwin doctrine that judges had to investigate and establish criminal responsibility before deciding whether to apply the amnesty. It continued, by the turn of the century, with the legal equation of disappearance and permanent kidnapping—a crime that continued past 1978 unless proved otherwise. The most recent tool was argument on the primacy of international law of human rights. In 2006, Chilean jurisprudence consolidated the new doctrine. For human rights crimes, amnesty (or immunity by other means) was inferior in standing to the body of international treaties, conventions, and law that outlawed it and to which Chile subscribed. The will to gut the amnesty was already clear in June 2006, when the Supreme Court used permanent-kidnap doctrine to overturn a ruling by the Santiago Court of Appeals judge Víctor Montiglio, one of the last civilian magistrates who continued to apply amnesty. The internationalist aspect of jurisprudence came to a head on 14 October, when the Inter-American Human Rights Court ruled in a suit brought by relatives of Luis Alfredo Almonacid Arellano, a schoolteacher and Communist summarily executed by carabineros in September 1973. Relatives opened a criminal case in the 1990s, only to see the Supreme Court hand it to a military court that applied amnesty in 1997. The Inter-American Court found for the family, ruled that amnesty laws for crimes against humanity themselves violated rights, and reasoned in part from the 1978 American Convention on Human Rights signed by Chile. The Chilean state had an obligation to act to prevent future use of the Amnesty Law to block criminal justice.[10]

The ruling consolidated a political climate that turned the Amnesty Law into the impermissible relic of a bygone era. Given that Chile subscribed to the Inter-American Court, that its internationalist political and economic strategy rested in part on a return to good reputation on human rights, and that President Bachelet's own values and interests aligned with the politics of human rights, the ruling could not be ignored. Also, the Concertación held for the first time a majority in both houses of Congress, a situation that diminished excuses for inaction. Bachelet warmly accepted the ruling as a mandate for legislation to comply—the most likely path was not annulment or repeal, but interpretive law on the primacy of international norms—but a year later she and political elites had still not reached agreement. The devil was in the details, particularly the constitutional viability of nullification and the potential effects in opening new cases.[11]

What the ruling *did* boost were sensibilities supportive of the emerging internationalism of Chilean jurisprudence. The human rights community and activist-victims had long promoted internationalism, but could now count on more support. Earlier in October, the newest member of the Supreme Court, Justice Sergio Muñoz, issued a treatise citing over ten treaties and international conventions to which Chile subscribed as superior in legal effect to amnesty—and as justification for Pinochet's loss of immunity in the Villa Grimaldi case. In December, Judges Alberto Chaigneau and Julio Torres ruled the Geneva Conventions applied to political prisoners, and set aside the Amnesty Law to find three policemen guilty in the 1973 deaths of two student-activists, Mario Superby and Hugo Vásquez. And so it went. In January 2007, the Supreme Court ruled the coup amounted to "an act of war." The Geneva Conventions on prisoner treatment applied, as did international law on the impermissibility of amnesty for war crimes. The case went back to October 1973, when the navy lieutenant Sergio Rivera Bozzo summarily executed José Matías Ñanco, a fisherman identified with twelve others as activist troublemakers in the indigenous Lafkenche community of Maiquillahue, in the Valdivia Region. Matías Ñanco had resisted arrest by Rivera's band, and his murder turned into a lesson. The other prisoners were forced to load the body into the helicopter that tossed it into the Pacific Ocean. The failure to achieve a legislative solution still kept the door somewhat open for inconsistent rulings by judges in the future, but the direction of change was clear and decisive.[12]

The bottom line that emerged from the push-pull dynamics of justice—no great spiral effect based on the Valech Commission in 2004, a hurry-up warning but no massive closure of cases by Supreme Court decree in 2005, a final tearing down of amnesty in the internationalist jurisprudence of 2006—was steadiness of scale and effect. Human rights trials increased but remained in the hundreds, not the thousands. They proceeded without dramatic acceleration, cumulatively broke down boundaries of impunity that once shielded military-police perpetrators, but left most civilians untouched. The idea of closure through institutional engineering lost its remaining politicocultural foundation. The program to create specialized judges and the insistent push by the human rights community began yielding results. In 2005, defendants on trial for disappearances, executions, or torture numbered 351; by year's end, the cumulative count of state agents found guilty and sentenced—mostly retired, mostly from the army and carabineros—numbered 94. The guilty-and-sentenced count continued its slow upward crawl, to 109 persons by October 2006. Most important, justice ensnared once untouchable officers. Three dozen army generals (retired) faced proceedings in 2005. Among them was Pinochet, whose medical escape hatch had declined into a device of appeal and postponement, not a solution. Also among them, and sentenced to jail, were Manuel Contreras and Hugo Salas Wenzel, the former heads of the secret police (DINA and CNI respectively). In 2006, Alvaro Corbalán, the former operative head of the CNI, was sentenced to jail, in a quadruple murder that ensnared thirteen other former agents. Meanwhile, Contreras kept piling up jail sentences—129 years by January 2007.[13]

In sum, several aspects of the transition in its early 1990–92 phase, even if unavoidable at the time, had turned into anachronisms fifteen years later. The specific areas of reform—antidemocratic constitutional engineering that weakened presidential authority and the popular vote, the institutional bias toward judicial closure and its socially forceful backing, the weight of the 1978 Amnesty Law—mattered greatly. But so did a larger change of cultural tone. Even in the mainstream political class, people could acknowledge more readily that the 1990s transition had pushed baggage into the future and that the time had arrived to address unfinished work.

The bag of the unfinished included not only the postponed reckonings of 2004–06: torture via the Valech Commission, criminal justice via specialized human rights judges, corruption masked as patriotism via the Riggs case. It also contained poignant mistakes. Among the most searing: misidentification of bodies buried at Patio 29 in Santiago's General Cemetery. In 1991, the return of democracy and pressure by relatives of victims launched a process of exhumation to identify 126 anonymous bodies. By 1998, the personnel of the Medical Legal Institute thought they had identified 96 people. Among them: Fernando Olivares Mori, a middle-class worker at a United Nations demography office. His saga of disappearance, anonymous disposal, exhumation, identification, and dignified reburial inspired the film director Silvio Caiozzi to produce a moving 1998 documentary, *Fernando Has Returned*. Doubts about accuracy began surfacing by 2003 and Olivares was reexhumed in 2005. By April 2006, the institute conceded that much of its Patio 29 work was unreliable—plagued by technical errors and overstated claims of certainty. Half the identifications were mistakes, and most of the rest at best provisional. Caiozzi released a new edition of the documentary with a coda: *Has Fernando Disappeared Again?* Agave Díaz, the widow, spoke angrily and tearfully as she told her saga. We relatives of the disappeared do not matter. "We are bothersome junk" (somos un cacho). First she was certain that she found and buried Fernando, then not certain, and finally overwhelmed by a 2006 PowerPoint presentation of technical doubts. "I felt humiliated."

The uncertainties about Patio 29 continued. In 2006, staff at the Human Rights Program of the Interior Ministry sought to find a way forward. Reliable results proved elusive. In May 2007, the Medical Legal Institute announced it would create a new DNA database.[14]

A SHIFTING AGENDA:
THE MEMORY QUESTION STRETCHED AND TRANSFORMED?

The more open climate had a corollary: changing times meant a shifting agenda of public issues, with paradoxical effects on the memory question. First, as sensibilities of constraint weakened and the world market price of copper boomed, Chileans pushed harder at "other" legacies of military rule, particularly the socioeconomic inequalities and insecurities of neoliberalism. This aspect enlarged the memory issues in serious play to include socioeconomic injustice, and critique of continuities of economic policy between the outgoing military regime and the Concertación-led transition. But diversifying the legacies under challenge could also diminish the role of human rights memory as "the" strategic heart of democratic legitimacy and contrast with military rule. Second, by the late 1990s (see chapter 4), sociocultural transformation and high sustained economic growth had already built some distance from the civic sensibilities of an "older" Chile, and reframed in part the relation of society and the individual. The "new" Chile featured a privatized culture of self-actualizing individuals—consumers— and a heightened appreciation of newer values: environmentalism, gender equality, tolerance of plural sexualities, unrestrained self-expression. The shift, a marker of openness not only to world markets but to global culture and tourism, did not suddenly stop at the turn of the century. Here too was a paradoxical effect. The new Chile tolerated a wider range of legitimate politicocultural expressions including a less self-censored politics of memory.

Precisely for that reason, however, human rights memory could make new inroads yet prove less strategic to the future of public culture and debate.

The early presidency of the Socialist Michelle Bachelet, who took office in March 2006 after winning (with 54 percent of the vote) the January runoff, captured the politicocultural mix: the enlargement of legacies of military rule and 1990s transition under challenge; the new inroads of human rights memory as continuing unfinished work; the less strategic place of the memory question in the overall agenda of issues shaping politicocultural contention and legitimacy. Her 2005 run as the Concertación's candidate for president had blended loyalty to human rights memory with symbolism of remarkable cultural change. Bachelet embodied the memory question—and an appealing will to face it squarely, without rancor, to build a morally healthier society. She was a former political prisoner at Villa Grimaldi, an exile who found a home in diaspora communities of Australia and Europe before returning to Chile, and the daughter of the air force general Alberto Bachelet, a Constitutionalist whose imprisonment and torture induced a fatal heart attack. Yet she also embodied sociocultural changes reshaping values, tolerance, and respectability. Bachelet was a religious agnostic, a woman, a single mother of three children, a feminist—a torrent of disqualifications for president in the old Chile. She also promised a new political style, more participatory and driven by citizens than by top-down accords among elites, and an agenda emphasizing benefits to the socially excluded and insisting on equality for women.[15]

A detailed review of politics and culture in the early Bachelet presidency is unnecessary. Suffice it to observe that the agenda that took shape in her first year of office—partly by top-down design, partly by bottom-up surprise—brought "other" legacies under fire, but *also* highlighted themes irreducible to memory of military rule or early democratic transition. We consider each briefly.

New Legacies under Challenge

Bachelet pushed reform of the social security pension system, privatized under Pinochet into an investment account model funded by worker contributions, with minimal regulations or competitive incentives to drive down fund fees. The practical result: The system bred insecurity while generating large profits for pension fund companies. Half the laboring population did not qualify for pensions or received only the minimum level, and the norm for retirees, income between a third and half their wage rates, fell short. In her major address to Congress on 21 May (the time when presidents report on the state of the nation and put forth a legislative agenda), Bachelet welcomed recent laws that raised minimum pensions by 10 percent and widened coverage but noted that the nation had to aim higher than stop-gaps. The system needed an overhaul. Her newly appointed Advisory Commission on Pension Reform was to create "a security system that covers all workers . . . permanent employees and temporary workers, professionals and micro-entrepreneurs." The point was universal coverage—"social security is a right of all women and men"—and a design of guaranteed minimums, gender equity, and transparency to assure "dignified and decent" pension levels. In December, the administration proposed a mixed public-private model, with modest universal minimums backed by public funds (in phases, rising to US$143 monthly by 2009), equity rules including child bonuses for women outside the formal labor force, and stronger competition to reduce fund fees and widen access.[16]

Other legacies of the Pinochet era came under fire in more unruly ways. Student protest rocked Chile in May 2006. High school students organized walkouts and building takeovers, called for major educational reform, and held a national strike—some 600,000 took to the streets in Santiago and other cities on 30 May. The students eschewed political party organizing and caught the political elite by surprise. Bachelet had included education in her congressional address as one of four transformations to be pursued in her presidency, alongside social security reform, research and incentive programs to boost entrepreneurship, and upgrading of housing and neighborhood quality of life. But her education agenda had emphasized preschool support and was overtaken by a student movement with its own dynamic. Protests that had begun in April with a narrow focus—the cost of bus passes and university entrance exams—expanded into a demand for universal quality education, regardless of social class.

The turbulence targeted another key legacy of the Pinochet regime, the education law known as LOCE (Ley Orgánica Constitucional de Enseñanza, or Organic Constitutional Law of Education), whose rank as "organic law" made repeal difficult. The law deregulated education, within a framework that minimized public spending and legitimated the profit motive as an organizing engine within a three-tier system of schools: private, subsidized private, and municipal. In the 1990s, the Concertación did not enjoy congressional blocs sufficient to abolish LOCE, and the climate of demobilization limited street pressure. Public spending increased, and significant initiatives including curriculum reform took shape by 1997–98, but the LOCE system—and its tolerance for cutting corners in subsidized, profit-driven schools—could not be challenged directly. In June, Bachelet defused the student movement by appointing a commission to replace LOCE and by promising new spending to resolve quickly specific discontents—bus fare costs, exam fees, shoddy infrastructure—raised by the students.[17]

Whether one pinned the responsibility for extreme social inequality on the military regime or the Concertación-led transition or both, the emerging climate made it less politically and culturally tolerable. The state revenue windfall from surging world market copper prices—from US$0.81 per pound in 2003, to $1.67 in 2005, to over $3.00 by mid-2006—had the same effect. In August 2006 serious labor strikes paralyzed state-owned La Escondida, the largest copper mine complex in the world. In October the treasury minister, Andrés Velasco, announced an 11.2 percent increase in social spending for the next budget. Beyond the specific sectoral and budgetary pressures, what proved evident was disintegrating tolerance of a trade-off associated with the 1990s. The earlier model accepted extreme socioeconomic inequality—including low pay, and insecure conditions of labor and subcontracting—as the price of a strong market-driven growth engine (average annual rates over 7 percent) that, in combination with public policy programs, sustained fast reduction of poverty. The growth engine also sustained rises in jobs and social spending. As we have seen (chapter 4), disillusion sensibilities had already set in by the late 1990s. After 1998, moreover, the era of 7 percent growth expectations ended. By 2005–06, earlier sensibilities of disappointment or postponement morphed into something tougher: impatience, and moral scandal. The climax came in August 2007, when the Rancagua bishop Alejandro Goic galvanized debate on an "ethical wage" for all including subcontracted workers. Goic's moral prestige derived from his double role, as president of the Episcopal Conference of (Catholic) Bishops, and as the mediator who negotiated an end to bitter labor conflicts in El Teniente and other copper mines. Goic and trade unionists pushed for a sharp upgrade of the minimum wage standard, from ca. US$280 per month (145,000 pesos) proposed in officialist circles, to ca. $480 (250,000 pesos).[18]

The debate culminated a push since 2005 by the Catholic Church and a newly restive labor movement to change the terms of moral and political discussion. In April 2005, on the eve of a new presidential election campaign, the Episcopal Conference worried about "the injustice of insufficient salary, retirement or pensions," decrying "scandalous levels" of inequality in housing, wages, health, education, and access to consumer goods. As candidate and newly elected president, Bachelet tapped into the climate by making social exclusion, especially the insecurities of the pension system, a calling card. In 2006 and beyond, workers responded to surging copper prices and a new president with strikes and insistence on new standards for subcontracted labor. The conflicts in the copper mines were the most serious, economically and politically, but the climate of moral critique was especially sharp when it extended to lower-paid sectors and women workers. Release of figures showing huge 2006 profits (128 billion pesos, nearly US$250 million) by the supermarket and retail holding company Cencosud sparked a stinging denunciation of wage hypocrisy and abuse by the labor leader Marianela Fernández. In August 2006, Cencosud fired from its newly acquired Economax chain 500 people at the top of the worker wage scale (at 381 thousand pesos monthly), only to rehire them at lower wages. "I make 202 thousand pesos and I am head of household. I cannot live on that pay, let alone 150 thousand, which is what some workers make." Cencosud sometimes even resorted to pretend-pay—by compensating laborers "with off-days instead of money. Like in the [days of the] nitrate mines."

In short, Cencosud abused the legal loopholes of a rigged system to pay workers—including women heads of household, about half the labor force in supermarkets—at poverty or near-poverty levels while running very high profits and paying amazing incomes at the top. In 2006, the average monthly salary for 544 executives exceeded 6.5 million pesos (about US$12,400, compared with a worker base rate of less than $300). The disparity between the highest executive salary and the worker base wage at Cencosud, a ratio of over 200 to 1, compared poorly with reported norms (5–8 to 1) for Europe and Japan.[19]

What gave force to such denunciations was the difficulty on the Right and in the business class of ignoring a moral debate ignited by Catholic bishops. In addition, a climate of civil society impatience and mobilization, supported by at least some sectors of the Concertación, could disrupt business expectations. Social peace required a new initiative. In August 2007, Bachelet announced a presidential advisory commission including representatives on the Right to recommend a new equity framework for labor policy. Meanwhile, some 300 trade union leaders intended to meet with legislators in October to push for a new deal.[20]

The unfinished memory question had stretched to include socioeconomic injustice more insistently by 2005–06, and the insistence did not fade. One result was a somewhat revised perspective on the 1990s transition. Goic put the point—rather diplomatically—in 2005. "We knew what it was to live in dictatorship, where there was just one voice. The transition to democracy in Chile, with all its limitations, has been extraordinary, but there remains this other step: that the riches can be distributed more equitably without having enterprise stop producing. If we do not begin to solve this, the mobilizations will continue."[21]

Themes Irreducible to Memory

Some themes central in the reshaping of politics and culture were not reducible to the memory question. Consider two examples: women's equality, including sexuality and reproduction; and mass transit in Santiago.

Bachelet, a committed feminist, sought to open doors for women. She began with an immediate bold step: gender parity among high presidential appointees. Half the twenty new cabinet ministers and half the ministerial subsecretaries and intendants were women. Bachelet used her own parity policy as a bully pulpit example to challenge Congress, the political parties, and the business class to end gender discrimination. The message: times are changing, talented women are in the pipeline, but one needs to push affirmatively for equality. In truth, participation by women in upper layers of the executive branch had grown since 1990, and the Aylwin government had established a cabinet-level ministry, SERNAM (Servicio Nacional de la Mujer, National Women's Service), to promote women's equality and to create programs to advise women of their rights, assist them as heads of household, curb domestic violence, and diminish adolescent pregnancy. It did its work, however, within an environment of constraint including small budgetary authority and a masculinist political culture. Bachelet's gender parity was a more unsettling challenge to the elite world of masculinist political leadership, patronage, and expectation.[22]

The most controversial new step, however, involved sexuality and reproduction. The influence of the Catholic Church (nominally the nation was still 73 percent Catholic in 2001), the overrepresentation of the Right in Congress, the fear of a split between Christian Democrats and the Left within the Concertación, all meant constraint on such issues. In 1989, moreover, prospects for liberal social policy took a step back when the outgoing Pinochet regime stripped away a key legal loophole: "therapeutic abortion" to protect the life or health of the prospective mother. Liberalized public policy on other aspects of sexuality, family, and marriage also proved tough to achieve. The Church and its allies managed to block legalization of divorce until 2004, and even then secured separation time and counseling provisions that injected expense and uncertainty. Meanwhile, sociocultural transformation generated new values and expectations that *in the long run* eroded Catholic Church hegemony. In 1990, nearly half the Chilean population (46.1 percent) thought divorce could never be justified. By 2000, only a quarter (26.8 percent) held to this view, and four-fifths (79.0 percent) supported legalization of divorce, regardless of personal belief. Chileans also invented resourceful adaptations—some 6,000 annulments per year based on legal defect in the original marriage, including deliberate improper signings of documents.

In short, on sexuality, marriage, and reproduction, a notable breach emerged between the political balance of forces and the sociological realities and expectations. In the 1990s and beyond, marriage rates declined, while rates of cohabitation, adult single living, and single parenting all rose. By 2002–03, the rate of childbirth outside wedlock had risen to nearly half (47 percent, compared to 34 percent in 1990), and visible labor force participation by women ages 15 to 60 had increased to nearly half (48 percent, compared to 36 percent in 1990). Values of family attachment remained strong, but family forms had diversified and the structure of expectations about female work, sexuality, reproduction, coupling, and separation had shifted.[23]

Bachelet did not challenge the legal prohibition on abortion, but she pushed a hot-button issue nearly as contentious—and which opponents framed as abortion or a step toward it. Beginning in September 2006, the Health Ministry promoted free distribution in public health clinics of the morning-after birth control pill to women, including female adolescents fourteen years or older, the age of legal sexual consent. Bachelet defended the program on equity grounds—the realities of social class that defined women's life chances. The state should not impose a particular view of sexuality on people, but it should "provide a choice to all, so that people have real possibilities, in this area like others, to move forward with equity." Bachelet and her allies pointed out that women and teenagers of upper-class and middle-class families could buy contraception and the morning-after pill, but the same was not true for the poor. In upper-class barrios, only 3 of 100 female adolescents (eighteen years old or younger) got pregnant. Nearly all adolescent mothers, who gave birth to some 40,000 babies annually, came from modest class backgrounds and depended on public health programs. Unequal access to contraception condemned women of modest means to lack of choice—and poverty. The new program catalyzed heated debate, a struggle at once cultural and legal and political, about the scientific boundaries of abortion versus contraception; about the rights of parental control over the sexuality of minors; about the sociological realities of sex, birth control, and abortion. (One key sociological reality was an estimated abortion rate, notwithstanding legal prohibition, of 150,000 per year.) The government stance sparked tension with the Catholic Church, the Right, and Christian Democrats, and legal challenges, but the political will to push access to contraception persisted. In October 2007, the Health Ministry fined Chile's top three pharmacy chains—Cruz Verde, Ahumada, Salcobrand—for failing to stock and sell the morning-after pill. Cruz Verde and Ahumada, the most important chains, backed down. Salcobrand, whose owners identified with Opus Dei, continued to resist.[24]

In short, the shifting public agenda came to include volatile issues irreducible to the memory question. The politics of gender and sexuality was not the only such arena. Among the most explosive was Transantiago, an overhaul of mass transit in Santiago. Conceptualized and designed in 2005–06 by the outgoing Lagos administration, it was launched early in 2007. The point was to replace the capital city's notoriously polluting and dangerous buses. In the old system, drivers rushed to complete as many routes as possible to increase their pay, and the competing bus companies had no incentive to ameliorate air pollution. Transantiago sought to rationalize and modernize mass transit by replacing the dirty buses with larger and cleaner vehicles; by limiting concessions to a few companies whose capital, costs, and technical capacities met the system's requirements; by designing a leaner routing system coordinated with Santiago's excellent subway system; and by organizing payment of fares via predeposits on electronic swipe cards. At least that was the theory.[25]

For many commuters, particularly from poor and working-class families who could not switch to autos, the technocratic utopia turned out to be a nightmare. There were not enough routes and not enough buses, the timing was less frequent and not predictable, and information about routes was elusive. The money spent on swipe card deposits was often lost. Some vendors sold bogus cards—and many buses even lacked swipe card machines. Whatever the theoretical appeal of the design, the debut showed poor connection to user realities, poor oversight of concession companies, and poor implementation. A cascade of unintended consequences followed.

Commuters flooded the subway system, the only reliable mass transit in the capital city, but the crush of people strained the system and produced serious ventilation problems and health incidents. Meanwhile, disgusted bus passengers refused to pay for poor quality of service—they boarded for free by entering through the back doors for passenger exit. At the height of the early troubles, in May 2007, a crowded subway line failed and police deployed tear gas to disperse people when angry passengers exiting to the street blocked a major downtown artery. Juana Alvarez Soto, a flower vendor who had to commute downtown from Pudahuel in western Metropolitan Santiago, voiced the exasperation of poor and working-class commuters. "It's not fair. I go by the Metro [subway] because there's no bus anymore, and then this happens. My eyes are really stinging. The Transantiago is a disgrace—and it's all the Concertación's fault."[26]

The cascade continued. The intended self-financing aspect failed, and the system began to require hefty subsidies—nearly us$1.2 billion in 2007, including rush orders to add 1,800 buses to the initial stock of 4,600. The political consequences of Transantiago also proved serious. Government approval ratings sunk hard in Metropolitan Santiago, from a 55–65 percent range early in 2007 to only 43 percent by year's end. The fallout of public anger, and unanticipated and regionally inequitable transportation subsidies, produced tensions within the Concertación as well with the opposition, weakening Bachelet's leverage in Congress.[27]

In sum, by 2006–07, key public policy issues that sparked politicocultural controversy did not reduce to the memory question—whether in the form of classic human rights violations under military rule that required recognition, repair, and prevention, or in the broader sense of unjust socioeconomic legacies that softened the contrast of pre-1990 and post-1990 society. Gender parity and liberalized contraceptive rights, technocratic rationalization and foul-up of mass transit—such issues connected to transformations of Chilean society that had crystallized in the late 1990s and early 2000s. Political responsibility, benefit, and critique homed in on the mature Concertación, and bore tenuous connection to memory politics, that is, contentious reckonings with unjust legacies and social debts bequeathed by military rule and constrained early transition.

The shifting politicocultural agenda had reshaped the meaning of the "memory question" by 2006, and the reshaping "gelled" and proved enduring into the future. Not only did the memory issues in play since 2004 stretch to include human rights and socioeconomic issues beyond the contentious core themes as defined in the early 1990s. Not only did new key issues arise that were irreducible to legacies of military rule. Not only did the classic version of the memory question—violent trampling of human rights and bodily dignity under military rule that required recognition, repair, and prevention—recede from the strategic place it held in 1990–91 and most recently in 2003–04. In addition, some controversial aspects of the updated "memory question" connected more tightly to legacies of the mature Concertación—the transformation of Chile on its watch—than to those of military rule.

The Mapuche question concentrated in acute form the revised texture of memory conflict. As we have seen (Afterword to chapter 4), relations between the state and Mapuche peoples in the South, especially in the Ninth Region, had entered a period of strain and disillusion by the late 1990s. After 1998, Mapuche and environmental activists denounced with increasing forcefulness a business-government alliance of depredation, especially in the forestry-cellulose sector in the case of indigenous peoples, and the hydroelectric energy sector in the case of ecological activists. (The distinction is one of emphasis. Crossover effects happened, and as seen in the Afterword to chapter 4 Mapuche social actors played a lead role in pre-1998 conflicts about hydroelectric projects.) They pointed the finger of responsibility at the mature Concertación, particularly the Lagos administration of 2000–06. Mapuche protesters, desperate about the strangulation of communities—not only loss of land, but also water sucked up by pine forests owned by powerful investors—embarked on a path of direct action tactics. Most such incidents amounted to nonviolent demonstrations including occupations of pine estates, but some militants also set fire to forests and attacked lumber trucks. Within the Mapuche movement, where issues of political autonomy rights intersected with those of resource rights, even those who did not endorse the most radical actions understood why they took place. The problem was not only injustice, but also perpetual postponement. After all, the declaration of good intentions and some modest steps forward in the early 1990s under Aylwin had not led to sustained practical results. In recent years, the difficulty of luring the state and investors into serious negotiation about socially responsible forestry and energy projects proved more notorious than ever. When it came to Mapuche issues, the Lagos administration relied on militarization and criminalization to contain protest and protect property. Carabineros guarded the pine estates against potential occupations, and the state used draconian antiterrorism law—inherited from the Pinochet regime, no less—to convert a political problem into a criminal one.

To be sure, relations between the state and Mapuche peoples had long been something of a sore point within the mystique of democratic transition —they exposed a state tilt toward powerful investor groups, and an ethnocentrism that marginalized Mapuche communities and leaders from the circle of effective dialogue. But in recent years the ante had escalated. The state criminalized protest. Mapuche activists had their internal differences, but the Mapuche movement did not recede. Activists pressed for greater political autonomy, for demilitarization of the community-forest territories, for rights of assembly and protest, and for release of political prisoners. They also founded an autonomist political party, Wallmapu, in 2006. Meanwhile, world market demand for cellulose, fueled by soaring per capita consumption in China, continued to boom. Chilean cellulose exports surpassed $1.7 billion in 2006, and kept soaring—to US$2.5 billion in 2007. Companies such as CELCO, owned by the powerful Angelini group, had plenty of incentive to keep expanding forestry-cellulose production.[28]

The Mapuche crisis finally came to a head in the Chilean summer of 2007–08. In the early dawn of 3 January, a group of about thirty activists from Yupeco-Vilcun sought to perform a symbolic occupation of lands lost to the Santa Margarita estate, about thirty kilometers southwest of Temuco. The carabinero Walter Ramírez shot Matías Valentín Catrileo Quezada, an agronomy student at the local Universidad de la Frontera. Catrileo died quickly. The other activists took the body away and refused to turn it over to police for investigation until Catholic Church mediators worked out a solution. The use of brute force, far out of proportion to any plausible threat and at odds with democratic policing, turned into a cause célèbre. At least two previous live fire incidents against Mapuches had also happened in 2006–07. Meanwhile, prisoners protested police abuses including torture, and several launched hunger strikes in October 2007. One prisoner-activist,

Patricia Troncoso, carried on into January despite the severe health risk. Her case, like that of Catrileo, became a cause célèbre. She drew international attention including thousands of visits to an eloquent declaration posted on the Web at YouTube. Finally, on 4 February, a negotiated liberalization of prison conditions brought an end to Troncoso's fast, and her transfer to a hospital in Temuco. The hunger strike had lasted 112 days. The pressure, both national and international, had become too important to ignore. In the second half of January, Bishop Goic, still president of the Episcopal Conference, observed that violence against Mapuches reflected failure to address root causes and truly "to listen to the voices of Mapuche leaders." Meanwhile, the government tried for a fresh start by appointing a presidential commissioner for indigenous issues.[29]

Mapuche activists inserted current protest within longer arcs of memory —the consistent trampling of indigenous rights and resources by the state and non-Mapuche Chileans since the nineteenth century, and the resort by democratic governments of Pinochet's antiterrorist laws to criminalize and repress radical Mapuche protest. In other words, although the Pinochet regime had launched the privatized forestry boom, stripped away community resources, and sparked a Mapuche movement, the memory aspect of the Mapuche struggle did not reduce either to the Pinochet regime or to the constraints of transition in the early 1990s. The problem was the mature Concertación. As Gustavo Quilaqueo Bustos, the leader of Wallmapu put it, the fact that government promises and declarations of intention in 2007 so closely resembled those at the start of transition revealed much. "One realizes that it is the democracy that owes a debt to the Mapuche people."[30]

The conflictive Mapuche question embodied, perhaps in extreme form, the memory paradox of Bachelet's Chile. Memory mattered in 2006 and beyond, but not in the same ways. The era of slowly rolling impasse—fiercely divided memory, accompanied by structural gap between desire resting on soft power and constraint resting on hard power—had given way to that of shared tragedy and unfinished work. New advances in the politics of human rights memory had reshaped the terrain of the possible since 2003. Chileans addressed the torture question, approached the pre-1973 era with less taboos, witnessed the emergence of human rights judges who tenaciously pursued their cases, saw a gutting of the 1978 amnesty by interpretive doctrine, and experienced a less restrained and self-censored civil society. Citizen testimony and insistence on the memory question had contributed powerfully to the changes of recent years. A new president made a special point of memory solidarity, by commemorating victims during anniversaries of human rights crimes, by visiting the house of the Agrupación of Relatives of the Detained and Disappeared, by returning to the former Villa Grimaldi, by acknowledging that much work remained to be done.[31]

At the same time, however, the stretching of the memory question to include what had once been marginalized coincided with a larger reshuffling of that which mattered in politics and culture. The reshuffling consigned human rights memory as traditionally understood to a less strategic place for building a future, and pushed to the fore issues irreducible to memory. Even when memory mattered, the specific issues had shifted. The historical focus that seared might be the legacy of promise and frustration linked to the Concertación, rather than that of the Pinochet regime itself. Could the memory box of Pinochet's Chile finally be put aside?

Maybe not always. When Pinochet died, curious things happened.

❅

The Curious Burial of Augusto Pinochet

The medical crisis lasted a week. Augusto Pinochet entered the Military Hospital of Santiago early Sunday morning, 3 December 2006, after a heart attack. Doctors performed two procedures, including an angioplasty to clear an artery. By Monday, they declared his medical condition "fairly stable" and its evolution "very favorable." They noted he had recognized and spoken with visitors, including the Santiago archbishop, Francisco Javier Errázuriz, and suggested he might go home after ten days. The prognosis seemed on the mark when doctors released Pinochet from the intensive care unit on Thursday. Given the history of medical arguments as an escape hatch or delaying tactic in criminal cases, followed by acts showing a Pinochet more fit or lucid than thought, the initial reports fed suspicions of a "show." After all, Pinochet's legal problems had heated up again. On 30 October, Judge Alejandro Solís, who had interrogated Pinochet and found him lucid, ordered his house arrest for thirty-six kidnap-disappearances, one murder, and twenty-three tortured persons at Villa Grimaldi. On 25 November, Pinochet released a letter accepting "political responsibility for all that was done" while pointedly rejecting the injustice of criminal trials, that is, "persecution and vengeance" against soldiers who helped him save the country. Just days before the hospitalization, Judge Víctor Montiglio ordered another house arrest, for the murder of two bodyguards of Salvador Allende. It turned out, however, that the medical crisis was real. On Sunday, 10 December, Pinochet's heart failed for the last time. He was ninety-one years old. Ironically, his death coincided with International Human Rights Day.[1]

Pinochet's final medical crisis brought the divided and passionate aspects of the memory question back into the open. The journalist Patricia Verdugo, who lost her father in the repression and whose famous book on the Caravan of Death proved important in truth telling at the outset of the transition and in Pinochet's legal troubles in 2000, stated the desire of many veteran human rights activists. They hoped for his recovery, not to send an ailing old man to jail, but to arrive at a formal sentence for the historical-legal record. "I need Pinochet alive so that he can be found guilty, in order to feel that I live in a decent country . . . with minimal ethical standards." She surmised his death would mean "political relief" for the Concertación and the opposition; they would no longer have to provide de facto impunity to someone whose criminality and corruption had become so obvious. The most revealing reactions, however, occurred on the streets. In spite of all that had changed since 2002—the disintegration of heroic versions of memory as salvation, the final discrediting of Pinochet as corrupt and un-bounded in the use of violence, his fall into irrelevance as an active political figure—many people still cared deeply about Pinochet. He was still *the* savior and founding father to be thanked, still *the* violent tyrant to be repudi-ated. Supporters gathered at the Military Hospital within hours of news of his heart attack. They bore national flags and picture-posters of their hero, and some continued their vigil through the night. By Monday, the street scene included counterdemonstrations, sometimes with a theatrical twist. A red-devil figure hovered near a military church as congregants inside prayed for Pinochet's health. Demonstrators from the opposed camps gen-erally kept their distance, but some scuffles broke out when they shared physical space or tried to talk directly to one another.[2]

The tension was not reducible to divisions between the memory camps as defined in the 1990s. Pinochetistas who kept up a street vigil near the hospital were *also* upset by leaders of the army and the political Right who had "abandoned" their hero. Protesters screamed "traitor" and "hypocrite" while kicking and throwing water on the car of General (retired) Juan Emilio Cheyre, when he visited the hospital. Their chants voiced betrayal by a Right whose leaders ducked hospital visits: "Derecha/dormida/Pinochet salvó tu vida" (The Right/Asleep/Pinochet Saved Your Life). After Pinochet died, such tensions continued: "Derecha/dividida/y mal agradecida" (The Right/Divided/and Ungrateful).[3]

The divided responses to medical crisis were a mere prologue. The wake, funeral, and burial of Augusto Pinochet galvanized memory theater. Death created a time-space for sacred ritual and performance that drew out how the country and its memory question had changed and not changed. What had changed: the politicocultural context and balance of forces shaping the memory question. As we saw (chapters 6–7), the terms of the memory debate and its relative weight in setting an agenda for the politicocultural future had shifted strongly by 2006. What had *not* changed: memory as a matter that was moral and existential and heartfelt, not simply political. The memory question had reshaped lives and values. The long Pinochet regime had proved formative across several generations: not only for the mature and young adults mobilized during the Frei-Allende era, and who experienced directly the crisis of 1973 and the turn to massive state violence, but also for children of the 1970s who "came of age" during the turbulent era of protest, repression, and plebiscite in the 1980s. About four of ten Chileans were under twenty-five years old and therefore lacked direct conscious memory of military rule in its most violent phases, through 1986. About four of ten, however, were thirty-five years or older. That is, they were people whose generational experiences—if they cared to remember them—could resonate with memory as a matter of the heart. The call to bear witness might still connect to deeply felt, formative moments—discoveries of moral community and moral awakening, imperatives that were intimate and personal and experiential. For some, indifference to memory or weariness with it might be the everyday habit that suddenly—even surprisingly—turns precarious. In addition, some who came of age during democratic transition were profoundly affected by post-1990 struggles over memory, truth, and justice that sensitized people to human rights as a core value.[4]

In short, even if the overall politicocultural context redefined the meanings of the memory question and dampened its capacity to take over the public agenda, Chilean society still included large numbers of people who did not remain impermeable to memory's call—once it broke out into the open again. Pinochet's death functioned as a classic memory knot. It broke the unthinking habits of daily life. It drew back to the surface, at least for a while, the moral potency and intergenerational aspects that made memory irreducible to politics. If memory was political, it was not *only* political.

That memory remained a matter of the heart, not easily set aside, became obvious after Pinochet's death. On Monday and into the early morning hours on Tuesday—the day of the public funeral—Pinochet lay in wake at the Military Academy. The upper portion of the coffin cover lay open to expose a glass cover that enabled visitors to see his face and shoulders and the fact that he was dressed in highest military uniform (captain-general rank). The surprise was the huge number of people who went to the Military Academy. They stood patiently, for up to six or seven hours, in lines that stretched for blocks and continued on past midnight until they finally passed through the metal detectors to say goodbye and mark their gratitude, sometimes tearfully. Some 60,000 people passed through by 2 AM on Tuesday. Some had traveled in from the provinces. Elderly women withstood the summer heat to pay their respects. "I do it with great love and thankfulness," said seventy-six-year-old Eva Núñez. "Neither my family nor I would be here if not for him and what he gave us. Now my children and grandchildren are professionals." Added Gladys Jorquera, "During the [Unidad Popular] my husband and I had nothing to eat, until my general liberated us." Outside, the crowds occasionally broke into song-chants: "We will never forget you / Liberator of Chile / Augusto Pinochet."[5]

Love, however, cut both ways. Also waiting in line with the Monday night visitors was Francisco Cuadrado Prats, the grandson of former army commander general Carlos Prats and his wife, Sofía Cuthbert, assassinated by a DINA car bomb in Buenos Aires on 30 September 1974. Cuadrado had been six years old when his grandparents were murdered. Upon approaching the coffin, Cuadrado gathered up his saliva and spat on the face-window. Military police moved in quickly to prevent an attack and remove him from the scene. Prats, a Constitutionalist opposed to the coup and brought into Allende's Cabinet in a failed effort to find a path to stability, was forced to resign as commander under pressure of an army split as the political crisis sharpened in August 1973. Pinochet, at the time considered a Constitutionalist, replaced him. Prats went into exile in Argentina after the coup, retained a strong prestige in some opposition circles, had insider knowledge of army social networks, and completed a memoir that revindicated the Constitutionalist military tradition shortly before the murder. The car bomb killing was the first of several spectacular assaults on foreign soil—in Rome and Washington, D.C., as well as Buenos Aires—to eliminate influential persons abroad who could pose problems for the regime. When the identity of Cuadrado came out, he explained his motives. "I spat on him as an act of contempt, because he assassinated my grandparents and because it hit me hard to see the exaggerated honors he received from the Army."[6]

The mix of emotions—gratitude to the savior, anger at the assassin, resentment toward ungrateful former allies who abandoned the hero, regret that death allowed an escape hatch from trial—injected the culturally strange into the familiar theater of goodbye. People violated protocols and sensibilities that otherwise applied. In the human rights camp, it was not just that a grandson felt compelled to spit on the corpse of the tyrant whose violence came down on his elders. It was also the euphoria and relief that took hold in some quarters. The culturally proper stance was solemnity: regret that Pinochet had escaped the final stages of formal justice, or alternatively, observation that enough had transpired to prove his knowing responsibility for massive crimes and achieve a justice of cultural humiliation. In this context, one might acknowledge that for the family his passing was a time of personal loss and grieving.[7]

But what if the death provoked exuberant joy and relief? News of Pinochet's passing produced not only street crowds to grieve the loss and thank the hero, but also crowds pouring into the plazas of Santiago and other cities for street parties. The agony of living with Pinochet was finally over! Luisa Toledo, a Christian base activist mother in the población of Villa Francia who had lost three sons to the military regime, noted the exceptionalism of her own reaction. "It is the first time that I am happy about someone's death. What most bothers me is his cowardice. He should have acknowledged everything that happened." Revelers drank champagne, danced, and waved flags and memory banners. In some Santiago neighborhoods they set up street barricades and lit bonfires. Street clashes between protesters and police occurred, especially in outlying districts, and some nihilist groups provoked fights and destroyed property downtown. The dominant tone, however, was joy and relief. The downtown Plaza Italia area drew thousands into a party of youthful euphoria similar to that which greeted the "No" victory in the 1988 plebiscite. Some in the crowds had taken their 1988 "No" placards and rainbows to the party. On the day of the funeral, several thousand persons at Constitution Plaza to celebrate the memory of Salvador Allende cheered when youths showed up carrying a mock coffin and burning the photo of Pinochet, and sang the upbeat protest-party song of the 1980s, "Adios general, adios carnaval" (Goodbye General, Goodbye Carnival).[8]

Meanwhile, jokes about problems when Pinochet arrives in the next world began to circulate. Pinochet goes down to Hell after a failed attempt to enter Heaven, but realizes he forgot his briefcase with his curriculum vitae at the gates of Heaven. Lucifer tells him not to worry. They know him well in Hell. They do not need his curriculum vitae and have prepared a party to welcome him. Two little devils will go up to Heaven to retrieve the briefcase. After a while, the telephone rings. It is Saint Peter calling for Lucifer. "Listen, Lucifer, be careful because Pinochet has been with you only a half hour, and already I have two little devils asking for political asylum."[9]

Mainstream political elites, with an interest in respecting rules of propriety and navigating a divisive memory terrain, criticized inappropriate behavior. Significantly, however, some also acknowledged the complexity and legitimacy of the sentiments in play. Elites declared an understanding of Cuadrado's motives, even if they did not endorse the act and rejected outright the partying at Plaza Italia. The defense minister, Vivianne Blanlot, skillfully walked the tightrope. She declared personal sympathy for the Pinochet family's loss, distinguished it from her critique of regime policy—suppression of human rights—and performed the role of the unpopular but necessary face of civilian authority at the military funeral. There, as we shall see, she exhibited an iron discipline of her own emotions, and insisted on institutional discipline in the soldier ranks. Yet she also declined to denounce civilians who expressed their inner reactions, on the contrary declaring she could appreciate what drove them. She could understand why the grandson of Carlos Prats and Sofía Cuthbert did not suppress his contempt. The celebrants at the Plaza Italia did not express her style, but she realized why they went to the street party. "I would not have done it, but I understand them. I cannot condemn them."[10]

The funeral service itself mixed the surreal with the familiar, as if to underscore that saying goodbye to Pinochet was different. The controversial could not be suspended, nor masked within the rites of a sorrowful collective goodbye by family, friends, and admirers. The nature of the funeral itself sparked debate. Bachelet rejected a state funeral and a decree to fly flags at half-mast. Pinochetistas and opposition critics as well as street demonstrators wanted the official tribute to a former president. The administration's stance: Even if one set aside the problem of the legal status of Pinochet's presidency, to provide state honors to a former ruler indicted for massive human rights crimes was unacceptable. The government would allow the army to hold a service at the Military Academy in recognition of Pinochet as former army commander, not as former president, and to fly the flag at half-mast on military installations. At the same time, the government would insist on the protocol of military subordination to civilian authority. Defense Minister Blanlot would attend the funeral, notwithstanding objections by family members, because it was an institutional rather than a private family ceremony. Blanlot added her own symbolism. She held to a demeanor of elegant stoicism—an unshakable calm of authority—despite the jeers and turned backs that greeted her. Her formal white suit contrasted with the traditional black of grieving; she attended as an institutional superior, not as a personal friend and mourner.[11]

The most controversial moment came when the army captain Augusto Pinochet Molina seized a moment on stage to deliver an impassioned defense of his grandfather's rule—and a critique of Chilean justice. At the height of the Cold War, his grandfather defeated Marxist totalitarians intent on seizing power "not by vote, but rather by straight force of arms." But the struggle did not stop after victory. "The battle was tougher in his old age. It was this enemy that hit him the hardest . . . [striking] the emotional life, forcing him to see how his wife and family were humiliated by judges more interested in renown than justice." Pinochet Molina, an active duty officer dressed in uniform, was not a scheduled program speaker. He violated military discipline by speaking without permission of superiors and by engaging in political speech. In short, he allowed the role of grandson—and his sense that the army was no longer a friendly career home anyway—to take over that of military officer. Within hours of the ceremony, Blanlot announced the unacceptability and her expectation that the army would take "pertinent measures." A day later, the army commander, Oscar Izurieta, who himself took care to avoid a political tone and to reiterate respect for human rights in his funeral speech, had an expulsion decree on Blanlot's desk for approval. The army general Ricardo Hargreaves also fell. As commander of the Fifth Division in Punta Arenas (just before promotion to a higher position in Santiago), he gave a newspaper interview praising Pinochet's work as a president who rescued a country in ruins, and declaring allegiance. "He took that responsibility. . . . I was a participant in that cause. I shared it fully and continue to do so." The bottom line of the expulsions: public speech that violated army discipline and institutional interest would not be tolerated, even if Pinochet's passing drew out strong emotions at a human level.[12]

In the end, what was most curious—and revealing—about the death of Augusto Pinochet was the disposition of the remains. Pinochet had requested cremation, a wish easy to honor, but deciding on a final resting point was another matter. The remains could function as a memory knot galvanizing opposed memories, passionately felt, if at a place too accessible. A heroic mausoleum was pointless. The army did not want a crypt at the Military Academy, and family members no longer saw the army as reliably loyal. The government also did not want a spot that would convene loyalists and protesters. The final disposition of the amphora with his ashes had not been decided before Pinochet's death, but within a day the family leaned toward the family's private landed estate, "Los Boldos," as the best option. There Pinochet could be protected from public access and surrounded by relatives who appreciated him.

But even a basic decision—privacy and protection from the world of divided memory—begs other smaller decisions. What else had to take place to assure privacy and protection? The cremation did not take place in Santiago, as originally announced, but in a more remote private cemetery in the Fifth Region. The transport to the Fifth Region was by helicopter, not by road. Finally, at 2 AM on Wednesday, Pinochet's sealed case of ashes arrived at Los Boldos, on a road heavily guarded by special *carabinero* forces. Their equipment included a water cannon truck in case they contended with protesters. Near the road, at the private chapel Pinochet had built for the estate, some fifty persons—relatives and friends, some retired military officers, and a few current army officers including Commander Izurieta—celebrated mass and a private funeral. In the end, however, Pinochet's ashes did not remain at the chapel. It was too close to the public road! Pinochet's widow, Lucía Hiriart, decided that the best adaptation was to have the ashes protected by permanent guard in a more remote interior area of the fifty-one-hectare estate, and to move them back to the chapel only when celebrating mass.[13]

Pinochet's final resting spot—more precisely, his travel back and forth between interior spot and private chapel—symbolized solitude. The leader's heroic facade had fallen away, even while controversy had not. Family members and loyalists comforted themselves by waiting for the judgment of History. "As time passes," asserted the former interior minister Sergio Fernández, "the stature of General Pinochet will grow immensely."[14]

The death of Pinochet was a cautionary note about the contingency of history. Even if the memory question was not strategic to the politicocultural future, one never knew what event might bring it roaring back into prominence, at least temporarily. Precisely because memory was moral and existential, not just political, it had a volatility irreducible to narrow rationalist calculation. Nor did one know for certain the consequences of memory-galvanizing events, if politicocultural elites treated them too casually. After all, notwithstanding the continuing work of civil society activists, the memory question had been cornered into marginal status before, in the mid-to-late 1990s, until key events in 1998—Pinochet's retirement as army commander, his arrest in London—opened up new possibilities. The icons of memory struggles since 1973 were passing into history, and death called forth moral witness. In this sense, the dialectics of containment and insistence—the effort to acknowledge yet hold the memory question in check, precisely because some social forces pushed to enlarge it—did not necessarily end in 2006. Pinochet's passing mobilized the remaining loyalists for a goodbye of sorrow, and the once suppressed for a party of relief tinged by the regret of incomplete trials. But such expressions did not necessarily cancel the paradox of memory—unprecedented advance, alongside growing risk of marginality—in Bachelet's Chile. Were the mobilizations that accompanied Pinochet's final crisis a brief and misleading timeout? The final resting spot and the reassertions of army discipline and civilian authority aimed at an affirmative answer. Yet precisely because the memory question seared so deeply, who knew for sure if the answer was final?

Conclusion

※

Reckoning with Pinochet

Reckoning with Pinochet and his legacy: this was the dramatic challenge faced by democratic Chileans after winning the "No" vote, against continuing rule by the general, in the plebiscite of October 1988. The defeat of Pinochet created not a democracy, but a democratic opening. It yielded not an outgoing regime in disarray, but an embattled leader determined to protect his regime's legacy and sustained by a powerful social and institutional base—a disciplined army under his command, an investor class that was loyalist and indeed grateful for the economic model, two-fifths voter support in an electoral system that enlarged its congressional weight, a conservative legal-constitutional order and a judiciary that built strong barriers to democratic reform. An interim of nearly a year and a half before transition to civilian rule also allowed time to prepare new laws and restrictions. In short, the plebiscite victory created not an opportunity to build from scratch, but structural tension between the "soft power" of an electoral majority and moral and cultural influence, and the "hard power" of force, economic resources, and institutions. To build the reborn yet constrained democracy was a project, not an outcome, and it had to be undertaken in a society of divided memory.

What made the transitional environment of 1989–90 and beyond so volatile was precisely the memory question. The reality and meaning of the crisis of 1973, and the violent rule of Pinochet and the junta thereafter: these, and the attendant debates over denial and misinformation and forgetting, had shaped the struggle for "hearts and minds"—politicocultural legitimacy—during military rule itself. During the 1970s and 1980s (as seen in Book Two of this trilogy), memory of military rule as salvation of the country from ruin and civil war, and its transformation into an orderly modern society of prosperity, competed for influence with memory as cruel rupture, the "open wound" of lethal state terror—killings and disappearances at the margins of law, profoundly aggravated by secrecy and misinformation to cover up the crime. The salvation narrative also came to compete with another dissident framework, memory as a narrative of multifaceted persecutions that sparked a new awakening. To witness or experience the varied repressive injustices that came down sparked moral awakening or even rage—a transformation as one learned new values or acquired a new determination to overcome dictatorship. The problem was not only the denied disappearances and executions aimed mainly at leftists and social activists, but also so much more: the massive imprisonments of dissidents and suspected dissidents, the pervasive torture and denial of due process that shaped imprisonment, the abusive roundups and raids in the *poblaciones*, the employment purges of the suspect, the mass flight into exile and the transfer of some citizens to internal exile, the random shootings and troop occupations to stamp out urban protest, the struggle of women to hold families together while coping with the poverty and repression that came down on neighborhoods, the morality shocks when police killed street priests or burned youngsters or vilified Catholic solidarity groups—and the pretense that one could deny that such things mattered much, if they had happened at all. Precisely because a struggle over what was important to remember and why proved dangerous to the regime's moral legitimacy, and its original narrative of salvation, a new memory framework had also emerged by the late 1970s—a reading of the past that called for mindful forgetting and resonated with its legal parallel—the Amnesty Law of 1978. The phase of dirty war, necessary to save the country, was thankfully completed. To revisit that phase was dangerous. It would harm the country and the patriots who saved it. To move forward rather than promote rancor, the country needed to close its memory box.

At first, in the early-to-mid 1970s, the struggle to frame the facts and meaning of the past-within-the-present boosted the regime, which quickly took control of the public domain and found a willing public for its official story. Even at the start, however, the regime contended with a more contested international domain of truth seeking, open to testimony and influence by Chilean exiles seeking to blunt the repression and defend human rights. Inside Chile, the struggle over how to understand and act on the memory of shocking times eventually wore down the regime's moral legitimacy; turned the idea of "memory" into a cultural code word and sacred value; energized and fused with mass opposition in the 1980s; and set the stage for regime defeat in 1988, in a vote originally conceptualized as a ratification exercise. By the time of the plebiscite vote, memory as rupture, persecution, and awakening had merged into a majority memory camp.[1]

The strategic character of memory struggles under military rule meant they could not be put aside in the new democracy. They had left a legacy. They had mobilized people and reframed values. They had made human rights and the immorality of forgetting a rallying cry. They tied the legitimacy and health of the new democracy to the idea of human rights—and a reckoning of some sort with truth and justice. The moral foundation of democracy would prove weak if it did not address the violent trampling of victims and their relatives, and if it did not draw a bright line of contrast between rule by brute force and rule by law and decency. The memory question was not simply unavoidable, but explosive. For many, it was a personal and moral issue, not just a political problem. Precisely because the basic facts had been so disputed, and regime denial and cover-up so pervasive, people had built a testimonial foundation that entangled the personal and the emblematic—my family's experience, my neighbor's experience, is the reality of Chile—as they struggled to find and assert their truth. Precisely because the memory question focused on life-and-death struggles with so much at stake—the shocks of violent atrocity and intense fear, the fierce dispute about facts and responsibilities, the agonizing uncertainty about the fate of abducted prisoners, the searing reflection on one's basic values—it resisted reduction to an amoral calculation. Yet it was *also* a political issue and danger. The moral legitimacy and political glue that held together the ruling Center-Left Concertación and gave it a strong electoral base rested greatly on the human rights critique of Pinochet and the dictatorship. Yet if society was so divided about Pinochetismo—for some he was a hero, for others an assassin—and if Pinochet retained considerable power and a strong social base as guardian of a proud legacy, how much reckoning could really happen? Would "hard power" sweep aside "soft power" and destroy democratic transition?[2]

This book has sought to understand how Chileans wrestled with the dramatic memory question—unavoidable, passionate, dangerous, strategic—as they built a reborn yet divided and constrained democracy, and with what consequences. Here I first focus on three major conclusions that stand out when analyzing the 1989 to 2006 period as a whole. I then step back to enlarge the space-time perspective—to consider what the democratic memory-reckoning story means if set within a longer view and within a transnational or world culture perspective. These reflections yield two additional conclusions, and in the end inspire a question. What does the Chilean story ask us to consider when acting in our own times?

A first conclusion leaps out if one considers, from a human rights perspective, the cumulative consequences of memory struggle during the difficult democratic transition. *Over time, the strains between soft and hard power produced both a structure of impasse, and a shifting center of gravity.* In other words, on memory issues Chilean democracy yielded not impasse once and for all, but a "rolling impasse." The specific points of contention that embodied the standoff between soft and hard power changed over time, and eventually, the structure of impasse itself began unraveling. What was unthinkable or impossible in 1990—that Manuel Contreras, the former head of the DINA, could be jailed while Pinochet continued as army commander —was not so unthinkable in 1995. Likewise, the unthinkable in 1995—that Contreras would turn out to be the first in a string of high officers prosecuted for human rights crimes, rather than the exception that proved the rule of impunity—was indeed imaginable in 2005. Yet at each key step along the way, tough standoffs occurred.

The transitional democracy of the 1990s rested on a paradox. On the closely related issues of memory, truth, and justice, this was a society where "soft hegemony" and "hard hegemony" pulled fiercely in contrary directions. Each memory camp sought not only to mold public policy, but also to shape the very language of politicocultural understanding and debate. The effort to set the terms of debate, and the large influence wielded by each camp, meant that the standoffs between them were not reducible only to a tension between soft and hard power. Each side sought to "hegemonize" politics and values in the Gramscian sense of seeking not only to impose but to educate—that is, to draw society as a whole and adversaries in particular into its preferred rules of engagement and language of memory discussion.[3] In the volatile transitional environment, the shapers of soft hegemony—the arena of cultural influence and electoral majorities, dominated by Center-Left political elites, grassroots activists, professionals, and celebrities sympathetic to human rights—remembered the Pinochet regime as persecution and rupture of life that sparked a new appreciation of democracy and human rights. This memory camp valued finding some way to hold people accountable for an atrocity-filled past, even though differences emerged over the relative weight and particular mechanisms of truth telling, criminal justice, and symbolic acts within an overall strategy of social repair and accountability. The wielders of hard hegemony—the arena of influence backed by force, dominated by a still powerful military and elite sectors crucial for economic growth and stability—framed the Pinochet regime as heroic rescue of Chile from Marxist disaster. This memory camp also saw Pinochet as the architect of successful modernization, and valued letting go of the human rights issue.

Structurally, the situation was a recipe for standoff, and it bred both conflict and ambivalence. The same persons and political camps could swing from the impulse to move forward on questions of memory, truth, and justice, *and* the impulse to retreat on such issues in the interests of stability or as a concession to practical constraint. As we have seen (chapter 3), from the start the structure of power and division over the memory question yielded the frustrating sensation of living within a circle. Forward movement on matters of truth or justice suddenly gave way to impasse and danger, that is, a return back to the problem of force and de facto power. As we have also seen (chapter 4), even within the camp ostensibly committed to human rights, the debilitating effects followed: there was cultural weariness with the memory question, and loss of political will to engage it, yet it was inflected by the moral impossibility of declaring openly its abandonment. One result was a kind of moral schizophrenia: swings in the public domain between the politics of everyday prudence and the moments of convulsion, when the latest outrage or polemic erupted and aroused all over again the impossibility of forgetting the past. Another result, by the mid-to-late 1990s, was that civil society activists felt increasingly alone, abandoned by the state, and responsible for forging initiatives and pressure on their own. Even after the events of 1998—Pinochet's retirement as army commander, his arrest in London—scrambled the lines of effective power, the human rights question remained volatile and bred ambivalence. As we have seen (chapter 6), during the Lagos administration major advances occurred, partly in response to grassroots pressure, but the political culture of conflicting impulses—forward movement and retreat—remained strong.

The paradoxical structure of post-1990 society yielded repeated impasse and frustration, but what it did *not* yield is also significant. It yielded not a society of amnesia but one of contradiction and ambivalence. For the human rights–oriented memory camp, it yielded not an absence of gains, but a dynamic of hard-fought limited gains—always inadequate, always at risk of becoming the last gain, yet also a potential stepping stone. In the perspective of time, each issue that yielded a limited gain was also a point of contention that drew out the adversity of it all—the underlying structure of impasse. The strains of hard versus soft power resurfaced, with a reminder that any concession to the human rights camp that had to be tolerated this time was also a boundary that should not be crossed in future time. The responses of Pinochet, the army and navy and *carabineros*, and the Supreme Court to the Rettig Commission Report—the most important human rights initiative of the Aylwin administration—made the point clearly. The truth commission report called forth not the remorse and follow-up sought by the president, but the proud offended intransigence that says, "You have had your moment. Make it the last one. Do not expect more."

Over time, however, the achievement of hard-fought limited gains did not stop, and a certain cumulative effect—in which one advance served as point of entry for another or at least shifted the boundaries of debate—also became evident. The process was not inexorable or linear. It was not inevitable that each modest advance laid a foundation for a new one (a point to be analyzed in more depth in the third conclusion later in the chapter). As we have seen throughout this book, some gains were subject to major setbacks, and they occurred despite periods of sapped political will. They required that people mobilize pressure, negotiate alliances, maneuver among currents of soft and hard hegemony, and regather their efforts after circular return to a state of impasse. Yet the once unthinkable or impossible happened, and produced a slow cumulative effect. Consider a few examples: In 1990–91, a truth commission process, focused on killings and disappearances, established as undeniable fact the reality of massive atrocities as state policy. In 1991–93, the Aylwin doctrine and the impact of the Alfonso Chanfreau case launched debate about proper interpretation of the 1978 Amnesty Law and the responsibility of judges to investigate rather than dismiss criminal cases. In 1995, the final phase of a judicial and political drama ended with the imprisonment of the DINA head Manuel Contreras, sentenced for the murder of Orlando Letelier and Ronni Moffitt. In 1997, Villa Grimaldi, the largest DINA torture center, was inaugurated as a memory site rather than a commercial property obliterating the past. In 1998–99, changes included major judicial reform, cultural "outings" of torturers, filing of domestic criminal complaints against Pinochet, and his arrest in London under universal jurisdiction theory. In 2000, the military-police forces formally recognized via the Dialogue Table that massive killings and disappearances had to be addressed. Domestic criminal investigation and prosecution also took place, leading to a house arrest order against Pinochet. After 2002, grassroots pressures culminated in a truth commission on torture, assignment of specialized criminal judges to hundreds of open human rights cases, and jail sentences reaching into the high officer ranks of "dirty war."

Significantly, each step provoked resistance and required facing down the reality or shadow (threat) of impasse, especially before 2002. The truth commission initiative in 1990–91 required a presidential decision by Aylwin against the instincts of his inner circle of advisors. The inauguration of Villa Grimaldi as a peace park in 1997 required that civil society activists overcome the idea, influential in political elite circles after the cat-and-mouse chase of Contreras in 1995, that the polity would not withstand new memory initiatives on torture and disappearance. Even after 1998, when the old structure of impasse began unraveling and a new generation of army leaders began to draw distance from Pinochetismo, old habits and anxieties and contentiousness did not disappear. The peaking grassroots and political pressures of 2003 to establish a torture commission contended with fears that to break *this* boundary of memory containment might backfire—by producing a snowball effect on criminal justice and in cultural discourse that would complicate the consolidation of a military culture emancipated from Pinochetismo, or by producing expectations of legal justice by torture victims that would culminate in a new frustration. The specter of impasse endured throughout 1990–2003, but the center of gravity—the issue that focused the contentiousness, as well as the balance of power among the actors—shifted over time.

If one steps back from discrete events to consider process, one also sees a certain cumulative effect. Consider, for example, the eventual gutting of the 1978 Amnesty Law via doctrinal interpretation. On one level, the human rights camp was continuously frustrated and defeated. Formal repeal, annulment, or nullification did not happen—not even as late as 2006. The law remained on the books, as a bitter symbol of impunity and as a legal option judges could invoke in specific cases. On another level, the substantive meaning and consequences of the law shifted, slowly and inconsistently but in the long run drastically. Notwithstanding the agonizing pace and the zigzag of adoption and retreat by judges, new layers of doctrinal interpretation accumulated, narrowed the legal zone for effective application of amnesty, and eroded the culture of impunity. The Aylwin doctrine—that judges had to investigate and reach conclusions about the facts and responsibilities of the crime before they could apply amnesty—turned out to be only a first step in launching a debate and eventually, a new judicial praxis. The doctrine that unsolved disappearances were, for legal purposes, kidnapping crimes that continued past 1978 and therefore ineligible for amnesty, unless judicial investigation proved an earlier endpoint, constituted the second major interpretive blow. The coup de grâce came as judges found legal reasoning within national constitutional law to grant primacy to international human rights law when it conflicted with domestic law. Each step reflected and contributed to a shifting climate—the balance of forces in an ongoing memory struggle—and each used earlier steps as precedent. For example, the launch of the Aylwin doctrine and the developments in the judicial investigation of the Alfonso Chanfreau case, whose scandalous termination in turn raised the heat on judges to apply the Aylwin doctrine to new cases, were directly linked to the evidentiary findings and politico-cultural impact of the Rettig Commission. If, as Florencia Mallon has argued, hegemony must be analyzed as conflictive process as well as outcome, the import of the cumulative layering effect is all the more striking.[4]

Tracing the history of memory impasse *and* its shifting center of gravity is the double lens that enables one to see the more subtle dynamics of democratic transition. The strain that issued from the contrary pulls of soft hegemony and hard hegemony created frustration among state and civil society actors aligned with the memory camp oriented toward human rights. In the heat of battle, and from the very start, each advance could seem only a quarter of the proverbial loaf. The 1990–91 truth commission, for example, had no subpoena powers, did not identify perpetrators by name, did not address torture thoroughly, and did not secure military leaders' acknowledgment of atrocity as state policy. In the perspective of time, however, each advance galvanized the soft hegemony camp, widened the influence of a language of human rights, and built a foundation for future legal and cultural struggles. The ultimate irony of the story comes through in the following contrast. To democrats and victim-survivors, the meager results of memory struggles reaffirmed impunity; to military regime loyalists, they created the slippery slope of vulnerability.

A second conclusion draws out implications of memory struggles for the ways we conceptualize the democratic transition. *To see the strains that produced both a structure of impasse and a shifting center of gravity offers a way to move beyond the influential idea of a "pacted transition." The idea remains useful, but it obscures as much as it reveals.* The idea's academic genealogy is rooted in political science, but it has also become a common sense that crosses disciplines. As dictatorships gave way in southern Europe (Greece, Portugal, Spain) in the 1970s, and in South America (among others, Argentina, Brazil, Uruguay, and finally Chile) in the 1980s, scholars studied the dynamics and prospects of democratic transition. To "move beyond" pacted transition means not to discard the core insight but to refine it—by considering more precisely the boundaries of pacts, their necessary fictions, and their consequences over time, when placed alongside other social dynamics. Political scientists have engaged in the task, for example, by balancing the explanatory weight of "founding conditions" of civilian-military power relations, as Felipe Agüero has argued in a superb analysis, against subsequent bargaining dynamics that unfold over time but are also constrained by the transition paths set in the founding moment. The task here is to nuance the discussion from a distinctive angle: historical research on memory reckoning in Chile.[5]

The concept of pacted transition (or "transactional transition") has staying power for good reason. The transitions to electoral democracies in southern Europe and South America rarely took the path of Greece in 1974 or Argentina in 1983—defeated military regimes in disarray. What usually occurred was more mixed, in terms of the initial balance of power between outgoing regimes and their social base on the one hand, and the opposition on the other. Internal regime fissures between "hard-liners" and "soft-liners," or a political crisis in which neither opposition nor regime could win decisively, or a strategy to protect military institutional needs or its national project long into the future: such considerations could push even a powerful regime to shape an exit path. Whether the exit was a proactive effort at controlled political liberalization from above, or a strategy under pressure of economic troubles or declining political strength, the point was to negotiate or impose the fundamental rules of the game in the future. In other words, the price of exit is some sort of transaction—an elite accord or understanding, whether explicit or implicit. In the scholarship of pacted transition, the case of Spain has loomed large as paradigm. Here indeed, political elites negotiated explicit accords, in the succession crisis following Francisco Franco's 1975 death. Here, too, the politics of elite consensus building was related to a politics of forgetting. Spaniards on all parts of the political spectrum agreed to put aside the conflicts and passions of the Spanish Civil War and the early Franco regime. As Paloma Aguilar has shown, the mem-

Conclusion: Reckoning with Pinochet   365

ory that mattered was the horror and madness of fratricide. The point was to forget mindfully—to leave the era behind, rather than risk reviving it. This was Spain's version of "memory as a closed box."[6]

The Chilean case also features in the scholarship of pacted transition, sometimes as a classic South American case for comparison with Spain. The reasons are obvious and up to a point valid. As we have seen, the democratic opposition faced enormous adversity: the dilemma of having to play within institutional rules set by a very strong outgoing regime. Yet it also could use the pressure of its 1988 plebiscite victory and its moral-political legitimacy to negotiate some revisions to Pinochet's 1980 Constitution, and to pull a democratic Right into apparent understandings on additional constitutional reforms. Pact making, backed by citizen vote in the case of the 1989 constitutional reforms, was fundamental but also a "devil's bargain" (to use Peter Winn's apt phrase). The incoming government's respect for the inherited legal institutionality—the revised 1980 Constitution, the decree-laws on the books—narrowed Pinochet's room for maneuver and enhanced the likely resilience of transition. To move against his own institutional legacy risked Pinochet's legitimacy and legal protection, even within his own social base. At the same time, though, Pinochet continued as army commander in chief, the legal levels of autonomous military prerogative were high, and the rules of the game would make it very difficult to overcome "authoritarian enclaves," such as the binomial election system that, along with designated Senator seats, assured overrepresentation of the Right. In short, room for maneuver to alter the inherited institutionality was narrow. Continuity of economic policy was also considerable. The Concertación made no secret that it would promote a privatized growth engine, aggressively open to and competitive in diverse world markets and unencumbered by dramatic shifts in the state share of the economy, albeit inflected by stronger commitments to social spending and equity. The latter were to be negotiated as accords with the congressional opposition and business, as well as the Center-Left parties and labor leaders.

Given the negotiations amidst adversity that produced an agreement on constitutional law, the emphasis on top-down accords, and an overall climate of demobilization in the 1990s, it is small wonder that the idea of pacts, some explicit and some unacknowledged, gained currency as "the" explanation of political immobility in memory politics, too. If one considers the retreat of state actors from expressive memory politics by the mid-1990s, the returns to impasse that bedeviled advances on truth and justice, and the culture of ambivalent swings between everyday prudence and passing convulsion, the sensation of struggling against a pact of forgetting and silence—of living within a "conspiracy of consensus," as Alexander Wilde has perceptively put it—was almost inescapable. Yet it is precisely on the memory question that the notion of transition pacts must be cut down to more modest explanatory size.[7]

Three problems arise. First, the pacts were partial and limited, more focused on constitutional and economic rules of the game than on human rights memory. Even before the conflicts around Pinocheques, the Rettig Commission, the Aylwin doctrine, and criminal investigations by judges during 1990–93, Pinochet had wanted to have the junta legislate a second amnesty in 1989 to cover human rights violations in the post-1978 period. He could not get it. The air force and navy realized that the moral and political legitimacy of human rights memory was too strong; to push through another amnesty would be an admission of guilt and undermine the military—that is, destroy the fragile social compact of transition. Even on economic matters, the understandings were partial. The amnesty the junta *did* pass in 1989, as an imposition rather than an agreement, was an economic one—a law that prohibited congressional audit and investigation that might undermine the 1980s privatizations favoring regime allies including former officials. The second problem is that at first no one trusted the pacts really to "hold." This was why the incoming democratic government saw governability, a strong economic track record, and building a new *convivencia* including broad portions of the Right as fundamental to block the danger of a failed transition or "regression." This was why Pinochet and the army worried that any weakness on the memory question would invite another shove down the slippery slope. This was why, amidst the necessary fictions of agreement on rules of the game, a struggle to redraw the lines of effective power also unfolded—whether in high public dramas such as the Pinocheques affair and the criminal investigations dragging officers into courtrooms, and followed by the hard push-backs of military alert, or in more subtle inside games, such as the push-pull over whether the president or the army commander had the last say on approving proposed promotion of generals.[8]

The third problem is that elites did not act in a vacuum, even in a climate of social demobilization. They came under the moral pressure of grassroots victim-activists in a society sensitized to human rights by a long history of memory struggles, and under the political pressure of realizing that human rights tensions affected the internal relations and the electoral base of the

Concertación coalition. Civil society activists, too, were seeking to redraw the lines of effective power—or at least keep alive the memory question as a central moral reckoning for a democratic society. We will analyze later the conflictive synergies and logics that unfolded between state and civil society actors.

The double lens needed to see the strains of memory reckoning—the structure of impasse, and its moving center of gravity—illuminates how the pacted aspect of transition, while real, is insufficient. It cannot alone explain the dynamics shaping the most explosive and strategic issue of the early transition, nor the cumulative consequences of memory struggle over time, nor the retreat by political elites into a more complacent stance by the mid-to-late 1990s. Power mattered more than pacts, and pacts had a history of ups and downs and countervailing pressures. Ironically, Pinochet himself gave bitter testimony to the point, in a then private interview with the historian James Whelan in February 2001. Only three weeks had passed since his house arrest by order of Judge Juan Guzmán, after loss of a court appeal—reinforced by a personal communication from the army commander Ricardo Izurieta that he would not support defiance of judges. Pinochet thought Patricio Aylwin Chile's "worst president" and "a creep" [*un desgraciado*] who always sought to harass and undermine him. He was equally contemptuous but less angry with Eduardo Frei Ruíz-Tagle, whom he considered "harmless." As for the loyalty of General Izurieta, "I will not say anything."[9]

A third conclusion addresses the deeper dynamics of advance in democratic memory reckonings—despite frustration, returns to impasse, and a political elite that often proved divided, reactive, or reluctant. *Frictional synergies of civil society actors and select state actors proved fundamental for major advances in human rights memory, and for preventing closure of its politicocultural relevance.* It was precisely the articulation of the social and the political, notwithstanding a climate of elitism and demobilization, and notwithstanding the structurally adverse conditions of transition, that allowed for creative moments of memory reckoning. It was also the insistence of civil society actors, and revived articulations with state and political actors, that kept the door open—or pried it back open—for new moments of reckoning.

What "synergy" did *not* imply is important. Synergy did not mean harmony of purpose, or a unified logic of action, among state actors and civil society actors within the human rights camp. The dynamics were frictional and at times openly conflictive, as well as collaborative and mutually dependent. Nor did synergy imply stable dynamics over time. As we shall see, synergies had a history of ups and downs—peak moments, deterioration, collapse, and rebirth under altered conditions. The social geography of relevant actors also shifted. Among state actors, for example, executive branch actors were crucial in 1990–91 while judges proved increasingly relevant after 1998. Finally, synergy did not imply return to an older model of state-society dynamics of support and conflict, based on mobilizing mass demonstrations, protests, and direct-action initiatives by powerful social movements or organizations linked to political parties, and thereby able to pressure the state for changes or to show strong support for a government program or project. The older model shaped political culture in pre-1973 Chile and was to an extent reborn—albeit temporarily, in a radically altered context and with a different balance between social movement dynamics and political party dynamics—in the 1980s. The dynamics of conflictive synergy during democratic transition unfolded as a subtle blend of collaboration, moral pressure, and protest.[10]

What frictional synergy *did* imply was mutual dependence of partners driven by distinct logics but who also needed one another—morally, politically, practically—to accomplish a goal considered fundamental by all. For some, the goal was in a sense sacred, that is, moral and transcendent, therefore irrenunciable. As important, no partner could alone achieve the goal or the legitimacy that flowed from it. The social actors were (to adapt the fine phrase of Heidi Tinsman) "partners in conflict," whose collaboration was crucial but also yielded tension.[11] The subtleties of frictional synergy were evident in the first major memory initiative of the new democracy: the Rettig Commission. The goal in common was a definitive public reckoning with the truth—the indisputable factuality—of massive executions and disappearances of unarmed citizens by agents of the military state. As we have seen, the objective was unachievable without collaborations of state and civil society actors that rippled out widely. Presidential and political backing launched the project as an urgent work of moral and civic repair—high-profile, strategic, newsworthy—without which the new democracy would be stillborn. Human rights activists had the expertise and archives needed to orient the project, and to undergird citizen-testimony with a documentary foundation. A sense of civic duty pulled lawyers, social workers, and others—only some had prior experience in the human rights community—into the role of state functionary on a truth commission. Relatives of the disappeared and the executed mobilized their memories and documents, gave their excruciating citizen-testimonies, and pulled complementary witnesses into the process. They had long pressed for the moment of social recognition rather than denial of the cruel violence that came down on their families, and for accountability. Surviving political prisoners whose own ordeals were not within the formal scope of the Rettig Commission but who had seen disappeared victims on the "inside" knew they had precious knowledge and felt compelled to organize it and testify.

Yet as we have also seen, the sense of collaboration in a sacred civic cause did not imply an absence of pressure and friction among collaborating parties. Motivations and goals overlapped, but only partially. The logics of action could diverge. State and civil society actors might come together to achieve an irrefutable truth they all considered indispensable, but could also part company on the longer vision of how to sort out relationships of truth and justice and how to continue the work of memory making. Consider, for example, the logic of Concertación political elites aligned with the human rights camp in the early 1990s. On the one hand, they could not act in a self-referential vacuum, regardless of the climate of demobilization and fragile transition. Much of the moral and electoral base of the Center-Left government and its project of successful democratic transition—convivencia—rested on achieving a fundamental moral contrast between democracy and rule of law, and its antithesis, dictatorship and state terror. This imperative was rendered all the more powerful by the culturally sensitizing effect of memory struggles by victim-activists during the long years of military rule, and by the fact that the parties of the Center-Left Concertación included people and social circles directly affected by repression. In this sense, Aylwin exerted a very powerful moral leadership, attuned to democratic legitimacy in a society hungry for some sort of human rights reckoning and also attuned to the internal health of his own coalition. On the other hand, the sheer adversity of the transition—its structure of impasse and the explosiveness of memory that could place other goals at risk—also produced elite retreat, caution, and ambivalence. In addition, it produced a great temptation: address the memory question quickly and define it narrowly, then declare it closed or marginal to the future. As we saw, Aylwin himself succumbed partially, by declining to support the Rettig Commission's recommendation on criminalizing the cover-up of information and by prematurely declaring the transition over in 1991—although his challenge to judges and insistence they had a duty to investigate crimes and responsibilities before declaring amnesty cut in the other direction.

For members of the Agrupación of Relatives of the Detained and Disappeared and many other activists in the human rights memory camp, the logic of action was distinct. The Rettig Commission's achievement was real and important, but what also mattered was that it turn into the first essential step of a more profound and relentless politicocultural journey, toward full truth and justice. The point was to keep exerting moral pressure to realize this vision.

The tension that emerged repeatedly, notwithstanding the synergies that also proved important, was that between memory work as formula and as wedge. The tendency of political elites, not only in the early Rettig Commission moment but subsequently, was to search for the formulaic—a path to take care of the memory question of the moment, declare it settled, and move on. This was the impulse dramatically evident when political elites visited Judge Juan Guzmán, commended him on his tenacious pursuit of justice, and commented that it would serve social peace if a medical exam released Pinochet from jeopardy. The tendency of civil society activists, on the other hand, was to see each initiative as a wedge to keep cracking open the wall of impunity—to widen the reach of truth and justice, to turn memory reckonings into the ongoing push for a healthier and more accountable democracy. This was the engine driving the soaring number and diverse kinds of criminal complaints filed against Pinochet after his retirement as army commander and his arrest in London.

The tension of formula versus wedge produced moral pressure and peak moments of creative synergy, but it also produced frustration, disenchantment, and open conflict. In short, it shaped the historicity of synergies—their ups and downs and shifting social dynamics, and the search for new partners. The high tides of creative yet frictional synergy among state and civil society actors were relatively rare: in 1990–92, during the launch of the Rettig Commission and varied social repair initiatives, and again in 2003–05, when specialized human rights judges and the Valech Commission widened the scope of truth and justice reckonings, and when lower-level judges and civil society activists beat back a Supreme Court effort to achieve rapid closure of most human rights cases. (One might arguably extend the period to the early months of the Bachelet administration in 2006.) As we have seen, "high tide" periods did not endure easily. Synergistic memory dynamics between high executive branch actors and civil society actors deteriorated notably during the late Aylwin administration, especially after the *boinazo* of 1993, and collapsed during the Frei administration, by 1996–97.

Even in the latter period, however, collapse implied not a definitive end to synergistic dynamics, but redirection. As we saw (chapter 5), activists searched, under hostile conditions that placed the burden of initiative on them, for new or more reliable partners within a differentiated state system. In the domain of politics, they relied increasingly on lower-level state actors. The 1997 inauguration of Villa Grimaldi as a Peace Park succeeded in part because activists had drawn municipal government and congressional actors, as well as some executive branch actors, into their struggle. The lower-level synergies mattered; they provided some political resilience and magnified moral pressure, despite retreat from the memory question at the apex of the political system and in the overall tone of cultural life. In another domain, the search for new synergies placed greater accent on judicial actors, and on an expanded notion of the relevant state system. If the point was to pull Chilean judges into taking responsibility for human rights justice, the method in part was to extend the legal spheres in play. By promoting innovations, such as universal jurisdiction theory, and by seeking and celebrating international judges as actors within a transnational state system, pressure also increased on the higher levels of the national judiciary to perform justice—or to allow lower-level judges to do so.

In sum, synergies were historical and dynamic, not stable or placid. Even at their nadir, a persistent if discouraging search to re-create synergies continued, precisely because civil society activists understood that articulation to state action was fundamental to accomplishing goals of truth and justice and to promoting cultural sensitization. When synergies did re-emerge, their strength and social dynamics did not simply reproduce earlier moments. The cumulative history of struggles and disappointments and necessities inflected new expectations and tensions, and created new relevant actors and roles. As we have seen, the Dialogue Table initiative pushed by Defense Minister Edmundo Pérez Yoma in 1999–2000 pulled in military partners in a manner inconceivable in 1990, as well as pulling in significant participation by the human rights community. Without such joint effort, the initiative had little point. But as we have also seen, the victim-activist community was much more divided about participation, compared to responses to the Rettig Commission. The state-society synergies were weaker, and the internal dynamics among Dialogue Table members also more strained. The aftermath, in terms of moral capital and good faith assumptions, also proved more problematic since new information on the disappeared provided as a result of the Dialogue Table accord proved unreliable. When more vigorous synergies returned in 2003–5, the actors in play and the cultural tone of relationships had shifted substantially. Consider the social geography of the collaborating partners, compared to 1990–92. Judges now had a leading role as state actors in memory reckonings, compared to the dominance of high executive branch actors at the start of transition. The new truth-telling project, the Valech Commission, had emerged only after considerable grassroots pressure, including "outings" of torturers, and ended up mobilizing citizen-testimony on a vastly different scale compared to the Rettig Commission. It placed prisoner-survivors in a new role, as victims in their own right rather than as witnesses to an ordeal that came down on the dead and disappeared, that is, those who could not speak for themselves.

The conflictive dynamics had also evolved. If "frictional" synergy captures the subtleties of advocacy—a blend of collaboration, moral pressure, and protest—that defined partnership and tension among civil society and state actors in the early 1990–92 period, the phrase requires some adjustment for the later period. At the outset, all the partners were conscious of the fragility and adversity of transition, and the uncertainties of the future. The mix of good faith partnership and mutual dependency on the one hand, with justified skepticism and mistrust on the other, could prove delicate and ambiguous. In the later period, the balance of good faith and mistrust among partners had shifted—the "frictional" aspect of synergy had hardened and turned more openly "conflictive." As we have seen, it took persistent and morally forceful grassroots pressure, accompanied by lawsuits against the state and inflected by a sense of unfair postponement and indecision by executive branch actors, before a truth-telling initiative to reckon with torture finally took center stage. In this stage of truth telling, compared to 1990–92, tensions among partners flared up more readily, even bitterly, notwithstanding mutual dependence.

The frictional synergies of state and civil society actors help explain an aspect of democratic memory reckonings that might otherwise remain mysterious. If the structure of impasse proved resilient and wearying, what social forces drove the insistent push that kept opening up new centers of gravity for conflictive memory reckonings? If ambivalence and frustration produced retreat by political elites—the temptation to address the memory question quickly and narrowly, more or less reactively, only to declare it closed or marginal—why did such temptation keep turning into an illusion? Put another way, if a climate of demobilization generally prevailed, how and when and to what extent did civil society activists prove effective anyway? It is the history of synergies, especially the creative persistence in seeking them and the ways they concentrated tensions of formula versus wedge, that helps one understand both the frustrations of memory work oriented toward human rights, and the cumulative advances. Left alone, in a culture of pact making sealed off from moral and grassroots pressures for social accountability, most elites would have settled on the formulaic. Caught in the ambivalent dialectics of necessary synergies, however, they found the memory question inescapable. It was like the cat with nine lives, somehow returning—not just active again but making trouble. In the long run the wedge effect proved real and enduring, even if the snapshot view, at a given moment, also exposed the risk of formulaic closure.

The dialectic, neither smooth nor automatic, might be expressed in a certain maxim: "Without a formula, there is no wedge; without pressure for a wedge, there is no formula." The formula can provide a new cornerstone to keep building the house of truth and justice, but without strong pressure to keep on building, elites are liberated from having to respond or continue.[12]

Some implications of the Chilean experience with memory reckoning after dictatorship emerge more clearly if one steps back to enlarge the space-time parameters. Consider a comparative perspective on articulations of the social and the political. Among the former dirty-war dictatorships of South America in 2006, at the close of this study, Argentina and Chile had made the strongest cumulative strides in establishing not only indisputable factual truths of human rights violations and their morally unjustifiable status, but also a praxis of criminal justice that gutted amnesty and ensnared hundreds of agents of dirty war including high leaders. They had also established a culture of legitimacy (as well as debate) for ongoing social repair programs and memory work. Advances in Brazil and Uruguay were more limited and vulnerable, despite admirable human rights activism and the election of Left-leaning presidents (Luiz Inácio "Lula" Da Silva and Tabaré Vásquez, respectively). The point holds if one extends the comparison to include Bolivia and Paraguay—the other major "Operation Condor" countries—or if one considers countries undergoing transitions from genuine civil war experiences—as in Peru, El Salvador, and Guatemala. What is notable in the Argentine and Chilean cases is that their relative convergence happened *despite* such contrasting initial paths and such distinct political cultures. Argentina moved dramatically from a military in disarray and a junta on trial in the mid-1980s, to a military that regrouped and used saber rattling and rebellion to press the civilian political leadership into retreat. New final-stop and due obedience laws, and presidential pardons, brought back a culture of impunity in the late 1980s and early 1990s. Chile had its own dramas, as we have seen, but the swings were less extreme, in part because military power and coherence were so strong from the outset and therefore boxed democratic political elites into trying to find a road to moderate cumulative advance.

Yet the deep structure of memory politics and culture in the two societies also produced a key pattern in common. Both countries came out of dictatorship with strong human rights memory camps—highly mobilized, internationally well connected, morally influential and legitimate in wide sectors of society, symbolically critical for democratic legitimacy. These were memory camps capable of producing insistent and resilient civil society actors whose moral call would resonate politically and culturally, even after setbacks. In short, the longer-term history of memory struggles that sunk roots before the end of dictatorship and shaped the culture of transition meant that retreat by political elites and judges, when it came, did not constitute the last word. A revival of interplays between the social and the political on memory matters was more likely in the medium run, precisely because it built on a stronger cultural foundation. When climate and opportunity shifted, the networks of civil society activists emerged to push a groundswell of human rights conversation and cultural and legal initiatives that resonated—as happened in Argentina, after shocking perpetrator confessions launched by Adolfo Scilingo in 1995, and in Chile, after Pinochet stepped down as army commander in 1998 and ended up under arrest in London.

Given the adversities and structures of impasse that hounded transition in both societies, advances did not flow automatically nor were they immune to setback, especially on the explosive issue of criminal justice. But the relative strength of their human rights cultures and networks, along with renewed creative efforts to mesh international with national law and to raise cultural awareness, did mean that select state actors (including judges) had more incentive—or necessity—to seek moral legitimacy and political capital through human rights. Readers of this book are already familiar with the Chilean version of such events, but this is clearly what also happened in the Argentine judiciary and among lower-level state actors during 1995–2002. Cultural work—mobilizations on anniversaries that served as "memory knots," public outings of torturers, searches to find grandchildren robbed from families of disappeared pregnant prisoners and adopted into regime-tied families, creation of memory museums with funds or political support by provincial or municipal political elites—shifted the climate, converging with painstaking on-the-ground work with judges to bring international law to bear on Argentine legal culture. The focus on child kidnappings was particularly important, not only for the profoundly poignant moral symbolism and sociopsychological quandaries, but also because child kidnappings (technically, appropriation of minors and false creation of identity) had not been covered in the 1987 due obedience laws. Between 1998 and 2000, some 100 criminal investigations of infant kidnapping unfolded and placed a dozen officers under arrest. The interplays of the social and the political, with important juridical effects, turned more forceful after the election of Néstor Kirchner as president in 2003 and came to a head in 2005. The Argentine Supreme Court used constitutional reasoning to ratify a lower court ruling and congressional laws that voided the final-stop and due obedience laws of 1986–87.

In sum, each society turned out not quite as exceptional as first appearances and national mythologies might suggest. Notwithstanding the sharply distinct "founding conditions" of transition, the contrasts of early memory-reckoning strategies, such as criminal trials of junta members in Argentina, and other important specificities—only Chile had a personalized dirty-war icon of the stature of Pinochet, only Argentina had a large mass of infants robbed from disappeared prisoners and adopted into a culture of perpetrator families—from a wider comparative perspective a certain convergence effect also took hold and set the two countries apart from other cases. This is all the more notable, given the contrasts of political culture, especially on elite levels, that shaped the transition paths and at times verged on national stereotypes: Chile as more moderate and cumulative and consensus oriented, if necessary by resorting to the euphemism that "nothing happened," and Argentina as more dramatic and openly confrontational, more theatrical and vulnerable to inconsolable setback. What the two cases had in common was a foundation of strong civil society activism around human rights memory that profoundly shaped the culture of moral legitimacy and would not go away—even when times changed and activists found themselves in the political wilderness of impunity and a trend toward closure. Eventually, the cultural foundation built by memory activists could reinflect political and judicial dynamics at upper layers of society. Each society showed that cumulative human rights advances could not fairly be ascribed to the wisdom of political elites or reduced to a self-congratulatory narrative of social engineering, even though a few individuals (e.g., Patricio Aylwin) for a time exerted strong leadership. Left to their own reactive instincts, and to the logic of state survival and stability, political elites would be too inclined to settle for quick closure and narrow definition of the memory question when the going got rough. The *refusal to settle* that built a foundation for cumulative advance, wider accountability and wider sensitization to human rights, was an accomplishment of civil society activists.

At the same time, however, the ups and downs of memory work in each society, and the cumulative contrasts with other Latin American cases, also show that even dedicated groups of activists with a strong social following could not make much headway unless they somehow pulled select state actors—judges, politicians, executive branch leaders, even sectors of the military leadership—into memory work.[13]

A fourth major conclusion to this study emerges from the foregoing: *From a comparative standpoint, building persistent and insistent connections, whether confrontational or synergistic or both, of civil society action and state action proved crucial for cumulative advance in memory reckonings.* Social movement or network strategies were necessary but insufficient. The dialectic of formula versus wedge required a dancing partner.

Comparison is only a first step toward considering Chile's memory reckoning within an enlarged space-time perspective. In truth, each unit of analysis is not completely isolated from the other. As we have seen, Chilean actors in all the memory camps—from Augusto Pinochet to Patricio Aylwin, from seasoned human rights professionals at the outset of transition to young funa activists who later outed torturers—sought to learn from the experiences and lessons of Argentina. As we have also seen (in Book Two of this trilogy), the culture of dissident memory and defense of human rights in the 1970s relied in part on transnational connections and solidarity. Pinochet quickly turned into an icon of dirty-war dictatorships in international culture, and conversely, the campaign of DINA extermination extended beyond national borders. What further conclusion may be reached when considering the transnational context of memory reckoning, or when setting the 1989–2006 period within a longer perspective?

The two questions are not unrelated. The synergies that shaped creative moments of memory making in Chile involved transnational advocacy and action and efforts to apply and "bring home" international law standards, as well as domestic relationships of collaboration, conflict, and moral pressure. As Ellen Lutz and Kathryn Sikkink have shown brilliantly, a certain "justice cascade" took effect in international human rights culture during the quarter-century since the mid- to late-1970s. The environment of judicial possibility and expectation in 2000 contrasted sharply to that in 1980, and Latin America, notably Argentina and Chile, figured prominently in the normative and practical shifts. The normative shift—the necessity for seeing and responding to mass atrocity that violates human rights as a world problem, even when happening among "Third World" peoples or "less developed" countries—began gaining traction in the 1970s and was related to the rise of transnational advocacy networks on human rights. Although the post–World War II moment laid down crucial foundational documents for international culture and law—notably, the 1948 United Nations Universal Declaration of Human Rights, a related convention on genocide, and the Geneva Conventions on treatment of prisoners—it is also true that the sweeping vision fizzled. The pressure of the Cold War proved too much, along with assumptions in the powerful nations that peoples of the colonized world and the global South mattered less, and reliance for enforcement on the elite club of interstate diplomacy without pressure of a strong activist-professional base. By the 1950s, the early international human rights regime was more exhortatory than practical, more transitory than resilient, more politicized and entangled in Cold War dynamics than transcendent. If the 1970s built on the earlier intellectual and normative foundation, it also marked the beginning of a new cycle—toward a more genuine universalization, toward a wider social base of advocacy backed by professionalization, and eventually toward new instruments of legal norm and precedent. By this time, too, the emphasis had shifted toward a more exclusive focus on rights of bodily integrity, rather than the more expansive 1940s vision including socioeconomic rights.[14]

The quantitative and qualitative markers of the international culture shift are clear. International nongovernmental organizations working on human rights grew explosively: from 41 NGOs in 1973, to 79 in 1983, and doubling again to 168 in 1993. Memberships shot up—from 3,000 in Amnesty International USA in 1974, for example, to 50,000 by 1976. Domestic human rights NGOs in Latin America also gained critical mass and proliferated—from 220 in 1981, to 550 in 1990. They included transnationally networked professionals, "rooted cosmopolitans" in the apt phrase of Sidney Tarrow. Local activists and victim-activists came to envision their work, potential effectiveness, and moral claims as part of a wider project of transnational values and solidarity. The qualitative markers of change are equally striking, whether one considers individual life histories of moral awakening by activists who moved into international NGO or solidarity work, or institutional histories and precedents. On both levels, the Chilean case figured prominently. As Joseph Eldridge, director of WOLA (Washington Office on Latin America) during 1974 to 1986, put it, "Human rights entered my vocabulary on September 11, 1973, when it was suddenly denied to one-third of the Chilean population." The "defining moment" set him on a long journey into understanding and acting on human rights. On a more institutional level, too, the United Nations culture of the 1970s built a foundation of attention to human rights investigation and exposure as an urgent world problem. The Chilean case played a leading role in the new culture of UN awareness and debate, via three institutions: the Commission on Human rights, which served as an umbrella committee for annual review and report; the Ad Hoc Working Group on the Situation of Human Rights in Chile, a special team to aid the commission in view of the gravity of the repression in Chile and the strong international concern about it; and the General Assembly, which received reports on the annual balance of grave human rights violations from the other two bodies, and which issued resolutions of condemnation in the Chilean case every year from 1974 to 1989.[15]

Argentina also figured significantly in the evolving world culture of human rights. It constituted a pressure point in the Jimmy Carter administration's politics of human rights in South America in the late 1970s, for example, and an inspiration for high-profile human rights achievement awards in the early-to-mid 1980s, when Adolfo Pérez Esquivel won the Nobel Peace Prize for his daring peace-and-justice work with an NGO amidst dictatorship, and when *The Official Story* (directed by Luis Puenzo) won an Academy Award for its portrait of moral complicity and awakening in a child-kidnapping story. Argentina also proved significant in the blurring of lines between national and transnational work, thereby contributing to the larger epistemic and practical shifts. Argentina's experience with forensic investigation of human remains and disappeared people, for example, created a cadre of professionals in demand as truth-telling and justice struggles arose elsewhere, notably El Salvador and Guatemala.[16]

Of course, the emerging international culture of human rights awareness and action cannot be reduced only to the impact of Chile or Argentina, although both proved important as symbols and as contributors to and beneficiaries of a larger transnational trend. In the 1970s, the controversy over the United States war in Vietnam, the politics of human rights in Eastern Europe, and the post-Watergate exposures of U.S. covert interventions (in which Chile, again, figured prominently) all played into the new sensibilities and traction. In the 1980s, much human rights focus and controversy on Latin America turned to the Central American wars—to slaughter by state agents and allied paramilitary forces in El Salvador and Guatemala, and to the contra war promoted by the United States in Nicaragua. In the 1990s, the former Yugoslavia and Rwanda drew attention for ethnic cleansing and genocide, and South Africa drew attention as it charted a transition from apartheid and launched a high-profile truth-telling experience.[17]

The larger point is that world culture passed through a major epistemic and practical shift, between the 1970s and early 2000s, on matters of human rights and memory reckoning after times of atrocity. Transnational social activity—norms, learning experiences, social networks, institutional vehicles for accountability—became a force in its own right, both as an external pressure point and as a resource for democrats and activists within nationally anchored memory struggles.

Three consequences follow, when considering the implications of the Chilean story. First, during and after the dictatorship, Chile's human rights drama and its memory struggles constituted one key engine driving the shift in international culture: *Symbolically and politically*, it was a cause that inspired transnational human rights activists during the foundational 1970s and persisted into the 1980s and 1990s and which generated an international icon of dirty war. *Socially and culturally*, it was a source of witness testimonies, solidarity activism, and professional knowledge that fed the new networks of transnational solidarity, in part because so many Chileans fled into exile after a formative era of social and political mobilization, and adapted their activism to the emergency back home and to their own politicocultural learning. *Legally and institutionally*, it was a highly notorious case of human rights repression creating new vehicles of accountability and precedent, from the United Nations culture of investigation and debate in the 1970s, to the emphasis on the primacy of international law and on new routes to criminal justice via international tribunals and universal jurisdiction theory in the late 1990s.[18]

Second, for Chilean political elites and democrats, and for their counterparts in other societies undergoing transitions from times of atrocity, to gain legitimacy within international culture and its state system rested in part on transnational assessments of the society's reckoning with the past.

The epistemic and practical shift between the 1970s moment and the turn-of-century moment is clear if one compares broad international assent to the closed-box syndrome (mindful forgetting) in the interests of social peace that marked Spain's post-Franco transition, with the later insistence on truth telling and transitional justice as constitutive for social peace. Examples are the proliferation of truth commissions in South Africa, Central America, Peru, and elsewhere; the flurry of precedents created by the London arrest of Pinochet; and the launch of tribunals for Rwanda and Serbia, and the International Criminal Court. In Chile as elsewhere, the relationship of domestic memory reckonings to international legitimacy and justice became a factor within domestic politicocultural calculation and struggle. Put another way, in the dance of formula versus wedge, there was by the end of the century a key third partner: transnational actors.[19]

For the Chilean case, the point came through dramatically in the arrest of Pinochet in London in 1998. As we have seen, it goes too far to say that post-1998 changes in Chile can all be laid at the door of the transnational event. Chilean activists themselves experimented with and promoted new international juridical strategies, in part as a consequence of their own frustrations with the internal balance of forces, and were therefore not isolated from the making of the precedent-setting event in another land. Also, shifts in power and cultural sensibilities—including Pinochet's loss of direct army command upon retirement from the post in March 1998, renovation of the judiciary and military leadership ranks, disenchantment issues that began infusing the culture and electoral base of the Concertación—were already under way. Nonetheless and as we also saw , the foreign event did serve as a great catalyst accelerating change and prompting new initiatives at both elite and grassroots levels of society.

The third implication comes through when considering the advent of the Chilean transition within a long-term perspective. The foundational moment of 1989–90—after Pinochet's defeat in a plebiscite, but under very adverse conditions for democratic forces—came only *midway* in the transition of world culture, not in the culminating phase of emphatic insistence on truth telling and transitional justice. In other words, the international scenario at the moment of transition added to the adversity. Set within a dual long-term perspective on Chilean history and international history, what stands out is the discontinuity achieved by democratic forces in Chilean society, compared to earlier ways of reckoning, and the difficult odds of achieving the discontinuity. In a pioneering set of studies, Brian Loveman and Elizabeth Lira have documented how Chilean political elites managed their many moments of intraelite ruptures and violence, from political massacres to civil war, since the independence wars of the nineteenth century. They forged legal instruments—amnesty, self-amnesty, and pardons, and pensions and political reincorporation—and a language of restoring concord within the metaphorical national family that together constituted a "Chilean path of political reconciliation." The resilience of political culture and institutions came to rest on the ability of political elites to declare and enforce a reconciliation. Juridically and politically if not culturally, the point was to consciously forget the past—and thereby end intraelite strife or at least postpone fundamental antagonism for another day or another election.[20]

Loveman and Lira perhaps overstate the case, given simultaneous sociopolitical dynamics of mobilization and claim and struggle that cut in distinct directions, but their insight into a powerful tendency within elite gentleman politics is real. They are aware, too, of the difficulties of the amnesty-into-oblivion project, especially with the rise of mass politics, competitive elections, and new ideologies in the twentieth century. The horrifying 1907 massacre of nitrate workers at Escuela Santa María de Iquique, for example, turned into an important memory symbol in popular culture, especially Left and worker circles. Likewise, the outlawing of the Communist Party in the 1948 law of "permanent defense of democracy"—a convergence of domestic political strife and international Cold War history—left behind a bitter legacy of persecution of political and trade union activists. Yet notwithstanding the difficulties, as street protests and strikes related to fiscal austerity and falling wages broke out, and as the 1958 elections approached, an amnesty erased alleged political crimes as well as crimes of repression, an electoral reform reinscribed on the voting rolls those expunged earlier, and the 1948 law was repealed. In sum, although not everyone could agree on a language of forgetting or a myth of reconciliation, the arrival of competitive elections that engaged a widening circle of political parties and social actors provided incentive to accept its practical effect. Loveman and Lira argue that this tradition of national reconciliation reemerged powerfully in the Chilean transition, and their point resonates with the tendency toward formulaic handling of the memory question analyzed in this book.[21]

Against this long-term backdrop, what stands out is the fundamental *discontinuity* that took hold in post-1990 society. The tools used to try to put the past behind sometimes bore uncanny resemblance to those of earlier times, whether one considers the simple amnesty-into-*olvido* formula when the junta passed its 1978 Amnesty Law, or the more complex language of reconciliation founded in truth and repair in 1990–91. Yet the continuities proved more formal and superficial than substantive. More than any previous president, Aylwin staked the prestige and success of his presidency on a direct sorrowful reckoning with the truth of violent and morally unacceptable persecution, accompanied by a stinging challenge to the judiciary. As important, sectors inside his political coalition and human rights actors and networks in civil society resisted judicial impunity fiercely. The tension between dynamics of formula and wedge kept resurfacing throughout the 1990s and into the 2000s, and kept going to the heart of the moral and political legitimacy of the new order. Whatever the inclinations of political elites, and the ambivalences derived from a structure of adversity and impasse, coming to terms with the past could not translate into an exit formula for politicocultural closure.

Once one sets Chilean memory reckonings within a transnational framework and a longer timeline, a final major conclusion to this study comes into view. *The sensitization to human rights as a core value in the public culture, irrenunciable regardless of a crisis that once served as justification for atrocity or looking away from it, was a major achievement against the odds, and a reciprocally constituted one when considering world culture.* Chilean memory struggles had an influential place in the epistemic and practical transformation of international culture, and likewise, the transnational advocacy networks inspired in part by Chilean experience came back to exert important consequences inside the home country. Given the country's long historical tradition of elite reconciliation through closure formulas, and its tough tensions of memory reckoning in the 1990s—a persistent structure of impasse alongside a struggle shifting its center of gravity, a recurrent tendency to turn memory work into a formula for closure alongside insistence on a wedge effect—the reciprocal interplay of the national and the transnational was a crucial resource. For civil society activists and select state actors who resisted closure of the memory question, it provided leverage to press for accountability.[22]

One need not overstate the accomplishment nor overlook the undersides. As we have seen (chapter 6), memory sensibilities turned toward the idea of unfinished work—not mission accomplished, not complacency or closure or mere nostalgia—by the early 2000s. Contentious truth-and-justice reckonings remained, even if the focus of conflict continued to shift. New ironies and risks emerged. Even as new advances unfolded in truth-and-justice reckonings as traditionally understood, and even as the memory question stretched to include socioeconomic legacies, such developments took place within larger cultural and political transformations that could prove perilous —toward a more privatized and individualistic culture that weakened the call of community responsibility, toward an agenda of public issues that seemed to push the memory question into a less strategic role. In the long run, as Greg Grandin and others have argued, the new international regime of human rights that took hold by the turn of the century proved compatible with a neoliberal vision that tended to strip social rights down to the minimum: the bodily integrity of the rights-bearing individual, rather than visions of social democracy and community responsibility influential during the 1940s to 1970s.[23]

In the Chilean case, and as we have seen, the point about the degree to which the new order was "neoliberal" proved politically contentious. Many Center-Left political actors saw themselves as charting a path toward social equity and reduction of poverty, alongside an engine of economic dynamism; critics and civil society activists used accusations of neoliberalism to press their claims in a society marked by scandalous concentration of income at the top. They were in a sense both right—precisely because what was taking place was a struggle for legitimacy and social rights, because the balance of that struggle shifted over time, and most especially, because mediation and balancing dynamics were unevenly distributed among regions and among the disadvantaged. As we saw (chapter 7), an exceptionally one-sided balance emerged between powerful neoliberal advantage backed by the state on one side, and social disadvantage and discrimination aggravated by state policy on the other, in the case of Mapuche peoples contending with the forestry-cellulose industry. The struggle turned so bitter and lopsided that even human rights in its restricted sense proved a sore point— a violent failing and injustice by a democratic state—by the early 2000s. For many Mapuche peoples, the historical periodization of social exclusion and democratic inclusion, the memories of continuity and discontinuity on matters of state repression and human rights, could depart radically from those that seemed germane to others.[24]

The undersides are important, but they do not imply an absence of achievement. They *do* imply that structures of adversity and struggle persisted, for those promoting human rights in its restricted and enlarged senses. Given that some social rights and claims linked back to longer-term experiences of repression or exclusion, and that some key critiques focused on the mature Concertación as well as the legacy of dictatorship, one might expect new versions of a "memory question" to reemerge as a language of cultural argument—a new "Battle of Chile," as María Angélica Illanes has suggested, to shape in the future.[25] A key wrinkle might also emerge: How should one interpret or draw meaning from the pioneering early struggle for human rights and memory under dictatorship? In a sense, the transformation of international culture means that the question belongs not only to Chileans but to everyone.

On 21 December 1976, Cardinal Raúl Silva Henríquez marked the completion of one year of work by the new Vicaría de la Solidaridad (Vicariate of Solidarity) with a religious celebration. A year earlier Pinochet had forced the closure of the ecumenical human rights group known as the Pro-Peace Committee. They had pressed too hard—they exposed misinformation; they pushed for habeas corpus; they made it harder for official stories to stick and for dirty war to proceed unmolested. Silva Henríquez had consented to the shutdown of Pro-Peace, but he reorganized its humanitarian and solidarity functions as a vicariate under the protection of the Santiago Catholic Church and incorporated non-Catholics into the work. The work involved not only the immediate human emergencies of repression—mystery abductions, imprisonment, and disappearance—but also the social, psychological, and economic problems that flowed when families lost people to the repression, the additional needs that flowed from economic shock policies and social welfare dismantling that consigned many families to poverty, and the denials of truth that made credible information and moral appeal about the true reality of Chile so urgent. Times remained rough and frightening. The secret police— the DINA of Manuel Contreras—still seemed unstoppable and kept disappearing people in 1976.

To the crowd of Vicaría associates, religious and international dignitaries, and human rights activists and persons of conscience, Silva Henríquez had a message. The work of the Vicaría was difficult. The motives and purposes of solidarity work were not always well understood, not even by those receiving assistance. The critique of solidarity as "political" and therefore illegitimate was misplaced. But amidst it all, something important had happened. "It seems incredible, but it is beautiful. In a world where violence [and] hate seem to reign, there are paths of love, charity, understanding."

Silva acknowledged the enormous difficulties of solidarity work, given the realities of power, ideology, and accusation in a violent dictatorship. He proceeded to ask the question that arises inexorably for persons of conscience and social justice activists in discouraging times. "What are we going to do?" His reply: "We shall continue." Amidst adversity, he saw signs of progress. Also, there was work to be done—not only emergency solidarity but also "in the arena of human promotion, development, help to those who do not have work . . . who also do not have what is needed to live." This work mattered. "We will continue to do it," he said, "with all the generosity possible, with all the goodwill and effectiveness we can, thanks to the help of so many." He had little to add, because the call to persist in what mattered, amidst trial and tribulation, did not reduce to one person: "It is the work of all of us."[26]

How shall we remember Silva's words? In religious terms, was he a Good Samaritan indifferent to politics? Was he a Prophet who saw acutely the sociopolitical failings, and galvanized a moral call to justice?[27] Shall we consider his words nostalgic epitaph to the best of humanity in the violent twentieth century, but not so pertinent now? Are they words of moral wisdom, a call to hope and action against despair and injustice in our new century? The answers are yet to be written. Memory and learning from the past are a work for every generation. Meanwhile, the Chilean story of memory reckoning continues to move, frustrate, and inspire. It is, as Silva might have put it, the story of all of us.

Abbreviations Used in Notes
and Essay on Sources

※

AAVPS	Archivo Audiovisual de la Vicaría del Pastoral Social (Santiago)
ACNVR	Archivo de la Comisión Nacional de Verdad y Reconciliación (as incorporated into Archivo de la Corporación Nacional de Reparación y Reconciliación)
ACPPVG	Archivo, Corporación Parque Por La Paz Villa Grimaldi
AFDD	Agrupación de Familiares de Detenidos-Desaparecidos
AFDDCD	AFDD, Centro de Documentación
AGAS	Archivo Gráfico del Arzobispado de Santiago
AGPHH	Archivo Gráfico Personal de Helen Hughes
AGPMAL	Archivo Gráfico Personal de Miguel Angel Larrea
AICT	Archivo Intendencia Cautín (Temuco; subsequently incorporated into Archivo Regional de Araucanía, Temuco)
APAF	Archivo Personal de Alicia Frohmann
APDPC	Archivo Personal de Diego Portales Cifuentes
APER	Archivo Personal de Eugenia Rodríguez
APJCC	Archivo Personal de Juan Campos Cifuentes
APHEM	Archivo Personal de María Eugenia Hirmas
APMM	Archivo Personal de "MM"
APSS	Archivo Personal de Sol Serrano
APTV	Archivo Personal de Teresa Valdés
ASVS	Arzobispado de Santiago, Vicaría de la Solidaridad
ASXX	Archivo Siglo XX del Archivo Nacional
BF	Biblioteca de FLACSO (Facultad Latinoamericana de Ciencias Sociales—Chile)
BF, AEH	BF, Archivo Eduardo Hamuy
BN	Biblioteca Nacional
CODEPU	Comité de Defensa de los Derechos del Pueblo
CODEPUCD	CODEPU, Centro de Documentación
DETDES	ASVS, *Detenidos desaparecidos: Documento de trabajo*, 8 vols. (Santiago: ASVS, 1993)
ECO	Educación y Comunicaciones
ECOCD	ECO, Centro de Documentación
FASIC	Fundación de Ayuda Social de las Iglesias Cristianas

FAV	Fundación de Documentación y Archivo de la Vicaría de la Solidaridad, Arzobispado de Santiago
FSA	Fundación Salvador Allende, Centro de Documentación (Santiago)
FSA, ASI	FSA, Archivo Sergio Insunza
ICNPPT	Comisión Nacional sobre Prisión Política y Tortura, *Informe de la Comisión Nacional sobre Prisión Política y Tortura* (Santiago: La Nación–Ministerio del Interior, 2004)
ICNVR	Comisión Nacional de Verdad y Reconciliación, *Informe de la Comisión Nacional de Verdad y Reconciliación*, 2 vols. in 3 books (Santiago: Ministerio Secretaría General del Gobierno, 1991)
ICTUSCD	Ictus, Centro de Documentación
LHORM	Ascanio Cavallo Castro, Manuel Salazar Salvo y Oscar Sepúlveda Pacheco, *La historia oculta del régimen militar: Chile, 1973–1988* (1988; reprint. Santiago: Antártica, 1990)
LHOT	Ascanio Cavallo, *La historia oculta de la transición: Memoria de una época, 1990–1998* (Santiago: Grijalbo, 1998)
PIDEE	Fundación para la Protección de la Infancia Dañada por los Estados de Emergencia
PIDEECD	PIDEE, Centro de Documentación
PUC	Princeton University Library Pamphlet Collection, Chile ("Main" and "Supplement" collections, as microfilmed by Scholarly Resources, Inc., by agreement with Princeton University Library)
SHSWA	State Historical Society of Wisconsin Archives
TVNCD	Televisión Nacional, Centro de Documentación

Notes

A few comments on the citing of quotations and website documents. (1) Citations for quotations are labeled to clarify the sources of multiple quotes or if there would be any question about which source goes with a particular quote; when there are multiple quotes without labels, it can be assumed that the order of the quotes in the chapter text matches the order of the sources in the notes. (2) Page numbers are generally omitted for quotes from newspaper articles but included for magazines. (3) Unless otherwise noted, translations of quotes are my own. (4) Unless otherwise noted, website documents and press accounts were accessed within a month of the date of the document or press account.

Introduction to the Trilogy: Memory Box of Pinochet's Chile

1   Guillermo O'Donnell's pioneering work is a fine guide to social science scholarship on bureaucratic authoritarianism, and (to a more limited extent) subsequent literatures on transitions and democratization. See esp. *Modernization and Bureaucratic-Authoritarianism: Argentina, 1966–1973*, 2nd ed. (1973; Berkeley: University of California Press, 1979); *Bureaucratic Authoritarianism: Argentina, 1966–1973, in Comparative Perspective* (Berkeley: University of California Press, 1988); and the adapted reprints and mature reflections in *Counterpoints: Selected Essays on Authoritarianism and Democratization* (Notre Dame, Ind.: University of Notre Dame Press, 1999). Cf. David Collier, ed., *The New Authoritarianism in Latin America* (Princeton, N.J.: Princeton University Press, 1979); Manuel Antonio Garretón, *El proceso político chileno* (Santiago: FLACSO, 1983); Guillermo O'Donnell, Phillippe Schmitter, and Laurence Whitehead, eds., *Transitions from Authoritarian Rule: Prospects for Democracy*, 4 vols. (Baltimore: Johns Hopkins University Press, 1986); and Scott Mainwaring, Guillermo O'Donnell, and J. Samuel Valenzuela, eds., *Issues in Democratic Consolidation: The New South American Democratization in Comparative Perspective* (Notre Dame, Ind.: University of Notre Dame Press, 1992). It should be noted that a comparative spirit marks this social science literature and often includes consideration of authoritarian regimes and democratic transitions in southern Europe.

For fine work that built on this literature while extending it in new directions

—toward themes such as the culture of fear, the fate and resilience of labor, and the dilemmas of transitional justice—see Juan E. Corradi, Patricia Weiss Fagen, and Manuel Antonio Garretón, eds., *Fear at the Edge: State Terror and Resistance in Latin America* (Berkeley: University of California Press, 1992); Paul W. Drake, *Labor Movements and Dictatorships: The Southern Cone in Comparative Perspective* (Baltimore: Johns Hopkins University Press, 1996); and A. James McAdams, ed., *Transitional Justice and the Rule of Law in New Democracies* (Notre Dame, Ind.: University of Notre Dame Press, 1997).

For a superb recent reflection, rooted in Holocaust history, on the larger connections of modernity, technocracy, and state terror in the twentieth century, see Omer Bartov, *Mirrors of Destruction: War, Genocide, and Modern Identity* (New York: Oxford University Press, 2000).

2 For a bottom-up perspective in which protest becomes the obverse social phenomenon—an explosion and realization of an underground potential amidst top-down control and repression—see, e.g., Cathy Lisa Schneider, *Shantytown Protest in Pinochet's Chile* (Philadelphia: Temple University Press, 1995). For the recent conceptual turn by historians of Latin America that eschews the analytical dichotomy of top down versus bottom up, in favor of a focus on more interactive, mutually constituting, and mediated political dynamics, see Steve J. Stern, "Between Tragedy and Promise: The Politics of Writing Latin American History in the Late Twentieth Century," in *Reclaiming the Political in Latin American History: Essays from the North*, ed. Gilbert M. Joseph (Durham, N.C.: Duke University Press, 2001), 32–77, esp. 41–47. Mexican historians have been very prominent in this turn: e.g., Gilbert M. Joseph and Daniel Nugent, eds., *Everyday Forms of State Formation: Revolution and the Negotiation of Rule in Modern Mexico* (Durham, N.C.: Duke University Press, 1994); Florencia E. Mallon, *Peasant and Nation: The Making of Postcolonial Mexico and Peru* (Berkeley: University of California Press, 1995); Mary Kay Vaughan, *Cultural Politics in Revolution: Teachers, Peasants, and Schools in Mexico, 1930–1940* (Tucson: University of Arizona Press, 1997).

3 The death-and-disappearance figures have received the most attention and require a detailed explanation. For tabulation of individual deaths and disappearances documented by Chile's two official commissions (the Truth and Reconciliation Commission of 1990–91, often nicknamed the Rettig Commission after its chair, and the follow-up organism known as Corporation of Repair and Reconciliation), see Comisión Chilena de Derechos Humanos (hereinafter CCHDH), *Nunca más en Chile: Síntesis corregida y actualizada del Informe Rettig* (Santiago: IOM, 1999), esp. 229. The state-certified figures run as follows: 2,905 cases documented as death or disappearance by state agents or those in their hire, and 139 deaths by political violence, which in most instances involved the shooting of civilians by state agents in curfew hours.

The conservative methodology for an estimated toll of 3,500–4,500 deaths and disappearances is based on several factors, beyond the slowly growing pile of anecdotal evidence of individual cases evident through newspaper accounts, my field research, and knowledge acquired in human rights and lawyer circles. On the latter point, see, e.g., the testimony of the former chair of Chile's Truth and Reconciliation Commission, Raúl Rettig, in Margarita Serrano's interview-book, *La historia de un "bandido": Raúl Rettig* (Santiago: Los Andes, 1999), 83, 89.

First among the factors I have considered is an important account by Adam Schesch, a U.S. survivor of arrest at the National Stadium in September 1973, which documents probable deaths of some 400 additional persons at the National Stadium. Schesch and his then wife, Pat Garret-Schesch, were detained in a part of the stadium that enabled them to count meticulously squads of prisoners taken out for execution and to hear the machine-gun fire cutting them down (in some instances, the prisoners sang just before execution), despite the use of the stadium's large ventilator fans to muffle sounds in the holding cells and lockers away from the field. Schesch returned to Chile in May 2002 to provide sworn testimony in criminal investigations by Judge Juan Guzmán. See his interview in *El Siglo*, 24-v-02; cf. the 1973 press conference and congressional testimony documents in SHSWA, Adam Schesch Papers, tape 823A, reel 3 (press conference, 2-x-73), and Manuscript 534. I am also grateful to him for numerous conversations about his experiences in Chile and at the National Stadium. Schesch's testimony raises the estimate toward 3,500, even if one does not assume that for each session of group execution, about an equal number of prisoners were taken out to the central field from the other side of the stadium. (In one instance, Schesch was able to infer such a two-sided grouping practice, by subtracting the number of people he saw removed from his side from the total number of prisoners mentioned by a soldier returning to his area.)

Second, the fear factor inhibited presentation of cases (or adequate corroboration of them), especially in countryside and provincial settings and in cases of persons not prominent in political party or other activism. The case of the roundup of leftists and peasants in Quillota in January 1974 is extremely suggestive because it offers a rare opportunity to document the rural anonymity and fear problem in quantitative terms. The documentary trail for specific individuals enabled the state's Truth and Reconciliation Commission to demonstrate definitively the deaths or disappearances of eight individuals in the Quillota roundup and massacre, but the Catholic Church's Vicariate of Solidarity files had inside information (two anonymous conscript testimonies) indicating the massacred group numbered thirty-three. In this instance, the ratio of anonymous to known deaths is chilling: about three to one! For detailed discussion and documentation, see Book One, chapter 3, of this trilogy.

Compounding the anonymity and fear problem were ethnic social barriers, and indigenous cultural interpretations of links between social relationships and events of death and misfortune, in southern areas that had substantial Mapuche populations and were subject to fierce repression. For an important in-depth study, see Roberta Bacic Herzfeld, Teresa Durán Pérez, and Pau Pérez Sales, *Muerte y desaparición forzada en la Araucanía: Una aproximación étnica* (Temuco and Santiago: Ediciones Universidad Católica de Temuco and LOM, 1998). If one sets aside the Santiago Metropolitan Region and assumes that elsewhere the fear-and-anonymity factor screened out definitive individual documentation by the democratic state of only one-third of actual deaths and disappearances, the toll in the provinces rises by about 587. This pushes the conservative estimate up to the 4,000–4,100 zone. (For a breakdown of official figures by regions, see CCHDH, *Nunca más en Chile*, 231.)

Last, assigning a more modest fear-and-anonymity factor (15–20 percent) to the Santiago Metropolitan Region, while setting aside the National Stadium figures modified by the Schesch testimony to avoid double counting, pushes the estimate toward 4,500.

Under the circumstances, a 3,500–4,500 estimate is quite conservative. The reality may have been higher. It is noteworthy that this estimate squares well with testimony given to the Chilean State Human Rights Commission in 1999 by former agents of the military government, stating that actual disappearances amounted to more than 2,000 (about 800 beyond the cases documented by the state). See the disclosure by the chair, Senator Jorge Lavandero, in *La Tercera*, e-ed.: www.tercera.cl, 13-VII-00; see also *Clarín* (Argentina), 14-VII-00. This estimate also squares well with the assumption that in at least half the 1,289 alleged cases of death or disappearance by human rights violations or political violence presented to the two commissions, and for which the commissions could *not* establish definitive proof, the cases were genuine rather than frivolous. For statistics on cases presented but not definitively proved, see Corporación Nacional de Reparación y Reconciliación, *Informe a Su Excelencia el Presidente de la República sobre las actividades desarrolladas al 15 de mayo de 1996* (Santiago: La Nación, 1996), 19 (Cuadro 1).

Finally, it should be noted that this rather conservative estimate in no way disparages the superb work of Chile's Truth and Reconciliation Commission and its follow-up Corporation of Repair and Reconciliation. Based on the 3,500–4,500 estimate, the two organisms managed under adverse circumstances to account, on a definitive and individualized basis, for some 65–85 percent of the toll—without subsequent disproof of a single case. This is a remarkable achievement. It also sufficed to demonstrate the systematic and massive quality of repression.

The other figures do not require as detailed a discussion here. For the technically complex issue of torture estimates by rigorous definition, a full documented discussion is offered in trilogy Book Three, chapters 2, 6. For documented political arrests, the 82,000 baseline figure is based on the 42,386 arrests acknowledged by the regime as of 6 February 1976, and an additional 40,043 arrests registered by the Santiago Catholic Church's Vicariate of Solidarity once it began operating in 1976, cited in FAV, Caja A.T. 2, Casos, "Algunas cifras sobre atentados a los derechos humanos durante el régimen militar [1990?]." The more realistic yet conservative estimate of 150,00 to 200,000 is based on discussion with José Zalaquett, 27-X-01, who is exceptionally well informed and rigorous in methodology and who has included short-term political detentions (at least a day) via crackdowns and roundups in the poblaciones, along with the more long-term cases. Zalaquett's background and expertise, and his penchant for conservative methodology, are documented in Books Two and Three of this trilogy. For exile estimates, which include both an initial wave impelled by political persecution and later waves impelled by mixed political and economic motives, see Thomas Wright and Rody Oñate, *Flight from Chile: Voices of Exile* (Albuquerque: University of New Mexico Press, 1998), esp. 8 (note); for a serious estimate as high as 400,000, see Carmen Norambuena Carrasco, "Exilio y retorno: Chile 1973–1994," in *Memoria para un nuevo siglo: Chile, miradas a la segunda mitad del siglo XX*, ed. Mario Garcés et al. (Santiago: LOM, 2000), 178 esp. n. 13.

4 The assumptions about a "soft" coup in a fundamentally law-abiding and democratic Chile, and the related issue of voluntary compliance with arrest lists and orders, are thoroughly documented in the trilogy. See Book One, chapter 3; Book Two, chapters 1–2. For the pattern of voluntary compliance, see also the case files assembled in *DETDES*.

5 The Brazilian case gave rise to a pioneering early study that documented political nonradicalism and conservatism among a substantial sector of shantytown dwellers, a finding that seemed counterintuitive at the time. See Janice E. Perlman, *The Myth of Marginality: Urban Poverty and Politics in Rio de Janeiro* (Berkeley: University of California Press, 1976), esp. 162–91.

6 North of Chile, Peru also succumbed to a "new" style of military government in 1968. The Peruvian military, however, followed a different path, albeit one influenced by the climate of mobilization and polarization about injustice. Led by General Juan Velasco Alvarado, it launched a "revolution" of Left-leaning reforms, including expropriation of foreign oil holdings, an agrarian reform in the highlands and coastal provinces, and worker cooperatives. Nonetheless, the result was a giant swath of military regimes in South America by the early-to-mid 1970s. Another important result was that the Nixon administration saw Peru and Chile, after Allende's election in 1970, as a large contiguous territory hostile to U.S. interests and propitious to Left politics. The recent books by John Dinges, *The Condor Years: How Pinochet and His Allies Brought Terrorism to Three Continents* (New York: New Press, 2004), and Peter Kornbluh, *The Pinochet File: A Declassified Dossier on Atrocity and Accountability* (New York: New Press, 2003), cast fresh light on transnational aspects of the rise of "dirty war" re-

gimes, in large part through declassified U.S. documents released in the Clinton administration and through use of the Freedom of Information Act.

The Southern Cone experience gave rise to a small industry of fine analytical and comparative writings by political scientists and sociologists, first about authoritarianism and the new style of dictatorships and subsequently about problems of democratic transition. See note 1 in this chapter.

7 See Kathryn Sikkink, "The Emergence, Evolution, and Effectiveness of the Latin American Human Rights Network," in *Constructing Democracy: Human Rights, Citizenship, and Society in Latin America*, ed. Elizabeth Jelin and Eric Hershberg (Boulder, Colo.: Westview Press, 1996), 59–84, esp. 63–64. Cf. Margaret E. Keck and Kathryn Sikkink, *Activists beyond Borders: Advocacy Networks in International Politics* (Ithaca, N.Y.: Cornell University Press, 1998); for more on Chile and transnational human rights agendas, *NACLA Report on the Americas* 36, no. 3 (November–December 2002); thematic issue on "NACLA: A 35 Year Retrospective"; and Book Two, chapter 3, of this trilogy.

8 The myth of Chilean exceptionalism is well known to scholars. For a striking example of Allende's effort to invoke it, amidst grave crisis, see trilogy Book Two, Afterword to chapter 1. Cf. Marc Cooper, *Pinochet and Me: A Chilean Antimemoir* (London: Verso, 2001), 81. The myth was most influential in middle-class urban society and in political elite circles; the new study by Florencia E. Mallon, *Courage Tastes of Blood: The Mapuche Community of Nicolás Ailío and the Chilean State, 1906–2001* (Durham, N.C.: Duke University Press, 2005), along with recent research by Claudio Barrientos and Lessie Jo Frazier (see note 9 below), do much to clarify the implicit regional, class, and ethnoracial parameters of such beliefs.

9 Two of the finest works that argue along these lines, and from which I have learned much, are Tomás Moulian, *Chile Actual: Anatomía de un mito* (Santiago: LOM, 1997); and Tina Rosenberg, *Children of Cain: Violence and the Violent in Latin America* (1991; repr., New York: Penguin, 1992), 333–87. Cf. Cooper, *Pinochet and Me*. Significantly, Rosenberg also ponders the German problem. "Sophistication," she writes, "was not the solution . . . The more cultured the Chileans were, the more willing they appeared to blind themselves to what was going on around them" (380).

For recent work on Chile that evinces both the pervasiveness of the memory-versus-forgetting dichotomy and intellectual efforts to break out of its confines, see Mario Garcés et al., *Memoria para un nuevo siglo*. Cf. Nelly Richard, ed., *Políticas y estéticas de la memoria* (Santiago: Cuarto Propio, 2000). On memory as a process of competing selective remembrance within a society's wider political and cultural struggles, see, aside from chapter 4 in Book One of this trilogy, the seminal theoretical essay by Argentine scholars Elizabeth Jelin and Susana G. Kaufman, "Layers of Memories: Twenty Years After in Argentina," in *The Politics of War Memory and Commemoration*, ed. T. G. Ashplant, Graham

Dawson, and Michael Roper (New York: Routledge, 2000), 89–110; and the fuller reflections in Jelin, *Los trabajos de la memoria* (Madrid: Siglo XXI, 2002). New research on Chile with a regional focus informed by similar theoretical perspectives includes Lessie Jo Frazier, *Salt in the Sand: Memory, Violence, and the Nation-State in Chile, 1890 to the Present* (Durham, N.C.: Duke University Press, 2007), and Claudio Barrientos, "Emblems and Narratives of the Past: The Cultural Construction of Memories and Violence in Peasant Communities in Southern Chile, 1970–2000" (PHD diss., University of Wisconsin, Madison, 2003).

10 My fuller reflection on the problem of representing the impossible, a theme that haunts discussion of relationships between "history" and "memory," is presented in trilogy Book Three, Afterword to chapter 2. There I explore searing human experiences and inherent narrative dilemmas as they related to the work of Chile's National Truth and Reconciliation Commission. For the history-versus-memory problem as conceptualized by Pierre Nora, see his multivolume memory project, *Realms of Memory: The Construction of the French Past*, ed. Lawrence C. Kritzman, trans. Arthur Goldhammer (French ed. 7 vols., 1984–92; English ed. 3 vols., New York: Columbia University Press, 1996–98), esp. "General Introduction: Between Memory and History," 1:1–23, cf. xv–xxiv. For helpful context and critique, less bound to a history-versus-memory dichotomy, see Natalie Zemon Davis and Randolph Starn, "Introduction," to *representations* 26 (spring 1989), thematic issue "Memory and Counter-memory," 1–6; and Tony Judt, "A la Recherche du Temps Perdu," *New York Review of Books* (3-XII-98), 51–58. Cf. the history-memory problem as developed in Yosef Hayim Yerushalmi, *Zakhor: Jewish History and Jewish Memory* (Seattle: University of Washington Press, 1982). See also related reflections by Amos Funkenstein, "Collective Memory and Historical Consciousness," *History and Memory* 1, no. 1 (1989): 5–26; and David Myers, "Remembering *Zakhor*: A Super-Commentary," *History and Memory* 4, no. 2 (1992): 129–46 (with a reply by Funkenstein, 147–48). For a perceptive and multifaceted brief reflection on the relationship of history and memory, see Jelin, *Los trabajos de la memoria*, 63–78. For a fuller discussion and guide to literature, and the related problem of representation, an excellent starting point is recent work by Dominick LaCapra, *History and Memory after Auschwitz* (Ithaca, N.Y.: Cornell University Press, 1998); and *Writing History, Writing Trauma* (Baltimore: Johns Hopkins University Press, 2001). Cf. Michael Bernard-Donals and Richard Glejzer, *Between Witness and Testimony: The Holocaust and the Limits of Representation* (Albany: State University of New York Press, 2001).

11 Benedetti's phrase ("el olvido está lleno de memoria") appears on the wall of remembrance of known political prisoners killed or disappeared at the largest torture camp of the DINA (secret police, formally Dirección de Inteligencia Nacional), Villa Grimaldi, inaugurated as a Peace Park in 1997. See also the contribution of Mireya García Ramírez, a leader-activist of the Agrupación de

Familiares de Detenidos-Desaparecidos (AFDD; Association of Relatives of the Detained-Disappeared), in Garcés et al., *Memoria para un nuevo siglo*, 447–50. The notion of "obstinate memory" was coined by documentary filmmaker Patricio Guzmán, in his moving *Chile: La memoria obstinada* (1997, available on video via First Run Icarus Films).

Introduction to Book Three: Reckoning with Pinochet

1 For theoretical elaboration on "memory knots," see Book One in this trilogy: Stern, *Remembering Pinochet's Chile: On the Eve of London 1998* (Durham, N.C.: Duke University Press, 2004), chapter 4, esp. 120–24 (and notes to chapter 4 for additional theoretical foundation and commentary). For pertinent case studies and theoretical reflection in South American contexts, see the research series published by Siglo Veintiuno (Madrid, also Buenos Aires and Mexico City) during 2002–06 under the umbrella title "Memorias de la Represión," based on a Social Science Research Council graduate training and research project for Latin American fellows, directed by Elizabeth Jelin and Eric Hershberg with Carlos Iván Degregori during 1998–2001, and with which I had the privilege of collaborating. The focus of the project was memory, political repression, and democratization in the Southern Cone countries and Peru. See esp. Elizabeth Jelin, *Los trabajos de la memoria* (2002); Elizabeth Jelin, ed., *Las conmemoraciones: Las disputas en las fechas "in-felices"* (2002); Elizabeth Jelin and Victoria Langland, eds., *Monumentos, memoriales y marcas territoriales* (2003); Ponciano del Pino and Elizabeth Jelin, eds., *Luchas locales, comunidades e identidades* (2003); and María Angélica Cruz, *Iglesia, represión y memoria: El caso chileno* (2004). Also of interest in the same series are Claudia Feld, *Del estrado a la pantalla: Las imágenes del juicio a los ex comandantes en Argentina* (2002); Ludmila da Silva Catela and Elizabeth Jelin, eds., *Los archivos de la represión: Documentos, memoria y verdad* (2002); Elizabeth Jelin and Federico Guillermo Lorenz, eds., *Educación y memoria: La escuela elabora el pasado* (2004); Elizabeth Jelin and Ana Longoni, eds., *Escrituras, imágenes y escenarios ante la represión* (2005); Eric Hershberg and Felipe Agüero, eds., *Memorias militares sobre la represión en el Cono Sur: Visiones en disputa en dictadura y democracia* (2005); Elizabeth Jelin and Diego Sempol, eds., *El pasado en el futuro: Los movimientos juveniles* (2006); Elizabeth Jelin and Susana G. Kaufman, eds., *Subjetividad y figuras de la memoria* (2006); and a parallel volume in Peru published as part of the "Memorias" series, Carlos Iván Degregori, ed., *Jamás tan cerca arremetió lo lejos: Memoria y violencia política en el Perú* (Lima: Instituto de Estudios Peruanos, 2003).

2 In the Latin American history field, Gilbert M. Joseph has done pioneering work by organizing or co-organizing team-based scholarly projects that promote integrative analysis—to move from dichotomy to mutual engagement

when considering top-down, bottom-up, and mediating dynamics; and likewise, to foster mutual engagement between subfields sometimes held apart (e.g., "political history" vs. "social history," the latter two vs. "cultural history," or "Latin American history" vs. "Cold War history"). See Gilbert Joseph and Daniel Nugent, eds., *Everyday Forms of State Formation: Revolution and the Negotiation of Rule in Modern Mexico* (Durham, N.C.: Duke University Press, 1994); Joseph, Catherine C. LeGrand, and Ricardo Salvatore, eds., *Close Encounters of Empire: Writing the Cultural History of U.S.-Latin American Relations* (Durham, N.C.: Duke University Press, 1998); Joseph, ed., *Reclaiming the Political in Latin American History: Essays from the North* (Durham, N.C.: Duke University Press, 2001); and Joseph and Daniela Spenser, eds., *In from the Cold: Latin America's New Encounters with the Cold War* (Durham, N.C.: Duke University Press, 2008). For evolution of Latin American historiography since the social history movement (which emphasized the history of "ordinary people") and its initial emphasis on bottom-up versus top-down social experience, and movement toward intellectual interest in integrative analyses that can overcome such dichotomies and consider, as well, mediating social dynamics, see Steve J. Stern, "Between Tragedy and Promise: The Politics of Writing Latin American History in the Late Twentieth Century," in Joseph, *Reclaiming the Political in Latin American History*, 30–77; cf. Thomas Skidmore, "Studying the History of Latin America: A Case of Hemispheric Convergence," *Latin American Research Review* 33, no. 1 (1998): 105–27.

3 An additional irony also emerges late in this book. Even when memory claims reemerged powerfully and led to unprecedented advances after 2002, the call to redress harmful legacies stretched to include demands for socioeconomic rights. The stretching of the memory question to include newly insistent issues, however, also placed classic human rights claims at risk of becoming more marginal to public life in the future. See chapter 7 in this volume.

4 For discussion of emblematic memory as well as memory lore and related issues of social voice and silence, see trilogy Book One, esp. the Afterword to chapter 2, chapter 4 and its Afterword, and the Conclusion. For powerfully researched and subtly conceptualized insight into community secrets and silences—in theoretical terms, critical as a key underside or counterpoint to emblematic memory making—see the research of Ponciano del Pino Huamán on the history of communities in Ayacucho (Peru) before, during, and after the Shining Path War: " 'Looking to the Government': Community, Politics, and the Production of Memory and Silences in Twentieth-Century Peru, Ayacucho" (PHD diss., University of Wisconsin, Madison, 2008); cf. del Pino, "Uchuraccay: Memoria y representación de la violencia política en los andes," in Degregori, *Jamás tan cerca arremetió lo lejos*, 49–93.

5 For a deeper reflection on what political science scholarship of democratic transitions may have to say to historians, especially if seeking to set the Chilean

case in a larger comparative perspective, see the conclusion to this book. Three fine starting points for wide-ranging and insightful social science reflections on democracy and constraint in Latin American transitional contexts marked by continuities of authoritarianism are Guillermo O'Donnell, *Counterpoints: Selected Essays on Authoritarianism and Democratization* (Notre Dame, Ind.: Notre Dame University Press, 1999), and for dialogue with Robert Dahl's concept of polyarchy, esp. 175–94; Manuel Antonio Garretón, *Incomplete Democracy: Political Democratization in Chile and Latin America*, trans. R. Kelly Washbourne with Gregory Horvath (Chapel Hill: University of North Carolina Press, 2003); and Katherine Hite and Paola Cesarini, eds., *Authoritarian Legacies and Democracy in Latin America and Southern Europe* (Notre Dame, Ind.: University of Notre Dame Press, 2004).

Chapter 1: The Perils of Truth

1 Patricia Verdugo, interview, 2-IV-97 (quote); cf. Verdugo, *Bucarest 187* (Santiago: Editorial Sudamericana, 1999), 202–3.

2 Patricia Verdugo, *Los zarpazos del puma* (1989; rev. ed., Santiago: CESOC, 1994). For the larger context and purposes of the Caravan of Death operation, and public controversy that began the 1980s, see Books One and Two of this trilogy. For a brief account and comparative perspective with another massacre, see Book One: Stern, *Remembering Pinochet's Chile: On the Eve of London 1998* (Durham, N.C.: Duke University Press, 2004), 94–101, 196 nn. 13–14; for timing, political uses, and relation to the "Plan Z" conspiracy, Book Two: Stern, *Battling for Hearts and Minds: Memory Struggles in Pinochet's Chile, 1973–1988* (Durham, N.C.: Duke University Press, 2006), 47–56, also 310–11 for controversy in the 1980s.

3 Lucía M., interview, 21-I-97.

4 *El Mercurio*, 3-XII-89.

5 For sales and bestseller lists, I am grateful to the late Patricia Verdugo for sharing news clippings from her personal archive. The cited bestseller list was from a photocopy (the periodical was unidentified) dated 8-IV-90; the breaking of the 100,000 sales mark was widely reported. The estimate of at least 25,000 pirate edition sales is conservative. On 24-11-90, e.g., *La Epoca* reported about 75,000 legal sales and a total estimate of 100,000. At that ratio, the figure of 100,000 sales of legal copies would translate into an additional 33,000 pirate edition sales. Cf. Verdugo, *Bucarest 187*, 202. The other books on the bestseller list were (in rank order) René García Villegas, *Soy testigo: Dictadura-tortura-injusticia* (Santiago: Amerinda, 1990); Eugenio Ahumada et al., *Chile: La memoria prohibida*, 3 vols. (Santiago: Pehuén, 1989); Patricia Politzer, *Altamirano* (Santiago: Melquíades, 1989); Carlos Jorquera, *El Chicho Allende* (Santiago: Bat,

1990); *LHORM*. As a control, I checked the list cited against that of *El Mercurio*, 8-IV-90, which used a more highbrow selection of bookstores (and notably excluded "Feria Chilena del Libro"). *El Mercurio*'s list was reasonably consistent. A just published novel of Isabel Allende (*Cuentos de Eva Luna*) was in the first position; the other books cited were in the top six, except for the García testimonio on torture, which failed to make the list; and the inside history by Cavallo et al. (*LHORM*), which appeared ninth. In tenth place was another memory book, interviews with Pinochet by Raquel Correa and Elizabeth Subercaseaux, *Ego Sum Pinochet* (Santiago: Zig-Zag, 1990).

6   My interpretation of the project of convivencia is based on discourses and actions: Aylwin's discourses in 1989–90, and the political priorities and actions of the new government during 1990–91. Specific speeches and acts that illustrate the point will be presented later. My understanding relied especially on the following sources: Patricio Aylwin Azócar, *La transición chilena: Discursos escogidos, Marzo 1990–1992* (Santiago: Andrés Bello, 1992); Aylwin, interview, 20-VI-97; Edgardo Boeninger, *Democracia en Chile: Lecciones para la gobernabilidad* (Santiago: Andrés Bello, 1997), esp. 367–523; *LHOT*; and Rafael Otano, *Crónica de la transición* (Santiago: Antártica, 1995). See also Andrés Allamand, *La travesía del desierto* (Santiago: Aguilar, 1999); presidential speeches and campaign documents in PUC, Main Collection, Politics in Chile, Rolls 26, 42. A new interview-book with Aylwin by Margarita Serrano and Ascanio Cavallo, *El poder de la paradoja: 14 lecciones políticas de la vida de Patricio Aylwin* (Santiago: Grupo Editorial Norma, 2006), is consistent with this interpretation. For superb analytical perspective about the convivencia-based approach to democracy and development, and its limitations over time, see Paul Drake and Iván Jaksic, eds., *El modelo chileno: Democracia y desarrollo en los noventa* (Santiago: LOM, 1999).

7   PUC, Main Collection, Politics in Chile, Roll 26, Aylwin speech, 15-XII-90 (quote); for a clear statement about the political costs and benefits of collaboration with Renovación Nacional from an Aylwin-Concertación perspective, see Boeninger, *Democracia en Chile*, 389.

8   Aylwin, interview, 20-VI-97 (long quote; the short "common sense" quote was from comment before taped portion of interview); cf. his speech on politics and ethics, 23-X-90, in Aylwin, *La transición chilena*, 88–96.

9   PUC, Main Collection, Politics in Chile, Roll 42, "Programa de Gobierno de la Concertación de Partidos por la Democracia [1989]," pp. 3–4. Pinochet incidents, in FAV, "Informe Mensual, Mayo–Junio 1989," 41–43 (41 for quotes); Allamand, *La travesía del desierto*, 254. Cf. *La Epoca*, 11-X-89; and for slightly different wording, Otano, *Crónica de la transición*, 100.

10 For this chapter paragraph and the following five, on the human rights and justice advisory commission and initial political context and pressures, see FAV, "Informe Mensual, Diciembre 1988," 85–86; "Informe Mensual, Marzo–

Abril 1989, 39–41, 54; and "Informe Mensual, Mayo–Junio 1989," 36–43. For Zalaquett's analysis over time, the key articles are "From Dictatorship to Democracy," *New Republic*, 16-XII-85, pp. 17–21; "Confronting Human Rights Violations Committed by Former Governments: Principles Applicable and Political Constraints," paper at Conference of Justice and Society Program of Aspen Institute, 4–6-XI-88, Wye Center, Maryland, as published in *State Crimes: Punishment or Pardon* (New York: Aspen Institute, 1989), 23–69 (46, 30, for "lost legitimacy" and "pernicious effects" quotes); and "Balancing Ethical Imperatives and Political Constraints: The Dilemma of New Democracies Confronting Past Human Rights Violations," Mathew O. Tobriner Memorial Lecture, 1991, University of California, in *Hastings Law Journal* 43, no. 6 (August 1992): 1425–38 (theoretical anchor in Weber). For critique of Zalaquett's framework within the human rights community, see Juan E. Méndez, "Accountability for Past Abuses," *Human Rights Quarterly* 19, no. 2 (1997): 255–82. My understanding of Zalaquett's views, international experience, and influence on the advisory commission also benefited from our interview, 23-IV-97, and a background document (copy in possession of author) considered by the commission. For the broader currency of Weber's ethical distinction within the culture of Concertación leaders, see, e.g., Juan Gabriel Valdés, "Comisarios, jerarcas y creativos," *La campaña del NO vista por sus creadores* (Santiago: Melquíades, 1989), 98–99; Aylwin, *La transición chilena*, 95; and Boeninger, *Democracia en Chile*, 410. For additional context on the Argentine and Uruguayan cases and for comparative analysis of militaries and transitions to civilian government, excellent starting points are, for Argentina, Carlos H. Acuña et al., *Juicio, castigos y memorias: Derechos humanos y justicia en la política argentina* (Buenos Aires: Ediciones Nueva Visión SAIC, 1995); and Deborah L. Norden, *Military Rebellion in Argentina: Between Coups and Consolidation* (Lincoln: University of Nebraska Press, 1996). See also, for fascinating cultural impact and uses of the junta trials, see Claudia Feld, *Del estrado a la pantalla: Las imágenes del juicio a los ex comandantes en Argentina* (Madrid: Siglo Veintiuno, 2002). For Uruguay, see Alexandra Barahona de Brito, *Human Rights and Democratization in Latin America: Uruguay and Chile* (New York: Oxford University Press, 1997); and for Uruguay and Brazil, Lawrence Weschler, *A Miracle, A Universe: Settling Accounts with Torturers*, rev. ed. (Chicago: University of Chicago Press, 1998). For comparative insight and the relative adversity of the Chilean transition case, see Katherine Hite and Paola Cesarini, eds., *Authoritarian Legacies and Democracy in Latin America and Southern Europe* (Notre Dame, Ind.: University of Notre Dame Press, 2004); also, for the related issue of military memories of "dirty war," Eric Hershberg and Felipe Agüero, eds., *Memorias militares sobre la represión en el Cono Sur: Visiones en disputa en dictadura y democracia* (Madrid: Siglo Veintiuno, 2005).

11 *LHOT*, 19; Patricio Aylwin, interview (quote), 20-VI-97.

12 U.S. Chilean Embassy to State Department, "Pinochet Looks Ahead," 23-11-89, esp. items 1, 9 (pp. 1–2, 6–7), at U.S. State Department, Freedom of Information Act Electronic Reading Room, http://foia.state.gov/default.asp, link path: Declassified/ Released Document Collections; State Department Collections— State Chile Declassification Project Tranche III (1979–1991). See also Augusto Pinochet Ugarte, *Camino recorrido: Memorias de un soldado*, 3 vols. in 4 books (Santiago: Instituto Geográfico Militar, 1990–94), III, 2:267; and Pinochet press interview, 12-VIII-1989, in Raquel Correa and Elizabeth Subercaseaux, *Ego Sum* (Santiago: Planeta, 1996), 124–27. Cf. the blunt public remarks in June and October 1989 mentioned earlier in this chapter and also press interviews in March 1990 and September 1991, in Correa and Subercaseaux, *Ego Sum*, 136–40, 185–86. I am also grateful to José Zalaquett, conversation, 22-VIII-02, for insight on Pinochet's interest in an additional 1989 amnesty law and internal junta opposition. That Pinochet's interest in amnesty was also stoked by a wider fear of prosecutions among soldiers and by meetings he held with them to analyze the situation and boost morale after the 1988 plebiscite defeat is evident in the "Pinochet Looks Ahead" memo cited earlier in this note; see also Serrano and Cavallo, *El poder de la paradoja*, 179–80.

13 See note 6 in this chapter for works that have influenced my overall interpretation. On Chilean military forces' interest in and relative success in achieving a very high level of autonomy, excellent starting points are Claudio Fuentes Saavedra, *La transición de los militares: Relaciones civiles-militares en Chile, 1990–2006* (Santiago: LOM, 2006), which also offers analysis of (somewhat surprising) results over time; and Felipe Agüero, "Authoritarian Legacies: The Military's Role," in Hite and Cesarini, *Authoritarian Legacies and Democracy in Latin America and Southern Europe*, 233–62, on the importance of "founding conditions" on subsequent democratic transitions.

14 For the 1980 Constitution, from juridical and political engineering points of view, see José Luis Cea Egaña, *Tratado de la Constitución de 1980: Características generales, garantías constitucionales* (Santiago: Editorial Jurídica de Chile, 1988); and Peter M. Siavelis, *The President and Congress in Postauthoritarian Chile: Institutional Constraints to Democratic Consolidation* (University Park: Pennsylvania State University Press, 2000), esp. 3–42. See also note 15 sources on the negotiations of 1989.

15 For illuminating memoirs and analysis by key actors, see Allamand, *La travesía del desierto*, 169–88 (180–81 for political implications of technical blunder); Allamand, "Las paradojas de un legado," in Drake and Jaksic, *El modelo chileno*, 169–90; and Boeninger, *Democracia en Chile*, 348–51, 362–66. Cf. Otano, *Crónica de la transición*, 82–84; Pamela Constable and Arturo Valenzuela, *A Nation of Enemies: Chile under Pinochet* (New York: W. W. Norton, 1991), 311–13; Carlos Andrade Geywitz, *Reforma de la Constitución Política de la República de Chile* (Santiago: Editorial Jurídica de Chile, 1991), esp. 233–34 for technical

language change regarding Consejo de Estado (National Security Council) role. For a striking example of the unsatisfied who nonetheless voted yes in the reform plebiscite, see Sergio Fernández, *Mi lucha por la democracia* (Santiago: Los Andes, 1994), 310–13.

16 See Allamand, *La travesía del desierto*, 184–87; Boeninger, *Democracia en Chile*, 364–65; and Otano, *Crónica de la transición*, 82–84. Some technical notes about the agreement to eliminate designated senators are relevant. Aylwin excised, as part of the reform package, constitutional language requiring immediate filling of vacant designated seats—a technical sign that the institution would not last beyond one term. Renovación Nacional did not agree to eliminate the ascension of former presidents to designated senator status. Aylwin was not slated to become a designated senator; his four-year transitional term of office fell short of the minimum required period. This prohibition did not matter to him, because he opposed the institution in principle and believed it would not last.

17 For the 1989 breakdown of congressional election results, see Siavelis, *The President and Congress in Postauthoritarian Chile*, 46–49; for a succinct guide to the presidential campaign and results, Constable and Valenzuela, *A Nation of Enemies*, 313–16.

18 For the previous four paragraphs, see, for data on privatizations, María Olivia Mönckeberg, *El saqueo de los grupos económicos al Estado chileno* (Santiago: Ediciones B, 2001), 21–160 (on the individual beneficiary cases cited, see, for de Castro, 34–35, 61; Piñera, 46–47, 61, 109, 113; Philippi, 38–40, 108, 121–27; Büchi [Richard], 32, 140–42; and Ponce Lerou, 44–46, 86–89); and Eduardo Bitrán and Raúl E. Sáez, "Privatization and Regulation in Chile," in *The Chilean Economy: Policy Lessons and Challenges*, ed. Barry Bosworth et al. (Washington, D.C.: Brookings Institution, 1994), 341–46 (346 for $500 million value of ENDESA foreign debt transfer). For privatizations as part of the larger project of restrictions to tie down the incoming regime politically, and to assure strategic continuities and silences protective of the legacy of military rule, see Carlos Huneeus, *El régimen de Pinochet* (Santiago: Editorial Sudamericana, 2000), 599–622. See also Otano, *Crónica de la transición*, 85, 99–103; Constable and Valenzuela, *A Nation of Enemies*, 316–18; and FAV, "Informe Mensual, Enero–Febrero 1989," 81–82 (Law 18,771). For operations in secret grave sites in the late 1970s and again the late 1980s, see sources and discussion in trilogy Book Two, 427–28 n. 2. For the Villa Grimaldi affair specifically, Pedro Matta (historian-archivist of Corporación Parque por la Paz), conversation, 12-1-97, supplemented by documents from ACPPVG: "Proyecto Parque por la Paz [1996]"; "Villa Grimaldi: Un Parque por la Paz, Por el Derecho a la Memoria" (1996), 8–9, 13–19; and "Parque por la Paz en Villa Grimaldi: Una experiencia social viable contra la impunidad en Chile," presented by Asamblea por los Derechos Humanos at Seminar on Impunity, Santiago, December 1996. Cf. *LHOT*, 53.

19 See Otano, *Crónica de la transición*, 85; and *Hoy*, 2-IV-90, pp. 16–17 (16 for statistics and "white elephant"). Cf. *ojo con la* TV, July–August 1989; and Mönckeberg, *El saqueo de los grupos económicos al Estado chileno*, 176–88.

20 The standard harassment technique against journalists in 1989 was to ensnare them in lawsuits for defamation or injury of high officials, although mystery assaults of property (home, car) of select journalists also happened. The television campaign was marred by advantaged distribution of air time in news reporting and by censorship of a portion of a Televisión Nacional interview with Patricio Aylwin in August, when he observed that he had not expected a coup in 1973, because Pinochet had been appointed by Allende and had a reputation of loyalty toward Allende. FAV, "Informe Mensual, Mayo–Junio 1989," 57–58, "Informe Mensual, Julio–Diciembre 1989," 85–89 (85–86 for Aylwin incident); APHEM, Hirmas, "Noticieros de TV: Cobertura de la campaña presidencial y parlamentaria, Chile, 1989," November 1990; and *ojo con la* TV, September–October 1989.

21 Aylwin, *La transición chilena*, 17–24 for speech (17, 18, 20, 21 for quotes below); see also note 23 in this chapter for departure from text. For events, tone, and choreography, see *El Mercurio*, 13-III-90 (cf. *La Tercera*, *La Epoca*); *Qué Pasa*, 15-III-90, pp. 34–35; and AFDDCD, "Recuento de actividades 1990" (copy in possession of author, courtesy of AFDD), 24–25.

22 For John Paul II's visit and the ways it catalyzed an effort to express the true face of Chilean reality on national television, see trilogy Book Two, 336–44.

23 For Aylwin's departure from the prepared text, I compared the speech as given in Aylwin, *La transición chilena*, 18; and in *El Mercurio*, 13-III-90 (whose punctuation is truer to the orality of the event), with the prepared version reproduced in PUC, Main Collection, Politics in Chile, Roll 26, 2. See also Otano, *Crónica de la transición*, 112.

24 See Otano, *Crónica de la transición*, 111. I am also grateful to Sol Serrano, who worked with Aylwin's team on public speeches and events, for insight on the care taken in organizing the event.

25 Curiously, the phrase is not in the published text of *El Mercurio*, 13-III-90, nor in Aylwin, *La transición chilena*, 17–24, but Aylwin recalled saying it (interview, 20-VI-97). What is indisputable is that he used the phrase (even if informally or improvisationally, at first) soon after he took office, and that it gained such currency as a cultural abbreviation that Aylwin came back to it in his 21-V-90 presidential address to Congress. His human rights policy, he declared, would be "consecuente con mi reiterada afirmación de que la conciencia moral de la nación exige que se esclarezca la verdad, se haga justicia en la medida de lo posible." Aylwin, *La transición chilena*, 33. By the time of our interview, the phrase had become a sensitive point, a code phrase in critiques that misunderstood, in Aylwin's view, his meaning and intentions.

26 Aylwin, *La transición chilena*, 113–19 (113, 116–17, 114, 118–19, for quotes). On

the advisors' reluctance, *LHOT*, 20; Sol Serrano, conversation, 31-VII-96; and Serrano and Cavallo, *El poder de la paradoja*, 273. I am also grateful to Sol Serrano for a copy of videotape that helped me understand the solemnity of the presentation. For background on Commission members, see *El Mercurio*, 25-IV-90; on Vial as minister of education, also trilogy Book Two, 186–87. Aylwin's insistence on finding four people from the Right came through strongly in our interview, 20-VI-97. The importance of achieving a unified and empirically unimpeachable report was not lost on the members of the Commission I interviewed: Jaime Castillo, 5-VI-97; Gonzalo Vial, 10-VI-97; José Zalaquett, 23-IV-97.

27 See Allamand, *La travesía del desierto*, 211–51 (212 for "keys" quote); Boeninger, *Democracia en Chile*, 433–42, 463–91; *LHOT*, 57–60; and Otano, *Crónica de la transición*, 134–47 (chapter title for "soup" quote). For additional analysis of neoliberalism versus growth-with-equity as policy and as discourse, in the early transition years, see Andrés Velasco, "The State and Economic Policy: Chile, 1952–1992," in Bosworth et al., *The Chilean Economy*, 408–11; and James Petras and Fernando Ignacio Leiva, with Henry Veltmeyer, *Democracy and Poverty in Chile: The Limits to Electoral Politics* (Boulder, Colo.: Westview, 1994). For analysis over a longer posttransition cycle, see Drake and Jaksic, *El modelo chileno*, 11–166; and Peter Winn, ed., *Victims of the Chilean Miracle: Workers and Neoliberalism in the Pinochet Era, 1973–2002* (Durham, N.C.: Duke University Press, 2004). See also chapter 4 in this volume. For acute analysis of the mix of reality and mythology in the politics of parties and consensus accords, depending on the issues in play, see Claudio Fuentes, "Partidos y coaliciones en el Chile de los '90: Entre pactos y proyectos," in Drake and Jaksic, *El modelo chileno*, 191–222.

28 Carmen Norambuena Carrasco, "Exilio y retorno: Chile 1973–1994," in *Memoria para un nuevo siglo: Chile, miradas a la segunda mitad del siglo XX*, ed. Mario Garcés et al. (Santiago: LOM, 2000), 173–87 (182 for quote, 178 n. 13 for 400,000 end of estimate range); Thomas Wright and Rody Oñate, *Flight from Chile: Voices of Exile* (Albuquerque: University of New Mexico Press, 1998), esp. 1–10 (note on 8 for 200,000 estimate), 198–225; Aylwin, *La transición chilena*, 115; and Elizabeth Lira and Brian Loveman, *Políticas de reparación: Chile, 1990–2004* (Santiago: LOM, 2005), 241–99, esp. 251–82. I am indebted, as well, to Roberto N., conversation, 11-IX-96, about his relationships with *retornados* and others upon return to Chile, and to materials in PIDEECD about mental health and retorno experiences since the mid-1980s.

29 For the previous three paragraphs, see *LHOT*, 45–46, 235; Lira and Loveman, *Políticas de reparación*, 55–65; *Qué Pasa*, 19-IV-90, pp. 6–9, 14–15; Otano, *Crónica de la transición*, 367; and Allamand, *La travesía del desierto*, 258–62. Cf. Serrano and Cavallo, *El poder de la paradoja*, 45–47; and Brian Loveman and Elizabeth Lira, *El espejismo de la reconciliación política: Chile, 1990–2002* (San-

tiago: LOM, 2002), 38–71. The other general shot in the Leigh episode was Enrique Ruiz.

30 PUC, Main Collection, Politics in Chile, Roll 26, Aylwin speeches, 15-v-90 ("Creación del Servicio Nacional de la Mujer"), 17-v-90 ("Creación de la Comisión de Pueblos Indígenas," also printed in Aylwin, *La transición chilena*, 166–69). For illuminating analysis placing such events in context, see Lisa Baldez, "La política partidista y los límites del feminismo de Estado en Chile," and Florencia E. Mallon, "Cuando la amnesia se impone con sangre, el abuso se hace costumbre: El pueblo mapuche y el Estado chileno, 1881–1898," both in Drake and Jaksic, *El modelo chileno*, 407–33, 435–64, respectively. For additional background on pre-1990 struggles by women and Mapuche peoples that informed the early transition years, see Temma Kaplan, *Taking back the Streets: Women, Youth, and Direct Democracy* (Berkeley: University of California Press, 2003), 73–101; and Florencia E. Mallon, *Courage Tastes of Blood: The Mapuche Community of Nicolás Ailío and the Chilean State, 1906–2001* (Durham, N.C.: Duke University Press, 2005).

31 Azun Candina Polomer, "El día interminable: Memoria e instalación del 11 de septiembre de 1973 en Chile (1974–1999)," in *Las conmemoraciones: Las disputas en las fechas "in-felices,"* ed. Elizabeth Jelin (Madrid: Siglo Veintiuno, 2002), 9–48; trilogy Book Two, 70–73, 135, 271–72, 279–80, 316–17, 326–27.

32 For previous six paragraphs, see *El Mercurio, La Tercera, Fortín Mapocho, La Epoca*, 4–5-ix-90; Aylwin, *La transición chilena*, 85–87 (Aylwin quotes); AGPHH, photos and notes on crowds; FSA, *Allende, Allende, Allende* (video, FSA and Cinco Producciones, 1992 funeral), includes quotes of crowd signs and chants; Otano, *Crónica de la transición*, 150; and LHOT, 48–49.

33 The fusion of memory struggle with mass experience, and the impact on the sustainability of dictatorship, are analyzed and documented in trilogy Book Two, part II.

34 AFDDCD, "Recuento de Actividades 1990," esp. 34, 39 ("moral constancy" and "mission" quotes), 46, 75, 92, 97 ("take decisions"), 125–27, 136, 140 (for joint meeting of AFDD and AFEP, the organization of relatives of the politically executed, with Aylwin), 149–50; Sola Sierra, interview, 26-iii-97 ("first frustration"). On Supreme Court ruling, see also Barahona de Brito, *Human Rights and Democratization in Latin America*, 176; and for additional context on courts and justice, Jorge Correa Sutil, in collaboration with Francisco Jiménez, " 'No Victorious Army Has Ever Been Prosecuted . . .': The Unsettled Story of Transitional Justice in Chile," in *Transitional Justice and the Rule of Law in New Democracies*, ed. A. James McAdams (Notre Dame, Ind.: University of Notre Dame Press, 1997), 123–54.

35 Julia Paley, *Marketing Democracy: Power and Social Movements in Post-dictatorship Chile* (Berkeley: University of California Press, 2001), 114–17; for wider context, note 36.

36 Ibid., 3–6, III–81, 203–4; Mallon, *Courage Tastes of Blood*, 182 ("writing grants"). On FOSIS and the fate of grassroots movements, see also Petras and Leiva, *Democracy and Poverty in Chile*, 140–66, esp. 148–51; cf. Aylwin's own vision of work to mute social protest mobilizations and to buy time for social programs and political accords to take effect, Serrano and Cavallo, *El poder de la paradoja*, 274–75, 278–80.

37 I am especially grateful to Patricia Politzer, interview, 8-IV-97, for insights on work and change at Televisión Nacional. For immediate speculation about implications of the transition for the station, see, e.g., *Qué Pasa*, 22-III-90, pp. 6–9.

38 *Hoy*, 2-IV-90, cover ("lying"), pp. 2–5, 11-VI-90, pp. 14–16 (esp. revealing on key role of former political prisoner of Pisagua, Dr. Alberto Enrique Neumann Lagos), 18-VI-90, pp. 4–18 (13 for Matthei quote), 20–21, and 25-VI-90, pp. 5–7; Otano, *Crónica de la transición*, 169. Cf. *Apsi*, 6-VI-90, pp. 12–13, and 20-VI-90, pp. 5, 11–13, 19–24. For the 1990 discovery within the wider frame of Pisagua as symbol in local and national memory lore, see the perceptive study by Lessie Jo Frazier, *Salt in the Sand: Memory, Violence and the Nation-State in Chile, 1890 to the Present* (Durham, N.C.: Duke University Press, 2007); and also trilogy Book Two, 289–94.

39 TVNCD, Cinta 30461: Noticias, 11-VI-90. For background on Toro, the controversy about his remarks, and the shadow of Pisagua, see Sergio Marras, *Confesiones de soldado* (Santiago: Ornitorrinco, 1989), 97–140; and *Hoy*, 25-VI-90, pp. 5–11.

40 Politzer, interview, 8-IV-97. Significantly, the legal ability of high officials to ensnare journalists and activists for defamation continued on well into the transition. For an exposition of the problem that itself turned into a cause célèbre, see Alejandra Matus, *El libro negro de la justicia chilena* (Santiago: Planeta, 1999); and Matus, *Injusticia duradera: Libro Blanco de "El Libro Negro de la Justicia chilena"* (Santiago: Planeta, 2002).

41 TVNCD, Cinta 037838: *Informe Especial*, 25-X-90.

42 Aylwin, *La transición chilena*, 81–84 (84 for quote). Cf. *El Mercurio*, *La Epoca*, 23–24-VI-89; and Otano, *Crónica de la transición*, 148.

43 Interview in *Apsi*, 23-V-90, p. 25 (Correa quote). On political memory and its generational aspects, trilogy Book Two, 196–205; Katherine Hite, *When the Romance Ended: Leaders of the Chilean Left, 1968–1998* (New York: Columbia University Press, 2000); and Patricio Aylwin, interview, 20-VI-97. For the political sensitivity of symbolic courtesies during the act of presidential transmission, see Aylwin's defense of same in 12-III-90 speech at the National Stadium, in Aylwin, *La transición chilena*, 19; and on Lagos and discrepancies on political strategy, Otano, *Crónica de la transición*, 114–16.

44 Aylwin, *La transición chilena*, 143–45 (143–44 for quotes).

45 My argument about Aylwin's ambivalent lack of obsession with an early Pinochet resignation is an interpretation based both on the logic of the actual

events described in the following eight paragraphs and documented in notes 46–50, and on explicit discussion of the topic by Aylwin and the political strategist Edgardo Boeninger. See Serrano and Cavallo, *El poder de la paradoja*, 159–60, cf. 146–47; and Boeninger, *Democracia en Chile*, 379–410, esp. 381, 392, 409.

46 Serrano and Cavallo, *El poder de la paradoja*, 148, 153.

47 On Ballerino and the Advisory Committee, and the inside political game related to the "Cutufa" and "Pinocheques" affairs, see *LHOT*, 29–37, 67–85; and Otano, *Crónica de la transición*, 124–30, 148–59. On muckraking in the 1980s, see trilogy Book Two, 297–311. On corruption and illicit enrichment by military insiders and select civilian beneficiaries, the layers turned out to be more widespread than initially realized and included traffic in drugs and arms. See, in addition to note 18 in this chapter, Rodrigo de Castro and Juan Gasparini, *La delgada línea blanca: Narcoterrorismo en Chile y Argentina* (Buenos Aires: Ediciones B, 2000); Víctor Osorio and Iván Cabezas, *Los hijos de Pinochet* (Santiago: Antártica, 1995); and Hernán Millas, *La familia militar* (Santiago: Planeta, 1999). Cf. Hugh O'Shaughnessy, *Pinochet: The Politics of Torture* (New York: New York University Press, 2000), 144–50.

48 Otano, *Crónica de la transición*, 104–5 (quote). Cf. *LHOT*, 16; *Ercilla*, 7-III-90, cover, pp. 6–7; and *Qué Pasa*, 8-III-90, p. 3.

49 Augusto Pinochet Ugarte, *Camino recorrido: Memorias de un soldado*, 3 vols. in 4 bks. (Santiago: Instituto Geográfico de Chile, 1990–94), see esp. 1:5–7 (prologue by Rafael Valdivieso), cf. vol. 3, bk. 2:285–92, 301–8. The congealing of this layer of memory as salvation was pervasive in interviews and conversations with Chileans who sympathized with the military regime in 1996–97, and among former high officials who had worked with the regime as far back as the crises of the 1970s: e.g., Sergio Fernández, *Mi lucha por la democracia* (Santiago: Los Andes, 1994); and Jorge Cauas, interview, 9-VI-97.

50 See *LHOT*, 49 (quote), 52–56; Otano, *Crónica de la transición*, 151–55, 333–34; Serrano and Cavallo, *El poder de la paradoja*, 154–56; and, for perspective on blockage of promotions, Fuentes Saavedra, *La transición de los militares*, 113.

51 For blunt assessment of the "ejercicio de enlace" affair by a top administration strategist, and his understanding of the final arrangement as a painful instance of the Weberian ethic of responsibility, see Boeninger, *Democracia en Chile*, 408–10; cf. Serrano and Cavallo, *El poder de la paradoja*, 156–60. See *La Segunda*, 19-XII-90, for a headline and report on "Pinocheques" testimony, accompanied by speculation on retirement, that Pinochet found inflammatory. After the incident, the newspapers and magazines of late December were filled with news and speculation; the best investigative journalism is *LHOT*, 67–85 (77 for Pinochet quote); and Otano, *Crónica de la transición*, 153–59. Jarpa's own account of the affair is a fine example of the cultural tendency of elites to create a language of normalcy, after settling a conflict, that retrospectively drains

drama from a tense event: Patricia Arancibia Clavel, Claudia Arancibia Floody, and Isabel de la Maza Cave, *Jarpa: Confesiones políticas* (Santiago: La Tercera-Mondadori, 2002), 428–30, which contrasts usefully with the more dramatic, "younger" style of his party comrade Andrés Allamand, *La travesía del desierto*, 266–68.

Afterword to Chapter 1: "My Dear President"

1 *El Mercurio*, 5-IX-90.
2 The fundamental sources for the description above are artifacts and documents in FSA, Caja "Testimonios Mausoleo de Salvador Allende," supplemented by Teresa Rubio (head of the FSA's Centro de Documentación in the late 1990s), conversation, 13-III-97; and AGPHH, photo collection and notes related to 1990 Allende funeral. All quotes in the text that follows are from letters in the notebook in the FSA's "Testimonios Mausoleo" box entitled "Testimonios depositado en el mausoleo de Salvador Allende (1990–1992)." The spelling mistakes in English are approximations of the spelling mistakes in Spanish. The custodian of the grave also turned over notes and letters, collected in a second notebook corresponding to 1993–94. My comment on the greater prevalence of notes in the first two years is based on comparison of the notebooks and on additional orientation by Teresa Rubio.
3 For Allende's last radio address, the sense of a "coup foretold" that enabled him to anticipate it, and his symbolism in the memory conflicts of the 1980s, see Book Two in this trilogy: Stern, *Battling for Hearts and Minds: Memory Struggles in Pinochet's Chile, 1973–1988* (Durham, N.C.: Duke University Press, 2006), 11–28, 173, 253, 255, 316–17, 325. For a full account of his last day, see Ignacio González Camus, *El día en que murió Allende* (Santiago: CESOC, 1990).

Chapter 2: Toward Memory Impasse?

1 ACNVR, Carpeta Antonio Arturo Barría Araneda (Ester Barría quotes). Technically, Ester Barría was Arturo's cousin but she considered him a brother. They had grown up together and he had been raised by his aunts, whom he later supported in adult life, after his mother had died.
2 ASXX, Ministerio de Educación, Reservados 1974, tomo 5 ("Antecedentes, 1974–75"), Del Jefe Supremo de la Nación al Señor Ministro de Educación [Pinochet to Castro], 28-VIII-74.
3 *DETDES*, 3:1080–85, esp. 1080–81.
4 The case of the 119 MIRistas and the DINA's "Operation Colombo," a misinformation effort intended as a cover story, is analyzed and documented in Book Two

of this trilogy: Stern, *Battling for Hearts and Minds: Memory Struggles in Pinochet's Chile, 1973–1988* (Durham, N.C.: Duke University Press, 2006), 108–12.

5 BF, Encuestas Collection, CERC, "Informe de Encuesta Nacional," April 1989, cuadros 26, 27 (*n* = 2988).

6 For comparative thinking in Chile in the late 1980s and the influence of José Zalaquett, see chapter 1 in this volume. For more on Argentina, good starting points are Carlos Santiago Nino, *Radical Evil on Trial* (New Haven, Conn.: Yale University Press, 1996); C. H. Acuña et al., *Juicio, castigos y memorias: Derechos humanos y justicia en la política argentina* (Buenos Aires: Nueva Visión, 1995); Deborah L. Norden, *Military Rebellion in Argentina: Between Coups and Consolidation* (Lincoln: University of Nebraska Press, 1996); and the pioneering cultural and media analysis of Claudia Feld, *Del estrado a la pantalla: Las imágenes del juicio a los ex comandantes en Argentina* (Madrid: Siglo Veintiuno, 2002). For comparative political science scholarship on military politics, democratic transition, and wider sociopolitical contexts, see Alfred Stepan, *Rethinking Military Politics: Brazil and the Southern Cone* (Princeton, N.J.: Princeton University Press, 1988); Leigh Payne, *Uncivil Movements: The Armed Right Wing and Democracy in Latin America* (Baltimore: Johns Hopkins University Press, 2000); and Katherine Hite and Paola Cesarini, eds., *Authoritarian Legacies and Democracy in Latin America and Southern Europe* (Notre Dame, Ind.: University of Notre Dame Press, 2004). For militaries and their framing of the memory question in South America, see Eric Hershberg and Felipe Agüero, eds., *Memorias militares sobre la represión en el Cono Sur: Visiones en disputa en dictadura y democracia* (Madrid: Siglo Veintiuno, 2005).

7 FAV, Caja A.T. 2, Casos, "Algunas cifras sobre atentados a los derechos humanos durante el régimen militar [1990?]." For upper and lower end exile estimates respectively, see Carmen Norambuena Carrasco, "Exilio y retorno: Chile, 1973–1994," in *Memoria para un nuevo siglo: Chile, miradas a la segunda mitad del siglo XX*, ed. Mario Garcés et al. (Santiago: LOM, 2000), 178 esp. n. 13; and Thomas Wright and Rody Oñate, *Flight from Chile: Voices from Exile*, (Albuquerque: University of New Mexico Press, 1998), 8. On technical aspects of international human rights and humanitarian law, and their relation to the Rettig Commission mandate, see ICNVR, vol. 1, bk. 1: 15–19. For technical discussion of the sometimes vexed figures of repression, see the "Introduction to the Trilogy" in this volume, esp. note 3.

8 José Zalaquett, interview, 23-IV-97 (for estimate of dozens of thousands of likely torture cases that would have needed review in 1990). Cf. FAV, Caja A.T. 2, Casos, "Algunas cifras sobre atentados a los derechos humanos durante el régimen militar [1990?]"; LHOT, 201; and a figure of some 28,000 cases documented in a torture commission report in 2004 (see chapter 6 in this volume).

9 BF, Encuestas Collection, CERC, "Informe de Encuesta Nacional," April 1989, p. 16.

10 *LHOT*, 21–22; Andrés Allamand, *La travesía del desierto* (Santiago: Aguilar, 1999), 262–63; Patricio Aylwin, interview, 20-vi-97; Gastón Gómez Bernales, interview, 20-11-97. Cf. Margarita Serrano, *La historia de un "bandido": Raúl Rettig* (Santiago: Los Andes, 1999), 80–81, 109–13; and Margarita Serrano and Ascanio Cavallo, *El poder de la paradoja: 14 lecciones políticas de la vida de Patricio Aylwin* (Santiago: Editorial Norma, 2006), 37–38.

11 For doubts among advisors and from within the Center-Left, see the discussion and sources cited in this volume's chapter 1. For frank acknowledgment of initial worries about effectiveness and composition, among persons strongly identified with human rights work, I am grateful among others to Jaime Castillo, interview, 5-vi-97; and Carmen Garretón, interview, 24-vii-97. See also *LHOT*, 20; Rafael Otano, *Crónica de la transición* (Santiago: Planeta, 1995), 163–64; and Mark Ensalaco, *Chile under Pinochet: Recovering the Truth* (Philadelphia: University of Pennsylvania Press, 2000), 183–84, 188–89.

12 For chronology and statistics in previous two paragraphs, see *ICNVR*, vol. 1, bk. 1: 4–7, vol. 1, bk. 2, anexos 1–3. For a fuller vision of institutional process and consultations, see WOLA (Washington Office on Latin America), paper no. 2, "The Ethics of Responsibility . . . Transcript of a seminar with José Zalaquett Daher, April 17, 1991" (copy in possession of author); FAV, Caja A.T. 61, "Informe Rettig: Comentarios, Aportes"; *LHOT*, 26–27; Otano, *Crónica de la transición*, 166–67; and interviews with the Commission members Jaime Castillo (5-vi-97), Gonzalo Vial (10-vi-97), and José Zalaquett (23-iv-97) and the staff members Gastón Gómez (20-11-97) and Paula Serrano (21-1-97). For a lucid overall characterization of the Commission's work by its executive secretary, Jorge Correa Sutil, see "Dealing with Past Human Rights Violations: The Chilean Case after Dictatorship," *Notre Dame Law Review* 67, no. 5 (1992): 1457–85, also available in abridged form in Neil J. Kritz, ed., *Transitional Justice: How Emerging Democracies Reckon with Foreign Regimes*, 3 vols. (Washington, D.C.: U.S. Institute for Peace, 1995), 2:455–61, 478–94. The importance of the documentary foundation previously established by the Vicaría, relatives of victims, and other human rights groups was obvious in the ACNVR case records I read when granted temporary access in 1996.

13 The qualitative aspects discussed below emerged from the interviews cited in note 12 in this chapter. See also WOLA, paper no. 2: "The Ethics of Responsibility . . . April 17, 1991"; *ICNVR*, vol. 1, bk. 2: 765–85 (quotes from hearings with relatives). Except in cases when the source of a quote is unclear in the text, or where a point did not emerge consistently from multiple interviews, I will avoid additional (repetitive) notes.

14 The story of Señora Herminda Morales is presented and documented in Book One of this trilogy: Stern, *Remembering Pinochet's Chile: On the Eve of London 1998* (Durham, N.C.: Duke University Press, 2004), 39–53. For new research on her community of La Legua, resistance on the day of the coup, and participa-

tion by her sons, see also Mario Garcés and Sebastián Leiva, *El Golpe en La Legua: Los caminos de la historia y la memoria* (Santiago: LOM, 2005).

15 *ICNVR*, vol. 1, bk. 1: 6.

16 To respect privacy, I have withheld the relevant names. The declaration was given on 12-VII-90 and appears in the ACNVR case file of a person disappeared in September 1974.

17 The declining relevance of political background within the Commission emerged from the interviews cited in note 12 in this chapter. On Novoa and Zalaquett, see also *LHOT*, 43, 89; Ensalaco, *Chile under Pinochet*, 206; and *El Mercurio*, 25-IV-90.

18 See esp. *ICNVR*, vol. 1, bk. 1: 7–9, for responses by military and police; occasional (anonymous) conscript testimony was directly confirmed by my research in ACNVR.

19 This is a point well known to Commission members and staff and personally confirmed in my research in ACNVR.

20 I am deeply grateful to Erika Hennings for sharing her experience (all quotes from interview, 5-VI-97). Chanfreau held dual Chilean and French citizenship, and the latter conferred a right of French citizenship upon Hennings.

21 On ad hoc aspects of the early DINA, see *ICNVR*, vol. 1, bk. 2: 464–65; on the sense of duty to memory, I am deeply grateful to the former political prisoners Claudio Durán, Erika Hennings, and Pedro Matta for sensitizing me. On women and pressure to collaborate, see Luz Arce, *El infierno* (Santiago: Planeta, 1993); and Marcia Alejandra Merino Vega, *Mi verdad: "Más allá del horror, yo acuso . . ."* (Santiago: A.T.G., 1993).

22 For the previous two paragraphs, Erika Hennings, interview, 5-VI-97 (quotes, size of network); testimonial discussion of the witness-survivor experience at the Comisión 4 group ("Métodos de lucha y experiencias de superación de la impunidad") of the Seminario Internacional "Impunidad y sus efectos en los procesos democráticos," organized by CODEPU (Comité de Defensa de los Derechos del Pueblo, Committee for Defense of the Rights of the People), FASIC (Fundación de Ayuda Social de las Iglesias Cristianas, Social Assistance Foundation of the Christian Churches), and SERPAJ-Chile (Servicio de Paz y Justicia, or Peace and Justice Service), Santiago, 13–15-XII-96; and *Análisis*, 9-VII-90, pp. 30–33, esp. 32–33.

23 On the "gray zone," see Primo Levi, *The Drowned and the Saved*, trans. Raymond Rosenthal (1986; New York: Vintage, 1989), esp. chap. 2, 36–69. On Merino and Arce specifically, see note 24.

24 Arce, *El infierno*; Merino, *Mi verdad*. For perceptive commenting on Arce's forcefulness of personality, see Merino, *Mi verdad*, 53–54; on Arce in a proactive role and accused of volunteering false information, ACNVR, Carpeta Oscar Castro Videla, declaration of Doña Heddy Olenka Navarro Harris, originally given 3-VIII-78; on Merino and body language, the remarkable video by the

director Carmen Castillo (the widow of the MIR's Miguel Enríquez), *La Flaca Alejandra* (France 3 and Institut National de L'Audiovisuel, 1994), copy at ECOCD; and on Arce as a catalyst of publicity, e.g., early publication of testimony in *Hoy*, 18-III-91, pp. 26–40. Cf. media stories upon her 1992 return to Chile, e.g., *La Epoca*, 15-II-92, 19-II-92, 10-III-92; and Merino's comments on intimidation and cautiousness (*Mi verdad*, 131–33). For tensions among former political prisoners about collaboration and relations of mutual acceptance with Arce and Merino, see note 26 in this chapter.

25 On activation of personal remorse and personal self-justification by perpetrators in the politicocultural environment of 1990, and the sharing of such sentiments with clergy, see FAV, Caja A.T. 61, "Informe Rettig: Comentarios, Aportes," Bishop Carlos González, "Verdad y reconciliación" (Talca, 1-VI-90). On personal crises of Arce and Merino, and the nexus of Christian rebirth and collaboration with the Rettig Commission and the courts, see Arce, *El infierno*, esp. 337–51 (347 for quote); and Merino, *Mi verdad*, esp. 131–38.

26 For this discussion, parts of it sensitive and off-the-record, I have drawn on participant-observation at the Comisión 4 group ("Métodos de lucha y experiencias de superación de la impunidad"), comprising survivor-witnesses and other human rights activists at the Seminario Internacional on "Impunidad" cited in note 22 of this chapter; also communications with Erika Hennings (including interview of 5-VI-97) and Pedro Matta; Arce, *El infierno*, 348–50; and ECOCD, *La Flaca Alejandra*.

27 There were other significant debates, e.g., how to characterize the death of Allende, whether to classify particular cases as human rights violations by the state or as death in circumstances of political violence, and how best to phrase the rather sensitive historical background section. For internal debate, I am indebted to interviews with the five Commission and staff members listed in note 12 in this chapter. See also *LHOT*, 88 (interpretation of no-name policy); Ensalaco, *Chile under Pinochet*, 188–210. For conceptual and substantive discussion of torture in the final report, see *ICNVR*, vol. 1, bk. 1: 16, 25, 29–30, 111–14; and vol. 1, bk. 2: 463–74, 478–80, 627, 651–53, 769–70.

28 For workloads and dynamics, and individual draft responsibilities, see *LHOT*, 88–90; Otano, *Crónica de la transición*, 166–67; Ensalaco, *Chile under Pinochet*, 181–211; and interviews (esp. Vial and Zalaquett) cited in note 12 in this chapter. For the narrative on justice, see *ICNVR*, vol. 1, bk. 1: 79–104.

29 For discussion of history prior to September 1973, see *ICNVR*, vol. 1, bk. 1: 19–20, 33–42 (37, 38, 39, 20 for quotes); and for process of drafting and discussion, Gonzalo Vial, interview, 10-VI-97; Jaime Castillo, interview, 5-VI-97; and José Zalaquett, interview, 23-IV-97. An insightful comparative reflection on truth commissions and nation building in Argentina, Chile, and Guatemala homes in on the treatment of history—both "structural analysis and causal history"— as precisely the unusual feature in the Guatemalan case. There, "state terror

was so brutal, so successful in destroying political opposition, that it shattered the conceit that future social solidarity could be constructed from a description of past human rights transgressions." Greg Grandin, "The Instruction of Great Catastrophe: Truth Commissions, National History, and State Formation in Argentina, Chile, and Guatemala," *American Historical Review* 110, no. 1 (February 2005): 46–67 (65 for quotes). Grandin's argument occasionally lapses into error, as when he claims the Rettig Report "mythologized the coup that brought Pinochet to power as a regrettable yet necessary measure" (64). His point about the sidestepping of deeper historical analysis is accurate, however, and later in the 1990s Chilean historians would write a "manifesto" that argued for the necessity of a deeper—more historicized, structural, and long-term—vision of the roots of the 1973 crisis and military era. See chapter 5 in this volume.

30 The Commission explicitly discussed, however, the classic distinctions and the rationale behind its approach in a chapter on norms, concepts, and criteria: *ICNVR*, vol. 1, bk. 1: 15–30. For the summary statistics, see ibid., vol. 1, bk. 2: 883 (anexo 2).

31 All the qualitative statements in this chapter section are based on my reading of the full report. The statistics are derived from the numbers given in *ICNVR*, vol. 1, bk. 2: 883–87 (anexo 2); and from the dates given for individual military and police victims in ibid., vol. 1, bk. 1: 432–41. Working right up to the deadline led to very slight counting errors in the report (e.g., the victim total should have been 2,298, not 2,279; *LHOT*, 91), but they were negligible for purposes of scale and proportion.

32 Patricio Aylwin, interview, 20-VI-97; remarks at 8-11-91 ceremony reprinted in Patricio Aylwin Azócar, *La transición chilena: Discursos escogidos, Marzo 1990– 1992* (Santiago: Andrés Bello, 1992), 123–25.

33 The speech is in Aylwin, *La transición chilena*, 126–36; all quotes follow this text, except that I changed the punctuation of the opening slightly to capture its orality, and I deleted the parenthetical citation of pages for Aylwin's quotes of the report on the judiciary. All observations of his voice and body language are from the videotape copy of the speech broadcast (with an additional hour of postspeech commentary) on Televisión Nacional, 4-III-91, in AAVPS, "Patricio Aylwin, Presentación Rettig" (video copy of Televisión Nacional broadcast of speech and follow-up program). The television audience was huge: two-thirds (64.6 percent) of adults (eighteen years old or higher) in the nation, according to BF, Encuestas Collection, CERC, "Evaluación del primer año del gobierno democrático [1991]," p. 9 (*n* = 1,500, based on 29 cities of 40,000 or higher, representing 62.9 percent of national population).

34 Otano, *Crónica de la transición*, 172.

35 I thank Sol Serrano, who worked on Aylwin's preparation of speeches, for the point about his more solitary preparation of the Rettig speech. The authenticity of the speech as a reflection of Aylwin's own values and sentiments as a leader

came through again, over a year and a half later, when *Qué Pasa* reported (12-XII-92, p. 47) that Aylwin cried when he viewed the Rettig speech in the company of intimate friends. He had taped the speech and could therefore view it at the "live" moment along with the rest of the nation.

36 Sola Sierra, interview, 26-III-97; Erika Hennings, interview, 5-VI-97.

37 Violeta E., interview, 26–27-VIII-96, 5–6-IX-96; Ramiro I. and Claudia de I., interview, 6–7-II-97; also interviews in note 36. For impact on the Right, the caution of comments on Televisión Nacional after the speech was revealing: AAVPS, "Patricio Aylwin, Presentación Rettig" (video copy of Televisión Nacional broadcast of speech and follow-up program); I am also grateful on this point to Father José Aldunate, interview, 10-I-97. To be sure, some persons were so skeptical of the Rettig Commission, they were not drawn in to the emotions and implications of the moment—even if they later saw the report and speech in a different light. Tonya R., interview, 13-XII-96, 2-I-97; Luz M., interview, 21-I-97.

38 At the time this chapter draft was revised for publication, over seventeen years after delivery of the report, there was still not a single case of disproof.

39 Corporación Nacional de Reparación y Reconciliación, "Informe a Su Excelencia el Presidente de la República . . . 15 de Mayo de 1996" (copy in possession of author: Santiago: La Nación, 1996), esp. cuadro 15.

40 BF, Encuestas Collection, CERC, "Evaluación del primer año del gobierno democrático [1991]," pp. 18–19, cuadros 20, 22 ($n = 1,500$).

41 BF, Encuestas Collection, "Los chilenos y la democracia" series, 1991–1994, by M. A. Garretón et al. and Corporación Participa, "Informe 1993," p. 67, cuadro 46 ($n = 1,498$). An elastic definition of "middle class" (including even a sector of the prosperous top 20 percent) probably had the effect of diluting the middle-class share that defined memory as dictatorship.

42 Text in *El Mercurio*, 9-III-91.

43 For texts of the statements, and related events, see *El Mercurio*, 28-III-91 for army, navy, 29-III-91 for carabineros; cf. *La Epoca* on same dates.

44 *El Mercurio*, 28-III-91.

45 Patricio Aylwin, interview, 20-VI-97.

46 See editorials in *El Mercurio*, 4-III-91, 6-III-91 (quotes). For a similar way of adapting to the truth of the Rettig Report by Doña Elena, a partisan of the regime, see trilogy Book One, 148, cf. 7–34.

47 *El Mercurio*, 28-III-91 (quotes).

48 LHOT, 95; Otano, *Crónica de la transición*, 182; FAV, Caja A.T. 56a, Tortura, *El Popular*, March 1991.

49 I owe thanks to colleagues—particularly Alfredo Riquelme, Sol Serrano, Teresa Valdés, and participants in two seminars, at Tulane University, 2-X-04, and at Pontificia Universidad Católica de Chile, 21-VIII-06—for discussions that helped me refine my understanding of the tension of formula versus wedge. I wish to acknowledge, too, Serrano's incisive formulation of the dialectical dynamic: "with-

out a formula there is no wedge" (sin fórmula no hay wedge). Over the years, José Zalaquett has been an advocate for building on initial steps in ways that create a certain wedge effect, and I am grateful to him for a suggestive metaphor, that of an icebreaker ship. A recent illuminating study of the "mirage" of reconciliation may be interpreted as a narrative of the unresolved tension, especially at the level of political elites, between the yearning for a formula leading to a closure and the impossibility of achieving it, that is, the formula/wedge problem at an institutional level. See Brian Loveman and Elizabeth Lira, *El espejismo de la reconciliación política: Chile, 1990–2002* (Santiago: LOM, 2002).

50 For background, context, and sources on political trajectories dividing the Communist Party and the renovated Left in the 1980s, see trilogy Book Two, 196–230, esp. 197–205, 214–16; for a major leader's memoir of Communist political life and ambiguities through the 1990s, Luis Corvalán, *De lo vivido y lo peleado: Memorias* (Santiago: LOM, 1997); for electoral base prior to 1973, Germán Urzúa Valenzuela, *Historia política de Chile y su evolución electoral (Desde 1810 a 1992)* (Santiago: Editorial Jurídica, 1992), esp. 620–21, 685 (18.0 percent of valid Senate vote and 16.8 percent of valid Representative vote in 1969 elections; geographical distribution of Communist voting strength, 1937–69); for the contrast with 1993 elections, *LHOT*, 229; for the complexity of social mobilization in the 1990s—real, but weaker and less visible compared to an earlier Chile—excellent studies are in Paul Drake and Iván Jaksic, eds., *El modelo chileno: Democracia y desarrollo en los noventa* (Santiago: LOM, 1999), pt. 3 (esp. essays by Gonzalo de la Maza E. and Lisa Baldez); for a pioneering grassroots study, Julia Paley, *Marketing Democracy: Power and Social Movements in Post-Dictatorship Chile* (Berkeley: University of California Press, 2001); and for perspective on labor, once a major social movement category and central to Communist politics, Paul W. Drake, *Labor Movements and Dictatorships: The Southern Cone in Comparative Perspective* (Baltimore: Johns Hopkins University Press, 1996). Participant-observation provided examples of persons who voted for realistic candidates in national elections yet opted for Communist candidates or rallies in trade union or other grassroots contexts. On the Frente Patriótico and guerrillas, see note 51.

51 An overview of the intertwined themes of political prisoners, guerrilla groups, police work, and unwanted army "help" may be gleaned from *LHOT*, 30–31, 38–47, 96–114. On the Frente and the reality and symbolism of armed struggle, see Hernán Vidal, *Frente Patriótico Manuel Rodríguez: El tabú del conflicto armado en Chile* (Santiago: Mosquito, 1995); I have also been assisted by APMM: copies of radio broadcast interventions (undated, internal evidence indicates 1991 or later); and on prevention in the broader sense, Patricio Aylwin, interview, 20-VI-97. See also Serrano and Cavallo, *El poder de la paradoja*, 47–53.

52 See *El Mercurio*, *La Epoca*, and the press more generally, 2–7-IV-91; and Otano, *Crónica de la transición*, 174–86. See also *LHOT*, 96–97.

53 On Guzmán in political and human contexts, see Carlos Huneeus, *El régimen de Pinochet* (Santiago: Editorial Sudamericana, 2000), 63–67, 85–87, 122 n. 42, 153–60, 213–28, 256 n. 11, 270–71, 279–315, 382 n. 70; trilogy Book Two, 57–58, 119, 139–40, 318; Rosario Guzmán Errázuriz, *Mi hermano Jaime* (Santiago: Editorial VER, 1991); Jaime Guzmán Errázuriz, *Escritos personales* (Santiago: Zig-Zag, 1992), esp. 31–67, 86–91; and Renato Cristi, *El pensamiento político de Jaime Guzmán: Autoridad y libertad* (Santiago: LOM, 2000). For wider history of conservative thought, see also Renato Cristi and Carlos Ruíz, *El pensamiento conservador en Chile: Seis ensayos* (Santiago: Editorial Universitaria, 1992), esp. 109–39. On the obvious need for Televisión Nacional coverage of the funeral, I am grateful to Patricia Politzer, interview, 8-IV-97.

54 On the changed atmosphere and its consequences, FAV, Caja A.T. 61, "Informe Rettig: Comentarios, Aportes": Comisión Chilena de Derechos Humanos, "Proposiciones para una política sobre la violencia" (Santiago, 16-IV-91), pp. 15–17; Otano, *Crónica de la transición*, 181–85; and numerous interviews and conversations. For recommendation to criminalize cover-up, see *ICNVR*, vol. 1, bk. 2: 873–74.

55 Jaime Castillo, interview, 5-VI-97; cf. speculation about the CNI, in Otano, *Crónica de la transición*, 185.

Afterword to Chapter 2: The Futility of History?

1 Lawrence Langer, *Holocaust Testimonies: The Ruins of Memory* (New Haven, Conn.: Yale University Press, 1991); James Young, *At Memory's Edge: After-Images of the Holocaust in Contemporary Art and Architecture* (New Haven, Conn.: Yale University Press, 2000); Hannah Arendt, *The Human Condition: A Study of the Central Dilemmas Facing Modern Man* (orig. 1958; Garden City: Doubleday Anchor, 1959), 212–19 (216 for quote); Arendt, *Eichmann in Jerusalem: A Report on the Banality of Evil*, rev. and expanded ed. (New York: Viking Press, 1964).

    For full appreciation of Langer's argument and focus on "ordinary witness" testimony, it is helpful to read, too, the searing and insightful published literature of memoir and testimony by survivor-witnesses. See esp. Charlotte Delbo, *Days and Memory*, trans. Rosette Lamont (1985; Marlboro, Vt.: Marlboro Press, 1990); Primo Levi, *Survival in Auschwitz*, trans. Stuart Woolf (1958; repr., New York: Touchstone [Simon and Schuster], 1966); Levi, *The Drowned and the Saved*, trans. Raymond Rosenthal (1986; New York: Vintage, 1989); and Elie Wiesel, *The Night Trilogy*, trans. Stella Rodawy (orig. pub. as *Night*, 1958; New York: Hill and Wang, 1987). Delbo was a source of particular inspiration to Langer, whose work was in part a brilliant elaboration of her testimonial insight. For background on memorialization before the countermonument or antimemory aesthetic gained traction, see also the earlier study of James Young, *The Texture of Memory: Holocaust Memorials and Meanings* (New Haven, Conn.: Yale University Press, 1993). For helpful reflection on "radical evil" and the problem of justice in its twentieth-century South American context, see Carlos Santiago Nino, *Radical Evil on Trial* (New Haven, Conn.: Yale University Press, 1996); and for recent insightful philosophical treatment of atrocity and evil, in dialogue with Kant and the history of moral philosophy, see Claudia Card, *The Atrocity Paradigm: A Theory of Evil* (New York: Oxford University Press, 2002). For discussion of the contrasting historical contexts of Kant and twentieth-century writers on radical evil, see Book One of this trilogy: Stern, *Remembering Pinochet's Chile: On the Eve of London 1998* (Durham, N.C.: Duke University Press, 2004), 178–80 (esp. 180) n. 26. On the unresolved tensions between radical evil and banality of evil in Arendt's thought, see *History and Memory* 8, no. 2 (autumn/winter 1996): thematic issue, "Hannah Arendt and *Eichmann in Jerusalem*," esp. the essays by Adi Ophir, "Between Eichmann and Kant: Thinking on Evil after Arendt," 81–136; Seyla Benhabib, "Identity, Perspective and Narrative in Hannah Arendt's *Eichmann in Jerusalem*," 35–59, esp. 44–48; and José Brunner, "Eichmann, Arendt and Freud in Jerusalem: On the Evils of Narcissism and the Pleasures of Thoughtlessness," 61–88.

For the related problem of historical representation, see also note 3 in this chapter.

2 For key works on "ordinary" persons committing genocide and the Jedwabne and Rwanda cases, see Christopher Browning, *Ordinary Men: Reserve Battalion 101 and the Final Solution in Poland* (New York: HarperCollins, 1992); Jan T. Gross, *Neighbors: The Destruction of the Jewish Community in Jedwabne, Poland* (Princeton, N.J.: Princeton University Press, 2001); Philip Gourevitch, *We Wish to Inform You that Tomorrow We Will Be Killed with Our Families: Stories from Rwanda* (New York: Farrar, Straus and Giroux, 1998); and for important caution about ideology-of-genocide assumptions, Scott Straus, *The Order of Genocide: Race, Power, and War in Rwanda* (Ithaca, N.Y.: Cornell University Press, 2006). For additional work that illuminates and complicates historical context, see, for the Rwandan case, Jan Vansina, *Antecedents to Modern Rwanda: The Nyigina Kingdom* (Madison: University of Wisconsin Press, 2004); Robert Lyons and Scott Straus, *Intimate Enemy: Images and Voices of the Rwandan Genocide* (New York: Zone Books, 2006); and, for the Holocaust, note 3.

3 Arno Mayer, *Why Did the Heavens Not Darken? The "Final Solution" in History* (New York: Pantheon, 1988), 31 ("war-cum-crusade"), xv ("incomprehensible"). For historicization from an "outside reader" perspective that serves as a fine introductory guide to historical scholarship and problematization, see Inga Clendinnen, *Reading the Holocaust* (New York: Cambridge University Press, 1999); cf. Browning, *Ordinary Men*. For an interdisciplinary review of Holocaust-related debates and scholarship since the 1950s, in dialogue with the

expanding field of genocide studies, a good introduction and reflection is Herbert Hirsch, *Genocide and the Politics of Memory: Studying Death to Preserve Life* (Chapel Hill: University of North Carolina Press, 1995). The problem of representation and language has generated a large interdisciplinary literature. For a theoretically informed and insightful guide to issues and scholarship, see—in addition to the works of Clendinnen, Hirsch, Langer, and Young cited earlier—Dominick LaCapra, *Representing the Holocaust: History, Theory, Trauma* (Ithaca, N.Y.: Cornell University Press, 1994); and Michael Bernard-Donals and Richard Glejzer, *Between Witness and Testimony: The Holocaust and the Limits of Representation* (Albany: State University of New York Press, 2001). I wish to acknowledge that LaCapra's critique of Mayer (69–90, esp. 81–83) in some respects parallels my own, although I do not share the dismissive aspect. For implications on how we may write history, an acutely sensitive and well-balanced essay relevant to this Afterword on the apparent "futility" of history is Saul Friedlander, "Trauma, Transference, and 'Working Through' in the Writing of the *Shoah*," *History and Memory* 4, no. 1 (spring–summer 1992): 39–59, esp. 51–53.

4 For ways that issues of representation figure in the Chilean and South American context, and on the question of disappearance, see Nelly Richard, ed., *Políticas y estéticas de la memoria* (Santiago: Cuarto Propio, 2000), esp. Richard, "Imagen-recuerdo y borraduras," 163–72; and Sergio Rojas, "Cuerpo, lenguaje y desaparición," 177–86. Cf. Michael J. Lazzara, "Tres recorridos de Villa Grimaldi," in *Monumentos, memoriales y marcas territoriales*, eds. Elizabeth Jelin and Victoria Langland (Madrid: Siglo Veintiuno, 2003), 127–47. On Jews and Communists, Tutsis and colonizers, see, e.g., Gross, *Neighbors*; and Gourevitch, *We Wish to Inform You that Tomorrow We Will Be Killed with Our Families*. On *genocide* in world vocabulary, Lemkin's thought and evolution, and the vexed question of political groups targeted for annihilation, see Raphael Lemkin, *Axis Rule in Occupied Europe: Laws of Occupation, Analysis of Government, Proposals for Redress* (Washington, D.C.: Carnegie Endowment for World Peace, 1944), 79–95, cf. xi–xiii; Lemkin, *Les actes constituant un danger general (interétatique) consideres comme déclites des droit des gens* (Paris: A. Pedone, 1933), also available in English translation as "Acts Constituting a General (Transnational) Danger Considered as Offences against the Law of Nations," trans. James T. Fussell, www.preventgenocide.org, "Key Writings of Raphael Lemkin" link; and Herbert Hirsch, *Genocide and the Politics of Memory: Studying Death to Preserve Life* (Chapel Hill: University of North Carolina Press, 1995), 181–211, esp. 197–99.

5 For discussion of "policide" as an analytical category, see trilogy Book One, 31–32, 180–81 n. 27, cf. xxii–xxiii; and for the broader significance of "atrocity" as a family of related issues in the moral philosophy of evil, regardless of where one draws the definitional boundary on "genocide," Card, *The Atrocity Paradigm*.

6 Gonzalo Vial, interview, 10-VI-97.

7 The cases of guards who were more "humane" in approach left a strong im-

print in the folklore of prison memory. Two of the most poignant cases were DINA agents disappeared by their comrades: ACNVR, Carpeta Rodolfo Valentín González Pérez, Carpeta Carlos Alberto Carrasco Matus; their cases are summarized in *ICNVR*, vol. 1, bk. 2: 589–90.

8 Gaston Gómez, interview, 20-11-97.

9 ACNVR, Carpeta Henry Francisco Torres Flores for letter and declaration by mother; *niño* was the term used by Gómez in our interview, 20-11-97. Lack of known militancy characterized 46.0 percent of victims identified by the Rettig Commission: see *ICNVR*, vol. 1, bk. 2, 885.

10 William Styron, *Sophie's Choice* (New York: Random House, 1979); Paula Serrano, interview, 21-1-97.

11 Paula Serrano, interview, 21-1-97.

Chapter 3: Circle of Truth, Justice, and Force

1 For the original recommendations of the Rettig Commission on justice in its variety of senses, see *ICNVR*, vol. 1, bk. 2: 823–72; and for Aylwin's reliance on the commission proposals as an anchor for his actions and recommendations, Patricio Aylwin Azócar, *La transición chilena: Discursos escogidos, Marzo 1990–1992* (Santiago: Andrés Bello, 1992), 129–30, 133–36. On justice after times of atrocity, a rich literature emerged for Latin America and other world regions experiencing "transition" from violent rule or conflicts in the 1990s. See, aside from the discussion of José Zalaquett in this volume's chapter 1 (see note 10 for his key writings), Carlos Santiago Nino, *Radical Evil on Trial* (New Haven, Conn.: Yale University Press, 1996); Juan E. Méndez, "Accountability for Past Abuses," *Human Rights Quarterly* 19, no. 2 (1997): 255–82; A. James McAdams, ed., *Transitional Justice and the Rule of Law in New Democracies* (Notre Dame, Ind.: Notre Dame University Press, 1997); Martha Minow, *Between Vengeance and Forgiveness: Facing History after Genocide and Mass Violence* (Boston: Beacon Press, 1998); and Nigel Beggar, ed., *Burying the Past: Making Peace and Doing Justice after Civil Conflict* (Washington, D.C.: Georgetown University Press, 2001). Of course, the extreme social inequalities and other forms of injustice and social demands in Latin America mean that the justice issue cannot be confined to the question of human rights atrocities by dictatorships or in war. For justice in this broad sense and its relation to citizenship and social movements, good starting points are Elizabeth Jelin and Eric Hershberg, eds., *Constructing Democracy: Human Rights, Citizenship, and Society in Latin America* (Boulder, Colo.: Westview Press, 1996); and Susan Eva Eckstein and Timothy P. Wickam-Crowley, eds., *What Justice? Whose Justice? Fighting for Fairness in Latin America* (Berkeley: University of California Press, 2003).

2 For social repair within a broader policy on human rights, an excellent short

guide is Elizabeth Lira and Brian Loveman, "Derechos humanos en la transición 'Modelo': Chile, 1988–1999," in *El modelo chileno: Democracia y desarrollo en los noventa*, eds. Paul Drake and Iván Jaksic (Santiago: LOM, 1999), 339–74; and for a comprehensive official report, Corporación Nacional de Reparación y Reconciliación (hereinafter CNRR), "Informe a Su Excelencia el Presidente de la República . . . 15 de Mayo de 1996" (copy in possession of author: Santiago: La Nación, 1996), esp. 42–55 for statistics on pension, health, and educational benefits and beneficiaries. For a more detailed discussion of public policy and debate, see Elizabeth Lira and Brian Loveman, *Políticas de reparación: Chile, 1990–2004* (Santiago: LOM, 2005).

The monthly pensions to relatives of the disappeared and the executed were meaningful but modest supplements, when considered within a context of lower middle-class and middle-class family incomes. The initial 1992 baseline used in the calculation of pension shares for surviving relatives was 140,000 pesos monthly (US$368), was adjusted in tandem with other pension programs, and grew to 212,733 pesos monthly (US$520) by December 1995. The 1992–95 baseline translated into a monthly pension range of US$148–208 for spouses (40 percent share); $110–56 for mothers, or fathers if mothers were absent (30 percent share); and $55–78 for each child under twenty-five years of age, or for a disabled child of any age (15 percent share). Each child had a right to a 15 percent share even if the total family share exceeded 100 percent of the baseline; if there was only one beneficiary, that person had a right to a 71.43 percent share, or a range of $263–372. In addition, recipients received a one-time lump sum equivalent to twelve monthly pension payments. For calculation of the U.S. dollar value of monthly pension rates above and below, I used the December averages observed for 1992 and 1995 in the dollar-peso exchange rates by Banco Central de Chile, www.bcentral.cl, "Base de Datos Estadísticos, Precios, Indices del tipo de cambio" link; for Chilean peso amounts, CNRR, "Informe a Su Excelencia . . . ," 48–49.

It is useful to place these figures—a baseline of about US$370–520 monthly, an expected minimum family share of about US$260–375 monthly—in the context of Chilean gross domestic product and household incomes. In the early 1990s, monthly per capita gross domestic product was about US$400, distribution of income highly unequal, and the monthly minimum wage under $100. At the close of the Aylwin presidency, in 1994,the household income of the bottom quintile amounted to $184. The middle quintile—in Chilean terms, lower middle class or solid working class—received $488, roughly on a par with the baseline calculation for pensions. The second-from-top quintile (solid middle class) received $747, and the top quintile $2,256. (Within the top quintile, comprised of upper middle-class and wealthy families, income was highly concentrated. The top tenth received three times the income of the second tenth.) In Chilean cultural terms, a minimum family share of $260–375 monthly translated into a nonextravagant but meaningful *supplement* to household income for a middle-class family, but would not by itself substitute for a need to work or for a strategy of multiple family income streams to achieve a dignified lower middle-class or middle-class life. For 1994 quintile figures (in pesos), and concentration within top quintile, see Patricio Meller, "Pobreza y distribución del ingreso en Chile (Década de los noventa)," in Drake and Jaksic, *El modelo chileno*, 57, 54; cf. the lower 1991 baseline and per capita figures in James Petras and Fernando Ignacio Leiva, with Henry Veltmeyer, *Democracy and Poverty in Chile: The Limits to Electoral Politics* (Boulder, Colo.: Westview Press, 1994), 129. Total spending on pensions including related health and lump sum payments settled in (after a bulge in the start-up year of 1992) to an annual rate of about us$14–14.5 million by 1994–95. CNRR, "Informe a Su Excelencia . . . ," 51. (A mistaken decimal placement mars dollar figures in the otherwise fine work by Lira and Loveman, *Políticas de reparación*, 162.)

For dissent on benefits and beneficiaries, FAV, Caja A. T. 22, Detenidos Desaparecidos, AFDD, "Observaciones al 'Proyecto de Ley Relativo a Reparaciones . . . ," 15-IV-91; focus group with Comando de Exonerados Militares, Santiago, 30-X-96; and Lira and Loveman, *Políticas de reparación*. On mixed personal responses to receiving a pension, I am grateful to Sola Sierra, interview, 26-III-97.

3 Aylwin, *La transición chilena*, 134 (quote); and for concession of gravity of findings, interviews including political conservatives on Televisión Nacional, 4-III-91, after Aylwin's speech, AAVPS, "Patricio Aylwin, Presentación Rettig" (video copy of Televisión Nacional broadcast of speech and follow-up program).

4 On gridlock, one needs to refine the point. For purposes of "ordinary government" such as routine legislation setting up budgets, the institutional design of the Constitution granted the Executive great authority relative to Congress. For other goals, such as institutional or constitutional reforms and symbolic acts, gridlock was more potent. Awareness of the gridlock problem on major objectives reinforced the cautious government strategy of building agreements with sectors of the Right. On the complexities of institutional design and strategy, see Peter M. Siavelis, *The President and Congress in Postauthoritarian Chile: Institutional Constraints to Democratic Consolidation* (University Park: Pennsylvania State University Press, 2000); on political pacts and their limits, depending on the specific theme in play, and comparison with the mythology of consensus, Claudio Fuentes, "Partidos y coaliciones en Chile: Entre pactos y proyectos," in Paul Drake and Iván Jaksic, *El modelo chileno*, 191–222.

5 AFDD, *Recuento de actividades 1990* (Santiago: AFDD, 1991[?]), 102–7 (copy given to author, but also at AFDDCD); AFDD, *Un camino de imágenes . . . que revelan y se rebelan contra una historia no contada: 20 años . . .* (Santiago: AFDD, 1997), III, 132–33; Fundación Memorial del Detenido Desaparecido y del Ejecutado Político, "Para que nunca más: Memorial del Detenido Desaparecido y

del Ejecutado Político" (flier, in possession of author). For background on Precht, the Vicariate of Solidarity, and its predecessor, the Pro-Peace Committee, see Pamela Lowden, *Moral Opposition to Authoritarian Rule in Chile, 1973–1990* (New York: St. Martin's Press, 1996); Eugenio Ahumada et al., *Chile: La memoria prohibida*, 3 vols. (Santiago: Pehuén, 1989); and Book Two of this trilogy: Stern, *Battling for Hearts and Minds: Memory Struggles in Pinochet's Chile, 1973–1988* (Durham, N.C.: Duke University Press, 2006), 81–230.

6   For the original cultural symbolism suggested by the Agrupación, which embraced a wide range of projects, see FAV, Caja A.T. 61: "Informe Rettig: Comentarios, Aportes," letter from AFDD (Sola Sierra et al.) to Comisión Rettig (Raúl Rettig Guissen and Jorge Correa Sutil), Santiago, 9-x-90; on the distinction between "memorial" and "monument," whose conflation had become so common I had fallen into it, Sola Sierra, interview, 26-III-97. On tension and delay, see Otano, *Crónica de la transición* (Santiago: Antártica, 1995), 356; and *LHOT*, 220.

7   Key documents are in FSA, Carpetas "Monumento a S. Allende," and include the following: *Punto Final*, 26-II-90, *La Epoca*, 20-VI-90, for start-up campaign by Left and Allendistas; Proyecto de Ley, Cámara de Diputados, 14-V-91; *El Sur* (Concepción), 26-VI-91 (for Vicealmirante Fernando Navajas Irigoyen "most terrible" quote); and Chilean press accounts (esp. *El Mercurio*, *La Tercera*, *La Epoca*), 5-VI-92, 10-VII-92 (cf. *La Segunda*, 4-VI-92, 9-VI-92), for boycott and eventual approval in House of Deputies, and 15-VI-94 for Senate approval. The administrative procedures set in motion were such that technically, another year passed before final authorization by the Consejo de Monumentos Nacionales for a statue of Allende along with those of Presidents Frei and Alessandri on the Plaza de la Constitución: see *El Mercurio*, 15-IV-95. More delay set in because it took years to complete approval procedures, raise funds, and commission and complete the work. For a fine discussion through inauguration of an Allende statue in June 2000, see Katherine Hite, "El monumento a Salvador Allende en el debate político chileno," in *Monumentos, memoriales y marcas territoriales*, ed. Elizabeth Jelin and Victoria Langland (Madrid: Siglo Veintiuno, 2003), 19–55; and for insight on memorialization in South American postdictatorship contexts, the other essays in the same volume, esp. the sensitive conceptual discussion by Hugo Achugar, "El lugar de la memoria, a propósito de monumentos (motivos y paréntesis)," 191–216.

8   For the Santa Rosa and Alemania proposals, see *La Epoca*, 10-VII-92; and *El Diario Austral* (Temuco), 20-IV-92. The larger pattern of proposals, tensions, and results was gleaned from documents and press clippings gathered in FSA, Cuaderno "Lugares llamados Salvador Allende, América del Sur."

9   FAV, Caja A.T. 61, Subsection "Informe Rettig: Comentarios, Aportes," Aylwin to President of Supreme Court, 4-III-91; *El Mercurio*, 10-III-91 (press conference quote).

10 Aylwin, *La transición chilena*, 159–65 (160 for quote); see also note 11 for broader context.

11 For the judiciary and politics in the 1990s, I have relied especially on the superb analytical overview by Jorge Correa S., "Cenicienta se queda en la fiesta: El poder judicial chileno en la década de los 90," in Drake and Jaksic, *El modelo chileno*, 281–315; and the remarkable investigation of inside details of professional decay and corruption, and court responses to the political environment and executive branch pressure, from the 1960s to the 1990s, by Alejandra Matus, *El libro negro de la justicia chilena* (Santiago: Planeta, 1999). See also Jorge Correa S. in collaboration with Francisco Jiménez, " 'No Victorious Army Has Ever Been Prosecuted . . .': The Unsettled Story of Transitional Justice in Chile," in *Transitional Justice and the Rule of Law in New Democracies*, ed. James McAdams (Notre Dame, Ind.: Notre Dame University Press, 1997), 123–54; Lisa Hilbink, "Un Estado de derecho no liberal: La actuación del poder judicial chileno en los años 90," in Drake and Jaksic, *El modelo chileno*, 317–37; Hilbink, "An Exception to Chilean Exceptionalism? The Historical Role of Chile's Judiciary," in Eckstein and Wickham-Crowley, *What Justice? Whose Justice*, 64–97; Louis Bickford, "Strengthening Democracy: Stakeholder Institutions, Public Policy, and Democratic Quality. The Case of Chile, 1990–1998" (PHD diss., McGill University, 1999), esp. chap. 7; and Patricia Politzer, *Chile: ¿de qué estamos hablando? Retrato de una transformación asombrosa* (Santiago: Editorial Sudamericana, 2006), 277–311. For the Chilean case in comparative perspective, see Alexandra Barahona de Brito, *Human Rights and Democratization in Latin America: Uruguay and Chile* (Oxford: Oxford University Press, 1997); and Barahona de Brito, "Passion, Constraint, Law, and *Fortuna*: The Human Rights Challenge to Chilean Democracy," in *Burying the Past: Making Peace and Doing Justice after Civil Conflict*, ed. Nigel Biggar (Washington, D.C.: Georgetown University Press, 2001), 150–83 (esp. 164).

12 FAV, Caja A.T. 61, Subsection "Informe Rettig: Comentarios, Aportes," Corte Suprema de Chile al Presidente de la República, Santiago, 13-v-91, public letter released to media.

13 For the previous two paragraphs related to the Chanfreau case, Erika Hennings, interview, 5-VI-97; Matus, *El libro negro de la justicia chilena*, 99–100; Luz Arce, *El infierno* (Santiago: Planeta, 1993), 348–74; *La Epoca*, 15-11-92, 19-11-92, 10-111-92 (Arce's return and court confrontation with Godoy); *LHOT*, 184–93; and AFDD, *Un camino de imágenes*, 122. On the notoriousness of Krassnoff and Romo, which was confirmed to me by their repeated mention in the case files I researched at ACNVR, good starting points are Arce, *El infierno*; and Marcia Alejandra Merino Vega, *Mi verdad: "Más allá del horror, yo acuso . . ."* (Santiago: A.T.G., 1993). Cf. the chilling interview book by Nancy Guzmán, *Romo: Confesiones de un torturador* (Santiago: Planeta, 2000), esp. 148–49 for Krassnoff's fusion of anti-Semitism and anti-Communism; and for comparative analysis,

see Leigh Payne, *Unsettling Accounts: Neither Truth nor Reconciliation in Confessions of State Violence* (Durham, N.C.: Duke University Press, 2008).

14 Arce, *El infierno*, 369; I am also grateful to Erika Hennings, interview, 5-VI-97, for discussing the difficulties of court testimony and confrontations.

15 *LHOT*, 185–86.

16 On the Patio 29 affair, see *LHOT*, 125–26; and also note 28 in this chapter. For a summary of 1991–92 activities by relatives of the disappeared, see AFDD, *Un camino de imágenes*, 112–23; for the Chanfreau case and the subsequent stream of court cases, notes 13, 17 in this chapter.

17 For the specific points cited, see Edgardo Boeninger, *Democracia en Chile: Lecciones para la gobernabilidad* (Santiago: Editorial Andrés Bello, 1997), 412–13; *LHOT*, 218; Correa, "Cenicienta se queda en la fiesta," 300–301; Correa, " 'No Victorious Army Has Ever Been Prosecuted . . . ,' " 135–42; Hilbink, "Un Estado de derecho no liberal," 325–26, cf. 319 n. 13; and Hilbink, "An Exception to Chilean Exceptionalism?" 80–83. Also illuminating and pertinent are Barahona de Brito, *Human Rights and Democratization in Latin America*, 175–84; and Brian Loveman and Elizabeth Lira, *El espejismo de la reconciliación política: Chile, 1990–2002* (Santiago: LOM, 2002), 94–97.

18 For growth statistics and Chile's reputation as a "model" in the early 1990s, see Barry P. Bosworth, Rudiger Dornbusch, and Raúl Labán, eds., *The Chilean Economy: Policy Lessons and Challenges* (Washington, D.C.: Brookings Institution, 1994), 32–33 for GNP growth; and for approval ratings and citizen optimism in surveys, Otano, *Crónica de la transición*, 295–97. Cf. BF, Encuestas Collection, "Los chilenos y la democracia" series, 1991–1994," by M. A. Garretón et al. and Corporación Participa, "Informe 1992" (*n* = 1503), cuadros 12, 14. See also Carlos Huneeus, *Chile, un país dividido: La actualidad del pasado* (Santiago: Catalonia, 2003), 130–31 and figs. 4.2, 4.3.

19 On the Cereceda affair and the new political environment on justice, see Matus, *El libro negro de la justicia chilena*, 100–24; *LHOT*, 184–93 (including 193 n. 16); Correa, "Cenicienta se queda en la fiesta," 303–4; and Loveman and Lira, *El espejismo de la reconciliación política*, 97–107. Cf. this chapter's notes 17, 20.

20 For more detail on the May 1993 events, their aftermath, and the second round of the Pinocheques affair, see Otano, *Crónica de la transición*, 306–35; and *LHOT*, 194–226. See also Boeninger, *Democracia en Chile*, 410–17; and note 25 in this chapter.

21 See this chapter's notes 20, 25.

22 On the August 1991 announcement and broader political strategy, the best journalistic treatment is Otano, *Crónica de la transición*, 187–92 (190 for Aylwin quote); and for the infrastructure project, see Aylwin, *La transición chilena*, 288–94. Otano emphasizes the role of the "end of transition" announcement as political maneuver to puncture trial balloon speculation—and to signal an end to Aylwin's temptation—that the president might, in view of administra-

tion success, seek an extension of his presidency. Otano's account is perceptive but too narrow. The larger issue in play was overall political strategy and the desire for a second-phase agenda of the Aylwin presidency. The latter would enable the administration to avoid falling into political stagnation and repetition, according to the strategic advising group coordinated by Edgardo Boeninger. For political strategy, see Boeninger, *Democracia en Chile*, 379–526, esp. 379–82, 407–8, 428–33; and for the role of polling data, *LHOT*, 124–25. I am grateful to Sol Serrano for pushing me to understand the desire to develop a new political agenda. For state-society relations and a new model of citizen participation, see the searching critical analysis of Julia Paley, *Marketing Democracy: Power and Social Movements in Post-dictatorship Chile* (Berkeley: University of California Press, 2001); cf. James Petras and Fernando Ignacio Leiva with Henry Veltmeyer, *Democracy and Poverty in Chile: The Limits to Electoral Politics* (Boulder, Colo.: Westview Press, 1994), 148–52. For a more positive presentation, see Aylwin, *La transición chilena*, 204–7.

23 My account is an interpretation based on the entire record of the Aylwin presidency, but it also relies on the indispensable and lucid exposition of administration strategy by Boeninger, *Democracia en Chile*, 379–90, 400–408, also 408–33, 445–46. For the ups and downs of judicial policy specifically, see note 11 in this chapter. Barahona de Brito, "Passion, Constraint, Law, and *Fortuna*," 150–83 (151 for quotes), analyzes how the multiplicity of pertinent variables including law and *fortuna* (the latter in the sense invoked by Machiavelli) opened up a breach between intention and result. In this perspective, she sees the quest for truth and justice during the Aylwin years as a mainly "political phase" that did not give way to a mainly "judicial phase" until the Frei presidency of 1994–2000.

24 For Pinochet's proposals, see *LHOT*, 218–19; and for Aylwin's sense that he was trying to balance the justice imperative on one side, and the stability imperative on the other, his personal note (30-VI-93) to Patricia Verdugo, *Bucarest 187* (Santiago: Editorial Sudamericana, 1999), 246.

25 For Aylwin's proposal and its unraveling, FAV, Recortes, "Ley Aylwin" (press clippings file), esp. *El Mercurio, La Epoca, La Nación*, 4–5-VIII-93, *El Siglo*, 4-VIII-93 (Aylwin speech, immediate reactions); *La Epoca, La Nación, El Mercurio*, 8-VIII-93 (additional reactions and synthesis; *La Nación* for Andrés Aylwin interview, and advertisements by AFDD and CODEPU, and AFDD quote); *La Tercera*, 12-VIII-93, and *La Epoca*, 16-VIII-93 (hunger strike); *El Mercurio*, 2–3-IX-93 ("urgency" status retired); AFDD, *Un camino de imágenes*, 128–29; and Patricio Aylwin, interview, 20-VI-97 (quote). See also *Qué Pasa*, 12-VI-93, pp. 14–18, for anticipation of a "true final stop" in the Center-Right; and Loveman and Lira, *El espejismo de la reconciliación política*, 109–26, for a fine account with additional detail.

26 See Otano, *Crónica de la transición*, 356.

27 For memory as politicocultural "work," see the astute reflections by Elizabeth Jelin, *Los trabajos de la memoria* (Madrid: Siglo Veintiuno, 2002).

28 On human rights as public value and indifference to human rights as public taboo, one might draw an analogy to the problem of racism in the United States. The civil rights revolution of the 1950s and 1960s did not eliminate racism or racial discrimination, which persisted as issues requiring political attention and justice. But among its (limited) achievements, the civil rights revolution did delegitimize racism and drive it to a more underground status. I am grateful to Father José Aldunate for discussions (interview, 10-1-97, and several conversations before and after the interview) about changes in Chilean culture and ethical sensibilities related to human rights.

On Pinochet as the great exception and on the Patio 29 controversy, see *LHOT*, 125–26. Cf. Otano, *Crónica*, 199–200; and *Punto Final*, 9-IX-91. The exhumed bodies of the disappeared at Patio 29 inspired two important documentary films: *Patio 29: Histories of Silence [edition with English subtitles]*, directed by Esteban Larraín (VHS, sponsored by FONDART Chile [Fondo del Desarrollo de las Artes y la Cultura] and Ford Foundation, 1998), which includes footage of Pinochet's "economizing" remark; and *Fernando ha vuelto*, directed by Silvio Caiozzi (1998; DVD expanded ed., Andrea Films, 2006), which focuses on the story of Fernando Olivares Mori, whose remains at Patio 29 were finally positively identified and returned to the family and who was buried on 22-IV-1998. In April 2006, however, serious doubt arose about the validity of identification; the 2006 edition of the documentary includes a powerful interview, shortly after the notification, with Agave Díaz, the widow.

29 On memory struggles and their politicocultural consequences during the dictatorship years, and on the targeting and evolution of the Left specifically, see trilogy Book Two. For Rettig Commission findings on targets of repression, see chapter 2 of this book; and for political experience and evolution of Left leaders, Katherine Hite, *When the Romance Ended: Leaders of the Chilean Left, 1968–1998* (New York: Columbia University Press, 2000).

30 The explosive expansion and symbolic diversification of the dissident memory camp in the 1980s are analyzed in trilogy Book Two, part II.

31 BF, Encuestas Collection, CEP: "Estudio social y de opinión pública No. 21," Octubre 1993 (*n* = 1820), cuadro 9; M. A. Garretón et al. and Corporación Participa, "Los chilenos y la democracia. La opinión pública, 1991–1994: Informe 1993" (*n* = 1498), cuadro 13e; *LHOT*, 229. For additional data on approval ratings and optimism about the future, see note 18 in this chapter.

32 Zalaquett, interview, 23-IV-97; cf. Margarita Serrano and Ascanio Cavallo, *El poder de la paradoja: 14 lecciones políticas de la vida de Patricio Aylwin* (Santiago: Editorial Norma, 2006), 272–73. I should add that in our interview (20-VI-97), Aylwin also observed that Justice Minister Francisco Cumplido was a close

collaborator in formulating initiatives and policy on truth and justice issues; the accounts in LHOT, Matus (*El libro negro de la justicia chilena*), and Otano (*Crónica de la transición*) are consistent with this statement.

33 Aylwin interview in *Mensaje*, January–February 1994, pp. 27–35; Otano, *Crónica de la transición*, 353–55, 366–67, to whom I am greatly indebted for this interpretation of Aylwin's final months. Cf. Serrano and Cavallo, *El poder de la paradoja*, 276–77. On political prisoners, see also chapter 1 in this volume.

34 Sola Sierra, interview, 26-III-97.

35 FAV, Iglesia de Santiago, "Separata," no. 15, October 1991, "Gracias, Vicaría de la Solidaridad," (Aylwin speech and quotes), copy supplied to author; AFDD, *Un camino de imágenes*, 123 (commemoration and plaque). For a superb study of distinct memory frameworks about the Catholic Church and human rights within Catholic communities in the 1990s, and the ways the closing down of the Vicaría figured in the politics and culture of Catholic memory, see María Angélica Cruz, *Iglesia, represión y memoria: El caso chileno* (Madrid: Siglo Veintiuno, 2004).

36 AFDD, *Recuento de actividades 1990*, 85.

Afterword to Chapter 3: The Sound of Tick-Tock

1 On the three foreign assaults discussed in this and the next three paragraphs, including the international and judicial aspects, background on the leaders targeted, and the ways the assaults played out as memory knots inside Chile, a starting point is Book Two of this trilogy: Stern, *Battling for Hearts and Minds: Memory Struggles in Pinochet's Chile, 1973–1988* (Durham, N.C.: Duke University Press, 2006), 100–101, 106–8, 137–78 (esp. 144–48), also 22, 55, 63. On the Letelier case and its wider context, the fundamental sources are John Dinges and Saul Landau, *Assassination on Embassy Row* (New York: Pantheon, 1980); Taylor Branch and Eugene Propper, *Labyrinth* (New York: Viking, 1982); Alejandra Matus Acuña and Francisco Javier Artaza, *Crimen con castigo* (Santiago: Ediciones B, La Nación, 1996); Peter Kornbluh, *The Pinochet File: A Declassified Dossier on Atrocity and Accountability* (New York: New Press, 2003), 341–412, 429–42 (including documents 1–5), 462–68; and John Dinges, *The Condor Years: How Pinochet and His Allies Brought Terrorism to Three Continents* (New York: New Press, 2004). See also Manuel Salazar, *Contreras: Historia de un intocable* (Santiago: Grijalbo, 1995). Unless otherwise noted, the following discussion of the Letelier and other assaults and the ways they played out are gleaned from the sources in this note.

2 ASXX, Ministerio de Educación, Reservados 1974, tomo 5, DINA, "Síntesis informativo no. 6 (Período . . . Noviembre)," Santiago, 11-XII-74, 7.

3 The political turbulence of 1978 and the amnesty law and idea of institutionalization as part of a new memory strategy are analyzed and documented in trilogy Book Two, 137–78, esp. 146–54.

4 See for "favor" and "warned" quotes, respectively, U.S. Department of State FOIA [Freedom of Information Act] Electronic Reading Room, http://foia.state.gov, link paths: Declassified/Released Document Collections, Chile Declassification Project Tranche III: *State*, Memorandum, "Issuance of Visas," 1-IX-76 (document number 13 if one queries "Stroessner," cf. document 8); and CIA, report on "Indictment of Former DINA Director," 24-VIII-78. The "bottom line" strategy of Pinochet and his negotiated exclusion from personal accountability in the Letelier case is a sensitive point, first put forth forcefully in 1980 by Dinges and Landau, *Assassination on Embassy Row*, 337–38, 364–66, 391–92, also 329–32; cf. Branch and Propper, *Labyrinth*, 435–82 (esp. 435–36, 471–72, 474–76), also 351–54, 598–600. The irony is that Landau smelled foolishness and ultimately blocked the Paraguayan route; the agents ended up relying on Chilean passports. It is fair to note, too, that not all officials and agencies of the U.S. government were inclined to handle the Letelier-Moffitt case in the same way. The case mobilized multiple logics—the most obvious was justice versus diplomacy, but even within the latter, the interest in asserting the unacceptability of foreign state terrorism on United States soil competed with reluctance to press the Pinochet regime *too* hard. The officials in play derived from multiple agencies including the Justice Department, FBI, State Department, CIA, and national security apparatus. Nonetheless, the documents cited above and the superb research of Peter Kornbluh and John Dinges have documented Pinochet's involvement not only in the murder conspiracy, but also the strategy of cover-up and damage control. See Kornbluh, *The Pinochet File*, 397–401; and Dinges, *The Condor Years*, 175–77, 192–93, 247. Cf. trilogy Book Two, 432 n. 35.

5 On the exhausting legal maneuvers of the 1980s, I am grateful to Fabiola Letelier, conversation, 27-V-97. See also Matus Acuña, *Crimen con castigo*, 212–14; and the chronology of the Letelier case in Salazar, *Contreras*, 181–93, esp. 185–86.

6 The time bomb metaphor was already invoked for the human rights theme in 1989 by the conservative magazine *Qué Pasa*, 5-1-89 (see cover and lead story); cf. its use as a framing device in the fine study of Brian Loveman and Elizabeth Lira, *El espejismo de la reconciliación política: Chile, 1990–2002* (Santiago: LOM, 2002), 175–221 (and which also reproduces the *Qué Pasa* cover on 176).

7 An account of Lonquén and its handling by Bañados, with guide to documents and sources, is in trilogy Book Two, 156–67; on Bañados as judge, see also Alejandra Matus, *El libro negro de la justicia chilena* (Santiago: Planeta, 1999), 57–59, 72–73, 117.

8 See chapter 1 in this volume on the Pisagua episode and tensions about media reports.

9 TVNCD, Cintas BT9–000517 and BTC6–3838, *Informe Especial*, 16-VIII-93 (program and quotes): "Michael Townley: Las confesiones de un asesino." On the larger media and political aspects, see note 10.

10 For the wider political and media context, including the postponement question and Bañados as judge, see *LHOT*, 220; Otano, *Crónica de la transición*, 329–30; Matus, *El libro negro de la justicia chilena*, 57–59, 72–73, 117; *La Tercera*, 18-VIII-93 (33-point television rating); for minor scandal and tension of Enrique Correa, e.g., *El Siglo*, 4-VIII-93; *El Mercurio*, 5-VIII-93; *La Tercera*, 11-VIII-93; *El Mercurio*, 17-VIII-93; and for detailed file of press accounts in August on the Letelier case, FAV, Recortes Letelier, Cajas 3-III-93–20-VIII-93, 21-VIII-93–13-XI-93.

11 TVN, *Informe Especial*, 11-IX-93, video copy viewed courtesy of Teresa Valdés.

12 TVNCD, Cintas BT6–4420 and BT6–4421, *Informe Especial*, 18-XI-93. Bañados ruled on 12-XI-93; see *El Mercurio*, 13-XI-93.

Chapter 4: Between Prudence and Convulsion

1 Joaquín Lavín, *Chile: Revolución silenciosa* (Santiago: Zig-Zag, 1987). The characterization of supermarkets and book corners in the 1990s is based on personal observations, July 1996 to August 1997.

2 Conversations with Alicia M., esp. 29-VII-96. On litigation, a good starting point is Patricia Verdugo, *Los zarpazos del puma* (1989; rev. ed., Santiago: CESOC, 1994), 289–353.

3 For a compelling and concise discussion of the hegemony concept, its relationship to cultural languages of dispute, and relevant scholarly genealogy, see William Roseberry, "Hegemony and the Language of Contention," in *Everyday Forms of State Formation: Revolution and the Negotiation of Rule in Modern Mexico*, ed. Gilbert M. Joseph and Daniel Nugent (Durham, N.C.: Duke University Press, 1994), 355–66; cf. Florencia E. Mallon, *Peasant and Nation: The Making of Postcolonial Mexico and Peru* (Berkeley: University of California Press, 1995), esp. 6–20.

4 See the revealing retrospective by Andrés Allamand, *La travesía del desierto* (Santiago: Aguilar, 1999), 352–61, on the scandal in 1993, when he openly complained about "poderes fácticos," and the turn in conservative circles to more matter-of-fact and public usage by 1996.

5 On the intimacy of the memory question in the mid-to-late 1990s and for fuller portraits of the people just mentioned, see Book One of this trilogy: Stern, *Remembering Pinochet's Chile: On the Eve of London 1998* (Durham, N.C.: Duke University Press, 2004).

6 See Alex Wilde's pioneering essay, "Irruptions of Memory: Expressive Politics in Chile's Transition to Democracy," *Journal of Latin American Studies* 31 (1999): 473–500. Wilde (475) defines memory irruptions as "public events that break in

upon Chile's national consciousness, unbidden and often suddenly, to evoke associations with symbols, figures, causes, ways of life which to an unusual degree are associated with a political past that is still present in the lived experience of a major part of the population." His irruptions are either "haphazard events," such as political assassinations or discovery of cadavers, that suddenly revive the "sinister past," or events triggered by state actors, especially the military, beyond democratic control (486). My use of the term *convulsions* includes a wider range of events and social actors triggering charged debate and agitation in the public domain, but our conceptual overlap is obvious and I gratefully acknowledge my debt to his valuable reflection.

7   An example of unforeseen deep upset occurred in my interview with Magdalena U., 26-v-97, a human rights activist. We had scheduled the interview for a date that coincided with the loss of a disappeared friend. When the day arrived, it functioned as a memory knot. She was notably agitated and found herself needing to tell people about the fate of her friend.

8   On Frei's personal style, background, and priorities, see *LHOT*, 237, cf. 304–5; and for acute analysis of tensions between "pact" and "project" in the politics of the 1990s, and the Frei administration's emphasis on modernization in this context, Claudio Fuentes, "Partidos y coaliciones en el Chile de los '90: Entre pactos y proyectos," in *El modelo chileno: Democracia y desarrollo en los noventa*, ed. Paul Drake and Iván Jaksic (Santiago: LOM, 1999), 191–222. For modernization of the state and social policy, as well as society at large, as a key leitmotif in wide-ranging discussions about public policy, including international aspects, see, e.g., FLACSO-Chile (Facultad Latinoamericana de Ciencias Sociales—Chile), *Chile 96: Análisis y opiniones* (Santiago: FLACSO, 1997); FLACSO-Chile, *Chile 97: Análisis y opiniones* (Santiago: FLACSO, 1998); and Cristián Toloza and Eugenio Lahera, eds., *Chile en los años noventa* (Santiago: Presidencia de la República and Dolmen Ed., 1998). See also José Miguel Insulza, *Ensayos sobre político exterior de Chile* (Santiago: Los Andes, 1998), esp. 1993 concept paper reprinted on 31–49, for the international dimension as conceptualized by an architect of Frei policies.

9   *LHOT*, 255 (quote). Illustration of the broader shift in tone will become evident in the remainder of this chapter.

10 See *LHOT*, 255, 245–53; and for the 1980s context and significance of the murder of the "three professionals," Book Two of this trilogy: Stern, *Battling for Hearts and Minds: Memory Struggles in Pinochet's Chile, 1973–1988* (Durham, N.C.: Duke University Press, 2006), 282–83, 310, 322, 328–29.

11 The Supreme Court later approved counting as time served 472 days of prior arrest, mostly preventive detention at the Military Hospital in 1978–79 during resolution of an extradition request by the United States. *La Nación*, 19-VIII-93 (quote and defiance). Cf. *Ultimas Noticias*, *El Mercurio*, 21-VIII-93; and *La Tercera*, 22-VIII-93. For 1995 sentencing and consequences, see note 12; and for

the inside story on the Punta Peuco arrangement, LHOT, 264–72. See also Margarita Serrano and Ascanio Cavallo, *El poder de la paradoja: 14 lecciones políticas de la vida de Patricio Aylwin* (Santiago: Editorial Norma, 2006), 51–52.

12 For the quotes that follow, see *El Mercurio*, 31-V-95 ("not going"); and *La Epoca*, 1-VI-95 ("wounded"). For the Pinochet interview, see *El Mercurio*, 5-VI-95. The chronology provided is synthesized from press accounts, well organized in FAV, Recortes, 4.7.15.2 (Caso Letelier). On the day after specific dates cited, see *El Mercurio*, *La Epoca*, *La Nación*, which may be supplemented by *La Tercera*, *Ultimas Noticias*, and on a same-day basis, the afternoon newspaper *La Segunda*. For information and context, I also drew on the following: *Latin America Weekly Report* (London), esp. 15-VI-95, p. 253, 29-VI-95, p. 284, 3-VIII-95, p. 339, 10-VIII-95, p. 359, and 31-VIII-95, p. 388 (events including tacit or off-the-record pressures); Ramiro I. and Claudia de I., interview, 6–7-11-97 (rumors, Osorno area); Fabiola Letelier, conversation, 27-V-97 (uncertainty and tension in political circles about whether to allow Contreras to serve out his sentence at a military base); LHOT, 273–303 (esp. 280–81, 283–84, on Pérez Yoma's secret consent to transfer to Talcahuano; cf. *Qué Pasa*, 24-VI-95, p. 17, and "Anuario 1995," p. 25); and Alejandra Matus Acuña and Francisco Javier Artaza, *Crimen con castigo* (Santiago: Diario La Nación, 1996), esp. 271–95. See also note 13; and for an early reflective essay, José Rodríguez Elizondo, *La ley es más fuerte: Civiles y militares chilenos a la luz de un proceso histórico* (Buenos Aires: Editorial Zeta, 1995).

13 See *El Mercurio*, 27-VII-95; *New York Times*, 20-VI-95 ("technical coup"); and Camilo Escalona, *Una transición de dos caras: Crónica crítica y autocrítica* (Santiago: LOM, 1999), 86–87 (86 for "crazy"). I am also grateful to Juan Pablo Letelier, conversation, 1-XI-99, for insight on varied Socialist responses to political pressures and anxieties of the Contreras case.

14 Significantly, those who thought Contreras would actually go to jail *declined* to 42 percent in September. For CERC (Centro de Estudios de la Realidad Chilena) poll results of July and the September decline, see Carlos Huneeus, *Chile, un país dividido: La actualidad del pasado* (Santiago: Catalonia, 2003), 187, 186, 194–95. The CERC results—with the notable exception of findings on whether people *thought* Contreras would go to jail—were at the time widely publicized: see, e.g., *La Tercera*, 21-VII-95.

15 On interests of both Pinochet and the Frei administration in avoiding the logic of a coup undermining the transition, and on the military process of pressuring and persuading Contreras that he would have to accept another patriotic sacrifice for the larger good, see the retrospectives by *La Epoca* and *El Mercurio*, 22-X-95. Cf. *Qué Pasa*, 24-VI-95, p. 17, "Anuario 1995," pp. 25, 42; and LHOT, 273–303, esp. 277–78.

16 On Frei and the Consejo, see LHOT, 291–94 (293 for quote); on the administration's human rights proposal in the larger juridical and political context, press

clippings assembled by FAV, Recortes, "Derechos humanos 1995–1996"; FAV, Subsection "Banco de datos de la prensa sobre derechos humanos," June–December 1995; and Allamand, *La travesía del desierto,* esp. 435–64. Cf. Escalona, *Una transición de dos caras,* 80–85. For a close and reliable analysis of the Frei proposal, the Figueroa-Otero accord, and public domain debate, see Brian Loveman and Elizabeth Lira, *El espejismo de la reconciliación política: Chile 1990–2002* (Santiago: LOM, 2002), 148–72. Frei shrewdly proposed two other reform projects simultaneously—one a restoration of presidential power to retire generals, the other a package of democratic reforms of the 1980 Constitution including abolition of designated senator seats. For the original formulation, see *El Mercurio, La Epoca, La Tercera,* 21–22-VIII-95; and for shrewd analysis of the three-way proposals in political context, *Hoy,* 21-VIII-95, pp. 8–10. On linkage to the Contreras affair, see also *Qué Pasa,* "Anuario 1995," pp. 25, 42; and on prisoners at Punta Peuco in 1996, Loveman and Lira, *El espejismo de la reconciliación política,* 181–82, and Jorge Correa Sutil with Francisco Jiménez, "'No Victorious Army Has Ever Been Prosecuted . . .': The Unsettled Story of Transitional Justice in Chile," in *Transitional Justice and the Rule of Law in New Democracies,* ed. A. James McAdams (Notre Dame, Ind.: University of Notre Dame Press, 1997), 146–47.

17 The description given in the three preceding paragraphs is synthetic, based on many conversations and field observations in 1996–97, in addition to the specific "convulsion" incidents discussed in the next two sections of this chapter. I should also acknowledge my debt to Erica Eppinger, a student researcher of the Agrupación de Familiares de Detenidos-Desaparecidos, conversations, esp. 22-VIII-96; the Agrupación leaders Viviana Díaz and Sola Sierra, conversations, esp. 3-IX-96, and interview with Sierra, 26-III-97, for insights on the relatively sophisticated ways political elites ambivalently sought to close the memory box in the 1990s—through postponed meetings, nonverbal signs of weariness, verbal affirmations of a split between political heart (desire for truth and justice) and political head (calculation of the realistic and the possible), and the like.

18 On the Soria affair, see esp. *La Epoca,* 25-VIII-96; and for political fallout, including a failed constitutional accusation against Supreme Court justices, *El Mercurio,* 15-IX-96.

19 See *El Mercurio, La Epoca,* 23–24-VII-96 (24-VII-96 for quotes).

20 See *El Mercurio, La Epoca,* 30–31-VII-96 (*La Epoca,* 30-VII-96 for quotes).

21 See *El Mercurio,* 1-VIII-96; *La Epoca,* 2-VIII-96; *Hoy,* 5-VIII-96, pp. 4–10, for an excellent and broad review.

22 *La Epoca, El Mercurio,* 4-IX-96 (quotes).

23 *La Epoca,* 5-IX-96 (quotes; cf. *Ultimas Noticias*); and also *La Epoca, El Mercurio,* 8-IX-96.

24 I attended the 11-IX-96 protest march and speeches. The Communist Party newspaper *El Siglo,* 13-IX-96, was the only press publication I could find that

quoted the "monument" remark (prominently, on the front page version, with a slightly less dramatic phrasing in the prepared text reprinted inside). For the additional quotes cited, see *La Epoca*, 30-x-96; and for the tenor of press coverage, *El Mercurio*, *La Epoca*, *La Tercera*, *Ultimas Noticias*, 30-x-96–1-xi-96. On the lack of wisdom of the Marín arrest, I also benefited from an off-the-record conversation with a prominent journalist influential in Concertación circles. The estimate of 10,000 marchers follows a conservative methodology. It compromises between the lowball figure (8,000) of conservative newspapers and the higher one (12,000) of experienced activists, and is consistent with my own street observations but much smaller than the 20,000 given by *El Siglo*. For Gladys Marín's life story in her own words, see *La vida es hoy* (Santiago: Edebé, 2002), 186–92, for her account of the September 1996 speech and subsequent arrest. On the abduction and disappearance of her husband, Jorge Muñoz, see also *DETDES*, 5:1765–68.

25 The first quote came from Pinochet's appearance on the Megavisión channel, on the program *Meganoticias* with Alicia de la Cruz, 21-ix-95. For the quote, I used the version given in *Ultimas Noticias*, 22-ix-95, but publicity was very widespread. See also *El Mercurio*, *La Epoca*, *La Cuarta*, 22-ix-95. See also Pinochet's comments on the virtues of olvido and amnesty in the expanded version of his interview-book with Raquel Correa and Elizabeth Subercaseaux, *Ego Sum* (Santiago: Planeta, 1996), 124–25, 185–86, 224. The second set of quotes came from a widely promoted and publicized interview on the La Red channel, by the sports and television personality Eduardo Bonvallet on his *Noche de Bomba* program, 7-vi-97. I watched the program and took notes. For news coverage, see *El Mercurio*, 7-vi-97; and *La Epoca*, 8-vi-97. Ironically, notwithstanding Pinochet's complaints of olvido, his reference to 15,000 foreign guerillas sent to arm and train Chileans to commit a bloodbath was itself a memory allusion easily recognizable to middle-aged and elderly Chileans. It evoked the apocryphal "Plan Z" conspiracy, heavily publicized in 1973. For analysis of Plan Z's veracity and uses as propaganda and "inside-game" politics, see trilogy Book Two, 41–55. Theoretical perspective on memory struggles in history as a pitting of one selective framework of "meaning of the past" against another, rather than flat struggle of memory against forgetting, is developed in trilogy Book One; cf. Elizabeth Jelin, *Los trabajos de la memoria* (Madrid: Siglo Veintiuno, 2002).

26 See *El Mercurio*, *La Epoca*, *La Tercera*, 31-xii-96 for initial reports on the escape, and extensive press coverage and controversy about state security and intelligence over the next month; cf. *Punto Final*, January 1997. For connections to internal Frente political dynamics, see *El Rodriguista*, December 1996–January 1997; and *Hoy*, 13-1-97, pp. 12–15. On television news, see Giselle Munizaga, "Qué vieron los chilenos en la agenda televisa del año 1996," in FLACSO-Chile, *Chile 96*, 57–65, esp. statistics on 60, 62.E

27 The Chilean newspaper that broke the story (the original interview was in *Excelsior* [Mexico City], 29-III-97) and promoted it aggressively was the afternoon daily *La Segunda*, 31-III-97 (initial quotes); and 1-IV-97, for reprint of interview and quotes of army reaction (cf. *El Mercurio*, 2-IV-97, for full army text). For ongoing polemics, see esp. *La Segunda*, 2-IV-97 (public letter of former ministers); *El Mercurio*, 3-IV-97 (polemics on whether army reply is political interference); 6-IV-97 (off-the-record quote from La Moneda); 8-IV-97 (political speculations); and *Hoy*, 7-IV-97, pp. 4–5 (political speculations and moral sensibilities). I also wish to thank Jorge Cauas, interview, 9-VI-97, who signed the letter of former ministers, and Patricio Aylwin, interview, 20-VI-97, for discussing the incident with me. Cauas considered divisive remarks about the past by a former president negative for the future of Chile and, not coincidentally, the legacy of military rule as very positive. Aylwin considered the reaction to the interview a sign that the recent past was still traumatic, an experience of profound consequence in the generations that lived the rupture of 1973 and subsequent military rule. In Pinochet's June 1997 television appearance, he was specifically asked about Aylwin's remarks.

28 For theoretical discussion and specific historical application to the case of Mexican history, see Joseph and Nugent, eds., *Everyday Forms of State Formation*; for the related idea of conflictive synergies, see chapters 1–3 in this volume.

29 On the dangers of generational stagnation and ritual repetition, see the illuminating essay on Argentina by Elizabeth Jelin, "La política de la memoria: El movimiento de derechos humanos y la construcción democrática en la Argentina," in *Juicio, castigo y memoria: Derechos humanos y justicia en la política argentina*, ed. Carlos H. Acuña (Buenos Aires: Nueva Visión SAIC, 1995), 101–46, esp. 143. The sense that memory activities were being deemed less notable and newsworthy by media, and the necessity to break out of impasse and stagnation, was a subtext that loomed in a number of activities involving members of the Agrupación de Familiares de Detenidos Desaparecidos (AFDD) and other activists in 1996–97. In this regard, comments at three forums I attended were significant—Seminario Internacional "Impunidad y sus efectos en los procesos democráticos," organized by CODEPU, FASIC, and SERPAJ, activist comments at Comisión 4, "Métodos de lucha y experiencias de superación...," Santiago, 13–15-XII-96; AFDD, *Un camino de imágenes... que revelan y se rebelan contra una historia no contada: 20 años...* (Santiago: AFDD, 1997), book launch at BN, 26-III-97, conversation with Sola Sierra about news media responses to AFDD faxes and book launch activities; and public discussion and comment at forum-panel on impunity, organized by AFDD, Santiago, 5-VI-97.

30 See *La Epoca*, 31-VII-96, 6-VIII-96; *El Mercurio*, 6-VIII-96; and *Punto Final*, 4-VIII-96. The Spanish judicial proceedings were considered in most quarters not likely to produce tangible results, but the procedural steps in the case did produce small intermittent notices in the Chilean press in 1997.

31 Seminario Internacional "Impunidad y sus efectos en los procesos democráticos," Santiago, 13–15-XII-96. I was present throughout as a participant-observer. Data cited are from the conference documents (including the "Comunicado" issued as a final report on January 1997; in possession of author), in addition to my field notes. Statistics are from participant list; the Pérez Esquivel quote is from prepared text version of speech; organizer quotes are from the program booklet, p. 13. For press coverage in Chile, which was modest, see *Ultimas Noticias, La Nación, La Epoca,* 16-XII-96.

32 The paper given by Richard J. Wilson at the Seminario Internacional, "Un tribunal penal internacional permanente: La impunidad pierde otro round," informed conference activists about developments related to the UN and the International Criminal Court. For the basics on ratification and pressures from the United States in 2002, see *New York Times,* 1-VII-02, 3-VII-02, also 28-VI-02, 10-VIII-02, 7-IX-02. I wish to acknowledge my intellectual debt to Yvonne Geerts, whose research as an undergraduate at the University of Wisconsin, Madison, illuminated my understanding of the International Criminal Court and of Third World networks of participation and influence in its creation. Analytical issues about world culture and politics raised by creation of the court—the emergence of new kinds of transnational activist and advocacy networks in the late twentieth century, the role of human rights issues and globalization itself in generating such communities—lie beyond the scope of this chapter. Two fine starting points from political science and sociology perspectives are Margaret E. Keck and Kathryn Sikkink, *Activists beyond Borders: Advocacy Networks in International Politics* (Ithaca, N.Y.: Cornell University Press, 1997); and Sidney Tarrow, *The New Transnational Activism* (New York: Cambridge University Press, 2005). Cf. Peter M. Haas, "Introduction: Epistemic Communities and International Policy Coordination," *International Organization* 46, no. 1 (winter 1992), 2–35.

33 For prizewinning theses published by the ex-Vicaría documentation center known as the Fundación de Documentación y Archivo de la Vicaría de la Solidaridad (FAV), see, e.g., Consuelo Pérez Mendoza, *Los protagonistas de la prensa alternativa: Vicaría de la Solidaridad y Fundación de Ayuda Social de las Iglesias Cristianas* (Santiago: FAV, 1997); Graciela Alejandra Lúnecke Reyes, *Violencia política (Violencia política en Chile. 1983–1986)* (Santiago: FAV, 2000); and María José Reyes Andreani and María Francisca Jurcic Cerda, *El Sí-No de la reconciliación: Representaciones sociales de la reconciliación nacional en los jóvenes* (Santiago: FAV, 2000). For activities and projects of relatives of the disappeared, and for the photo-book project, see AFDD, *Un camino de imágenes;* and for the annual round of permanent commemorations, November 1996 AFDD pamphlet (in possession of author), entitled "AFDD: Agrupación de Familiares de Detenidos-Desaparecidos." Additional accounts of AFDD activities are summarized in the monthly bulletin (published since 1994) *Informativo* (copies in

possession of author). The additional dates marking permanent commemorative activities were International Week of the Detained-and-Disappeared, 25–31 May; Romería to Cemetery of Isla de Maipo (remembrance of Lonquén), 7 October; and Romería to Memorial at Santiago General Cemetery, 1 November. For the journalism testimonial, see Ernesto Carmona, ed., *Morir es la noticia: Los periodistas relatan la historia de sus compañeros asesinados y/o desaparecidos* (Santiago: J&C Productores, 1997); and for an interview with Carmona on the project, *La Epoca*, 29-III-97. I attended the book launch at the BN, 20-III-97.

34 The "Primer Festival Internacional de Cine Documental" took place in Santiago at the Goethe Institute, 6–17-v-97; the number of screenings is based on the institute's festival flyer and calendar (in possession of author); the 300–500 figure for well-attended screenings is based on personal observation and notes; Guzmán's *La batalla de Chile* had been produced in three parts, 1974–78. For related press reports, see *La Epoca*, 9-v-97, 12-v-97; and *El Mercurio*, 14-v-97, 17-v-97. For an insightful appraisal by a literary and cultural studies scholar, see Nelly Richard, "Con motivo del 11 de septiembre: Notas sobre La Memoria Obstinada (1996) de Patricio Guzmán," orig. 1998, repr. in *Escrituras, imágenes y escenarios ante la represión*, Elizabeth Jelin and Ana Longoni (Madrid: Siglo Veintiuno, 2005), 121–29.

35 On memory organizing and sensibilities in Iquique and Pisagua during the dictatorship and democratic transition, see Lessie Jo Frazier, *Salt in the Sand: Memory, Violence, and the Nation-State in Chile, 1890 to the Present* (Durham, N.C.: Duke University Press, 2007), esp. 158–89. For Concepción, I relied on my field notes, 20-XII-96, and related photos. For regional memory sensibilities, see Alejandra Brito Peña, "Concepción: Un antes y un después," in *Memoria para un nuevo siglo: Chile, miradas a la segunda mitad del siglo XX*, ed. Mario Garcés et al. (Santiago: LOM, 2000), 463–68. Note that the militant coal-miner tradition in nearby Lota also figured in the fierce 1973 repression and that the alleged "Plan Z" conspiracy was first broken as a news story and conspiracy anchored in Concepción. See trilogy Book Two, 42–43, 98.

36 On La Victoria and commemoration of Jarlan, see the superb study of María Angélica Cruz, *Iglesia, represión y memoria: El caso chileno* (Madrid: Siglo Veintiuno, 2004), 83–119. Cruz's participant-observation took place in 2000, but the community's commemorative tradition began immediately upon Jarlan's death and continued through the 1990s, albeit with declining vigor in the mid-1990s. For additional background and sources, see trilogy Book Two, 270–72, 331, 456 n. 37.

37 My description of Villa Francia, Bolton, and Vergara is based on field notes, interviews, and historical research recounted and documented in Books One and Two of this trilogy: on the celebration of Father Bolton, see Book One, 65–67; and on the role of Rafael Vergara and his brother Eduardo as symbols of community memory, the bond of Rafael with Bolton, and Bolton's own role in

memory struggles, Book Two, 265–67, 455 n. 28, 90, 259–61, 270, 355. It should be noted, too, that some scholar-activists actively worked to encourage recuperation of community memories and histories in the mid-to-late 1990s. Especially impressive was the nongovernmental organization ECO (Educación y Comunicaciones), directed by Mario Garcés, whose work has encompassed Santiago, Valparaíso, and Concepción. A documentary record of its work is at ECOCD; see also www.eco-educacionycomunicaciones.cl, and for origins, trilogy Book Two, 207, 215–16. In 1998, ECO incorporated its tradition of local work into a national cultural intervention on memory in collaboration with the History Department of USACH (Universidad de Santiago), and drawing in a wide range of social actors and artists as well as scholars in the "preseminars" culminating in the conference: see Garcés et al., *Memoria para un nuevo siglo*. I should acknowledge that I collaborated with the committee that formulated the project, and gave a keynote lecture at the conference. The work on popular memory by ECO continued; I am grateful to Mario Garcés for inviting me to attend a community memory workshop held in La Legua in 2000, as part of a project to reconstruct with the community the events and experiences there of 11 September 1973, which included a rare instance of armed confrontation and had become legendary but about which basic facts were at the time uncertain. See the fascinating book that resulted: Mario Garcés and Sebastián Leiva, *El Golpe en La Legua: Los caminos de la historia y la memoria* (Santiago: LOM, 2005). For additional evidence of community interest in recovery of local memory via interaction with historians, in a rural and indigenous context, see the study of Nicolas Ailío and the methodology of work, begun in 1997, recounted by Florencia E. Mallon, *Courage Tastes of Blood: The Mapuche Community of Nicolás Ailío and the Chilean State, 1906–2001* (Durham, N.C.: Duke University Press, 2005).

38 On Villa Grimaldi's history, lore, and transformation into a memory site, I relied on Pedro Matta (a former Villa Grimaldi prisoner and historian-archivist of the Corporación Parque por la Paz Villa Grimaldi), conversation and tour of Peace Park site during final phase of construction, 12-1-97; ACPPVG: "Proyecto Parque por la Paz [1996]," and "Villa Grimaldi: Un Parque por la Paz, Por el derecho a la memoria [1996]," which is especially comprehensive and reproduces documents and brief oral testimonies (photo on 12 for wall mural quote); Asamblea por los Derechos Humanos, "Parque por la Paz en Villa Grimaldi: Una experiencia social viable contra la impunidad en Chile," presented at Seminario Internacional "Impunidad y sus efectos en los procesos democráticos," Santiago, 13–15-XII-96, organized by CODEPU, FASIC, and SERPAJ-Chile; *LHOT*, 53; Carlos B., conversation, 22-11-97 (neighborhood lore, restless spirits); and Helen Hughes, conversation, 12-1-97 (lore, windows). See also background in newspaper reports cited in note 39. An important novel in 1996 resonated with the Villa Grimaldi events and lore, through the eyes of a young couple given the gift of a home—once

abandoned, now put to new purpose, but also strangely haunted by spirits and legacies of a terrible past: Carlos Cerda, *Una casa vacía* (Chilean ed., Santiago: Aguilar, 1996). On the elusiveness of memory and representation of the horror at Villa Grimaldi, see the novel by Germán Marín, *El palacio de la risa* (Santiago: Planeta, 1995); and the related insightful essay of Michael J. Lazzara, "Tres recorridos de Villa Grimaldi," in *Monumentos, memoriales y marcas territoriales*, ed. Elizabeth Jelin and Victoria Langland (Madrid: Siglo Veintiuno, 2003), 127–47.

39   Field notes from inauguration, 22-III-97 (including Gho quote), supplemented by *La Epoca*, 22-III-97 (Frei attendance expectations); *La Epoca*, 23-III-97 (Ortega quote); and *El Mercurio*, 23-III-97 (Alvear reply).

40   Field notes from inauguration, 22-III-97.

41   ACPPVG: "Proyecto Parque de la Paz [1996]"; "Villa Grimaldi: Un Parque por la Paz, Por el derecho a la memoria [1996]," supplemented by *ICNVR* vol. 1, bk. 2: 465–67; conversations with Pedro Matta and field notes on site tours, 1996–2006, esp. 12-1-97, 3-IX-06; Pedro Alejandro Matta, "Villa Grimaldi, Santiago de Chile: A Visitor's Guide" (brochure, 2000, in possession of author). Internal debates among ex-prisoners and the victim-activist community about the aesthetic of the Peace Park were marked by several currents: literalist reconstruction of the camp and its ruins; a human rights park with a distinct symbolic aesthetic, to induce reflection and encounter without reproducing the physical image of horror; and an intermediate position that would use some reconstruction or salvaged remains of the physicality of the center to inspire memory encounters and reflection. The latter approach prevailed but also explains why reconstruction of the Tower would over time prove important. For insight on aesthetics and internal debates, and contrasting perspective, I am especially grateful to Pedro Matta, conversation and site tour, 3-IX-06; and Sola Sierra, interview, 26-III-97. Cf. *La Epoca*, 1-X-96; *El Siglo*, 4-IV-97 (Laura Atencio Abarca, "La verdad de los de Villa Grimaldi"); Lazzara, "Tres recorridos," 130–35; and description of Villa Grimaldi and the Tower, www.villagrimaldicorp.cl (accessed February 2007), which dates the beginning stage of the reconstruction of the Tower in 2000–2001. That reconstruction of the Tower had more to do with political will than with cost is indicated by the modesty of funds needed through private appeal. In late 2002, the London-based solidarity group known as Proyecto Internacional de Derechos Humanos appealed for funds to assist with the second stage of reconstruction (e-mail to author from Nicole Drouilly, 20-XI-02, on behalf of Proyecto International). At the time, fundraising for the first stage of reconstruction (the outer shell of the wood tower) was completed and amounted to 2 million pesos; the second-stage effort (interior reconstruction) was estimated at 2.3 million pesos. The combined total amounted to less than US$10,000. By 2005, the Tower was fully reconstructed and accessible to visitors: "Santiago Times": www.santiagotimes.cl, 17-VIII-05; by then, the politicocultural environment was also quite different: see chapter 6 in this volume.

42 For figures on G D P, exports, and national savings, and for an overview of the Chilean economy as of 1997 taking into account corrected figures issued by the Chilean Central Bank in February 1998, see Oscar Muñoz Gomá, "La economía chilena en 1997," in FLACSO-Chile, *Chile 97*, 139–57, esp. 157, 139–40 n. 1; and for comprehensive technical analysis in long-term perspective, Ricardo Ffrench-Davis, *Entre el neoliberalismo y el crecimiento con equidad: Tres décadas de política económica en Chile*, 3rd rev. ed. (Santiago: J.C Sáez, 2003), and specifically for international trade strategy and figures on export market geography and foreign direct investment, 280–94 (esp. 292–93), 351–52. See also the overviews of foreign relations and commercial integration as of 1997 by Paz Milet, Andrés Angulo, and Alicia Frohmann, in FLACSO-Chile, *Chile 97*, 161–87; and for comparative context, Barbara Stallings and Wilson Peres, *Growth, Employment, and Equity: The Impact of the Economic Reforms in Latin America and the Caribbean* (Washington, D.C.: United Nations Economic Commission for Latin American and the Caribbean, 2000), and specifically for inflation, 52. For common-sense expectations of per capita G D P of about $6,000 by 2000, see, e.g., *Hoy*, 16-XII-96, p. 5; cf. the more exaggerated expectation ($7,500) cited by Patricio Meller, "Pobreza y distribución del ingreso en Chile (Década de los noventa)," in Drake and Jaksic, *El modelo chileno*, 56. The "Asian flu" meant that expectations fell somewhat short. In 1999 U.S. dollars, per capita G D P amounted to about 5,000 (or 9,000 in purchasing power parity). For figures in long-term perspective (1960–2000) and alongside other quality-of-life indicators, see Programa de las Naciones Unidas para el Desarrollo (hereinafter PNUD), *Desarrollo humano en Chile 2002: Nosotros los chilenos: un desafío cultural* (Santiago: PNUD, 2002), anexo II, esp. Table 1. For the troubling underside of these achievements, see the next two sections of this chapter and esp. notes 50–53.

43 See Ffrench-Davis, *Entre el neoliberalismo y el crecimiento con equidad*, 357, 353; *Qué Pasa*, 3-VIII-96, p. 94 (de Castro quote); and *New York Times*, 17-XI-96 ("easier to buy").

44 Stallings and Peres, *Growth, Employment, and Equity*, 120, 121; for poverty and social spending figures, and causes of reduction, Meller, "Pobreza y distribución del ingreso en Chile (Década de los noventa)," 43–50. The figures cited in the text on the annual reduction rate are different from those in Meller because I used a different time frame (1990 rather than 1987 as the point of departure). The standard international measure of poverty and indigence is well known and over the years has been used in annual United Nations statistical reports on Latin America and the Caribbean, issued by CEPAL (Comisión Económica para América Latina y el Caribe); for its use in the Chilean context, see Ffrench-Davis, *Entre el neoliberalismo y el crecimiento con equidad*, 308.

45 For an articulate and comprehensive vision of political governability in relation to economic strategy and international integration, by a key architect of Concertación governing strategy, see Edgardo Boeninger, *Democracia en Chile: Lecciones*

para la gobernabilidad (Santiago: Editorial Andrés Bello, 1997), 367–526, esp. 499–503, 474–76. For a searching reexamination and critique of Chile as "model," see Drake and Jaksic, *El modelo chileno*; on social concertation and consensus building in relation to workers, see also Volker Frank, "Politics without Policy: The Failure of Social Concertation in Democratic Chile," in *Victims of the Chilean Miracle: Workers and Neoliberalism in the Pinochet Era, 1973–2002*, ed. Peter Winn (Durham, N.C.: Duke University Press, 2004), 71–124.

46 For perceptive contemporary essays (most are based on articles that originally appeared during 1995–98 in *Qué Pasa*) on unease as an aspect of Chile's larger sociocultural transformation and new "spirit of the 90s," see Eugenio Tironi, *La irrupción de las masas y el malestar de las élites: Chile en el cambio de siglo* (Santiago: Grijalbo, 1999), and note reference to leaving behind the "paradigm of Arturo Prat" (p. 19). For other data cited, see *New York Times*, 17-XI-96; *Hoy*, 16-XII-96, p. 4 ("Argentines" quote, attributed to Andrés Allamand); and *El Mercurio*, 8-XII-96 ("beautiful women").

47 For a review of the Lota shutdown and the conflict that surrounded it, see *Hoy*, 21-IV-97, pp. 20–22 (cf. 5-VIII-96, pp. 16–19); on Enacar versus Chilgener and investment in Colombia, Hugo Fazio R., *Mapa actual de la extrema riqueza in Chile* (Santiago: LOM, 1997), 77–81; and for credit cards and malls in the 1990s, PNUD, *Desarrollo humano en Chile 2002*, 99, 104–5. For consumer culture and its consequences, see also note 48.

48 For the shift toward consumer culture and implications for subjectivity, three perceptive but varied interpretations by social scientists in the late 1990s were —in order from most welcoming to least welcoming—Tironi, *La irrupción de las masas y el malestar de las élites*; Norbert Lechner, "Condiciones de gobernabilidad democrática en América Latina," in FLACSO-Chile, *Chile 97*, 9–23; and Tomás Moulian, *Chile Actual: Anatomía de un mito* (Santiago: LOM, 1997). Cf. José Joaquín Brunner, *Bienvenidos a la modernidad* (Santiago: Planeta, 1994), who anticipated some of Tironi's arguments. For a much commented study documenting the tensions of modernization and subjectivity, and the paradoxes of rising opportunities and rising insecurities, see PNUD, *Desarrollo humano en Chile—1998: Las paradojas de la modernización* (Santiago: PNUD, 1998), and specifically on sociability and religious communities, and on sectorial analysis of debt and carrying loads, 136–48, 187–88; and for average debt data and typology of consumers, PNUD, *Desarrollo humano en Chile 2002*, 99–101. The typology was based on a survey in 2001, after the effects of the 1998 economic downturn. Arguably, percentage results might have been a bit more satisfied in 1997—notwithstanding the turn toward economic pessimism evident, and discussed below, already taking place in 1996–97. The late Lechner was a pioneer of studies of politics and subjectivity since the 1980s and important in the work of the PNUD: see, for fuller context of his thought, *Los patios interiores de la democracia: Subjetividad y política* (Santiago: FLACSO, 1988); and

Las sombras del mañana: La dimensión subjetiva de la política (Santiago: LOM, 2002).

49 For the impact of accelerated modernization on exclusivity and social values, see Tironi, *La irrupción de las masas y el malestar de las élites*; and for data on hotels and flights, PNUD, *Desarrollo humano en Chile 2002*, 153–55.

50 Meller, "Pobreza y distribución," 51–55; cf. Ffrench-Davis, *Entre el neoliberalismo y el crecimiento con equidad*, 305–46, esp. 321–22, on the impact of imputing or not imputing rent in calculating distribution of income (and of spending) in Greater Santiago. The bottom line result is the same, insofar as taking into account social spending (including its impact on housing) finds a significant impact on material life and income share of families in the bottom quintile, but only a slight impact in the share of overall income concentrated in the top quintile. What renders this result less than paradoxical is precisely the high concentration of income—for example, a 2 percent shift in national income directly from top to bottom quintile would boost income by 50 percent for a bottom quintile whose share is otherwise about 4 percent, but would decrease income by only 3.6 percent in a top quintile whose share is otherwise 58 percent.

51 The observation of pervasive ostentatious flaunting as well as growing disillusion is based in part on cumulative field experience in Chile, July 1996 to August 1997. It is worth noting that for many persons of modest means, images of wealth were based not only in media but also direct experience in service-sector work—not only domestic service but also the commercial service sector—from food preparation to cleaning to security, in restaurants, hotels, apartment buildings, and office buildings. For pioneering analyses of workers in the industries cited, with insights on both political economy and subjectivity, see Winn, *Victims of the Chilean Miracle*, and for a striking "no miracle for us" comment by a worker, 125. On relativization of poverty—specifically, a cultural shift from an understanding of poverty based on lack of resources, to a concept more tied to relations of inequality and insecurity—see Jorge Manzi and Carlos Catalán, "Los cambios en la opinión pública," in Toloza and Lahera, *Chile en los años noventa*, 523–55, esp. 526–33, 537–39, 555. Cf. PNUD, *Desarrollo humano en Chile—1998*, 47–48, 183–86; and Meller, "Pobreza y distribución del ingreso en Chile," 56. See also note 52. For sentiment of disappointment and continuing poverty in poblaciones, see the discussion in the next paragraph and following chapter section, and notes 53, 58, and 62 below.

52 For statistics cited, see Huneeus, *Chile, un país dividido*, 130–31, 134 (121–65, for additional context); and Manzi and Catalán, "Los cambios en la opinión pública," 534. Cf. CERC and Adimark polls as reported in *La Epoca*, 20-XII-96, 5-IV-97.

53 For the Copeva episode and excellent overall appraisal of social policy, see María Pía Martin, "Integración al desarrollo: Una visión de la política social," in

Toloza and Lahera, *Chile en los años noventa*, 313–52, esp. 340–41. For social policy from the angle of urban pobladores and activists, see Gustavo Rayo and Gonzalo de la Maza, "La acción colectiva popular urbana," in ibid., 427–69 (435 for quote).

54 That late modernity (or postmodernity, if one prefers) renders fragile a sense of connection to the past and social community tradition, and also to the future, is well known and drew attention by scholars in the 1980s and 1990s: for astute comment and relevant references, see, e.g., Norbert Lechner, "Ese desencanto llamado posmoderno," in Lechner, *Los patios interiores de la democracia*, 163–89. Cf. Eric Hobsbawm, *The Age of Extremes: A History of the World, 1914–1991* (New York: Pantheon, 1994), 15–16, 558–85. From one angle, one might say that Chile in the 1990s partook of the postmodern aspect of world culture at the turn of the twenty-first century, insofar as the declining credibility of political metanarratives and the idea of progress, the experience of increased individuality and reordering and fragmentation of relevant social community, and the increased crossing of cultural borders all decentered social identities—especially those tied to nation-state communities and myths. (In the case of the former Soviet Union, however, note the reordering and fragmentation of community also implied creation of new nation-state communities and myths.) The rise of transnational values and social networks promoting such varied causes and identities as human rights, women's empowerment, indigenous peoples' rights, environmentalism, and gay sexuality had a similar effect. It is beyond the scope of this chapter to take on the issue of whether the postmodern phenomenon, especially in Third World contexts where social hybridity of distinct "historical moments" (in the perspective of advanced Western countries) has long been common, is best understood as an aspect of "late" modernity and its always incomplete and socially hybrid character, or as an era of "postmodernity." For purposes of this chapter, the nomenclature problem is moot, in part because the postmodern aspects of world culture did not come into bolder relief in Chile until after 1998.

55 De Castro interview in *Qué Pasa*, 3-VIII-96, pp. 92–94. For the business class of the 1990s, and its formative years under military rule remembered with gratitude, see Tironi, *La irrupción de las masas y el malestar de las élites*, 57–86, esp. 60–64, 72–74. See also note 56.

56 For the mission accomplished idea and the claiming of credit for Concertación success by Pinochetistas, see, aside from note 55, chapter 1 above. I am also grateful to the businessman and former minister under the junta Jorge Cauas, interview, 9-VI-97, who saw as a fundamental accomplishment of military rule the laying of a long-term foundation for Chilean success, rather than reactive government responding to transitory short-term crises of the moment. Cauas was also a signer of the public letter defending Pinochet after Aylwin's March 1997 interview in *Excelsior*.

57 From the angle of the Concertación, the debate between Center-Left elites known as *auto-complacientes* (self-satisfied) and those considered *auto-flagelantes* (self-scourging) that unfolded early in 1998 was revealing: as Tironi notes, *La irrupción*, 51–56, cf. 134–38, 205–11, the Asian downturn and its consequences later that year interrupted the debate. I am also grateful to Emilio Filippi, interview, 3-IV-97, for sensitizing me to a certain pride of accomplishment, albeit tempered by a sense of unfinished agendas. The tempering of pride with acknowledgment of deficiency was especially evident in face-to-face meetings by Concertación officials with grassroots groups such as pobladores, as in the focus group discussions cited in note 58.

58 For the previous two paragraphs, see Julia Paley, *Marketing Democracy: Power and Social Movements in Post-dictatorship Chile* (Berkeley: University of California Press, 2001); field notes, focus group discussions with pobladoras, "I Conferencia de Participación Ciudadana en Evaluación de Políticas Públicas," Santiago, 26-IX-96, and "II Conferencia de Participación Ciudadana en Evaluación de Políticas Públicas," Santiago, 9-I-97, both convened by FLACSO. The "bury us" quote is from the first meeting, Comisión de Género group; the "makě us content" quote is from the second meeting, also Comisión de Género group.

Some caveats are also in order. That it is too neat to reduce tension over social equity to a simple split between political elites and grassroots activists is apparent, on an elite level, in Eugenio Lahera and Cristián Toloza, "La Concertación de Partidos por la Democracia: Balance y perspectivas," in Toloza and Lahera, *Chile en los años noventa*, 705–19, esp. 705–11; in the nascent debate between "auto-complacientes" and "auto-flagelantes" (see note 57); and on a grassroots level, from field observations in 1996–97. It is also too simple to reduce disappointment only to shifts of the moment during the 1990s. For trenchant analysis of disappointment in the 1990s, based on dialogue between public opinion polls, broad considerations of political culture, and comparative national surveys, see Marta Lagos, "Latin America's Smiling Mask," *Journal of Democracy* 8, no. 3 (July 1997): 123–38; and for subtle early explorations of the potential for *desencanto*, in dialogue with questions of modernity and postmodernity as well as the culture of dictatorship, see Lechner, *Los patios interiores de la democracia.*

59 Sola Sierra, interview, 26-III-97.

60 Field notes and video recording (in possession of author) of panel-forum convened by AFDD, "Necesidad de anular los efectos de la Ley de Amnistía," Santiago (Centro El Agora), 5-VI-97. I am grateful to Juan Cifuentes Campos of the AFDD for videotaping the forum and providing me a copy.

61 Chapters 1–3 in this volume (events in Aylwin presidency); *Hoy*, 7-IV-97, pp. 4–5 (Cavallo quote and reflection).

62 The "we were better in dictatorship" idea, meant not as a statement that life was better under military rule but as ironic observation about a turn from an ethos of solidarity toward greater egotism, recurred during my fieldwork in 1996–

97, and at focus groups with pobladoras at "I Conferencia de Participación Ciudadana en Evaluación de Políticas Públicas" and "II Conferencia de Participación Ciudadana en Evaluación de Políticas Públicas," FLACSO, Santiago, 26-IX-96, 9-1-97. Suggestions of declension, at times with a hint of nostalgia, also began to inform memories of Aylwin; some who had been quite critical during his presidency retrospectively nuanced their assessment or softened the critique, to a greater or lesser degree, in light of the deterioration perceived in the Frei years. I am especially grateful to Tonya R., interview, 24-1-97, for clarity and in-depth discussion of this point, but similar sensibilities occurred in other interviews including Herminda Morales, 11-IX-96; and Marisa T., 8-X-96. Cf. Sola Sierra's views on the shifting meaning of olvido, cited in the previous section of this chapter.

63 Huneeus, *Chile, un país dividido*, 105, and for additional context of perceptions of democracy, and attitudes of trust and mistrust, 93–119, 205–47; cf. PNUD, *Desarrollo humano en Chile—1998*, 127–53.

64 Tomás Moulian, *Chile Actual*, 31, 37 (quotes); Alexandra Barahona de Brito, "Passion, Constraint, Law, and *Fortuna*: The Human Rights Challenge to Chilean Democracy," in *Burying the Past: Making Peace and Doing Justice after Civil Conflict*, ed. Nigel Biggar (Washington, D.C.: Georgetown University Press, 2001), 174. The memoir of Jorge Lavandero, *El precio de sostener un sueño* (Santiago: LOM, 1997), also expressed the more open climate of debate on the nature of the transition. It should be noted that an earlier book by the journalist Rafael Otano, *Crónica de la transición* (Santiago: Planeta, 1995), anticipated some of the sensibilities put forth strongly in Moulian and that the 1998 arrest of Pinochet in London (chapter 5 in this volume) also stimulated books on the nature of the transition.

65 Moulian, *Chile Actual*, esp. 7–11 on academic conventions, 102–14 on "ciudadano credit-card."

66 Alfredo Jocelyn-Holt's books garnered a prize, celebrity interviews in newspapers, and reprint editions. In *El peso de la noche: Nuestra frágil fortaleza histórica* (Buenos Aires and Santiago: Planeta/Ariel, 1997) and *El Chile perplejo: Del avanzar sin transar al transar sin parar* (Santiago: Planeta/Ariel, 1998), Jocelyn-Holt debunked cherished historical mythology, turning it into "our fragile historical fortress." Myths of Chilean exceptionalism used one facet of Chilean history to deny the tensions and consequences—and perplexity—created by countervailing undersides. Portales, the revered nineteenth-century Giver of Law, was actually a dictator wedded to the state as means rather than end, and reliant on force over institutions to contain barbarism. The dominant self-definition of Chile as a culture that prized order and moderation actually rested on fear of the savagery that accumulated, like the energy of earthquakes, below the surface. Chilean history and culture were less a story of advances than of frustration, betrayals, and resentment as epic projects gave way to political

pragmatism, opportunism, and impasse. In this context, the Unidad Popular represented not an aberration but a dense accumulation and playing out of dynamics profoundly historical and Chilean. In Jocelyn-Holt's vision, the frustration, gridlock, and public relations mythology of the transition fit the pattern of betrayal and self-deception. The No campaign of the 1988 plebiscite distilled this perplexing and perplexed Chile, and its resort to mythological sleight of hand. Pinochet was personally criticized and defeated but at the cost of accepting the new Chile created under military rule. "He left and he did not leave. It fell and it did not fall." The Rettig Report's lament and Aylwin's pardon plea were ritual devices to bury the past by spreading responsibility to all, rather than pinning crimes on specific individuals. See esp. *El Chile perplejo*, 214 (quote), 206–8. Jocelyn-Holt's vision of the underside of Chilean mythology is worth comparing and contrasting with Left visions of the role of violence in Chilean history. See esp. Gabriel Salazar, *La violencia política popular en las Grandes Alamedas: Chile, 1947–1987* (Santiago, SUR, 1987), for a much discussed and influential interpretation (see *Proposiciones* 20 [1991]) during the early transition years.

67 Faride Zerán, *Tiempos que muerden: Biografía inconclusa de Fernando Castillo Velasco* (Santiago: LOM, 1998), 161–72; trilogy Book Two, 175–76, 178, on the symbolism of Morandé 80 and changes to La Moneda; field observations of dynamics of masked youths and carabineros, 11-IX-96 (supplemented by press accounts, 1994–96 anniversary disturbances); *Qué Pasa*, 10-V-97, p. 14 (statistics).

68 On the 1988 plebiscite and youth, see trilogy Book Two, 360–77, esp. 365, 374. On youth culture, alienation, the barra brava phenomenon, and linkages to collective memory issues in the 1990s, excellent studies include Alfredo Riquelme Segovia, "¿Quiénes y por qué 'no están ni ahí'? Marginación y/o automarginación en la democracia transicional. Chile. 1988–1997," in Drake and Jaksic, *El modelo chileno*, 261–79; Pedro Lembel, "Soccer and Devotion in the Barrios of Santiago," NACLA *Report on the Americas* 32, no. 1 (July/August 1998): 36–42; and Reyes Andreani and Jurcic Cerda, *El Sí-No de la reconciliación*. I also benefited from conversation and ethnographic observation in poblaciones and middle-class settings, especially Father Roberto Bolton, interview, 21-X-96; Marisa T., interview, 8-X-96; and Luz M., interview, 21-I-97. For additional context on sociability, and the significance of religious communities and sport identities, see PNUD, *Desarrollo humano en Chile—1998*, 138, 144–45.

69 See Enrique Cañas, "Los partidos políticos," in Toloza and Lahera, *Chile en los años noventa*, 53–90 (60, 80, 56, 87–88 for specific figures cited).

70 Figures based on lower chamber election (percentages were slightly different for Senate voting), are derived from *La Tercera*, e-ed.: www.tercera.cl, 13-XII-97; and also Peter M. Siavelis, *The President and Congress in Postauthoritarian Chile: Institutional Constraints to Democratic Consolidation* (University Park: Pennsylvania State University Press, 2000), 182 (null and blank vote figures, 1988–

97). The tiny institutional result is evident in comparison of Concertación legislative seats yielded by the 1993 and 1997 elections: in the House of Deputies, 70 of 120 seats both times; in the Senate, comprising seats by election and by appointment, 20 of 48 in 1997 compared to 21 of 47. The increase in total seats for the new 1998 Congress occurred because Pinochet was scheduled under the Constitution to become a lifetime senator. On comparative election outcomes within a broader reflection on the party system, see Peter M. Siavelis, "Continuidad y transformación del sistema de partidos en una transición 'modelo,'" in Drake and Jaksic, *El modelo chileno*, 223–59 (229–30 for figures on seats).

71 Field notes at Santiago Cemetery, 1-xi-96. The reductionism was pervasive, not unusual, during my field research in Chile during July 1996 to August 1997. Indeed, it sometimes led interviewees who were less than maximal victims of repression to say to me that they did not have a noteworthy story to tell, and it went hand in hand with the sense of cultural and media isolation that marked the panel-forum on amnesty held by relatives of the disappeared in June 1997. See note 60 in this chapter.

72 The emergence of the memory frameworks mentioned and their explosive expansion in the 1980s is recounted in Book Two of this trilogy.

73 The risk that struggle to put forth emblematic memories in a struggle for primacy had become exhausted and would give way to more privatized memory, culturally isolated and loosened from wider social meaning, was one of the fears in play at the panel-forum organized by relatives of the disappeared in June 1997. See note 60 in this chapter. During my fieldwork in 1996–97, more than one dedicated activist spoke to me of exhaustion and temptation to retreat into or at least accept a more private memory domain. The issue also arose in discussion at the Seminario Internacional "Impunidad y sus efectos en los procesos democráticos," organized by CODEPU, FASIC, and SERPAJ, activist comments at Comisión 4, "Métodos de lucha y experiencias de superación . . . ," Santiago, 13–15-xii-96. But the problem was not one limited to classic victims, and even when major emblematic memory frameworks were vibrant, they privileged some social voices over others. See, e.g., the story of the conscript "Cristián" in trilogy Book One, 134–42. For a turn in 1998 toward a discourse of plural and private ("loose") ways of remembering as preferable, particularly in reference to the 11 September anniversary, see chapter 5 in this volume.

74 *La Epoca*: e-ed., www.laepoca.cl, 5-xi-97; *LHOT*, 349–56.

75 On the Pinochet case and diplomatic repercussions, including an awkward moment when the Chilean government granted Patricio Aylwin temporary diplomatic status to prevent testimony, see *Qué Pasa*, 31-v-97, p. 21; and *La Epoca, El Mercurio*, 26-vi-97. Cf. Hugh O'Shaughnessy, *Pinochet: The Politics of Torture* (New York: New York University Press, 2000), 159–61; and Paz Rojas B.

et al., *Tarda pero llega: Pinochet ante la justicia española* (Santiago: LOM-CODEPU, 1998), esp. 5–33. Early in 1998, testimony on the case by the Lutheran bishop Helmut Frenz before the Spanish judge Manuel García Castellón drew publicity in Chile. Frenz indicated that Pinochet justified torture ("de otra manera, no cantan" [otherwise, they don't sing]) when he and the Catholic bishop Fernando Ariztía as co-presidents of the Pro-Peace Committee, saw Pinochet in 1974 to discuss the case of disappeared Spanish priest Antonio Llidó. *La Epoca*, e-ed.: www.laepoca.cl, 10-11-98. On Chilean Supreme Court shifts and military complaints cited, see Barahona, "Passion, Constraint, Law, and *Fortuna*," 161; Alejandra Matus, *El libro negro de la justicia chilena* (Santiago: Planeta, 1999), 309–14, esp. 309; and *El Mercurio*, e-ed.: www.elmercurio.cl, 24-IX-97. The legal, political, and cultural fallout of Caso Albania was substantial and continued for years. For a dramatic instance, see "El Mostrador": www.elmostrador.cl, 24-1-01.

76   *El Mercurio*, 27-X-96. The broader context of the interview was a discussion of Chilean television. On *La pequeña historia*, see the Afterword to this chapter. That a psychiatrist was a playwright was no accident. For background on connections between theater, medical students, and alternative cultural activity under the dictatorship in the 1970s, see the illuminating study of the Agrupación Cultural Universitaria by Víctor Muñoz Tamayo, *ACU: Rescatando el asombro* (Santiago: La Calabaza del Diablo, 2006).

Afterword to Chapter 4: The Joys of "Not Too Much"

1   For disenchantment in the mid-to-late 1990s, and for characterization of the lead-up to the 1973 crisis in the Rettig Report issued in 1991, see chapters 4 and 2 in this volume, respectively. For background on Center-Left renovation under the pressure of military rule, and the role of memory of the Unidad Popular, see Book Two of this trilogy: Stern, *Battling for Hearts and Minds: Memory Struggles in Pinochet's Chile, 1973–1988* (Durham, N.C.: Duke University Press, 2006), 197–205. For additional insight, see Katherine Hite, *When the Romance Ended: Leaders of the Chilean Left, 1968–1998* (New York: Columbia University Press, 2000); Jeffrey M. Puryear, *Thinking Politics: Intellectuals and Democracy in Chile, 1973–1988* (Baltimore: Johns Hopkins University Press, 1994); Kenneth Roberts, *Deepening Democracy? The Modern Left and Social Movements in Chile and Peru* (Stanford, Calif.: Stanford University Press, 1998), esp. chaps. 4–6, 9; and Ignacio Walker, *Socialismo y democracia: Chile y Europa en perspectiva comparada* (Santiago: CIEPLAN-HACHETTE, 1990).

2   For television preferences over time, and differences according to rates of television watching, see Flavio Cortés, "Modernización y concentración: Los medios de comunicación en Chile," in *Chile en los años noventa*, ed. Cristián

Toloza and Eugenio Lahera (Santiago: Presidencia de la República y Dolmen Ed., 1998), 602–4. On youth and the soccer clubs known as *barras bravas*, a good introduction is Pedro Lemebel, "Soccer and Devotion in the Barrios of Santiago," *NACLA Report on the Americas* 32, no. 1 (July–August, 1998), 36–42.

3 I acknowledge gratefully my intellectual debt, in what follows, to the superb interpretation (as well as descriptive material) of the actress and theater professor Violeta Espinoza, "1988 La Negra Ester 1998," in *Memoria para un nuevo siglo: Chile, miradas a la segunda mitad del siglo XX*, ed. Mario Garcés et al (Santiago: LOM, 2000), 369–77; to conversations with Sol Serrano, who added nuance to my analysis by prodding me to consider the relation of *La Negra Ester* to the culture of the 1988 plebiscite; and to the interview with the director Andrés Pérez by Faride Zerán, in *La Epoca* ("Temas de La Epoca" section), 26-1-97. On betrayal, my interpretation below diverges modestly from that of Espinoza, since I see only a diffuse resonance—compatible with the seductiveness of art put forth without resentment—whereas she suggests more specific political connections, and since I also see multiple messages and sources of appeal whose balance could shift over time. For the work itself and quotes, see the 1996 theater text edition, adapted by the director Andrés Pérez, in Roberto Parra, *Poesía popular, cuecas choras y La Negra Ester*, ed. Catalina Rojas (Santiago: Fondo de Cultura Económica, 1996), 127–202 (157, 142, 129 for quotes); cf. the original *décimas* text in Roberto Parra, *Décimas de La Negra Ester y otras yerbas* (Santiago: Editorial Fértil Provincia, 1992), 37–62. The theater version was first published in Escuela de Teatro de la Pontificia Universidad Católica de Chile, *Revista Apuntes* 98 (autumn–winter 1989): 33–54, with reflections, testimonios, and poetry on 2–31 (see esp. Carmen Romero, 9–11, and Marco Antonio de la Parra, 23–26).

Significantly, theater culture and book culture allowed for more play of pointed humor and pointed memory experience than television, which was more cautious and vulnerable to pressure. Among the bestselling novelists of the 1990s, e.g., were Isabel Allende and Marcela Serrano. There were differences, of course, in style between the authors and in the evolution of their writing. Allende first established herself in the 1980s, Serrano in the 1990s; Allende leaned more toward the magical realism tradition to express and capture truths, Serrano toward personal introspection and memory by key characters; Allende would publish a major memoir in addition to novels. What both had in common was an ability to focus on woman-centered experiences and longings, in dialogue with Chilean memory and experience and laced with cultural "recognition value" and moments of humor as well as sorrow. For Marcela Serrano's works popular through the mid-to-late 1990s, see *Nosotras que nos queremos tanto* (Santiago: Los Andes, 1991); and *Para que no me olvides* (Santiago: Los Andes, 1993), where the Rettig Commission and discovery of a "different" Chile, marked by torture and disappearance, figure prominently. For

Isabel Allende's, see *The House of the Spirits* (1982; New York: Bantam ed., 1986), in which a family saga becomes inseparable from memory of what led Chile to its 1973 coup; *Of Love and Shadows* (1984; New York, Bantam ed., 1988), a novelistic version of the Lonquén affair; *Eva Luna* (1987, New York: Knopf, 1988); *The Stories of Eva Luna* (1990; New York: Atheneum, 1991); and the moving memoir of her late daughter, *Paula* (1994; New York: HarperCollins, 1994), whose range of memories includes the personality and times of her uncle Salvador Allende Gossens.

Some television shows were exceptions to the climate of caution on political humor. Most notable was the *Plan Zeta* program (television station Rock & Pop), whose title evoked the "Plan Z" conspiracy propaganda of 1973 and which caused a scandal during my field research period in 1996–97 by having Pinochet appear as an obsequious servant waiting on Salvador Allende. The scene brilliantly cast and mocked Pinochet as a secret traitor, and arguably cast Allende as a dupe. For an exceptionally thoughtful essay on the wider cultural scene in the 1990s, see Roberto Merino, "Microclimas culturales," in Toloza and Lahera, *Chile en los años noventa*, 681–701 (esp. 687–88 for *La Negra Ester*, 693–94 for television); and for insightful reflections on culture, memory, and representation since the military period through the 1990s, Nelly Richard, ed., *Políticas y estéticas de la memoria* (Santiago: Editorial Cuarto Propio, 2000).

4 For the undercurrents of betrayal in the memory culture and politics of the 1970s and 1980s, see trilogy Book Two.

5 For the text of the play and illuminating commentary by de la Parra, historian Sol Serrano, theater professor Consuelo Morel Montes, and four theater students, see Escuela de Teatro de la Pontificia Universidad Católica de Chile, *Revista Apuntes* 109 (winter 1995): 3–39 (18, 19, 31–32, 35, 36 for quotes that follow). Chile's Círculo de Críticos de Arte awarded it the prize for the best national theater in 1996: *El Mercurio*, 9-XII-96.

6 For the previous five paragraphs, excellent analysis set within the frame of a longer historical vision is in Florencia E. Mallon, "Cuando la amnesia se impone con sangre, el abuso se hace costumbre: El pueblo mapuche y el Estado chileno, 1881–1998," in *El modelo chileno: Democracia y desarrollo en los noventa*, ed. Paul Drake and Iván Jaksic (Santiago: LOM, 1999), 435–64; for principles enunciated by Aylwin at congresses of the Comisión Especial de Pueblos Indígenas in 1990 and 1991, Patricio Aylwin Azócar, *La transición chilena: Discursos escogidos, Marzo 1990–1992* (Santiago: Editorial Andrés Bello, 1992), 166–69, 193–99; and for Mapuche social movement in the run-up to democratic transition, and inadequate resources and administrative follow-through in the 1990s, Florencia E. Mallon, *Courage Tastes of Blood: The Mapuche Community of Nicolás Ailío and the Chilean State, 1906–2001* (Durham, N.C.: Duke University Press, 2005), esp. 174–248. Cf. José Bengoa, *Historia de un conflicto: El estado y los mapuches en el siglo XX* (Santiago: Planeta, 1999); and Rosa Isolde Reuque Paillalef, *When a*

Flower Is Reborn: The Life and Times of a Mapuche Feminist, ed. and trans. Florencia E. Mallon (Durham, N.C.: Duke University Press, 2002). I am also grateful to Mallon for conversations about the political identities and aspects of the dismissed CONADI directors.

Energy scarcity was part of everyday news and concern about blackouts or brownouts in Santiago (personal observations, Chilean summer of 1996–97), and the conflicts with Mapuches over lands, forests, and hydroelectric projects connected with broader environmental and public policy issues. Two excellent —and contrasting—starting points are Tonci Tomic and Fernando Toledo, "Modernización, desarrollo y medio ambiente," in Toloza and Lahera, *Chile en los años noventa*, 253–82; Thomas Miller Klubock, "Labor, Land, and Environmental Change in the Forestry Sector in Chile, 1973–1988," in *Victims of the Chilean Miracle: Workers and Neoliberalism in the Pinochet Era, 1973–2002*, Peter Winn, ed. (Durham, N.C.: Duke University Press, 2004), 337–87, esp. 373–80. On several principles in play in the Ralco affair, and trade-offs from ecological and economic viewpoints, as understood by Ricardo Lagos, who was minister of public works in the late 1990s, see Patricia Politzer K., *El libro de Lagos* (Santiago: Ediciones B, 1998), 278–84.

7 *Hoy*, 23-IV-96, p. 59.

Chapter 5: The Turn: Consequences of 1998

1 See Thomas Kuhn's brilliant study, *The Copernican Revolution: Planetary Astronomy in the Development of Western Thought* (Cambridge, Mass.: Harvard University Press, 1957), 99–184, esp. 82–82, 134–35, and for his somewhat different formulation of the metaphor I have adapted, 181. Kuhn showed that situated in his own time and intellectual context, Copernicus was in many ways the last of the great astronomers working within the tradition of Ptolemy and the Aristotelian universe, even as his 1543 *De Revolutionibus* also turned out to be a revolution-making work that opened up a new astronomical science that destroyed Aristotelian cosmology. I gratefully acknowledge Alexander Bird, *Thomas Kuhn* (Princeton, N.J.: Princeton University Press, 2000), for applying the metaphor to Kuhn himself (see 278–80) and alerting me to the original usage.

2 For press coverage, see esp. *El Mercurio, La Epoca*, 12-III-98, 10-IV-98 (*La Epoca*, e-ed.: www.laepoca.cl, 12-III-98 for quote); cf. *New York Times*, 12-III-98. One legacy of the Pinochet regime was the split location of government branches: the Executive in Santiago, Congress in Valparaíso.

3 The synopsis of October events in this and following paragraphs in this section is drawn from the enormous international press coverage generated by the arrest. Below I provide additional specific citations for October 1998 events only for quotations. For press coverage in Chile, Spain, England, and the

United States, I relied especially on www.tercera.cl, www.elpais.es, www.el-mundo.es, http://reports.guardian.co.uk, 15–18-x-98; and *New York Times*, 18–21-x-98 (also 24–25-x-98). See also Hugh O'Shaughnessy, *Pinochet: The Politics of Torture* (New York: New York University Press, 2000), esp. 1–7; and continuing October press coverage in the newspapers cited and in *El Mercurio*. I also benefited from being a recipient of e-mail alerts as the Pinochet case unfolded in October 1998, and from Juan Pablo Letelier, conversation, 1-xi-99. For background on the international jurisdiction strategy, see chapter 4 in this volume; for limited hopes for success from the vantage point of 1997, field notes, forum-panel convened by AFDD, "Necesidad de anular los efectos de la Ley de Amnistía," Centro El Agora, Santiago, 5-vi-97. For more extensive political and cultural chronicling of the London arrest, and analysis of its international and Chilean consequences, superb starting points are Madeleine Davis, ed., *The Pinochet Case: Origins, Progress, and Implications* (London: Institute of Latin American Studies, 2003); and Ariel Dorfman, *Exorcising Terror: The Incredible Unending Trial of General Augusto Pinochet* (New York: Seven Stories Press, 2002). See also Naomi Roht-Arriaza, *The Pinochet Effect: Transnational Justice in the Age of Human Rights* (Philadelphia: University of Pennsylvania Press, 2005); Roger Burbach, *The Pinochet Affair: State Terrorism and Global Justice* (New York: Zed Books, 2003), esp. 95–160; and for a loyalist defense of Pinochet against the trap set by the "European Left," Hermógenes Pérez de Arce, *Europa vs. Pinochet: Indebido proceso*, 2nd ed. (Santiago: El Roble, 1998), 3 (quote).

4 Quotes were from *La Tercera*, e-ed.: www.tercera.cl, on the following dates: Artaza, 21-x-98; Frei, 18-x-98; Insulza, 23-x-98; Troncoso, 21-x-98; Izurieta, 22-x-98.

5 For quotes, see *La Tercera*, e-ed.: www.tercera.cl, 23-x-98.

6 Coverage in *New York Times*, 29-x-98 (quotes).

7 Among the 1998 press articles on the effects of Izurieta's command and judicial reform, an excellent starting point is the Sunday "Reportajes" section by *La Tercera*, 13-ix-98, "Un '11' viejo con rostro inédito" and "La deuda del '11'"; see also chapter 4. The tendency toward an army leadership taking distance from Pinochetismo, begun under Izurieta as commander in chief, turned more full-blown under his successor, General Juan Emilio Cheyre (who served as Izurieta's chief of staff and who was therefore deeply involved in the initial turn). For superb and original analysis of change that sets the military within the wider context of politics, power, and society since 1990, see Claudio Fuentes Saavedra, *La transición de los militares: Relaciones civiles-militares en Chile, 1990–2006* (Santiago: LOM, 2006); cf. Patricia Politzer, *Chile: ¿de qué estamos hablando? Retrato de una transformación asombrosa* (Santiago: Editorial Sudamericana, 2006), 15–72. To assess the change over time, it is helpful to set Chile within a comparative context of power balances during the founding moments of transi-

tion. See Felipe Agüero, "Authoritarian Legacies: The Military's Role," in *Authoritarian Legacies and Democracy in Latin America and Southern Europe*, ed. Katherine Hite and Paola Cesarini (Notre Dame, Ind.: University of Notre Dame Press, 2004), 233–62; and Agüero, "Institutions, Transitions, and Bargaining: Civilians and the Military in Shaping Postauthoritarian Regimes," in *Civil-Military Relations in Latin America: New Analytical Perspectives*, ed. David Pion-Berlin (Chapel Hill: University of North Carolina Press, 2001), 194–222. For the relationship to military memory and education, see Eric Hershberg and Felipe Agüero, eds., *Memorias militares sobre la represión en el Cono Sur: Visiones en disputa en dictadura y democracia* (Madrid: Siglo Veintiuno, 2005), esp. Agüero and Hershberg, "Las Fuerzas Armadas y las memorias de la represión en el Cono Sur," 1–34, and María Eva Muzzopappa, "Savia nueva de un árbol eterno: Ejército, jóvenes y memoria en la Escuela Militar (Chile, 1971–2002)," 107–42.

8 For Alvear's determination and leadership style, see Politzer, *Chile: ¿de qué estamos hablando?*, 277–311, esp. 278–84. For the reform within the wider context of politics and the judiciary, see Jorge Correa S., "Cenicienta se queda en la fiesta: El poder judicial chileno en la década de los 90," in *El modelo chileno: Democracia y desarrollo en los noventa*, ed. Paul Drake and Iván Jaksic (Santiago: LOM, 1999), 281–315; Lisa Hilbink, "Un estado de derecho no liberal: La actuación del poder judicial chileno de los años 90," in Drake and Jaksic, *El modelo chileno*, 317–37; Alejandra Matus, *El libro negro de la justicia chilena* (Santiago: Planeta, 1999), 309–25; and Louis Bickford, "Strengthening Democracy: Stakeholder Institutions, Public Policy, and Democratic Quality: The Case of Chile, 1990–1998" (PHD diss., McGill University, 1999), esp. chap. 7. Cf. *La Epoca*: e-ed.: www.laepoca.cl, 11-1-98.

9 *La Epoca*: e-ed., www.laepoca.cl, 29-XII-97, 21-1-98; Brian Loveman and Elizabeth Lira, *El espejismo de la reconciliación política: Chile 1990–2002* (Santiago: LOM, 2002), 206–7, 207 n. 68, cf. 229, 288–91; Juan Guzmán Tapia (with collaboration of Olivier Bras), *En el borde del mundo: Memorias del juez que procesó a Pinochet*, trans. from the orig. 2005 French ed. by Oscar Luis Molina S. (Barcelona: Editorial Anagrama, 2005), 136–40.

10 See year-end review in *La Tercera*, 16-1-00, for statistics through 1999; I tracked 2000–2001 statistics via the continuous summary reports in the *Economist* (for the still significant link between Chile's macroeconomic fortunes and the world market price of copper, see the *Economist*, 1-XII-00, p. 37). For Lavín's political style and premises, a good starting point is his interview in *El Mercurio*, 8-IX-98; and for Lagos, Patricia Politzer K.'s interview book, *El libro de Lagos* (Santiago: Ediciones B, 1998).

11 On letting go of efforts to hegemonize memory, see the editorial in *El Mercurio*, 11-IX-98, cf. Frei's own statement on the subject in his 21-V-1999 address to Congress, as reprinted in *El Mercurio*: e-ed., www.elmercurio.cl, 22-v-99, p. 40.

On abolition of the 11 September holiday and its subtexts, see *El Mercurio*, *La Tercera*, 20-VIII-98, cf. 19-VIII-98; *Qué Pasa*, 29-VIII-98, pp. 20–22, 24; and interviews with Pinochet in *El Mercurio*, 6-IX-98, *Cosas*, 9-IX-98, pp. 11–14. On a theater of gestures, see notes 12–13.

12 See *La Segunda*, 2-IX-98, and *El Mercurio*, *La Tercera*, 3-IX-98. For clarification of army mass by Izurieta, see *El Mercurio*, 6-IX-98; on Izurieta's approach to September memory season, *Hoy*, 31-VIII-98, pp. 4–7; and on GAP, *La Nación*, 4-IX-98. Cf. *La Tercera*, 5-IX-98.

13 Pinochet on Radio Cooperativa, 3-IX-98, *La Segunda*, 3-IX-98 (quote); *La Tercera*, 4-IX-98, *El Mercurio* 4-IX-98, 8-IX-98.

14 "Homilía en la Sta. Misa celebrada en el Santuario de Nuestra Señora del Carmen de Maipú, Fiesta da la Natividad de la Sma. Virgen, 1998 [8-IX-98]," copy kindly provided to author by Arzobispado de Santiago (quotes). Cf. *El Mercurio*, 8–9-IX-98; and *La Tercera* and *La Nación*, 9-IX-98. For speculation on new information on the disappeared fostered by Catholic and other religious channels, see *La Tercera*, 10-IX-98, 14-IX-98; *El Mercurio*, 11-IX-98, 13-IX-98; and *Ultimas Noticias*, 11-IX-98.

15 For symbolic presences and absences, see *Ultimas Noticias*, 11-IX-98, and note 14; and also, flier by "Movimiento por la Dignidad Nacional," distributed in protest demonstrations on 11 September 1998 (in possession of author). On the Morandé 80 march and the Escuela Militar demonstration on 11-IX-98, I relied on personal observation (I could witness both demonstrations because repression of the first occurred so quickly that it gave me time to take the subway to the second), supplemented by *La Tercera*, *El Mercurio*, 12-IX-98; television coverage (esp. Televisión Nacional), nights of 11–12-IX-98; and casualty statistics, *El Mercurio*, 13-IX-98.

16 Vial in *La Segunda*, 1-IX-98; Zalaquett (quotes) in *La Tercera*, 8-IX-98.

17 *El Mercurio*, 5-IX-98; *La Tercera*, 12-IX-98, cf. 13-IX-98. Technically, it was the Supreme Court's Segunda Sala Penal (Second Criminal Chamber) that made the Geneva Convention ruling.

18 For La Victoria commemoration, see *La Nación*, 4-IX-98; and *La Tercera*, 5-IX-98, 7-IX-98 (cf. *La Cuarta*, 6–7-IX-98); for other activities and news from provinces, see *El Siglo*, 11-IX-98; and *La Tercera*, 12-IX-98. All are from APAF, and I am grateful to Alicia Frohmann for sharing her meticulously prepared September 1998 newspaper clippings file. For perspective on La Victoria and Jarlan commemorations in the context of Catholic Church memory currents in the 1990s, see María Angélica Cruz, *Iglesia, represión y memoria: El caso chileno* (Madrid: Siglo Veintiuno, 2004), esp. 83–119. The number of new titles published on memory themes during August–October 1998 is too staggering to list completely. Notable books of varied genres, from memoirs to documentary or testimonial publications to imaginary public letters to historical and legal analysis, included, among works critical of military rule and in some instances

the 1990s transition, Patricio Aylwin Azócar, *El reencuentro de los demócratas: Del golpe al triunfo del No* (Santiago: Ediciones B, Grupo Zeta, 1998); Marco Antonio de la Parra, *Carta abierta a Pinochet* (Santiago: Planeta, 1998); Fernando D. García and Oscar Sola, eds., photo-book with text by Alejandra Rojas, *Salvador Allende: Una época en blanco y negro* (Buenos Aires: El País, 1998); Roberto, Manuel Antonio, and Carmen Garretón Merino, *Por la fuerza sin la razón: Análisis y textos de los bandos de la dictadura militar* (Santiago: LOM, 1998); Tomás Moulian, *Conversación interrumpida con Allende* (Santiago: LOM, 1998); Miguel Orellana Benado, *Allende, alma en pena* (Santiago: Demens and Sapiens, 1998); Roberto Parra, *El Golpe* (Santiago: LOM, 1998); Hernán Soto, ed., *Voces de muerte* (Santiago: LOM, 1998); Paz Rojas B. et al., *Tarda pero llega: Pinochet frente a la justicia española* (Santiago: LOM, 1998); Armando Uribe, *Carta abierta a Patricio Aylwin* (Santiago: Planeta, 1998); Patricia Verdugo, *Interferencia secreta: 11 de septiembre de 1973* (Santiago: Sudamericana, 1998), with compact disc recording attached; José Antonio Viera-Gallo, *11 de septiembre: Testimonios, recuerdos y una reflexión actual* (Santiago: CESOC, 1998); and Faride Zerán, *Tiempos que muerden: Biografía inconclusa de Fernando Castillo Velasco* (Santiago: LOM, 1998). The period also witnessed a significant albeit smaller flurry of publications favorable to the military past: e.g., Julio Canessa Robert and Francisco Balart Páez, *Pinochet y la restauración del consenso nacional* (Santiago: Arquén, 1998); Gustavo Cuevas Farren, *Pinochet: Balance de una misión (1973–1990)* (Santiago: Arquén, 1998); Alfonso Márquez de la Plata Yrarrázabal, *Mirando al futuro* (Santiago: Arquén, 1998); and José Toribio Merino, *Bitácora de un almirante: Memorias* (Santiago: Andrés Bello, 1998).

19 My discussion of the 4 September concert is based in large measure on participant-field observation, facilitated by the Fundación Salvador Allende's (FSA's) gracious incorporation of me into the group of "técnicos" assigned logistical responsibilities before and during the event, and free to move about and observe. For relevant press reports, see *La Tercera*, 3-IX-98, 5-IX-98; *La Nación*, 4-IX-98; and *El Mercurio*, 5-IX-98. Cf. *La Cuarta*, 5-IX-98. Other efforts to break out of earlier memory molds included imagined open-letter or "conversation" books with historical figures (de la Parra, *Carta abierta a Pinochet*; Moulian, *Conversación interrumpida con Allende*; Uribe, *Carta abierta a Patricio Aylwin*); and an innovative memory conference that integrated pre- and post-1973 perspectives and an unusually wide variety of performative, testimonial, and analytical perspectives: "Memoria para un nuevo siglo," held in Santiago on 4–6-XI-98, and cosponsored by the History Department of the University of Santiago and the nongovernmental organization ECO, Educación y Comunicaciones. I am grateful for the privilege of working with the organizing committee and participating in the conference. Many of the contributions were subsequently published in Mario Garcés et al., eds., *Memoria para un nuevo siglo: Chile, miradas a la segunda mitad del siglo XX* (Santiago: LOM, 2000).

20 For media dynamics and concentration in the 1990s, see Guillermo Sunkel and Esteban Geoffroy, *Concentración económica de los medios de comunicación* (Santiago: LOM, 2001), esp. 46 for data from which media concentration figures in text were adapted, 31 for media closures; and Flavio Cortés, "Modernización y concentración: Los medios de comunicación en Chile," in *Chile en los noventa*, ed. Cristián Toloza and Eugenio Lahera (Santiago: Dolmen, 1998), 557–611 (580–81 for pre-1998 media closures). Cf. Hugo Fazio R., *Mapa actual de la extrema riqueza en Chile* (Santiago: LOM, 1997), 427–38. I also relied on author field observation for 1998 media closures.

21 For the radio and television environment of the 1990s, see Cortés, "Modernización y concentración," 583–607 (590 for radio ratings). Cf. Sunkel and Geoffroy, *Concentración económica*, 57–105; Fazio, *Mapa actual*, 428–38; and *La Epoca*: e-ed.: www.laepoca.cl, 6-XII-97 (Guzmán quote). A new directorship system for Televisión Nacional had been established in 1992, in line with the idea of independent public television. Those named to the board could not be removed by political fiat, but on the other hand, the Senate approval needed for the initial appointments and the president's power to appoint the board president implied potential sensitivity to political controversy by the oversight body. For additional information on the ousting of Navarrete and Politzer, I am grateful to Patricia Politzer, interview, 8-IV-97.

22 The events cited and their Chilean ramifications may be tracked in next-day print editions, and a mix of same-day and next-day reports in e-editions, of *La Tercera* (www.tercera.cl); and *El Mercurio* (www.emol.com). For international perspectives, see *New York Times* (www.nytimes.com); *El País* (www.elpais.es); and *Guardian* (http://reports.guardian.co.uk). For a useful event calendar of the Pinochet case, see www.tercera.cl, 2-III-00, "Casos: Pinochet" link, and for a key early document on the case for universal jurisdiction, Amnesty International, "The Case of General Pinochet: Universal jurisdiction and the absence of immunity for crimes against humanity," October 1998, www.amnesty.org, Report EUR 45/21/98 at AI Index.

23 I am grateful to Eliza Tanner, a journalism scholar who conducted dissertation research in Chile during 1998 and 1999, for conversations on media coverage that enhanced my own tracking and visits to Chile during 1998–99. For fine analysis of television news and the shaping of politicocultural climate, see Giselle Munizaga, "Augusto Pinochet en Londres: El caso Pinochet en los noticiarios de televisión," in *Nuevo gobierno: Desafíos de la reconciliación, Chile 1999–2000*, ed. FLACSO-Chile (Santiago: FLACSO, 2000), 221–30.

24 Eliza A. Tanner, " 'Las Grandes Alamedas': The Paradox of Internet and Democracy in Chile" (PHD diss., Journalism, University of Wisconsin, Madison, 2000), 121, 178, 81 for statistics cited, and chaps. 3–5, 7. I am also grateful for insights by Miguel Angel Larrea, the leader of *La Epoca*'s Internet operation, interview, 3-IV-97.

25 Tanner, "'Las Grandes Alamedas,'" for statistics 265 (cf. 266–67), 278–79 (my "comments" category combines Tanner's "commentaries" and "exclamations" messages, which add up to 60.6 percent), and for quotes, 283 (message no. 816), 284 (message no. 1511). The e-letter count was 1670 by 23-1-99.

26 See *La Tercera*, e-ed.: www.tercera.cl, 6-iv-99, 25-iv-99 (quote); cf. the cracking of military silence briefly recounted by Tina Rosenberg in *New York Times*, 22-viii-00.

27 See *New York Times*, 2-xii-98, 13-11-00; and also note 28. Cf. Margaret E. Keck and Kathryn Sikkink, *Activists beyond Borders: Advocacy Networks in International Politics* (Ithaca, N.Y.: Cornell University Press, 1998), 22, 88–92, 97–102 (esp. 101); and Book Two in the trilogy: Stern, *Battling for Hearts and Minds: Memory Struggles in Pinochet's Chile, 1973–1988* (Durham, N.C.: Duke University Press, 2006), 92–97, 100–101, 106–7, 417 n. 17.

28 Sensitive postcoup disclosures began with the first release of documents, which showed FBI cooperation in tracking associates of Chilean Left: see *New York Times*, 10-11-99. On the Contreras payment, see "Hinchey Report" (after the New York Democratic congressman Maurice Hinchey), formally Section 311 of Intelligence Authorization Act for Fiscal Year 2000, section on "Relationship with Contreras," reproduced by National Security Archive, www.nsarchive.org, and at U.S. State Department site, www.foia.state.gov, and Archivo Nacional de Chile site, www.dibam.renim.cl/ISCI45). Cf. press coverage on new document batch, www.elmostrador.cl, www.emol.com, www.tercera.cl, 13–14-xi-00. For denial by Contreras, see www.emol.com, 22-ix-00. Key documents on Contreras and Corbalán were reproduced by "El Mostrador": www.elmostrador.cl, 14-xi-00, including a memo documenting the CIA's destruction of its security file on Contreras: Special Investigations and Support Group, Office of Security to General Counsel, 21-v-91, subject: "Name Trace Request—Juan Manuel Contreras Sepulveda, Pedro Espinosa Bravo, et al." On the Pinochet case, the National Security Archive, declassification, and use of the Freedom of Information Act, as seen by Peter Kornbluh, the key leader of the disclosure effort at National Security Archive, see *Nation*, 21-xii-98, pp. 11–24; 9-viii-99, pp. 21–24; cf. www.nsarchive.org, press release 13-xi-00. For background on Corbalán, identified in court in October 2000 by Major Carlos Herrera Jiménez as having given orders to assassinate the carpenter Juan Alegría Mundaca to cover up the Tucapel Jiménez assassination, see www.elmostrador.cl, 31-x-00, cf. 27–28-x-00; and www.emol.com, 1-xi-00. Cf. Benedicto Castillo Irribarra, *El cóndor quiere carne: Emblemático crimen de Tucapel Jiménez* (Santiago: Editorial Mare Nostrum, [2005?]), esp. 122–31.

29 Televisión Nacional, *Informe Especial*, 16-xi-00 (APAF video copy in possession of author, kindly supplied by Alicia Frohmann).

30 Peace Park quotes are from e-mail announcement, "Sitio web de la Corporación Parque por la Paz Villa Grimaldi," 5-vii-99, from pajaropardo@xoom

mail.com to author and others; see also Villa Grimaldi Peace Park website, www.villagrimaldicorp.cl. Adam Rosenblatt, " 'You will find your name, absent now from all terror': Chileans Remember Their Disappeared on the World-Wide Web" (senior essay in the literature major, Yale University, 2000), offers additional insight on the early history of World Wide Web use by Villa Grimaldi and other human rights activists; I am grateful to him for sharing the essay. The links cited for the "Derechos Chile" site, www.derechoschile.com, were as of 7-x-99, and included the "Nizkor" group's comprehensive site on human rights issues in Latin America as a whole: www.derechos.org/nizkor. For background to the "Derechos Chile" site, I am grateful to conversations in 1998 with Alex Wilde, then head of the Ford Foundation office in Santiago. Data from the Pinochet Foundation site, www.fundacionpinochet.cl, were as of 6-x-99, by which date the site had recorded 46,258 visitors.

31 See www.elmostrador.cl, 18-x-00 with links to Berríos documents, cf. 11-x-00; and subsequent full account by "El Mostrador" reporter Jorge Molina Sanhueza, *Crimen imperfecto: Historia del químico* DINA *Eugenio Berríos y la muerte de Eduardo Frei Montalva* (Santiago: LOM, 2002). For a subtle example of the importance of "El Mostrador" as a source for other newspapers, note the discreet acknowledgment of a scoop in the secondhand report of *El Mercurio*, e-ed.: www.emol.com, 13-xi-00, on United States documents about a plot to kill Aylwin and penetration of the Frente Patriótico Manuel Rodríguez, "in accord with the translation by a local electronic newspaper."

32 Mónica González, *Chile: La conjura. Los mil y un días del golpe* (Santiago: Ediciones B, Grupo Zeta, 2000), for investigative journalism; Camilo Escalona, *Una transición de dos caras: Crónica crítica y autocrítica* (Santiago: LOM, 1999), 7 (quote); Adolfo Cozzi Figueroa, *Estadio Nacional* (Santiago: Sudamericana, 2000); and Patricia Verdugo, *Bucarest 187* (Santiago: Sudamericana, 1999). On Guzmán's 1997 documentary, youth culture, and commercial diffusion (esp. through video rental), I am grateful to Claudio Barrientos for conversations based on field observations, 1999–2001; cf. "El Mostrador": www.elmostrador .cl, 27-ix-00.

33 *The Clinic*, 30-xi-00 (quotes, torture stories, essay by Viviana Díaz on her father, Víctor Díaz López). Other new media of politicocultural interest included *Rocinante* (1998–); and *La Firme* (1999–).

34 See Alejandra Matus, *El libro negro de la justicia chilena* (Santiago: Planeta, 1999), and on Jordán specifically, 23, 111–18; and Matus, *Injusticia duradera: Libro blanco de "El libro negro de la justicia chilena"* (Santiago: Planeta, 2002). For the tone of mainstream press coverage and editorials at the outset of the scandal, see *El Mercurio, La Tercera, Ultimas Noticias, La Segunda*, 15-iv-99 and over the subsequent week. The clearly anachronistic aspect of the Law of Internal Security, by February 2001, was underscored when the commanders of the army and air force declined, for the sake of political peace with the Lagos

administration, to invoke it against obstruction of justice charges (*La Tercera*, e-ed.: 24-11-01; cf. interview with the secretary general of government Carolina Tohá in *El Mercurio*: e-ed., 18-11-01). At the time, the air force general Hernán Gabrielli resorted to its provisions in the wake of torture charges, but to no avail. On the Gabrielli affair, see the final section of this chapter.

35 My understanding of the funas is based principally on the following: interviews with the young activists Patricia Lobos and Alejandra López, 8-xii-00 (Lobos joined the group as an act of solidarity, López as a child of a disappeared person); interview with Pedro Matta (an older activist and former political prisoner who assisted with research), esp. 4-xii-00; Manuel Rivas Díaz, dina agent, telephone interviews, 5-xii-00, 6-xii-00 (supplemented by telephone interview with Pedro Valdivia, prefect, Policía de Investigaciones, 6-xii-00); Dr. Alejandro Forero, telephone interview, 5-xii-00; conversation with Carmen Vivanco of the afdd, 7-xii-00; funa-related flyers, media clippings, and photos from three archives: fav, funa documentation folder, and court documents, including copies of legal testimony on Rivas and Forero, as cited more specifically in note 36; funa documents and press clippings in personal archives of Pedro Matta and Claudio Barrientos. Media and e-mail reports were helpful for establishing chronology, verifying basic events, and considering social responses: *La Segunda*, 18-viii-00, 24-viii-000; *La Nación*, 21-viii-00; "El Mostrador": www.elmostrador.cl, 19-viii-00, 21-viii-00, cf. 1-vi-00; *La Tercera*, 3-ix-00; *La Firme*, 18-viii-00; *The Clinic*, 7-ix-00; *La Funa: Boletín de la Comisión Funa* No. 2 [June 2000 (?)]; *SurDA* 26 (September–October 2000): 30–31, 39 (the latter three publications kindly supplied by C. Barrientos); e-mail reports from the British-based "War Resisters International," www.gn.apc.org/warresisters, esp. 18-ix-00, 18-x-00. Fliers (in possession of the author) focus on José Aravena Ruíz, Germán Jorge Barriga Muñoz, Alejandro Jorge Forero Alvarez, Miguel Krassnoff Martchenko "Capitán Miguel o Caballo Loco," and Manuel Rivas Díaz. The Lobos and López interviews were the sources for all following activist quotes unless otherwise indicated. To set the Chilean funas in comparative generational contexts with Argentina and Uruguay, see Temma Kaplan, *Taking back the Streets: Women, Youth, and Direct Democracy* (Berkeley: University of California Press, 2004), 152–75; and Elizabeth Jelin and Diego Sompol, eds., *El pasado en el futuro: Los movimientos juveniles* (Madrid: Siglo Veintiuno, 2006), esp. 143–220 (essays by Pablo Daniel Bonaldi and Diego Sompol).

36 Bathroom story and clinic conversation as leaked by staff employee to funa activists; Alejandro Forero, telephone interview, 5-xii-00 (quote); flier (in possession of author); fav, Casos Judiciales, Caso Cerda, Rol 2–77, Juzgado del Crimen de Santiago, Ministro en Visita Dn. Carlos Cerda, 14-viii-86 arrest order and key documents at xix: doc. 340-f (cf. vii: fols. 2434, 2471v; viii: fols. 3017, 3064; xvii: fols. 7220, 7233); and fav, Casos Judiciales, Rol 10.161–11,

Juez José I. Contreras Pérez, Cuarto Juzgado del Crimen de San Miguel, Denunciado Carol Flores Castillo, Forero's testimony in 1991 and 1992 at 111: fol. 354, 11: fol. 806. For a helpful guide to the legal process, see *DETDES*, 6:2143–50. For additional context on the Comando Conjunto and Forero's role as medical collaborator, see Mónica González and Héctor Contreras, *Los secretos del Comando Conjunto* (Santiago: Ornitorrinco, 1991), esp. 103, 199, 255–56; cf. *Apsi*, 18-XI-91, pp. 40–44.

37 In the case of Zanghellini, I personally checked on his withdrawal from public life on 5-XII-00 by calling his last-known telephone contacts: his office at Clínica Santa Lucía (335–2644) and his home telephone (208–4852). The office contact yielded a new number and a telephone message for a doctor of a different name. The house telephone yielded an out-of-service message ("se encuentra temporalmente fuera del servicio"). A noteworthy aspect of the culture of the funas was not only investigation to assure a defensible selection of targets, and openness rather than anonymity among the joyfully raucous and angry youth who demonstrated, but also a sidelining of partisan political identity. Activists agreed not to allow political party flags and slogans to muddy the issue of human rights and justice. Youths from the Communist Party, Socialist Party, and Christian Democratic Party all participated, but party stances were not the point.

38 The high-end estimate of 2,000 at the Claro demonstration was from Pedro Matta, interview, 4-XII-00.

39 Manuel Rivas Díaz, telephone interviews 5-XII-00, 6-XII-00 (quotes); and Prefect Pedro Valdivia, telephone interview, 6-XII-00. On 1993 court declaration, see FAV: "Detención y destino final de detenidos desaparecidos por la DINA (1974–1977): Un estudio preliminar," study for Corporación Nacional de Reparación y Reconciliación, September 1995, by Erika Hennings, Viviana Uribe, and Gabriel Guajardo based on declarations of 45 ex–DINA agents, pp. 28, 47, 53–54, 67, 72. The congressional representative Maximiano Errázuriz (of Renovación Nacional) did at one point announce a criminal suit for illicit association to defame persons, but failed to press the matter. It is possible, of course, that the point of suggestion and speculation about lawsuits was not to follow through, but to push activists to end the cycle of funa outings sooner than might otherwise have been the case.

40 *La Segunda*, 18-VIII-00.

41 *La Tercera*, e-ed.: www.tercera.cl, 27-X-98 (Aylwin quote); *La Tercera*, 3-XI-98 (Zalaquett quote).

42 For a fine inside account, see José Zalaquett, "La Mesa de Diálogo sobre derechos humanos y el proceso de transición política en Chile," *Estudios Públicos* 79 (winter 2000): 5–30, and note the same issue's "Documents" section, including interviews and the final Dialogue Table agreement; for opening statements by members showing distinct views of the agenda and languages of

discussion, see www.mesadedialogo.cl, "Intervenciones" link. For mainstream press coverage, see *El Mercurio, La Tercera,* initially 21–22-VIII-99, with extensive reports in subsequent months; and for well-contextualized analysis of the impact of increased judicial pressure, Loveman and Lira, *El espejismo,* 250–67.

43 Composition as given at www.mesadedialogo.cl, "Integrantes" link. Cf. Zalaquett, "La Mesa de Diálogo," 14; and Pereira incident and quote, *El Mercurio,* 22-VIII-99. I have given the spelling of her father's maternal surname as it appeared in *El Mercurio,* not the slightly different spelling used by the Rettig Commission report.

44 Texts reproduced at the Mesa de Diálogo website, www.mesadedialogo.cl, "Integrantes: Intervenciones" link; Salgado, 31-VIII-99, p. 5 (quote); Waghorn, 7-IX-99, pp. 5, 3–4 (quotes). Significantly, two days before the first session of the Mesa, Commander Izurieta stated publicly that as an institution the army did not have secret records on the fate and remains of the disappeared; *El Mercurio*: e-ed., www.elmercurio.cl, 30-VIII-99.

45 Texts reproduced at www.mesadedialogo.cl, "Integrantes: Intervenciones" link; Pereira, 31-VIII-99, p. 1 (quote); also Lira, personal communication, 14-IX-99.

46 Quotes are from text of Pinochet's December 1998 "Carta a los chilenos," as posted in 1999, www.fundacionpinochet.cl, "Documentos históricos" link.

47 For documents and commentary, see Sergio Grez and Gabriel Salazar, eds., *Manifiesto de historiadores* (Santiago: LOM, 1999), esp. documents on 7–44 (16 for quotes), 49 (Mario Garcés on Concepción incident), 89–90 (Leonardo León on the powerful impact of public knowledge and testimony by Gabriel Salazar on his torture at Villa Grimaldi). For a succinct version of Vial's vision of the 1973 crisis, see his "Causas y antecedentes del 11 de septiembre de 1973," in *Análisis crítico del régimen militar,* ed. Gonzalo Vial (Santiago: Universidad Finis Terrae, 1998), 15–21, cf. 263–72 (Vial on Pinochet). Vial went on to produce a biography of Pinochet that depicted him as a flawed hero and giant, within the "Great Man" genre of historical writing: *Pinochet: La biografía,* 2 vols. (Santiago: El Mercurio, 2002). Vial's critique of human rights violations implied that they were gratuitous rather than integral for the regime's project of saving, rebuilding, and modernizing Chile on a new foundation.

48 Text as reproduced at www.mesadedialogo.cl, "Integrantes: Intervenciones," Serrano, 7-IX-99, pp. 1, 2 (quotes). I am also grateful to Serrano for an illuminating conversation about the Mesa de Diálogo and conceptions of history in play, 23-VIII-02.

49 On Agrupación demonstration, see *El Mercurio,* 22-VIII-99; and on FASIC versus CODEPU, particularly useful was a statement of FASIC on the Mesa de Diálogo, 23-VI-00, originally published by the "Nizkor" group and forwarded to author by warresisters@gn.apc.org, 24-VI-00. For an example of collaboration between FASIC and CODEPU on matters of impunity, see chapter 4 in this volume; and on MIRista, Communist, and generational aspects of ambivalence and tension, for

useful (albeit somewhat simplified) investigative journalism, the "Los que apoyan mesa" article in *El Mercurio*, e-ed.: www.elmercurio.cl, 5-IX-99.

50 Text as reproduced at www.mesadedialogo.cl, "Integrantes: Intervenciones," Garretón, 24-IX-99, p. 1 (quote).

51 For the previous two paragraphs, the best starting point is Zalaquett, "La Mesa de Diálogo," esp. 23–27; but also *La Tercera*, e-ed.: www.tercera.cl, 5-III-00, 7-III-00, 6-IV-00, 11-V-00 (the latter a flap about comments on Izurieta by human rights lawyer and Dialogue Table member Héctor Salazar). My awareness of the sense of mockery linked to the March welcome ceremony was also assisted by e-mail communications.

52 Quotes in previous three paragraphs are from "Declaración de la Mesa de Diálogo sobre Derechos Humanos," 12-VI-00, www.mesadedialogo.cl, "Sesiones de la Mesa" link; see also Zalaquett, "La Mesa de Diálogo," 27–30. Cf. the remarks by Lagos on 13-VI-00, reproduced by *La Tercera*, e-ed.: www.tercera.cl, "Casos: Mesa de diálogo: Documentos" link.

53 See Carlos Huneeus, *Chile, un país dividido: La actualidad del pasado* (Santiago: Catalonia, 2003), 74, 82, 79 for figures cited, also 71–80 for broader context. For more detail from the revealing April 1999 survey, see www.cerc.cl, "Encuesta Nacional CERC, Abril de 1999" link; cf. a government poll in October 1998 (reported at *La Tercera*, e-ed.: www.tercera.cl, 1-XI-98) showing that three-fifth majorities both backed the Frei government's initial responses (63 percent) *and* wanted Pinochet judged in Chile, while three-quarters (75 percent) wanted him judged in some form by some jurisdiction. Early in the October 1998 crisis, the government floated three arguments: sovereignty, the capacity of Chilean justice institutions and their higher right to judge him, and a possible humanitarian rationale for Pinochet's return. For shifts in relative weight among arguments, see esp. *La Tercera*, e-ed.: www.tercera.cl, 27-1-99, and the one-year retrospective, 17-X-99; and also *El Mercurio*, e-ed.: www.elmercurio.cl, 4-IV-99. For Pinochetista interest, by 1999, in at least outward signs of a vigorous Chilean judiciary, see the revealing incident in Guzmán Tapia, *En el borde del mundo*, 166.

54 For repercussions of the Supreme Court ruling, see esp. *La Tercera*, e-ed.: www.tercera.cl, 26-VII-99; and also Loveman and Lira, *El espejismo*, 271 (cf. 250–67; and Fuentes, *La transición de los militares*, esp. 116–29, for broader perspective on increased judicial pressure). For the new doctrine's implications for the Dialogue Table, see *El Mercurio*, 29-VIII-99; and on the Dialogue Table list, Zalaquett, "La Mesa de Diálogo," 12 n.7. On arrests of top architects of dirty war and key judicial cases, see *La Tercera*, e-ed.: www.tercera.cl, 4-XI-99, 16-XI-99; and *El Mercurio*, e-ed.: www.elmercurio.cl, 4-IV-99, 15–16-IX-99, 24-IX-99. Cf. *New York Times*, 3-X-99 and note 55. For succinct background on the events and origins of the three reactivated cases, see trilogy Book Two, 26, 51, 226–28 (also 450 n. 47), 310–11 (also 466–67 n. 29), 347 (also 475 n.26).

55 See esp. *El Mercurio*, e-ed.: www.elmercurio.cl, 16-ix-99; and www.emol.com (in the shifting cyber-map of media, the "emol" address emerged in 2000 as the stable new website address for *El Mercurio*), 11–13-xi-00. Cf. "El Mostrador": www.elmostrador.cl, 18-xi-00, 20-xi-00.

56 For background on the initial Pinochet case filed with Guzmán (the court classification for this and subsequent cases was Rol No. 2.182–98), see earlier in this chapter, including note 9. For the subsequent chronology of Pinochet cases, I relied on the systematic tracking calendar by FASIC, published at *La Tercera*, e-ed.: www.tercera.cl, 2-III-00, "Casos: Pinochet: Documentos: Querellas" link.

57 For facsimile copies of Guzman's letter, 4-x-99, Pinochet's reply, 28-x-99, see "El Mostrador": www.elmostrador.cl, 7-XII-00, links at article "Pinochet sí respondió . . ."; for the other events cited and initial Court of Appeals vote approving Guzmán's request, *La Tercera*, e-ed.: www.tercera.cl, and *El Mercurio*, e-ed.: www.elmercurio.cl (also www.emol.com), 4-XI-99, 7-III-00, 6-VI-00, 9-VIII-00 (cf. *New York Times*, 9-VIII-00); and for Judge Guzmán's own account, *En el borde del mundo*, esp. 161–62 (also 148–49 on related 1999 actions). It is worth noting that the putative purpose of parliamentary immunity was to block frivolous lawsuits, not to provide absolute immunity against prosecution for serious criminal offense, if justified by well-founded evidence. The distinction provided the legal basis for a request to strip a congressional official of immunity on a case-by-case basis. In practice, overall politicocultural climate and the balance of de facto power also mattered as judges deliberated; legal reasoning and its likely effectiveness were not disembodied from wider contexts. . .

58 On AFDD difficulties getting an appointment, see Lira and Loveman, *El espejismo de la reconciliación política*, 270–71 (also, author conversations with Sola Sierra and Viviana Díaz).

59 *New Yorker*, 19-x-98, pp. 44–57; Patricia Verdugo, *La caravana de la muerte: Pruebas a la vista* (Santiago: Editorial Sudamericana, 2000). See also note 60.

60 An illuminating measure of softening belligerence is the contrast between, first, Pinochet's open letter to Chileans from London in December 1998, when he presented a proud historical narrative of salvation and complained that self-defined enemies subjected him to "a political-judicial plot, cunning and cowardly, without any moral value": "Carta a los chilenos," www.fundacionpinochet.cl, "Documentos históricos" link; and, second, his short "Day of Unity" message of September 2000. The latter abandoned a memory narrative of salvation for an expression that he had acted in good faith to serve Chile and hoped that "the pain of yesterday" had been superseded. The main point, symbolized by the public reading of the message by his granddaughter María José Martínez, was the appeal that Chileans set aside the past and look to a future of unity, peace, and progress: *El Mercurio*, e-ed.: www.emol.com,

5-IX-00. For additional context, see discussion in the chapter about Izurieta's visit to Pinochet in January 2001, and about the drawing of political distance by the Right.

61 For early reports on the initial arrest order, see *La Tercera*, e-ed.: www.tercera.cl, 1-XII-00, "Extras" link; and "El Mostrador": www.elmostrador.cl, 1-XII-00. The latter usefully notes that at the time of the arrest order, Guzmán had come under pressure because of controversy related to a courtesy note of appreciation to the state's legal representative Clara Szczaranski (president of the Consejo de Defensa del Estado), considered improper by Guzmán's critics; cf. www.tercera.cl, 30-XI-00. A documentary leak that critics attributed to Guzmán also contributed to pressure on him, and a certain danger in the form of discipline by the Supreme Court or pressure to recuse himself. In this perspective, and in view of Pinochet's refusal to submit to face-to-face interrogation, Guzmán had reason to act quickly—to launch the legal shot across the bow— once the legal elements for a justified arrest order were in place. See Guzmán Tapia, *En el borde del mundo*, 177–99, for the judge's account of the arrest decisions, the pressures and maneuvers in play, and the impact of General Lagos's interview. See also www.tercera.cl; and *El Mercurio*, e-ed.: www.emol .com, 2–6-XII-00. For review of the new legal developments, in relation to the Dialogue Table process and a "justice with clemency" idea floated by José Zalaquett, see *El Mercurio*, 10-XII-00, Sunday "Reportajes" section on "El golpe de Guzmán al gobierno"; cf. *New York Times*, 2-XII-00, 13-XII-00. For decisions ratifying the stay of the arrest order, see www.tercera.cl, 12-XII-00, 20-XII-00; and on General Lagos's testimony on Televisión Nacional, 25-I-01, www.elmos trador.cl, www.tercera.cl, 26-I-01.

62 Guzmán Tapia, *En el borde del mundo*, 175–79, on discipline. We have already traced and documented shifting court doctrine and practice in this chapter, and in previous ones, but for a succinct visual chart of Court of Appeals and Supreme Court tendencies toward case closures invoking amnesty versus reopenings based on interpretive doctrine undermining the amnesty's immediate definitive application, during the years 1990–2004, see Fuentes Saavedra, *La transición de los militares*, 128.

63 Presidential speech text reprinted in "El Mostrador": www.elmostrador.cl, 7-I-01; on numerical error in the speech and related polemics, see also *La Tercera*, e-ed., www.tercera.cl, 9-I-01.

64 For the doubts cited, see "El Mostrador": www.elmostrador.cl, 8-I-01, 13-I-01; and *La Tercera*, e-ed.: www.tercera.cl, 8-I-01, 10-I-01, cf. 13–14-I-01. For a good overview of the first week of reaction, see *El Mercurio*, e-ed.: www.emol.com, 14-I-01; and all three newspapers, 5–14-I-01.

65 See *La Tercera*, e-ed.: www.tercera.cl; and "El Mostrador": www.elmostrador.cl, 25-IV-01, 7-V-01. I have assumed that the French-Chilean family members who attended in January were the same as those who arrived in May.

66 See *La Tercera*, e-ed.: www.tercera.cl, "El Mostrador": www.elmostrador.cl, 25-IV-01, 7-V-01.

67 I tracked the twists and turns of the Pinochet case between January and July 2001 in three media: *La Tercera*, e-ed.: www.tercera.cl; "El Mostrador": www .elmostrador.cl; and *El Mercurio*, e-ed.: www.emol.com. For a sample of key controversies and turning points, see the accounts (especially of "El Mostrador") on the following dates: for January medical exams and interrogation, and new house arrest order, 6–7-1-01, 16–18-1-01, 21–24-1-01, 29–30-1-01; narrowing of charges, 8-III-01; fingerprinting issues, 5-IV-01; Pinochet's medical drama, rumors of imminent death, suspension of legal case, 7-VII-01, 9–10-VII-01 (also reports by Mónica González in *Clarín* [Argentina], e-ed.: www .clarin.com.ar, 10–11-VII-01, and retrospective interview of Interior Minister Insulza, www.emol.com, 15-VII-01). See also Guzmán Tapia, *En el borde del mundo*, 190–95, 200–202.

68 Guzmán Tapia, *En el borde del mundo*, 188–90 (cf. 163–69), 203.

69 For intellectually respectable efforts to boost memory as salvation, see, e.g., Víctor Farías, *La izquierda chilena (1969–1973): Documentos para el estudio de su línea estratégica*, 6 vols. (Santiago: Centro de Estudios Públicos, 2000); Cristián Pérez, "Guerrilla rural en Chile: La batalla del Fundo San Miguel (1968)," *Estudios Públicos* 78 (autumn 2000): 181–208; and Pérez, "Salvador Allende, Apuntes sobre su dispositivo de seguridad: El Grupo de Amigos Personales (GAP)," *Estudios Públicos* 79 (winter 2000): 31–81. For a work less serious as scholarship but significant as a marker of counterattack in ongoing memory wars, see Patricia Arancibia Clavel, ed., *Los orígenes de la violencia política en Chile. 1960–1973* (Santiago: Fundación Libertad y Desarrollo, 2001). For the cruder effort of Manuel Contreras Sepúlveda, see *La verdad histórica: El ejército guerrillero, Primer período de la guerra subversiva, abril de 1967 al 10 de setiembre de 1973* (Santiago: Ediciones Encina, 2000), esp. 29–30 (foreigner statistics), 129–36 (casualties statistics); and the follow-up volume, *La verdad histórica II: ¿Desaparecidos?* (Santiago: Ediciones Encina, 2001). For doubt, see *El Mercurio*, e-ed.: www.emol.com, 28-IX-00.

70 The website addresses (which no longer exist) were www.manuelcontreras .com, www.despiertachile.netfirms.com. See *La Tercera*, e-ed.: www.tercera.cl, 28-VII-01 (Contreras site), 22-VIII-01 (Insulza on CNI), 22–25-VIII-01 (Piñera; cf. for same dates "El Mostrador": www.elmostrador.cl, *El Mercurio*, e-ed., www .emol.com). For controversy on the role of Alvaro Puga, an advisor of the military regime and a supportive news commentator from its 1973 inception, see also www.elmostrador.cl, 4-IX-01.

71 For Guzmán's ruling on the DINA, see *El Mercurio*, e-ed.: www.emol.com, 15-VII-01 ("El 'otro' fallo"); cf. "El Mostrador": www.elmostrador.cl, 9-VII-01, and *La Tercera*, e-ed.: www.tercera.cl, 10-VII-01. For the ironic expansion of inquiry, see "Santiago Times": www.santiagotimes.cl, 30-VIII-01. For Izurieta-

Pinochet quotes, *La Tercera* broke the story a half-year later: www.tercera.cl, 15-VII-01 ("Exclusivo: el día que Pinochet se quedó solo"; cf. 6-1-01).

72 On torture estimates and microlevel changes, see the report in the *New York Times*, 3-1-00, cf. 1-VII-99 on College of Medicine estimate. By 2004, torture would become a center-stage cultural issue, and an object of official government inquiry; see chapter 6 in this volume for this development and for complexities of definition and statistics. The highest estimate during the 1998–2001 period was 300,000 ("Primera Línea": www.primeralinea.cl, 5-VII-01). My own estimate is that a methodologically conservative, minimal baseline is that between 50,000 and 70,000 persons suffered torture for political reason under military rule, based on a conservative baseline of 150,000 to 200,000 political detentions under military rule. If one included cruel and degrading treatment (also prohibited under international law) that arguably shades off into torture, the range might well be higher. I am grateful to José Zalaquett for illuminating conversations (27-XI-01, 29-XI-01) on statistics of imprisonment and maltreatment, and on the issue of mass roundup arrests in poblaciones leading to short imprisonments in the 1980s. Responsibility for the estimate, however, is mine alone.

73 The witnesses, in order of occupations given above, were Carlos Bau, Héctor Vera, Juan Ruz, and Ricardo Navarro Valdivia. For key press reports, see "El Mostrador": www.elmostrador.cl, *La Tercera*, e-ed.: www.tercera.cl (cf. *El Mercurio*, www.emol.com), 27-XI-00 (Ruíz-Tagle remains), 8–18-11-01 (wave of witness testimonies, and responses by Interior Minister Insulza), 5-X-01 (denouement and retrospectives).

74 *La Tercera*, e-ed.: www.tercera.cl, 14–15-11-01, 18-11-01 (Insulza); 4-111-01 (Aylwin).

75 *New York Times*, 8-IX-01 (quote). For a thorough treatment that charts events and significance beyond 2001, see Patricia Verdugo, ed., *De la tortura no se habla: Agüero versus Meneses* (Santiago: Catalonia, 2004); and also chapter 6 in this volume.

76 For presidential and congressional election results, 1999–2001, see *La Tercera*, e-ed.: www.tercera.cl, *El Mercurio*, e-ed.: www.emol.com, 13-XII-99 (first round, presidential election), 17-1-00 (second round), 17-XII-01 (congressional election). Cf. comments and analysis in these media during the subsequent week. The UDI's voting share (25.2 percent) in the congressional election jumped sharply from its 1997 vote (14.4 percent) and converted it into the nation's largest political party. On Concertación vulnerability and the UDI's new image, see www.tercera.cl, 14–15-X-01; and for insight on the turn-of-century elections and the Lagos campaign within a context of broader politicocultural changes, Eugenio Tironi, *El cambio está aquí* (Santiago: La Tercera-Mondadori, 2002).

77 See *La Tercera*, e-ed.: www.tercera.cl, 15-VII-01: "Exclusivo: El día que Pinochet se quedó solo" (scoop and related analysis); and 2-IV-01 (Longueira quote).

78 For cultural privatization and transformation, see chapter 4 in this volume. In theoretical terms, one may conceptualize "structure of common sense" as a naturalization of practical experience (and its underlying structure of power relations) embodied in cultural assumptions about what is true, moral, or credible. I gratefully acknowledge my intellectual debt to the work of two pioneers of culture-as-practice theory: Raymond Williams, *Marxism and Literature* (New York: Oxford University Press, 1977), esp. 128–35 on "structures of feeling"; and Pierre Bourdieu, *Outline of a Theory of Practice*, trans. Richard Nice (New York: Cambridge University Press, 1977), esp. 165–69 on "doxa." Of course, a major challenge, particularly when considering Bourdieu's doxa and his closely related concept of the "habitus," is to remain attentive to the fissures, conflicts, and dynamics driving major change. In this regard, the turn in the 1990s toward visions of culture as argument and driven in part by gender dynamics, and of hegemony not only as outcome but as an ongoing contentious process that of necessity incorporates the counterhegemonic, is a crucial analytical complement. For new ways of conceptualizing hegemony, see Florencia E. Mallon, *Peasant and Nation: The Making of Postcolonial Mexico and Peru* (Berkeley: University of California Press, 1995); and William Roseberry, "Hegemony and the Language of Contention," in *Everyday Forms of State Formation: Revolution and the Negotiation of Rule in Modern Mexico*, eds. Gilbert Joseph and Daniel Nugent (Durham, N.C.: Duke University Press, 1994), 355–66, and the anthology more generally. For rethinking "culture as argument" in relation to gender, and to politics and social movements more generally, see Steve J. Stern, *The Secret History of Gender: Women, Men, and Power in Late Colonial Mexico* (Chapel Hill: University of North Carolina Press, 1995); and Sonia E. Alvarez, Evelina Dagnino, and Arturo Escobar, eds., *Cultures of Politics, Politics of Cultures: Re-visioning Latin American Social Movements* (Boulder, Colo.: Westview Press, 1998).

79 On conceptualizing memory and subjectivity (more precisely, intersubjectivity), incisive reflection that also historicizes memory from a social actor perspective is Elizabeth Jelin, *Los trabajos de la memoria* (Madrid: Siglo Veintiuno, 2002). Cf. Elizabeth Jelin and Susana G. Kaufman, "Layers of Memories: Twenty Years After in Argentina," in *The Politics of War Memory and Commemoration*, ed. T. G. Ashplant, Graham Dawson, and Michael Roper (New York: Routledge, 2000), 89–110; and Jelin and Kaufman, eds., *Subjetividad y figuras de la memoria* (Madrid: Siglo Veintiuno, 2006). For "little memories" and the retreat from hegemonizing, see note 80; cf. "little history," in Afterword to chapter 4 in this volume.

80 Matías Rivas and Roberto Merino, eds., *¿Qué hacía yo el 11 de septiembre de 1973?* (Santiago: LOM, 1997), 7 (quotes by editors), 60 (for drizzle and sign: essay by Hernán Soto); Frei's address to Congress on 21-v-99, as reprinted in *El Mercurio*, e-ed.: www.elmercurio.cl, 22-v-99, p. 40 (quote). Beyond the scope of this

study are shifts in education curriculum related to acceptance of plural memory and retreat from hegemonizing claims, yet also cognizant of the politics of curriculum and texts in circumstances of divided memory. For announcement in March 2000 by the Ministry of Education that it would recommend readings and documents, for secondary school students, that brought forth varied contending perspectives about the 1973 crisis and military rule, see *La Tercera*, e-ed.: www.tercera.cl, 4-III-00; and for critical analysis, Leonora Reyes Jedlicki, "Actores, conflicto y memoria: Reforma curricular de Historia y Ciencias Sociales en Chile, 1990–2003," in *Educación y memoria: La escuela elabora el pasado*, ed. Elizabeth Jelin and Federico Guillermo Lorenz (Madrid: Siglo Veintiuno, 2004), 65–93.

81 Dates of death were, for Merino, 30-VIII-96; Mendoza, 13-IX-96; Leigh, 29-IX-99; Silva, 9-IV-99; Sierra, 1-VII-99. For ceremonies, street crowds, and cultural commentary, see *El Mercurio*, *La Tercera* during the week following each date. For Sola Sierra's homage to Cardinal Silva only months before her own passing, see AFDD, *Informativo* 63 (April 1999); and for the ways Silva's passing was a memory knot that mobilized contending memories about Silva, the Church, and human rights—notably, the legacy of "Good Samaritan" versus that of "Prophet"—Cruz, *Iglesia, represión y memoria*, 67–81.

82 Percentages are based on the population and age group estimates at midyear, 30-VI-00, in Chile, Instituto Nacional de Estadísticas (hereinafter INE), *Anuario de estadísticas vitales 2000* (Santiago: INE, 2002), 51, cuadro 1.2.1–3. Rounding off explains why the total percentage given in the text for Chileans under 25 years old is 44.7, not 44.8. The national census of 2002 showed that the age-structure estimates given in 2000 were sound. See INE, *Anuario de estadísticas vitales 2002* (Santiago: INE, 2004), 31, cuadro 1.2.1–2; and for additional orientation, www.ine.cl.

83 "El Mostrador": www.elmostrador.cl, 1-X-01, 29-X-01, for Caravan of Death re-enactment; 15-VIII-01, 31-VIII-01, for youth survey results (Tercera Encuesta Nacional de Juventud, conducted in September 2000). Overall among youth, the "discriminatory" and "classist" characterizations were given by 61.2 and 66.7 percent, respectively. Among young people of voting age (eighteen to twenty-nine years old), weariness with human rights also reflected a more general skepticism about civic and political life. Only four in ten (38 percent) had registered to vote; the number who identified with the Concertación declined from 43 percent in 1994 to only 16 percent in 2000.

Afterword to Chapter 5: Covering History with History?

1 I personally reviewed changes in civic geography during a field visit to Chile in December 2000 and in the National History Museum during a field visit in

. August 2002, and compared these observations with field notes from July 1996. For background on the project to update the National History Museum exhibit, and cultural tensions sparked by the project, see the excellent account by Tina Rosenberg, "Through Allende's Broken Glasses: A View of Chile Today," in *New York Times*, 13-III-02.

2 On the 1980–81 refurbishing of civic Santiago and La Moneda, see Book Two of this trilogy: Stern, *Battling for Hearts and Minds: Memory Struggles in Pinochet's Chile, 1973–1988* (Durham, N.C.: Duke University Press, 2006), 173–76; and on the presidential statues debates, Katherine Hite, "El monumento a Salvador Allende en el debate político chileno," in *Monumentos, memoriales y marcas territoriales*, ed. Elizabeth Jelin and Victoria Langland (Madrid: Siglo Veintiuno, 2003), 19–55. See also chapter 3 in this volume; *Hoy*, 15-V-95, pp. 17–19; and *La Segunda*, 5-V-95.

3 *La Tercera*, e-ed.: www.tercera.cl, 27-VI-00 (quote); Hite, "El monumento a Salvador Allende," 42–52. Cf. *El Mercurio*, e-ed.: www.emol.com, 27-VI-00.

4 The description is based on field notes and photographs, 8-XII-00, supplemented by aesthetic commentary by the sculptor Arturo Hevia in Hite, "El monumento a Salvador Allende en el debate político chileno," 42–47.

5 I am grateful to Florencia Mallon for sharing her 2001 field observations and photographs of the Temuco Peace Park, and for insight on the significance of the canelo. Also helpful was a report by CODEPU (Committee for Defense of the Rights of the People) about the Temuco Peace Park, inaugurated on 16-VI-01 after seven years of work: www.codepu.cl, "Resumen de prensa 11 al 17 de junio de 2001." I thank War Resisters International for alerting me to CODEPU reports via e-mail, 25-VI-01, 6-IV-01. The Temuco project was not the only significant new memorialization project in the south. In Valdivia, in 2001, activists apparently secured government assistance and approval in principle for an enlarged regional memorial to the executed and disappeared at the local cemetery. On the Valdivia project, I am grateful to Claudio Barrientos for sharing field-based observations; and www.codepu.cl, "Resumen de prensa 26 a 31 de marzo de 2001." For additional insight on the history of repression and memory in these regions, see Mallon, *Courage Tastes of Blood: The Mapuche Community of Nicolás Ailío and the Chilean State, 1906–2001* (Durham, N.C.: Duke University Press, 2005), esp. 136–248; and Barrientos, "'Y las enormes trilladoras vinieron [. . .] a llevarse la calma': Neltume, Liquiñe y Chihuío, tres escenarios de la construcción cultural de la memoria y la violencia en el sur de Chile," in *Luchas locales, comunidades e identidades*, ed. Ponciano del Pino and Elizabeth Jelin (Madrid: Siglo Veintiuno, 2003), 107–44.

6 For elaboration of the ways the making of memory is also a making of silence, in dialogue with the theoretical framework that informs this trilogy and with pertinent scholarly literature, see Book One in this trilogy: Stern, *Remembering Pinochet's Chile: On the Eve of London 1998* (Durham, N.C.: Duke University

Press, 2004), 149–52, cf. 133–42; and for a brilliant case study of the making of memory and silence, in a Peruvian community context, Ponciano del Pino, "Uchuraccay: Memoria y representación de la violencia política en los Andes," in *Jamás tan cerca, arremetió lo lejos: Memoria y violencia política en el Perú*, ed. Carlos Iván Degregori (Lima: Instituto de Estudios Peruanos, 2003), 49–93 (a similar version is in del Pino and Jelin, *Luchas locales, comunidades e identidades*, 11–62).

7 For background and context on the Eternal Flame of Liberty and its subsequent history of conflict and shifting locations, see trilogy Book Two, 70–73, 326–27; and also Ximena Tocornal Montt, "Escenarios de la memoria en conflicto: A propósito de la Llama de la Libertad y/o Altar de la Patria y del Memorial del Detenido Desaparecido y del Ejecutado Político," paper for Social Science Research Council fellowship project on "Memoria colectiva y represión," February 2000. My site visits included the former location at Cerro Santa Lucía (December 1977) and that facing the rear of La Moneda (July 1999, December 2000).

8 For early use of Londres 38 by the DINA, see trilogy Book One, 45–47; and for a good summation of conditions there, *ICNVR*, vol. 1, bk. 2: 464–65. Cf. *ICNPPT*, 442–43. For additional insight, I am especially grateful to Erika Hennings, interview, 5-VI-97. For a 1995 site demonstration by relatives of the disappeared publicizing the reality of the building whose address had changed to "Londres 40," see AFDD, *Un camino de imágenes . . . que revelan y se rebelan contra una historia no contada: 20 años de historia . . .* (Santiago: AFDD, 1997), 140.

9 I first visited the interior of the Londres 38/Londres 40 site of the O'Higgins Institute on 2 September 1998. I am grateful to a member of the staff—to whom I presented only a selective truth, that I was a historian interested in the Chilean past and memory of O'Higgins—for a tour, orientation, and permission to spend time in the upstairs reading room to review institute pamphlets and its magazine, *Revista Libertador O'Higgins*. I based the "readiness" date for transfer on the July 1988 starting date in the visitor log, "Libro de Visitantes y Lectores de la Biblioteca." A number of smaller rooms or cubicles upstairs had not been refurbished since the times of horror—they were locked, with views of the inside hidden by opaque glass on the doors. On General Carrasco and repression in Lota, see trilogy Book Two, 98, cf. 42–43, 325. For new developments and the post-2004 drive to reclaim Londres 38 as a memory site, see Afterword to chapter 6 in this volume.

Chapter 6: Memory as Unfinished Work

1 See the Chilean press (esp. *El Mercurio, La Tercera, La Nación*, "El Mostrador"), 2–7-VII-03; but for an especially revealing inside account of the decision to

retire within the broad context of the Supreme Court decision and legal strategies, *El Mercurio*, e-ed., www.emol.com, 7-VII-03 ("La 'carta bomba' del general"). For reflection by the prosecuting judge on the consistency of the Court decision with urgings to him by visitors, and with preparation of the public for a medical exit from the Pinochet problem, see Juan Guzmán Tapia, *En el borde del mundo: Memorias del juez que procesó a Pinochet* (Barcelona: Anagrama, 2005), 202–3; cf. chapter 5 in this volume.

2 "Declaración de la Mesa de Diálogo sobre Derechos Humanos," 12-VI-00, www.mesadedialogo.cl (subsequently available at www.ddhh.gov.cl and reprinted at *Estudios Públicos* 79 [winter 2000]: 481–87); Elizabeth Lira and Brian Loveman, *Políticas de reparación: Chile, 1990–2004* (Santiago: LOM, 2005), 40–41, 163–67, 209–12; Brian Loveman and Elizabeth Lira, *El espejismo de la reconciliación política: Chile, 1990–2002* (Santiago: LOM, 2002), 310, 330–31, 334–38, 377–78, 418–19, 422. See also note 3.

3 Universidad Diego Portales, Facultad de Derecho (hereinafter UDPFD), *Informe anual sobre derechos humanos en Chile 2004 (Hechos de 2003)* (Santiago: Universidad Diego Portales, 2004), 114–33 (which also takes note of court decisions that cut in the other direction), 184, 191; Lira and Loveman, *Políticas de reparación*, 172–77, 203–4, 460–62. Another important judicial case was that of the 1982 murder of the labor leader Tucapel Jiménez and the related cover-up. In 2002, Judge Sergio Muñoz found various officers guilty; the case also exposed responsibility at the highest levels of the secret police (CNI). The subsequent debate was not about whether justice should be served but about whether the sentences were adequately severe, given the crime. Since the murder of Jiménez took place after the amnesty period, I have not devoted space to it in the text. See Benedicto Castillo Irribarra, *Emblemático crimen de Tucapel Jiménez: El Cóndor quiere carne* (Santiago: Editorial Mare Nostrum, 2005). For a sense of impact in 2002, see also reports and documentary links (including judicial sentence) in "El Mostrador," www.elmostrador.cl, 5-VIII-02, 9-VIII-02; *El Mercurio*, e-ed., www.emol.com, 5–8-VIII-02; and interview article with Judge Muñoz, *Siete + 7*, 24-VIII-02, pp. 12–15. For significance of the murder in its original 1980s context, see Book Two of this trilogy: Stern, *Battling for Hearts and Minds: Memory Struggles in Pinochet's Chile, 1973–1988* (Durham, N.C.: Duke University Press, 2006), 226–28.

4 UDPFD, *Informe anual . . . (Hechos de 2003)*, 187–89, which also takes useful note of the distinct dispositions of Judge Valdovinos and Judge Urrutia to press forward the case in which they ended up sharing responsibility; Lira and Loveman, *Políticas de reparación*, 170–72. For more background on Lonquén as a memory knot and the effort to erase evidence through second disposals of bodies, see trilogy Book Two, 156–67, 137, 427–28 n. 2.

5 Tension over the Campos cover-up and the push for resignation of Ríos heated up in September and October of 2002. The best starting point, with useful

retrospective and links, is "El Mostrador": www.elmostrador.cl, 11-x-02, 14–15-x-02. See also mainstream coverage as the problematic nature of the air force information began emerging, e.g., *La Tercera*, e-ed., www.tercera.cl, 22-ix-02 ("La semana en que Lagos perdió paciencia"); and *El Mercurio*, e-ed., www.emol.com, 27-ix-02 ("La Moneda pide más precisión"). For the 2003 ruling, see UDPFD, *Informe anual . . . (Hechos de 2003)*, 189.

6 Guzmán Tapia, *En el borde del mundo*, 206–22. For the Estadio Nacional case and impact of foreign witnesses, see also *El Mercurio*, e-ed.: www.emol.com, 15-v-02; *La Tercera*, e-ed.: www.tercera.cl, 15-v-02; "El Mostrador": www.elmostrador.cl, 14-v-02 (also 11-v-02); *El Siglo*, 24-v-02; and Steven Volk, "Judgment Day in Chile," *NACLA Report on the Americas* 36, no. 1 (July–August 2002), 4–6, 43–44. For Guzmán and the helicopter flights, the breakthrough account by Jorge Escalante was in *La Nación*, e-ed.: www.lanacion.cl, 23-xi-03 (see *El Mercurio*, *La Tercera*, "El Mostrador" during the last week of November for reactions and press attention).

7 Juan Emilio Cheyre, "2003: Un desafío de futuro," in *La Tercera*, 5-1-03 and in Army Press Communiqué, 6-1-03, www.ejercito.cl (quotes); for additional analysis and press reaction, "El Mostrador": www.elmostrador.cl, 5-1-03, and the rest of Chilean press, 6-1-03 and over the subsequent week; for excellent analysis of Cheyre's stance within the shifting context of civil-military relations and judges' emergence as key actors, Claudio Fuentes Saavedra, *La transición de los militares: Relaciones civiles-militares en Chile, 1990–2006* (Santiago: LOM, 2006), esp. 122–23, 130–33, 139–46 for budgetary aspects; and for Cheyre's court testimony about his own relation to a human rights case, Loveman and Lira, *El espejismo de la reconciliación política*, 426. Cf. Cheyre's stance when Judge Muñoz sentenced officers in the Tucapel Jiménez murder case, in *El Mercurio*, e-ed.: www.emol.com, 7-viii-02.

8 Cheyre quotes from *El Mercurio*, 14-vi-03, 6-vi-03, respectively, as reprinted in www.memoriaviva.com, "Boletín" 68 link, 1–15-vi-03.

9 On Bachelet and symbolism, see esp. *El Mercurio*, 13-1-02. Cf. *El Mercurio*, *La Tercera*, and "El Mostrador," e-editions at www.emol.com, www.tercera.cl, and www.elmostrador.cl, respectively, 8–9-1-02; *Latin America Weekly Report*, 15-1-02, p. 36; and on the circumstances of General Bachelet's death, *ICNVR*, vol. 1, bk. 2: 498.

10 Guzmán Tapia, *En el borde del mundo*, 215.

11 UDPFD, *Informe anual . . . (Hechos de 2003)*, 190.

12 See, in addition to chapter 5 in this volume, Lira and Loveman, *Políticas de reparación*, 71–73; and Anne Pérotin-Dumon, "El pasado vivo de Chile en el año del Informe sobre la Tortura: Apuntes de una historiadora," *Nuevo Mundo Mundos Nuevos*, http://nuevomundo.revues.org 5 (2005): 7, 34 n. 41.

13 For a thorough account of the Agüero-Meneses affair—including chronology, legal aspects, internal dynamics and strains at Catholic University, and media

treatment—see Patricia Verdugo, ed., *De la tortura no se habla: Agüero versus Meneses* (Santiago: Catalonia, 2004), esp. Verdugo, "Los protagonistas," 17–44; Carmen Hertz, "El proceso, 61–89; Claudio Fuentes, "Golpe a la cátedra," 91–116; and Sebastián Brett, "El caso en la prensa," 117–40. The conflict also yielded reports in United States media: see *New York Times*, 8-IX-01; and *Chronicle of Higher Education*, 17-VIII-01, also 13-1-03.

14 "Primera Línea," primeralinea.cl, 5-VII-01, 25-VI-02; Inter Press Service News Agency, www.ipsnews.net, 19-VI-02 ("Activists Demand Reparations"); "El Mostrador": www.elmostrador.cl, 25-VI-03 (quote); *La Nación*, e-ed., www .lanacion.cl, 9-VI-03; and "No aceptamos más verdad a cambio de impunidad," 24-VIII-03, posted 31-VIII-03 at Argenpress, www.argenpress.info, and note twenty-four organizations as cosigners (in comparison to twelve founding organizations in 2001). Publicity about torture in 2003 also included an account of Pinochet's blunt comments about the topic to the Lutheran bishop Helmut Frenz, who attended the June 2003 meeting with Lagos, in *El Siglo*, 10-VII-03; cf. Frenz, *Mi vida chilena: Solidaridad con los oprimidos* (Santiago: LOM, 2006), 9–11.

15 Lira and Loveman, *Políticas de reparación*, 74 (quote, citing *El Mercurio*, 10-XII-02); UDPFD, *Informe anual . . . (Hechos de 2003)*, 194–97.

16 For the initial Alegría-Mery events, I relied principally on the electronic news clipping service in the bimonthly human rights news bulletins, July to September 2003, published at www.memoriaviva.com, "Boletín" link. For chronology and data cited, see the articles therein from *El Mercurio*, 11-VII-03, 13–14-VIII-03; *La Nación*, 14-VII-03, 17-VII-03, 20-VII-03 (the best investigative report, and also for Alegría quote); *La Tercera*, 15-VII-03, 22–23-VII-03, 12-IX-03; and for September denouement, "El Mostrador," 27-IX-03. For events after September 2003, see also note 17.

17 Quotes are from author's copy of the "Declaración Pública" of the women, dated 23-VII-03, circulated on the Internet. I am grateful to Karin Rosemblatt for forwarding me the copy. The examples of solidarity by former political prisoners are from *La Nación*, 20-VII-03, *El Mercurio*, 13-VIII-03, as reproduced in the electronic bulletin cited in note 16. For the Alegría-Mery court case after the resignation, a related court case by other political prisoners, and Mery's eventual rehabilitation as a figure important in human rights work, *La Nación*, e-ed.: www.lanacion.cl, is systematic and useful: see 29-IX-03 (initiation of case against Alegría), 27-IV-04 (ruling against Alegría), 20–21-v-04 (legal appeal initiated), 27-VIII-04 (Mery's release from complaint by other prisoners), 10-IX-04 (Mery after favorable Supreme Court review), 17-X-04 (early rehabilitation: report on tensions between Investigations Police and Army during democratic transition), 8-VI-06 (reduction of sentence against Alegría in view of good behavior and psychological suffering), and 29-VII-07 (rehabilitation: interview of Mery as expert on important pending human rights matters).

18 Carlos Huneeus, *Chile, un país dividido: La actualidad del pasado* (Santiago:

Catalonia, 2003), 49, 56, 194–95, 174, for survey data; for 11 September anniversary as memory knot, Azun Candina Polomer, "El día interminable: Memoria e instalación del 11 de septiembre de 1973 en Chile (1974–1999)," in *Las conmemoraciones: Las disputas en las fechas "in-felices,"* ed. Elizabeth Jelin (Madrid: Siglo Veintiuno, 2002), 9–48. See also Afterword by Jelin, 49–51; Marcelo Casals Araya, "Silencios, memorias y poder: Los vaivenes de la conmemoraciones del 'Once' chileno, 2001–2006" (unpublished paper, history graduate seminar on "Memoria, violencia política y actores sociales," Pontificia Universidad Católica de Chile, 2006); and Alfred Joignant, *Un día distinto: Memorias festivas y batallas conmemorativas en torno al 11 de septiembre en Chile, 1974–2006* (Santiago: Editorial Universitaria, 2007), esp. 79–119. It is worth noting that the "Day of Unity" holiday created in 1998 as an alternative failed to resonate much and was repealed in 2001. For August and September as a memory season, both for the army and nation, see chapter 1 in this volume.

19 Juan Emilio Cheyre, "2003: Un desafío de futuro," in *La Tercera*, 5-1-03 and in Army Press Communiqué, 6-1-03, www.ejercito.cl (cf. admiring article on Cheyre's political skills, *El Mercurio*, e-ed.: www.emol.com, 6-VI-03); *La Nación*, e-ed.: www.lanacion.cl, 5-VI-03. See also, for "commemorative anxieties" context, Joignant, *Un día distinto*, 81–87.

20 On television, other media, and cultural events, I am particularly indebted to Huneeus, *Chile, un país dividido*, 249–50, 252–63 (253 for survey data cited); Marcela Ríos Tobar, "La explosión de la memoria: Conmemoraciones del 30mo aniversario del Golpe Militar en Chile" (unpublished paper, history graduate seminar on "Political Violence and Memory in Latin America," University of Wisconsin, Madison, 2003); Casals Araya, "Silencios, memorias y poder," 20–21 (quotes from *The Clinic*, 21-VIII-03, 11-IX-03); and *La Nación*, e-ed.: www.lanacion.cl, 11-IX-03 ("Como los medios abordarán el 11"). For interest in the human and authentic, through themes such as sound, music, sport, film, and technology, see also Claudio Rolle, ed., *1973: La vida cotidiana de un año crucial* (Santiago: Planeta, 2003). For the continued influence of political polarization as a framing narrative in television in 2003, and incisive discussion of the politics and plurality of social memory, see Mario Garcés and Sebastián Leiva, *El Golpe en La Legua: Los caminos de la historia y la memoria* (Santiago: LOM, 2005), 9–27.

21 For previous two paragraphs, aside from sources in note 20, see audio-visual documentation, *El sueño existe, Estadio Nacional 5 y 6 de septiembre 2003, Chile y el mundo recuerdan a Salvador Allende*, directed by Carmen Luz Parot (DVD, Alerce, 2005; copy in possession of author); for Angel Parra rap, *¡Venceremos! Homenaje a Salvador Allende, 11 septiembre 1973–11 septiembre 2003* (CD, EMI, 2003; copy in possession of author); and for events at La Moneda and in Plaza de la Constitución, widely covered in the Chilean press on 10–11-IX-03, *El Mercurio*, e-ed., www.emol.cl, 10-IX-03 (Insulza quote). For original context of

erasure of the Morandé 80 door, see trilogy Book Two, 173–76; for continued symbolic potency and contentiousness in the 1990s, chapter 4 in this volume; and for a perceptive argument on Allende's transformation from martyr of the Left into icon of the Republic, and the contrasting fate of Pinochet, Joignant, *Un día distinto*, 97–119.

22 The estimate of 12,000 follows "El Mostrador," www.elmostrador, 11-IX-03; the traditionally low estimate by carabineros was 6,000, while some organizers claimed a turnout of 40,000. On Lagos and symbolic politics of La Moneda in a larger context, see the apt comments of Pérotin-Dumon, "El pasado vivo de Chile en el año del Informe sobre la Tortura," 4–5.

23 *La Nación*, e-ed.: www.lanacion.cl, 14-IX-03 (quote). Three youths had started a hunger strike but were hospitalized after seventeen days; a half-dozen women of the Agrupación continued the fast on a rotating basis.

24 On human rights matters and a tendency toward the reactive in the early Lagos years, see note 25. The annual real growth rates (i.e., at constant prices) in GDP are based on the 1996–2005 series and the 2003–06 series (for verified rather than preliminary figures for 2004–06) that are given, along with unemployment and the copper statistics cited later in this note, in Banco Central de Chile, "Base de Datos Estadísticos" link (accessed 12-VI-07), www.bcentral.cl. The overall three-year annual average growth for 2004–06 was 5.2 percent (which reflected a softened growth rate of 4.0 percent in 2006). The surging world market price for copper, facilitated by the roaring growth (ca. 10 percent sustained growth) and raw material needs of the Chinese economy, was in part responsible for the boom. Calculated on a base where the 2003 price = 100, copper prices amounted to only 82.5 in 2002 but soared to 210.0 in 2005, and 367.3 in 2006. The Lagos government also moved aggressively to expand international trade and reached free trade agreements with the European Union, the United States, South Korea, and China during 2003–05. For return in 2003–06 to a fast reduction of poverty (from 18.7 percent to 13.7 percent), after a sluggish reduction in 1998–2003 (from 21.6 percent to 18.7 percent), and for somewhat improved income distribution, see the 2006 household survey of Mideplan (Ministerio de Planificación y Cooperación), www.mideplan.cl, CASEN 2006 (Encuesta de Caracterización Socioeconómica Nacional) link, published June 2007 (accessed 23-VII-07), Serie 1: "Pobreza en Chile 2006," esp. Table 1, and Serie 2, "Distribución del ingreso e impacto distributivo del gasto social 2006," esp. Tables 1–2, 5–6, 13. The results on poverty and distribution, while encouraging, still showed very high income concentration and did not imply that labor or the poor received a "fair share" in an economy heavily tilted toward capital and export markets. See commentary summarized in "Santiago Times": www.santiagotimes.cl, 3-VII-07; and for analytical critique, Hugo Fazio Rigazzi, *Lagos: El presidente "progresista" de la Concertación* (Santiago: LOM, 2006). Cf. Hugo Fazio et al., *Gobierno de Lagos: Balance crítico* (Santiago: LOM, 2005); and Peter Winn, ed., *Victims of the Miracle:*

Workers and Neoliberalism in the Pinochet Era, 1973–2002 (Durham, N.C.: Duke University Press, 2004). For politicocultural implications of transition from an era of 7 percent growth expectations to 4 percent expectations, see Eugenio Tironi, *El cambio está aquí* (Santiago: La Tercera-Mondadori, 2002), 85–136; for the impact of corruption charges late in 2002 and early 2003 on ability to pursue a human rights initiative, UDPFD, *Informe anual . . . (Hechos de 2003)*, 169 n. 3; and for fizzling of high-profile corruption charges against the Ministry of Public Works officials Carlos Cruz and Sergio Cortés, and Congressman Juan Pablo Letelier, see, e.g., *La Nación*, e-ed.: www.lanacion.cl, 11–12-111-03, 18-VI-03, 28-VIII-03. For the role of 2003 in the political turnaround by Lagos, see the useful retrospective by Justin Vogler in "Santiago Times": www.santiagotimes.cl, 11-111-06.

25   For nonresponsiveness, see Lira and Loveman, *Políticas de reparación*, 79–87; UDPFD, *Informe anual . . . (Hechos de 2003)*, 168–69 and n. 3; and for acute observation and insight on reactive versus pro-active tendencies within political elite culture, José Zalaquett, " 'No Hay Mañana Sin Ayer': Análisis de la propuesta del Presidente Lagos sobre derechos humanos," *Estudios Públicos* 92 (spring 2003): 62–63.

26   See UDPFD, *Informe anual . . . (Hechos de 2003)*, 167–73; and Lira and Loveman, *Políticas de reparación*, 188–94. See also "El Mostrador": www.elmostrador.cl, 21-VI-03, for protest march; and Huneeus, *Chile, un país dividido*, 259, for UDI and credibility on human rights with about a quarter of voters. For lucid discussion of the rationale for incentives, within a broader discussion of moral refounding after times of denied or secret atrocity and in a context differentiated from the UDI's time deadline, see Zalaquett, " 'No Hay Mañana Sin Ayer': Análisis de la propuesta," 29–75, esp. 47–48, 54, 66–69, 71–72.

27   For the previous three paragraphs, Lagos speech and quotes, 12-VIII-03, Ministerio del Interior, Programa de Derechos Humanos, www.ddhh.gov.cl, "No Hay Mañana Sin Ayer" link; and for debates and legislative follow-ups, Lira and Loveman, *Políticas de reparación*, 194–204, 471–77 (472 for Pizarro quote); UDPFD, *Informe anual . . . (Hechos de 2003)*, 173–83. See also *La Nación*, e-ed.: www.lanacion.cl, 18-VIII-03, for related debates over 1978 amnesty; and *El Mercurio*, 7-XI-04, for profiles of the commissioners. The bulk of social repair spending had gone to compensate over 85,000 people politically purged from jobs under military rule. The conversion to U.S. dollars is based on average exchange rate (691.4 pesos) for 2003, as given by Banco Central de Chile, www.bcentral.cl, "Base de Datos Estadísticos" link (accessed 17-1-08).

28   *ICNPPT*, 21–29, 24–25 (quote), also published in electronic format, www.comi siontortura.cl (accessed 1-XII-04).

29   The "zombie" analogy is from Pedro Matta, 3-IX-06, in the context of a site visit by Chilean students to Parque Por la Paz Villa Grimaldi. For scholarship on torture, the best starting point is the brilliant reflection by Elaine Scarry, *The Body in Pain: The Making and Unmaking of the World* (New York: Oxford Univer-

sity Press, 1985). For additional perspective attentive to psychological and historical aspects, especially in South America and the United States, see Lawrence Weschler, *A Miracle, A Universe: Settling Accounts with Torturers*, rev. ed. (Chicago: University of Chicago Press, 1998); and Alfred W. McCoy, *A Question of Torture: CIA Interrogation, from the Cold War to the War on Terror* (New York: Metropolitan Books, 2006). Cf. A. J. Langguth, *Hidden Terrors: The Truth about U.S. Police Operations in Latin America* (New York: Pantheon, 1978).

30 *ICNPPT*, 22.

31 Ibid., 29–79 (68–69, 73–74, 76–77 for statistics cited), 87–92; for the 2005 follow-up qualifications, in the context of wider debates, UDPFD, *Informe anual sobre derechos humanos en Chile 2006 (Hechos de 2005)* (Santiago: Universidad Diego Portales, 2006), 285–86. Despite the culture of cover-up and make-believe truth under military rule, in the early phase before secret police units organized more sophisticated targeting and techniques of repression and misinformation, and for prisoner-survivors compared to the disappeared, some state agencies generated documents acknowledging the detention. Hence, documents from military offices or a state agency such as SENDET (Secretaría Ejecutiva Nacional de Detenidos, or National Executive Secretariat of Prisoners) could be useful. For examples, see *ICNPPT*, 93–107. Even in the acknowledged cases, however, the archives of the human rights and victim communities were important, since they gathered information on taboo aspects such as torture.

32 For influential and cogent reasoning on the problem of proof of torture in individual cases, see Zalaquett, "'No Hay Mañana Sin Ayer': Análisis de la propuesta," 42, 52–53. Cf. *ICNPPT*, 74; and Lucas Sierra, "Hechos y contexto," originally in *El Mercurio*, 6-XII-04, reprinted in *Estudios Públicos* 98 (autumn 2005): 378–80. For reasoning and standards on political imprisonment as violation of human rights, cross-check methodology, and detention sites, see *ICNPPT*, 26–29, 42–46, 259–466; cf. Pérotin-Dumon, "El pasado vivo de Chile en el año del Informe sobre la Tortura," 18–20, on the high truth-value of the Valech Commission's findings—including those on the pervasiveness of torture—by the standards of historical methodology and reasoning.

33 *ICNPPT*, 74, 223–57, cf. 259–466.

34 Ibid., 177–78 (178 for quotes), cf. 159–221. On the chronology of detentions, discrepancies appear in the absolute number of detentions given on 177, 201–21, but do not change the order of magnitudes over time.

35 See Ascanio Cavallo, "Tres claves sobre el Informe Valech," originally in *La Tercera*, 5-XII-04, reprinted in *Estudios Públicos* 98 (autumn 2005): 373–77, for perceptive early comment by an influential observer on complicity and culture.

36 *ICNPPT*, 493–513 (504 for quotes), cf. 17–18.

37 For the link between double life and memory as rupture, in a context of dialogue with Holocaust scholarship and literature, see Book One of this trilogy:

Stern, *Remembering Pinochet's Chile: On the Eve of London 1998* (Durham, N.C.: Duke University Press, 2004), 108–9, 203–4 n. 8.

38 Interview, Cristián Correa, 8-1-07 ("silence"); *ICNPPT*, 17–18, 243, 493–513; Pérotin-Dumon, "El pasado vivo de Chile en el año del Informe sobre la Tortura," 8–10 (10 for quote). For baseline estimates, see also chapter 5, note 72, in this volume.

39 *ICNPPT*, 17–18 (quotes).

40 Figures in the last two paragraphs are based on the statistics in *ICNPPT*, 467–89. On masculinity and politics in the early 1970s, see the pioneering studies of Heidi Tinsman, *Partners in Conflict: The Politics of Gender, Sexuality, and Labor in the Chilean Agrarian Reform, 1950–1973* (Durham, N.C.: Duke University Press, 2002); and Florencia E. Mallon, "Barbudos, Warriors, and Rotos: The MIR, Masculinity, and Power in the Chilean Agrarian Reform, 1965–74," in *Changing Men and Masculinities in Latin America*, ed. Matthew C. Gutmann (Durham, N.C.: Duke University Press, 2003), 179–215.

41 *ICNPPT*, 242–43 (quotes), 251–57, 507–8. The Valech Commission defined "sexual aggressions and violence" as coerced "realization or suffering of acts of a sexual character" (242). Such acts thereby encompassed, e.g., forced witness and threats and simulations of rape, as well as acts of violent penetration.

42 Ibid., 252.

43 Ibid., 244 ("testicles"), 252, 254–56 (256 for "being a person" quote).

44 Particularly insightful on the increasing necessity of a postheroic defense that separated Pinochet the person from the work and legacies of military rule is the report by *El Mercurio*, 8-VIII-04, "La semana en que se quebró el pinochetismo." See also notes 45–46.

45 *El Mercurio*, 6-XI-04 (Cheyre quote). I am grateful to CEDOP (Centro de Documentación Política of the Pontificia Universidad Católica de Chile) for allowing me to consult its press clippings file (especially tema no. 14, Derechos Humanos—Chile) to track responses and press coverage. Also helpful are the articles and reprinted newspaper columns in *Estudios Públicos* 98 (2005), the issue entitled "Reacciones al Informe sobre Prisión Política y Tortura" (e-edition at www.cepchile.cl). The articles included examples of more skeptical reaction to the "proof value" of the Valech Report, including a cranky critique by Gonzalo Vial, 354–72, who compared its methodology unfavorably with that of the Rettig Commission but seemed unmindful of comparative scholarship on truth commissions that demonstrates the unusual scale and methodological options available to the Rettig Commission. See Priscilla Hayner, *Unspeakable Truths: Facing the Challenge of Truth Commissions* (New York: Routledge, 2002). Interestingly, Vial had written a biography of Pinochet that resorted to a "mixed record" approach and comparison with other historical figures, within a "Great Man" tradition of historical writing, to build a nuanced version of heroic salvation memory. The work acknowledged Pinochet's limitations and the human

rights record while envisioning him as a leader of great and positive consequence. Gonzalo Vial, *Pinochet: La biografía*, 2 vols. (Santiago: El Mercurio, 2002).

46 *El Mercurio*, 13-XI-04 (editorial quote), 14-XI-04 (García testimonio).

47 *El Mercurio*, 4-XII-04 (poll; cf. Pérotin-Dumon, "El pasado vivo de Chile en el año del Informe sobre la Tortura," 8, 35 n. 17); "Manifiesto de historiadores: Contra los que torturan en nombre de la patria," dated 16-XII-04 and reprinted in *El Siglo*, 24-XII-04 (quote).

48 On the impact of Riggs Bank revelations, see the Chilean press (esp. *El Mercurio*, *La Tercera*, *La Nación*, "El Mostrador") during 16-VII-04 to 8-VIII-04, which is well summarized in "Santiago Times": www.santiagotimes.cl; see also note 49 in this chapter. Cf. *New York Times*, 19-VII-04.

49 Fuentes Saavedra, *La transición de los militares*, 90–92 (91 for Larraín and Cardemil quotes); *El Mercurio*, 8-VIII-04 (Pinochetismo quote). Cf. editorials in *El Mercurio*, *La Tercera*, 18-VII-04.

50 For events and figures cited, based on reporting gleaned from Chilean press, see "Santiago Times": www.santiagotimes.cl, 10-1-05, 24-1-05, 11-VIII-05, 15-VIII-05, 25-1-06, 23-V-06; see also *New York Times*, 24-XI-05.

51 For Miami interview and quotes, see "Santiago Times": www.santiagotimes.cl, 26-XI-03. For Operation Condor arrest, see *El Mercurio*, e-ed.: www.emol.com ("historic"), *La Nación*, e-ed.: www.lanacion.cl, "El Mostrador": www.elmostra dor.cl, 14-XII-04; and Guzmán Tapia, *En el borde del mundo*, 216–22 (cf. Guzmán on Pinochet's health in "El Mostrador," 15-XI-04). For superb research on Operation Condor, including U.S. aspects, see John Dinges, *The Condor Years: How Pinochet and His Allies Brought Terrorism to Three Continents* (New York: New Press, 2004); and also Peter Kornbluh, *The Pinochet File: A Declassified Dossier on Atrocity and Accountability* (New York: New Press, 2003), 323–94.

52 See *La Nación*, e-ed.: www.lanacion.cl, 4-1-05 (Martínez Busch quote). For Pinochet's legal trouble in 2005–06, a useful timeline of "Desafueros y caso Riggs" appeared after his death in *El Mercurio*, 11-XII-06, special section entitled "La era de un general"; see also "Santiago Times": www.santiagotimes.cl, 21-XI-05 (Operation Colombo, Contreras testimony), 23-1-06 (Villa Grimaldi, Lawrence testimony), 19-VII-06 (reopening of Caravan of Death, Campos testimony). For background on Contreras's falling-out with Pinochet, see also *La Tercera*, e-ed.: www.tercera.cl, 13-V-05. For summary of the mixed legal results for Pinochet in mid-2005, see "Santiago Times": www.santiagotimes.cl, 11-VII-05; cf. "Mixed day in court for Pinochet" and "Pinochet 'stable' after fainting" reports, BBC World News Service, http://news.bbc.co.uk, "Americas" link, 7-VI-05, 21-VI-05.

53 CERC (Centro de Estudios de la Realidad Chilena), www.cerc.cl, August 2006 survey. In 1997, two-thirds of the Right (68 percent of UDI voters, 66 percent of Renovación Nacional voters) thought Pinochet would be remembered as one of the greatest rulers: September 1997 survey (both surveys accessed 26-VIII-06).

54 For publicity and controversy about Frei's death, I relied on press clippings, television programs, and field notes during my stay in Chile in August–September 2006, particularly Televisión Nacional (hereinafter TVN) *Informe Especial* programs "La muerte de Eduardo Frei: Una conspiración secreta," 23-VIII-06 ("history of a crime"), and "La muerte de Eduardo Frei: Capítulo final," 30-VIII-06; TVN, *24 Horas de la Mañana*, 24-VIII-06 (morning news program, interview with the former senator Carmen Frei, daughter of Eduardo Frei Montalva); Chilevisión, *Tolerancia cero*, 27-VIII-06 (television talk show, interview with the senator and former president Eduardo Frei Ruíz-Tagle, son of Frei Montalva); press accounts in *El Mercurio, La Tercera, La Nación, La Segunda, Ultimas Noticias*, 17-VIII-06–1-IX-06 (see esp. the 27-VIII-06 Sunday edition treatments by the first three newspapers above), *The Clinic*, 24-VIII-06; *El Mercurio*, "Wikén" section, 1-IX-06 (rating and estimated viewers, initial TVN program). For the context of Frei's death in its own time, and in relation to the death of the most formidable labor adversary of the regime, Tucapel Jiménez, see trilogy Book Two, 196–230, esp. 226–28.

55 For defense based on evidence cutting in two directions and supportive of the medical negligence hypothesis, see, e.g., *El Mercurio* (quote); and *La Tercera*, 27-VIII-07. For the Leyton and Frei cases in 2007, see *La Nación*, 24-VII-07, 26-VII-07, and Nelson Mery interview, 29-VII-07; and "Santiago Times": www .santiagotimes.cl, 25-VII-07, 27-VII-07, 8-VIII-07 (the latter by Mónica González, originally in *The Clinic*). As of June 2009, Madrid had not announced a conclusion in the Frei investigation.

56 On the 1964–73 era and especially the Unidad Popular as trump card in memory as salvation, from the 1970s to the 1990s, and for the use of historical context as exculpation that cast human rights denunciation as propaganda, see the earlier volumes in this trilogy: Book One, esp. chapters 1, 3, 4; Book Two, esp. chapters 2–3, 8.

57 The semitaboo status of the Unidad Popular is a complex topic precisely because "sect memory" under dictatorship did include rethinkings of the past as part of a process of adjusting strategies of resistance and conceptualizing political renovation, and because the merging of memory struggle and mass mobilization in the 1980s eroded taboos in some street mobilization contexts. Nonetheless, that the era and its upheavals remained a potent symbol of rejection and a trap to be avoided came through strongly in the 1988 plebiscite campaign. For annotated discussion, see trilogy Book Two, esp. chapters 5, 8.

58 Unless otherwise indicated, the discussion of *Machuca* in this and subsequent paragraphs in this section is based on the following: *Machuca* directed by Andrés Wood (Wood Producciones [Chile] and Tornasol Films [Spain], 2004; DVD ed. in possession of author); Andrés Wood, interview, 31-VIII-06; Chilean press coverage, commentary columns, and letters to editor, 5–12-VIII-04, esp. *El Mercurio, La Tercera*, but also commentaries of John Müller, Javier Campos,

and Roberto Castillo S. in "El Mostrador": www.elmostrador.cl, 9-VIII-04, 3–4-VIII-05, cf. Daniel Villalobos, 11-VIII-04, at "CivilCinema," www.civilcinema.com (at /critica.cgi?c=137), and interview of Andrés Wood by Francisca Babul G. and Sofía Hasbún K., *Perspectivas*, Radio Universidad de Chile, 27-IX-04, www.radio.uchile.cl (at /notas.aspx?idnota=12506, accessed 17-X-07); and Televisión Nacional, *Chile Elige*, 24-VIII-06 (viewed by author during field visit). Box office record figures in the initial four-day weekend cycle are from *El Mercurio*, 10-VIII-04; cumulative viewership is from *Chile Elige* (also noted on cover of DVD edition). Wood's coauthors of the screenplay were Roberto Brodsky and Mamoun Hassan; for technical specifications and actors, www.producciones.com, "Machuca" link. All the following quotes from Wood are from the interview, 31-VIII-06, and all screenplay quotes were checked by author directly.

59 In Chilean Spanish, the two boys' last names introduce some wordplay worth noting. Infante means "prince" and "infant," and is in Chile a respectable family name. It resonates implicitly with notions of innocence and social privilege. Machuca in Chilean usage is an adjective for someone bothersome. The related verb forms (*machucar, machucarse*) are stronger: "to bruise or get bruised." The term implicitly evokes notions of the socially and physically annoying—the kind of persons from whom one wishes to draw distance. I am grateful to Florencia Mallon for a conversation about Infante, which prodded me to think about these issues.

60 In my interview with Wood, 31-VIII-06, he told me that the mediocrity of the adults in Gonzalo's mind was also his own view of irresponsibility by "a world of child adults" (niños adultos) in 1973. He was also conscious that the depiction of Allende with Brezhnev had the effect of creating some emotional distance.

61 For Wood, the connection with Colegio Saint George was also personal. He had been a student at Saint George in the era of mixed social geography; one of his son's teachers turned out to be Amante Eledín Parraguez; and research for the film catalyzed reencounters with old classmates. Wood, interview, 31-VIII-06. For tracking down of real-life "Machucas," see *La Tercera*, 5-VIII-04; and for the memoir, Amante Eledín Parraguez, *Tres años para nacer: Historia de un verdadero Machuca*, 2nd ed. (Santiago: Pentagrama Editores, 2004), 82 (Whelan quote). For the junta's clarity that it wished to bring about social class segregation in metropolitan Santiago, see ASXX, Ministerio de Educación, Reservados 1974, tomo 2, Acta No. 33, Junta de Gobierno en Sesión Secreta, 12-XI-73; and for eventual implementation, Eduardo Morales and Sergio Rojas, "Relocalización socioespacial de la pobreza: Política estatal y presión popular, 1979–1985," in *Espacio y poder: Los pobladores*, ed. Jorge Chateau (Santiago: FLACSO, 1987), 75–121 (including maps 1 and 2, between 118 and 119). For Colegio Saint George, high-level interest by military officials including Pinochet, and the ways military intervention of the school generated a struggle that included

international tensions with the owner, the Congregation of the Holy Cross in Indiana, there are fascinating materials in ASXX, Ministerio de Educación, Reservados 1974, tomos 1, 4, 5; see esp. tomo 5 ("Antecedentes 1974–75"), Colonel Manuel Contreras, Director of DINA, to Minister of Education Rear Admiral Hugo Castro, 5-VII-74, for chronological summary as seen by the DINA; and for continuing tensions, tomo 1 ("Oficios"), Minister Castro to Supreme Chief of the Nation [Augusto Pinochet], 9-X-74, 6-XII-74.

62 A revealing contrast of artistic strategy, and of cultural climate of reception, occurs when one considers the masterful and moving 1997 film documentary of Patricio Guzmán, *Chile: La memoria obstinada*: see chapter 4 in this volume. The point of view in Guzmán's film is that of the returning middle-aged artist and *compañero*, sympathetically linked to generational peers who were leftist victim-survivors of repression and believed in Allende but who are marginalized and forgotten in the transformed Chile of the 1990s. The film garnered an enthusiastic response among those struggling in civil society to take initiative to push forward the memory question, at a time when political elites were retreating from it and when the sense of impasse was strong. Precisely for this reason, however, the documentary could not break out from the film festival circuit into commercial theater or television. I hope to develop a fuller analysis of this point in a future research project on cinema.

63 For insight on muted ambivalence about the film's capacity to reinforce social prejudice, particularly as this aspect unfolded over time, I am grateful to Claudio Barrientos, conversation, 18-VIII-06. Wood observed (in our interview of 31-VIII-06, where he also discussed the e-mail messages from youths) that in Spain, in contrast to Chile, he had received a critique of the film as "reactionary" because it allegedly equated Allende's government with chaos. Even there, the critique was given personally, not in written or public form. In Chile, people on the Left recognized that the film filled a void, and they refrained from criticizing a lack of didactic political correctness. In Wood's perception, what emerged was something more mixed—the Left "gets on board, but does not get on board." Perhaps the shrewdest critique, from a Center-Left perspective, came from Ascanio Cavallo, who warned—in a context of great admiration—that by mixing a classic personal coming-of-age story with that of the coup, the film "ends up seeming less a political conflict than the interruption of a process of interclass integration." *El Mercurio* (Revista "El Sábado"), 7-VIII-04. For examples of the other critiques, see press coverage and columns cited in note 58 in this chapter.

64 In addition to Wood, interview, 31-VIII-06, see the DVD edition, which includes copies of the movie trailers and television ads that skillfully used international acclaim in Spain and a 2004 Cannes Film Festival Prize to help promote the film.

65 See Julio Pinto Vallejos, ed., *Cuando hicimos historia: La experiencia de la Unidad*

Popular (Santiago: LOM, 2005), and note his framing (5) of the essays as an attempt to address the neglected "fiesta" aspect originally noted by Tomás Moulian; Rolle, ed., *1973: La vida cotidiana de un año crucial*; and Florencia E. Mallon, *La sangre del copihue: La comunidad Mapuche de Nicolás Ailío y el Estado chileno, 1906–2001* (Santiago: LOM, 2004). The studies by Garcés and Mallon, in particular, built on grassroots community collaborations. Like Mallon, the historians cited did not conceptualize the Unidad Popular period as neatly sealed off from histories that preceded and followed it; for important related books by authors in the anthology by Pinto that make this point clear, see Mario Garcés, *Tomando su sitio: El movimiento de pobladores de Santiago, 1957–1970* (Santiago: LOM, 2002); Garcés and Leiva, *El Golpe en La Legua*; María Angélica Illanes, *La batalla de la memoria: Ensayos históricos de nuestro siglo, Chile, 1900–2000* (Santiago: Planeta, 2002); and Verónica Valdivia Ortiz de Zárate, *El golpe después del golpe: Leigh vs. Pinochet, Chile 1960–1980* (Santiago: LOM, 2003).

Afterword to Chapter 6: Unsettled Monuments

1 Hugo Achugar, "El lugar de la memoria, a propósito de monumentos (motivos y paréntesis)," in *Monumentos, memoriales y marcas territoriales*, ed. Elizabeth Jelin and Victoria Langland (Madrid: Siglo Veintiuno, 2003), 191–216 (191 for quote). For a striking example of the problem of fixity from another angle, when ruins meant to preserve an authentic space-time of atrocity are in danger of being overrun by nature (weather, vegetation), see Sarah Farmer, *Martyred Village: Commemorating the 1944 Massacre of Oradour-sur-Glane* (Berkeley: University of California Press, 1999), esp. 193–205. For historicization of the problem of monuments and memory, see Jelin and Langland, *Monumentos, memoriales y marcas territoriales*; and the pioneering work of James Young: *The Texture of Memory: Holocaust Memorials and Meanings* (New Haven, Conn.: Yale University Press, 1993), and *At Memory's Edge: After-images of the Holocaust in Contemporary Art and Architecture* (New Haven, Conn.: Yale University Press, 2000). For cautionary notes about Young and related influential work of Pierre Nora when considered in South American contexts, however, see Book One of the trilogy: Stern, *Remembering Pinochet's Chile: On the Eve of London 1998* (Durham, N.C.: Duke University Press, 2004), 3–4, 199–202, note 2.

2 My tracking of major memorial projects linked to a more coherent policy by the Human Rights Program of the Interior Ministry was based on three "snapshot" reviews over time—in June 2005, January 2007, and February 2008—and also the narrative of policy and funding produced by the program. The works completed and still under construction, the calls for artistic competitions, a narrative of policy (including the funding figure approved by Lagos), and related news were recorded and updated at the program's website. See www.ddhh.gov

.cl, "Obras simbólicas" link (accessed 19-11-08, with parallel reports first accessed 14-VI-05). I am also grateful to the program staff member Pamela Mewes Urrutia, interview, 9-1-07, for insight on memorialization policy and progress, a copy of the January 2007 database on projects, and permission to reproduce photos of the memorials. See also the stunning photo-book by the photographer Alejandro Hoppe, *Memoriales en Chile: Homenajes a las víctimas de violaciones a los derechos humanos*, 2nd ed. (Santiago: Ocho Libros, 2007).

3   For insight on issues of memory sites as civic awareness and as symbolic repair, the tensions among the two functions, and contested ownership of memorialization, ca. 2006, I am especially grateful to Cristián Correa, interview, 8-1-07, and Pamela Mewes Urrutia, interview, 9-1-07, from the perspective of the Presidential Advisory Commission on Human Rights and the Program on Human Rights, respectively, at the Interior Ministry; Erika Hennings, interview, 11-1-07, for activist perspective related to Londres 38; and Pedro Matta (multiple conversations and interviews over the years including 2006–08) and Margarita Romero (multiple e-mail exchanges about a museum project at Villa Grimaldi, December 2007–January 2008, and in-person conversations, March 2009), for activist perspective related to Villa Grimaldi. See also the Londres 38 saga recounted in the following section.

4   Katherine Hite, "Estadio Nacional: Monumento y lugar de conmemoración," in Verdugo, *De la torture*, 213–27; *Estadio Nacional*, directed by Carmen Luz Parot (2001; DVD ed., Alerce, 2002).

5   For early uses of Londres 38 and Tejas Verdes, see trilogy Book One, 45–47; for concise description of Londres 38 in the context of other secret sites by the DINA in Metropolitan Santiago, and for eventual eclipse by Villa Grimaldi, see *ICNPPT*, 442–46. The classic account of Tejas Verdes is Hernán Valdés, *Tejas Verdes: Diario de un campo de concentración en Chile* (1974; repr., Barcelona: Editorial Laia, 1978; new Chilean ed., Santiago: LOM, 1996). For fuller description and sources on Operation Colombo, see Book Two of this trilogy: Stern, *Battling for Hearts and Minds: Memory Struggles in Pinochet's Chile, 1973–1988* (Durham, N.C.: Duke University Press, 2006), 108–11.

6   The narrative of Londres 38 during 2005–7 here and in subsequent paragraphs is based on media reports, interviews, website research, and field visits, esp. *La Nación*, e-ed., www.lanacion.cl, 12-X-05, 3-III-06, 3-VIII-06, 24-VIII-06, 26-IX-06, 15-VIII-07, 26-VIII-07; *La Tercera*, e-ed.: 19-VII-05, 16-II-06, 2-III-06, 14-VIII-07; "El Mostrador": www.elmostrador.cl, 2-VIII-06 (interview article with Romy Schmidt, reproduced at www.memoriaviva.com, link at "Boletín" no. 143, 1–14-VIII-06); field site visits, 19-VIII-06, 12-1-07; Erika Hennings, interview, 12-1-07, and head secretary of O'Higgins Institute, conversation, 12-1-07, esp. for insights on activist memory projects, new civilian leadership at the institute, and their interplay; www.londres38.cl, "Londres 38: La Persistencia de la Memoria" and "Proyecto Integral: Un espacio para la memoria" links (accessed 21-11-08);

and www.institutoohigginiano.cl, for new address in 2008 (Londres 25), and for insight on budgetary vulnerability to presidential pressure, in "Reglamento Orgánico y de Funcionamiento" (see Article 15), reprinted on home page (last consulted 2-III-08). For additional information on Carrasco, see trilogy Book Two, 97–98. I am also grateful to Alison Bruey for insightful and well-informed conversation (19-VIII-06) on Londres 38 and related efforts to memorialize other torture sites, including José Domingo Cañas. I will confine the following notes to quotes or particular aspects whose sources would not otherwise be obvious from the list above.

7 *La Nación*, e-ed.: www.lanacion.cl, 12-X-05 (quote).

8 "El Mostrador": www.elmostrador.cl, 2-VIII-06 (quote; from original article reprinted at www.memoriaviva.com, link at "Boletín" no. 143, 1–14-VIII-06).

9 The archaeology-of-struggle description is based on field notes, 19-VIII-06.

10 *La Nación*, e-ed.: www.lanacion.cl, 24-VIII-06 (quotes).

11 *La Nación*, e-ed.: www.lanacion.cl, 15-VIII-07 (Hennings quote); www.londres 38.cl, "Londres 38: La Persistencia de la Memoria" link (Auschwitz quote, dated 23-IX-07).

Chapter 7: Reframing Democratic Transition

1 Lagos speech and quotes, www.comisiontortura.cl. See also *El Mercurio, La Tercera*, 29-XI-04; and for legislative aspects and debate, Elizabeth Lira and Brian Loveman, *Políticas de reparación: Chile, 1990–2004* (Santiago: LOM, 2005), 496–97. Lagos's three paths of repair followed the outlines proposed by the Valech Commission, but with some differences. The Valech Commission, e.g., proposed the Institute for Human Rights take a more active role in justice-seeking and that the silence rule apply for thirty rather than fifty years: *ICNPPT*, 515–31, esp. 522–31.

2 Priscilla Hayner, *Unspeakable Truths: Facing the Challenge of Truth Commissions* (New York: Routledge, 2002), for comprehensive comparative analysis. I researched the irony of 2004 as the "year of torture" in which the United States and Chile went in opposite directions for an op-ed column ("Closure on Rogues and Accountability") in *Chicago Tribune*, 22-XII-04. I am also grateful to Seymour Hersh for sharing insights, while preparing and publishing his path-breaking 2004 reports in the *New Yorker* on the Abu Ghraib atrocities and undersides of the Iraq war, 1-III-04, during a lecture visit to Madison.

3 On Cheyre, other military figures, and between-the-lines reporting on reactions by high political elites, see *El Mercurio*, 6-XI-04, 11-XI-04, 18–19-XI-04, also *La Tercera*, 12-XI-04; for analysis of the army stance in wider context, Claudio Fuentes Saavedra, *La transición de los militares: Relaciones civiles-militares en Chile, 1990–2006* (Santiago: LOM, 2006), 111–37, esp. 130–37; and

on the government's eventual public stance that it would neither promote nor block lawsuits by individuals against torturers, *El Mercurio*, 29-XI-04, 5-XII-04, 7-XII-04.

4 For useful review of the four-year evolution of Lagos on human rights and on political completion of the transition and its memory reckoning, see *El Mercurio*, 28-XI-04 ("La jugada final de Lagos").

5 *El Mercurio*, 30-XI-04, 2–5-XII-04; *La Tercera*, 30-XI-04, 4-XII-04; "El Mostrador": www.elmostrador.cl, 7-XII-04; *La Nación*, e-ed.: www.lanacion.cl, 5-XII-04 (in e-ed., the top-ten story was under title "Los imperdonables"), 6-XII-04, 10-XII-04, 12-XII-04; *El Siglo*, 10-XII-04 (torture list), 24-XII-04 (historians' manifesto); Coordinadora de Ex-Presas y Ex-Presos Políticos de Santiago, "Nosotros, Los Sobrevivientes Acusamos," December 2004, www.memoriaviva.com, "Tortura" link. For related controversy about editorial line and fact-checking, see "El Mostrador": www.elmostrador.cl, 5-1-05 (editorial), and letter exchanges between Liliana Mason Padilla of the Coordinadora and the editors, 14-1-05. For a pioneering study of the ways a truth commission experience also opens up spaces for alternative truth telling and critiques, for the case of Peru, see Cynthia E. Milton, "At the Edge of the Peruvian Truth Commission: Alternative Paths to Recounting the Past," *Radical History Review* 98 (spring 2007): 3–33; cf. Ksenija Bilbija et al., eds., *The Art of Truth-Telling about Authoritarian Rule* (Madison: University of Wisconsin Press, 2005).

6 On program implementation and critiques, and initial cost estimates, see Lira and Loveman, *Políticas de reparación*, 497–98; *La Tercera*, 29–30-XI-04; *El Mercurio*, 30-XI-04; for persistence of such critiques, Letter to Bachelet from five human rights organizations, 16-VIII-06, www.fasic.org, "Documentos" link: "Demandas de organizaciones de D D . H H . a la Presidenta Michelle Bachelet." The letter also pushed for a new period in which victims of political prison and torture uncertified by the Valech Commission process could present their case, and for a lifting of the secrecy-of-information rule for judges.

7 Colectivo de Memoria Histórica Corporación José Domingo Cañas, *Tortura en poblaciones del Gran Santiago (1973–1990)* (Santiago: Corporación José Domingo Cañas, 2005), esp. 15–16, 21–22, 27–28, 70, 79–80, 118–26, 165–67 (167 for quote), and apéndice. I thank Alison Bruey, who worked with the colectivo, for graciously supplying a copy of the report.

8 For the 2005 reforms in the context of military-civilian balance of power, see Fuentes Saavedra, *La transición de los militares*, esp. 33–34, 56–57; for protest of what the reforms failed to include, "Santiago Times": www.santiagotimes.cl, 20-IX-05; and on the binomial election system, under public debate in 2005–06 as a bulwark of the old Constitution that escaped reform, Carlos Huneeus, ed., *La reforma al sistema binomial en Chile: Propuestas para el debate* (Santiago: Catalonia, 2006).

9 The events cited in the previous three paragraphs are gleaned from the elec-

tronic news-clipping service on human rights coverage in the Chilean press provided by www.memoriaviva.com, "Boletín" link, Nos. 106–13, 16-1-05 to 15-v-05; and quotes are from *El Mercurio*, e-ed.: www.emol.com, 20-1-05 ("worried"), and "El Mostrador," www.elmostrador.com, 26-1-05 ("mistaken"), 2-11-05 ("due process"), 7-iv-05 ("surpassed"). See also Universidad Diego Portales, Facultad de Derecho (hereinafter udpfd), *Informe anual sobre derechos humanos en Chile 2006 (Hechos de 2005)* (Santiago: Universidad Diego Portales, 2006), 263–69.

10 For internationalist jurisprudence, the Almonacid case, and Inter-American Court ruling, see udpfd, *Informe anual sobre derechos humanos en Chile 2007 (Hechos de 2006)* (Santiago: Universidad Diego Portales, 2007), 97–136. See also "Santiago Times": www.santiagotimes.cl, 1-vi-06 on Supreme Court and Montiglio; and notes 11–12 for politicocultural effects of Inter-American Court ruling.

11 For the increasing climate of obsolescence surrounding amnesty, even as technical aspects proved contentious and legislation elusive, Chilean press coverage of October to December 2006 offers ample evidence. See esp. the amnesty-related reports in *La Nación*, e-ed., www.lanacion.cl, 4-x-06, 15-x-06, 24-x-06, 29-x-06 (including interview of José Zalaquett by Mirko Macari), 1-xi-06, 22-xi-06 (including op-ed by Federico Aguirre Madrid of codepu); cf. *New York Times*, 24-xii-06.

12 For useful press reports, see *La Nación*, e-ed., www.lanacion.cl, 5-x-06 (Muñoz); "Santiago Times": www.santiagotimes.cl, 18-xii-06 (Chaigneau, Torres); and "El Mostrador," www.elmostrador.com, 20-1-07 (Supreme Court).

13 Cumulative guilty sentences (115 in 2005) exceeded the number of cumulative perpetrators (94 in 2005), because some persons were found guilty in multiple cases. For statistics and the secret police chiefs, see Fundación Social de Ayuda Social de las Iglesias Cristianas, "Derechos Humanos en Chile: Balance 2005," released 2-11-06, www.fasic.org, "Documentos" link; Human Rights Watch, World Report 2007, Chile Report, hrw.org/wr2K7/index.htm, "Americas" link, then "Chile" link; for Corbalán, *La Nación*, e-ed., www.lanacion.cl, 29-xii-06; and for cumulative sentences of 129 years for Contreras, *El Mercurio*, e-ed.: www.emol.com, 30-1-07, and "El Mostrador": www.elmostrador.cl, 31-1-07. In 2007, the Supreme Court confirmed the life sentence of Salas Wenzel in the 1987 murders of a dozen dissidents known as Operación Albania; "Santiago Times": www.santiagotimes.cl, 30-viii-07.

14 *Fernando ha vuelto*, directed by Silvio Caiozzi (1998; dvd expanded ed., Andrea films, 2006), quotes from coda ("¿Fernando ha vuelto a desaparecer?"; copy in possession of author); see also *Patio 29: Historias de silencio*, directed by Esteban Larraín (vhs, fondart [Fondo de Desarrollo de las Artes y la Cultura] and Ford Foundation, 1998; copy in possession of author); and on dna, "Santiago Times": www.santiagotimes.cl, 23-v-07. For continuing uncertain state in 2007

of the prior identifications, I am grateful to staff with the Human Rights Program and presidential advisory group at the Interior Ministry: Cristián Correa, interview, 8-1-07; Carmen Garretón, conversation, 8-1-07.

15   Bachelet's symbolism and ascent—a personal and nonrancorous fusion of the inherited and troubled memory question on the one hand, and the winds of change on women's opportunities, social issues, and leadership style on the other—caught international as well as national attention; see *New York Times*, 15–16-1-06. See also Elizabeth Subercaseaux and Malú Sierra, *Michelle* (Santiago: Catalonia, 2005); Andrea Insunza and Javier Ortega, *Bachelet: La historia no oficial* (Santiago: Random House Mondadori, 2005); and Bachelet's inaugural speech, in a sense also her last campaign speech, www.gobiernodechile.cl, "Discursos" link, "Primer discurso oficial desde el balcón del Palacio de La Moneda," 11-III-06 (cf. "Intervención en Acto Ciudadano," Casablanca, 11-III-06; "Participación en el acto cultural," 12-III-06); and sources in chapter 6, note 9 in this volume.

16   Bachelet's speech, text at *La Nación*, e-ed., www.lanacion.cl, 21-v-06; for new plan, 15-XII-06, and passage into law, 11–12-III-08 (with minimums of about US$140 in 2008 and US$175 in 2009). Cf. international coverage and interest in the fate of privatized social security: *Latin American Weekly Report* (U.K.), 19-XII-06; and *New York Times*, 26-XII-06.

17   For a good synthesis on the student movement, LOCE, and media coverage, see"Santiago Times": www.santiagotimes.cl, esp. 31-v-06, 5-VI-06, 13-VI-06, 16-VI-06; and for eventual fate of LOCE and student movement, 1-v-07, 12-IV-07, 10-IV-07.

18   For the ethical wage debate, Goic's role, and responses by labor, entrepreneurs, and political elites, the Chilean newspaper media in the month of August 2007 is the best source. Especially useful (and worth comparing with *El Mercurio* on same dates) is *La Nación*, e-ed., www.lanacion.cl, 30–31-VII-07, 1–2-VIII-07, 5-VIII-07, 9-VIII-07, 12-VIII-07, 21-VIII-07, 23–24-VIII-07, 26-VIII-07, 29-VIII-07, also 2-x-06 for Velasco's budget speech; see also note 19. For pioneering analysis of labor policy and worker experiences during 1973–2002, important for understanding the impatience and mobilizations that burst forth so powerfully in 2005–07, see Peter Winn, ed., *Victims of the Miracle: Workers and Neoliberalism in the Pinochet Era, 1973–2002* (Durham, N.C.: Duke University Press, 2004); and for acute comparative insight, Paul Drake, *Labor Movements and Dictatorships: The Southern Cone in Comparative Perspective* (Baltimore: Johns Hopkins University Press, 1996).

19   For quotes, see www.iglesia.cl, "Documentos" link: "Hemos visto al Señor . . . ," by Los Obispos de Chile, Punta de Tralca, 22-IV-05; and *La Nación*, e-ed., www.lanacion.cl, 21-VIII-07; see also 19-VIII-07, 27-VIII-07, 30-VIII-07. For stances by Catholic Church bishops on labor, see also www.iglesia.cl, "Documentos" link, by Bishop Alejandro Goic Karmelic, "La persona humana es lo

primero," Rancagua, 30-IV-05; "Por un Chile más justo," Santiago, 11-VII-07; and "Desafíos de fondo en los recientes conflictos laborales" (with Mons. Cristián Contreras Villarroel), 18-VII-07. Cf. "Por la dignidad del trabajo humano," by Comisión Nacional de Pastoral de Trabajadores, Padre Hurtado, 13-VII-07. For contextual insight on the politics of the Catholic Church and its effort to stake out moral authority while facing tougher times in struggles over sexuality and reproduction, see note 23 in this chapter.

20 *La Nación*, e-ed., www.lanacion.cl, 21-VIII-07; see also 19-VIII-07, 27-VIII-07, 30-VIII-07.

21 *La Nación*, e-ed., www.lanacion.cl, 5-VIII-05 (Goic quote).

22 For public promotion of gender parity, see, e.g., www.gobiernodechile.cl, Bachelet speeches (use website's search function with "Discurso" or "Seminario," and date of speech): "Intervención en Acto Ciudadano," Casablanca, 11-III-06; "Seminario sobre Paridad y Participación Pública," Vitacura, Santiago, 5-X-06; and her 2006 congressional agenda and state-of-the-nation speech, text in *La Nación*, e-ed., www.lanacion.cl, 21-V-06. My understanding of the unsettling effects of gender parity on the masculinist world of politics and patronage is based in part on field visits, August–September 2006 and January 2007. For Sernam's accomplishments and constraints in the gender politics of the 1990s, see note 23 (esp. the works of Valdés and Htun).

23 For sociocultural trends and statistics cited, and political and Catholic Church contexts, see Teresa Valdés, "Entre la modernización y la equidad: Mujeres, mundo privado y familias," in *Chile en los noventa*, ed. Cristián Toloza and Eugenio Lahera (Santiago: Dolmen, 1998), 471–519 (502, out-of-wedlock births; 478–79, on distinction between visible and invisible paid labor force participation); J. Samuel Valenzuela, Eugenio Tironi, and Timothy R. Scully, eds., *El eslabón perdido: Familia, modernización y bienestar* (Santiago: Taurus, 2006), esp. Osvaldo Larrañaga, "Participación laboral de la mujer, 1958–2003," 177–224 (180, labor force rates), and M. Soledad Herrera and Eduardo Valenzuela, "Matrimonio, separaciones y convivencia," 225–63; Mala Htun, *Sex and the State: Abortion, Divorce, and the Family under Latin American Dictatorships and Democracies* (New York: Cambridge University Press, 2003), esp. 102–3, 111 (annulments, out-of-wedlock births), 135–40, 164–67; and William Lies and Mary Fran T. Malone, "The Chilean Church: Declining Hegemony?" in *The Catholic Church and the Nation-State: Comparative Perspectives*, eds. Paul Christopher Manuel, Lawrence E. Reardon, and Clyde Wilcox (Washington, D.C.: Georgetown University Press, 2006), 89–100 (94 for attitudes on divorce). See also *La Tercera*, 15-I-07, *New York Times*, 30-I-05, for obstacles to divorce in practice, after legalization. For proportion of population at least nominally Catholic, which declined somewhat from 1990, I relied on the 2001 survey of Programa de las Naciones Unidas para el Desarrollo (hereinafter

PNUD), *Desarrollo humano en Chile 2002: Nosotros los chilenos: un desafío cultural* (Santiago: PNUD, 2002), 237.

24 On the September 2006 debate, legal and politicocultural struggles culminating in a presidential decree in January 2007, and the tussle with pharmacy chains and settlement in November 2007, helpful starting points within the ample press coverage (and also sources for the statistics cited) are the Sunday feature story ("La toma de pastilla") on adolescent sexuality by *La Nación*, e-ed., www.lanacion.cl, 10-IX-06; the January snapshot of contention reported in *El Mercurio*, 18-1-07 (Bachelet quote), cf. *La Nacion*, 19-1-07 (for related abortion issues including an effort to revive legal therapeutic abortion); and synthesis of legal and political events including pharmacy conflict, in "Santiago Times": www.santiagotimes.cl, 3-11-07, 8-XI-07. For international notice, see *New York Times*, 17-XII-06.

25 The Transantiago account in this and the following two paragraphs is gleaned from extensive continuous reporting in Chilean media: for useful starting points (and statistics cited on buses and subsidies), see "Santiago Times": www.santiagotimes.cl, 27-III-07 (Bachelet apology in early difficult phase), 15-V-07 (commuter anger), 20-XII-07 (congressional inquiry), 4-1-08, 17-1-08 (continuing political fallout, budget subsidies, and bus additions).

26 "Santiago Times": www.santiagotimes.cl, 15-V-07 (quote).

27 Survey results, as cited and tracked in Centro de Estudios de la Realidad Chilena (often known by the acronym CERC), "Informe de Prensa, Encuesta Nacional, Diciembre de 2007," www.cerc.cl.

28 For the previous two paragraphs, good starting points are, for national-level media and reporting, "Santiago Times": www.santiagotimes.cl, 22-V-06 (hunger strikes, antiterrorist laws), 21-III-07, 28-III-07 (arrest of José Huenchunao Mariñán and related debates), and 5-IX-07 (campaign by Observatory on the Rights of Indigenous Peoples, comments by former President Aylwin), also 21-1-08 (cellulose exports, Angelini group). See also note 29. For Mapuche-centered reports and reflections, see articles in *AZkintuWE* (online version is at www.nodo50.org) by José Marimán, "Estado chileno y Pueblo Mapuche," in two parts, nos. 11–12 (December 2004–January 2005, February–March 2005); Marimán, "Para qué un partido nacionalitario?" no. 20 (June–July 2006); Víctor Naguil, "Wallmapu tañi kizungünewün," no. 14 (June–July 2005); Naguil, "Hacia la creación de un partido mapuche," no. 15 (August–September 2005); Antonio Valencia, "Wallmapu: La patria mapuche," no. 22 (October–November 2006); Pedro Cayuqueo (interview with Gustavo Quilaqueo Bustos), and "La democracia chilena está en deuda con nuestro pueblo," no. 26 (July–August 2006). For a thorough report on the Lagos administration's resort to antiterrorism law and military courts to suppress Mapuche protest and the consequent abuse and sidestepping of due process, see Human Rights Watch

and Observatorio de Derechos de Pueblos Indígenas, "Undue Process: Terrorism Trials, Military Courts and the Mapuche in Southern Chile" (2004), www .hrw.org, "country reports" link (accessed 14-11-08). For additional background, see sources cited in Afterword to chapter 4, note 6 in this volume. I am grateful to Florencia E. Mallon for illuminating discussions of Mapuche history and contemporary conflicts, and for graciously lending me her clipping file from *AZkintuWE*.

29 For the summer crisis, see reports (including interview of Catrileo's mother, and editorial by *La Tercera*) in "Santiago Times": www.santiagotimes.cl, 4-1-08, 7-1-08, 16-1-08 (Goic quote), 21-1-08, 24-1-08, 25-1-08, 5-11-08; and for Troncoso's declaration, posted 26-XII-07, www.youtube.com, at extension/watch ?v=Fy6_ZQgCZAY&Nr=1.

30 Quilaqueo quote from interview by Pedro Cayuqueo, "La democracia chilena está en deuda . . . ," in *AZkintuWE* 26 (July–August 2006).

31 On the sense of a changed level of support and sensitivity from the presidency once Bachelet came into power, I am grateful to Viviana Díaz, conversation, 12-1-07, also Erika Hennings, 12-1-07; on human rights symbolism and visits to the Agrupación and Villa Grimaldi, see "Santiago Times": www.santiagotimes .cl, 29-V-06, 12-III-07. Cf. Bachelet's remarks at human rights commemorations, as reprinted at www.gobierno.cl, e.g., "Inauguración del monumento 'Un lugar para la memoria': Nattino—Parada—Guerrero,'" Quillicura, Santiago, 29-III-06. At the same time, the sense of the unfinished and of the need to keep pushing remained strong in the human rights camp; see, e.g., the letter to Bachelet, 16-VIII-06, from five Chilean human rights groups (Sergio Laurenti for Amnistía Internacional—Sección Chile; Simona Ruy-Pérez Bravo for CINTRAS: Centro de Salud Mental y Derechos Humanos; Paz Rojas Baeza for CODEPU: Corporación de Promoción y Defensa de los Derechos del Pueblo; Claudio González Urbina for FASIC: Fundación de Ayuda Social de las Iglesias Cristianas; and María Eugenia Rojas Baeza for PIDEE: Fundación de Protección a la Infancia Dañada por los Estados de Emergencia), www.fasic.org, "Documentos" link, posted as "Demandas de organizaciones de DD.HH. a la Presidenta Michelle Bachelet," 17-VIII-06; cf. AFDDCD, memo-letter from AFDD to President Bachelet, 25-V-06.

Afterword to Chapter 7: The Curious Burial of Pinochet

1 For the medical crisis, death, and funeral events, I relied principally on Chilean media coverage in electronic web editions during 3–17-XII-06, and hard-copy editions of *El Mercurio* for the week of 11–17-XII-06, for which I thank Carolina Sciolla. For thoughtful and meticulous analysis, see also Alfredo Joignant, *Un*

día distinto: Memorias festivas y batallas conmemorativas en torno al 11 de septiembre en Chile, 1974–2006 (Santiago: Editorial Universitaria, 2007), 129–73. Throughout the afterword I provide specific citations only for quotes, key aspects not reported in multiple media outlets, or pertinent background. For "stable" and "favorable" quotes, see *La Nación*, www.lanacion.cl, 4-xii-06; for "show," medical chronology in *El Mercurio*, 11-xii-06; for "political responsibility" letter of 25-xi-06, *El Mercurio*, e-ed., www.emol.com, 26-xi-06, also reprinted in *Ercilla*, 1-i-07, supplement on "Documentos históricos de la Junta Militar y el general Augusto Pinochet," p. 18. For Pinochet's legal troubles in October–November and debate on his public letter, see *La Nación*, e-ed., www.lanacion.cl, 30–31-x-06, 25–26–27-xi-06, cf. 18-x-06, 24-x-06, 27-x-06.

2 "El Mostrador": www.elmostrador.cl, 5-xii-06 (Verdugo quotes); "Santiago Times": www.santiagotimes.cl, 5-xii-06 (red-devil suit).

3 Joignant, *Un día distinto*, 143–44 (quotes); *El Mercurio*, 11-xii-06. I have changed punctuation to capture better the chanting rhythm in Spanish.

4 For the personal and existential aspects of memory well into the 1990s, and the relationship to emblematic memory frameworks and social process, see Book One of the trilogy: Stern, *Remembering Pinochet's Chile: On the Eve of London 1998* (Durham, N.C.: Duke University Press, 2004); and for historical dynamics and memory as mass experience in the 1980s, see Book Two: Stern, *Battling for Hearts and Minds: Memory Struggles in Pinochet's Chile, 1973–1988* (Durham, N.C.: Duke University Press, 2006). On population statistics, I relied on the projections for 2005 (the last census was in 2002) constructed by the Instituto Nacional de Estadísticas, www.ine.cl, "Demografía y Vitales, Demografía" link, then "Chile: Estimaciones y proyecciones de población por sexo y edad: País urbano-rural, 1990–2020" link, cuadros 2, 5 (pp. 21, 27), originally published June 2004 (accessed 18-iii-08). Summing the five-year age group percentages yielded 42.0 percent of the national population younger than 25 years, and 43.1 percent at least 35 years old.

5 *El Mercurio*, 12-xii-06 (quotes and visitor estimate).

6 Radio Cooperativa, www.cooperativa.cl, 13-xii-06 (Cuadrado quote). For more background on the incident, and Cuadrado's subsequent dismissal from his job as artist and cultural consultant for the municipality of Las Condes, see *La Nación*, e-ed., www.lanacion.cl, 12-xii-06, 21-xii-06. See also "El Mostrador": www.elmostrador.cl, 20-xii-06; and *El Mercurio*, e-ed., www.emol.com, 15-xii-06. For the high-profile assaults in 1974–76, see trilogy Book Two, 106–8, 100–101; and for wider analysis of Chilean organization of international dirty war, see John Dinges, *The Condor Years: How Pinochet and His Allies Brought Terrorism to Three Continents* (New York: New Press, 2004).

7 For a good sampling of properly solemn commentary by elites, including rebukes of joyful reaction by some to Pinochet's death, see *El Mercurio*, 11-xii-06.

For expressions of regret that his death blocked completion of justice, see *El Mercurio*, e-ed.: www.emol.com, 10-XII-06; and "El Mostrador," 11-XII-06. Cf. 5-XII-06 interview of Patricia Verdugo.

8 *El Mercurio*, 11-XII-06 (Toledo quote, photo with "No" banner); *La Nación*, e-ed., www.lanacion.cl, 12-XII-06 (for street theater and "Adios general"). That the party atmosphere was not confined to downtown Santiago came through in a fine report on La Victoria, a población that suffered much repression during the dictatorship, in "Santiago Times": www.santiagotimes.cl, 12-XII-06. For background on Toledo, her sons the Vergara brothers, and the memory symbolism when the first two (of three) murders of her sons took place, see trilogy Book Two, 265–67.

9 The Lucifer–Saint Peter joke circulated on e-mail within a day of Pinochet's death (author received copy on 11-XII-06). Another joke used Spanish wordplay ("Sata" as shorthand for Satan, "Tata" for "the big daddy") to talk about upset in Hell. "Hubo cambio de mando en el infierno. Sale el Sata, entra el Tata" (There was a change of rule in Hell. Out with the Sata, in with the Tata). Joignant, *Un día distinto*, 129. The Argentine newspaper *Página/12* came up with a similar twist ("What did hell do to deserve this?"), cited in *Latin American Weekly Report* (U.K.), 12-XII-06, p. 8.

10 *El Mercurio*, 17-XII-06 (Blanlot interview and quote); for Concertacionista elites taking a sterner view of celebration at Plaza Italia, yet expressing sympathy with Cuadrado, see also 11-XII-06, and e-ed.: www.emol.com, 15-XII-06. Cf. Bachelet's discussion of Cuadrado, Pinochet Molina (whose case is discussed in the next section), and human reactions to loss, *La Nación*, e-ed., www.lanacion.cl, 23-XII-06.

11 For a succinct guide to the official line and the controversy, see interview of Blanlot in *El Mercurio*, 17-XII-06, cf. 11–12–13-XII-06; and for subtleties of protocol, Joignant, *Un día distinto*, 131–40. I am also indebted to Teresa Valdés for an illuminating conversation in January 2007 about the funeral and Blanlot.

12 Pinochet Molina quotes from *El Mercurio*, e-ed., www.emol.com, 12-XII-06; and for more extensive review, and Blanlot and Hargreaves quotes, respectively, print editions, 14-XII-06, 15-XII-06, and for additional background on Pinochet Molina, his interview, 16-XII-06 (in magazine *El Mercurio Sábado*, 14–18).

13 For the previous two paragraphs, see *La Tercera*, 11-XII-06, for early family and state deliberations; *El Mercurio*, 13–14-XII-06, for transfers and water cannon truck; *Qué Pasa*, 19-1-07, p. 4, on the roadside chapel problem; and for shrewd analysis of the symbolic significance of the final resting place, along with the funeral protocols and cremation, as "metamorphosis of the cadaver" and a marker of precarious status, Joignant, *Un día distinto*, 141–43.

14 "El Mostrador": www.elmostrador.cl, 11-XII-06 (quote). For other admirers and collaborators who invoked history and the passage of time, see the commentaries in *El Mercurio*, 11-XII-06, special section on "Pinochet, 1915–2006: La

era de un general"; and for assessment in this vein by conservative historian Gonzalo Vial, his "Augusto Pinochet, 1915–2006," published by the newspaper *La Segunda* as a December 2006 supplement (and distillation of Vial's earlier two-volume biography).

Conclusion: Reckoning with Pinochet

1 The memory struggles and transformations just summarized are documented and analyzed in detail in Book Two of this trilogy: Stern, *Battling for Hearts and Minds: Memory Struggles in Pinochet's Chile, 1973–1988* (Durham, N.C.: Duke University Press, 2006).

2 The intimate aspects of memory that made it an issue that was personal, moral, and even existential persisted well into the 1990s, and also fed interplays of "loose" personal memories and "emblematic" memory, the latter understood as frameworks of meaning. These aspects are developed via ethnographic portraits and theorization in Book One of this trilogy: Stern, *Remembering Pinochet's Chile: On the Eve of London 1998* (Durham, N.C.: Duke University Press, 2004).

3 For a compelling discussion of the hegemony concept, its relationship to cultural languages of dispute, and relevant scholarly genealogy, see William Roseberry, "Hegemony and the Language of Contention," in *Everyday Forms of State Formation: Revolution and the Negotiation of Rule in Modern Mexico*, ed. Gilbert M. Joseph and Daniel Nugent (Durham, N.C.: Duke University Press, 1994), 355–66; cf. note 4.

4 Florencia E. Mallon, *Peasant and Nation: The Making of Postcolonial Mexico and Peru* (Berkeley: University of California Press, 1995), esp. 6–20.

5 Felipe Agüero, "Institutions, Transitions, and Bargaining: Civilians and the Military in Shaping Postauthoritarian Regimes," in *Civil-Military Relations in Latin America: New Analytical Perspectives*, ed. David Pion-Berlin (Chapel Hill: University of North Carolina Press, 2001), 194–222; cf. his nuanced and well-contextualized analysis of "Authoritarian Legacies: The Military's Role," in *Authoritarian Legacies and Democracy in Latin America and Southern Europe*, ed, Katherine Hite and Paola Cesarini (Notre Dame, Ind.: University of Notre Dame Press, 2004), 233–62. For seminal early treatment of transitions and pacts, see Guillermo O'Donnell, Philippe C. Schmitter, and Laurence Whitehead, eds., *Transitions from Authoritarian Rule: Prospects for Democracy*, 4 vols. (Baltimore: Johns Hopkins University Press, 1986), esp. vol. 4: O'Donnell and Schmitter, *Tentative Conclusions and Uncertain Democracies*, 37–47. See also Guillermo O'Donnell, "Transitions to Democracy: Some Navigation Instruments," in *Democracy in the Americas: Stopping the Pendulum*, ed. Robert A. Pastor (New York: Holmes and Meier, 1989), 62–75; and Guillermo O'Donnell

and J. Samuel Valenzuela, eds., *Issues in Democratic Consolidation: The New South American Democracies in Comparative Perspective* (Notre Dame, Ind.: University of Notre Dame Press, 1992), esp. essays by O'Donnell, "Transitions, Continuities, and Paradoxes," 17–56, and Scott Mainwaring, "Transitions to Democracy and Democratic Consolidation: Theoretical and Comparative Issues," 294–341. For new directions in study of authoritarian legacies that placed pacts in a new perspective (directly or indirectly) and in which comparisons of South America and southern Europe remained prominent, see Juan J. Linz and Alfred Stepan, *Problems of Democratic Transition and Consolidation: Southern Europe, South America, and Post-Communist Europe* (Baltimore: Johns Hopkins University Press, 1996); Paul W. Drake, *Labor Movements and Dictatorships: The Southern Cone in Comparative Perspective* (Baltimore: Johns Hopkins University Press, 1996); Omar G. Encarnación, "The Legacy of Transitions: Pact-Making and Democratic Consolidation in Spain," *Estudios / Working Papers* 193 (2003) of Centro de Estudios Avanzados en Ciencias Sociales of Instituto Juan March de Estudios e Investigaciones, www.march.es; Omar Sánchez, "Beyond Pacted Transitions in Spain and Chile: Elite and Institutional Differences," *Democratization* 10, no. 2 (summer 2003): 65–86; and Hite and Cesarini, eds., *Authoritarian Legacies*. For the international dimension of pact making by Latin Americans in the 1980s and the sense of their positive value, relative to the alternatives, see the insightful study of Alicia Frohmann, *Puentes sobre la turbulencia: La concertación política latinoamericana en los 80* (Santiago: FLACSO, 1990).

6 For the comparative comments, see note 5 in this chapter (esp. the works of O'Donnell and Mainwaring); and on Spain and memory, Paloma Aguilar, *Memory and Amnesia: The Role of the Spanish Civil War in the Transition to Democracy*, trans. Mark Oakley (New York: Berghahn books, 2002). For perspective on Spain as paradigmatic, see Linz and Stepan, *Problems of Democratic Transition and Consolidation*; Felipe Agüero, *Soldiers, Civilians, and Democracy: Post-Franco Spain in Comparative Perspective* (Baltimore: Johns Hopkins University, 1995); and Encarnación, "The Legacy of Transitions."

7 For previous two paragraphs, aside from empirical descriptions of the Chilean case based on this book's chapters, and for comparison and contrast of Chile with Spain (a comparison made by Pinochet, who admired Franco), see Sánchez, "Beyond Pacted Transitions"; and Paloma Aguilar and Katherine Hite, "Historical Memory and Authoritarian Legacies in Processes of Political Change: Spain and Chile," in Hite and Cesarini, *Authoritarian Legacies*, 191–231. See Peter Winn, "The Pinochet Era," in *Victims of the Miracle: Workers and Neoliberalism in the Pinochet Era, 1973–2002*, ed. Winn (Durham, N.C.: Duke University Press, 2004), 49, for "devil's bargain" quote, applied to the 1988 plebiscite. For "authoritarian enclaves," see Manuel Antonio Garretón, "Human Rights in Democratization Processes," in *Constructing Democracy: Human*

Rights, Citizenship, and Society in Latin America, eds. Elizabeth Jelin and Eric Hershberg (Boulder, Colo.: Westview, 1996), 39–56; *La posibilidad democrática en Chile* (Santiago: FLACSO, 1989); and *Incomplete Democracy: Political Democratization in Chile and Latin America*, trans. R. Kelly Washbourne with Gregory Horvath (Chapel Hill: University of North Carolina Press, 2003). For "conspiracy of consensus" sensation, see Alexander Wilde, "Irruptions of Memory: Expressive Politics in Chile's Transition to Democracy," *Journal of Latin American Studies* 31, no. 2 (May 1999): 473–500 (476 for quote); cf. insights on political elites and the role of trauma itself in their 1990s stances, in Katherine Hite, "La superación de los silencios oficiales en el Chile posautoritario," in *Historizar el pasado vivo en América Latina*, ed. Anne Perotín-Dumon (Santiago: Universidad Alberto Hurtado, Centro de Etica, 2007), e-book, www.etica.uahur tado.cl, posted as link at Centro de Etica home page, also at www.historizarel pasadovivo.cl. For stinging critiques of Concertación elites as engaged in a kind of conspiracy of olvido, transactional sell-out, and myth-making, see Tomás Moulian, *Chile Actual: Anatomía de un mito* (Santiago: LOM, 1997); and Alfredo Jocelyn-Holt Letelier, *El Chile perplejo: Del avanzar sin transar al transar sin parar* (Santiago: Planeta, 1998). For more subtle analysis of political actors caught between "pacts" and "projects," see Claudio Fuentes, "Partidos y coaliciones en el Chile de los '90: Entre pactos y proyectos," in *El modelo chileno: Democracia y desarrollo en los noventa*, ed. Paul Drake and Iván Jaksic (Santiago: LOM, 1999), 191–222.

8   Aside from the events recounted in chapters 1–3 in this volume, see also the revealing report by Pilar Molina A., "Qué se pactó en la transición: Del presidente intocable al Pinochet en los tribunales," in *El Mercurio*, e-ed.: www.emol .com, 26-III-00. On "economic amnesty," by virtue of a 1989 law by the junta to block congressional audit and reversal of privatization, see interview of Jose Zalaquett by Mirko Macari ("Muchos caballeros se lavan las manos"), in *La Nación*, e-ed.: www.lanacion.cl, 29-x-06. Cf. Aylwin's account of frustration on this point, in the interview-book by Margarita Serrano and Ascanio Cavallo, *El poder de la paradoja: 14 lecciones políticas de la vida de Patricio Aylwin* (Santiago: Editorial Norma, 2006), 282–83. On failure to secure a 1989 human rights amnesty law, and alternative shielding adaptations, see chapter 1 in this volume, including the sources in note 12.

9   Pinochet interview with Whelan ("La entrevista más franca de Augusto Pinochet"), in *La Tercera*, e-ed.: www.tercera.cl, 14-IX-03 (quotes), cf. 21-IX-03 for more background. That Pinochet's vision of Aylwin and Frei extended to other members of the family is evident in the interview of Augusto Pinochet Molina, Pinochet's grandson who had spoken out at his grandfather's funeral, in *El Mercurio*, 16-XII-06 (*Sabado* magazine, 18).

10   For the climate of demobilization and the turn toward subtle frictional synergies rather than traditional social movement dynamics, from two very distinct per-

spectives—grassroots oriented, and elite oriented, respectively—see Julia Paley, *Marketing Democracy: Power and Social Movements in Post-dictatorship Chile* (Berkeley: University of California Press, 2001); and Aylwin's account in Serrano and Cavallo, *El poder de la paradoja*, 274. For a perceptive revindication of street movements and a lament of demobilization, within an older paradigm less inclined to see or analyze the synergies described here, see Temma Kaplan, *Taking back the Streets: Women, Youth, and Direct Democracy* (Berkeley: University of California Press, 2004). For related debate on the transition's lack of support for a plural and feisty press, see *La Nación*, e-ed.: www.lanacion.cl, 8-xii-06; and Juan Pablo Cárdenas, "El periodismo y el proceso político chileno," in *Frágiles suturas: Chile a treinta años del gobierno de Salvador Allende*, ed. Francisco Zapata (Mexico City and Santiago: El Colegio de México/Fondo de Cultura Económica, 2006), 479–88.

11 Heidi Tinsman, *Partners in Conflict: The Politics of Gender, Sexuality, and Labor in the Chilean Agrarian Reform, 1950–1973* (Durham, N.C.: Duke University Press, 2002). The historical context and focus of her study were quite distinct, but it is provocative to consider Tinsman's phrase when one remembers that the metaphor of restoring unity to the Chilean national family was common during the early transition.

12 I acknowledge gratefully the insight of Sol Serrano—she pushed my thinking by observing that "sin fórmula no hay wedge"—at a seminar I gave on truth commissions and tensions of "formula versus wedge" at the Instituto de Historia of the Universidad Católica in Santiago, 22-viii-06. I am also grateful to Alfredo Riquelme and Claudio Rolle for observations that refined my thinking.

13 For the preceding subsection on Chile and Argentina, as case studies in their own right, and as arenas of example and action influential in the transnational history of human rights, a superb study and guide to relevant scholarship is Thomas C. Wright, *State Terrorism in Latin America: Chile, Argentina, and International Human Rights* (Lanham, Md.: Rowman and Littlefield, 2007). For additional insight on Argentina, particularly grassroots and media activity, see Federico Lorenz, "¿De quién es el 24 de marzo? Las luchas por la memoria del golpe de 1976," in *Las conmemoraciones: Las disputas en las fechas "in-felices,"* ed. Elizabeth Jelin (Madrid: Siglo Veintiuno, 2002), 53–100; Claudia Feld, *Del estrado a la pantalla: Las imágenes del juicio a los ex comandantes en Argentina* (Madrid: Siglo Veintiuno, 2002); Leigh Payne, "Perpetrators' Confessions: Truth, Reconciliation, and Justice in Argentina," in *What Justice? Whose Justice? Fighting for Fairness in Latin America*, ed, Susana Eva Eckstein and Timothy P. Wickham-Crowley (Berkeley: University of California Press, 2003); and Naomi Roht-Arriaza, *The Pinochet Effect: Transnational Justice in the Age of Human Rights* (Philadelphia: University of Pennsylvania Press, 2005), esp. 5–25, 97–117, but also notable for intertwined justice dynamics in Chile and Argentina. For human rights justice as an aspect setting the two countries apart, from an

international journalism perspective, see *The Economist*, 14-IV-07, pp. 39–40. My understanding of the other cases mentioned derives in part from media tracking, in part from discussions with regional experts at scholarly seminars and conferences, and in part from published scholarship informed by truth-and-justice issues while setting them in broader contexts such as balance-of-power assessments, grassroots experiences, and cultural developments. See, e.g., for Southern Cone cases, Alexandra Barahona de Brito, *Human Rights and Democratization in Latin America: Uruguay and Chile* (New York: Oxford University Press, 1997); cf. Lawrence Weschler, *A Miracle, A Universe: Settling Accounts with Torturers*, 2nd ed. (Chicago: University of Chicago Press, 1998). For more recent twists related to Uruguay's amnesty-granting "Ley de Caducidad," see *Latin American Weekly Report* (U.K.), 20-XII-07, p. 10; Eric Hershberg and Felipe Agüero, eds., *Memorias militares sobre la represión en el Cono Sur: Visiones en disputa en dictadura y democracia* (Madrid: Siglo Veintiuno, 2005), esp. Agüero and Hershberg, "Las fuerzas armadas y las memorias de la represión en el Cono Sur," 1–34, and Aldo Marchesi, "Vencedores vencidos: Las respuestas militares frente a los informes 'Nunca Más' en el Cono Sur," 175–210; Leigh A. Payne, *Unsettling Accounts: Neither Truth nor Reconciliation in Confessions of State Violence* (Durham, N.C.: Duke University Press, 2008), whose case studies include South Africa as well as South American societies. For Peru, see Raynald Belay et al., eds., *Memorias en conflicto: Aspectos de la violencia política contemporánea* (Lima: Instituto de Estudios Peruanos and Instituto Francés de Estudios Andinos, 2004), esp. Carlos Iván Degregori, "Heridas abiertas, Derechos esquivos: Reflexiones sobre la Comisión de la Verdad y Reconciliación," 75–85, but note that the book is not limited to Peru; Jo-Marie Burt, *Political Violence and the Authoritarian State in Peru: Silencing Civil Society* (New York: Palgrave Macmillan, 2007); Cynthia E. Milton, "At the Edge of the Peruvian Truth Commission: Alternative Paths to Recounting the Past," *Radical History Review* 98 (spring 2007): 3–33; Kimberly Theidon, *Entre prójimos: El conflicto armado interno y la política de la reconciliación en el Perú* (Lima: Instituto de Estudios Peruanos, 2004); and Coletta Youngers, *Violencia política y sociedad civil en el Perú: Historia de la Coordinadora Nacional de Derechos Humanos* (Lima: Instituto de Estudios Peruanos, 2003). For Central America, see Leigh Binford, *The El Mozote Massacre: Anthropology and Human Rights* (Tucson: University of Arizona Press, 1996); Ellen Moodie, " 'El Capitán Cinchazo': Blood and Meaning in Postwar San Salvador," in *Landscapes of Struggle: Politics, Society, and Community in El Salvador*, ed. Aldo Lauria-Santiago and Leigh Binford (Pittsburgh: University of Pittsburgh Press, 2004), 226–44; Elizabeth Oglesby, "Educating Citizens in Postwar Guatemala: Historical Memory, Genocide, and the Culture of Peace," *Radical History Review* 97 (winter 2007): 77–98; Margaret Popkin, *Peace without Justice: Obstacles to Building the Rule of Law in El Salvador* (University Park: Pennsylvania State University

Press, 2000); and Rachel Sieder, "War, Peace, and the Politics of Memory in Guatemala," in *Burying the Past: Making Peace and Doing Justice after Civil Conflict*, ed. Nigel Biggar (Washington, D.C.: Georgetown University Press, 2007), 184–206.

14 Ellen Lutz and Kathryn Sikkink, "The Justice Cascade: The Evolution and Impact of Foreign Human Rights Trials in Latin America," *Chicago Journal of International Law* 2, no. 1 (spring 2001): 1–33. See also the seminal account of transnational activism by Margaret E. Keck and Kathryn Sikkink, *Activists beyond Borders: Advocacy Networks in International Politics* (Ithaca, N.Y.: Cornell University Press, 1998), which sets the human rights and Latin American aspects within a broader framework, including the rise of environmental and women's advocacy networks; Wright, *State Terrorism in Latin America*; Sidney Tarrow, *The New Transnational Activism* (New York: Cambridge University Press, 2005); and Roht-Arriaza, *The Pinochet Effect*. For the related but distinct topic of epistemic communities (distinct because the focus is on transnational expertise communities and their relations with states, but not on advocacy dynamics and networks as such), see Peter M. Haas, "Introduction: Epistemic Communities and International Policy Coordination," *International Organization* 46, no. 1 (winter 1992): 1–35. For the more expansive 1940s vision of human rights and the role of Latin Americans and NGOs in pushing for it, see Greg Grandin, *Empire's Workshop: Latin America, the United States, and the Rise of the New Imperialism* (New York: Metropolitan Books, 2006), 37–38; and Keck and Sikkink, *Activists beyond Borders*, 85–86. For long-term views of the impact of Cold War politics on visions and practice of human rights, both in its restricted and expansive senses, see Grandin, *Empire's Workshop*, and *The Last Colonial Massacre: Latin America in the Cold War* (Chicago: University of Chicago Press, 2004). See also Lesley Gill, *The School of the Americas: Military Training and Political Violence in the Americas* (Durham, N.C.: Duke University Press, 2004); and Alfred W. McCoy, *A Question of Torture: CIA Interrogation from the Cold War to the War on Terror* (New York: Metropolitan Books, 2006). For reframings of Cold War history from a Latin American angle emphasizing grassroots experiences and culture, see Gilbert M. Joseph and Daniela Spenser, eds., *In from the Cold: Latin America's New Encounter with the Cold War* (Durham, N.C.: Duke University Press, 2008), esp. Joseph, "What We Now Know and Should Know: Bringing Latin America More Meaningfully into Cold War Studies," 3–46; cf. Daniela Spenser, ed., *Espejos de la guerra fría: México, América Central y el Caribe* (Mexico City: CIEAS, 2004). For knotty issues including the imperial perils of universal claims and the paradoxical relationship of human rights and revolution, see also Jeffrey N. Wasserstrom, Lynn Hunt, and Marilyn B. Young, eds., *Human Rights and Revolutions* (New York: Rowman and Littlefield, 2000).

15 Keck and Sikkink, *Activists beyond Borders*, 11, 89–92 (statistics and Eldridge

quote); Tarrow, *The New Transnational Activism*, 29, defines rooted cosmopolitans as "people and groups who are rooted in specific national contexts, but who engage in contentious political activities that involve them in transnational networks of contacts and conflicts." He sees transnational activists as a "subgroup" of this larger category. For the role of Chile in 1970s transnational activism, including solidarity networks in Europe and the Americas, and institutional vehicles, including the United Nations and the Organization of American States, see trilogy Book Two, 81–128.

16 See Wright, *State Terrorism in Latin America*, 118–25; Keck and Sikkink, *Activists beyond Borders*, 103–10; and Binford, *The El Mozote Massacre*, 122–34, 229 n. 10. See also Popkin, *Peace without Justice*, 142, 201–2. Pérez Esquivel received the Nobel Prize in 1980; *The Official Story* received the Academy Award for best foreign film in 1986. The forthcoming dissertation of Vanessa Walker, a graduate student in United States international history at the University of Wisconsin, will do much to uncover further aspects of Carter administration policy on human rights in South America.

17 The larger trends, in terms of world regions that drew wide attention, are well known. For a fine work that embraces developments in Europe and Africa as well as the Americas, and analyzes in this context the theory, experiences, and upsurge of truth commission activity of varying effectiveness, see Priscilla B. Hayner, *Unspeakable Truths: Facing the Challenge of Truth Commissions*, 2nd ed. (New York: Routledge, 2002); cf. Biggar, ed., *Burying the Past*. For the prominence of Chile in post-Watergate Congressional and media investigation, see trilogy Book One, 169–70 n. 8, 172–73 n. 16.

18 See, in addition to intersections of Chilean and transnational developments recounted in this volume and in trilogy Book Two, Wright, *State Terrorism in Latin America*; and Roht-Arriaza, *The Pinochet Effect*. Cf. Madeleine Davis, ed., *The Pinochet Case: Origins, Progress, and Implications* (London: Institute of Latin American Studies, 2003). I wish to thank Yvonne Geerts, who deepened my understanding as she worked on her fine Senior Thesis, "Access and Agency in Latin America: The Politics of International Civil Society and the Creation of the International Criminal Court" (University of Wisconsin, Madison, 2006).

19 See, in addition to sources cited in note 18, the contrast between the Spanish case, grounded in the 1970s, in Aguilar, *Memory and Amnesia*, and shift-of-era developments as described by Hayner, *Unspeakable Truths*; Lutz and Sikkink, "The Justice Cascade"; and Keck and Sikkink, *Activists beyond Borders*.

20 Brian Loveman and Elizabeth Lira, *La suaves cenizas del olvido: Vía chilena de reconciliación política, 1814–1932* (Santiago: LOM, 1999); *Las ardientes cenizas del olvido: Vía chilena de reconciliación política, 1932–1994* (Santiago: LOM, 2000); *El espejismo de la reconciliación política: Chile, 1990–2002* (Santiago: LOM, 2002), the last of which balances emphasis on continuity of the "vía chilena" by taking account of discontinuities in post-1990 society. For recent synthesis and up-

date, see Loveman and Lira, "Truth, Justice, Reconciliation, and Impunity as Historical Themes: Chile, 1814–2006," *Radical History Review* 97 (winter 2007): 43–76.

21 For subtle analysis of Iquique and the North, the massacre, and interplays of memory making, state violence, and political subjectivities, see Lessie Jo Frazier, *Salt in the Sand: Memory, Violence, and the Nation-State in Chile, 1890 to the Present* (Durham, N.C.: Duke University Press, 2007). Cf. Pablo Artaza Barrios et al., *A 90 años de los sucesos de la Escuela Santa María de Iquique* (Santiago: LOM, 1998); and trilogy Book Two, 289–95. For outlaw of the Communist Party and subsequent reopening of the political system, see Loveman and Lira, *Las ardientes cenizas del olvido*, 125–98.

22 Wright, *State Terrorism in Latin America*, xv, makes a similar argument when invoking the notion of a "reciprocal relationship" between "the international human rights regime and state terrorism in Argentina and Chile, including its legacies." At a broader level, the issues in play are on the one hand, the search for mechanisms of social accountability that can complement or compensate the limited effects of electoral politics and "weak" democracy in the turn-of-century moment, and on the other, the search for transnational mechanisms of pressure on states and business practices in an age of globalized market dynamics that limit accountability through electoral processes within nation-states. For searching critical analysis of these themes and the politics of citizenship, see, respectively, Enrique Peruzzotti and Catalina Smulovitz, eds., *Enforcing the Rule of Law: Social Accountability in the New Latin American Democracies* (Pittsburgh: University of Pittsburgh Press, 2006); and Gay W. Seidman, *Beyond the Boycott: Labor Rights, Human Rights, and Transnational Activism* (New York: Russell Sage Foundation, 2007).

23 Greg Grandin, "The Instruction of Great Catastrophe: Truth Commissions, National History, and State Formation in Argentina, Chile, and Guatemala," *American Historical Review* 110, no. 1 (February 2005): 46–67. Cf. Grandin, *The Last Colonial Massacre*; and the essays in *Radical History Review* 97 (winter 2007): issue entitled "Truth Commissions: State Terror, History, and Memory." Such critique, while valid, is tempered if one also bears in mind practical issues and consequences that shape advocacy, not only in cases of human rights emergencies and legacies but also when promoting socioeconomic rights. Keck and Sikkink, *Activists beyond Borders*, found that transnational networks have proved most effective when framing advocacy as "bodily harm to vulnerable individuals, especially when there is a short and clear causal chain (or story) assigning responsibility," or as "issues involving legal equality of opportunity" (27). In this context, they note that boycott campaigning against business abuse and practice was relatively effective in the case of the Nestlé boycott, which contrasted the marketing of infant formula to poor women in the Third World as "modern" and "healthy" with actual effects that proved dangerous and un-

healthy, and for which causal responsibility was also clear (203–6, 209, cf. 14, 20–21, 28, 131–32, 158–63). They also noted the positive underside of liberalism for activists, insofar as it opened up spaces for effective contestation when activists "expose the gap between discourse and practice" (206). For stimulating historical comparison in the context of labor and anticolonialism in Africa in the 1940s–1950s, see Frederick Cooper, "Conditions Analogous to Slavery: Imperialism and Free Labor Ideology in Africa," in *Beyond Slavery: Explorations of Race, Labor, and Citizenship in Postemancipation Societies*, ed. Cooper, Thomas C. Holt, and Rebecca J. Scott (Chapel Hill: University of North Carolina Press, 2000), 107–49. For additional insight on the complexities and limits of transnational advocacy within world contexts framed by liberal or neoliberal rule making, see Seidman, *Beyond the Boycott*; and Daniel Jaffee, *Brewing Justice: Fair Trade Coffee, Sustainability, and Survival* (Berkeley: University of California Press, 2007).

24 For how the logic of historical periodization shifts, depending on social and regional vantage point, and can nuance standard visions of 1973 as rupture with the democratic past but without diminishing the extreme violence of the Pinochet dictatorship, see Florencia E. Mallon, *Courage Tastes of Blood: The Mapuche Community of Nicolás Ailío and the Chilean State, 1906–2001* (Durham, N.C.: Duke University Press, 2005). Cf. Claudio Barrientos, "'Y las enormes trilladoras vinieron [. . .] a llevarse la calma': Neltume, Liquiñe y Chihuío, tres escenarios de la construcción cultural de la memoria y la violencia en el sur de Chile," in *Luchas locales, comunidades e identidades*, ed. Ponciano del Pino and Elizabeth Jelin (Madrid: Siglo Veintiuno, 2003), 107–44, esp. 112–20; and Frazier, *Salt in the Sand*. Of course, the distinct logics of historical periodization and meaning anchored in regional geography should not be taken to construe an absence of conflicting visions when writing about the nation as a whole or adopting a Santiago-centric perspective. The relationships between national and regional vision on the one hand, and distinct narrative frameworks and emphasis on the other, are in this sense nuanced and dialectical. For distinct emphases within the democratic memory camp, during the dictatorship, about the long-term sweep of Chilean history and the role of violent rupture within it, see trilogy Book Two, 197–217, esp. 215–16. For innovative turn-of-the-century efforts at historical synthesis, influenced by the course of memory struggles in the late twentieth century as well as new trends in social and cultural historiography, but distinctive in overall interpretive approaches, see Sofía Correa et al., *Historia del siglo XX chileno: Balance paradojal* (Santiago: Editorial Sudamericana, 2001); and Gabriel Salazar and Julio Pinto, eds., *Historia contemporánea de Chile*, 5 vols. (Santiago: LOM, 1999–2002), which should be compared with the foundational study by Salazar, *Labradores, peones y proletarios: Formación y crisis de la sociedad popular chilena del siglo XIX* (Santiago: Ediciones Sur, 1985). See also note 25.

25 For insightful meditation on the "battle of memory" as a continuing project whose compass must include more than post-1973 history, see María Angélica Illanes, *La batalla de la memoria: Ensayos históricos de nuestro siglo, Chile, 1900–2000* (Santiago: Planeta, 2002), 16 (quote, which is itself a memory illusion to Patricio Guzmán's famous 1970s film documentary trilogy, *La batalla de Chile*). For a thoughtful "state of the literature" review on history and memory, see also Peter Winn, "El pasado está presente: Historia y memoria en el Chile contemporáneo," in Pérotin-Dumon, ed., *Historizar el pasado vivo en América Latina*. The introductory essay to the book (whose chapters emphasize Argentina, Chile, and Peru but also include other essays) by Anne Pérotin-Dumon, "Verdad y memoria: Escribir la historia de nuestro tiempo," offers a wide-ranging and perceptive reflection on the responsibilities and methodological challenges that living "battle of memory" issues pose to historians, in Europe as well as the Americas.

26 Transcript of Silva's speech in *Solidaridad* 12, (first half, January 1977): 20 (available at FAV; quotes); for background and context on the Pro-Peace Committee, the Vicariate of Solidarity, and dynamics of repression, misinformation, and solidarity in 1973–76, see trilogy Book Two, 81–136.

27 The posing of "Good Samaritan" versus "Prophet" memory is not by chance. This was precisely the tension that emerged in Catholic Church currents of emblematic memory making in the 1990s, especially upon Silva's death in 1999: see the superb study of María Angélica Cruz, *Iglesia, represión y memoria: El caso chileno* (Madrid: Siglo Veintiuno, 2004), esp. 69–76.

Essay on Sources

This essay provides a guide to the research sources I used for "The Memory Box of Pinochet's Chile." Since I conducted integrated research for the entire trilogy, and since each book is influenced by research findings of the others, it makes little sense to provide a distinct essay on sources for each book. As a courtesy to readers, this essay is reproduced in each volume.

The first research phase involved a year of intense field and archival investigations in Chile, from July 1996 to August 1997. The second phase involved supplementary research via five shorter visits to Chile during 1998 to 2002, and library, microfilm, and Internet work (mainly media tracking) in the United States. I read newly published books through 2001, the close of the period under study, as comprehensively as possible. After 2001, I continued to read widely, albeit less comprehensively, among new publications while completing the first draft of all three volumes. I also continued to track relevant media developments or findings. The third research phase, specifically to complete an improved draft of Book Three and to expand its chronological parameters to 2006, involved two additional field research visits to Chile in 2006–07, as well as readings of scholarship and relevant media and website tracking through 2007.

I relied on three streams of sources: (1) written documents—archival, published, and, more recently, electronic—that constitute the traditional heart of historical research; (2) audio and visual traces of the past and its memory struggles, in television and video archives, photojournalism, radio transcripts, and sound recordings; and (3) oral history including formal, semistructured interviews, less formal interviews and exchanges, and field notes from participant-observation experiences and focus groups. Participant-observation experiences also included visits to physical sites or ruins.

Below I divide the research sources somewhat differently, in order to consider traditional and nontraditional "media" sources in a more integrated fashion.

Readers should note that—with the exception of media—I do not offer a guide below to the vast published literature. The latter includes primary sources, especially an extensive *testimonio* and memoir literature; secondary sources on twentieth-century Chilean history; and rich comparative and theoretical literatures on memory in history. I have used these illuminating literatures extensively, but they are cited systematically in the notes, which often include commentaries for interested readers. To review these works again here would needlessly lengthen this essay, whose focus is on primary sources beyond the book publications available in major university libraries in the United States.

Before proceeding, however, I should note three aspects of the published literature that may be useful for other researchers. First, as is apparent in the notes, the testimonio and memoir genre is rich because it embraces social actors from a wide variety of social strata. They range from political and cultural elites with varied ideologies and experiences along Chile's Left-Center-Right spectrum, and in institutional niches (the Catholic Church, the military) more ambiguously related to specific political parties or identities; to grassroots actors from varied social worlds and experiences, that is, priests as well as Catholic lay activists, shantytown women indirectly affected by repression as well as direct victim-survivors and their relatives, former political prisoners as well as former agents of repression and prisoners coerced into collaboration. Second, two documentary publications require special mention, not only because of the quality of their data, but also because they serve as useful complementary guides for research in archives: Arzobispado de Santiago, Vicaría de la Solidaridad (hereinafter ASVS), *Detenidos desaparecidos: Documentos de trabajo*, 8 vols. (Santiago: ASVS, 1993), which provides meticulous accounts of key data (events of repression, witness testimonies, judicial trajectory) in the Vicariate of Solidarity's individual case files on disappeared persons, on a case-by-case basis for the entire country; and the Comisión Nacional de Verdad y Reconciliación, *Informe de la Comisión Nacional de Verdad y Reconciliación*, 2 vols. in 3 books (Santiago: Ministerio Secretaría General de Gobierno, 1991), which was the report of the Truth and Reconciliation Commission organized in 1990 by the newly elected administration of Patricio Aylwin Azócar. The 1991 Truth Commission report also presented a case-by-case analysis of individual victims, set within a reliable larger narrative on patterns. Below (and in the notes) these sources are cited as *DETDES* and *ICNVR*, respectively.

Finally, one must underscore that in research on contemporary and recent history of contentious memory, the conventional line between "primary" and "secondary" sources blurs and sometimes disintegrates altogether. A book by a reporter, about historical events that occurred well before the date of publication, for example, can become a crucial "primary" source or document because of the politicocultural responses it generates. In addition, the role of investigatory journalism, and the prominence of testimonio-style witnessing in the culture and politics of persuasion, mean that books that might at first sight seem a secondary source account may turn out to include substantial primary source material (interviews, testimonios, documents). An excellent example of both phenomena—strong responses that turn a book into a document of its era, narratives that mix primary and secondary source features—is the pioneering 1989 study of the Caravan of Death episode of 1973 by the journalist Patricia Verdugo, *Los zarpazos del puma* (1989; rev. ed., Santiago: CESOC, 1994). For context, see Book Three of this trilogy, esp. chapter 1.

The abbreviations used below after the first mention of archives, documentation centers, and library collections correspond to those provided in the abbreviation list that precedes the notes. To ease identification of distinct archives or sources (and comparison with the abbreviation list), I italicize their first mention here.

A. Archives, Documentation Centers, and Library Collections

The archives and collections mentioned in this section exclude repositories that pertain exclusively to the "Media" section below.

A1. Church and State Archives

Given the history of memory struggles and the role of the Santiago Catholic Church, the fundamental institutional starting point for research is *Fundación de Documentación y Archivo de la Vicaría de la Solidaridad, Arzobispado de Santiago* (FAV). The FAV is the most comprehensive and well-organized human rights and memory archive in Chile (and arguably, in the entire Southern Cone region of South America). Particularly useful for tracking human rights and memory themes over time is the Informe Confidencial series, whose inside-information aspect sometimes has the flavor of an intelligence service outside the formal state. The FAV's Caja A.I. and Caja A.T. series are also invaluable because they reproduce documents by theme and by organization. Much of the work and documents of other important human rights groups—among them AFDD (Agrupación de Familiares de Detenidos-Desaparecidos), FASIC (Fundación de Ayuda Social de las Iglesias Cristianas), and the Comisión Chilena de Derechos Humanos—are tracked and reproduced in these FAV series. Also collected are documents from the predecessor organization to the Vicariate of Solidarity, the Pro-Peace Committee (COPACHI). The FAV Recortes files contain amazingly comprehensive press clippings files (including radio and television transcripts), organized by theme and running back in time to 1973. They thereby facilitate media research. In the 1990s, the tracking function also came to include a useful computerized Banco de Datos (database) on human rights and judicial themes. The judicial case files are extensive (but often restricted) and are well-summarized, for disappearance cases, in the *DETDES*. The excellent library contains a full run of *Solidaridad* as well as other magazines and books.

State archives usefully complement the FAV holdings. Among the most important for me were case files from the 1990–91 Truth and Reconciliation Commission: *Archivo de la Comisión Nacional de Verdad y Reconciliación* (ACNVR). The case files from the original archive were not held separately but incorporated into the case files of the state's follow-up organism, Archivo de la Corporación Nacional de Reparación y Reconciliación, but for the sake of clarity I cite only case files from the original ACNVR. Theoretically, this archive is to be incorporated into Chile's national archive system and made available to researchers. The de facto reality has been that the materials are considered very sensitive and the archive remains under the control of the Interior Ministry. I was fortunate to secure access for a limited period (ca. six weeks) that enabled me to review and analyze the Commission's work through a sample of thirty case files. These were mainly Santiago Metropolitan Region cases, organized by two fundamental criteria: (1) several cases each chosen from the various political backgrounds in play (victims with militance in each of the distinct parties subjected to targeted repression, and also victims without identifiable militance), and (2) cases with cross-record linkage potential, based on my prior research. I supplemented these cases with several cases of special human or research interest (e.g., cases of the DINA [secret police] turning against its own agents or collaborators). The ICNVR was a crucial companion guide for this research.

I also made use of *Archivo Siglo XX del Archivo Nacional* (ASXX), which has volumes of papers on deposit from various ministries. Although the purge of sensitive papers by the outgoing military regime has hampered the ASXX collection on sensitive topics—it does not hold, for example, Interior Ministry documents from the 1970s—the state had many ministries, and the purge was far from complete. I focused especially on the Reservados volumes of the Education Ministry from the early-to-mid 1970s; they documented the pressure and means used to rid educational institutions of dissidents and "subversives," and they also reproduced copies of external documents—such as directives and reports from Pinochet and the DINA, and early minutes of junta sessions—that might have been more effectively purged or withheld in other branches of the state.

Courtesy of Florencia Mallon, I also consulted photocopied material from *Archivo Intendencia Cautín* in Temuco (AICT). This archive was subsequently incorporated into Archivo Regional de Araucanía, Temuco. The AICT provides unusual access to regional documents and correspondence with authorities tracing grassroots support for and concern about the incoming military regime.

A2. Nongovernmental Organizations (NGOs) and Social Actors

The FAV archive documents a good deal of memory-related work and struggles by many NGOs (not simply the Vicaría de la Solidaridad) and by social actors inside and outside the state. Nonetheless, numerous other NGO and social actor holdings also proved important in the research.

For transnational solidarity activities related to Chile's memory struggles, and synergies with struggles within Chile, a superb starting point is *Fundación Salvador Allende, Centro de Documentación* (FSA). Particularly valuable is its *Archivo Sergio Insunza* (FSA, ASI), a major archive built up in exile by Allende's last minister of justice, Sergio Insunza. As a former member of the Unidad Popular and in his work with the International Commission of Democratic Jurists, Insunza participated actively in European solidarity networks that crossed Cold War boundaries. His papers include witness-survivor testimonies, and mock trials of the junta held in various parts of the world; public declarations and pamphlets; confidential correspondence and communications among Democratic Jurist and Unidad Popular networks, and more generally between activists, diplomats, officials, and United Nations organisms; and extensive press clippings files organized by theme. The FSA also has, in addition to documents from Allende's life and presidency, collections of interest to memory work after 1973: messages and memorabilia left at Allende's tomb, the politics of street naming and monument projects to honor Allende's memory within and beyond Chile. With the assistance of Claudio Barrientos, at that time a graduate student at the University of Wisconsin, Madison, the cataloguing system of the FSA, ASI changed and became more rationalized after I did my work. My citation method corresponds to the older system, but the new system is sufficiently meticulous to enable one to find the cited documents.

For transnational solidarity, the strength of the FSA, ASI lies in its coverage of Europe and Latin America. For the U.S. side of the story, good complementary holdings are at *State Historical Society of Wisconsin Archives* (SHSWA), particularly its Community Action on Latin America Records, 1971–91, which documents grassroots activities in Madison, Wisconsin, and links out to other U.S.-based solidarity organizations and to U.S. congressional activity; and the survivor-witness testimony in the Adam Schesch Papers, 1965–74, which includes an important press conference reel (2 October 1973) about Schesch's imprisonment at the National Stadium in September 1973. As of 2004, researchers also have permission to utilize the SHSWA's Institute for Policy Studies Records, 1961–92, the important solidarity and think-tank NGO where Orlando Letelier worked before his assassination in Washington, D.C., in 1976.

Various Chilean NGOs have documentation centers whose holdings include a variety of published and unpublished sources including NGO bulletins related to their memory work. I benefited from documents, bulletins, and publications at the following: *Archivo, Corporación Parque Por La Paz Villa Grimaldi* (ACPPVG) documents the successful struggle in the 1990s to stop a project to obliterate the former torture-and-disappearance center Villa Grimaldi and transform it into a Peace Park. *Agrupación de Familiares de Detenidos-Desaparecidos, Centro de Documentación* (AFDDCD) focuses on the truth, justice, and memory struggles of relatives of the disappeared. *Comité de Defensa de los Derechos del Pueblo, Centro de Documentación* (CODEPUCD) is the working library of a human rights NGO important since the 1980s, with notable emphasis on torture and a policy explicitly embracing defense of the human rights of armed opponents of dictatorship. *Educación y Comunicaciones, Centro de Documentación* (ECOCD) documents ECO's trajectory in organizing grassroots history and memory of the labor movement, and in recovering popular memory and histories of struggle in local grassroots contexts. *Fundación para la Protección de la Infancia Dañada por los Estados de Emergencia, Centro de Documentación* (PIDEECD) is the working library of the PIDEE, an NGO that pioneered work on family and youth mental health issues related to repression. *Ictus, Centro de Documentación* (ICTUSCD) consists of a vast video repository with related print documents and bulletins on the cultural work of Ictus (originally an experimental theater group), whose staff and actors became heavily engaged with the world of alternative video forums in the 1980s. I should clarify that in the case of the AFDDCD and ACPPVG, I did not work directly in the repositories but rather was kindly given copies of bulletins and documents held by these organizations; as of 2002, a major reorganizing effort has been under way to reorder the AFDDCD holdings in a new building and to establish a computerized catalog or database.

Personal archives were also valuable for documenting some kinds of grassroots social activities: *Archivo Personal de Alicia Frohmann* (APAF), for ephemera related to underground bulletin work during the state of siege of 1984–85 and for initiatives by young historians in the 1980s; *Archivo Personal de Eugenia Rodríguez* (APER), for pro-junta clippings, magazines, and ephemera, and publications and activities of the Secretaría de la Mujer; *Archivo Personal de Juan Campos Cifuentes* (APJCC), for documents and videos related to the work of relatives of the disappeared, and a run of *carabinero-* and military-related documents; *Archivo Personal de Teresa Valdés* (APTV), the invaluable archive tracing the work of the women's human rights group Mujeres Por La Vida.

A3. Additional Special Libraries, Collections, and Ephemera

I benefited from several libraries and collections, in addition to the vast FAV library and the specialized documentation centers mentioned above. The *Biblioteca Nacional* (BN) has an invaluable repository of Chilean newspapers. I used it for targeted research, examining key dates (usually, a two-week period whose center point was the key date), to supplement gaps that remained after using thematically organized clipping files in repositories such as the FAV and FSA. Comprehensive reviews of major weekly magazines also helped me identify less obvious dates (events or anniversaries) that might need further newspaper examination at the BN, and sensitized me to ways memory played out during noncharged as well as charged seasons and moments. The *Biblioteca de* FLACSO (BF) includes an excellent collection of books and magazines related to memory and human rights issues, and it also has a fine collection of polling surveys by various organizations, including FLACSO (Facultad Latinoamericana de Ciencias Sociales–Chile). Its *Archivo Eduardo Hamuy* (BF, AEH) also offers a database that documents polling research performed by Eduardo Hamuy. The *Princeton University Library Pamphlet Collection, Chile* (PUC) is a treasure, in part because it includes so much ephemera related to social movements and politics under military rule (as well as more standard material, such as newspaper and magazine runs). I relied on microfilm copies (available from Scholarly Resources, Inc., by agreement with Princeton University Library) of both the "Main" and "Supplement" collections.

B. Media Sources: Print, Audio and Visual, and Electronic

Research on the recent history of memory struggles requires considerable attention to media, not only as a basic source for historical events (the traditional "first draft of history" role of journalists) but also as an object of analysis in its own right. The sources below are listed with both functions in mind, and therefore they include not only listings of media as historical sources but archives or collections oriented to analysis of media.

B1. Print Media

The list below combines newspapers and magazines. An asterisk (*) after the listing marks those media reviewed systematically, as distinguished from those used sporadically for specialized themes or purposes—for example, documentation of the publicity given to the alleged Plan Z conspiracy or of events and reactions related to the London arrest of Pinochet. When no city or country is listed in parentheses, the place of publication is Santiago and the publication is normally considered "national." City citations in parentheses refer to "de provincia" periodicals within Chile; country citations in parentheses mark foreign media. For some media, I relied in part on electronic (online) editions after 1997. In those cases, I have also supplied the online Web page location used. In a few instances, the medium is exclusively online. I note this by listing such media in quote marks rather than in italics (i.e., "El Mostrador" rather than *El Mostrador*).

I must underscore my appreciation for the extensive and well-organized clippings files at the FAV. Without that foundation (and the complementary clippings files at the FSA, ASI), I could not have reviewed as many media as systematically, nor pulled into my radar complementary media for specific cases or events, nor developed an efficient targeted methodology (see section A3 above) for media work at the BN and other collections.

To ease location and render common Spanish and English usages compatible, I retain *El* and *The* in the alphabetical listing below. The only exceptions are *Miami Herald*, *New York Times*, *Ultimas Noticias*, and *Washington Post*, which bow to contemporary conventions.

When a magazine or newspaper uses a week as its date of publication, I generally use the first day listed as the "date of publication" in the notes. For example, a magazine dated 3 to 10 September 1978 would simply be listed as 3-IX-78.

Readers should note that a number of the publications cited no longer exist. Some date to the Allende era and were closed by the dictatorship but were important for research on efforts to establish a memory script for a "coup foretold." Others played significant roles under dictatorship or during times of democratic transition but eventually succumbed to the difficulties of a concentrated and changing media market in the 1990s.

Amiga
*Análisis**
*Apsi**
AZkintuWE (Mapuche; also at www.nodo50.org, extension /azkintuwe)
BBC World News Service (U.K., at http://news.bbc.co.uk)
Cal y Canto
Caras
*Cauce**
*Chile-America** (Italy)
*Chile Hoy**
Clarín (Argentina; also www.clarin.com.ar)
Clarín (Santiago)
Concordia de Arica (Arica)
*Cosas**
Crónica (Concepción)
El Correo (Valdivia)
El Cronista
El Día (La Serena)
El Diario
El Diario Austral (Temuco)
*El Mercurio** (also at www.emol.com, formerly www.elmercurio.cl)
El Mercurio (Antofagasta)
El Mercurio (Valparaíso)
El Mercurio de Calama (Calama)
"El Mostrador"*. www.elmostrador.cl
El Mundo (Spain; also www.el-mundo.es)
El Observador (Quillota)
El País (Spain; also www.elpais.es)
El Rodriguista
*El Siglo**
El Sur (Concepción)
El Tarapacá (Iquique)
*Ercilla**
Estrategia
Fortín Mapocho
*Hoy**
"Inter-Press Service" (international): www.ips.org
La Bicicleta
La Cuarta

*La Epoca** (also www.laepoca.cl)
La Estrella (Valparaíso)
La Estrella de Iquique (Iquique)
La Estrella del Norte (Antofagasta)
La Firme
*La Funa**
*La Nación** (also www.lanacion.cl)
La Opinión (Argentina)
La Patria
La Prensa (Iquique)
La Prensa (Nicaragua)
La Prensa (Tocopilla)
La Prensa (Vallenar)
La Prensa de Santiago
*La Segunda**
*La Tercera** (also www.tercera.cl, formerly www.latercera.cl)
*Latin American Weekly Report** (U.K.)
Mensaje
Miami Herald (U.S.)
NACLA Report on the Americas (U.S.)
*New York Times** (U.S.; also www.nytimes.com)
Pluma y Pincel
Prensa
Prensa Libre (Guatemala)
"Primera Línea": www.primeralinea.cl
Proa (San Antonio)
*Punto Final**
Puro Chile
*Qué Pasa**
Realidad
*Revista Carabineros de Chile**
Rocinante
"Santiago Times"*: www.santiagotimes.cl (also link at www.derechoschile
    .com; formerly www.tcgnews.com, also "CHIP News," www.chip.cl)
*Solidaridad**
SurDA
*The Clinic**
The Economist (U.K.)
The Guardian (U.K.; also http://reports.guardian.co.uk)
The Nation (U.S.)
The New Republic (U.S.)
The New Yorker (U.S.)

Ultimas Noticias
Vea
Washington Post (U.S.)

B2. Audio and Visual Sources

Photojournalism played a significant role in memory struggles and is a marvelous point of entry into the 1973–2006 period. The print media listed above, of course, make ample use of photojournalism. The websites listed below (section B3) also provide visual documentation. I complemented these with photojournalism collections by professional photographers. The *Archivo Gráfico Personal de Helen Hughes* (AGPHH) has the work of the gifted photographer Helen Hughes, who has lived in Chile since 1977 and worked actively with the Vicaría de la Solidaridad and human rights networks. The archive generously allowed me to use selections from her photo collection in this trilogy. Her annotations to photos in her personal archive add valuable insight and context for work in visual sources. The *Archivo Gráfico Personal de Miguel Angel Larrea* (AGPMAL) is a fine personal collection by a working photojournalist and provides an excellent sense of the images important in oppositional journalism in the 1980s. The *Archivo Gráfico del Arzobispado de Santiago* (AGAS) complements the AGPHH and AGPMAL nicely, because it includes images that date back to the 1970s and that were important for the work of the Vicaría de la Solidaridad and in the early activities of relatives of the disappeared.

Radio, television, and alternative audiovisual networks (grassroots screenings and discussion forums) all proved important media streams and focal points of memory struggles. For radio, which was especially important in the 1970s, the FAV archive has transcripts of relevant news and commentary within its clippings files and bulletins on human rights and memory controversies. The coverage embraces pro-official, church-oriented, and dissent-oriented radio: *Radio Agricultura, Radio Balmaceda, Radio Chilena, Radio Cooperativa, Radio Minería, Radio Nacional, Radio Portales*. I complemented the FAV transcripts with documents from personal collections: Radio Agricultura recordings, from the APER; and clandestine radio broadcasts by the Frente Patriótico Manuel Rodríguez, from the APMM (*Archivo Personal de* "MM," whose name is withheld to preserve anonymity).

Sound as a medium of communication and memory struggles also circulated outside the sphere of radio and outside the genre of news-talk (i.e., news reports, commentary, and interviews). Particularly important as "alternative sound" was music (see trilogy Book Two, Afterwards to chapters 3, 7). Under the dictatorship, this included private cassettes circulating the repressed "New Song" music of the 1960s and early 1970s, such as the work of Violeta Parra, Víctor Jara, and Patricio Manns or of groups such as Inti-Illimani and Quilapayún. It also included newer music produced under conditions of dictatorship, by such groups as Congreso,

Illapu, Los Prisioneros, and Sol y Lluvia. Since the democratic transition in the early 1990s, such music has become readily available for purchase in new compact disc editions, circulates publicly, and feeds into ongoing memory work or struggles. For musical documentation, I relied on the personal collection Florencia Mallon and I have built up over the years, in dialogue with data from interviews and documents.

An additional source of alternative sound were cassettes of audio documents and testimonies that circulated extensively in the mid-1980s and which aired sounds then considered taboo on radio—for example, Allende's last speech and intercepts of communications between Pinochet, Gustavo Leigh, and other high military officials on 11 September 1973. The most important production was *Chile: Entre el dolor y la esperanza* (1986), directed by journalists Mónica González and Patricia Verdugo, in the series *El Sonido de la Historia* and kindly copied for me by a person in exile. Here, too, I relied on my personal collection.

My research on television and on alternative audiovisual media drew on several sources. Most important were *Televisión Nacional, Centro de Documentación* (TVNCD), *Archivo Audiovisual de la Vicaría de Pastoral Social (Santiago)* (AAVPS), and the ICTUSCD. At the TVNCD, the working video and documentary center of Televisión Nacional, I was able to review news reporting in the 1980s, as well as specific media events and spectacles in the 1980s and 1990s—including the television strips (*franjas*) by both sides in the 1988 plebiscite, and news interviews and programs (especially the *Informe Especial* news magazine) that sparked attention and controversy during the 1990s.

The purging of archives conducted by the outgoing military regime made 1970s programming more scarce at the TVNCD. Fortunately, the 1970s transcripts included in the clippings files and bulletin reports at the FAV included news and commentary at Televisión Nacional (Canal 7) and at Televisión de la Universidad Católica de Chile (Canal 13).

Both the AAVPS and ICTUSCD were crucial for understanding the world of alternative audiovisual media. The AAVPS not only contained video copies of key public events (such as President Patricio Aylwin's televised 1991 speech to the nation about the report of the Truth and Reconciliation Commission), thereby allowing me to concentrate on other matters during my limited access time at the TVNCD. It also contained a run of the forty-six highly professional and counterofficial news programs in the *Teleanálisis* series of 1984–89, barred from television but distributed in videos for viewing and discussion forums in shantytowns and popular settings, with church and NGO assistance. The ICTUSCD collection rounded out the street world of alternative audiovisual programming via its marvelous holdings of videos (movies, documentaries, and theater, produced by Ictus and other alternative media groups) used in popular screening-forum events in the 1980s, and via its records on the distribution and popularity of specific works.

Additional viewing of significant audiovisual productions, some from the world of public programming and some from the semiunderground world of communications, came from various sources. I was assisted in this way by the ECOCD, FSA, APAF, APJCC, APTV, and *Archivo Personal de Sol Serrano* (APSS).

Finally, I should mention personal archives that offered important insight on television and audiovisual communications. *Archivo Personal de Diego Portales Cifuentes* (APDPC) allowed me access to published and unpublished reports by the NGO media group ILET, Instituto Latinoamericano de Estudios Transnacionales. The ILET was crucial in the emergence of sophisticated audiovisual analysis and experience in Chile in the years leading up to the 1988 plebiscite. Similarly, *Archivo Personal de María Eugenia Hirmas* (APHEM) offered copies of her extensive and astute media analyses, including her influential and insightful studies of television publicity and propaganda related to the 1988 plebiscite. An interview with María Elena Hermosilla, 14-III-97, also offered sharp analysis of the world of alternative communications and pointed me toward promising leads and personal archives.

B3. Electronic Sources

The Internet and World Wide Web emerged as a world media phenomenon during the last nine years covered by this study (1998–2006) and had implications for the course of memory struggles. The theme receives explicit attention in Book Three of this trilogy. For my purposes, the most important research implication was the ability to track from abroad media reports and spectacles in online editions of newspapers, which also came to include links to documents or exposés of interest. Since 1998, the early leaders in newspapers with links to memory archives and documents were "El Mostrador" (www.elmostrador.cl) and *La Tercera* (www.tercera .cl), which could be usefully supplemented by "Santiago Times" (www.santiagotimes.cl). In the pre-1998 phase of Internet adoption in Chile (see trilogy Book Three, chapter 5), the now defunct *La Epoca* (www.laepoca.cl) also played a pioneering role.

Beyond electronic newspapers and their links to archives of back-articles and thematically organized documents, other websites have organized memory-related information, documents, forums, and testimonios. In other words, they have become memory "players" in ongoing struggles. A note of caution is in order. Website addresses change and evolve. A few sites have been shut down—either because the flux of business and markets rendered them untenable, as in the case of *La Epoca*, or because questions of politics, legality, or timeliness undermined them, as in the case of Despierta Chile, organized by former secret police agents and sympathizers to publish "confessions" by tortured prisoners.

The list below is organized by World Wide Web address, with parenthetical notes to identify the organizing group and to add, if needed, a brief annotation. The list is necessarily selective, reflects only sites I consulted and found useful, and offers a spread of memory frameworks and political perspectives. Rather than provide lengthy extensions in the address, I generally provide the point of entry, since links to the Chile-related memory sectors of the site are easy to find.

Unless otherwise noted, all addresses below begin with the conventional *www.* prefix. I simply provide the remainder of the address.

amnesty.org (Amnesty International, international human rights NGO)

argenpress.info (Argenpress; news clippings service for Latin America, emphasis on critique of status quo including Left and human rights perspectives)

bcentral.cl (Banco Central de Chile; useful statistical data bank)

cerc.cl (Centro de Estudios de la Realidad Contemporánea; polling)

chipsites.com (Chile Information Project; links to memory issues)

codepu.cl (CODEPU; human rights NGO in Chile)

comisiontortura.cl (Comisión Nacional sobre Prisión Política y Tortura; see also links at ddhh.gov.cl)

ddhh.gov.cl (Ministerio del Interior, Programa de Derechos Humanos; many links to key documents and programs related to human rights since 1990)

derechoschile.com (Derechos Chile; fairly comprehensive map of memory and human rights issues and history in Chile)

derechos.org/nizkor (Equipo Nizkor; human rights, Latin America)

despiertachile.netfirms.com (Despierta Chile; former secret police)

ejercito.cl (Chilean Army)

fasic.org (FASIC; human rights NGO in Chile)

foia.state.gov (U.S. State Department, Freedom of Information Act documents; begins address as http://)

fundacionpinochet.cl (Fundación Presidente Augusto Pinochet Ugarte)

geocities.com, at /Athens/Delphi/9574/grimaldi.htm (Villa Grimaldi Peace Park; also, http://members.xoom.com/grimaldi, and recently www.villagrimaldicorp.cl)

gn.apc.org/warresisters (War Resisters International, U.K.)

gobiernodechile.cl (home page of presidential administration, executive branch; also gobiernochile.cl)

guillo.cl (Guillo Bastías; brilliant political cartoons)

hrw.org (Human Rights Watch; international human rights NGO)

iglesia.cl (Chilean Catholic Church; includes documents by bishops)

ine.cl (Instituto Nacional de Estadísticas; Chilean government statistical research)

institutoohiggiano.cl (Bernardo O'Higgins Institute, for a time housed at the former torture house Londres 38, as part of a cover-up)

londres38.cl (Colectivo Londres 38; NGO, survivors of Londres 38 torture house)

manuelcontreras.com (Manuel Contreras; former head of the DINA) memoriaviva.com (Memoria Viva; memory and human rights NGO, organized by Chilean exiles in the United Kingdom; "Boletín" link provides human rights news clippings service on Chile; related international tree-planting project at ecomemoria.com)

mesadedialogo.cl (Mesa de Diálogo sobre Derechos Humanos; 1999–2000 dialogue initiative encompassing military and civilians; see also ddhh.gov.cl above)

mideplan.cl (Ministerio de Planificación y Cooperación; household survey research)

nsarchive.org (National Security Archive; NGO, systematic work with U.S. government documents and Freedom of Information Act, major link to Chile documents via Clinton administration's Declassification Project and Freedom of Information Act; also at gwu.edu/nsarchiv; see also foia.state.gov above)

villagrimaldicorp.cl (Villa Grimaldi Peace Park)

C. Oral History Sources

In addition to written documents and audio and visual traces of the past, I used oral sources. Below I first consider the basic purpose and parameters of the oral research, then turn to more subtle issues of method, relationships with informants, and representation.

C1. Purpose and Parameters of Oral Research

The fundamental purpose of my oral research was to explore in depth the ways people from diverse memory camps and walks of life defined meaning and memory of the 1973 crisis and the violence of military rule, both in terms of their own lives and in terms of the wider society. Of course, I also used many oral interviews to help me hypothesize or reconstruct empirical historical facts that could be corroborated or cross-checked with other sources, and to ask informants, in turn, to react to hypotheses and findings based on my work in written or other sources. My main quest, however, was to establish relationships, interviews, and participant-observation experiences—in the spirit of an ethnographer or a journalist involved in field immersion—that might enable me to achieve an in-depth human exploration of memory and meaning in Chilean society.

For purposes of historical analysis, the oral historical research served two objectives: understanding the human faces of memory and meaning since the mid-to-late 1990s, especially among ordinary rather than well-known Chileans; and integration of what I learned via oral research and field immersion since the mid-to-late 1990s into the analysis of memory creation and struggle over time, as a process traced through historical records from the 1970s through the early 2000s.

Several consequences followed for my oral research strategy. First, I gave priority to semistructured life history interviews, not to the design of formal questionnaires for statistically valid analysis or representative population samples modeled in the manner of social science opinion surveys. I relied on survey data by Chilean pollsters and social scientists—they are of good quality from the mid-to-late 1980s on—to help me understand wider public opinion contexts and to serve as a check against misleading findings through historical and oral research. The semistructured life history interviews walked us through the interviewee's personal background and history, as well as key events or turning points significant for collective memory—while remaining sufficiently open-ended to let the interviews move toward the experiences my collaborators thought meaningful and important.

At its best, the method in semistructured yet open-ended interviews is a bit like playing jazz with a partner. One must be attentive and sensitive to the place one's partner wants to go and must therefore improvise. One needs to "listen and learn" rather than stick to a rigid scripting. One welcomes and adjusts to the unexpected flow or riff. At the same time, one bears in mind a leitmotif—the basic research questions and a sequence of themes for discussion—and therefore finds the moment when one can fruitfully return or build a conversational bridge to still unaddressed and pertinent questions or topics. See also section C2 below for the importance of deliberate insertion of "off-balance" moments in the interview process.

Second, I sought to develop a multilayered rather than monodimensional approach to "interview" research. Because I sought depth, I wanted not only to compare oral research with findings from other source streams (especially written documents but also visual, audio, and audiovisual) but also to develop different kinds of oral experiences and evidence. I complemented the formal semistructured life history with less formal—more "spontaneous" and opportunistic—interviews and exchanges and kept track of these exchanges in a field notebook. I supplemented the one-on-one approach with focus-group meetings. I valued participant-observation experiences such as joining in a workshop, a demonstration, or a commemoration, and again kept track of what I learned or observed in a field notebook. I kept relationships going by returning transcripts to persons interviewed, soliciting reactions to the transcript, and in some instances following up with additional interviews. In cases where "key informants" emerged—people who offered exceptionally rich possibilities for in-depth reflection—I supplemented my information not only with cross-record research in written sources but also ethnographic work and conversation with friends or relatives of the informant who could help me diversify and contextualize my understanding of the person and my interviews. (I do not include such conversations in the "interview count" given below.)

Third, while I made no pretense of building a scientifically valid cross-section of society as my interviewee universe, I *did* actively seek out persons from a wide variety of memory camps, social backgrounds, and political perspectives. After all, my purpose was to understand how memory struggles and issues played out in society as a whole, not simply in one or another memory camp of a divided society. My informal working goal was to assure that I had achieved "good" in-depth interview experiences with at least several examples of almost every relevant social perspective I could imagine—by social class, political alignment, memory camp, degree of direct connection to repression, and the like. Thus I ended up interviewing persons from very different walks of life and experiences of military rule. I interviewed women from working-class poblaciones, from middle-class neighborhoods, and from elegant upscale sectors. As to social status and class, there were low-status laborers, such as electricians, carpenters, and security guards; middle-class or lower middle-class workers, such as secretaries, schoolteachers, and librarians; professionals, such as journalists, lawyers, and therapists; and persons of high wealth or power, such as financiers, journalism directors, and political leaders. Most important for my purposes, I interviewed persons across the social boundaries that have historically defied "memory conversation" within Chile—across the various memory camps I discovered in my research; across the social roles of victim, perpetrator, and bystander; and across identities as civilian or military.

Even within a superficially homogenous social type, I sought diversity. My "priests," for example, included a cerebral intellectual who offered inspiring theological insight, in addition to experience in the world of human rights; a street priest living in a shack in a población, and whose insights into everyday life added texture to research on memory events and controversies in the población; and a former military chaplain who went on to serve a church in an upscale neighborhood and who drew me into the world of conservative Catholic Church outlooks and experiences. Similarly, my "military and police folk" included not only former officers but also former conscripts, not only defenders and participants in military rule but also those purged or marginalized as dissenters and unreliables. Among victim-survivors, I sought out not only the persistent activist who stays involved with a group such as the relatives of the disappeared through thick and thin, but also the person who had become discouraged and dropped out, or dropped in and out.

Fourth, my interest in understanding "ordinary" Chileans meant that with some exceptions, I gave priority to gaining access to lesser-known or unknown individuals, rather than celebrities or public figures whose memory voices and views were available in a host of other sources—and who were not likely to deviate in interviews from already-established positions or to move into the personal. The exceptions were that for specific organizations or groups who played large roles in memory struggles or the politics of truth, I did seek out leaders and public figures. For example, I interviewed three members (the late Jaime Castillo, and Gonzalo Vial and José Zalaquett) of Chile's Truth and Reconciliation Commission and the former president Patricio Aylwin, who staked his presidency and its legitimacy on the work of the

Commission, and I also interviewed well-known journalists (Emilio Filippi, Patricia Politzer, the late Patricia Verdugo, Cristián Zegers). But even in such cases, I also sought out the lesser-known faces—not simply the Truth Commission's voting members but the staff that laid the groundwork for meetings with relatives of victims, gathered and analyzed records, implemented the approach framed by the Commission, and prepared summary memos and files for the deliberations by Truth Commission members. Even when focusing on persons who worked with human rights organizations such as the Vicaría de la Solidaridad, I granted strong priority to learning the perspective of a secretary, a social worker, or a photojournalist.

From my own point of view, the biggest weakness of the oral research was concentration of the interview work on Greater Santiago and on urban rather than rural experiences. Fortunately, regionally based research by superb scholars such as Claudio Barrientos, Lessie Jo Frazier, Florencia Mallon, and Heidi Tinsman have done much to compensate for this weakness.

I used three methods to identify and connect to potential interviewees: social contacts, social location, and proactive opportunism. (1) To build an initial network of collaborators ("interviewees"), I mobilized the full range of my social contacts to connect with distinct sorts of people. My Chilean colleagues and human rights contacts played important roles in opening up the world of human rights networks, grassroots social organizations, and professionals such as journalists. My wonderful extended Chilean family of *tías, tíos,* and *primos* helped me connect to more conservative and traditionalist slices of Chilean society. As my web of contacts expanded, I used the snowball method—asking people to help me identify other promising persons—to expand my map of possibilities and establish initially elusive contacts, such as former soldiers. (2) I also benefited from social location. Precisely since certain places and activities draw persons involved in one or another sort of memory work or struggle, my research provided possibilities for expanding social networks and connections. For example, everyday research at the FAV archive created opportunities to meet people such as the former political prisoner and memory activist Pedro Matta, who also showed up at the FAV day after day, eventually became a close friend, and opened up new layers of oral, written, and field site research possibilities. Similarly, attending a forum (organized by my social science colleagues and friends at FLACSO) of pobladora women provided opportunities to meet and learn from poor women in a working-class neighborhood. (3) Proactive opportunism is perhaps the most difficult method to explain to the noninitiated. It involves a state of hyperalertness—like a journalist obsessively pursuing and sniffing out a story—that enables one to notice and "seize" any opening that emerges at any moment and to create verbal lures to observe reactions and actively create openings. For example, running away from tear gas in a demonstration commemorating 11 September 1973 created a bond and an opportunity to ask about the life of a Chilean exile recently returned from Canada. Consider a more subtle example. My trips to the "Israeli Stadium" for exercise and family activity prompted a person to ask how Jews relate to Israel. I channeled the conversation toward the idea of diasporas and mentioned that Chileans would of course understand the diaspora concept, since so many ended up wandering to so many places in the world. Then I watched for body language, verbal reaction, possible engagement.

These methods yielded ninety-three interviewees, whom I prefer to think of as collaborators in a conversation, through 2002. Among these collaborators, fifty-four participated in formal semistructured interviews, virtually all of them tape-recorded. (A few declined to speak with a tape recorder on.) In almost every case, the interview lasted at least an hour and a half; in some cases, the taped conversations lasted more than four hours and actually involved several interview sessions. In almost all instances, I also learned from my collaborators via informal interviews and exchanges, both before and after the formal interviews. The thirty-nine remaining collaborators followed more "opportunistic" interview formats of informal exchanges. To help readers distinguish between the semistructured formal interviews (almost always taped) and more opportunistic or informal conversations (usually recorded or summarized in field notebooks), I gloss the former as *interview* and the latter as *conversation* in the notes. By Chilean cultural standards, however, almost all such exchanges would be considered "interviews." The supplementary field research for Book Three in 2006–07 added five new interviewees, along with some follow-ups among the original ninety-three.

The focus group–style discussions that supplemented the one-on-one approach took place in five forums. In some, "memory" was the central issue for explicit discussion; in others, memory was an informing issue, an aspect of experience or identity that came up and conditioned discussion formally organized around a distinct topic. The groups and topics assembled in the forums, all in 1996–97, were the following: shantytown women discussing their needs and experiences as women and as poor people, a testimonio-style workshop of human rights survivors and activists discussing memory, truth, and justice strategies in dialogue with personal experience; shantytown men and women discussing educational and economic needs; military veterans, purged for their Constitutionalist rather than pro-coup inclinations in 1973, discussing the possibility of securing dignity and reparation within democracy; and members of the organization of relatives of the disappeared discussing the problem of legal impunity after an initial panel presentation by invited human rights lawyers and political figures.

To preserve privacy, and also to make clear for non-Chileans the distinction between public figures and "ordinary" Chileans, I use the following naming convention in the text. For public figures, I use the authentic first and last names. For nonpublic figures, I respect privacy by using a pseudonym given as a first name and the initial of a last name. In a few instances, when a person expressed special concern about identification, I also introduced small changes (for example, occupation) that would not affect the larger analysis. An exception to this naming convention is that some "ordinary" persons had reason to prefer use of their true names, regardless of the implications for privacy. For example, for a person such as Herminda Morales, a mother of disappeared sons who waged a long struggle against official lies, to use a pseudonym would play into the hands of the culture of secrecy and misinformation against which she battled. An additional exception occurs when some ordinary persons became transformed for a time, for reasons beyond their control, into figures linked to public events, as in the case of Paulina Waugh (see trilogy Book Two), the owner of a fire-bombed art gallery.

C2. Methods, Relationships, and Representation

Some aspects of method, particularly the nature of oral "truths" and one's relationships with "informants," raise subtle issues that have become an object of scholarly discussion and debate. Here I wish to offer my approach to these questions.

As noted above, I emphasized the semistructured, yet open-ended interviewing method that places a premium on "listening" and "conversation," a collaboration akin to a jazz performance. My option for this approach—rather than, say, the prescripted survey with multiple choice answers that lends itself to statistical analysis, or the "hunt for facts" interview that prioritizes isolating and discarding the fallacies of memory—aligns me with the approach to oral truths and method outlined by historians such as Alessandro Portelli. See *The Death of Luigi Trastulli and Other Stories: Form and Meaning in Oral History* (Albany: State University of New York Press, 1991). As Portelli brilliantly demonstrates, if one "accepts" one's collaborator and the idea that oral research connects most fundamentally to meaning, one can discover truths elusive in other sources. One need not take the interviewee's narrative of facts at face value—on the contrary, one must subject all sources, written or oral, to critical appraisal and corroboration. But in oral research and especially for study of memory in history, the gap between the verifiable empirical historical record of events and the ways they are remembered and interpreted itself turns into empirical information, becoming a source of "truth" for investigation. As Portelli puts it, "the diversity of oral history consists in the fact that 'wrong' statements are still psychologically 'true'" (51).

Three subtle issues of method and representation arise within this approach and require comment. First, building a conversational collaboration requires finding a basis for mutual acceptance. As a practical matter, I used any true facet of my own background, interests, personality, and social experiences that might help me connect with people and build a relationship of credibility or confidence. Of course, with some individuals I was more successful than with others, and in some social contexts I found the process easier than in others. The fact that I am a second-generation Holocaust survivor, and that this aspect of my family history has shaped me to the core of my soul—my sense of self, my social sympathies, my anxieties and ideals—made me feel most at ease with persecuted people who had passed through intense life-and-death experiences. I did not use my Holocaust background crudely or wave a banner of horror (tender loyalties to my own relatives and their memory preclude such vulgar instrumentalism), but it is also true that in some instances, my Holocaust background provided a bridge of credibility, empathy, and intuitions useful in conversation. In the end, and although this may sound strange to others, I am most "at home" with people who have experienced or witnessed social injustice or violent persecution.

In other contexts, other facets of my background helped me find bridges of intuition, connection, or acceptance for a conversational collaboration. In the world of human rights professionals, my background as an intellectual who leans Left and supports human rights solidarity provided a way to connect. With elders, the manners I learned from my parents helped. With conservatives, the value I place on family, the genuine affection and social embeddedness I experienced with my Chilean family, and my general ability to embrace individuals unlike myself all helped me find ways to connect and accept. (My ability to enjoy people quite different from me may derive partly from the fact that I have long been an outgoing social climber from modest origins—a tailor's son and a first-generation college student at an Ivy Leave university—as well as a "stranger" from a Holocaust refugee family. I am long used to being both an "outsider" and a social traveler who enjoys navigating, connecting with, and learning from people of radically different backgrounds.) Perhaps most important, when personal connection proved elusive, was sheer intellectual curiosity. I have long taken intellectual delight in discovering the "logic" of other people's thought and experiences, and as a foreigner I could ask innocent or delicate questions—in a sense, seek cultural mentoring—without necessarily giving offense.

A second subtle issue involves striking a balance between "listening" with an open mind for the authentic truth embedded in a person's story or memory, and using one's critical facilities to "push" for more or to "test and critique" the narrative. Notwithstanding the collaborative aspect of the conversation, there also emerges, to a greater or lesser degree, a potential tug-of-war. One wants to hear and understand people's stories in their integrity, but at times one also wants to move discourses away from the preferred narrative, toward unintended or taboo areas. I took care in my interviews to insert the occasional decentering or uncomfortable question (for example, "when did you come to accept the death of your disappeared loved one?"), or to engage in some "arguing back" with the logic of the narrative ("but some people might say . . ." or "I saw some documents that said . . ."), or to organize a follow-up interview or conversation that pursued a new line of discussion. The goal here was not to obstruct the interviewee or to prevent us from getting back, after a detour, to the story the person wanted to tell but to achieve greater depth and to find the balance between "listening" and "probing."

For similar reasons (and as mentioned above), I found it helpful to do complementary research on key informants who offered exceptional possibilities for indepth reflection. I supplemented the oral information they provided with cross-record research in written sources, and with ethnographic work and conversation with friends or relatives who might help me diversify and contextualize my understanding of the person and the interviews.

A third difficult issue when making use of oral sources is representation. Since the late 1980s, scholarly controversies about ethnographic authority in anthropological writings, and about the uses and misuses of testimonial writings, have drawn great attention to issues of truth and representation in oral history and anthropology. A salient issue is how to represent relationships between researchers and "informants." See James Clifford, *The Predicament of Culture: Twentieth-Century Ethnography, Literature, and Art* (Cambridge, Mass: Harvard University Press, 1988); Georg M. Gugelburger, ed., *The Real Thing: Testimonial Discourse and Latin America* (Durham, N.C.: Duke University Press, 1996); and the recent Rigoberta Menchú controversy in David Stoll, *Rigoberta Menchú and the Story of All Poor Guatemalans* (Boulder, Colo.: Westview Press, 1999), and Arturo Arias, ed., *The Rigoberta Menchú Controversy* (Minneapolis: University of Minnesota Press, 2001).

The most satisfying response to the problem of representation occurs through the genre of life history writing. The scholar or collaborating partners can pursue in depth a person's life experience, the analysis of interview transcripts, and the dynamics of the relationship between scholar and "informant." The genre can lend itself to thoughtful sections or essays, separate from the life history narrative or transcripts, explicitly analyzing the relationship of "author" and "subject" and its representation, as well as the nature of the "truths" available in the interview transcripts. The Latin American history field has recently witnessed two superb examples of this response: Daniel James, *Doña María's Story: Life History, Memory, and Political Identity* (Durham, N.C.: Duke University Press, 2000); and Rosa Isolde Reuque Paillalef, with Florencia E. Mallon, ed. and trans., *When a Flower Is Reborn: The Life and Times of a Mapuche Feminist* (Durham, N.C.: Duke University Press, 2002). As Mallon has pointed out, moreover, the life history genre has a long and distinguished tradition—it reaches back to the 1950s fieldwork of Oscar Lewis and Sidney Mintz—in Latin American anthropology.

The new life history studies have been instructive and have informed the critical eye I bring to my interview sources. For my purposes, however, these wonderful studies have not solved the problem of representation. Several obstacles arise. First, the goal of this project is to understand and trace systematically the making of memory struggles. It is not primarily an oral history. It requires mobilizing such a huge array of sources from multiple genres—written, audio and visual, and oral—that a life history approach inviting explicit extended reflections on relationships and representation related to particular oral sources and interviews is not practical. Just as some research topics require that a social historian glean historical truths from thousands of critically analyzed documents, rather than focusing especially (as a literary scholar might) on a singularly rich text, so it is that I would find it reductionist and misleading to home in on a single life for this project.

Second, I have a "Holocaust problem." To enter into extended in-depth reflections about myself and my relationships in the text—beyond the reflections in this essay on sources—would risk violating the integrity of my collaborators and the Chilean story. My own family story is so dramatic and relates so tightly to one of the overwhelming symbols of our times that to dwell on it at length, in a study about Chile, seems ethically and professionally irresponsible. To do so would risk turning the searing Chilean experience into a kind of one-dimensional foil, rather than a human story worth analyzing in its own right. The "memory box of Pinochet's Chile" would subtly morph into the story of "a Holocaust Jew in Pinochet's Chile." There may be another time and another venue for a more extended personal reflection, but not in this trilogy.

Third, precisely because Pinochet's Chile is an example of "radical evil," it issues a challenge to representation far more extreme and intractable than the issues that attach to oral history as such. In this sense the difficulties of representation that bedevil this book belong to a stream of scholarly and philosophical reflections on representation provoked by the Holocaust and other examples of radical evil in world history. The design of this history—the use of an introductory volume focused on human stories, the use of Afterwords that extend and sometimes unsettle the main chapters that immediately precede them, the sobering "futility of history" reflection in the Afterword (to chapter 2 of Book Three of this trilogy) that follows analysis of the Truth and Reconciliation Commission—prioritizes this larger issue of representation. The big issue is, How do we represent, historicize, and analyze social relations and atrocities so extreme they defy our imagination, our assumption of moral order, and our notion of humanity?

Rather than including in the text extended reflections on oral sources and my relationships with them, I have resorted to a more subtle compromise and approach. In Book One, the introductory volume emphasizing human portraits of a society caught in memory impasse, and the book most "literary" or ethnographic in texture, I allow my role in interviews and conversations to emerge here and there, as an organic part of the story. In chapter 2 and its Afterword, I also allow glimpses of the dialogue between my family's Holocaust background and the professional research experience in Chile. In all three books, when relevant for the analysis I allow skepticism about specific informant stories or memories to become part of my own narrative strategy. An obvious example occurs in the story of Colonel Juan (Book One, chapter 3). A more subtle example occurs when I critique activist memories that draw too strong and linear a line between "ant's work" activism prior to 1983 and the eruption of major street protests during 1983–86 (Book Two, chapter 5).

In all three books as well, I have used the notes as a vehicle for commentary as well as documentation. This allows room for more extended critical appraisal of specific methodological problems or historical sources, whether written or oral.

Index

Page references in italics refer to illustrations. A "t" following a page number denotes a table.

Allende, Salvador (*cont.*)
267, 422n7; vilification of, 38. *See also*
coup of 11 September 1973
Allende Bussi, Isabel, 39, 163, 212, 267
Alliance for Progress, xxvi–xxvii
Almonacid Arellano, Luis Alfredo, 332
Al Qaeda, 274
Altamirano, Carlos, 15, 141
Altar to the Fatherland, 269
Alvarez Soto, Juana, 343
Alvear, Soledad, 171, 216
ambivalent culture, 361–62, 383. *See also*
triumphalism and disenchantment
American Convention on Human Rights
(1978), 332
amnesty: Aylwin on, 88, 113; for crimes
against humanity, 332; forum on, 187;
"full stop," 121, 123–24, 128, 130, 134;
international law/treaties vs. national
law on, 275; memory box closed via, 7,
129–30; *El Mercurio* on, 93; Pinochet
on, 18–19, 22, 123, 367, 401n12,
433n25; Supreme Court appointments'
effects on, 197–98; for war crimes, 333.
See also under Pinochet Ugarte, Augusto
Amnesty International, xxvii, 19, 160, 213,
378
Amnesty Law (1978), 382–83; Aylwin doctrine on, 88, 113, 118, 121, 127–28, 154,
252, 332, 362–64; as crisis measure,
138; disappearance-as-kidnap doctrine
as eroding, 117–18, 127–28, 217, 247,
275, 332, 364; disappearance cases
affected by, 32, 45, 117, 217; end date of,
22; impunity undermined by legal
interpretation of, 196, 363; international law as eroding, 221, 275, 332, 364;
Letelier-Moffitt murder as exempt
from, 136, 138, 196; nullification of, 18–
19, 332–33, 363; penal justice hampered
by, 113, 116–17
Amunátegui, Miguel Luis, 289
Análisis, 223
Anderson, John Lee, 249
Angelini group, 345
anti-Communism, xxvii
Antofagasta, 13, 251
APEC (Asia-Pacific Economic Cooperative),
149

Apsi, 223
Arancibia, Jorge, 257
Arce, Luz, 78–80, 115–16
Arellano Stark, Sergio, 13–15, 144, 247–
48, 251
Arendt, Hannah, 99–100
Argentina: border crisis of, with Chile,
138; Chilean views of Argentines and,
179–80; democratic transition in, 365;
final stop/due obedience laws in, 19–
20, 376; human rights advances in,
374–77, 379; military in, xxv, 19–20,
68, 374–75; perpetrator confessions in,
375; political transition in, 165; truth
commission in, 68
Armed Forces Building (Santiago), 119
army: arrests by, 293; arrests of officers in,
247–48, 334; boinazo maneuver by,
119–21, 123; institutional responsibility
for abuses accepted by, 298, 326–28;
on Law of Internal Security, 457–58n34;
response of, to Rettig Report, 91–93,
362. *See also* "ejercicio de enlace" affair;
justice; military
Army Day, 38
Army Month, 51
arrests/detentions, political: acknowledged cases of, 476n31; hold-and-
release detentions, 290; number of,
xxiii–xxiv, 68, 292–93, 392–93n3,
465n72, 476n34. *See also*
deaths/disappearances; political prisoners; Valech Commission
arrogance, perils of, 179–80
Artaza, Mario, 214
Asian financial crisis, 177–78, 217,
439n42
Association of Former Concentration
Camp Prisoners (Agrupación de ex
Prisioneros de Campos de Concentración), 280
Association of Relatives of Executed Political Prisoners (Agrupación de Familiares de Ejecutados Políticos), 45, 162–
63
Association of Relatives of the Detained
and Disappeared. *See* Agrupación de
Familiares de Detenidos-Desaparecidos

Democracia y Progreso, 25, 26t
democracy: accountability required for,
66; books raising awareness of, 190–
91, 444n64; competing visions of, 132–
33; disappointment with, 185–86, 190;
military dictatorship vs., xxii–xxiii, 126,
132; moral foundation of, 359; permanent defense of, 382; as return to rule
of law, 67; scholarship on, xxii, 394n6;
weak, 500n22. *See also* convivencia
democratic transition, 324–47; in Chile
vs. Spain, 366; founding conditions of,
365, 376; impatience with limitations
of, 330–35, 338–40, 486n13; memory
of, 324–25; memory paradox of Bachelet's Chile and, 344–47, 356; pacted,
364–66; shifting agenda of public
issues during, 335–44, 349–50, 487n15;
soft vs. hard hegemony during, 189,
193, 210, 249, 360–61, 364; Valech
Report responses to, 325–29, 484n1,
485n6; volatility in, 357–58
demonstrations. *See* protests
"Derechos Chile," 229
detentions. *See* arrests/detentions,
political
Dialogue Table, 239, 242–47, 250–55,
274–79, 362, 372
Díaz, Agave, 335, 426n28
dictatorships, South American: democracy
vs., xxii–xxiii, 126, 132; "dirty war," xxiv,
xxvii, 19, 138, 393–94n6; scholarship
on, xxii; social debt following, 34, 37–
38, 46, 185–86, 207, 343; U.S. support
of, 136; "we were better in dictatorship"
idea, 189, 443–44n62
Diez, Sergio, 118
dignity: Movement for National Dignity,
220; Vial on, 102; of victims, 103, 109,
294–95, 418–19n7
DINA (Dirección de Inteligencia Nacional): arrests by, 65–66, 293; Caravan of
Death role of, 14; CNI as replacing, 14,
138; Colonia Dignidad's collaboration
with, 197; cover stories about disappeared, 166; exiled leaders targeted by,
136–42, 351; Halcón I group, 116; helicopter flights used by, to disappear pris-

oners, 276–77; history of, 14; as an
illicit association, 257; misinformation
campaign by, 319; spying by, 141; tor-
ture/detentions and deaths/disap-
pearances by, 85, 102, 116, 141, 303, 385,
395n11, 419n7; Townley's testimony
about, 141; Tucán group under, 116. *See
also* Letelier, Orlando: murder of;
Londres 38/40; Villa Grimaldi
Dirección de Inteligencia Nacional. *See*
DINA
disappeared persons, 165–66, 195; declaration of death of, 89; Dialogue Table
report on fate of, 253–55, 274–75, 279;
female, 240, 276; hunger strikes by relatives of, 137–38; memorials to, 109–
10, 111–12, 265, 468n5; relatives of, as
victims, 103. *See also* Agrupación de
Familiares de Detenidos-
Desaparecidos; deaths/disappearances;
General Cemetery; Patio 29
disenchantment. *See* triumphalism and
disenchantment
divorce, 341
"The Dream Exists" concert festival, 285
DuBois, Pierre, 167

ECO (Educación y Comunicaciones),
437n37, 454n19
Economax (supermarket chain), 339
economic growth and inequality, 177–84,
286, 338–40; Mapuche aspects of,
206–8, 344–46. *See also* triumphalism
and disenchantment
*Educación y Comunicaciones, Centro de
Documentación* (ECOCD), 507
educational reform, 337–38
Edwards, Agustín, 115, 328
Edwards, Cristián, 115
egotism vs. solidarity, 189, 443–44n62
Eichmann, Adolf, 100
"ejercicio de enlace" affair, 59–60, 106,
121, 407–8n51
Eldridge, Joseph, 379
Elecmetal, 235
elections, binomial system of, 23, 25, 26t,
29–30, 95, 145, 192, 212, 330
Eledín Parraguez, Amante, 307, 480n61

Pinochet Ugarte, Augusto (*cont.*)
inet reshuffled by, 138; *Camino recorrido*, 55–56; Caravan of Death and, 13, 247–51, 257–58, 273, 300–302; Carrasco and, 322; Communists ordered arrested by, 65; Contreras and, 151, 153, 158, 228, 302; corruption of, 54, 57, 106, 204, 298–300, 349; crimes against humanity charges against, 164; criminal complaints/lawsuits against, 217, 247–49, 280, 327–28, 334, 348, 362; criticism of, 159–60; "Day of Unity" message of, 462n60; death of, xxi, 273, 348–56, 492n9; dictatorship of, overview of, xxi; on 11 September anniversary, 218–19; Frei Montalva's death and, 302–3; final health crisis of, 348–49; on Frei Ruíz-Tagle, 368; funeral/wake of, 349–53; Grade One troop alert ordered by, 59, 106, 121, 407–8n51; health of, 213, 225, 230–31, 245, 249–50, 255–56, 273, 300–301; under house arrest, 251, 348, 363, 463n61; humor/satire about, 250, 352, 449n3, 492n9; as icon of brutal dictatorship, 136, 377; as icon of U.S. anticommunism, xxvii; immunity of, 212–13, 215, 224, 248–50, 301–2; insensitivity of, to human rights violations, 127; Izurieta's caution to, not to defy courts, 258, 260, 368; legal roller coaster of, 301, 348; Letelier-Moffitt murder and, 138–39, 141, 428n4; "Letter to Chileans," 240–41, 244, 249, 251, 462n60; loyalty to, 27, 29–30, 53, 212, 260, 277, 300–302, 349, 356, 478n53; memory remarks by, 158–59; military promotions by, 56–57; "Mission Accomplished" campaign by, 55–56, 185; on olvido, 161, 433n25; Operation Condor and, 301; plebiscite defeat of, xxxii, 1, 6, 14, 185, 445n66; power of, 7, 226, 248–49, 260–61, 277, 359; prosecutions opposed by, 22, 401n12; public opinion on rule of, 90, 302, 478n53; public opinion on prosecution of, 246–47, 461n53; resignation of, 3, 50–53, 57–59, 406–7n45; return of, to Chile, 225–26, 230–31,

245, 279–80; secret police dissolved by, 28; as a senator, 212–13, 216, 248; softened belligerence of, 251, 462n60; Spain's case against, 197, 213, 446–47n75; Supreme Court base of, 26; on torture, 472n14; torture complaints against, 327–28; Villa Grimaldi and, 302; war thesis embraced by, 92, 240. *See also* boinazo and "taking back" the transition; Concertación; coup of 11 September 1973; Pinocheques case; Riggs Bank case

Pisagua: annual march to, 167; human remains found at, 48–50, 54, 60, 117, 129, 140; memory wall in, 316, *317*; prisoner camp at, 103–4, 280

Pizarro, Lorena, 279, 289

Plan Z, 14, 433n25, 436n35, 449n3, 509

Plan Zeta (television program), 449n3

Plaza de Armas (Santiago), 265–66

plazas, 180–81, 265–66

pobladores (shantytown residents), 30, 167, 169, 185–86, 310–11, 329. *See also* shantytowns

Poblete Córdova, Pedro, 221

poderes fácticos (fact-of-life powers), 145, 429n4

polarization, xxiv–xxv, 16, 83, 240–42, 253, 393n6

policide, xxv, 102

political prisoners: associations of, 280–81; definition of, 290; exile/release of, 36–37, 134, 159; lawsuits filed by, 281; number of, 281, 292–93, 476n34; pregnant women as, 240, 297; protests by, 36–37, 129; sociology of, 295; torture of, 36–37, 76, 291–92; women as, 76–77, 295–97. *See also* arrests/detentions, political; torture: sexual; Valech Commission

politics as war by other means, 52–57

Politzer, Patricia, 47–49, 56–57, 224; *Altamirano*, 398n5

Ponce Lerou, Julio, 27, 59

El Popular, 94

Portales, Diego, 266–67, 444n66

poverty, 178–79, 183–84, 193, 338, 439n44, 441n51, 474n24

power: fact-of-life powers (poderes fácticos), 145, 429n4; hard vs. soft, 53, 126, 129, 145, 212, 346, 357, 359–60, 362; of Rettig Commission, 69–70, 80
Prat, Arturo, 179
Prats, Carlos, 136–37, 141, 162, 164, 351
Prats, Sofia, 142
presidential election day, 38–39, 222
presidents (Chile), 24, 30, 330; election of 1999, 217–18; memorialization of, 110, 113; statues of, 267. *See also under names of individual presidents*
private memory. *See* loose/private memory
privatization: of culture, 9, 11, 195, 261–62; modernization via, 149, 176, 184–85; of public enterprise, 26–27, 180, 195
Progressive Union of Prosecuting Attorneys, 164
Pro-Peace Committee (COPACHI; Comité Pro-Paz), 135, 385, 447n75, 505
Propper, Eugene, 137–38
protests: commemorative marches as, 166; criminalization of, 345–46; at General Cemetery, 191; by Mapuche, 344–46; over Londres 38, 320–21; after Pinochet's death, 352; against Pinochet, 212–15, 225, 226, 267; by political prisoners, 36–37, 129; right to demonstrate, 238; on 11 September anniversaries, 191, 220, 286, 474n23; student demonstrations for educational reform, 337–38; via voting, 192, 446n70. *See also* hunger strikes
prudence/convulsions produced by memory struggles, 146–48, 151, 155–62, 188, 193, 429–30n6, 430n7, 432n17, 432–33n24, 433n25, 434n27. *See also* turn in Chilean life
Puenzo, Luis, *The Official Story*, 379, 499n16
Punta Arenas, 316, *317*
Punta Peuco prison (near Santiago), 150–52, 155
Purdy, Frederick, 276

Quercia, Boris, 202
Quilaqueo Bustos, Gustavo, 346
Quillota massacre (1974), 391n3

radical evil. *See* crimes against humanity
Radical Party, 17
Radio Cooperativa, 28, 223
Ralco hydroelectric project, 208–10, *209*
Ramírez, Rosa, 202
Ramírez, Walter, 345
Ramírez Hald, Hernán, 247–48
Rebolledo, Miguel Angel, 116
Renovación Nacional: "clean hands" slogan of, 157–58; on designated senators, 402n16; on discovery of human remains, 48; on economic reform, 35; as flexible/democratic, 17; on memorials to Allende, 110; on political prisoners, 37; on Punta Peuco, 150–51; response of, to Rettig Report, 93; on Truth and Reconciliation Commission, 69. *See also* Concertación
repression: awakenings prompted by, 193–94; barbarism of, 15, 390–93n3; economic privation caused by, 108; health toll of, on victims' relatives, 73; imminent war as justification for, 14–15, 21, 55, 82–85, 91–93, 109, 127, 161, 256; as institutionalized, 239–40; as massacres' goals, 14; multilayered, 131; reductionist approach to, 193–94, 446n71; scale of, xxiii–xxiv, xxviii, 131–32, 239–40; secrecy vs. truth about, 21; sociology of targets of, 295; trials for perpetrators of, 333–34, 486n13. *See also* arrests/detentions, political; atrocities; Contreras, Manuel; deaths/disappearances; exiles; Pinochet Ugarte, Augusto; torture
reproduction, politics of, 340–41
Rettig, Raúl, 34
Rettig Commission. *See* Truth and Reconciliation Commission
returnees, 35–36
revolution, xxiv–xxv
Riggs Bank case, 57, 299–302, 311, 334
Ríos, Chino, 198
Ríos, Patricio, 276, 470n5
Rivadeneira, Ricardo, 69
Rivas Díaz, Manuel, 235, 237
Rivera Bozzo, Sergio, 333
Rivera Matus, Juan Luis, 255

Index   543

Soviet Union's collapse, 95, 442n54
Spain, 365–66, 381
Spanish judicial proceedings on crimes against humanity, 164, 434n30
Special Commission on Indigenous Peoples, 38, 207
speech, powers to discipline, 159, 231–32, 457–58n34
Stange, Rodolfo, 150, 196
state and civil society, 156–57, 162–76, *172, 174, 377,* 438n41
Stevin Groep, 136
Straw, Jack, 225, 245
Stroessner, Alfredo, xxv, 139
Styron, William, *Sophie's Choice,* 104
subways, 342–43
success cult. *See* triumphalism and disenchantment
Sudamericana Vapores, 235
Superby, Mario, 333
supermarkets, 143–44, 339
Supreme Court (Chile): amnesty affected by appointments to, 197–98; on Aylwin doctrine, 117, 252, 274; Contreras/ Espinoza sentences upheld by, 150–51, 430n11; coup ruled act of war by, 333; National Security Council and, 23; Pinochet's base in, 26; on progress of human rights cases, 330–31; reform of, 35–36, 114–15, 118, 122–24, 127–28, 149, 163, 216–17; renovation of, 197–98, 246–47; on Rettig Report, 115, 140; Segunda Sala Penal and, 453n17; truth-and-justice barrier passed by, 274
survivor-witnesses. *See* victim-survivor-witnesses
synergies, frictional, 8–9; adversity's subtleties captured by, 373; definition of, 163; formula/wedge problem as producing, 371, 374; frictional dynamics of, 368–69, 371–72; human rights advances explained by, 373–74; mutual dependence of partners in, 369–70, 496n11; between political elites and human rights activists, 43–45, 47, 77–78, 93–94, 119, 128, 130, 132, 162–63, 371; relevant actors in, 369, 372–73; renewal of, 312–13
Szczaranski, Clara, 463n61

Talcahuano Naval Hospital, 151–52
Tarrow, Sidney, 378, 499n15
tax reform, 17, 34–35
Tejas Verdes, 318
telecommunications deregulation, 227
television, 47–48, 223–24, 284, 448–49n3, 455n21. *See also* Televisión Nacional
Televisión Nacional (TVN): Allende funeral broadcast by, 39; Aylwin interview on, 403n20; on Aylwin's Rettig Report speech, 414n37; on coup, 142; debt of, 28–29; directorship system for, 455n21; on Frei Montalva's death, 302–3; human rights journalism by, 132; leadership of, 47; Letelier-Moffitt case covered by, 140–42; news tradition of, 224; on Pisagua, 49–50; Politzer–Toro interview on, 48–49, 140; on U.S. intervention in Chilean politics, 229. See also *Informe Especial*
Temuco Peace Park, 268, *268,* 468n5
La Tercera, 28, 223, 227, 307, 514
"Te recuerdo Amanda" (Jara), 31
Teruggi, Frank, 276
theater culture, 201–4, 448–49n3
"There Is No Tomorrow Without Yesterday" proposal, 286, 288–90
"the three professionals" murder, 150, 196
Toledo, Luisa, 352
top-down/bottom-up social dynamics, 7–9, 396–97n2
Toribio Medina, José, 262–63
Toro, Horacio, 48–49, 54, 140
Torres, Julio, 333
Torres Flores, Henry Francisco, 103–4
Torres Silva, Fernando, 117
torture: allanamientos (search raids) as, 328–29; archives and, 476n31; civilian complicity in, 328; deaths due to, 290–91; definition of, 68, 290; evidence of, 68; in floating jails, 328; humiliation of, 99, 146, 279, 281, 293, 295–96; institutionalized, 292–93, 298; international laws against, 290; at Londres 38, 76, 270, 318–19; memorialization of sites of, 318; as memory knot, 237, 253, 258; number of victims of, xxiii–xxiv,

torture (*cont.*)

68–69, 131, 258, 294, 409n8, 465n72; personhood destroyed by, 99, 290; pervasiveness/moral significance of, 81, 291–92; of political prisoners, 36–37, 76, 291–92; pressure to address, 279–81, 472n14; rebuilding life after, 293–94; sexual, 281–83, 293–95, 477n41; techniques of, 292, 296; torturers confronted by victims, 116; torturers identified by Vicaría, 94; torturers outed, 232–38, 236, 253, 258–59, 263, 459n37, 459n39; torturers sued, 485n3; in the Tower, 175; trials for perpetrators of, 333–34, 486n13; Truth and Reconciliation Commission's investigation of, 69, 80–81; Valech Report and, 327–28; victims' silence about, 293; at Villa Grimaldi, 28, 66, 76, 169–70, 173, 240, 395n11; of women, 240, 276. *See also* Contreras, Manuel; Londres 38/40; Pinochet Ugarte, Augusto; Valech Commission; Villa Grimaldi Peace Park

tourism, 181–82

Tower, the (Villa Grimaldi), 175–76, 438n41

Townley, Michael, 137–42

trade agreements, 149, 177–78, 474n24

trade unions, 181, 338–39, 382

Transantiago, 342–43

transitions, xxii, 7–8, 364–68, 394n6. *See also* Aylwin, Patricio: transition from Pinochet to; democratic transition

treason, 204, 288

Tres Alamos prison camp, 76

triumphalism and disenchantment, 176–189, 190–93, 440n48; in book culture, 190–91, 444n64, 444–45n66; congressional elections, skepticism expressed in, 192, 446n70; de la Parra on triumphalism, 198–99; disillusionment produced by, 182–83, 193, 441nn50–51; memory in making of, 147, 184–89, 443n57

Troncoso, Patricia, 345–46

Troncoso, Raúl, 214–15

Truth, 18–19, 52–57, 72; justice and, 18–19, 66–67, 106. *See also* convivencia

Truth and Reconciliation Commission (Rettig Commission), 65–98; Agrupación's collaboration with, 44–45, 162–63; Aylwin's speech on findings of, 85–89, 97, 108–9, 413–14n35, 414n37; Barría case examined by, 65–66; cathartic aspect of testimony of, 71–74; civic duty felt by members of, 74, 84; commemoration of, 166; completion deadline of, 83–84; confrontation with, 67–75; criticism of/skepticism about, 93–94, 414n37; cultural follow-up to, 94–95, 97–98, 121, 126–27, 131–32; deaths/disappearances tabulated by, 89, 131, 390n3, 392n3; debates/unity in, 78–84, 412n27; documentation of, 60, 70–71, 82–83, 128, 410n12; establishment of, 8, 33, 45–46, 369; findings of, as irreversible, 75, 81; as formula/wedge, 94, 132, 188–89; good faith within, 81, 84; historical analysis by, 82–83, 91, 413n29; on judicial failure, 114–15; lawyers on staff of, 71–74, 103, 369; limited power of, 69–70, 80; makeup of, 34, 404n26; mandate of, 33, 68–70, 80, 84, 131–32; necessity of work of, 53; no-naming policy of, 80, 94; nonmilitant victims identified by, 103–4, 419n9; Pisagua site inspected by, 48; political background as irrelevant on, 74–75; pressure on/skepticism about, 68–69; publication/dissemination of, 93–94; on Quillota massacre, 391n3; responses to, 84–93, 115, 129, 327–28, 362, 370–71, 414n38; restrained tone of, 102; scope of, 33, 94, 131; social repair aspect of hearings of, 71–72; social workers on staff of, 71–72, 103, 369; success of, 98, 121, 126–27; survivor-witnesses' collaboration with, 75–80, 162–63, 369–70; testimony by military officers, 75; torture cases investigated by, 69, 80–81; truth, president, and nation and, 84–90; Valech Report vs., 477n45; workload of, 70

truth commissions, 67–68, 326–27. *See also* Valech Commission

turn in Chilean life (1998–2001), 211–64;

STEVE J. STERN

is the Alberto Flores Galindo Professor of History at the University of Wisconsin, Madison.

In addition to the first two volumes of his trilogy, *The Memory Box of Pinochet's Chile,*

Remembering Pinochet's Chile: On the Eve of London 1998 and *Battling for Hearts and Minds:*

Memory Struggles in Pinochet's Chile, 1973–1988, his recent publications

include *Shining and Other Paths: War and Society in Peru, 1980–1995*, also

published by Duke University Press.

Library of Congress Cataloging-in-Publication Data

Stern, Steve J., 1951–
Reckoning with Pinochet : the memory question in democratic Chile,
1989–2006 / Steve J. Stern.
p. cm. — (Latin America otherwise)
"Book three of the trilogy: The memory box of Pinochet's Chile."
Includes bibliographical references and index.
ISBN 978-0-8223-4712-5 (cloth : alk. paper)
ISBN 978-0-8223-4729-3 (pbk. : alk. paper)
1. Pinochet Ugarte, Augusto. 2. Chile—History—1973–1988. 3. Chile—History—1988–
4. Chile—History—Coup d'état, 1973—Psychological aspects. 5. Collective memory—Chile.
I. Title. II. Series: Stern, Steve J., 1951– Memory box of Pinochet's Chile ; bk. 3.
III. Series: Latin America otherwise.
F3100.S824 2010
983.06'5—dc22   2009043780